The

MANRIQUE de LARA and HOPKINS

FAMILY

From

Spain to Leon, Guanajuato, Mexico

And

England to the Island of Saint Helena,
a British Territory,

To

California, United States of America

With

MANRIQUE de LARA,

GOMEZ (of Portugal), MEDINA, CALDERON, HERRERA, ALCARAS,
LOPES, BOCANEGRA, GONZALES, DURAN, ESPARZA and LOZANO
Family Ties, including 1576 Leon, Guanajuato, Mexico Founder Ancestors,

And

English Translation of
Manrique de Lara Lineage
by Don Luis de Salazar y Castro,
Historia Genealogica de la Casa de Lara

By:

Anne Louise Manrique

Copyright © 2024, Anne Louise Manrique

ALL RIGHTS RESERVED.
No part of this publication may be reproduced, stored in a retrieval system or transmitted in any form or by any means whatsoever, whether electronic, mechanical, magnetic recording, or photocopying, without the prior written approval of the Copyright holder or Publisher, excepting brief quotations for inclusion in book reviews.

Published by:

Janaway Publishing, Inc.
Santa Maria, California 93454
www.janawaypublishing.com

2024

Disclaimer: Information accuracy depends entirely on its sources and how they were recorded.

Front Cover: Former Serapio Manrique Oakdale farmland
(tree planted by author's grandfather)
Photo credit: Anne Louise Manrique

ISBN: 978-1-59641-486-0
Library of Congress Control Number: 2024945664

Made in the United States of America

MANRIQUE de LARA - HOPKINS FAMILY

TABLE OF CONTENTS

Introduction		1
JOSEPHA GOMEZ MANRIQUE de LARA	(GEN1)	9
GASPAR ANTONIO MANRIQUE de LARA	(GEN2)	11
JOSEPH MANUEL MANRIQUE de LARA	(GEN3)	13
JOSEPH URBANO MANRIQUE de LARA	(GEN4)	15
JOSE ISIDRO MANRIQUE	(GEN5)	19
SIMON MANRIQUE	(GEN6)	21
CLEMENTE MANRIQUE	(GEN7)	23
SERAPIO MANRIQUE	(GEN8)	24
Biography of Serapio Manrique		28
DANIEL EDWIN HOPKINS, Island of St. Helena, UK		31
FLORA FELIPA-PHILOMENA RAMIREZ, San Francisco, CA, USA		35
HOPKINS-RAMIREZ children and biography		37
MARY HOPKINS - SERAPIO MANRIQUE		42
MANRIQUE-HOPKINS children	(GEN9)	50
MANRIQUE-HOPKINS grandchildren	(GEN10)	52
MANRIQUE de LARA	(10 Generations +)	55
HOPKINS FAMILY	(3 Generations)	56

APPENDIX

I.	California, USA		61
	A.	Anderson	61
	B.	Cayton	61
	C.	Cottle	62
	D.	HOPKINS, ROBERT	62
	E.	HOPKINS, CARRIE	64
	F.	HOPKINS, GUADALUPE PAULINE	65
	G.	HOPKINS, DANIEL SANTIAGO	66
	H.	Ramirez, Joseph	67
	I.	Silva	69
II.	PETRA DURAN (1866-)		70
III.	SERAPIA GONZALES (1839-1888)		76
IV.	BOCANEGRA		79
V.	ANA RITA ALCARAS (1730-)		83
VI.	Manuel Manrique (de Lara) (4)		87
VII.	Rita Marmolejo (1715-1753)		95

VIII.	Godparents for children of GASPAR MANRIQUE de LARA and FRANCA. CALDERON de HERRERA	101
IX.	FRANCA. XAVIER(A) CALDERON de HERRERA (1707-)	110
	Map A	142
	Map B	143
X.	Ruiz de Esparza	144
XI.	Lozano Isla	161
XII.	PEDRO GOMEZ and CATALINA MANRIQUE de LARA	170
XIII.	MEDINA	191
XIV.	Manrique de Lara (Surnames) (1600-1788, Mexico)	193
XV.	MANRIQUE de LARA (Spain)	201
XVI.	Gomez (Surnames) (1580-1663, Guanajuato, Mexico)	251
XVII.	Gomez of Portugal (Jalisco & Guanajuato, Mexico)	260
XVIII.	Manrique de Lara y Arias de Guzman	290
XIX.	History of Leon	298
XX.	New Spain History	300

REFERENCE MATERIAL

Map of Nueva Espana	304
Translation of Urbano Manrique/Melchora Lopes marriage record	305
1864 Island of St. Helena marriage record: Essex to Hopkins	305
MARY HOPKINS, birth notice page 11, Tues., 31 July 1900, The *SF Call*	306
HOPKINS-RAMIREZ, marriage, page 13, Fri., 25 Oct. 1901, The *SF Call*	306
DANIEL E. HOPKINS (sailor/musician), 1902, SF, CA, USA (photo)	307
DANIEL, FLORA and MARY HOPKINS, 1902, SF, CA, USA (photo)	308
HOPKINS-RAMIREZ, 1909, St. Mary's Stockton, CA, marriage record	309
FLORA (RAMIREZ) HOPKINS, 1918, *Stockton Record* obituary	310
FLORA (RAMIREZ) HOPKINS, 1918 San Joaquin Cemetery card	310
SERAPIO MANRIQUE farmland, 1950, Oakdale, CA, USA (photos)	311
LINDA, JOE, JULIUS, TONY, ALICE, ED & MADELINE MANRIQUE (photo)	312
JOE, MARY (HOPKINS), LAWRENCE & SERAPIO MANRIQUE (photo)	312
MANRIQUE FAMILY PHOTOS	313
WW2 Memorial Honoree VINCENT MANRIQUE	314
WW2 Memorial Honoree LAWRENCE MANRIQUE	314
WW2 Memorial Honoree JOSEPH MANRIQUE	314
(WW2 plaques from *American Battle Monument Collection*)	
ACKNOWLEDGMENTS	315
BIOGRAPHY	316

THE MANRIQUE de LARA - HOPKINS FAMILY

Manrique de Lara - Hopkins descendants from Northern California, USA originated from ancestors born in many parts of the world including Leon, Guanajuato, Mexico, the Island of St. Helena, a British Overseas Territory, and Spain. This Manrique de Lara branch has resided in the New World for at least thirteen generations since their mid-1550 New Spain arrival. Originally, the "Manrique" surname was: Manrique de Lara.

The earliest Californian ancestors remain undetermined, a mystery even a team of California Genealogical Society genealogists could not certify. Joseph Ramirez, born California (abt. 1850), was the grandfather of Mary Hopkins born 1900, San Francisco, California. His lineage has yet to be discovered although it was speculated he may have Spanish or Native American (Northern Californian) heritage. Regardless, Joseph Ramirez, born California, is assumed to have married Francis Lopez who likely was born in either the Azores Islands or Spain given her lineage remains uncertain, as well. Joseph Ramirez and Francis Lopez were the parents of Flora (Philomena) Felipa Ramirez born 13 September 1882 in "California." Flora Ramirez married Daniel Edwin Hopkins on 24 October 1901 in San Francisco, California, USA. Conclusive Portuguese, Spanish and pre-1882 Northern California Native American heritage remain unfounded, if those are the origins of Joseph Ramirez and Francis Lopez.

However, the Manrique de Lara - Hopkins line does consist of three confirmed origins - Manrique de Lara ancestors born in Leon, Guanajuato, Mexico, Hopkins family members born at the Island of St. Helena, a British Overseas Territory, and early 1900 Northern California-born descendants.

The Manrique de Lara family emigrated from Spain to Leon, Guanajuato, Mexico during the mid-1550s and now spans more than thirteen generations after Serapio Manrique married Mary Hopkins on 26 December 1917 in Stockton, San Joaquin, California, USA. The genealogy of this line is as follows...

~~~~~

THE MANRIQUE de LARA FAMILY

From Leon, Guanajuato, Mexico to Oakdale, California, USA

JOSEPHA GOMEZ MANRIQUE de LARA, baptized 23 July 1677, Irapuato, Guanajuato, MX
GASPAR ANTONIO MANRIQUE de LARA, born 28 March 1702, Leon, Guanajuato., Mexico
JOSEPH MANUEL MANRIQUE de LARA, born 30 October 1734, Leon, Guanajuato, Mexico
JOSEPH URBANO MANRIQUE de LARA, born 25 May 1768, Leon, Guanajuato, Mexico
JOSE ISIDRO MANRIQUE, baptized 17 May 1804, Leon, Guanajuato, Mexico
SIMON MANRIQUE, baptized 19 February 1835, Leon, Guanajuato, Mexico
CLEMENTE MANRIQUE, baptized 24 November 1862, Leon, Guanajuato, Mexico
SERAPIO MANRIQUE, born 14 October 1891, Silao de Victoria, Guanajuato, Mexico
JULIUS CLEMENT MANRIQUE, born 8 April 1932, Oakdale, Stanislaus, California, USA
ANNE LOUISE MANRIQUE, born 31 October 1965, Modesto, Stanislaus, California, USA

~~~~~

The search for this Manrique de Lara branch began during 2015 with the intent to learn where my Manrique ancestors originated in Spain. Since obtaining 1550-1630 New Spain records proved difficult, while it is likely Gaspar Gomez Manrique de Lara is GEN1, his birth record was not located. As such, his great-grandchild, Josepha Gonzales Bravo, begins our line as per her documented birth and death records, facts that deem Manrique-Hopkins children GEN9 (*rather than GEN12*) and Manrique-Hopkins grandchildren GEN10 (*alternatively GEN13*) from this Leon Manrique de Lara branch. After 1800, the text, "de Lara," was eliminated from our Spanish surname: Manrique de Lara.

Our documented Manrique de Lara lineage begins with JOSEPHA GOMEZ MANRIQUE de LARA, born 1677 in Irapuato, Guanajuato, Mexico. Josepha Gomez Manrique de Lara married Nicolas de Medina, who was the son of Melchora de Medina and Diego de la Cruz. JOSEPHA MANRIQUE died in Mexico City and was buried in the parish of Santa Vera Cruz on 2 March 1718 (*Mexico, Distrito Federal, registros parroquiales y diocesanos, 1514-1970; Santa Veracruz/Guerrero Sureste, Defunciones y entierros, 1760-1822; Image 136/1091*). Josepha Gomez Manrique de Lara was listed as the widow of Nicolas de Medina (**Appendix XIII**).

Santa Vera Cruz, which became a monastery, was founded by Hernan Cortes as a brotherhood originally intended for conquistadores or noble families. When Josepha Manrique was buried at Santa Vera Cruz, the priest was Phelipe Manrique de Lara.

Josepha Gomez Manrique de Lara was the great-great-grandchild of Pedro Gomez and Catalina Manrique de Lara, founders of Leon, Guanajuato, Mexico (**Appendix XII**). Manrique de Lara lineage from our line via onomastics and documentation is:

PEDRO GOMEZ (born abt. 1520-1584)
(Founder - 1576 Leon, Guanajuato, Mexico)
CATALINA MANRIQUE de LARA (born abt. 1530-1585)
(Founder - 1576 Leon, Guanajuato, Mexico)
|
GASPAR GOMEZ MANRIQUE de LARA (born abt. 1550-)
(Founder - 1576 Leon, Guanajuato, Mexico)
MARIANA FERRER
|
CATALINA (GOMEZ) MANRIQUE de LARA (born abt. 1600, Leon, Gto., MX)
GARCI BRAVO de LAGUNAS
|
MARIA BRAVO de LAGUNAS y (GOMEZ) MANRIQUE (de LARA) (1630-)
PEDRO GONZALES de AGUIRRE y RULES
|
JOSEPHA GONZALES BRAVO (y GOMEZ MANRIQUE de LARA)
(born 23 July 1677, Irapuato, Gto., MX; buried 2 March 1718, DF, MX)
NICOLAS de MEDINA
|
GASPAR ANTONIO MANRIQUE de LARA (1702-1755)

Josepha Gomez Manrique de Lara's son took her surname as using the last name(s) of the mother was a naming pattern among Portuguese during this era. Also, in old Spanish families a man would use surnames from his mother's side if his maternal grandfather had no male children. Additionally, during this period, names were a mix of parent's surnames, and, as a result, siblings would have different surnames. Baptismal books, which were rare in Nueva Espana from 1550 until the late 1600s, often listed only first names and information such as: "Maria, of the villa, daughter of Pedro..." As villas were comprised by at most by only twenty-five Spanish or Portuguese families, links between one another likely but difficult to prove as per lost documentation. The Manrique de Lara surname was rare, and the Gomez-Manrique de Lara combination only found between Pedro Gomez and Catalina Manrique de Lara descendants within the entirety of New Spain (Mexico) 1575-1675. As per onomastics, and the fact that Gaspar Antonio Manrique de Lara (1702-1755) was buried *inside* Leon's El Sagrario church, our lineage connects to Pedro Gomez and Catalina Manrique de Lara.

1576 Leon founding families included Pedro Gomez and Catalina Manrique de Lara plus three of their children: twins, Baltasar Gomez and Gaspar Gomez (born abt. 1550) and Lucia Manrique. Gaspar Antonio Gomez (Manrique de Lara) (1550) shared the same first name as Gaspar Antonio (Medina) (y Gomez) Manrique de Lara (1702).

While documents relating to Nueva Espana settlers are unavailable, our early Leon, Guanajuato family history relates to Leon, Guanajuato's 1576 founding (**Appendix XII**).

PEDRO GOMEZ
(born abt. 1520 - 1585, Nueva Espana)
CATALINA MANRIQUE de LARA
(born abt. 1530 - died abt. 1585-1587, Nueva Espana)

As per Josepha Gomez Manrique de Lara's surname combination, the search for ancestors in Leon assumes our lineage connects to Pedro Gomez who married Catalina Manrique (de Lara) as they were the only individuals with that surname combination in Nueva Espana. While Catalina Manrique was listed without the "de Lara" on the founder list, her descendants took the Manrique de Lara surname until 1799. Unfortunately, the only genealogical information found in Mexico centered upon one of the twins, Baltasar Gomez Manrique rather than our ancestor, Gaspar Gomez Manrique (de Lara). Two biographies of Pedro Gomez were found: one written in 1961 and the other in 1990.

From: Fuente: Gonzalez Leal, Mariano. <u>Leon Trayectoria y Destino</u>. Pro Urbe. Leon 1990. Pages 5 & 6.

> "He resided in this region at least since 1564, the year the Royal court of Mexico awarded him the site of the Cerro Gordo - on August 13th. In the corresponding document reference is made to his merits in the war against the Chichimecas. He came with his wife, Catalina Manrique and three children: Baltasar and Gaspar Gomez, twins, and Lucia Manrique.

In the year 1581, Pedro Gomez held the position of Mayor of the First Church (...), a position that he held until his death in the year of 1584 or early 1585, and at least from 1582 to 1584 he was the ordinary mayor of the town of Leon as recorded in the protocol of the notary, Andres de Truijllo in the volumes corresponding to those years.

In a document dated March 21, 1585, it is stated Lucia Manrique, daughter of the founder and also founder, was married to PEDRO de ZAVALA, a resident of Irapuato.

Baltasar Gomez, called "Old Man" because he has a son of the same name, was born around 1550. He was still alive in 1624. He declared his age in the famous "big lawsuit" between the Mayors' Offices of Leon and Lagos. He inherited the Cerro Gordo Ranch and owned the Palenque ranch, close to the towns of Rincon - San Francisco and Purisima and the border with Nueva Galicia. He was married to MARIA ISABEL GALVAN, and left numerous descendants who later became linked to the AROCHA family."

As per the translation of, "Mayor of the First Church, according to Rodolfo Herrera Perez, Director (2023) of Leon's Archivo Historico, "stewards or treasurers of the Church were lay people who intervened in the economic life of the ecclesiastical corporations," ecclesiastical assets or financial matters upon which the clergy had no formal role. Pedro Gomez, as "Mayor of the First Church," was responsible for accounting expenses and assets of the church incurred by celebrations of the year and held an administrative role for church finances.

From a genealogical study listed in the <u>Memories of the Mexican Academy of Genealogy and Heraldry</u> (second period, Volume II, December 1961, pages 109-114), Lic. Gonzalo Torres Martinez outlined his lineal relationship to Pedro Gomez in: "Descendants of Pedro Gomez, Founder and First Settler of Villa de San Sebastian de Leon in Nueva Espana, today, Leon, Guanajuato." From Martinez' research, it can be confirmed our line did not descend from either Baltasar Gomez Manrique or Lucia Manrique (de Lara), but instead from Gaspar Gomez Manrique (de Lara).

"By Royal Decree given by the Audencia of Mexico on 13 August 1564, the Catholic Majesty of King Philip II rewarded the services rendered by Don Pedro Gomez in the war against the Chichimecas and Guachichiles in which he took part in providing men, arms and horses with his own money..." (*Martinez, Page 109*)

"The lands that comprised the original mercy and others that were acquired later by the descendants of Don Pedro Gomez, were in the hands of his descendants (*of Baltasar Gomez Manrique de Lara*) for three centuries..."(*Martinez, Page 109*)

"When, by the order of the Viceroy of New Spain, Don Martin Enriquez de Almanza, what is now the city of Leon was founded on 20 January 1576, Don Pedro, together with his wife, Dona Catalina Manrique (de Lara) and his twin sons Don Baltasar and

Don Gaspar Manrique, (who had) settled in Cerrogordo from the time it was granted, move to Leon, and in their capacity as Spaniards and first settlers they received plots of land in the layout of the new town to cultivate their houses and orchards." (*Martinez, Page 110*)

…"Elected councilors (during 1576 included) Pedro Gomez…" (*Martinez, Page 111*)

"In the year 1581, Don Pedro Gomez held the position of Mayor Domo of the First Church that existed in Leon, a position that he held until his death in the year 1584 or early 1585, and at least from 1582 to 1584 he was ordinary mayor of the Villa de Leon as stated in the Protocol of Notary Andres de Trujillo in the volumes corresponding to those years." (*Martinez, Page 111*)

"On 21 March 1585 Don Pedro Gomez, according to the declaration of his widow, Dona Catalina Manrique (de Lara) before the Notary Andres de Trujillo in notarial instrument of recognition of debt to her son-in-law Pedro de Zavala, a resident of Irapuato, by virtue of a clause in the will of Don Pedro Gomez that has not been found." (*Martinez, Pages 111-112*)

"As the parish archives began in 1646, since the previous books were lost, it is not possible to establish the date of Don Pedro Gomez' death nor that of his wife and his children Don Baltasar and Don Gaspar Gomez Manrique appear as her children and heirs, (individuals who) recognize (their) brother-in-law Pedro de Zavala's credit on the estate." (*Martinez, Page 112*)

From Martinez' account of the Pedro Gomez family, we confirm Pedro Gomez and Catalina Manrique de Lara were Spaniards and records were lost prior to 1646. Additionally, Martinez outlines the inheritance of Pedro Gomez land (Cerro Gordo and others) to his son, Baltasar Gomez Manrique de Lara. There is no mention of Gaspar Gomez Manrique, although he is listed as an heir in Pedro Gomez' will. Given our verified ancestor, Josepha Gomez Manrique de Lara, carried the two surnames, and few individuals existed in Guanajuato with the Gomez-Manrique de Lara surname combination, again, as per onomastics, our branch fits within the Pedro Gomez and Catalina Manrique de Lara line.

To put Spanish history into perspective during the time our ancestors left Spain (or Portugal) for Nueva Espana, then were gifted land (Cerro Gordo) by King Phillip II, the history of "Phillip the Prudent" (21 May 1527-13 September 1598) is necessary to review. King Phillip II was King of Spain (1556-1598), King of Portugal (1580-1598), King of Naples and Sicily (1555-1598) and "King of England and Ireland" after marrying Queen Mary I in 1554. As for other titles, including House of Habsburg (House of Austria) membership, he was the Duke of Milan (1540-1598) and Lord of Seventeen Provinces of the Netherlands.

Phillip II's parents were Emperor Charles V and Isabella of Portugal, and as such, he inherited the Spanish Empire in 1556 and the Portuguese throne in 1580 given no heirs existed in the line. The connection to Portugal was not just by title. Born on 21 May 1527 at Palacio de Pimentel in Valladolid, Castile, Spain, he was the son of Isabella of Portugal.

His first wife was Maria Manuela of Portugal who he married 1543 (she died in 1545). He married three more times (Mary, Queen of England; m. 1554; died 1558) (Elizabeth of Valois; m. 1559; d. 1568) (Anne of Austria; m. 1570; d. 1580). He died on 13 September 1598 at El Escorial, San Lorenzo de El Escorial, Castile, Spain.

Isabella of Portugal was born in Lisbon 24 October 1503, the child of King Manuel I of Portugal and his second wife, Maria of Aragon. While her son, Phillip II of Spain, was the only surviving son of his father, Emperor Charles V, he was also the grandson of Manuel I of Portugal, and as such, claimed the Portuguese throne. Phillip II was elder sibling to sisters Maria (born 21 June 1528, Madrid; married 15 September 1548 Archduke Maximillian; 16 children born; died 26 February 1603, Madrid, Spain) (Queen Consort of Hungary, Germany, Bohemia; Archduchess consort, Austria) and Juana (of Austria; Princess of Portugal) (born 24 June 1535; Married Joao Manuel, Prince of Portugal; died 7 September 1573) (married at age sixteen and widowed at age eighteen, she left her son, Sebastian of Portugal, with her mother-in-law in Portugal, and never saw him again after returning to Madrid).

King Phillipe II's first wife was his "double" first cousin, Maria Manuela, Princess of Portugal, the daughter of his maternal uncle, John III of Portugal and his paternal aunt, Catherine of Austria. Married in Salamanca on 12 November 1543, they had one son who died at age twenty-three without children. Maria Manuela died shortly after the birth of her son, Carlos, Prince of Asturias (8 July 1545-24 July 1568) in 1545.

When the King of Portugal (Sebastian of Portugal) died without heirs, his elderly granduncle succeeded, then also passed away without descendants. As such, Phillip II claimed the throne (Battle of Alcantara) in September of 1580 and was crowned Phillip I of Portugal in 1581. After his first wife died, he married Queen Mary I of England (who was thirty-seven years old) at Winchester Cathedral on 25 July 1554. His son, Phillip III of Spain, was born from his fourth wife, Anne of Austria, on 14 April 1578 in Madrid, Spain. Phillip III married Margaret of Austria in 1599 and died 31 March 1621, Madrid, Spain. Phillip III was also King of Spain, Portugal, Naples, Sicily and Sardinia plus Duke of Milan.

Two entities existed within the Spanish empire in Mexico - Nueva Galicia and Nueva Espana. Nueva Galicia, founded in 1550, comprised of three provinces - Nayarit, Jalisco and Sinaloa - and was ruled by its own governor and administration. Nueva Espana was larger than Nueva Galicia and ruled by a viceroy appointed by the Spanish king. The Kingdom of New Spain was founded on 18 August 1521 and ruled by the Crown of Castile.

Registered at birth as, "Gaspar Antonio," "Espanol de la villa (Spaniard of the village)," Gaspar Antonio Manrique de Lara was born on 28 March 1702 and baptized during April 1702, the son of Josepha Gomez Manrique de Lara and Nicolas de Medina. Gaspar Antonio Manrique de Lara's father, Nicolas de Medina, also took his mother's surname. During this period, names were listed using both parent's surnames with the most "important" often chosen thereby not including the father's surname. If a daughter was born to a Portuguese mother, the child would most always take the mother's maiden name. Gaspar Antonio Manrique de Lara's 1755 burial inside the Leon church denoted either wealth, perhaps as a silver merchant, or status as a descendant of 1576 founders of Leon and/or Spanish Manrique de Lara heritage (**Appendix XV + XVII**).

The Manrique de Lara surname originated from Pedro Manrique de Lara, the 4th Senor de Amusco, who was born abt. 1270 and died 1323 in Spain. He was a relation, for instance, to Queen Beatrix of the Netherlands and would be King Charles of England's 18x great-grandfather, his Royal Highness Albert of Monaco's 21x great-grandfather and is Majesty Juan Carlos of Spain's 18x great grandfather. The line is quite documented, and our specific link is from CATALINA MANRIQUE de LARA, the wife of Pedro Gomez. Our Manrique de Lara surname was found on Guanajuato, Mexico birth and marriage records until 1799 when the surname was shortened to, Manrique.

To emigrate from Spain to Mexico the head of the family would file a form with Spain's "Council of the Indes" which would list the name of the male principal family member along with a group of unnamed individuals leaving Spain such as, "wife, children and servants." The "Council of Indes" was established in 1524 by King Charles V to administer the "Indes," Spain's name for its territories.

Although our Manrique surname once was fully written as, Manrique de Lara, the "de Lara" did not denote the surname of the mother but designated an entire last name. The surname, Manrique de Lara, was rare from 1550-1700 Guanajuato, Mexico and originally indicated nobility tied to Spain. By the early 1800s, priests began to shorten the name Manrique de Lara to Manrique then added letters, "z" or "es." However, there were fewer than two hundred Manrique de Lara surnamed individuals living in Guanajuato, Mexico from 1595 until the late 1700s.

The House of Lara originated during the medieval Kingdom of Castile, Leon, Andalusia and Galicia, then members of the branches moved throughout the Spanish colonies, including Mexico. Castile became Spain in 1516 under King Charles V, the grandson of Ferdinand II of Aragon and Isabella of Castile. The House of Lara was prominent during the 11th and 14th centuries in Castile, Spain. Only one branch of the House of Lara survived the Middle Ages, and that was the Manrique de Lara branch. The Manrique de Lara branch was supported Catholic monarchs such as Queen Isabella of Castile and King Ferdinand II of Aragon. In 1520 Emperor Charles V appointed the House of Lara to a position of "grandee" or nobility. The original coat of arms for the Manrique de Lara branch represented two cauldrons which suggested the ability of the family to support many followers (**APPENDIX XV**).

Members of Spain's noble families who emigrated abroad were mostly not first-born sons given they would not lose valuable inheritances due to the laws of primogeniture. However, the use of the entire Manrique de Lara surname in Mexico is proof our branch left Spain for Nueva Espana. Manrique-Hopkins grandchildren are likely fifteen generations from their Spanish ancestors, descendants of Catalina Manrique de Lara (born abt. 1530) whose parentage has not been determined.

~~~~~

The MANRIQUE de LARA Family
Leon, Guanajuato, Mexico

To emigrate from Spain to New Spain (Mexico) the head of the family would file a form with Spain's "Office of the Indes" which would list the name of the senior male member of the family along with a group of unnamed individuals leaving Spain such as, "wife, children and servants." One could emigrate from Peru or the Philippines as a "Spaniard," regardless of a birth in Peru or Philippines. Our Manrique de Lara branch is recorded as, "Espanoles" within marriage/birth/death books until 1865 (when race specification on birth/marriage/death records ceased in Mexico), a notation confirming Spanish ancestry. During the Colonial period, priests would list children in baptismal books by the color of their parent's skin, and as such, such demarcations were not always authenticated. After the late 1700s the Council of Indies began listing women with their maiden names, as well as, the individual by age, sex and relation to family.

Our Manrique (de Lara) branch is noted by **bold** text (*abbreviation written - MdL*).

"Parroquia Del Sagrario" is the Leon church where most Manrique (de Lara) family members were baptized. The Leon church was also written as, "El Sagrario Parroquia."

Leon, which means "Lion" in Spanish, was first settled in 1552 and founded on 20 January 1576 by Juan Bautista de Orozco. When Leon was given city status in 1830, "de los Aldamas" was added to honor of Juan and Ignacio Aldama, brothers who fought in the Mexican War of Independence. "Aldama" is also a Basque town near Pagazta and Iperraga in Northern Spain whose translated name means "side slope" (alde) "location" (ama). "Leon de Los Aldama" is also known as "Lion of the Aldama."

The founding families of Leon, Guanajuato include individuals with the surnames of Manrique (Catalina Manrique de Lara, spouse to Pedro Gomez and their daughter, Lucia Manrique), Gomez (Pedro Gomez, the husband of Catalina Manrique de Lara, and their twin sons, Baltasar and Gaspar Gomez), Medina and (de la) Cruz. Additional founder family surnames include Arias, Duran and Torres - families our Leon ancestors married into generations later. Godparents with Marmejolo surnames were also part of the original fifty-plus early Leon settler family members (**Appendix XIX**).

Villa de Leon was the fourth viceroy of New Spain founded under the condition fifty residents would commit to staying for at least ten years. Among the Leon founding residents was Pedro Gomez who arrived in New Spain by 1564 with the intention to fight the Chichimeca Indians. Because of his efforts during the War of the Chichimecas, the Royal Court of Mexico awarded Pedro Gomez land in Leon named, Cerro Gordo (or Cerrogordo). There was also a river that ran through the land named Rio de los Gomez because it meandered through the large ranch then onward to Leon.

Undetermined is whether ALVARO MANRIQUE (de LARA) de ZUNIGA (1525, Seville, Andalucia, Spain -1604, Seville, Andalucia, Spain) was related to Catalina Manrique de Lara, the wife of Pedro Gomez. Alvaro Manrique de Zuniga was the 1st Marquis of Villamanrique and 7th Viceroy of New Spain. He governed from 17 October 1585 to 26 January 1590. The younger son of the 4th Duke of Bejar, Francisco de Zuniga y Sotomayor, King Philip II rewarded him for his service to the Spanish crown with the title of Marques de Villamanrique. Alvaro Manrique de Zuniga ended the Chichimeca War by forbidding Spanish soldiers to shoot at the Indians, and providing food and clothing, plus land for the Chichemecas to reside. His parents were Teresa de Zuniga y Manrique de Lara, the III Duquesa de Bejar, and Alonso de Zuniga y Sotomayor, the V Count of Bejar. In addition, a "Gomez of Portugal" line which originally settled in Lagos de Moreno, Nueva Galicia, connects with our lineage via godparents (**Appendix XVII**).

JOSEPHA GOMEZ MANRIQUE de LARA (1677-1718):

Josepha Gomez Manrique de Lara was christened on 23 July 1677 at Nuestra Senora de la Soledad, Irapuato, Guanajuato, Mexico, the legitimate daughter of Pedro Gonzalez de Aguirre and Maria Bravo. The margin text read: "Josepha, espanola." The document (*Family Search #004783806; Image 326/406*) lists her mother's name as MARIA BRAVO de LAGUNAS, which was the surname of her father (Garci Bravo de Lagunas). Her mother, Maria Manrique de Lara (born abt. 1630, Sante Fe, Guanajuato, Mexico), was the daughter of Catalina Manrique de Lara (born abt. 1600, Leon, Guanajuato, Mexico) and grandchild of Gasper Gomez Manrique de Lara. Given her parent's surname combinations, Josepha Gonzales Bravo, the last of thirteen children, was also, Josepha Gomez Manrique de Lara. (**Appendix XII**).

JOSEPHA GOMEZ MANRIQUE de LARA married NICOLAS de MEDINA by 1699.

NICOLAS de MEDINA was christened on 29 September 1680 in Salvatierra, Guanajuato, Mexico. His parents were MELCHORA de MEDINA and DIEGO de la CRUZ. The Salvatierra, Guanajuato, Mexico christening document (*Salvatierra Baptism Records August 28, 1679- January 9, 1686; Image 29/120*) margin text reads: "Nicolas, of the city." The record stated: "…Baptized, Nicolas, son of Diego de la Cruz and Melchora de Medina. Godparents Pablo de Caseres and Nicolasa Perez, of the villa." Nicolas de Medina took the surname of his mother, Melchora de Medina.

MELCHORA de MEDINA married DIEGO de la CRUZ on 17 July 1670 in Salvatierra, Guanajuato, Mexico. The birth records for their other son listed the child as an, "Espanol, of the villa (Salvatierra, Guanajuato, Mexico)." (**Appendix XIII**)

San Andres de Salvatierra was founded on 9 February 1644 by Spanish viceroy Don Garcia Sarmiento de Sotomayor, 2nd Count of Salvatierra and the Marquis of Sobroso. The town was granted title of city in 1646 and became the first city in the state of Guanajuato, Mexico. It was known for its agricultural properties and located on the Lerma River. Located one-hundred miles from Leon, Salvatierra was on route to Mexico City, a city where Josepha Gomez Manrique de Lara was buried.

No marriage record for NICOLAS de MEDINA to JOSEPHA GOMEZ MANRIQUE de LARA was found prior to their son, SEBASTIAN (MANRIQUE de LARA), whose christening on 20 January 1700 denoted the parents were both Spaniards.

The known children of Nicolas de Medina and JOSEPHA GOMEZ MANRIQUE de LARA were (a):

a1. SEBASTIAN (MEDINA MANRIQUE de LARA), birthdate 20 January 1700/christening 1700, Leon, Guanajuato, Mexico (Father: Nicolas de Medina/Mother: JOSEFA *GOMEZ*, wife) (ESPANOLES) (Godfather: Nicolas Manrique/Godmother: Maria de Olaes - *Ulloa*) (Priest: R. Nicolas de Salazar) (*Leon de los Aldama. Baptism Records 1695-1704; Image 33/174*).
Married: MARIANA ANTONIA ARIAS.
The known child of Sebastian Manrique (a) and Marina Antonia Arias was:
b1. ANDRES ANTONIO MANRIQUE ARIAS, christening 16 December 1729, San Jose y Santiago, Marfil, Guanajuato, Mexico.

Death/burial 14 August 1749, El Sagrario, Leon, Guanajuato, Mexico. (*Leon. Death Certificates 1820-1823; Image 271/648*). Spouse: MARIANA ANTONIA ARIAS Record: Sebastian Manrique, Espanol.

a2. **GASPAR ANTONIO (MEDINA MANRIQUE de LARA),** born 28 March 1702, Leon, Guanajuato, Mexico. Christened April of 1702, Leon, Guanajuato, Mexico (Father: NICOLAS de MEDINA/Mother: JOSEFA MANRIQUE de LARA) (Witnesses: Don Gaspar de Alvarado and Dona T. Jauil Manrique) (*Leon de los Aldema. Baptismal Records book from 1691-1715; Image 45/128*). Book margin text: "Gaspar Antonio, Espanol de la villa."

a3. FELIPE de SANTIGO (MEDINA MANRIQUE de LARA), christened during 1707, Leon, Guanajuato, Mexico (Father: Nicolas de Medina/Mother: Josefa Manrique) (Witnesses: Joseph de Gaona, Manuela Manrique, Joseph de Lara and Julio de Dios Marquez Ramirez). Book margin text: "Felipe de Santigo, Espanol."

Josepha Gomez Manrique de Lara was buried on 2 March 1718 at Santa Veracruz, Guerrero Sureste, Distrito Federal, Mexico (*Defunciones y entierros 1760-1822; entry number 10771*). Josepha Manrique was noted as the widowed spouse of Nicolas de Medina.

The Santa Veracruz Monastery was built during 1586 in the center of Mexico City, an area later known as Colonia Guerrero. It was established originally as a religious brotherhood of knights or nobles founded by Hernan Cortes to thank God for having reached land in 1519 (Veracruz, Mexico). A priest who practiced at Santa Veracruz from 1698 to at least by 1718 was named, Phelipe Manrique de Lara. The relationship between Josepha Gomez Manrique de Lara and Phelipe Manrique de Lara, if any, has yet to be determined. Santa

Veracruz Church was the third most important religious establishment in Mexico City during the 16th century.

GASPAR ANTONIO MANRIQUE de LARA (1702-1755):

GASPAR ANTONIO MANRIQUE de LARA was born 28 March 1702 in Leon, Guanajuato, Mexico. He was christened in early April 1702 and listed (*Leon de las Aldama. Baptismal Records 1691-1715; Image 45/128 - Family Search*) in margin text as: "Gaspar Antonio, Espanol de la villa." His mother was listed as JOSEPHA MANRIQUE de LARA and his father was recorded as NICOLAS de MEDINA. His godparents were noted as Don Gaspar de Alvarado and Dona T. Jauel Manrique.

Gaspar Manrique de Lara's father, Nicolas de Medina, died prior to his mother's March 1718 burial when Gaspar Antonio Manrique de Lara was younger than age sixteen.

Gaspar Antonio MEDINA MANRIQUE de LARA gave two children the MEDINA surname while the rest retained the surname, MANRIQUE (de LARA).

By 1729 he married FRANCA. XAVIER CALDERON de HERRERA who was born 1707 in Aguascalientes, Aguascalientes, Mexico. The baptismal record of their first child stated the parents were married. All of Gaspar Manrique de Lara and Francisca Xavier Calderon de Herrera's children were baptized at El Sagrario Church in Leon, Guanajuato, Mexico with noted godparents (**Appendix VIII**). Some children were recorded as Spaniards while others mixed race which represents Francisca de Herrera's ancestry because her parents were of mixed race. Also, it is assumed priests typecast a child based on a parent's features. One of Gaspar Antonio Manrique de Lara and Francisca Xavier Calderon Herrera's children was named, MARIA JOSEPHA, likely to honor his mother, (Maria) JOSEPHA GOMEZ MANRIQUE de LARA, while another child was given the surname of his grandfather, Diego de la CRUZ.

Gaspar Antonio Manrique de Lara died on 17 September 1755, Leon, Guanajuato, Mexico. His death record noted he was a "Spaniard by origin" (*Gaspar Manrique, Spaniard).* The document also stated Gaspar Antonio was buried in the basement of El Sagrario Church in Leon, Guanajuato which meant he was a person of significance or his family had status as most individuals were buried outside the church. The record was found in the book of "Deaths" ("*Defunciones de castas" 1743-1808/1820-1823 Guanajuato, Mexico, Catholic Church Records*) (*Family Search Microfilm 4782934; Image 297/648*). Gaspar Antonio Manrique de Lara was listed as married with his spouse on the burial record noted as, "Franca de Herrera." The name, Manrique de Lara, was shortened with the birth of Gaspar Antonio Manrique de Lara's children but reappears on his grandchildren's baptismal and marriage documents.

The baptismal record for Francisca Herrera or "*Franca. Xavier Calderon Herrera*," the wife of Gaspar Antonio Manrique de Lara, was recorded at El Sagrario Church on 18 December 1707 in Aguascalientes, Aguascalientes, Mexico (Father: Cristobal Calderon/Mother: Manuela de Herrera).

Francisca Calderon de Herrera lineage extends to Aguascalientes 1595 founding. The history of this branch is quite notable as it connects to Basque Esparza and Spanish Lozano-Lavezzari lineage, as well as Moctezuma heritage (**Appendixes IX, X & XI).**

~~~~~~

The known children (MANRIQUE de LARA HERRERA) of Gaspar Antonio Manrique de Lara (a) and Francisca Xavier Calderon de Herrera were:

b1. JUE (JOSUE/*JOSHUA*) ANTONIO MANRIQUE, baptized 16 June 1730, El Sagrario, Leon, Guanajuato, Mexico (Father: Gaspar Manrique/Mother: Franca de Herrera Manrique) (Godparents: Antonio Sanchez and Maria Herrera) (Margin text: "Jue. Antto., Espanol de la villa") (*Leon de los Aldama. Baptism Records 1718-1748; Image 60/119*).

b2. MARIA JOSEPHA ESTANISLAO MANRIQUE, baptized 25 November 1731, El Sagrario, Leon, Guanajuato, Mexico (Father: Gaspar Anto. Manrique/Mother: Franca de Herrera) (Godparents: Juan de Almaxas and Dona Maria Herrera de Oxnafe) (Margin text: "Espanola de la villa") (*Leon de los Aldama. Baptism Records 1718-1748; Image 69/119*).

b3. CARLOS VINCENTE de MEDINA, baptized 2 April 1733, El Sagrario, Leon, Guanajuato, Mexico (Father: Gaspar de Medina/Mother: Franca. Herrera) (Godparents: Don Nicholas Marmolejo and Dona Maxiana Gomez) (Margin text: "Carlos Vincente, espanol de la villa") (*Leon de los Aldama. Baptisms 1718-1748; image 81/119*).

b4. **JOSEPH MANUEL MANRIQUE**, baptized 4 November 1734, El Sagrario, Leon, Guanajuato, Mexico (Father: Gaspar Manrique/Mother: Franca. de Errera Manrique) (Godparent: Rita Getrudis Marmolejo, single, Spaniard) (Espanol). Married Ana Rita Alcaras (1730-).

b5. JOSEPH EUGENIO de MEDINA, baptized 19 September 1736, El Sagrario, Leon, Guanajuato, Mexico ("legitimate son") (Father: Gaspar de Medina, Espanol/Mother: Franca Xaviera, Mestiza) (Godparents: Mathias --, Maria Antonia Manrique) (*Baptismos de Indios, Mulatos y Mestizos, 1732-1736; Image 13/23*).

b6. MARIA MAGDALENA MANRIQUE, baptized 29 July 1738, El Sagrario, Leon, Guanajuato, Mexico (Father: Gaspar Manrique/Mother: Geronima Herrera) (Godparents: Joseph Guzman and Maria de la Encarnation) (Margin text: "Ma. Magdalena *Cartilla* de la villa") (*Bautismos de Indios, Mulatos y Mestizos, Leon Baptism Records, 1731-1741; Image 50/168*).

b7. JOSEPH MARIA MANRIQUE, baptized 9 July 1743, El Sagrario, Leon, Guanajuato, Mexico (Father: *JUAN* Antonio Manrique/Mother: Franca Xaviera Herrera) (Margin text: "Joseph Maria, mestizo de la villa") (*Bautismos de Indios, Mulatos y Mestizos, 1741-1749; Image 86/172*).

b8. JOSEPH FRANCISCO MANRIQUE, baptized 9 May 1744, El Sagrario, Leon, Guanajuato, Mexico (Father: Gaspar Manriquez/Mother: Maria Franca. Herrera) (Godparents: Gregorio Infante and Getrudis Espinosa) (Margin text: "Joseph Franc., mestizo de la villa") (*Bautismos de Indios, Mulatos y Mestizos, 1741-1749; Image 121/172*).

b9. MARIA de JESUS MANRIQUE, baptized 26 May 1746, El Sagrario, Leon, Guanajuato, Mexico (Father: Gaspar Manrique/Mother: Franca Xaviera de Bierrara) (Godparents: Don Francisco Abirgo and Dona Josepha Calvillo) (Margin text: "Maria de Jesus, espanola de la villa") (*Leon de los Aldama. Baptism Records 1718-1748; Image 55/73*).

b10. MARIANA de la CRUZ MANRIQUE, baptized 27 September 1747, El Sagrario, Leon, Guanajuato, Mexico (Father: Gaspar Antonio Manrique/Mother: Francisca Xaviera Herrera) (Godparents: Diego Joseph Manrique and Mariana Lopes) (Margin text: "Mariana de la Cruz, mestiza de la villa") (*Bautismos de Indios, Mulatos y Mestizos, 1741-1749: Image 120/212*).

b11. JOSEPH JOAQUIN MANRIQUE de HERRERA, christening 12 May 1749, Parroquia de Leon, Leon, Guanajuato, Mexico (Father: Gaspar Antonio Manriquez/Mother: Maria de Herrera) (Godparents: Don Juan Sanches and Maria de Herrera) (Margin text: "Joseph Joaquin, espanol de la villa") (*Leon de los Aldama. Baptism Records 1749-1777; Image 8/318*). Death or burial date on 17 May 1749, Leon, Guanajuato, Mexico. Buried at El Sagrario Church, Leon, Guanajuato, Mexico. Text reads: "Joseph Joaquin, Espanol, the son of Gaspar, Espanol."

b12. JUAN de DIOS MANRIQUE, christening year was 1751, Leon, Guanajuato, Mexico (Father: Gaspar Manrique/Mother: Franca de Errera) (Godparents: Don Ildefonso Navarrete and Dona Rosa Lopez) (Margin text: "Juan de Dios, espanol de la villa") (*Leon de los Aldama. Baptism Records 1749-1777; Image 18/318*).

JOSEPH MANUEL MANRIQUE de LARA (1734-):

JOSEPH MANUEL MANRIQUE de LARA was born on 30 October 1734, Leon, Guanajuato, Mexico and noted as of Spanish origin ("Joseph Manuel, legitimate son, Spaniard"). He was baptized on 5 November 1734 at El Sagrario Church, Leon, Guanajuato, Mexico. The record states Joseph Manuel's parents were "residents of the town and his father was GASPAR MANRIQUE, Spaniard, while his mother was FRANCA. de HERRERA, Spaniard. The document also denotes Joseph Manuel as the "son of legitimate spouses." The godparent was listed as "Rita Gertrudis Marmolejo, single, Spaniard" (*Book of Baptisms of Spaniards 1746-1777, 1806-1814*) (*Family Search 4777478; Image 91/382*) (**Appendixes VI & VII**). Joseph Manuel Manrique Herrera does not have a known death record, and zero records were found using his mother's surname as he was known as, Manuel Manrique.

Joseph Manuel Manrique de Lara married ANA RITA ALCARAS (Spaniard, resident of Leon) in Leon, Guanajuato, Mexico but the marriage record was not located nor were death records verified for Joseph Manuel Manrique de Lara and Ana Rita Alcaras. It was confirmed Joseph Manuel Manrique de Lara was not part of the Spanish military during the American Revolutionary years at either Leon or Mexico City presidios.

ANA RITA de ALCARAS was listed as of mixed race or a "mestiza," on her 16 April 1730, Church of El Sagrario, Leon, Guanajuato, Mexico baptismal record (*Book of Baptisms of Indians, Mulattos and Mestizos, 1717-1732*). Her father was LORENSO de ALCARAS,

Spaniard, and her mother was JUANA VARRERA. Godparents were listed on her baptismal record as: Alonso Varrera and Isabel Varrera. Ana Rita Alcaras was the only person with that unique name in Guanajuato City, Marfil, Silao and Leon in Guanajuato, Mexico during the time the below children were born as Alcaras was a very unusual surname (**Appendix V**). However, an Antonia Rita Manrique de Lara did exit.

Given the name "Manuel" listed as the father's name and "Ana Rita" as the mother's name on the baptismal record of Joseph Urbano Manrique, he is the only confirmed child of Joseph Manuel Manrique de Lara and Ana Rita Alcaras (**Appendix V**).

MA was an abbreviation which could mean either Maria or Manuel. However, if there was a superscript of "L (MAL)," then the name would be confirmed as, Manuel. While the children of Joseph Manuel and Ana Rita (Alcaras) Manrique may have been documented as the children of "Joseph Maria Manrique (de Lara)," the only proven child was Joseph Urbano Manrique de Lara. To add to this uncertainty, there were four individuals named Manuel Manrique, during his lifetime (**Appendix VI**). However, Urbano Manrique de Lara's lineage was confirmed by a certified genealogist.

The first marriage (m1) record of Joseph Manuel and Ana Rita (Alcaras) Manrique's son listed his name as, Joseph Urbano Manrique de Lara, a Spaniard of origin. It was the last time the "de Lara" was added to individuals of this Manrique de Lara branch. The second marriage (m2) of Joseph Urbano Manrique de Lara listed his name as, Joseph Maria Manrique, the only time Joseph Urbano Manrique de Lara was listed as such, because on his children's baptismal records and his death record, he was listed as, Urbano Manrique. Joseph Urbano Manrique named a son, Jose Maria Manrique. Joseph Manuel was also listed as "Joseph Maria Manrique" on many of his children's baptismal records. In these instances, father (Joseph Manuel Manrique de Lara) and son (Joseph Urbano Manrique de Lara) were recorded by priests as: Joseph Maria Manrique. Joseph Maria Manrique and Ana Rita Alcaras may have also a son born during 1743 named, "Joseph Maria Manrique" who shared his father's name, but this is unproven. On the baptismal record of Joseph Diego Manrique, Joseph Manuel Manrique de Lara was listed as Joseph Maria Manriques de Lara.

Regardless of speculated children in this line, the verified grandson of Gaspar Antonio Manrique de Lara was Joseph Urbano Manrique de Lara, the son of Joseph Manuel Manrique de Lara and Ana/Anna Rita Alcaras.

<u>The known child of Joseph Manuel (a) Manrique de Lara and Ana Rita Alcaras was:</u>
    JOSEPH URBANO de la LUZ MANRIQUE de LARA (Spaniard) (legitimate son), born 25 May 1768, Leon, Guanajuato, Mexico. Baptized 25 May 1768, El Sagrario Church, Leon, Guanajuato, Mexico (Father: Joseph Manuel Manrique, Spaniard/Mother: Anna Rita Alcaras, Spaniard) (Godparents: Juan Aparicio Torres and Maria Luz de las Nieves Torres, Spaniards of the villa) (Margin text: "Joseph Urbano de la Luz, Espanol") (*Family Search Microfilm 4777477; Image 471/598*) (*Leon de Los Aldama. Baptism Records 1749-1777; Image 191/318*). <u>Married</u> MARIA MELCHORA LOPES (1784-1847) on

18 May 1799, Silao, Guanajuato, Mexico. Death/burial: 3 September 1857, El Sagrario, Leon, Guanajuato, Mexico.

JOSEPH URBANO MANRIQUE de LARA (1768-1857):

JOSEPH URBANO de la LUZ MANRIQUE de LARA was noted as a Spaniard born 25 May 1768, Leon, Guanajuato, Mexico. He was baptized ("said day and month, 1768") on 25 May 1768 or before 29 May 1768 (*previous record date in baptismal book*) at El Sagrario Church, Leon, Guanajuato, Mexico. The text records "Joseph Urbano" as the "legitimate son" of (*Father*) JOSEPH MANUEL MANRIQUE, Spaniard, of the town (*Leon*) and (*Mother*) ANNA RITA ALCARAS, Spaniard, of the town (*Leon*). His godparents were listed as: Juan Aparicio Torres and Maria Luz de las Nieves Torres. His baptismal record states: "Joseph Urbano de la Luz, legitimate son of Joseph Manuel Manrique and Anna Rita Alcaras, Spaniards of the town" (*Family Search #4777477; Image 471/598*).

Joseph Urbano de la Luz Manrique de Lara Alcaras was known as, Urbano Manrique.

It is possible Joseph Urbano Manrique de Lara married (m1) ROSA LOPES on 29 August 1792 at Santa Fe Church, Sante Fe, Guanajuato, Mexico. The marriage document listed the full surname of: Manrique de Lara. However, there was no record for Urbano's possible first wife's death and an individual named, Jose Urbano Manrique, shared a similar age, but not the "de Lara" surname addition. Joseph Maria (Urbano de la Luz) Manrique (de Lara) married (m2) MARIA MELCHORA REYES LOPES on 18 May 1799 at Santiago Apostal Church in Silao, Guanajuato, Mexico.

Urbano Manrique died or was buried on 3 September 1857 at El Sagrario Church, Leon, Guanajuato, Mexico. His wife was listed as: Melchor Lopes.

The marriage document of Urbano Manrique de Lara and Maria Melchora Lopes reads:

In the congregation of Silao on the 18th of May of the year 1799, I the Bachelor Don Rafael de Servantes with permission from the Priest on duty, having preceded without impediment the three notices of the Council (of Trent) of Josef Maria Manrique, Spaniard by origin and resident of Rancho de Bonillas, and Dona Maria Melchora Lopes, Spaniard by origin and resident of La Canada de Amargura of this Parish, and being present in the Parish Church of said Congregation, I solemnly married and veiled in accordance with the order of our Holy Mother Church, having determined the mutual consent of both, and being Witnesses Don Josef Maria Aranjo and Josef Joaquin Garrea (?) Spaniards of this neighborhood, and godparents Francisco Manrique and Maria Catarina, residents of Rancho de Bonillas, and to certify I signed along with the Priest on duty, Signatures of Francisco (illegible surname) and Rafael Servantes."

From the Santiago Apostal Church, Silao, Guanajuato, Mexico record: "18 May 1799. Groom name: Josef Maria Manrique, of Spanish origin. Groom residence: Rancho de Bonillas. Bride name: Maria Melchora Lopes, of Spanish origin. Bride residence: La Canada de Amarguita of this parish. Godparents: Francisco Manrique and Maria Catarina, residents of Rancho Bonilla. Witnesses: Josef Maria Araujo and Josef Joaquin Larrea, Spaniards of this neighborhood." The record (*Family Search 4804705; Image 212/376*) denoted "Josef Maria Manrique" as groom which is likely an error of the recorder as all children of Maria Melchora Lopes are listed with a father named, Joseph Urbano Manrique (de Lara). As with Joseph Manuel and Ana Rita Alcaras possible children, the name "Joseph Maria" is substituted by the priest for Joseph Urbano.

MARIA MELCHORA REYES LOPES was born on or before the 17th of January 1784 in La Canada de Amargura, Guanajuato, Mexico. She was christened on 17 January 1784 at Parroquia de Silao, Guanajuato, Mexico, the daughter of NICOLAS NARCISO LOPES (born abt. 1750) and JUANA JOSEFA GERTRUDIS GONZALEZ (born abt. 1750). Extended family listed on her christening document included: "Godfather - Francisco Antonio Gonzales. Francisco Jaso Tieniente, B. Carlos de Aguirre and Francisco Jose." Maria Melchora Reyes Lopes died (at age 63) on 14 March 1847 in Leon, Guanajuato, Mexico and was buried at El Sagrario Church, Leon, Guanajuato, Mexico. Maria Melchora (Lopes) Manrique's death record states: "Urbana Manrique spouse: Melchor Lopez."

The father of Maria Melchora REYES Lopes was Nicolas Narciso (Reyes) Lopes who died 30 October 1804, Leon, Guanajuato, Mexico and was buried at Santiago Apostol Church, Guanajuato, Mexico. His spouse was: Maria Josefa (Gertrudis) Gonzales.

<u>The known children (LOPES GONZALEZ) of Nicolas Narciso Lopes (a) and Juana Josefa Gonzalez were</u>:
- b1. MARIA DOLORES JOSEFA ESPINOLA LOPEZ GONZALES, baptized 2 April 1778, Nuestra Senora de Guanajuato, Guanajuato, Guanajuato, Mexico (Father: Don Nicolas Lopes/Mother: Dona Josefa Gonzalez, wife) (Espanol).
- b2. MARIA MELCHORA REYES (LOPES), christening date was 17 January 1784 at Parroquia de Silao, Silao, Guanajuato, Mexico (Father: Nicholas Narciso Lopes/Juana Josefa Gonzales, wife). <u>Married</u> **JOSEPH URBANO MANRIQUE** on 16 May 1799, Silao, Guanajuato, Mexico, as "Dona MA Melchora Lopes, Spaniard, resident of Rancho de la Amargura." Death/burial 14 March 1847, Sagrario, Leon, Guanajuato, Mexico.
- b3. MARIA ANTONIA LOPES, born abt. 1786, La Canada de Amargura, Guanajuato, Mexico *(Godparent to Maria Francisca Manrique*, the daughter of sister, MA Melchora Lopes).*
- b4. MARIA TOMASA LOPEZ, born abt. 1788, Guanajuato, Mexico. <u>Married</u> JOSEF CESARIO GOMEZ (son of Josef Guillermo Gomez and Maria Josefa Esparza) on 1 May 1803 at Santiago Apostol, Santiago Maravatio, Guanajuato, Mexico (Father: Nicolas Lopez/Juana Josefa Gonzalez, wife).
- b5. JOSE MANUEL LOPES, christening date was 25 December 1791, Sante Fe, San Felipe, Guanajuato, Mexico (Father: Nicolas Lopes/Mother: Maria Josefa). Died 2 March 1792, Yuriria,

Guanajuato, Mexico (Father: Jose Lopes/Mother: Maria Josepha).

b6. MARIA JULIANA LOPES, born abt. 1792, Guanajuato, Mexico. Died 13 April 1795, Yuriria, Guanajuato, Mexico (Place: Nuestra Senora del Socorro, Yuriria, Guanajuato, Mexico. Marital Status: Single. Race: I [White]. Ethnicity: IRISH. Father: Nicholas Lopes. Mother: Maria Josefa).

b7. MARIA SINFORIANA ROMANA (RAMONA) LOPES, baptized 27 August 1795, Nuestra Senora de los Dolores, Dolores Hidalgo, Guanajuato, Mexico (Espanol) (Father: Nicholas Lopes/Mother: *Gertrudis Gonzales*). Married (m1) Salvador Guzman de Manzano on 20 February 1811, Nuestra Senora de los Dolores, Guanajuato, Mexico (Father: Nicholas Lopes/ Mother: MA Gertrudis Gonzales)/(m2) Engagement to JOSE LEOCADIO PICON GUERRA on 18 April 1818, Nuestra Senora de Guanajuato, Guanajuato, Guanajuato, Mexico (age 23/MA Ramona Lopez) (Father: Nicholas Lopez/Mother: Maria Gertrudis Gonzales). Married 1 May 1818 Nuestra Senora de Guanajuato, Guanajuato, Guanajuato, Mexico (Father: Nicholas Lopes/Mother: *Gertrudis Gonzales*).

b8. JOSE FRANCISCO MANUEL CASILDO LOPES, baptized 29 September 1797, Nuestra Senora de los Dolores, Dolores Hildalgo, Guanajuato, Mexico (Father: Nicholas Lopes/Mother: Gertrudis Gonzales). Died 12 February 1798, Yuriria, Guanajuato, Mexico (Place: Nuestra Senora del Socorro, Yuriria, Guanajuato, Mexico. Marital Status: Single. Race: I [White], Ethnicity: IRISH. Father: Nicolas Lopes. Mother: Maria Josefa, wife).

The known children (MANRIQUE de LARA LOPES) of Joseph Urbano Manrique de Lara (c) and Maria Melchora Lopes were:

d1. MARIA FRANCISCA MANRIQUE, born 18 February 1800, La Canada de Amargura, Guanajuato, Mexico. Baptized 19 February 1800, Santiago Apostal, Silao, Guanajuato, Mexico (Father: Urbano Manrique, resident La Canada de Amargura/Mother: Maria Melchora Lopes, resident La Canada de Amargura) (Godparents: Miguel Garivay y *Maria Antonia Lopez**).

d2. MARIA MICAELA MANRIQUE, baptized 20 June 1801, Santiago Apostol, Santiago, Maravatio, Guanajuato, Mexico (Father: Urbano Manrique/Mother: Melchora Lopes) (Document text: "Infante Espanola de la Canada de Amargura").

d3. **JOSE ISIDRO MANRIQUE**, baptized 17 May 1804, El Sagrario, Leon, Guanajuato, Mexico (Father: Urbano Manrique/Mother: Melchora Lopes). Married MARIA BIBIANA MORENO BOCANEGRA (1806-) on 27

February 1827, Leon, Guanajuato, Mexico (Espanol - birth/marriage records) **(Appendix IV)**.

d4. FELIPA ROZALIA MANRIQUE, baptized 5 May 1807, Santiago Apostol, Santiago, Maravatio, Guanajuato, Mexico (Parents: Urbano Manrique and wife, Melchora Reyes) (Espanol).

d5. CIRILA MANRIQUE, born abt. 1810, Leon, Guanajuato, Mexico. Married CECILIO RAMIREZ (b. 1790) on 30 January 1828, Guanajuato, Mexico. Died 17 June 1905 (age 95) in Leon, Guanajuato, Mexico (Father: Urbano Manrique/Mother: Melchor) (Espanol).

d6. JOSE INES RAMON MANRIQUE, baptized 23 January 1813, El Sagrario, Leon, Guanajuato, Mexico (Father: Urbano Manrique/Mother: Maria Melchora Lopez) (Manrique - Lopez) (Espanol).

d7. MARIA APOLONIA de SAN JUAN MANRIQUE, christening date was 13 April 1814, Purisima del Rincon, Guanajuato, Mexico (Father: Urbano Manrique/Mother: Maria Melchor Reyes) (Espanol). Married JOSE ANTONIO BOCANEGRA (b. 1804) (*Brother Isidro married, BIBIANA BOCANEGRA, sister to Jose Antonio Bocanegra*) on 20 June 1830, Leon, Guanajuato, Mexico (**Appendix IV**).

d8. JOSE MARIA MANRIQUE, baptized 30 November 1815, Leon de los Aldama, Guanajuato, Mexico (Father: Urbano Manrique/Mother: Melchora Mena) (Godparents: Pedro de Lara, Ignacia Manrique) (legitimate son) (Espanol) (*Leon de los Aldama. Baptism Records 1814-1821; Image 105/414*). Married MARIA TOMASA NUNES (baptized 25 September 1813, El Sagrario, Guanajuato, Guanajuato, Mexico) (Espanola) (Father: Vicente Nunes/Mother: Maria Dorotea Razo) (**Appendix II**).

The known children of JOSE MARIA MANRIQUE (d) and MARIA TOMASA NUNES (a) were:

e1. EVARISTO MANRIQUE, baptized 28 October 1836, El Sagrario, Leon, Guanajuato, Mexico (Father: Jose Ma. Manrique/Mother: Tomasa Nunes). Married MARIA de JESUS GARCIA (Father: Dioncio Garcia/Mother: Macedonia Reyes) on 29 September 1866, Nuestra Senora de Senora/San Miguel de Leon, Guanajuato, Guanajuato, Mexico (Father: J. Ma. Manrique/Mother: Tomasa Nunez).

e2. HIGINIA MANRIQUE, baptized 13 January 1838, El Sagrario, Leon, Guanajuato, Mexico (Father: Je. Maria Manrique/Mother: Tomasa Nunes).

e3. ZEPHARINA de los DOLORES RESPLANDON MANRIQUE, baptized 28 August 1841, El Sagrario, Leon, Guanajuato, Mexico (Father: Jose Maria Manrique/Mother: Tomasa Nunes) (*Leon de los Aldama. Baptism Records 1840-1846; Image 58/371*). Married MARTIN DURAN on 16 November 1861, Nuestra Senora de Guanajuato, Guanajuato, Guanajuato, Mexico.

e4. JOSE JULIAN de la LUZ MANRIQUE, baptized 19 February 1843, El Sagrario, Leon, Guanajuato, Mexico (Father: Jose Ma. Manrique/Mother: Tomasa Nunes) (*Bautismos de hijos legitimos*

1843-1844; b89/p25). <u>Married</u> MARIA CRISTOBAL SOLIS (daughter of Prudencio Solis and Juana Rodriquez) on 3 March 1856, Nuestra Senora de Guanajuato, Guanajuato, Guanajuato, Mexico (Father: Jose Ma. Manrique/Mother: Tomasa Nunes).

    e5.   JOSE CELEDONIO MANRIQUE, baptized 9 December 1844, El Sagrario, Leon, Guanajuato, Mexico (Father: Jose Ma. Manrique/Mother: Tomasa Nunes) (*Bautismos de hijos legitimos 1845-1846; b91/pp 9-10 December 1845*) (Father: Je. Ma. Manrique/Mother: Tomasa Nunes).

    e6.   MARIA PONCIANA MANRIQUE, baptized 20 November 1846, El Sagrario, Guanajuato, Guanajuato, Mexico (Father: Jose Ma. Manrique/Mother: Tomasa Nunes). Burial 28 November 1847 (Maria Ponciana Manrique) (age 1) Nuestra Senora de Guanajuato, Leon, Guanajuato, Mexico (Father: Je. Ma. Manrique/Mother: Tomasa Nunes).

    e7.   EULOGIA ANTONIA MANRIQUE, death/burial 12 March 1849, Nuestra Senora de Guanajuato, Leon, Guanajuato, Mexico (Father: Je. Ma. Manrique/Mother: Tomasa Nunes (*Leon. Death Certificates 1848-1850; Image 159/356*).

d9.   MARIA VIVIANA MANRIQUE, born abt. 1816, Leon, Guanajuato, Mexico. <u>Married</u> JULIAN REYNOSO on 2 February 1837, El Sagrario, Leon, Guanajuato, Mexico (Father: Urbano Manrique/Mother: MA Melchora Lopes) (Espanoles). Death/Burial 1 November 1849, El Sagrario, Leon, Guanajuato, Mexico.

d10.   MARIA GREGORIA RAMONA de JESUS MANRIQUE, baptized 21 November 1819, El Sagrario, Leon, Guanajuato, Mexico (Father: Urbano Manrique/Mother: Maria Reyes) (Espanol).

d11.   FRANCO del CARMEL MANRIQUE, baptized 14 October 1824, El Sagrario, Leon, Guanajuato, Mexico (Father: Jesus Urbano Manrique/Mother: Maria Reyes) (Espanol).

d12.   INIGIO MANRIQUE, born 1827, Leon, Guanajuato, Mexico. <u>Married</u> PAULINA BARAJAS (b. 1827) on 6 August 1845, San Diego de Alejandria, Jalisco, Mexico (La Immaculate Conception Church marriage record: Father: Urbano Manrique/Mother: Melchora Lopez).

JOSE ISIDRO MANRIQUE (1804-):

JOSE ISIDRO MANRIQUE was born on or before the 17th of May 1804, Leon, Guanajuato, Mexico and baptized on 17 May 1804 at El Sagrario Church, Leon, Guanajuato, Mexico ("*Bautismos de Espanoles, 1796-1809," El Sagrario, Leon Guanajuato; Image 135/257*). The book margin text states: "JOSE ISIDRO, Espanol of the villa." His father was listed as Urbano Manrique and mother was listed as Melchora Lopes. The godparents were Juan Espinosa and Antonia Lopes. Maria Antonia Lopes was Melchora Lopes' sister and Jose Isidro's aunt.

Isidro Manrique married MARIA DOLORES BIBIANA MORENO BOCANEGRA (born 1806) on 27 February 1827 at the (Sagrario) Parroquia de San Sebastian de la Villa in Leon,

Guanajuato, Mexico. The parents of the spouses were listed as (groom) Urbano Manrique and Melchora Lopes/(bride) Antonio Bocanegra and Rita Torres y Manrique (**Appendix IV**). The marriage record noted both bride and groom were Spaniards.

Jose Isidro Manrique Lopes was known as Isidro Manrique.

MARIA DOLORES BIBIANA BOCANEGRA was born 2 December 1806 and christened 7 December 1806 at Nuestra Senora de Guanajuato, Leon, Guanajuato, Mexico. Her father was Don Jose Antonio Bocanegra and her mother was Dona Rita Antonia Torres y Manrique ("infanta Espanola") (*Guanajuato Baptism Records 1806-1808; Image 62/141*). Her brother, JOSE ANTONIO BOCANEGRA, married Isidro Manrique's sister, Maria Apolonia Manrique.

No death records were found for Jose Isidro Manrique or Maria Dolores Bibiana Bocanegra y Manrique.

The known children (MANRIQUE BOCANEGRA) of Isidro Manrique (d) and Bibiana Bocanegra were:
- e1. SIMEON **(SIMON)** de JESUS **MANRIQUE**, baptized 19 February 1835, Sagrario, Leon, Guanajuato, Mexico (Father: ISIDRO MANRIQUE/Mother: VIBIANA BOCANEGRA). Married SERAPIA GONZALEZ (daughter of Luciano Gonzalez and Santos Ramirez) on 8 April 1856, El Sagrario, Leon, Guanajuato, Mexico. Died 29 March 1895, Sauz de Armenta, Guanajuato, Mexico (Spaniard).
- e2. AGAPITA MANRIQUE, born abt. 1837, Leon, Guanajuato, Mexico. Died age 0 on 27 August 1837, Leon, Guanajuato, Mexico. Buried El Sagrario, Leon, Guanajuato, Mexico (Father: Isidro Manrique/Wife: Viviana Moreno).
- e3. MARIA JUANA MANRIQUE, baptized 26 June 1844, El Sagrario, Leon, Guanajuato, Mexico (Father: Isidro Manrique/Mother: Bibiana Bocanegra). Married PLACIDO FUENTES (son of Salome Fuentes and Rosalia Buzo) on 6 November 1862, El Sagrario, Leon, Guanajuato, Mexico. Died 6 November 1889, Leon, Guanajuato, Mexico.
- e4. JOSE MIGUEL MANRIQUE, born abt. 1847, Leon, Guanajuato, Mexico. Baptized *(no date)* at El Sagrario, Leon, Guanajuato, Mexico (Father: Isidro Manrique/Wife: Vibiana Bocanegra). Married NARCISA REYNOSO. Died 6 September 1907, Leon, Guanajuato, Mexico (Father's name: Isidro Manrique/Mother's name: Bibiana).

    The known children of Jose Miguel Manrique (e) and Narcisa Reynoso were:
    - f1. AMBROSIA MANRIQUE, baptized 8 December 1871, San Miguel de Leon, Leon, Guanajuato, Mexico.
    - f2. VIDAL MANRIQUE, baptized 29 April 1873, San Miguel de Leon, San Miguel de Leon, Leon, Guanajuato, Mexico.

- f3. JOSE (M)NICANOR MANRIQUE, christening 11 January 1875, San Miguel de Leon, Leon, Guanajuato, Mexico. Birthplace: Mirasol, Guanajuato, Mexico.
- f4. JOSE JUBENCIO MANRIQUE, christening 26 January 1877, San Miguel de Leon, Leon, Guanajuato, Mexico.
- f5. JOSE GERARDO MANRIQUE, born 6 October 1878, San Miguel de Leon, Leon, Guanajuato, Mexico.
- f6. JOSE LUIS de JESUS MANRIQUE, born 22 June 1879, San Miguel de Leon, Leon, Guanajuato, Mexico.
- f7. JESUS LADISLADO MANRIQUE, baptized 29 June 1880, San Miguel de Leon, Guanajuato, Mexico.
- f8. MARIA CRUZ MANRIQUE, born 4 August 1881, Leon, Guanajuato, Mexico. Christening location: San Miguel de Leon, Leon, Guanajuato, Mexico.
- f9. MARIA SOLEDAD MANRIQUE, christening 11 April 1884, San Miguel de Leon, Leon, Guanajuato, Mexico.
- f10. JOSE WENCESLAO MANRIQUE, christening 29 September 1885, San Miguel de Leon, Leon, Guanajuato, Mexico.
- f11. BRIGIDO MANRIQUE, christening 12 October 1889, San Miguel de Leon, Leon, Guanajuato, Mexico.

SIMON (SIMEON) MANRIQUE (1835-1895):

SIMON de JESUS MANRIQUE was born on or before the 19th of February 1835 in Leon, Guanajuato, Mexico and baptized on 19 February 1835 at El Sagrario Church in Leon, Guanajuato, Mexico (*Leon de los Aldama. Baptism Records 1834-1835; Image 86/120*). His father was Isidro Manrique and his mother was Vibiana Bocanegra. Simon Manrique's godparents were Antonio Ramirez and Antonia Paz.

Simon de Jesus Manrique Bocanegra was known as, Simon Manrique.

Simon Manrique married SERAPIA GONZALEZ on 8 April 1856 at El Sagrario Church, Leon, Guanajuato, Mexico. The marriage was recorded in the book, "*Leon, Matrimonios de Espanoles 1854-1862 (Image 114/296)*." The groom's parents were listed as: Isidro Manrique and Bibiana Bocanegra. The bride's parents were recorded as: Luciana Gonzales and Maria Santos Ramirez. The godparents were Ignacio and Juana Rivas.

SIMON MANRIQUE died 29 March 1895 (age 80, born 1815) in El Sauz, San Francisco del Rincon, Guanajuato, Mexico (Death place: Sauz de Armenta, Mexico. Father: Isidro Manrique. Mother: Viviana Moreno. Spouse: SUAPIA GONZALES). The burial document noted the mother of Simon Manrique was BIBIANA BOCANEGRA.

MARIA SERAPIA de la TRINIDAD del MIRASOL GONZALEZ was born 13 December 1839, Leon, Guanajuato, Mexico. She was baptized 16 December 1839, El Sagrario, Leon, Guanajuato, Mexico. Her father was LUCIANO GONZALEZ, and her mother was MARIA SANTOS RAMIREZ. Her godparents were Rosario Sess-- and Vicente Ramirez) (*Leon de los Aldama. Baptism Records 1836-1840; Image 379/540) (Text: Day 16 baptized/3 days old - born 13 December).* Serapia Gonzalez' death registration took place on 6 December 1888 in Leon, Guanajuato, Mexico (Father: Luciano Gonzalez/Mother: Maria Santos Ramirez/ Spouse: Simon Manrique) (**Appendix III**).

<u>The known children (MANRIQUE GONZALEZ) of Simon Manrique (e) and Serapia Gonzales were:</u>

- f1. FELIX MANRIQUE, baptized 12 July 1857, El Sagrario, Leon, Guanajuato, Mexico (Father: Simon Manrique/Mother: Serapia Gonzalez).
- f2. MARIA BRAULIA MANRIQUE, baptized 28 March 1859, San Miguel de Leon, Leon, Guanajuato, Mexico.
- f3. BELEN MANRIQUE, baptized 24 January 1860, El Sagrario, Leon, Guanajuato, Mexico (Father: Simon Manrique/Maria Serapia Gonzalez, wife with Maria Braulia Manrique, daughter).
- f4. ESTANISLADO del MIRASOL MANRIQUE, baptized 7 May 1861, El Sagrario, Leon, Guanajuato, Mexico (Father: Simon Manrique/Mother: Serapia Gonzales).
- f5. **CLEMENTE MANRIQUE**, baptized 24 November 1862, El Sagrario, Leon, Guanajuato, Mexico (Father: SIMON MANRIQUE/Mother: SERAPIA GONZALES). <u>Married</u> PETRA DURAN (1866-). Died 6 January 1920, Leon, Guanajuato, Mexico.
- f6. JOSE de la CRUZ MANRIQUE, baptized 5 May 1866, San Miguel de Leon, Leon, Guanajuato, Mexico (Father: Simon Manrique/Mother: Serapia Gonzalez).
- f7. MARIA MAGDALENA MANRIQUE, christening 26 May 1867, San Miguel de Leon, Leon, Guanajuato, Mexico (Father: Simon Manrique/Mother: Serapia Gonzales).
- f8. MARIA SIXTO MANRIQUE, born abt. 1871, Leon, Guanajuato, Mexico. <u>Married</u> LUIS ROCHA (Parents: Antonio and Lucia Rocha) on 20 May 1889, Leon, Guanajuato, Mexico (Spouse's parents: Simon Manrique and Serapia Gonzalez).
- f9. ALTAGRACIA MANRIQUE, christening 7 February 1875, San Miguel de Leon, Leon, Guanajuato, Mexico (Father: Simon Manrique/Mother: Serapia Gonzalez). <u>Married</u> ANTONIO DIAZ. Died 26 February 1920, Leon, Guanajuato, Mexico (Father: Simon Manrique/Mother: Serapia Gonzales/Spouse: ANTONIO DIAZ).
- f10. JOSE EUGENIO ESTANISLAO MANRIQUE, christening 15 November 1876, San Miguel de Leon, Leon, Guanajuato, Mexico. Birthplace - Capellania (Father: Simon Manrique/Mother: Serapia Gonzalez).
- f11. MARIA de la LUZ MANRIQUE, baptized 26 May 1887, San Miguel del Leon, Leon, Guanajuato, Mexico. Died 23 September

1887 age 0 (three months), Leon, Guanajuato, Mexico (Father: Simon Manrique/Mother: Serapia Gonzalez).

CLEMENTE MANRIQUE (1862-1920):

CLEMENTE MANRIQUE was born on or before 24 November 1862 and baptized on 24 November 1862 at El Sagrario Church, Leon, Guanajuato, Mexico. His father was Simon Manrique. His mother was Serapia Gonzales. His godparent and maternal grandfather was Luciano Gonzales (*Leon. Baptism Records 1862; Image 291/322*). Clemente Manrique married PETRA DURAN (**Appendix II**) although the document was not found. Clemente Manrique died on 6 January 1920 in Leon, Guanajuato, Mexico. His death record noted his father was Simon Duran (*text should have recorded his father as, Simon Manrique*) and his mother was Zarapia Duran (*text should have recorded his mother as, Serapia Gonzales*) (*Mexico, Guanajuato, Civil Registration, 1862-1930, Guanajuato, Leon Defunciones 1920; Image 13/785*). The Duran surname was Clemente Manrique's wife's maiden name - Petra *Duran*.

Clemente Manrique Gonzales was known as Clemente Manrique. He was a farmer who owned a rancho which consisted of twenty acres (*My Mother's Garden*, page 4). This property was likely in Silao de la Victoria, an agricultural area near Leon where his son, Serapio Manrique, was born. It is also speculated, like many Leon residents, he was also a shoemaker.

MARIA PETRONILA DURAN was baptized on 31 May 1866 at San Miguel de Leon, Leon, Guanajuato, Mexico. Her father was Martin Duran and her mother was Zepharina Manrique. Martin Duran, the son of Juan Duran and Maria Dolores Gonzales, married Ceferina Manrique, the daughter of Jose Maria Manrique and Tomasa Nunes, on 16 December 1861 in Leon, Guanajuato, Mexico. Zeferina Manrique (**Appendix II**) was the daughter of Clemente Manrique's grandfather's brother. She was baptized Zepharina de los Dolores Resplandon Manrique on 28 August 1841, El Sagrario, Leon, Guanajuato, Mexico and died 10 April 1920 (age 75 born 1845) in Leon, Guanajuato, Mexico (Father's name: Jose Maria Manrique/ Mother: Tomasa Nunes/Spouse: Martin Duran).

The known children of Martin Duran (a) and Zeferina Manrique were:
b1. MARIA PETRONILA DURAN, baptized 31 May 1866, Leon, Guanajuato, Mexico. Married **CLEMENTE MANRIQUE**.
b2. JUANA DURAN, born abt. 1877, born Leon, Guanajuato, Mexico. Married DIONICIO BARAJAS (parents Vincente Barajas and Maria Guadalupe Fernandez) on 14 August 1893 in Leon, Guanajuato, Mexico (Spouse's parents: Martin Duran and Zeferina Manrique).

The known children (MANRIQUE DURAN) of Clemente Manrique (f) and Petra Duran were:
g1. JUAN MANRIQUE, born abt. 1889, Leon, Guanajuato, Mexico. Age 0 - Christening date: 10 January 1889, San Miguel de Leon, Guanajuato,

    Mexico (Father: Clemente Manrique/Mother: Petra Duran) (*Possible twin/triplet*).
g2. JOSE MANRIQUE, born 18 January 1889, Leon, Guanajuato, Mexico. Died 18 January 1889, Leon, Guanajuato, Mexico (Father: Clemente Manrique/Mother: Petra Duran) (*Possible twin/triplet*).
g3. MARIA LUZ MANRIQUE, born 1889, Leon, Guanajuato, Mexico. Died 11 November 1889, Leon, Guanajuato, Mexico (Father: Clemente Manrique/Mother: Petra Duran) (*Possible twin/triplet*).
g4. **SERAPIO MANRIQUE DURAN**, born 14 November 1891, Silao de la Victoria, Guanajuato, Mexico. Birth Registration: 23 November 1891, Silao, Guanajuato, Mexico (Father: Clemente Manrique/Mother: Petra Duran). Married (m1) JULIA MACHADO (b. 1896, San Francisco, California, USA; d. 23 April 1917, Oakdale, Stanislaus, California, USA) on 11 August 1913, Oakdale, Stanislaus, California, USA/(m2) MARY HOPKINS (b. 29 July 1900, San Francisco, California, USA; d. 27 February 1978, Oakdale, Stanislaus, California, USA) on 26 December 1917, Stockton, San Joaquin, California, USA. d. 29 December 1952, Oakdale, Stanislaus, California.

The children of Serapio (g) and (m1) Julia (Machado) Manrique were:

h1. PRIMITIVO MANRIQUE (b. 26 July 1914, Oakdale, Stanislaus, California, USA; d. 19 January 2011, Modesto, Stanislaus, California, USA). Married LULA BELLE WYATT.

The children of Primitivo (h) and Lula (Wyatt) Manrique were:
 i1. ROBERT MANRIQUE (b. 1938).
 i2. LOUISE MANRIQUE (b. 1940).
 i3. RICHARD MANRIQUE (b. 1941).
 i4. SHIRLEY MANRIQUE (b. 1942).
 i5. BEVERLY MANRIQUE (b. 1945).
 i6. JAMES MANRIQUE (b. 1948).
 i7. CHARLES MANRIQUE (b. 1950).

h2. DOLORES LAURA MANRIQUE (b. 2 May 1916, San Francisco, California, USA; d. 24 November 1997, San Francisco, California, USA). Married CASTOR PONGAN in 1936.

The children of Serapio (g) and (m2) Mary (Hopkins) Manrique were:

h3. VINCENT JOSEPH MANRIQUE (b. 5 April 1919, Oakdale, Stanislaus, California, USA; d. 31 December 2014, Tucson, Arizona, USA).

Married BERNICE MAYR on 1 October 1949, Alameda, California, USA.
The children of Vincent (h) and Bernice (Mayr) Manrique were:
i1. CYNTHIA MANRIQUE (b. 1950).
i2. GEORGE MANRIQUE (b. 1954).

h4. JENNY MANRIQUE (b. 17 July 1920, Oakdale, Stanislaus, California, USA; d. 15 January 1936, Oakdale, Stanislaus, California, USA).

h5. LAWRENCE MAXWELL MANRIQUE (b. 1 December 1921, Oakdale, Stanislaus, California, USA; d. 11 June 1981, Fremont, Alameda, California, USA).
Married IDA SANTANA in 1954.
The children of Lawrence (h) and Ida (Santana) Manrique were:
i1. DAVID MANRIQUE (b. 1946).
i2. ANITA MANRIQUE (b. 1948).
i3. LAWRENCE MANRIQUE (b. 1953).
i4. CHRISTOPHER MANRIQUE (b.1961).

h6. LEONA (LINDA) MANRIQUE (b. 23 March 1923, Oakdale, Stanislaus, California, USA; d. 17 January 2001, Concord, California, USA).
Married (m1) DAN GALLEGOS/(m2) THOMAS VALENCIA.
The children of Dan (m1) and Linda (h) Manrique Gallegos were:
i1. RAMONA VALENCIA (b. 1941).
i2. VIRGINIA VALENCIA (b. 1942).
The children of Thomas (m2) and Linda (h) (Manrique) Valencia were:
i3. NANCY VALENCIA (b. 1948).
i4. STEVE VALENICA (b. 1956).

h7. (ALBERT) STEVEN (FRANK) MANRIQUE (b. 5 September 1924, Oakdale, Stanislaus, California, USA; d. 17 October 1924, Oakdale, Stanislaus, California, USA).

h8. ARTHUR (ARTURO) HOPKINS MANRIQUE (b. 5 September 1924, Oakdale, Stanislaus, California, USA; d. 1926, Oakdale, Stanislaus, California, USA).

h9. JOSEPH HOPKINS MANRIQUE (b. 5 September 1924, Stanislaus, California, USA; d. 13 January 2009, Modesto, Stanislaus, California, USA).

Married SHARON AMARAL in 1959.

The children of Joseph (h) and Sharon (Amaral) Manrique were:

i1. ANDRE MANRIQUE (b. 1959).
i2. JEFFERY MANRIQUE (b. 1960).
i3. ANNETTE MANRIQUE (b. 1963).

h10. (JOHN) RAYMOND MANRIQUE (b. 16 May 1928, Oakdale, Stanislaus, California, USA; d. 12 April 1998, San Leandro, Alameda, California, USA).

Married DOROTHY BROWN in 1952.

The children of Raymond (h) and Dorothy (Brown) Manrique were:

i1. ROXANN MANRIQUE (b. 1953).
i2. JOHN MANRIQUE (b. 1955).
i3. DENISE MANRIQUE (b. 1957).
i4. ALLEN MANRIQUE (b. 1960).

h11. JULIUS CLEMENT MANRIQUE (b. 8 April 1932, Oakdale, Stanislaus, California, USA; d. 10 December 2023, Modesto, Stanislaus, California, USA).

Married BARBARA PINKHAM on 29 July 1963, Toronto, Ontario, Canada.

The children of Julius C. (h) and Barbara (Pinkham) Manrique were:

i1. ANNE MANRIQUE (b. 1965).
i2. Daughter MANRIQUE (b. 1967).

h12. EDWARD MANRIQUE (b. 12 April 1934, Oakdale, Stanislaus, California, USA; d. 14 December 2005, Oakdale, Stanislaus, California, USA).

Married (m1) VIOLA PORTER in 1955/(m2) ANNETTE LESHER in 1972.

The children of Edward (h) and (m1) Viola (Porter) Manrique were:

i1. EDDIE MANRIQUE (b.1955).
i2. MICHAEL MANRIQUE (b. 1957).
i3. WILLIAM MANRIQUE (b. 1959).
i4. JAMES MANRIQUE (b. 1960).
i5. SUSAN MANRIQUE (b. 1961).

h13. ALICE MANRIQUE (b. 22 October 1935, Oakdale, Stanislaus, California, USA).

Married ELMO GARCIA in 1951.

The children of Elmo and Alice (h) (Manrique) Garcia were:

i1. JOHN GARCIA (b. 1952).
i2. LORETTA GARCIA (b. 1955).

     i3. DONNA GARCIA (b. 1959).
   h14. STEVEN (RICHARD) MANRIQUE (b. 10 March 1937, Oakdale, Stanislaus, California, USA; d. 9 September 2018, Modesto, Stanislaus, California, USA).
     <u>Married</u> (m1) BRENDA SWINDELL in 1959/(m2) DONNA ELWESS.
   <u>The children of Richard (h) and (m1) Brenda (Swindell) Manrique were:</u>
   i1. KIMBERLY MANRIQUE (b. 1961).
   i2. KELLY MANRIQUE (b. 1964).
   <u>The child of Richard (h) and (m2) Donna (Elwess) Manrique was:</u>
   i3. RICHARD MANRIQUE (b. 1976).
   h15. TONY MANRIQUE (b. 13 June 1938, Oakdale, Stanislaus, California, USA).
     <u>Married</u> (m1) RICKY VAN ORSDALE in 1958/(m2) BARBARA WILKINSON in 1984.
   <u>The children of Tony (h) and (m1) Ricky (Van Orsdale) Manrique were:</u>
   i1. ANTHONY MANRIQUE (b. 1959).
   i2. JEANETTE MANRIQUE (b. 1960).
   h16. MADELINE VIOLET MANRIQUE (b. 13 January 1940, Oakdale, Stanislaus, California, USA; d. 27 December 1944, Oakdale, Stanislaus, California, USA).
 g5. PRIMITIVO MANRIQUE, christening 11 June 1892, El Sagrario, Leon, Guanajuato, Mexico (Listed on record: Justo Gonzales, Petra Duran, Zeferina Manrique, Martin Duran, Rafael Ortiz Justo, Clemente Manrique). <u>Married</u> ANTONIA BARRON.
  <u>The known children of Primitivo (g) and Antonia (Barron) Manrique were:</u>
  h1. REINALDO PUENTE MANRIQUE, baptized 31 January 1943, El Sagrario, Leon, Guanajuato, Mexico (Father: Primitivo Manrique/Mother: Antonia Barron).
  h2. PETRA MANRIQUE BARROS, baptized 27 November 1944, El Sagrario, Leon, Guanajuato, Mexico (Father: Primitivo Manrique/Wife: Antonia Barron).
  h3. AMALIA MANRIQUE, baptized 16 May 1946, El Sagrario, Leon, Guanajuato, Mexico (Father: Primitivo Manrique/Wife: Antonia Baron).
 g6. MARIA ALTAGRACIA MANRIQUE DURAN, born 6 January 1896, Sauz de Armenta, Guanajuato, Mexico.

      Baptized 18 January 1896, San Francisco de Asis, San Francisco del Rincon, Leon, Guanajuato, Mexico (Father: Clemente Manrique/Mother: Petra Duran). Birth Registration(s): 12 February 1896, El Sauz, San Francisco del Rincon, Guanajuato, Mexico/Sauz de Armenta, Guanajuato, Mexico (Father: Clemente Manrique/Mother: Petra Duran).

g7. JOSE LEON MANRIQUE DURAN, born 11 April 1898, Leon, Guanajuato, Mexico. Baptized 22 April 1898, El Sagrario, Leon, Guanajuato, Mexico. (Listed on record: Zeferina Manrique, Julio Juarez, Martin Duran, Petra Duran, Clemente Manrique). Birth Registration: 5 September 1898, Leon, Guanajuato, Mexico (Father: Clemente Manrique/Mother: Petra Duran).

g8. AMALIA MANRIQUE DURAN, born 9 July 1904, Leon, Guanajuato, Mexico. Baptized 11 July 1904, Leon, Guanajuato, Mexico (Listed on record: Rafael Ortiz Jose Santos Gomez, Zeferina Manrique, Petra Duran, Martin Duran and M. Santos Gonzales).

g9. MARIA DOLORES MANRIQUE DURAN, born 4 April 1905 (*year listed on record as 1805, incorrect*). Christening 6 April 1905, El Sagrario, Leon, Guanajuato, Mexico (Listed on record: Espiridon Reynoso, Rafael Ortiz, Vincenta Vera, Tomas F. Machinea, Petra Duran, Clemente Manrique).

SERAPIO MANRIQUE (1891-1952):

SERAPIO MANRIQUE was born 14 October 1891 in Silao de Victoria, Guanajuato, Mexico (record from "*1891 Guanajuato, Mexico, Civil Registrations, Births, 1862-1929; Silao - 1891*"). Serapio Manrique was likely the only member of his family born in Silao, a city founded in 1833 which is located within an agricultural area near Leon along the Silao River. Silao is known for a variety of crops such as strawberries, peaches, corn, avocado, beans and wheat. In a manner of coincidence, twenty years after his Silao birth, Serapio Manrique resided alongside Northern California's Stanislaus River growing strawberries and grapes on his property in the agricultural heartland of California's Central Valley.

Serapio Manrique left Mexico because he did not want to become a priest as per his mother's wish or join the army (*My Mother's Garden,* page 6). "There were 6,454 Mexicans in California in 1850, rising to 9,339 in 1900, which amounted to .5 percent of California's population. This was a surprising(ly) small percentage…California ranchers did not turn to Mexico labor in the Central Valley until 1910." (*Stanislaus Historical Quarterly,* Vol 7, Number 1, Spring 2014, Page 614.*)*

Serapio Manrique arrived in California during 1906 as recorded on a 1930 Oakdale census which is confirmed by another document stating he was a California resident by 25 September 1910. Serapio Manrique married Julia Machado (1896-1917) on 11 August 1913 in Oakdale, Stanislaus, California, USA. His eldest child, Primitivo Manrique, was born 26 July 1914 in Oakdale, Stanislaus, California, USA and named after his younger brother, Primitivo. Daughter Dolores Laura Manrique was born 2 May 1916 in San Francisco, California, USA. After the death of his first wife, Julia Machado ("Woman Found Murdered," *Oakdale Leader*, Vol XXVIII, Thursday, April 26, 1917, page 1, Oakdale, Stanislaus County, California, USA), Serapio married MARY HOPKINS on 26 December 1917 in Stockton, San Joaquin, California, USA. Julia Machado, Serapio's first wife, and her stepfather, Bonifacio Cayton, were godparents to Mary Hopkins' younger brother, Daniel Santiago Hopkins. The Daniel Hopkins family likely met Julia Machado's parents in San Francisco where both Mary Hopkins and Julia Machado were born. When Julia Machado's mother became a widow, she married an Oakdale resident (Cayton) then moved from San Francisco to the Central Valley. Serapio Manrique and Bonafacio Cayton, who married the widowed mother of Julia Machado, were farmers who resided in Oakdale, California.

Serapio Manrique, upon arrival in California's Central Valley, worked on the Sante Fe Railroad near Oakdale, California. He then managed land for (Francis) Marion M. Cottle (**Appendix I-C**), an Oakdale founding family originally from Missouri. Serapio's WW1 draft card stated he was a "farmhand" for Marion Cottle, married with two children, Caucasian and a citizen of Mexico. By 1920 Serapio owned (Indenture record dated June 7, 1917-purchase of Lot 1 and Lot 3 of Blocks 30 in the city of Oakdale for ten dollars in gold coin by Primotivo and Dolores Manrique from Margarita Toledo formerly known as Margarita N. Fuller of Colusa) a white farmhouse on 157 North 5th Avenue in Oakdale and rented thirty-four acres of farmland across the street from his North Fifth property, land he later owned. During the late 1940s, he also owned twenty-eight acres of land at 8400 Laughlin Road in Oakdale, California. As a farmer, he grew grapes, beans, tomatoes, strawberries and walnuts. At the edge of the Manrique Laughlin Road farmland was an operating dairy and a view of the Sierra foothills in the distance. Given the topography, Serapio cultivated his vineyard and crops using the terrace method of farming. He also had the talent for planting grape vines perfectly spaced apart without need for measurement.

An account of Serapio Manrique's Oakdale life was shared by his son within Julius C. Manrique's unfinished manuscript (2023) ("From 157 North Fifth Avenue to College Avenue and the Many Miles Between"):

> "From our 157 North Fifth Avenue house one could see an almond orchard half a block away to the north and to the east cotton fields which sometimes offered the view of their Midwestern-born caretaker cultivating his crop with a mule unless he had planted alfalfa. Across the street from our home was an unused swimming pool where my siblings and I would play inside the empty seventy-five feet long by twenty-five feet wide space. Eventually, my dad bought two lots next to the pool for fifty dollars. He used this property to grow vegetables for family meals and built a chicken coop to provide eggs and meat. He also raised rabbits which we would play

with until they mysteriously disappeared." Manrique, J. C. [Unpublished text], Pages 1 & 2 of 21.

"My father owned twenty-eight acres of farmland on Laughlin Road in Oakdale where he planted his prized vineyard. At the same time, he grew tomatoes, strawberries and black-eyed peas between the vines to make additional money. He died suddenly after a bout of pneumonia while I was registering for courses at San Jose State University. From this point on, the grapes were left on their own without a devoted farmer taking care of them. Although I vowed to my father I would never sell his land, on 31 May 1958, when I went to the ranch, I found the vines in ruin after a bitter frost left his vineyard looking as if a blowtorch had burned the vines to the ground. I called my oldest brother, a local farmer who was experienced with grape and fruit tree cultivation, and Primo suggested we trim the brown limbs off the vines, irrigate the property to encourage growth, then wait a few years for a crop to reappear. In the meantime, we paid taxes and property expenses while we afforded our non-farm lives. As my brothers had growing families to support by this point, we struggled to maintain the property between 1952-1960. Ultimately, we sold my father's beloved vineyard ..." Manrique, J. C. [Unpublished text], Pages 5 & 6 of 21.

Serapio Manrique Duran signed his name, "Serapio D.(Duran) Manrique" and chose the English name, Samuel or Sam. Census and phone records record him as: Sam D. Manrique. His children also used his English name on their records by listing, "Samuel Manrique" as their father's given name. Serapio was named for his grandmother, Serapia Gonzales, a noted "Spaniard" born Leon, Guanajuato, who married Simon Manrique, also a "Spaniard" born Leon, Guanajuato, Mexico.

The Modesto News Herald described Serapio Manrique as both a vintner and farmer. On Friday, 5 November 1931, he was involved in a prohibition liquor raid that netted three-thousand gallons of wine confiscated, including three-hundred-and-fifty gallons of wine at the Manrique North 5th residence. Serapio Manrique's sentence was suspended. United States prohibition laws banned the production, importation, transportation and sale of alcoholic beverages from 1920 to 1933. Although charges were dropped against Serapio Manrique, the barrels of wine were taken.

According to PBS News, "prohibition greatly expanded federal law enforcement powers and turned millions of Americans into scofflaws." Federal agents arrested 577,000 suspects between 1920-1930 with two out of three being convicted of minor infractions. The IRS created the "Prohibition Unit" which was staffed by agents who did not have to take Civil Service exams which meant local politicians and members of Congress could appoint their "cronies." The federal government provided funds for 1,500 agents across America to enforce Prohibition laws, but while these individuals were given guns and vehicles, many had no training.

Serapio Manrique married (m1) JULIA VERONICA MACHADO (born 1896, San Francisco, California, USA; d. 1917) on 11 August 1913 in Oakdale, Stanislaus, California, USA. Julia

Machado, born in San Francisco, California, USA, was the daughter of Mariana Gonzales (born California) and (unknown) Machado who died when Julia Machado was a child. Maria (Gonzales) Machado, a widow, married Boniface Cayton. The 1910 Oakdale, California United States census listed the Boniface Cayton family residing at 521 North 7th Street in Oakdale, California with his stepdaughter, Julia Machado (**Appendix I-B**).

The children of Serapio and (m1) Julia (Machado) Manrique were Primitivo Manrique (born 26 July 1914, Oakdale, Stanislaus, California, USA; d. 19 January 2011, Modesto, Stanislaus, California, USA) and Dolores Laura Manrique (born 2 May 1916, San Francisco, California, USA; d. 24 November 1997, San Francisco, California, USA). Julia (Machado) Manrique was godparent, along with Boniface Cayton, her stepfather, to Daniel Santiago Hopkins, the son of Daniel Edwin and Flora (Ramirez) Hopkins. After Julia (Machado) Manrique died in early 1917, widower Serapio Manrique married Mary Hopkins, sister to Daniel Santiago Hopkins, on 26 December 1917 in Stockton, California. The reason for the connection between the Stockton Hopkins family and Oakdale Manrique-Cayton families remains unproven, although likely San Francisco related. Primitivo (Primo) Manrique married Lula Belle Wyatt (b. 7 February 1917, Plainville, Lamar, Arkansas, USA; d. 7 March 2009, Modesto, Stanislaus, California USA). Primo was a life-long peach farmer in Modesto, California where he resided on his ranch and lived to the age of ninety-six years old. Dolores Manrique married Castor Evardo Pongan (b. 28 March 1904, Manilla, Philippines; d. 9 December 1996, San Francisco, California, USA) on 3 July 1936 in Tijuana, Mexico after he arrived on the ship, *President Lincoln*. Caspar and Dolores Pongan resided in San Francisco, California, USA. Both Primitivo and Dolores Manrique were buried in the Manrique family plot at Oakdale Citizens Cemetery with their spouses (Lula Belle Wyatt Manrique/Castor Evardo Pongan).

Given lack of documents (marriage record for Pedro Gomez and Catalina Manrique de Lara; baptismal record for Gaspar Gomez Manrique de Lara), it is my assumption Manrique-Hopkins children are GEN12/Manrique-Hopkins grandchildren are GEN13 from this line. However, given Josepha's Bravo's birth certificate, Manrique-Hopkins children *are* GEN9 and Manrique-Hopkins grandchildren GEN10 from this MdL branch.

HOPKINS FAMILY

ISLAND OF ST. HELENA, BRITISH OVERSEAS TERRITORY

The Island of Saint Helena is Britain's second-oldest overseas territory after Bermuda. The British East India Company was given a charter to govern Saint Helena in 1657 and the island was colonized by 1659. In 1981, *The British Nationality Act* re-classified Saint Helena as a British Dependent Territory. My *23&Me* DNA recorded "Southern England" origins likely correlate to Daniel Edwin Hopkins' ancestors as my maternal Canadian roots are confirmed from Northern England, Scotland and Ireland.

Research for DANIEL EDWIN HOPKINS' birth records (born 28 September 1872, Island of St. Helena, United Kingdom) via *Family Search* microfilmed baptismal records and documents from the St. Helena Archives (in the Island of St. Helena) resulted with proof both Hopkins and Essex families resided on the island for generations. Unfortunately, while there was no baptismal record for the St. Helena Island birth of Daniel Edwin Hopkins on 28 September 1872, the Hopkins surname proved uncommon in St. Helena. Additionally, the St. Helena Archives noted the island did not record every birth, resident or arrival to the island and historical documentation for the island began in 1853. Given zero Danial Edwin Hopkins' birth records, it can be assumed the non-Anglican Hopkins/Essex branch emigrated to St. Helena prior to 1853. The St. Helena Archives only had Anglican registers for births and marriages between the years 1860 and 1962, as other religious denominations were not recorded. Therefore, Daniel Edwin Hopkins was neither Catholic nor Anglican, as his birth records were not discovered at the St. Helena Archives and he needed a dispensation for the Canonical form to marry his Catholic wife, Flora Ramirez, at St. Mary's Catholic Church in Stockton, California, USA during 1909.

As noted by Daniel Edwin Hopkins' Stockton St. Mary's Catholic Church marriage record written in Latin, his father was "Caroli" which is the Latin cognate for the name, Charles or Carl. His mother was listed as Catherine, a fact that aligns to his declaration in Stockton after the loss of a child that the "mother," was "Catherine Essex" of England. Officially, the hospital attendant was likely asking the name of the child's mother (Flora Ramirez Hopkins, born California), but after the loss of his daughter, Daniel Hopkins provided a clue to his parentage: Daniel Hopkins' mother was born in "England" (or the Island of St. Helena) and named, Catherine Essex. The information was helpful as it confirmed his father was Charles/Carl Hopkins who married Catherine Essex. There were residents of St. Helena with the Essex surname and the St. Helena Archives did have a marriage listing for a Charles Essex to Catherine Harriet Hopkins.

(Please note, a "Daniel Edwin Hopkins" was born 2 February 1872 to William Hopkins and Elizabeth Benjamin who married at the Jamestown Baptist Chapel in St. Helena on 25 December 1871. Elizabeth Benjamin was a 28-year-old widow from Jamestown, St Helena. Elizabeth Hopkins died of epilepsy on 6 April 1887 at age 44. If William and Elizabeth Hopkins were the parents of Daniel Hopkins, their names would likely appear as he and Flora Hopkins' children's names - which they do not. Additionally, the birth of this Daniel Edwin Hopkins was 2 February 1872 which does not coincide with the birth date of Daniel Edwin Hopkins who married Flora Ramirez in San Francisco during 1901.)

There were Essex family marriage and birth records at the St. Helena Archives, however, the only one that connected a Hopkins to an Essex was a marriage which took place between Catherine Harriet Hopkins to Charles Essex on 9 June 1864 at the Jamestown, Island of St. Helena parish. The marriage correlated to both Daniel Hopkins' 1908 Stockton Catholic St. Mary's Church marriage license (father - Caroli Hopkins) and his statement that (his) the mother was, "Catherine Essex of England." However, in this 9 June 1867 St. Helena marriage record the surnames are switched - Catherine Hopkins/Charles Essex. If the transcriber made a mistake, it is impossible to prove. The marriage year of 1867 fits with Daniel Edwin Hopkins' birth year of 1872 and makes them likely parents if the text had stated: Charles Hopkins married Catherine Harriet Essex. Had that been the case, then it would prove, Charles Hopkins and Catherine Harriet Essex were the likely parents of Daniel Edwin Hopkins.

Catherine Harriet Hopkins was age eighteen at the date of her marriage to Charles Essex, which means her birth year was 1846. This does not make her a child of James Hopkins and Mary Jane Crowley who married 6 August 1858 and had a first-born child named, Daniel Hopkins born 12 November 1856. The Jamestown, Island of St. Helena parish church 9 June 1864 record reads: "*Charles Essex, age 23, Bachelor, Groom of Jamestown, married Catherine Harriet Hopkins, Spinster of Jamestown.*"

Daniel Edwin Hopkins (b. 28 September 1872, St. Helena Island, UK), father of Mary Hopkins and husband to Flora (Ramirez) Hopkins, may have been related to the Daniel Hopkins' Jamestown, St. Helena family. James and Mary Coley (Crowley) Hopkins had three daughters along with their first-born son, Daniel Hopkins who was born 12 November 1856. Given the first child of Daniel and Flora (Ramirez) Hopkins was, "Mary," this lends to the possibility of a family connection. Daniel Edwin Hopkins and Flora (Ramirez) Hopkins, also named a son, "Daniel," perhaps to honor a St. Helena Daniel Hopkins relative.

Mary Coley was likely, Mary Crowley. The father of Mary Jane Crowley was Richard Crowley, a stonemason who died in St. Helena on 21 October 1858 at the age of fifty-eight. Given names were transcribed phonetically during the 1800s, Mary Crowley may have also witnessed two St. Helena marriage records as, "Mary Coley."

The children of James Hopkins and Mary (Crowley) Coley baptized at the St. Helena Anglican Church in James Town (*Daniel & Elizabeth: 1849-1862 registrar; Edith Mira: 1862-1912 registrar; Charlotte: 1862-1884 registrar*) were:

~ DANIEL HOPKINS, born 12 November 1856, James Town, Island of St. Helena
~ ELIZABETH HOPKINS, born 16 June 1859, James Town, Island of St. Helena
~ EDITH MIRA HOPKINS, born 27 May 1862, James Town, Island of St. Helena
~ CHARLOTTE HOPKINS, born 13 March 1866, James Town, Island of St. Helena

In many families during this era, if a child died, they would name another later born child for the member who passed. If, for instance, Daniel Hopkins born 1856 died, and James and Mary Hopkins had a son during 1872, there is also the possibility to their naming this child, Daniel Hopkins. However, the "Carl" and "Catherine Essex" information makes the James and Mary Hopkins family likely St. Helena Island relatives.

There were only seventeen Hopkins' surnames found in St. Helena (Anglican) marriage and birth records. Hopkins was the sixty-third most popular name on this island with fewer than a thousand residents. The parentage of Daniel Edwin Hopkins born 28 September 1872 remains unknown, but likely: Charles Hopkins, born Island of St. Helena and Catherine Essex, born England (or the Island of St. Helena, a British Overseas Territory).

The Island of St. Helena is a five-hour plane ride from Johannesburg, South Africa and located in the South Atlantic Ocean between Brazil and Africa. According to the St. Helena tourism site, the island is the second oldest British territory next to Bermuda and resembles and English county village. Only 10.5 miles long and 6.5 miles wide, St. Helena is about the size of San Francisco, California. Given the location and dimensions of the island, it is home to at most three thousand residents annually. St. Helena is deemed one of the safest and most remote island in the world with pristine ecological land and marine environments. However, upon opening the first St. Helena airport in 2017, travel to this "top ten" most remote tourist destinations sites became easier. Family lore theorized Daniel Hopkins "sailed on a vessel around the world." This is likely true as St. Helena was a port for traveling ships and an original outpost for the British West India Company until 1832. The Island of St. Helena became a British Crown Colony in 1834. After the Suez Canal opened in 1869, many St. Helena jobs were eliminated so "Saints," as citizens of the Island of St. Helena are called, like Daniel Hopkins left the island to find vocations elsewhere.

Daniel Edwin Hopkins was noted on a California census record as a naturalized citizen who arrived in San Francisco, California during 1890 and voted (Republican) in both Stanislaus and Alameda counties of California. His naturalization record was not found in the Central Valley cities of Stockton or Sacramento. Likely, the document was destroyed during the 1906 San Francisco earthquake and fire along his daughter's (Mary Hopkins) birth record, information that may have given more clues regarding Daniel Edwin Hopkins' St. Helena Island heritage.

Hodges Alley, San Francisco, CA
The Hopkins Family resided here prior to September 1902.

HOPKINS-MANRIQUE

NORTHERN CALIFORNIA, USA

FLORA FELIPA (PHILOMENA) RAMIREZ was born 13 September 1882 in "California." She is the first documented Northern Californian in our line although her father, JOSEPH RAMIREZ was born "in California" likely during 1850-1860. In a (5 June 1900) United States Census record for Newman, Stanislaus County, California, "FELL RAMIZA" was listed as a border age seventeen born September 1882 in California. Her father was "born in California" and she could "read, write and speak English." Listed next to her on the same record was Frances Silva, a widow age thirty-three who was born 1867 in Mexico (*although likely Portugal*) and could "speak English," along with her son, Benjamin Silva, born 1884 Mexico who could "read, write and speak English." Both Frances and Benjamin Silva emigrated from Mexico to California during 1884. The relationship is unknown between Flora Ramirez and Frances Silva, if there was one at all. On the same page of the census, many "Silva" surname individuals were listed, all born Portugal (**Appendix I-I**).

Between 5 June 1900 and 29 July 1900, Flora (Fell-Felipa-Philomena) Ramirez traveled from Newman, California to San Francisco, California, one-hundred miles east from the Central Valley, where Mary Hopkins, her first child, was born on Sunday, 29 July 1900 and recorded in *The San Francisco Call,* the local newspaper, on page eleven of the Tuesday, 31 July 1900 edition:

"Hopkins - In this city, July 29, 1900, to the wife of F. D. Hopkins, a daughter."

The initials (F. D.) were incorrect as the text should have read: D. E. Hopkins. However, very few Hopkins surnamed individuals resided in 1900 San Francisco, and given the loss of records after the 1906 San Francisco earthquake, this is the only document noting Mary Hopkins's San Francisco, California birth. That the family celebrated Mary Hopkins birthdate on 22 October 1900 could coincide with her baptismal date, another piece of information lost during the 1906 SF earthquake and fire as the baptismal record was not located at St. Mary's in San Francisco or any San Francisco Catholic church, including archives at the Archdiocese of San Francisco in Menlo Park, California.

MARY HOPKINS was the eldest child of DANIEL EDWIN HOPKINS and FLORA FELIPA RAMIREZ. She was also her parent's only child born in San Francisco, California. Mary Hopkins used to share with her children that she was born in Patterson, California, but the town did not exist in 1900. Daniel Hopkins arrived in San Francisco, California at age eighteen in 1890 where he was recorded as a "sailor and musician." There is one family photo of Daniel Edwin Hopkins, Flora Hopkins and Mary Hopkins (likely age two) taken in San Francisco and another from the same day with Daniel Edwin Hopkins standing next to an accordion placed on the floor. Siblings Mary and Robert Hopkins were taught to play the piano by their father, Daniel Edwin Hopkins.

The marriage between Daniel Edwin Hopkins and Flora Ramirez took place in San Francisco, California. *The San Francisco Call* newspaper noted the Thursday, 24 October 1901 marriage license in the Friday, 25 October 1901 edition on page thirteen:

"*Daniel E. Hopkins, age 28, 2 Hodges Alley and Fell Ramirez, age 19, 2 Hodges Alley.*"

Hodges Alley, San Francisco is located near the Embarcadero (near the TransAmerica building), a residence by the port which would have been convenient for a sailor. 2 Hodges Alley was where Mary Hopkins lived during the first two years of her life. Both the property and alley exist today. Given Daniel Hopkins' birth year of September 1872, the article should have noted he was age 29 by October 1901.

The marriage date of 24 October 1901 is significant because likely Mary Hopkins was baptized on October 22nd, the day she regarded as her birthday. Perhaps, after the baptism (in 1901), Daniel Hopkins and Flora Ramirez married in San Francisco, California, USA. As Daniel Hopkins was a sailor, he could have been at sea until this time. Flora Ramirez may have returned "home" to her San Francisco Ramirez family members after having her first child if Daniel Hopkins was away. Regardless of speculation, Mary Hopkins was born 29 July 1900 in San Francisco, California and her parents, Dan and Flora Hopkins, married 24 October 1901 in San Francisco, California.

While searching for Flora Ramirez' father in 1880 San Francisco, there were two J(oseph). Ramirez-named individuals located - a SF cigar maker and a grocer in Alameda. Neither individual was confirmed as parents for Flora Felipa Ramirez, but few Ramirez surnames existed in 1880 San Francisco (**Appendix: I-H**). A hypothesis for Flora Ramirez is she was born in San Francisco on 13 September 1882, met Daniel Hopkins between 1890-1900 at her father's SF cigar or Alameda grocery store, worked in Newman during June of 1900, then returned to have her child, Mary Hopkins, in San Francisco by 29 July 1900. With family in San Francisco, Flora Ramirez was likely born in the city in September of 1882, but the 1906 San Francisco earthquake and fire eliminated documents to prove such background.

Daniel Hopkins, Flora Hopkins and Mary Hopkins moved from San Francisco to Stockton, California, another port city, by September 1902 as their daughter, Kate Hopkins, was born in Stockton. In Stockton, California, the family members were the only Hopkins surnamed individuals in town. While working as a "laborer," it was noted Daniel Hopkins was employed at a woolen mill. The addresses in Stockton and San Jose where the DANIEL E. HOPKINS family resided in rented homes include:
- ~1904: 518 Commerce Street, Stockton, CA (laborer)
- ~1905: 316 S. El Dorado Street, Stockton, CA (laborer)
- ~1906: 316 S. El Dorado Street, Stockton, CA (laborer)
- ~1907: 43 West Sonora Street, Stockton, CA (laborer)
- ~1909: 516 S. Commerce Street, Stockton, CA (laborer)
- ~1910: 40 West Church Street, Stockton, CA (laborer)
- ~1911: 28 Vine Street, San Jose, CA (laborer)
- ~1913: 348 Park Avenue, San Jose, CA (laborer)

~1913: 46 South Monroe, Stockton, CA
~1914: 46 South Monroe, Stockton, CA (cement worker)
~1915: 625 West Church, Stockton, CA (laborer)
~1916: 46 South Monroe, Stockton, CA (cement worker)
~1917: 46 South Monroe, Stockton, CA (cement worker)
~1918: 625 West Church, Stockton, CA (laborer)
~1919: 625 West Church, Stockton, CA (laborer)

On 10 September 1918, Daniel Edwin Hopkins registered for the WW1 draft. He was then age forty-five and born 28 September 1872, England. He listed his occupation as a laborer for MacDonald & Kahn. Daniel Hopkins stated his nearest relative was his wife, Mrs. Flora Hopkins, who resided at the same address as he did: 625 West Church Street. Daniel Hopkins' physical features were listed as: Tall with medium build, brown eyes and dark hair. Mary Hopkins married Serapio Manrique on 29 December 1917 in Stockton, California. Serapio Manrique's (m1) wife, Julia Machado, was Mary Hopkins' younger brother's godmother who passed away leaving behind two young children. Flora Hopkins died of the Spanish flu on 3 November 1918. The Daniel Hopkins family then moved to Oakdale nearby Serapio and Mary (Hopkins) Manrique after the death of Flora Hopkins. Daniel Edwin Hopkins, age fifty-seven, was noted in the 1930 Oakdale United States census as residing with his son, Robert Hopkins and his family, as well as, youngest son, Dan Hopkins, then age nineteen. The Robert Hopkins family moved later to Alameda, as did Robert Hopkins' father, Daniel Edwin Hopkins.

The children of Daniel Edwin and Flora (Ramirez) HOPKINS were:
1. MARY HOPKINS (b. 29 July 1900, San Francisco, California, USA; d. 27 February 1978, Oakdale, Stanislaus, California, USA).
2. KATE HOPKINS (b. 4 September 1902, Stockton, San Joaquin, California, USA; d. 3 September 1903, Stockton, San Joaquin, California, USA).
3. JENNIE HOPKINS (b. 14 October 1903, Stockton, San Joaquin, California, USA; d. 15 October 1903, Stockton, San Joaquin, California, USA).
4. ROBERT HOPKINS (b. 20 August 1904, Stockton, San Joaquin, California, USA; d. 8 October 1964, San Leandro, California, USA).
5. VICTORIA HOPKINS (b. 22 July 1905, Stockton, San Joaquin, California, USA; *d. 21 February 1907*, Stockton, San Joaquin, California, USA).
6. ROSE HOPKINS (b. 5 July 1906, Stockton, San Joaquin, California, USA; d. 15 October 1906, Stockton, San Joaquin, California, USA).
7. CARRIE HOPKINS (b. 30 December 1907, Stockton, San Joaquin, California, USA; d. 3 November 1952, Fairfield, Solano, California, USA).
8. FRANCIS HOPKINS (b. 14 December 1908, Stockton, San Joaquin, California, USA; d. 9 December 1909, Stockton, San Joaquin, California, USA).
9. JOSEPH EDWARD HOPKINS (b. 4 July 1910, Stockton, San Joaquin, California, USA; d. 25 November 1910, Stockton, San Joaquin, California, USA).
10. RUBY HOPKINS (b. 4 July 1910, Stockton, San Joaquin, California, USA; d. 23 April 1914, Stockton, San Joaquin, California, USA).
11. GUADALUPE PAULINA HOPKINS (b. 23 July 1911, San Jose, Santa Clara, California, USA; d. 31 March 1969, Alameda County, California, USA).

12. DANIEL SANTIAGO HOPKINS (b. 27 February 1913, San Jose, Santa Clara, California, USA; d. 16 April 1993, Sonora, Tuolumne, California, USA).
13. SARAH HOPKINS (b. 21 September 1916, Stockton, San Joaquin, California, USA; d. 21 September 1916, Stockton, San Joaquin, California, USA).

The Daniel and Flora (Ramirez) Hopkins children who survived childhood were (**Appendixes I-D, I-E I-F & I-G**):

~ MARY HOPKINS (b. 29 July 1900, San Francisco, California, USA; d. 27 February 1978, Oakdale, Stanislaus, California, USA).

Mary Hopkins was the only child born in San Francisco and does not have a baptismal record. Her birthdate is confirmed as per a *San Francisco Call* newspaper birth announcement which recorded: "Hopkins - in this city, July 29, 1900, to the wife of F. D. Hopkins, a daughter." She married SERAPIO D. MANRIQUE on 26 December 1917 in Stockton, San Joaquin, California, USA. Her parents were listed as: Mother, Flora Romilious (Ramirez) born California/Father, Dan Hopkins born England. Mary (Hopkins) Manrique died 27 February 1978, Oakdale, Stanislaus, California, USA.

~ROBERT HOPKINS (b. 20 August 1904, Stockton, San Joaquin, California, USA; d. 8 October 1964, San Leandro, California, USA).

Robert Hopkins was born on 20 August 1904 in Stockton, San Joaquin, California, USA. He was known as Tudi (*Uncle Tudi*). His baptismal record stated he was the child of Daniel Hopkins of California and Feliz Ramos of California. His godparents were Adolf Anderson and Mrs. Anderson (**Appendix I-A**). Robert Hopkins married (m1) JULIA SILVA and (m2) CATHERINE/MARY LOPEZ. Robert J. Hopkins, his family, father and brother moved to Eden Township, Alameda, California from Oakdale, California during the 1930s. Robert Hopkins died 8 October 1964 in San Leandro, Alameda, California, USA (**Appendix I-D**).

~CARRIE HOPKINS (b. 30 December 1907, Stockton, San Joaquin, California, USA; d. 3 November 1952, Fairfield, Solano, California, USA).

Carrie Hopkins was born 30 December 1907 in Stockton, San Joaquin, California, USA. Her baptismal (Latin) certificate stated her name was: Maria*m* Carmine*m*. Her father was Daniel Hopkins born St. Helena Insula and her mother was Flora Romidas born Teotia (*Terceira is a Portuguese Azores Island*). Carrie's godparents were Remundus Real and Julia Figueroa. Carrie Hopkins married (m1) PETE MENDEZ/(m2) ABEL MARTINEZ. Carrie (Hopkins) (Mendez) Martinez died 3 November 1952 in Fairfield, Solano, California, USA (**Appendix I-E**).

~GUADALUPE PAULINA HOPKINS (b. 23 July 1911, San Jose, Santa Clara, California, USA; d. 31 March 1969, Alameda County, CA).

Guadalupe Paulina Hopkins was born on 23 July 1911 in San Jose, Santa Clara, California, USA. She was known as Lupe Hopkins. She was one of two Hopkins-Ramirez children born in San Jose, California and does not have a located baptismal record. Guadalupe Pauline Hopkins married FELIPE MANUEL DURAN. Lupe (Hopkins) Duran died on 31 March 1969 in Alameda County, California, USA. The California Death Index lists Lupe H. Duran's mother's maiden name (Ramirez) as: ASCENCIO. While Hopkins-Duran children family lore included information that Daniel Edwin Hopkins traveled across Mexico and met Felipe Duran during this period, it is possible Serapio Manrique, husband to Mary Hopkins, the eldest sister of Lupe Hopkins, was Martin Duran's relation since Serapio's mother was, Petra Duran (**Appendix I-F**).

~DANIEL SANTIAGO HOPKINS (b. 27 February 1913, San Jose, Santa Clara, California, USA; d. 16 April 1993, Sonora, Tuolumne, California, USA).

Daniel Santiago Hopkins was born 27 February 1913 in San Jose, Santa Clara, California, USA. He was known as, Danny Hopkins. He was baptized on 15 June 1913 at Stockton's St. Mary's Catholic Church. His father was Daniel Hopkins born England and mother was Felipa Ramedes born California. His godparents were Boniface Cayton and Julia Machado, the first wife of Serapio Manrique who, as a widower, married Daniel Santiago Hopkins' sister, Mary Hopkins. Daniel Hopkins married (m1) CARRIE DOMINGUEZ and (m2) ROSARIO NUNEZ. His social security card stated his mother was Felipa Ramirez and father was Dan Hopkins. Daniel Santiago Hopkins died on 16 April 1993 in Sonora, Tuolumne, California, USA (**Appendix I-G**).

The Daniel and Flora (Ramirez) Hopkins children who died during childhood were:

~KATE HOPKINS (b. 4 September 1902, Stockton, San Joaquin California, USA; d. 3 September 1903, Stockton, San Joaquin California, USA).

Kate Hopkins was born 4 September 1902 in Stockton, San Joaquin, California, USA. She died on 29 September 1903 at the age of one year and twenty-five days in Stockton of "enteritis," a bacterial infection of the small intestine. The place of death is listed as 518 Commerce Street, Stockton, California.

~JENNIE HOPKINS (b. 14 October 1903, Stockton, San Joaquin California, USA; d. 15 October 1903, Stockton, San Joaquin California, USA).

Jennie Hopkins was born 14 October 1903 in Stockton, San Joaquin, California, USA. She died on 15 October 1903 in Stockton, California from "inanition" which means she "failed to thrive" or consume nutrients.

~VICTORIA HOPKINS (b. 22 July 1905, Stockton, San Joaquin California, USA; d. 21 February 1907, Stockton, San Joaquin California, USA).

Victoria Hopkins was born 22 July 1905 in Stockton, San Joaquin, California USA. She was baptized on 28 August 1905 at St. Mary's Catholic Church in Stockton, San Joaquin County, California. Victoria's baptismal record listed her name as - Victorera. Father: Daniel Hopkins, born Portugal. Mother: Felipa Ramires born Mexico. Godparents: Alfredus Morales and Christina Nunes. There was no San Joaquin County or California Death index record for Victoria, but family notes list a 21 February 1907, Stockton, California, USA death date.

~ROSE HOPKINS (b. 5 July 1906, Stockton, San Joaquin, California, USA; d. 15 October 1906, Stockton, San Joaquin, California, USA).

Rose Hopkins was born 5 July 1906 in Stockton, California, USA. She was baptized on 4 August 1905 at St. Mary's Church with an illegible first name. The document lists __LL Rose Hopkins, the daughter of Daniel Edwin Hopkins of Stockton and Phillipa Ramirez of Stockton. Rose Hopkins' death certificate reads: Place of death: 346 Market Street, Stockton (the family resided at El Dorado); Date of death: 15 October 1906; Age: 3 months/10 days. Rose Hopkins died of cerebral spinal meningitis. The informant was James Ford of Stockton. The parents were Daniel Hopkins and Flora Hopkins. Burial took place at San Joaquin Catholic Cemetery on 17 October 1906.

~FRANCIS HOPKINS (b. 14 December 1908, Stockton, San Joaquin, California, USA;
d. 9 December 1909, Stockton, San Joaquin, California, USA).
Francis Hopkins was born 14 December 1909 in Stockton, San Joaquin, California, USA. She was baptized on 2 May 1909 at St. Mary's Catholic Church in Stockton, San Joaquin County, California. The baptismal record stated her name was (*Latin*): Francis*cam*. She was born 14 December 1908 and baptized on 2 May 1909. Father: Daniel Hopkins born Santae Helenie Insula. Mother: Flora Remidas, born California. Godfather: Ezechiel Pablo. Francis Hopkins died at 40 West Church Street on 7 December 1909 at eleven months of pneumonia according to the death certificate. The burial certificate stated the father was Daniel Hopkins born England and mother Fell Ramirez born California. The informant was Fell Hopkins (*Francis Hopkins was likely named for Flora Ramirez' mother, Francis Lopez*).

~JOSEPH EDWARD HOPKINS (b. 4 July 1910, Stockton, San Joaquin, California, USA;
d. 25 November 1910, Stockton, San Joaquin, California, USA).
Joseph Hopkins was twin to Ruby Hopkins and born 4 July 1909, Stockton, San Joaquin County, California, USA. His birth certificate noted his father was Daniel Hopkins born St. Helena and his mother Flora Ramirez born California. He was baptized with his twin, Ruby Hopkins, at St. Mary's Church, Stockton on 15 November 1910. The Catholic baptismal record named him: Joseph Edward*um* born 4 July 1910 and baptized on 15 November 1910. His father was Daniel Hopkins born Anglia and his mother was Philomena Remond born California. His godfather was Francisco Duarte. Joseph Hopkins' death record stated: Place of death - 40 West Church Street, Stockton (at home); Death date - 25 November 1910; Age - four months and twenty-five days; Cause of death - "cholera infantum" - a fatal form of gastroenteritis that occurs in infants. The burial took place at San Joaquin Cemetery on 27 November 1910. The father was Daniel Hopkins born Isle of St. Helena and Flora Ramirez born California. The informant was Daniel Hopkins (*Joseph Hopkins was likely named for Flora Ramirez' father, Joseph Ramirez, and given a middle name, "Edwin," not "Edward," for his father, Daniel Edwin Hopkins*).

~ RUBY (REBECCA EVELYN) HOPKINS (b. 4 July 1910, Stockton, San Joaquin,
California, USA; d. 23 April 1914, Stockton, San Joaquin, California, USA).
Ruby Hopkins was twin to Joseph Hopkins, and born 4 July 1910 in Stockton, San Joaquin County, California, USA. She was baptized along with her twin, Joseph Edwin Hopkins, on 15 November 1910 at St. Mary's Catholic Church in Stockton, California. Ruby's baptismal record states her name is: Rebecca Ruby Evelin*an* Hopkins born 4 July 1910 and baptized 15 November 1910. Her father was Daniel Hopkins born Anglia and mother was Philomena Remond born California. Her godfather was Francisco Duarte. Ruby Hopkins' death certificate stated her place of death was 46 South Monroe Street, Stockton (at home); Death date - 23 April 1914: Age - three years and nine months. The cause of death was "acute nephritits" which is a kidney disorder. The parents on the death certificate were listed as Daniel Hopkins and Catherine Essex, born in the Isle of St. Helena. There was no burial information. The listing of "Catherine Essex" as the mother's name was likely Daniel Hopkins' mother's name which he gave when asked the name of "the mother" during a time of grief.

~ SARAH HOPKINS (b. 21 September 1916, Stockton, San Joaquin, California, USA; d.
21 September 1916, Stockton, San Joaquin, California, USA).

Sarah Hopkins was born 21 September 1916, Stockton, San Joaquin, California, USA. She was a stillbirth and died of hydrocephilis or water-on-the-brain. The location of her birth was 625 West Church Street in Stockton (at home). Her father was listed as Dan Hopkins born Island of St. Helena. Her mother was listed as Flora RHmere born California. Given the 1910 Stockton, San Joaquin, California, United States Census records listed Flora Hopkins as, "Sarah Hopkins," there is a possibility Sarah may have been named, "Flora" and named for her mother, who was listed on a Stockton census record as, "Sarah" Hopkins. Sarah Hopkins was buried on 22 September 1916 at the San Joaquin Cemetery. There was no informant given on the record.

Daniel Hopkins and Flora Ramirez received a marriage license in San Francisco on Thursday, 24 October 1901 (noted on page thirteen in the Friday, 25 October 1901 *The San Francisco Call* edition): Daniel E. Hopkins, age 28, 2 Hodges Alley and Fell Ramirez age 19, 2 Hodges Alley." A devout Catholic, Flora (Ramirez) Hopkins also was married to Daniel Hopkins in a Catholic church during 1909. The Stockton St. Mary's Catholic Church document noted witnesses were Ezechiel Pablo and Susan Terrano. The marriage was presided by Father Joe Sorasio. The marriage, recorded in Latin, listed the name of the spouse as DANIEL EDWARD (*not EDWIN*) HOPKINS, whose parents were CAROLI HOPKINS and CATHERINE HOPKINS. FLORA FELIPA RAMIREZ, the wife, parents were listed as JOSEPH RAMIREZ and FRANCIS LOPEZ.

The St. Mary's Stockton Catholic Church 23 May 1909 marriage document states:

> "*Hopkins et Remirez (516 S. Commerce Street, 23 May 1909)*
> *Matrimonio: Danielum Edwardum Hopkins (32) ex loco Saint Helena Insula -*
> *Fillium, Caroli Hopkins et Catherine Hopkins et Floretam Remirez (29), ex loco California, Fillium Joseph et Francisi Lopez.*"

The record stated a dispensation of the Canonical Form allowed the marriage to take place (between a non-Catholic to a Catholic) and was signed 31 January 1909, San Francisco, California, USA. This meant that Daniel Edwin Hopkins was not a baptized Catholic.

Translated, the marriage record states Daniel Edwin Hopkins, born in the Island of St. Helena, the son of Charles (Carl) Hopkins and Catherine Hopkins married Flora Ramirez, born in California, the daughter of Joseph (*Ramirez*) and Francis Lopez.

St. Mary's Church baptismal records noted Flora Felipa Ramirez' name in many formats including, Phillippa Ramirez, Feliz Ramos, Felipa Rameres, Flora Romidas, Philomena Remond and Felipa Ramedes. Daniel Hopkins' country of birth was listed as: Anglia and St. Helena Insula. Flora Ramirez country of birth was usually listed as "California" although it was also listed as, Portugal and Mexico.

The marriage document noted years of birth that are different for both Daniel Hopkins and Flora Ramirez. Daniel Edwin Hopkins was born in 1872, but his marriage document denoted a birth year of 1877. Flora Ramirez consistently stated her birth month-year was September 1882, but the St. Mary's marriage record listed her birth was 1880.

In the 1910 Stockton, San Joaquin, California, United States census, Sarah (Flora) Hopkins, wife of Dan Hopkins, stated the number of children born to her by 1910 was eight with the number of children living as three (Mary, Robert and Carrie Hopkins). By 1910, the children of Daniel Edwin and Flora (Ramirez) Hopkins who had died were Kate, Jennie, Victoria, Rose and Francis Hopkins. Twins, Joseph and Ruby Hopkins were born 4 July 1910 in Stockton, California, USA after the census date.

Flora Felipa (Ramirez) Hopkins died on 3 November 1918 of "influenza pneumonia" (Spanish flu) in the French Camp, San Joaquin County Hospital at age thirty-six. It is noted on her death certificate by the doctor informant that Flora Hopkins was born in California and had been hospitalized for twenty-one days. Flora Felipa Hopkins was buried at Stockton's San Joaquin Catholic Cemetery along with her children, Rose, Francis, Joseph Edwin, Ruby and Sarah Hopkins. The cemetery index card for Flora Hopkins lists her parents as natives of Spain. The Spanish flu epidemic of 1918-1919 was one of the most-deadly in modern history, infecting an estimated five-hundred million people worldwide and killing an estimated twenty to fifty million victims, more casualties than WW1. The 1918-1919 flu afflicted twenty-five percent of the United States population with 675,000 Americans dying during the pandemic.

The obituary from the *Stockton Record* for Flora Hopkins stated:
"HOPKINS - In Stockton, November 3, 1918, Flora Hopkins, wife of D. E. Hopkins, mother of Mrs. S. Manrique of Oakdale, Robert, Carrie, Lupe and Dave Hopkins of Stockton, a native of California, aged 36 years and 22 days. The funeral will take place Tuesday, November 5th at 2 pm at St. Mary's Church. Internment at San Joaquin Cemetery. Services private. Remains at Warren & Smiths."

Daniel Hopkins was listed in California Voter Registration logs: Hopkins, Daniel E., Rep (Republican) 1926, Stanislaus County and 1928 -1930, Alameda County. His children, (Robert Hopkins, Danny Hopkins, Carrie Hopkins and Lupe Hopkins) moved to Alameda by early 1930, along with Daniel Edwin Hopkins. Daniel Edwin Hopkins died on 23 December 1934 at age sixty-three and is buried in an unmarked grave at the Holy Ghost Cemetery, part of the historical Holy Spirit Church built during 1886 in Fremont, Alameda County, California. The church held services in Portuguese, leading credibility to Flora Hopkins' parents emigrating from Portugal. (*A "Joseph Ramirez" was buried at the same cemetery on 25 January 1944 - whether this was Flora Ramirez Hopkins' father is unknown.*) Daniel Hopkins hobbies included playing the accordion, piano and guitar, skills he taught his daughter, Mary (Hopkins) Manrique. A San Francisco directory (1891-1902) listed Daniel Hopkins as "sailor and musician."

The birth of Mary Hopkins was noted in the Tuesday, 31 July 1900 *San Francisco Call* edition on page eleven (HOPKINS - In this city, July 29, 1900, to the wife of F. D. Hopkins, a daughter.). She married Serapio Manrique on 26 December 1917 in Stockton, San Joaquin County, California. Serapio's first wife and her stepfather were the godparents to Mary's brother, Daniel Hopkins, Jr. By early 1917, Serapio Manrique was a widower with two young children. The children of Serapio and (m1) Julia (Machado), Primitivo and Dolores Manrique, resided with the Serapio and (m2) Mary Hopkins Manrique family at 157 North 5th

Avenue off Main Street in Oakdale, California. The 1910 farmhouse was also home to Vincent, Jenny, Lawrence, Linda, triplets Steven, Arthur and Joseph, Raymond, Julius, Edward, Alice, Richard, Tony and Madeline Violet Manrique, not to mention (m1) Primo and Dolores Manrique.

According to Julius Manrique, "Fifth Avenue was important to the cattlemen in the area because they would bring their cattle from the north grazing land across the old bridge south to the corrals on 5th Avenue near the cemetery."

A 1917 World War Draft Registration card listed Serapio Manrique as: White; Married; Born 14 November 1892, Mexico and resident of Oakdale, California. The document also noted he was a "farmhand" working for Marion Cottle and the married father of two children.

Mary Hopkins and Serapio Manrique married on 26 December 1917 in Stockton, San Joaquin County, California, USA. The marriage license listed Serapio Manrique's parents as: CLEMENTE MANRIQUE and PETRA DURAN. Mary Hopkins' parents were recorded as: DAN HOPKINS and FLORA ROMILOUS. The witnesses on the marriage document were Flora Amescua of Oakdale and Cyril Kenyon of Stockton, California, USA. Serapio and Mary (Hopkins) Manrique resided in Oakdale, California, a town situated alongside the Stanislaus River with fewer than one-thousand residents.

The 1920 Oakdale Township, Stanislaus County, California, United States Census listed "Sorophia Manrique" as age twenty-seven, owner of the house at 157 N. 5th Avenue, Oakdale, California, and head of the household for the 157 N. 5th Avenue residence. His wife was Mary Manrique born California to a father born England and mother born California; age 22. The children were: Primo Manrique (age 6), Laura (Dolores) Manrique (age 3 years and 9 months) and Vincent Manrique (age nine months) - all children born California.

The 1930 Oakdale Township, Stanislaus County, California, United States Census listed: Salvador Manrique age 28 as head of the household who immigrated to California in 1906 with wife, Mary Manrique, age 29 born California to a father born England and a mother born California and children: Primo (age 15), Dolores (age 13), Vincent (age 11), Jennie (age 9), Lawrence (age 8), Linda (age 7), Joe (age 5) and Raymond (age 1 and ten months) - all born California.

The *Modesto News-Herald*, dated Saturday, 7 November 1931 (Vol. XXXXIL, No. 267) and Sunday, 8 November 1931 (Vol. XXXXIL, No. 268) cover stories noted news which included the Sunday paper article titled, "Large Quantity of Liquor Seized in County Raids/County Raids Net Large Quantity of Wine, Whisky. Principle Hauls Made at Three Homes in Oakdale Area: Seven Arrested..."
> *"...Over 3,000 gallons of wine confiscated... In second raid, they found 150 gallons of wine under the house and three fifty-gallon barrels of wine in the house (of S. Manrique whose sentence was suspended) ..."*

The above November 1931 raid included Serapio Manrique and took place during the last two years of the prohibition when selling, making or distributing alcohol was a federal crime (although wine made for the church was overlooked and allowed).

The 1940 Oakdale Township, Stanislaus County, California, United States Census listed: Sam Manrique age 42 and head of the household with wife Mary Manrique age 40 and children: Vincent (age 21), Lawrence (age 18), Joseph (age 15) Raymond (age 11), Julius (age 8), Edward (age 6), Alice (age 4), Richard (age 2), Tony (age 1) and Violet (age four months) - all born California.

1942 World War Draft Registration: Serapio D. Manrique. Age - 50. Birthdate - 14 November 1892. Date - 1942. Residence Place - Ahwahnee, California. Serapio Manrique was recovering from tuberculosis at the Ahwahnee Sanatorium where they removed one of his lungs. Serapio Manrique listed his neighbor, Sam Kaufman (b. 1894/1940 residence - 904 Second Avenue, Oakdale, California) as his contact. The Ahwahnee in Madera, California was built in 1918, a property with four-hundred-and-eighty acres to provide rehabilitation for tuberculosis patients under the care of Dr. William Wheaton.

Serapio and Mary (Hopkins) Manrique's sons, Vincent Manrique (Army Air Force - Battle of the Bulge, France), Lawrence Manrique (US Army) and Joseph Manrique (Corporal Army; Papua New Guinea) fought in WW2.

Manrique-Hopkins children recall Serapio Manrique could plant grape vines perfectly spaced apart by doing math in his head, then making the calculations needed to envision the area needed to allow the crop to grow. They also remember the 157 North 5th Avenue home being the neighborhood gathering place for dancing and music where the children would hide under the kitchen table after the pocket doors slid out making the home an entire dance floor. Mary Manrique would play the piano while others would accompany her on the guitar. On occasions, Serapio and Mary Manrique would put their children in the back of the pickup truck and drive Hayward where Lupe (Hopkins) Duran, Mary's sister, lived on an apricot farm. There, the Manrique children would play with their cousins, the Duran children. Mary (Hopkins) Manrique crocheted any design without using templates, an art that has resulted in many family heirloom pieces.

The United States City Directory often listed "Serapio Manrique" as, "Sam" or "Samuel." United States social security applications for Dolores Manrique Pongan, daughter of (m1) Julia Machado, listed her father as "Serapio Manrique" while Linda Manrique's Social Security application stated her father was, "Sam Manrique." Raymond Manrique recorded his father as, "Sam D. Manrique" and mother "Mary Hopkins." The name, "Salvador," was once listed on a census record without accuracy.

> 1948 U. S. City Directory: *Samuel D. Manrique* residing at 5th Avenue North East in Modesto, a laborer married to Mary H. Manrique.
> 1950 U. S. City Directory: *Sam Manrique* residing at 157 N 5th Avenue in Modesto, California, a laborer married to Mary Manrique.

1952 U. S. City Directory: *Samuel Manrique* residing at RDI Box 624 in Modesto, California with Alice, Edward, Joseph, Julius, Mary, Primo, Raymond, Richard, Samuel and Tony Manrique.

After suffering from a bout of pneumonia, Serapio Manrique died (in the car on route to a doctor with his son, Edward, driving) on 29 December 1952 in Oakdale, California.

The California Death Index noted: Serapio Manrique. Birth Date: 14 November 1892, Mexico. Death date: 29 December 1952, Stanislaus County, California.

Serapio Duran Manrique's baptismal record confirmed his birth was 14 November 1891, information documented in an 1891 Silao, Guanajuato, Mexico baptismal record book. Serapio's younger brother, Primitivo Manrique, was christened on 11 June 1892 in Leon, Guanajuato, Mexico.

Mary (Hopkins) Manrique resided at 157 North 5th Avenue in Oakdale, Californian until her death on 27 February 1978 in Oakdale, California at age seventy-seven. Mary (Hopkins) Manrique was listed as:

1953 U. S. City Directory: *Widow of Samuel D. Manrique*, 157 N 5th, Modesto.
1965 U. S. City Directory: *Wid. Samuel D. Manrique*, 157 N 5th, Modesto, Stanislaus, California. Spouse: Mary H. Manrique.

Both Serapio Manrique and Mary (Hopkins) Manrique were buried at Oakdale Citizens Cemetery. To this day, Serapio Manrique's former Laughlin Road farmland remains untouched with a view of the Sierra foothills still visible while the property at 157 N. Fifth Avenue was sold by Manrique-Hopkins grandchildren and the house no longer exists.

The children of Serapio and Mary (Hopkins) Manrique were at least GEN4 Northern Californians given their great-grandfather, Joseph RAMIREZ (GEN1), was born "in California," their grandmother Flora (RAMIREZ) Hopkins (GEN2) was born September 1882 "in California," and their mother, Mary HOPKINS (GEN3) was born July 1900 in San Francisco, California. The grandchildren of Serapio and Mary (Hopkins) are GEN5 Northern Californians.

Twins and triplets were in the DNA of both Petra Duran and Flora Ramirez/Francis Lopes. Serapio Manrique's siblings, children of CLEMENTE and Petra (DURAN) MANRIQUE, born Leon, Guanajuato, Mexico included either triplets or twins. The first-born children were - JUAN MANRIQUE (b.1889), JOSE MANRIQUE (b. 1889) and MARIA LUZ MANRIQUE (b. 1889). Mary Hopkins' siblings, children of DANIEL and FLORA (RAMIREZ) HOPKINS born Stockton, California, were also twins: JOSEPH HOPKINS (b. 4 July 1910) and RUBY HOPKINS (b. 4 July 1910). Serapio and Mary (Hopkins) Manrique also likely had twins born 5 April 1919, California: VINCENT JOSEPH MANRIQUE b. 5 April 1919; d. 31 December 2014, Tucson, Arizona) and LINDRA MANRIQUE (b. 5 May 1919; d. 5 June 1919, Fresno, California). However, the death record for "Lindra Manrique" noted she was age 1/12 or one month old when she died in Fresno on 5 June 1919. If she was the twin of Vincent, she would have been 2/12 or two months old when she passed away. Likely the month age listed was incorrect, and Lindra was Vincent's twin, especially as the name, "Linda" was given to a daughter born years later and the surname, Manrique was rare in Northern California during the early 1900s. However, there is no birth record for Lindra Manrique to prove Vincent-Lindra Manrique twin status. Triplets were likely born Oakdale, California: (ALBERT FRANK) STEVEN MANRIQUE (b. 5 September 1924, ARTHUR (ARTURO H.) MANRIQUE (b. 5 September 1924) and JOSEPH HOPKINS MANRIQUE (b. 5 September 1924; d. 13 January). While it was noted the family had identical twins (Frank and Joseph Manrique), burial documentation notes possible triplets (Arturo H. Manrique - b. 1924; d. 1926). No birth record was found for Arturo (Arthur) Manrique who could have also been born between the years 1925-1926. Mary (Hopkins) Manrique and her sister, Lupe (Hopkins) Duran, both named sons, Frank and Arthur.

(Julius) Clement Manrique's 1932 birth certificate disclosed Mary Hopkins had given birth to twelve children. By April 1932, seven of her children were living and five children had died. Children who died were: *Lindra Manrique* (b. 5 April 1919; d. 5 June 1919, Fresno, California), Frank Manrique (b. 5 September 1924, Oakdale, California; d. 17 October 1924, Oakdale, California) and Arturo Manrique (born abt. 1924; d. 1926, Oakdale, California). Given Mary Hopkins adopted her husband's children from his first marriage, Primo and Dolores Manrique, her stepchildren were included within the total of twelve. All Manrique-Hopkins children were born at the 157 North 5th, Oakdale, California, USA house.

<u>The known children of Serapio and Mary (Hopkins) Manrique (a) were:</u>
b1. VINCENT JOSEPH MANRIQUE, born 5 April 1919, Oakdale, Stanislaus, California, USA. Died 31 December 2014, Tucson, Arizona, USA. Buried Holy Sepulchre Cemetery, Hayward, California, USA.
b2. JENNY MANRIQUE, born 17 July 1920, Oakdale, Stanislaus, California, USA. Died 15 January 1936, Oakdale, Stanislaus, California, USA. Buried Oakdale Citizens Cemetery, Oakdale, Stanislaus, California, USA.
b3. LAWRENCE MAXWELL MANRIQUE, born 1 December 1921, Oakdale, Stanislaus, California, USA. Died 11 June 1981, Fremont, Alameda, California, USA.
b4. LEONA (LINDA) MANRIQUE, born 23 March 1923, Oakdale, Stanislaus, California, USA. Died 17 January 2001, Concord, California, USA.
b5. (ALBERT) STEVEN (FRANK) MANRIQUE, born 5 September 1924, Oakdale, Stanislaus, California, USA. Died 17 October 1924, Oakdale, Stanislaus, California, USA. Buried Oakdale Citizens Cemetery, Oakdale, Stanislaus, California, USA.
b6. JOSEPH HOPKINS MANRIQUE, born 5 September 1924, Oakdale, Stanislaus, California, USA. Died 13 January 2009, Modesto, Stanislaus California, USA. Buried Oakdale Citizens Cemetery, Oakdale, Stanislaus, California, USA.
b7. ARTURO H. (ARTHUR) HOPKINS MANRIQUE, born abt. 5 September 1924, Oakdale, Stanislaus, California, USA. Died 1926 (age 2), Oakdale,

Stanislaus, California, USA. Buried Oakdale Citizens Cemetery, Oakdale, Stanislaus, California, USA.

b8. (JOHN) RAYMOND MANRIQUE, born 16 May 1928, Oakdale, Stanislaus, California, USA. Died 12 April 1998, San Leandro, Alameda, California, USA.

b9. (JULIUS) CLEMENT MANRIQUE, born 8 April 1932, Oakdale, Stanislaus, California, USA. Died 10 December 2023, Modesto, Stanislaus, California, USA. Buried Oakdale Citizens Cemetery, Oakdale, Stanislaus, California, USA.

b10. EDWARD MANRIQUE, born 12 April 1934, Oakdale, Stanislaus, California, USA. Died 14 December 2005, Oakdale, Stanislaus, California, USA. Buried Oakdale Citizens Cemetery, Oakdale, Stanislaus, California, USA.

b11. ALICE MANRIQUE, born 22 October 1935, Oakdale, Stanislaus, California, USA.

b12. STEVEN (RICHARD) MANRIQUE, born 10 March 1937, Oakdale, Stanislaus California, USA. Died 9 September 2018, Modesto, Stanislaus, California, USA. Buried Ceres Memorial Park, Ceres, Stanislaus, California, USA.

b13. TONY MANRIQUE, born 13 June 1938, Oakdale, Stanislaus, California, USA.

b14. MADELINE VIOLET MANRIQUE, born 13 January 1940, Oakdale, Stanislaus California, USA. Died 27 December 1944, Oakdale, Stanislaus, California, USA. Buried Oakdale Citizens Cemetery, Oakdale, Stanislaus. California, USA.

Many Manrique family members are buried at Oakdale Citizens Cemetery. Those include: Serapio D. Manrique (plot #122), Mary (Hopkins) Manrique (plot #120), Jenny Manrique, (Albert) Steven Manrique, Arthur (Arturo H.) Manrique, Edward Manrique, Joseph Manrique, Julius Clement Manrique and Madeline Violet Manrique. Other family members buried at the cemetery include Serapio and (m1) Julia (Machado) Manrique's children, Primitivo Manrique with his wife, Lula Belle (Wyatt) Manrique and Dolores Laura (Manrique) Pongan with her husband, Castor Evardo Pongan.

Proof of twins and triplets in the Manrique-Hopkins family include a <u>California Birth/Death Index</u> for a "Lindra Manrique" who was born May 1919 and died 5 June 1919 (age 1/12). The name, Linda, was later given to a Manrique-Hopkins daughter, and the year of birth matches that of the eldest child, Vincent Manrique. The <u>California Birth Index</u> also listed a "Frank Menriques" and "Joe Menriques" born on 5 September 1924 in San Joaquin, California. The mother's name was listed as, "Hopkins" proving Mary Hopkins was the mother of Frank Manrique. Somehow, "Frank," was translated into "Steven Albert Manrique" on a 17 October 1924, Oakdale, California death record. Born also on 5 September without a <u>California Birth Index</u> listing was, "Arturo H." or "Arthur Hopkins" Manrique who was buried at Oakdale Citizens Cemetery between the ages of one and two years old during 1926, therefore, likely, a 1924 birth year triplet (his gravestone lists: 1924-1926).

Three of Serapio and Mary (Hopkins) Manrique's sons served in the World War II Armed Forces. Vincent Manrique served in the 18th Army Air Force in England and France. He worked in England at an airport until the unit was deployed to France where he loaded bombs into B17s at an airfield located several miles from the Battle of the Bulge. Lawrence Manrique served in the Army Air Force while stationed in Florida. Joseph Manrique enlisted in the United States Army on 3 February 1942 at the Presidio of Monterey in California. He served as a Private in the United States Army and was stationed during WW2 at the South Pacific Island of Papua New Guinea, a post with extreme heat and humidity, as well as malaria outbreaks. Joseph Manrique served as Corporal in the Army until 1962.

Vincent Joe Manrique's WW2 registration card stated he was age 21 and born 5 April 1919 in Oakdale, California. His residence was 5th "E" Street, Oakdale, California. He listed his contact person ("*who will always know your address*") as his mother, Mrs. Mary Manrique of 5th "E" Street, Oakdale, California. His employer was M. Kamigaki. He signed his name as Vincent J. Manrique.

Lawrence Maxwell Manrique's WW2 registration card stated he was age 21 born 1 December 1921, Oakdale, California. His residence was 5th & "E" Street, Oakdale, California. His contact person ("*who will always know your address*") was Mrs. Lupe Durante, Hayward, California. He signed his name as Lawrence Maxwell Manrique.

Joseph H. Manrique's WW2 registration card (written as, "Joe H. Manrique") stated he was age 18 and born 5 September 1924 in Ripon, California. His contact person ("*who will always know your address*") was Samuel Manrique, Box 844, Oakdale, California. His employer was Kaufman Brothers, Pacific Packing Company, Oakdale, California. He signed his name as, "Joe Manrique." His veterans affairs file listed the name, Joseph H. Manrique. Joseph Manrique's "H" middle initial stands for, "Hopkins."

Raymond Manrique also enlisted for WW2 service and his registration card stated he was age 18 born 16 May 1928, Oakdale, California. His contact person ("*who will always know your address*") was Mrs. Mary Manrique, Box 844, Oakdale, California. He was listed as a student and signed his name as Ray Manrique.

The academic of the family was Julius Clement Manrique. The name, "Clement," was to recognize Serapio Manrique's father, Clemente Manrique. The name "Julius" was officially added as Clement's first name by Serapio and Mary (Hopkins) Manrique during 1951. Serapio Manrique hoped one of his children would become a doctor and J. C. achieved his father's dream by earning a Doctorate in Education. Julius Manrique graduated from Oakdale High in 1949 then Modesto Junior College in 1952 (AA degree) and San Jose State University (1955 BA, Social Studies with a minor in Spanish along with a teaching credential and 1965 MA degree), the first California State University established in 1857 and the oldest public institution established on the West coast. After working as a teacher then principal, Julius C. Manrique earned a Doctorate in Education in 1975 from Stockton's University of the Pacific, California's first private university established in 1851. Julius Manrique's children graduated from Stanford University (BA 1987/BA 1988).

Julius Manrique was an active member of Oakdale's Troop 43 Boy Scout group where he earned nineteen badges, the Order of the Arrow (Top Scouter in a Troop) and an Eagle Scout award as member of the Yosemite Area Council Boy Scouts. He became Assistant Scoutmaster and Scoutmaster of Troup 43 (six years as an adult) and the only Wood Badger (a fully trained Scoutmaster, first in the Yosemite Area Council) in the Yosemite Area Council. Julius C. Manrique also received the Silver Beaver Award. As Scoutmaster, he had a record eleven boy scouts earn Eagle Scout honors, and one year had twenty Eagle Scouts in his Oakdale Troop 43 Boy Scout group.

Alice Manrique married her "high school sweetheart" (*Vision*, Spring 2013, p. 17), Elmo Garcia, who became Oakdale City Council member (1968-1984) and Oakdale Mayor (1984-1994). Elmo Garcia also served as Oakdale City Treasurer from 2000-2004 and was nominated by then California Governor Jerry Brown and United States President Ronald Reagan to serve on the Stanislaus County Selective Service Board #61.

While it is theorized Serapio and Mary Hopkins had identical twin boys, Albert Steven and Joseph, the "twins," may have been triplets. Steven (Frank) died one month after his birth and was the first Hopkins-Manrique buried at Oakdale Citizens Cemetery. His brother Arthur (Arturo H.) followed his sibling to the cemetery in 1926 with a record that stated, "died age two.". If not a triplet, then Arthur Manrique may have been born between the years 1925-1926. Jenny Manrique passed away after a bout with pneumonia on 15 January 1936 when she was fifteen years old. Madeline Violet Manrique, the youngest child of Serapio and Mary, had enjoyed playing hide-and-go seek on the family farm with her siblings before she fell ill to meningitis. At age four, she found the ideal hiding location - inside the standing pipe of an irrigation ditch - where none of her brothers or sisters saw her. As the afternoon turned to dusk, her family called local officials - police and firemen - to seek her whereabouts. Eventually she was located, but after-hours breathing air in standing pool of water, she contracted bacterial spinal meningococcal meningitis, a disease whose first effective cure of penicillin was discovered the year of her death in 1944. Given the small town did not provide the opportunity for Madeline to receive care, like her sister Jenny, Madeline died shortly after becoming sick. Unfortunately, the first meningococcal vaccine was not available until 1970. Because of the contagious nature of the disease, Madeline Violet's belongings were burned, and the family was put under quarantine. While no one else in the family caught the deadly disease, Madeline's death remains a heartbreakingly sad moment in the family history.

As Manrique-Hopkins' family generations grow, it can be confirmed our ancestors left Spain for Leon, Guanajuato, Mexico during the mid-1500s and sailed from Britain to the Island of St. Helena, a British Overseas Territory by the 1700s. Both lines then settled in Northern California by the late 1880s to early 1900s, Californian lineage which has today resided in the state for over one-hundred-and-fifty years.

~~~~~~~~

MANRIQUE-HOPKINS CHILDREN

The known children of Serapio and Mary (Hopkins) Manrique were:

1. VINCENT JOSEPH MANRIQUE, born 5 April 1919, Oakdale, Stanislaus, California, USA. Died 31 December 2014, Tucson, Arizona, USA.
2. JENNY MANRIQUE, born 17 July 1920, Oakdale, Stanislaus, California, USA. Died 15 January 1936, Oakdale, Stanislaus, California, USA.
3. LAWRENCE MAXWELL MANRIQUE, born 1 December 1921, Oakdale, Stanislaus, California, USA. Died 11 June 1981, Fremont, Alameda, California, USA.
4. (LEONA) LINDA MANRIQUE, born 23 March 1923, Oakdale, Stanislaus, California, USA. Died 17 January 2001, Concord, California, USA.
5. (ALBERT) STEVEN (FRANK) MANRIQUE, born 5 September 1924, Oakdale, Stanislaus, California, USA. Died 17 October 1924, Oakdale, Stanislaus, California, USA.
6. JOSEPH HOPKINS MANRIQUE, born 5 September 1924, Oakdale, Stanislaus, California, USA. Died 13 January 2009, Modesto, Stanislaus, California, USA.
7. ARTURO H. (ARTHUR) HOPKINS MANRIQUE, born abt. 5 September 1924, Stanislaus, Oakdale, California, USA. Died 1926, Oakdale, Stanislaus, California, USA.
8. (JOHN) RAYMOND MANRIQUE, born 16 May 1928, Oakdale, Stanislaus, California, USA. Died 12 April 1998, San Leandro, Alameda, California, USA.
9. JULIUS CLEMENT MANRIQUE, born 8 April 1932, Oakdale, Stanislaus, California, USA. Died 10 December 2023, Modesto, Stanislaus, California, USA.
10. EDWARD MANRIQUE, born 12 April 1934, Oakdale, Stanislaus, California, USA. Died 14 December 2005, Oakdale, Stanislaus, California, USA.
11. ALICE MANRIQUE, born 22 October 1935, Oakdale, Stanislaus, California, USA.
12. (STEVEN) RICHARD MANRIQUE, born 10 March 1937, Oakdale, Stanislaus, California, USA. Died 9 September 2018, Modesto, Stanislaus, California, USA.
13. TONY MANRIQUE, born 13 June 1938, Oakdale, Stanislaus, California, USA.
14. MADELINE VIOLET MANRIQUE, born 13 January 1940, Oakdale, Stanislaus, California, USA. Died 27 December 1944, Oakdale, Stanislaus, California, USA.

The children of Serapio and Mary (Hopkins) (a) Manrique (*plus unconfirmed*) (a) were:

b1. VINCENT JOSEPH MANRIQUE, born 5 April 1919, Oakdale, Stanislaus, California, USA. Died 31 December 2014, Tucson, Arizona, USA. Buried Holy Sepulchre Cemetery, Hayward, California, USA.
b2. *LIND(R)A MANRIQUE, born 5 April 1919, Oakdale, Stanislaus, California, USA. Died 5 June 1919, Fresno, California, USA.*

b3. JENNY MANRIQUE, born 17 July 1920, Oakdale, Stanislaus, California, USA. Died 15 January 1936, Oakdale, Stanislaus, California, USA. Buried Oakdale Citizens Cemetery, Oakdale, Stanislaus, CA, USA,

b4. LAWRENCE MAXWELL MANRIQUE, born 1 December 1921, Oakdale, Stanislaus, California, USA. Died 11 June 1981, Fremont, Alameda, California, USA.

b5. (LEONA) LINDA MANRIQUE, born 23 March 1923, Oakdale, Stanislaus, California, USA. Died 17 January 2001, Concord, California, USA.

b6. (ALBERT) STEVEN (FRANK) MANRIQUE, born 5 September 1924, Oakdale, Stanislaus, California, USA. Died 17 October 1924, Oakdale, Stanislaus, California, USA. Buried Oakdale Citizens Cemetery, Oakdale, Stanislaus, California, USA.

b7. JOSEPH HOPKINS MANRIQUE, born 5 September 1924, Oakdale, Stanislaus, California, USA. Died 13 January 2009, Modesto, Stanislaus, California, USA. Buried Oakdale Citizens Cemetery, Oakdale, Stanislaus, California, USA.

b8. ARTURO H. (ARTHUR) HOPKINS MANRIQUE, born abt. 5 September 1924, Oakdale, Stanislaus, California, USA. Died 1926 (age 2), Oakdale, Stanislaus, California, USA. Buried Oakdale Citizens Cemetery, Oakdale, Stanislaus, California, USA.

b9. (JOHN) RAYMOND MANRIQUE, born 16 May 1928, Oakdale, Stanislaus, California, USA. Died 12 April 1998, San Leandro, Alameda, California, USA.

b10. JULIUS CLEMENT MANRIQUE, born 8 April 1932, Oakdale, Stanislaus, California, USA. Died 10 December 2023, Modesto, Stanislaus, California, USA. Buried Oakdale Citizens Cemetery, Oakdale, Stanislaus, California, USA.

b11. EDWARD MANRIQUE, born 12 April 1934, Oakdale, Stanislaus, California, USA. Died 14 December 2005, Oakdale, Stanislaus, California, USA. Buried Oakdale Citizens Cemetery, Oakdale, Stanislaus, California, USA.

b12. ALICE MANRIQUE, born 22 October 1935, Oakdale, Stanislaus, California, USA.

b13. (STEVEN) RICHARD MANRIQUE, born 10 March 1937, Oakdale, Stanislaus California, USA. Died 9 September 2018, Modesto, Stanislaus, California, USA. Buried Ceres Memorial Park, Ceres, Stanislaus, California, USA.

b14. TONY MANRIQUE, born 13 June 1938, Oakdale, Stanislaus, California, USA.

b15. MADELINE VIOLET MANRIQUE, born 13 January 1940, Oakdale, Stanislaus California, USA. Died 27 December 1944, Oakdale, Stanislaus, California, USA. Buried Oakdale Citizens Cemetery, Oakdale, Stanislaus. California, USA.

MANRIQUE-HOPKINS GRANDCHILDREN
Born California, USA

VINCENT MANRIQUE (b. 1919).
<u>Married</u>: BERNICE MAYR (b. 1923) in 1949.
<u>The children of Vincent and Bernice (Mayr) Manrique were</u>:
    1.   CYNTHIA MANRIQUE (b. 1950). <u>Married</u> BABCOCK.
    2.   GEORGE MANRIQUE (b. 1954).

LAWRENCE MANRIQUE (b. 1921).
<u>Married</u> IDA SANTANA (b. 1924) in 1954.
<u>The children of Lawrence and Ida (Santana) Manrique were</u>:
    3.   DAVID MANRIQUE (b. 1946; d. 12 December 2020). <u>Married</u> CONLEY.
    4.   ANITA MANRIQUE (b. 1948). <u>Married</u> BAKER.
    5.   LAWRENCE MANRIQUE JUNIOR (b. 1953). <u>Married</u> BACHMAN.
    6   CHRISTOPHER MANRIQUE (b. 1961).

LINDA MANRIQUE (b. 1923).
<u>Married</u> (m1) DAN GALLEGOS/(m2) THOMAS VALENCIA (b. 1923).
<u>The children of Dan (m1) and Linda (Manrique) Gallegos were</u>:
    7.   RAMONA VALENCIA (b. 1941). <u>Married</u> BODKIN.
    8.   VIRGINIA VALENCIA (b. 1942). <u>Married</u> JUDD.
<u>The children of Thomas (m2) and Linda (Manrique) Valencia were</u>:
    9.   NANCY VALENCIA (b. 1948). <u>Married</u> HARTMAN.
    10.   STEVE VALENICA (b. 1956). <u>Married</u> WILSON.

JOSEPH H. MANRIQUE (b. 1924).
<u>Married</u>: SHARON AMARAL (b. 1938) in 1959.
<u>The children of Joseph and Sharon (Amaral) Manrique were</u>:
    11.   ANDRE MANRIQUE (b. 1959; died 9 February 2024).
    12.   JEFFERY MANRIQUE (b. 1960).
    13.   ANNETTE MANRIQUE (b. 1962). <u>Married</u> McCARTHY.

RAYMOND MANRIQUE (b. 1928).
<u>Married</u>: DOROTHY BROWN (b. 1936) in 1952.
<u>The children of Raymond and Dorothy (Brown) Manrique were</u>:
    14.   ROXANN MANRIQUE (b. 1953).
    15.   JOHN MANRIQUE (b. 1955).
    16.   DENISE MANRIQUE (b. 1957). <u>Married</u> MARTINEZ.
    17.   ALLEN MANRIQUE (b. 1960).

JULIUS CLEMENT MANRIQUE (b. 1932).
<u>Married</u>: BARBARA ANNE PINKHAM (b. 1937) in 1963.
<u>The children of Julius Clement and Barbara (Pinkham) Manrique were</u>:
    18.   ANNE MANRIQUE (b. 1965).
    19.   Daughter MANRIQUE (b. 1967).

EDWARD MANRIQUE (b. 1934).
Married: (m1) VIOLA PORTER in 1955/(m2) ANNETTE LESHER (b. 1951) in 1972.
The children of Edward and (m1) Viola (Porter) Manrique were:
    20.   EDDIE MANRIQUE (b. 1955). Married McCRAY.
    21.   MICHAEL "MIKE" MANRIQUE (b. 1957; d. 16 February 1996).
    22.   WILLIAM MANRIQUE (b. 1959). Married JONES.
    23.   JAMES MANRIQUE (b. 1960). Married PARKER.
    24.   SUSAN MANRIQUE (b. 1961).
The child of Edward and (m2) Annette (Lesher) Manrique was:
    (#33)   TAMMY MANRIQUE (b.1969) *(Adopted)*.

ALICE MANRIQUE (b. 1935).
Married: ELMO GARCIA (b. 1935) in 1951.
The children of Elmo and Alice (Manrique) Garcia were:
    25.   JOHN GARCIA (b. 1952). Married (m1) ROBERTS/(m2) HAWTHORNE.
    26.   LORETTA GARCIA (b. 1955). Married LAUGHLIN.
    27.   DONNA GARCIA (b. 1959). Married BORGES.

RICHARD MANRIQUE (b. 1937).
Married: (m1) BRENDA SWINDELL (b. 1941) in 1959/(m2) DONNA ELWESS (b. 1935)
    in 1970.
The children of Richard and (m1) Brenda (Swindell) Manrique were:
    28.   KIMBERLY MANRIQUE (b. 1961). Married JASPER.
    29.   KELLY DAWN MANRIQUE (b. 3 May 1964; d. 22 February 2003).
The child of Richard and (m2) Donna (Elwess) Manrique was:
    30.   RICHARD MANRIQUE (b. 1976).

TONY MANRIQUE (b. 1936).
Married: (m1) Ricky Van Orsdale (b. 1940)/(m2) Barbara Ann Walton in 1984.
The children of Tony and (m1) Ricky (Van Orsdale) Manrique were:
    31.   ANTHONY MANRIQUE (b. 1959). Married LUND.
    32.   JEANETTE MANRIQUE (b. 1960). Married WILLHITE.

(Please note Manrique-Hopkins grandchildren's spouse surname list is incomplete)

SERAPIO AND MARY (HOPKINS) MANRIQUE GRANDCHILDREN
(Listed by birth order)

1.	Ramona Valencia	Linda Manrique	b. 1941
2.	Virginia Valencia	Linda Manrique	b. 1942
3.	David Manrique	Lawrence Manrique	b. 1946/d. 12 Dec. 2020
4.	Anita Manrique	Lawrence Manrique	b. 1948
5.	Nancy Valencia	Linda Manrique	b. 1948
6.	Cynthia Manrique	Vincent Manrique	b. 1950
7.	John Garcia	Alice Manrique	b. 1952
8.	Lawrence Manrique Jr.	Lawrence Manrique	b. 1953
9.	Roxann Manrique	Raymond Manrique	b. 1953
10.	George Manrique	Vincent Manrique	b. 1954
11.	Eddie Manrique	Edward Manrique	b. 1955
12.	John Manrique	Raymond Manrique	b. 1955
13.	Loretta Garcia	Alice Manrique	b. 1955
14.	Steve Valencia	Linda Manrique	b. 1956
15.	Denise Manrique	Raymond Manrique	b. 1957
16.	Michael Manrique	Edward Manrique	b. 1957/d. 26 Feb. 1996
17.	Andre Manrique	Joseph Manrique	b. 1959/d. 9 Feb. 2024
18.	Anthony Manrique	Tony Manrique	b. 1959
19.	Donna Garcia	Alice Manrique	b. 1959
20.	William Manrique	Edward Manrique	b. 1959
21.	Allen Manrique	Raymond Manrique	b. 1960
22.	James Manrique	Edward Manrique	b. 1960
23.	Jeanette Manrique	Tony Manrique	b. 1960
24.	Jeffery Manrique	Joseph Manrique	b. 1960
25.	Christopher Manrique	Lawrence Manrique	b. 1961
26.	Kimberly Manrique	Richard Manrique	b. 1961
27.	Susan Manrique	Edward Manrique	b. 1961
28.	Annette Manrique	Joseph Manrique	b. 1962
29.	Kelly Manrique	Richard Manrique	b. 1964/d. 22 Feb. 2004
30.	Anne Manrique	Julius Clement Manrique	b. 1965
31.	Daughter Manrique	Julius Clement Manrique	b. 1967
32.	Richard Manrique	Richard Manrique	b. 1976

MANRIQUE (de LARA) GENERATIONS 1-10 (*GEN1-13**)

Pedro Gomez - Catalina Manrique de Lara
|
Gaspar Gomez Manrique de Lara (*GEN1**) - Mariana *Ferrer*
|
Catalina Gomez Manrique de Lara - Garci Bravo de Lagunas
|
Maria Bravo de Lagunas - Pedro Gonzales de Aguirre y Rules
|

JOSEPHA GOMEZ MANRIQUE de LARA (GEN1)
Christening 23 July 1677, Irapuato, Gto.
Married: NICOLAS de MEDINA
Buried: 2 March 1718, Mexico City, MX.

GASPAR ANTONIO MANRIQUE de LARA (GEN2)
Born 28 March 1702, Leon, Gto., MX.
Married: FRANCA. XAVIER CALDERON de HERRERA
Died: 17 September 1755, Leon, MX.

JOSEPH MANUEL MANRIQUE de LARA (GEN3)
Baptized: 4 November 1734, Leon, MX.
Married: ANA RITA ALCARAS
Death unknown.

JOSEPH URBANO MANRIQUE de LARA (GEN4)
Born: 25 May 1765, Leon, Gto., MX.
Spouse: MARIA MELCHORA LOPES
Died: 3 September 1857, Leon, MX.

JOSE ISIDRO MANRIQUE (GEN5)
Baptized 17 May 1804, Leon, Gto., MX.
Married: MARIA DOLORES BIBIANA MORENO BOCANEGRA
Death unknown.

SIMON MANRIQUE (GEN6)
Baptized: 19 February 1835, Leon, MX.
Married: MARIA SERAPIA GONZALEZ
Died: 29 March 1895, Sauz de Armenta, Guanajuato, Mexico.

CLEMENTE MANRIQUE (GEN7)
Baptized: 24 November 1862, Leon.
Married: MARIA PETRONILLA DURAN
Died: 6 January 1920, Leon, Gto., MX.

SERAPIO MANRIQUE (GEN8)
Born: 14 November 1891, Silao de Victoria, Guanajuato, Mexico.
Married: MARY HOPKINS
Died: 29 December 1952, Oakdale, Stanislaus, California, USA.

JULIUS CLEMENT MANRIQUE (GEN9)
(Manrique-Hopkins children) (GEN12)*
Born: 8 April 1932, Oakdale, Stanislaus, California, USA
Died: 10 December 2023, Modesto, Stanislaus, California, USA.
Married: BARBARA PINKHAM

ANNE LOUISE MANRIQUE (GEN10)
(Manrique-Hopkins grandchildren) (GEN13)*
Born: 31 October 1965, Modesto, Stanislaus, California, USA

HOPKINS FAMILY TREE (GEN1-GEN3)

The children of Daniel Edwin (a) and Flora (Ramirez) HOPKINS were:

b1. MARY HOPKINS (b. 29 July 1900, San Francisco, California, USA; d. 27 February 1978, Oakdale, Stanislaus, California). Married SERAPIO MANRIQUE on 17 December 1917, Stockton, San Joaquin, California, USA.

The children of Serapio and Mary (HOPKINS) (b) Manrique were:

- c1. VINCENT JOSEPH MANRIQUE (b. 5 April 1919, Oakdale, Stanislaus, California, USA; d. 31 December 2014, Tucson, Arizona, USA). Married BERNICE MAYR on 1 October 1949, Alameda, California, USA.

  The children of Vincent (c) and Bernice (Mayr) Manrique were:
  - d1. CYNTHIA MANRIQUE (b. 1950). Married BABCOCK.
  - d2. GEORGE MANRIQUE (b. 1954).

- c2. JENNY MANRIQUE (b. 17 July 1920, Oakdale, Stanislaus, California, USA; d. 15 January 1936, Oakdale, Stanislaus, California, USA).

- c3. LAWRENCE MAXWELL MANRIQUE (b. 1 December 1921, Oakdale, Stanislaus, California, USA; d. 11 June 1981, Fremont, Alameda, California, USA). Married IDA SANTANA.

  The children of Lawrence (c) and Ida (Santana) Manrique were;
  - d1. DAVID MANRIQUE (b. 1946; d. 12 December 2020). Married CONLEY.
  - d2. ANITA MANRIQUE (b. 1948). Married BAKER.
  - d3. LAWRENCE MANRIQUE JR. (b. 1953). Married BACHMAN.
  - d4. CHRISTOPHER MANRIQUE (b. 1961).

- c4. (LEONA) LINDA MANRIQUE (b. 23 March 1923, Oakdale, Stanislaus, California, USA; d. 17 January 2001, Concord, California, USA). Married (m1) DAN GALLEGOS/(m2) THOMAS VALENCIA.

  The children of Dan (m1) and Linda (c) (Manrique) Gallegos were:
  - d1. RAMONA VALENCIA (b. 1941). Married BODKIN.
  - d2. VIRGINIA VALENCIA (b. 1942). Married JUDD SR.

  The children of Thomas (m2) and Linda (c) (Manrique) Valencia were:
  - d3. NANCY VALENCIA (b. 1948). Married HARTMAN.
  - d4. STEVE VALENICA (b. 1956). Married WILSON.

- c5. (ALBERT) STEVEN (FRANK) MANRIQUE (b. 5 September 1924, Oakdale, Stanislaus, California, USA; d. 17 October 1924, Oakdale, Stanislaus, California, USA).

- c6. JOSEPH HOPKINS MANRIQUE (b. 5 September 1924, Oakdale, Stanislaus, California, USA; d. 13 January 2009, Modesto, Stanislaus, California, USA). Married SHARON AMARAL.

  The children of Joseph (c) and Sharon (Amaral) Manrique were:
  - d1. ANDRE MANRIQUE (b. 1959; d. 9 February 2024).
  - d2. JEFFERY MANRIQUE (b. 1960).
  - d3. ANNETTE MANRIQUE (b. 1962). Married McCARTHY.

- c7. ARTURO H. (ARTHUR) HOPKINS MANRIQUE (born abt. 5 September 1924, Oakdale, Stanislaus, California, USA; d. 1926, Oakdale, Stanislaus, California, USA).
- c8. (JOHN) RAYMOND MANRIQUE (b. 16 May 1928, Oakdale, Stanislaus, California, USA; d. 12 April 1998, San Leandro, Alameda, California, USA). Married DOROTHY BROWN.

  The children of Raymond (c) and Dorothy (Brown) Manrique were:
  - d1. ROXANN MANRIQUE (b. 1953).
  - d2. JOHN MANRIQUE (b. 1955).
  - d3. DENISE MANRIQUE (b. 1957). Married MARTINEZ.
  - d4. ALLEN MANRIQUE (b. 1960).
- c9. JULIUS CLEMENT MANRIQUE (b. 8 April 1932, Oakdale, Stanislaus, California, USA; d. 10 December 2023, Modesto, Stanislaus, California, USA). Married BARBARA ANNE PINKHAM.

  The children of Julius Clement (c) and Barbara (Pinkham) Manrique were:
  - d1. ANNE MANRIQUE (b. 1965).
  - d2. Daughter MANRIQUE (b. 1967).
- c10. EDWARD MANRIQUE (b. 12 April 1934, Oakdale, Stanislaus, California, USA; d. 14 December 2005, Oakdale, Stanislaus, California, USA). Married (m1) VIOLA PORTER/(m2) ANNETTE LESHER.

  The children of Edward (c) and (m1) Viola (Porter) Manrique were:
  - d1. EDDIE MANRIQUE (b. 1955). Married McCRAY.
  - d2. MICHAEL MANRIQUE (b. 1957; d. 16 February 1996).
  - d3. WILLIAM MANRIQUE (b. 1959). Married JONES.
  - d4. JAMES MANRIQUE (b. 1960). Married PARKER.
  - d5. SUSAN MANRIQUE (b. 1961).

  The child of Edward and (m2) Annette (Lesher) Manrique was:
  - d6. *TAMMY MANRIQUE (adopted).*
- c11. ALICE MANRIQUE (b. 22 October 1935, Oakdale, Stanislaus, California, USA). Married ELMO GARCIA.

  The children of Elmo and Alice (c) (Manrique) Garcia were:
  - d1. JOHN GARCIA (b. 1952). Married (m1) ROBERTS/(m2) HAWTHORNE.
  - d2. LORETTA GARCIA (b. 1955). Married LAUGHLIN.
  - d3. DONNA GARCIA (b. 1959). Married BORGES.
- c12. RICHARD MANRIQUE (b. 10 March 1937, Oakdale, Stanislaus, California, USA; d. 9 September 2018, Modesto, Stanislaus, California, USA). Married (m1) BRENDA SWINDELL/(m2) DONNA ELWESS.

  The children of Richard (c) and (m1) Brenda (Swindell) Manrique were:
  - d1. KIMBERLY MANRIQUE (b. 1961). Married JASPER.
  - d2. KELLY MANRIQUE (b. 3 May 1964; d. 22 February 2003).

  The child of Richard (c) and (m2) Donna (Elwess) Manrique was:
  - d3. RICHARD MANRIQUE (b. 1976).

- c13. TONY MANRIQUE, (b. 13 June 1938, Oakdale, Stanislaus, California, USA). Married (m1) RICKY VAN ORSDALE /(m2) BARBARA ANN WALTON.

  The children of Anthony (c) and (m1) Ricky (Van Orsdale) Manrique were:
  - d1. ANTHONY MANRIQUE (b. 1959). Married LUND.
  - d2. JEANETTE MANRIQUE (b. 1960). Married WILLHITE.
- c14. MADELINE VIOLET MANRIQUE (b. 13 January 1940, Oakdale, Stanislaus, California, USA; d. 27 December 1944, Oakdale, Stanislaus, California, USA).

- b2. KATE HOPKINS (b. 4 September 1902, Stockton, San Joaquin, California, USA; d. 3 September 1903, Stockton, San Joaquin, California, USA).
- b3. JENNIE HOPKINS (b. 14 October 1903, Stockton, San Joaquin, California, USA; d. 15 October 1903, Stockton, San Joaquin, California, USA).
- b4. ROBERT HOPKINS (b. 20 August 1904, Stockton, San Joaquin, California, USA; d. 8 October 1964, San Leandro, California, USA). Married (m1) JULIA (Silva) (b. 1907) in 1924/(m2) MARY CATHERINE LOPEZ in 1934.

  The children of Robert Hopkins (b) and Julia (Silva) Hopkins were:
  - c1. ROBERT HOPKINS JUNIOR (b. 14 June 1924, Oakdale, Stanislaus, California, USA; resided Union City, CA; d. 2 February 2008, Pleasanton, Alameda, California, USA). Married SUSAN HISCOCK (b. 11 March 1929, London, England).

    The children of Robert Junior and Susan (Hiscock) Hopkins were:
    - d1. LILLIAN ELIZABETH HOPKINS (b. 22 February 1947, San Joaquin, California, USA).
    - d2. ROBERTA SUE HOPKINS (b. 10 June 1950, San Joaquin, California, USA).
    - d3. JULIE ANNE HOPKINS (b. 11 July 1953, San Joaquin, California, USA).
  - c2. ADELINE FRANCES HOPKINS (b. 27 December 1925, Oakdale, California, USA; d. 27 November 1982, Stanislaus, California, USA). Married CARPENTER.

  The children of Robert (b) and (m2) Mary Catherine (Lopez) Hopkins were:
  - c3. EVELYN (ROSALINE) HOPKINS (b. 18 October 1934, Alameda, California, USA). Married RODRIQUEZ.
  - c4. VALENTINA BEATRICE HOPKINS (b. 22 January 1936, Alameda, California, USA).
  - c5. GILBERT DANIEL HOPKINS (b. 14 May 1937, San Leandro, California, USA).
  - c6. GLORIA EVA HOPKINS (b. 21 August 1939, San Leandro, California, USA).
- b5. VICTORIA HOPKINS (b. 22 July 1905, Stockton, San Joaquin, California, USA; d. 21 February 1907, Stockton, San Joaquin, California, USA).
- b6. ROSE HOPKINS (b. 5 July 1906, Stockton, San Joaquin, California; d. 15 October 1906, Stockton, San Joaquin, California, USA).

b7. CARRIE HOPKINS (b. 30 December 1907, Stockton, San Joaquin, California, USA d. 3 November 1952, Fairfield, California, USA). Married (m1) PETE MENDEZ in 1923/(m2) ABEL MARTINEZ by 1927.
The children of Pete and Carrie (b) (Hopkins) Mendez were:
    c1. ROBERT MENDEZ (born abt. 1923, Stanislaus, California, USA).
    c2. MARGARET (MARGUERITE) MENDEZ (b. 17 October 1924, Ripon, San Joaquin, California, USA; d. 18 March 1971, Pittsburg, Contra Costa, California, USA). Married CERDA.
    c3. LOUIS GONZALES MENDEZ (b. 21 June 1926, Stanislaus, California, USA; d. 7 March 2009, Solano, California USA).
    c4. HELEN MENDEZ (b. 29 November 1927, Stanislaus, California, USA).
    c5. NATTIE MENDEZ (b. 27 July 1934, Stanislaus, California, USA).
The children of Abel (m2) and Carrie (Hopkins) Martinez (a) were:
    c6. ABEL MARTINEZ (b. 16 August 1936, Alameda, California, USA).
    c7. PAUL OCTAVIANO MARTINEZ (b. 2 March 1938, Alameda, California, USA).
b8. FRANCIS HOPKINS (b. 14 December 1908, Stockton, San Joaquin, California, USA; d. 9 December 1909, Stockton, San Joaquin, California, USA).
b9. JOSEPH EDWIN HOPKINS (b. 4 July 1910, Stockton, San Joaquin, California, USA; d. 25 November 1910, Stockton, San Joaquin, California, USA).
b10. RUBY HOPKINS (b. 4 July 1910, Stockton, San Joaquin, California, USA; d. 23 April 1914, Stockton, San Joaquin, California, USA).
b11. GUADALUPE PAULINA HOPKINS (b. 23 July 1911, San Jose, Santa Clara, California, USA; d. 31 March 1969, Alameda, California, USA). Married FELIPE MANUEL DURAN (b. 12 August 1884, Leon, Guanajuato, Mexico; d. 15 July 1966, California, USA).
The children of Felipe and Lupe (Hopkins) (b) Duran were:
    c1. PHILIP DURAN (b. 23 January 1934, Santa Clara, California, USA).
    c2. ARTHUR FRANK DURAN (b. 17 June 1935, Oakland, California, USA; d. 12 September 2008, Pueblo, Colorado, USA).
    c3. ASCENSION CINDY DURAN (b. 20 November 1936, Alameda, California, USA; d. 28 March 2011, Modesto, Stanislaus, California, USA).
    c4. JOSEPH DANIEL DURAN (b. 2 April 1938, Alameda, California, USA; d. 12 December 2013, Hayward, Alameda, California, USA).
    c5. PAULINE ADELINE DURAN (b. 8 April 1939, Alameda, California, USA; d. 19 June 2010, Pueblo, Colorado, USA).
    c6. MARY ANNIE DURAN (b. 16 June 1940, Alameda, California, USA; d. 17 August 2013, California, USA). Married MORENO on 31 May 1961, Santa Clara, California, USA.
    c7. ISABEL NATALIE DURAN (b. 21 November 1941, Alameda, California, USA; d. 12 April 2004, Hayward, Alameda, California, USA).
    c8. ADELINE (LENA) MARGARET DURAN (b. 13 December 1942, Alameda, California, USA; d. 11 May 2007, Hayward, Alameda, California, USA).

- c9. ROBERTA CLAUDIA DURAN (b. 6 June 1946, Alameda, California, USA).
- c10. CRUZ DURAN (b. 28 July 1947, Alameda, California, USA). <u>Married</u> HERNANDEZ on 12 November 1965, Modesto, Stanislaus, California, USA.

b12. DANIEL SANTIAGO HOPKINS (b. 27 February 1913, San Jose, Santa Clara, California, USA; d. 16 April 1993, Sonora, Tuolumne, California, USA). <u>Married</u> (m1) CARRIE DOMINGUEZ/ (m2) ROSARIO NUNES.

<u>The child of Daniel Santiago (b) and Rosario (Nunes) Hopkins was</u>:
- c1. DANIEL HOPKINS JUNIOR (born abt. 1948, Alameda, California, USA).

b13. SARAH HOPKINS (b. 21 September 1916, Stockton, San Joaquin, California, USA; d. 21 September 1916, Stockton, San Joaquin, California, USA).

APPENDIX I: CALIFORNIA, USA

A. Anderson

ANDERSON: On Robert Hopkins' baptismal record, it is reported his godparents were: Adolf Anderson and Mrs. Anderson. Adolf Valencia Anderson was born 1854 in California. He resided in 1904 a half-a-mile from the Hopkins' family residence. His mother's name was Paula Valencia and his spouse's (Mrs. Anderson) first name was Rafaelia.

B. Cayton

CAYTON: BONIFACE CAYTON was listed in the 1910 Oakdale United States Census as born 1877 in the Philippines and arriving in the America by 1900. He married MARY (GONZALES) MACHADO, a widow born 1880 California and mother to JULIA MACHADO (born 1896, California). Mary Gonzales's 1880 (likely, born San Francisco) birth year hints at a childhood friendship with Flora Ramirez (born 1882, likely San Francisco). Boniface Cayton and Julia Machado were godparents to DANIEL SANTIAGO HOPKINS, the child of DANIEL and FLORA (Ramirez) HOPKINS. While Boniface Cayton immigrated from the Philippines and lived in Oakdale, two Caton brothers immigrated from Portugal (b. 1872; b. 1870) and resided in 1910 Oakdale, California.

Julius Clement Manrique, son of Serapio and (m2) Mary (Hopkins) Manrique, remembered walking by "Gramma Mate's house" as a child. His mother, Mary Manrique, would insist he greet Mary (Gonzales) (Machado) (Cayton) Mate, as "Gramma." Gramma Mate was the mother of Julia Machado, Serapio Manrique's first wife and grandmother to both Primitivo and Dolores Manrique, children of Serapio and (m1) Julia (Machado) Manrique. Mary Gonzales (born 1880, California) married Bonifacio Cayton (born 1879, Manilla, Philippines) on 23 March 1904 in Oakdale, California. Mary Gonzales was a widow by 1904 with a daughter, Julia Machado (born 1896, California).

The 1910 Oakdale, Stanislaus, California United States Census listed Boniface Cayton as head of household with wife, Mary G. Cayton and stepdaughter, Julia Machado age 14 born 1896 with children:
- Jenny (Juanita) Cayton, age 9 born 1901, Oakdale, California, USA
- Stella Cayton, age 7 born 1903, Oakdale, California, USA
- Nattie Cayton, age 5 born 1905, Oakdale, California, USA
- Manuel Cayton, age 0 born 1910, Oakdale, California, USA

The 1920 Oakdale, Stanislaus, California United States Census listed Boniface Cayton age 46 born 1874, Philippines with wife Mary Cayton age 40, born California (1880) and children:
- Juanita (Jenny) Cayton age 19 born 1901, Oakdale, California, USA
- Stella Cayton age 17 born 1903, Oakdale, California, USA
- Nattie Cayton, age 14 born 1906, Oakdale, California, USA
- Manuel Cayton, age 10 born 1910, Oakdale, California, USA
- Victor Cayton, age 4 born 1916, Oakdale, California, USA
- Lawrence Cayton, age 1 born 1919, Oakdale, California, USA

On 6 June 1920 in Oakdale, California, Juanita Theodora (Jennie) Cayton married Gregario Vera age 26, born 1894, Philippines.

The <u>1930 Oakdale, Stanislaus, California, United States Census</u> listed Boniface Cayton age 53 with wife Mary Cayton age 49, born California (father born Chile) and children:
- Juanita Cayton, age 28 born 1902, Oakdale, California, USA
- Manuel Cayton, age 20, born 1910, Oakdale, California, USA
- Victor Cayton, age 14 born 1916, Oakdale, California, USA
- Lawrence Cayton, age 11 born 1919, Oakdale, California, USA

Boniface Cayton must have died shortly after the 1930 census was taken.

The <u>1940 Oakdale, Stanislaus, California, United States Census</u> listed the head of the household at "end of 5th and State" (near the North 5th Manrique home) as Mary (Gonzales) (Machado) (Cayton) Mate, age 57 (born 1883 California) with husband, Teofilo Mate age 41 (born 8 December 1892, Philippines; immigrated on ship *Governor Voy 4* in 1918). The children listed on the document were: Philip Mate age 14 born 1926 and Lawrence Cayton, age 21 (b.1919, CA).

C. Cottle

COTTLE: Francis Cottle (1887, Oakdale - 1971) signed the marriage document for Serapio and Mary (Hopkins) Manrique during December of 1917 in Stockton, San Joaquin, California, USA. The Cottle family - including Zora Cottle (1837-1894), wife Catherine Price Cottle & Francis Marion Cottle - arrived in Oakdale from Missouri then purchased a portion of the ferry and managed large herds of cattle. Francis Marion Cottle (1837, Missouri -1916, Oakdale) married Harriet Louise Kennedy (1848, Missouri - 1929, Oakdale) and purchased land where he raised fruit.

Serapio Manrique was recorded as a farmer working with (*Frances*) Marion M. Cottle in 1917. The Cottle family founded Oakdale Citizens Cemetery where many Manrique-Hopkins family members are buried and were Tuolumne County Pioneer Emigrants who crossed the Sonora Pass during 1853 then became founders of Oakdale. Serapio Manrique arrived in Oakdale during 1906, the year the town was incorporated as a city.

HOPKINS

D. Robert Hopkins

ROBERT HOPKINS:

ROBERT HOPKINS was born 20 August 1904 in Stockton, San Joaquin, California, USA. He was baptized on 20 August 1904 at St. Mary's Catholic Church in Stockton, California, USA. He died on 8 October 1964 in San Leandro, Alameda, California, USA at age sixty years old. Robert Hopkins was known to family members as, (Uncle) Tudi.

St. Mary's Church, Stockton, California Baptismal Record: August 20, 1904, Stockton, California, USA. Father - Daniel Hopkins of California; Mother - Feliz Ramos of California; Godparents - Adolf Anderson and Mrs. Anderson (*See Appendix I -Anderson*).

Married (m1) JULIA SILVA (born 1906, England-) in 1924/(m2) MARY CATHERINE LOPEZ (born 1914-) in 1934.

1930 Oakdale, Stanislaus County, California, United States Census: Robert Hopkins, head of household age 25 married (m1) to JULIA (SILVA) (age 23, born England, employed in cannery). Employment: General labor. Two children: ROBERT HOPKINS, JR. (born 1925, age five ½) and ADELINE (LENA) HOPKINS (age 4 ½). Father, Dan Hopkins (born 1873, *MASSACHUSETTS*), and brother, Dan Hopkins (born 1911 California, age nineteen) were also listed on the census report.

1940 Eden Township, Alameda County, California, United States Census: Robert Hopkins age 35, head of household, laborer at school building project. Married to CATHERINE (KATE) HOPKINS age 26. Children: Robert Hopkins Junior age 16, Adeline Hopkins age 14, Rosaline Hopkins age 5, Gilbert Hopkins age 2 and Gloria Hopkins age 1.

Eden Township, Alameda County, California spanned from the bay to the coastal ranges and used to include the city of Hayward, where brother, Daniel Hopkins, resided.

    The children of Robert (a) and JULIA (SILVA) HOPKINS were:
b1.   ROBERT HOPKINS JUNIOR (b. 14 June 1924, Oakdale, California, USA; resided Union City, CA; d. 2 February 2008, Pleasanton, Alameda, California, USA). Married SUSAN HISCOCK (b. 11 March 1929, London, England).
    The children of Robert Jr. (b) and (m2) MARY (LOPES) Hopkins born San Joaquin, California, USA were:
        c1.   LILLIAN ELIZABETH HOPKINS (b. 22 February 1947).
        c2.   ROBERTA SUE HOPKINS (b. 10 June 1950).
        c3.   JULIE ANNE HOPKINS (b. 11 July 1953).
b2. ADELINE FRANCES HOPKINS (b. 27 December 1925, Oakdale, California, USA; resided Manteca, California; died 27 November 1982, Stanislaus, California, USA). Married CARPENTER.

The children of Robert (a) and (m2) Mary Catherine (Lopez) Hopkins were:
b3.   EVELYN (ROSALINE) HOPKINS (b. 18 October 1934, Alameda, California, USA; resided Sacramento, California, USA). Married RODRIQUEZ.
b4.   VALENTINA BEATRICE HOPKINS (b. 22 January 1936, Alameda, California, USA).
b5.   GILBERT DANIEL HOPKINS (b. 14 May 1937, San Leandro, California, USA).
b6.   GLORIA EVA HOPKINS (b. 21 August 1939, San Leandro, California, USA).

California Death Index: Robert J. Hopkins, born 20 August 1904 in California and died 8 October 1964 in Alameda County.

The Daily Review Obituary (page 2; column 1) for Robert Hopkins on 10 October 1964:
"Robert Hopkins leaves a widow, Mary, a son, Robert Hopkins Junior of Union City, a daughter, Mrs. Adeline Carpenter of Manteca, a daughter, Mrs. Rosalie Rodriquez of Sacramento, (a son, Earnest R. Merlino of Stockton, a son, Joseph Stone Jr. of Stockton, a son, Frank D. Stone of Stockton, a daughter, Josephine R. Luskin of Alameda and a son, John J. Stone of Hayward). A sister, Mrs. Mary Manrique of Oakdale, a sister, Mrs. Lupe Duran of Manteca and a brother, Daniel S. Hopkins of Hayward. 27 Grandchildren. Buried at Lone Tree Cemetery, Hayward, Alameda County, California."

E. Carrie Hopkins

CARRIE HOPKINS:

CARRIE HOPKINS was born on 30 December 1907 in Stockton, San Joaquin County, California. She was baptized on 8 March 1908 in St. Mary's Catholic Church, Stockton, California. She died on 3 November 1952 at the age of forty-four in Fairfield, Solano County, California, USA.

St. Mary's Catholic Church, Stockton, California, baptismal record: 8 March 1908. Maria*um* Carmin*eum* (*Maria Carmine*) Hopkins, born 30 December 1907, residing at 229 W. Washington, the father Daniel Hopkins born in St. Helena Insula and mother Flora Romidas born in Scotia with godparents Romundas Real and Julia Figueroa.

Married (m1) Pete Mendez in 1923 in California, USA.

    The children of Pete and Carrie (a) (Hopkins) Mendez were:
- b1. ROBERT MENDEZ (born abt. 1923, Stanislaus County, California, USA).
- b2. MARGARET MENDEZ (b. 17 October 1924, Ripon, San Joaquin, California, USA; d. 18 March 1971, Pittsburg, Contra Costa, California, USA). Married JOE CERDA.
- b3. LOUIS GONZALES MENDEZ (b. 21 June 1926, Stanislaus, California, USA; d. 7 March 2009, Solano, California, USA).
- b4. HELEN MENDEZ (born 29 November 1927, Stanislaus, California, USA).
- b5. NATTIE MENDEZ (b. 27 July 1934, Stanislaus, California, USA).

1930 Oakdale Township, Stanislaus, California, United States Census: Pete Mendez, age 34 born 1896, Mexico (age at marriage 28 years), wife, Carrie Mendez (age 23 born California, age at marriage age 16), and children: Robert (age 6 born 1924), Margaret (age 5 born 1925), Louie (age 4 years and 9 months born 1926) and Helen (age 2 years and four months) Mendez.

Married (m2) ABEL MARTINEZ, a widower, by 1927.

The children of Abel (m2) and Carrie (Hopkins) (a) were:
b6. ABEL MARTINEZ (born 16 August 1936, Alameda, California, USA).
b7. PAUL OCTAVIANO MARTINEZ (b. 2 March 1938, Alameda, California, USA).

1940 Eden Township, Alameda, California, United States Census: Abel Martinez age 55 head of household with wife, Carrie Martinez age 32 and children: Levi Martinez age 19, Robert Mendez age 16, Margaret Mendez age 15, Louie Mendez age 14, Helen Martinez age 12, Clemente Martinez age 9, Nattie Mendez age 5 and Paul Martinez age 2.

California Death Index: Carrie *Savina* Martinez born 30 December 1907 in California; died 3 November 1952 in Solano County. Father's surname: HOPKINS.

Carrie Savina (Hopkins) Martinez was buried at the Suisun-Fairfield Cemetery, Solano County, California, USA.

F. Guadalupe Pauline Hopkins

GUADALUPE PAULINE HOPKINS:

GUADALUPE PAULINE HOPKINS was born on 23 July 1911 in San Jose, Alameda County, California. There was no Stockton St. Mary's Catholic Church baptismal record for Lupe because the Daniel Hopkins' family resided in San Jose, California between 1911-1913. Lupe Hopkins died on 31 March 1969 in Alameda County, California, USA. Guadalupe Pauline Hopkins was known to family members as, Lupe Hopkins.

Married FELIPE MANUEL DURAN.

Guadalupe Pauline Hopkins married Felipe Manuel Duran (born 12 August 1884, Leon, Guanajuato, Mexico; d. 15 July 1966, Stanislaus County, California). The Duran family resided in Manteca and at a Hayward apricot farm during the 1950s.

The children of Felipe and Lupe (a) (Hopkins) Duran were:
b1. PHILIP DURAN (b. 23 January 1934, Santa Clara, California, USA).
b2. ARTHUR FRANK DURAN (b. 17 June 1935, Oakland, California, USA; d. 12 September 2008, Pueblo, Colorado, USA).
b3. ASCENSION CINDY (CHONITA) DURAN (b. 20 November 1936, Alameda, California, USA; d. 28 March 2011, Modesto, Stanislaus, California, USA).
b4. JOSEPH DANIEL DURAN (b. 2 April 1938, Alameda, California, USA; d. 12 December 2013, Hayward, Alameda, California, USA).
b5. PAULINE ADELINE DURAN (b. 8 April 1939, Alameda, California, USA; d. 19 June 2010, Pueblo, Colorado, USA).
b6. MARY ANNIE DURAN (b. 16 June 1940, Alameda, California, USA; d. 17 August 2013, California, USA). Married JOSEPH MORENO on 31 May 1961, Santa Clara, California, USA.

b7. ISABEL NATALIE DURAN (b. 21 November 1941, Alameda, California, USA; d. 12 April 2004, Hayward, Alameda, California, USA).
b8. ADELINE (LENA) MARGARET DURAN (b. 13 December 1942, Alameda, California, USA; d. 11 May 2007, Hayward, Alameda, California, USA).
b9. ROBERTA CLAUDIA DURAN (b. 6 June 1946, Alameda, California, USA).
b10. CRUZ DURAN (b. 28 July 1947, Alameda, California, USA). Married CANDELAR HERNANDEZ on 12 November 1965, Modesto, California, USA.

California Death Index: Lupe H. Duran. "H." = Hopkins. Death date: 31 March 1969. Mother's maiden name: ASCENCIO (*rather than Ramirez*).

G. Daniel Santiago Hopkins

DANIEL SANTIAGO HOPKINS:

Daniel Santiago Hopkins was born 27 February 1913 in San Jose, Santa Clara, California, USA. He was baptized at Stockton's St. Mary's Catholic Church on 15 June 1913. He died 16 April 1933 in Sonora, Tuolumne, California, USA.

St. Mary's Catholic Church, Stockton, California Baptismal Record: 15 June 1913. Daniel Santiago Hopkins was born 27 February 1913 to father, Daniel Hopkins born England, and mother, Felipa Ramides born California. His godparents were Boniface Cayton and Julie Machado. Julie Machado was the first wife of Mary Hopkins' husband, Serapio Manrique.

Daniel Santiago Hopkins, Carrie Hopkins and Robert Hopkins, along with their father, Daniel Edwin Hopkins, moved to Alameda County by 1930s. Daniel Santiago Hopkins is noted as residing in Hayward, California within his brother Robert Hopkins' obituary text. Lupe Hopkins' children were also born in Hayward, California.

1930 Eden Township, Alameda County, California, United States Census: Dan Hopkins, age nineteen born California. Resided with brother, Robert Hopkins' family and father, Dan Hopkins (born 1873, *Massachusetts*).

1940 Eden Township, Alameda County, California, United States Census: Daniel Hopkins age 27, head of household, with wife, Carey Hopkins (age 32 born Texas).

Daniel Santiago Hopkins married (m1) CARRIE DOMINGUEZ and (m2) ROSARIA NUNEZ. His 10 October 1940 WW2 registration noted he was a resident of Decoto, Alameda, CA living at 617 5th Street. The name of the "person who will always know your address: was his wife, "Mrs. Carry Hopkins," which fits with 1940 census. The WW2 draft card listed his name as, Dan Santiago Hopkins born February 27, 1913 in San Jose, California, age - 27. His employer was recorded as: W. P. H. He signed his name as, Dan S. Hopkins.

August 1942 United States Army Enlistment: Daniel Santiago Hopkins. Single. Age twenty-nine. Army Warrant Officer.

Daniel Hopkins married (m2) Rosaria Nunez, whose name is listed as both "Eva" and "Pauline," and resided in 1949-1961 Stockton, California (from city directory records).

The child of Daniel (a) and Rosaria (Eva/Pauline) (Nunez) Hopkins was:
b1.   DANIEL HOPKINS JUNIOR (born abt. 1948, Alameda County, California).

California Death Index: Daniel Santiago Hopkins born 27 February 1913 in California. Died 16 April 1993, Tuolumne County, California. His mother's maiden name: RAMIREZ.

From the Modesto Bee dated 19 April 1993 (obituary): Daniel S. Hopkins.
"*Daniel Santiago Hopkins, 80 of Jamestown, died Friday at the Sonora Community Hospital. Mr. Hopkins was a native of San Jose. He lived in Jamestown for 29 years. He was a maintenance worker for the Sierra Railroad for 10 years. He served in the Army from 1942-1945. He is survived by his son, Daniel Hopkins of Stockton. The rosary will be recited at 7 pm today and Mass said at 10 am Tuesday at the Heuton Memorial Chapel in Sonora. Burial will be at Mt. Shadow Cemetery in Sonora. Visitation is scheduled from 9 am to 5 pm at the chapel.*"

H.   Joseph Ramirez

JOSEPH RAMIREZ:

The search for birth documents noting Flora Felipa Ramirez' 13 September 1882, California birth has not resulted in definitive parentage. However, given Flora Ramirez' child's birth in San Francisco in 1900 (Mary Hopkins, b. 29 July 1900, San Francisco, California) and the fact Daniel Edwin Hopkins was a sailor who arrived in San Francisco during 1890 where he resided while in port until September of 1902, it is likely, Flora Ramirez was born in San Francisco, records of which have been lost due to the 1906 San Francisco earthquake and fire.

There were many Joseph Ramirez individuals researched with likely possibilities listed below given their name and locations of businesses.

1) RAMIREZ & CO., cigar factory, San Francisco, California. Noted in the United States City and Business Directory is a "Ramirez" with a cigar factory at 308 Commercial, San Francisco, California between the years of 1882-1884. This would place (Joseph) and Francis (Lopez) Ramirez in San Francisco during their granddaughter, Mary Hopkins' 29 July 1900 San Francisco birth with their daughter, Flora Ramirez.

Ramirez & Co. was listed in the United States City and Business Directory during the years 1871-1874 in San Francisco, California as "Chinese cigar manufacturing" at 135 Commercial, San Francisco, California.

The cigar trade directory of 1867 stated there were 47 cigar factories in San Francisco, and 300 in the state of California. Most businesses were one-man units serving gold-rush mining camps. The 1875 Directory listed 187 San Francisco factories with the 1886 Directory listing 255 factories, and 120 around the state as by then, gold-rush towns were emptying. "Engelbrecht's Cigar" company claims three-quarters of the Chinese factories were hidden behind Spanish names as Chinese ownership was not allowed. The 1886 Directory does not confirm more than forty factories had Chinese names, while the others were of Caucasian or Spanish origins.

Founding a cigar company required little funds. A single person could start a factory with less than $5. To set up a storefront with twenty or thirty rollers could be accomplished with little than $300 capital. A Chinese factory was about 15' x 20' dividing a standard room with 9 or 10 foot ceilings in a two-story factory where fifty people worked. "After all," historical notes stated, "cigar rollers didn't need room to stand while working…"

It is possible Joseph Ramirez owned the San Francisco "Ramirez & Co." cigar factory during the time his daughter, Flora Ramirez was born. Given the business type, it is also likely his customer may have been Daniel Edwin Hopkins.

2) J. R. RAMIREZ: J. R. Ramirez was noted as owning a grocery and produce store at 1120 Center Street in Alameda, California from 1883 until 1890. His name also coincides with a Solano County Genealogical Society burial record: J. R. Ramirez, d. 25 April 1900, St. Mary's, Solano County, California. However, the Vallejo death book notes he was born in Mexico and his first name is not clarified by, "Joseph." The "California Death and Burial" certificate for J. R. Ramirez noted he was age 62 (born abt. 1838, Mexico) who resided at 626 Main Street in Vallejo, Solano County, California. He died 27 April 1900, Vallejo, Solano County, California. Catholic, he was buried in Oakland at St. Mary's in Alameda, California.

3) JOSEPH E. RAMIREZ: Listed as a farmer in Modesto, California with a residence directory from 1900-1916. A Joseph Ramirez is also listed in 1932 with a spouse of Josephine Ramirez. Undetermined is whether this is a relation of Flora Ramirez or if Joseph Ramirez Junior was the same person from 1900-1916. EULOJIA RAMIRES was listed as a Central Valley resident who was born 1830 and died in Stanislaus County, California at age 104 on 22 May 1934.

4) JOSEPH RAMOS: Flora Felipa Ramirez was also listed in a St. Mary's baptismal record with a Latin translation of the name, Ramirez: Ramos. There were three JOSEPH RAMOS named individuals buried at Holy Cross Catholic Cemetery where Daniel Edwin Hopkins was buried in 1934. While, "Ramos" is a common surname, the death dates fit with the timeline of Joseph Ramirez.
~ JOSEPH RAMOS, d. 19 May 1924, Holy Cross Catholic Cemetery, Alameda, CA
~JOSEPH RAMOS, d. 24 Nov. 1936, Holy Cross Catholic Cemetery, Alameda, CA
~JOSEPH RAMOS, d. 4 Dec. 1942, Holy Cross Catholic Cemetery, Alameda, CA

5). Possible Ramirez relation in Modesto, California: RICARDO/RICHARD N. RAMIREZ.

Richard Ramirez was born 1851 and resided in Stanislaus County by 1872. He married Angeline Armenta on 17 March 1875 in Stanislaus County, California. Richard and Angeline (Armenta) Ramirez had one child, DOLORES A. RAMIREZ. When Richard N. Ramirez died on 13 August 1906, he left a will giving his assets of $750 to his only heir, Dolores Ramirez, as his wife, Angeline (Armenta) Ramirez was also deceased.

I. Silva

SILVA: Frances Silva (b. 1886, Mexico) widow with son, Benjamin Silva (b. 1894, Mexico) was listed on the same 5 June 1900 Newman, California United States Census as Flora Ramirez (age 17, born September 1882). The next entry are two Silva-surnamed men - Ecelveta Silva (b. April 1864, Portugal) and Joaquin Silva (b. January 1872, Portugal). On this census page were also other Portuguese immigrants - John Jadez (b. 1877), Antoine Magellan (b. March 1860), Manuel Bettencourt (b. March 1860), Antoine Triguerro (b. May 1860), John Rubion (b. September 1851), Dionariano Dias (b. March 1854), Ignacio Ponicabe (b. August 1842), James Fieres and Monica Calvado (b. June 1860), Thomas Alves (b. June 1852), Manuel T. Rey (b. July 1875) and Ramundo Dias (b. 1854).

Flora Felipa Ramirez listed her mother as, "Frances Lopez" at her May 1909 Catholic marriage to Daniel Hopkins. Daniel and Flora (Ramirez) Hopkins named two children after Flora Ramirez' parents: Joseph and Francis Hopkins.

~~~~~

APPENDIX II: PETRA DURAN (1866-1920)
(Wife of CLEMENTE MANRIQUE)
(Connects Urbano Manrique de Lara's sons, Jose Isidro and Jose Maria Manrique)

```
                JOSEPH URBANO de la LUZ MANRIQUE de LARA (1768)
                                    m. (1799)
                          MARIA MELCHORA LOPES (1784)
                     |                                    |
    JOSE ISIDRO MANRIQUE (1804)    -    JOSE MARIA MANRIQUE (1815)
            m. (1827)                          m. (prior to 1833)
      BIBIANA BOCANEGRA (1806)              TOMASA NUNES (1813)
                     |                                    |
       SIMON MANRIQUE (1835)              ZEPHARINA MANRIQUE (1841)
            m. (1856)                              m. (1861)
      SERAPIA GONZALEZ (1832)                MARTIN DURAN (1840)
                     |                                    |
      CLEMENTE MANRIQUE (1862)  -m. (prior to 1889)-  PETRA DURAN (1866)
```

~~~~~~

MARIA IGNACIA MANRIQUE*
        (daughter of Jose Urbano Manrique and Alexandria Luz Garcia)
    (granddaughter of Antonio Marcelo Manrique and Maria Bernarda de la Rocha)
                                    |
                                Godmother
                                | |
                JOSE MARIA MANRIQUE m. TOMASA NUNES
                                    |
                ZEPHARINA MANRIQUE (1841) m. MARTIN DURAN
                                    |
                            PETRA DURAN (1866)
                         m. CLEMENTE MANRIQUE (1862)

~~~~~~

MARIA PETRONILA DURAN, baptized 31 May 1866, San Miguel de Leon, Leon, Guanajuato, Mexico (Father: Martin Duran/Mother: **ZEPHARINA MANRIQUE**). <u>Married</u> **CLEMENTE MANRIQUE**. Died 10 April 1920, Leon, Guanajuato, Mexico (*Death Registration - Page 211/Reg. #647*).

MARTIN DURAN (born abt. 1840) (son of Juan Duran and Maria Dolores Gonzales). <u>Married</u> **CEFERINA MANRIQUE** (daughter of Jose Maria Manrique and Tomasa Nunes) on 16 November 1861, Nuestra Senora de Guanajuato, Leon, Guanajuato, Mexico (*Leon. Religious Marriage Investigation Files 1861-1862; Image 326/522) (Page 311*).

MARTIN DURAN (son of Juan Duran and Dolores Gonzales) married CEFERINA MANRIQUE (daughter of Jose Maria Manrique and Tomasa Nunes) on 20 May 1912, Leon, Guanajuato, Mexico (*Leon de los Aldama. Marriage registration. Page #125; Reg. # 140*).

~~~~~

JOSE MARIA MANRIQUE, baptized 30 November 1815, Leon, Guanajuato, Mexico (Father: Urbano Manrique/Mother: Melchora Mena) (Godparents: Pedro de Lara, IGNACIA MANRIQUE*) (legitimate son) (Espanol) (*Leon de los Aldama. Baptism Records 1814-1821; Image 105/414*).

MARIA TOMASA (NUNES, baptized 25 September 1813, El Sagrario, Leon, Guanajuato, Mexico (ESPANOL) (Father: Vicente NUNES/Mother: Sebera Rosso) (Godparents: Pantaleon Perez and *MARIA IGNACIA MANRIQUE**) (*Leon de los Aldama. Baptism Records 1808-1814; Image 167/190*).

The known children of JOSE MARIA MANRIQUE and MARIA TOMASA NUNES (a) were:

a1. EVARISTO MANRIQUE, baptized 28 October 1836, El Sagrario, Leon, Guanajuato, Mexico (Father: Jose Ma. Manrique/Mother: Tomasa Nunes). Married MARIA de JESUS GARCIA (Father: Dioncio Garcia/ Mother: Macedonia Reyes) on 29 September 1866, Nuestra Senora de Senora/San Miguel de Leon, Leon, Guanajuato, Mexico (Father: J. Ma. Manrique/Mother: Tomasa Nunez).

a2. HIGINIA MANRIQUE, baptized 13 January 1838, El Sagrario, Leon, Guanajuato, Mexico (Father: Je. Maria Manrique/Mother: Tomasa Nunes).

a3. **ZEPHARINA de los DOLORES RESPLANDON MANRIQUE**, baptized 28 August 1841, El Sagrario, Leon, Guanajuato, Mexico (Father: Jose Maria Manrique/Mother: Tomas Nunes) (*Leon de los Aldama. Baptism Records 1840-1846; Image 58/371*). Married MARTIN DURAN on 16 November 1861, Nuestra Senora de Guanajuato, Leon, Guanajuato, Mexico.

a4. JOSE JULIAN de la LUZ MANRIQUE, baptized 19 February 1843, El Sagrario, Leon, Guanajuato, Mexico (Father: Jose Ma. Manrique/Mother: Tomasa Nunes) (*Leon de los Aldama. Bautismos de hijos legitimos 1843-1844; b89/p25*). Married MARIA CRISTOBAL SOLIS (daughter of Prudencio Solis and Juana Rodriquez) on 3 March 1856, Nuestra Senora de Guanajuato, Leon, Guanajuato, Mexico (Father: Jose Ma. Manrique/ Mother: Tomasa Nunez).

a5. JOSE CELEDONIO MANRIQUE, baptized 9 December 1844, El Sagrario, Leon, Guanajuato, Mexico (Father: Jose Ma. Manrique/Mother: Tomasa Nunes) (*Leon de los Aldama. Bautismos de hijos legitimos 1845-1846; b91/pp 9 - 10 December 1845*).

a6. MARIA PONCIANA MANRIQUE, baptized 20 November 1846, El Sagrario, Leon, Guanajuato, Mexico (Father: Jose Ma. Manrique/ Mother: Tomasa

Nunes). Burial 28 November 1847 (Maria Ponciana Manrique) (age 1) Nuestra Senora de Guanajuato, Leon, Guanajuato, Mexico (Father: Je. Ma. Manrique/Mother: Tomasa Nunes).

- a7. EULOGIA ANTONIA MANRIQUE, death/burial 12 March 1849, Nuestra Senora de Guanajuato, Leon, Guanajuato, Mexico (Father: Je. Ma. Manrique/ Mother: Tomasa Nunes (*Leon. Death Certificates 1848-1850; Image 159/356*).

The father of Tomasa Nunes was VICENTE NUNES (born abt. 1760) who died 17 February 1823, La Canada de *Amargua (Alfaro* listed) (*Leon. Death Certificates 1820-1823; Image 177/648*) (*Urbano Manrique's wife, Melchora Lopes resided in La Canada de Amargua*). Vincente Nunes married Maria Dorotea Razo.

The known children of VINCENTE NUNEZ and MARIA DOROTEA RAZO (a) were:
- a1. MARIA JACINTA NUNEZ, born abt.1790/1791. Married JOSE ANTONIO CAPIO (son of Lorenzo Capio and Maria Apolonia Ramirez) (age 16) (Father: Vincente Nunez/Mother: Maria del Razo) October 1806, Nuestra Senora de Guanajuato, Leon, Guanajuato, Mexico (*Leon. Religious Marriage Investigation Files 1806-1807; Image 269/698*).
- a2. MARIA LEONARDA NUNEZ, christening 16 April 1796, Leon, Guanajuato, Mexico ("Espanola in the Hacienda de la San - legitimate daughter of Vincente Nunes and Maria Rosa") (Godparents Diego Hinjosa and Maria Hinjosa (*Leon de los Aldama. Baptism Records 1777-1796; Image 242/256*).
- a3. ANASTACIA de la LUZ NUNEZ, christening 30 May 1798, El Sagrario, Leon, Guanajuato, Mexico (Father: Vicente Nunez/Mother: Maria del Razo) (Godparents: Bernabe Razo and Maria Razo) (Margin text: "Anastacia de la Luz, Espanola del Puerto de la Sanja") (*Bautismos de espanoles 1796-1809*).
- a4. JOSE SEBERIANO NUNES, baptized 27 April 1800, El Sagrario, Leon, Guanajuato, Mexico (Father: Vincente Nunez/Mother: Maria Raso) (*Leon de los Aldama. Bautismos de espanoles 1796-1809; Certificate #121*).
- a5. MARIA RUFINA NUNEZ married BASILO PEREZ (son of Vincente Perez and Teresa Lopes) (Father: Vincente Nunez/Mother: Maria Razo).
- a6. JOSE MARIA CANDIDO NUNEZ, baptized 20 December 1810, El Sagrario, Leon, Guanajuato, Mexico (Father: Vicente Nunez/ Mother: Maria Dorotea Razo) (*Bautismos de indios, mulatos y mestizos 1808-1813; certificate #73*) (Mestizo) (Godmother: Maria Josepha Gomez).
- a7. MARIA MATIANA NUNES, christening 1807, Leon, Guanajuato, Mexico (Father: Vincente Nunes/Mother: Maria Dorotea Raso).
- a8. **MARIA TOMASA (NUNES)**, baptized 25 September 1813, El Sagrario, Leon, Guanajuato, Mexico (Espanola) (Father: Vicente Nunes/ Mother: Sebera Rosso) (Godparents: Pantaleon Perez and *MARIA*

IGNACIA MANRIQUE*) (*Leon de los Aldama. Baptism Records 1808-1814; Image 167/190*).

~~~~~~~

The godmother to both Jose Maria Manrique and Tomasa Nunes, mother of Cepharina Manrique, was MARIA IGNACIA MANRIQUE whose grandfather was ANTONIO MARCELO MANRIQUE and father was JOSE URBANO MANRIQUE.

MARCELO ANTONIO MANRIQUE, christening 20 February 1744, Guanajuato, Guanajuato, Mexico (Espanoles) (Father: Juan de la Gasca/Mother: Juana de Dios Manrique) (Godparents: Nicolas de la Gasca and Maria de las Nieves Manrique).

ANTONIO MANRIQUE, burial 15 March 1824, Nuestra Senora de Guanajuato, Guanajuato, Guanajuato, Mexico (Spouse: Bernarda Rocha).

Married

Dona BERNARDA ROCHA, burial 6 April 1814, Nuestra Senora de Guanajuato, Guanajuato, Guanajuato, Mexico (Spouse: Antonio Marcelo Manrique).

The known children of Antonio Marcelo Manrique and Maria Bernarda de la Rocha (a) were:

a1. JOSE BERNARDO MANRIQUE, christening 13 April 1762, El Sagrario, Leon, Guanajuato, Mexico (Father: Marcelo Antonio Manrique/Mother: Maria Bernarda Rocha (Godparents: Joseph Maria and Maria de Losa) (Margin text: "Joseph Bernardo, Espanol de la villa") (*Leon de Los Aldama. Baptism Records 1749-1777; Image 101/318*). Married MARIA de la LUZ MARMOLEJO (daughter of Franco Mariano Marmolejo and Maria Josefa Moreno) on 30 April 1794 (son of Antonio Marcelo Manrique and Maria Bernarda de Rocha), Nuestra de Senora, Guanajuato, Guanajuato, Mexico.

a2. JOSEPH ANSELMO MANRIQUE ROCHA, christening 26 April 1763, Leon, Guanajuato, Mexico (Father: Marcelo Antonio Manrique/Mother: Maria Bernarda Rocha) (Witnesses: Marcos Antonio Echeveste, Joseph Franco Marmelejo, Ana Maria de Torres).

a3. JOSEPH LUCIANO MANRIQUE, christening 1764, Leon, Guanajuato, Mexico (son of Marcelo Antonio Manrique and Maria Bernarda Rocha). Married MARIA PETRA LARA (daughter of Miguel Lara and Maria Guadalupe Belmontes) on 7 February 1798, Nuestra Senora de Guanajuato, Leon Guanajuato, Mexico (Father: Antonio Marcelo Manrique/Mother: Maria Bernarda de la Rocha).

a4. JUANA MARIA HIGINIA de la LUZ MANRIQUE, christening 1767, El Sagrario, Leon, Guanajuato, Mexico (Father: Marcelo Antonio Manrique and Maria Bernarda Rocha) (Espanola).

a5. ANTONIO ONOFRO BETANA, christening 13 June 1770, Leon, Guanajuato, Mexico (Father: Antonio Manrique/Mother: Maria Bernarda de Rocha) (Witnesses: Joseph de Barze, Petronilla Duran, Joseph Antonio Barrena).

a6. JUAN JOSE MANRIQUE. Married TRINIDAD UFRACIA DURAN (daughter of Antonio Feliciano Duran and Maria Franca Pacheco) on 15 October 1794, Nuestra Senora de Guanajuato, Leon, Guanajuato, Mexico (Father: Antonio Marcelo Manrique/Mother: Maria Bernarda de la Rocha).

a7. MARIA IGNACIA MANRIQUE. Married LUIS ANTONIO SABEDRA (son of Don Franco Antonio Sabedra and Dona Catarina Lubian) on 8 February 1796, Nuestra Senora de Guanajuato, Leon, Guanajuato, Mexico (Father: Don Marcos Antonio Manrique/Mother: Dona Bernarda Rocha).

a8. MARIA ISIDRA MANRIQUE, born 1774 (Father: Antonio Marcelo Manrique/ Mother: Maria Bernarda de la Rocha). Married JUAN JOSE GARIVAY (son of Juan Agustin Garivay and Maria Conception Belmontes) on 5 September 1789, Nuestra Senora de Guanajuato, Leon, Guanajuato, Mexico.

a9. JOSE URBANO MANRIQUE (Espanol) (son of Antonio Marcelo Manrique and Maria Bernarda Rocha). Married MARIA ALEXANDRA LUZ GARCIA (Espanola) (daughter of Juan Garcia and Maria Isadora Dias) (born La Sanja 1780; death/burial 26 April 1832, Nuestra Senora de Guanajuato, Leon, Guanajuato, Mexico) on 4 February 1799, Nuestra Senora de Guanajuato, Leon, Guanajuato, Mexico (Godparents: Jose Bernardo Manrique and Maria Luz Marmolejo) (*Leon. Marriage Records 1729-1814; Image 102/370*).
Known as: (Jose) Urbano Manrique.

The known children of JOSE URBANO MANRIQUE and ALEXANDRIA LUZ GARCIA (a) were:

b1. **MARIA IGNACIA YLARIA MANRIQUE***, born 3 November 1799, La Sanja, Guanajuato, Mexico. Christening 9 November 1799, El Sagrario Leon, Guanajuato, Mexico (Father: Urbano Manrique/ Mother: Alexandra Garcia) (*Leon de los Aldama. Bautismos de espanoles 1796-1809; certificate # 108*).
Godparent to Jose Maria Manrique and to Maria Tomasa Nunes, who married Jose Maria Manrique, son of Joseph de la Luz Urbano Manrique de Lara and Maria Melchora Lopes.

b2. MARIA ANTONIA DAMIAN MANRIQUE, christening 1801, Leon, Guanajuato, Mexico (Father: Jose Urbano Manrique/Mother: Maria Alexandra Garcia).

b3. JOSE ONOFRE MANRIQUE, baptism 13 June 1804, El Sagrario, Leon, Guanajuato, Mexico (Father: Urbano Manrique/Mother: Alexandra Garcia).

b4. MARIA ANASTACIA MANRIQUE, christening 18 August 1805, Leon, Guanajuato, Mexico (Father: Urbano Manrique/Mother: Maria Alexandra Garcia).

b5. MARIA TRINIDAD MANRIQUE, born abt. 1810. Married SANTOS RIBERA (Father: Je. Bernardo Ribera/Mother: Ma. Juana Ramires) on 14 December 1825, Nuestra Senora de Guanajuato, Leon, Guanajuato, Mexico.

- b6. MARIA de la LUZ SOSTENES MANRIQUE, baptism 1 December 1811, El Sagrario, Leon, Guanajuato, Mexico (Father: Urbano Manrique/Mother: Alexandra Garcia).
- b7. MARIA EDUVIGE MANRIQUE, christening 1807, Leon, Guanajuato, Mexico (Father: Urbano Manrique/Mother: Maria Alexandra Garcia).
- b8. JOSE de los ANGS. MANRIQUE, baptized 3 October 1814, El Sagrario, Leon, Guanajuato, Mexico (Father: Urbano Manrique/Mother: Alexandra Garcia).

a10. JOSE RAFAEL MANRIQUE. Married Dona MARIA FELIS ALMAGUER on 21 August 1799, Nuestra Senora de Guanajuato, Leon, Guanajuato, Mexico (Father: Don Antonio Manrique/Mother: Dona Maria Bernarda Rocha).

a11. JOSE MATIAS MANRIQUE, born 25 February 1781, Monte, Tepatitlan de Morelos, Jalisco, Mexico. Christening 1781, Leon, Guanajuato, Mexico (Espanol) (Father: Antonio Marcela Manrique/Mother: Maria Bernarda). Married MARIA CARMEN LARA (daughter of Miguel de Lara and Maria Guadalupe Cervantes) on 19 April 1802, Nuestra Senora de Guanajuato, Leon, Guanajuato, Mexico (Father: Antonio Marcelo Manrique/Mother: Maria Bernarda Rocha).

~~~~~~~

APPENDIX III: SERAPIA GONZALES (1839-1888)
(Wife of Simon Manrique)

JUAN GONZALES
m. MARIA del CARMEN CARPIO
|
LUCIANO GONZALEZ (born abt. 1818)
m. MARIA SANTOS RAMIREZ (born abt. 1818)
|
MARIA SERAPIA de la TRINIDAD del MIRASOL GONZALEZ (1839-1888)
m. SIMON MANRIQUE (1835-1895)

~~~~~~

JUAN GONZALEZ (born abt. 1790) married MARIA del CARMEN CARPIO.

MARIA FRANCISCA del CARMEN CARPIO, baptized 23 July 1806, El Sagrario, Leon, Guanajuato, Mexico (Father: Jose Antonio Carpio/Mother: Maria Loza) (Godparents: Prudencio Gonzales and Petra Fuentes) (*Bautismos de espanoles 1796-1809*).

The known children of Juan Gonzalez and Maria Francisca del Carmen Carpio were:
a1. JE. CALDELARIO de JESUS GONZALEZ CARPIA, baptized 2 March 1817, El Sagrario, Leon, Guanajuato, Mexico (Father: Juan Gonzales/Mother: Maria Carmen Carpia).
a2. **LUCIANO GONZALEZ**, born abt. 1818, Leon, Guanajuato, Mexico (Father: Juan Gonzalez/Mother: Maria del Carmen Carpio). Married MARIA SANTOS RAMIREZ.
a3. MARIA TORIBIA GONZALEZ, born 1821, Leon, Guanajuato, Mexico. Burial 15 September 1825, El Sagrario, Leon, Guanajuato, Mexico (Father: Juan Gonzalez/Mother: Carmen Caruso).
a4. JOSE APOLINARIO GONZALEZ, baptized 26 July 1824, El Sagrario, Leon, Guanajuato, Mexico (Father: Juan Gonzalez/Mother: Carmel Carpio).
a5. MARIA CRISPIN GONZALEZ, baptized 29 October 1825, El Sagrario, Leon, Guanajuato, Mexico (Father: Juan Gonzalez/Mother: Maria Carpio).

LUCIANO GONZALEZ, born abt. 1818, Leon, Guanajuato, Mexico (Father: Juan Gonzalez/Mother: Maria del Carmen Carpio).

MARIA SANTOS RAMIREZ, born abt. 1818, Leon, Guanajuato, Mexico (Father: Jose Ramirez/Mother: Juana de Dios Roseno). Burial 15 March 1867, San Miguel de Leon, Guanajuato, Mexico (Spouse: Luciano Gonzalez).

Married: 7 February 1837, Nuestra Senora de Guanajuato, Leon, Guanajuato, Mexico.

The known children of Luciano Gonzalez (a) and Maria Santos Ramirez were:

b1. FRANCISCO GONZALEZ, baptized 12 December 1837, El Sagrario, Leon, Guanajuato, Mexico (Father: Luciano Gonzales/Mother: Santos Ramirez). Married SERAPIA SERRANO (Father: Faustino Serrano/Mother: TEODORA MANRIQUE) on 1 June 1867, San Miguel de Leon, Leon, Guanajuato, Mexico (Father: Luciano Gonzalez/Mother: Santos Ramirez/Son: Franco Gonzalez). Death Registration 4 February 1909, Leon, Guanajuato, Mexico (Father: Luciano Gonzalez/Mother: Santos Ramirez/Spouse: Serapia Gonzalez).

b2. **MARIA SERAPIA de la TRINIDAD del MIRASOL GONZALEZ**, born 13 December 1839, Leon, Guanajuato, Mexico. Baptized 16 December 1839, El Sagrario, Leon, Guanajuato, Mexico (Father: Luciano Gonzales/Mother: Maria Santos Ramirez) (Godparents: Rosario Sess--and Vicente Ramirez) (3 days old) (*Leon de los Aldama. Baptism Records 1836-1840; Image 379/540*) (*Text: Day 16 baptized/3 days old - born 13 December*). Married **SIMON MANRIQUE** (Father: Isidro Manrique/Mother: Bibiana Bocanegra) on 8 April 1856 (Father: Luciano Gonzales/Daughter: Serapia Gonzales). Death registration: 6 December 1888, Leon, Guanajuato, Mexico (Father: Luciano Gonzalez/Mother: Maria Santos Ramirez/Spouse: Simon Manrique).

b3. JULIAN GONZALEZ, born abt. 1841, Leon, Guanajuato, Mexico. Married MARIA REGINA VERA (Father: Tranquilino Vera/Mother: Dolores Quesada) on 12 May 1860, El Sagrario, Leon, Guanajuato, Mexico (Father: Luciano Gonzales/Mother: Maria Santos Ramirez/Son: Julian Gonzales).

b4. ANGELA GONZALEZ, born abt. 1842, Leon, Guanajuato, Mexico. Married CELSO SANCHEZ (Father: Dario Sanchez/Mother: Maria Cosme Serrano) on 17 November 1862, San Miguel de Leon, Leon, Guanajuato, Mexico (Father: Luciano Gonzalez/Mother: Maria Santos Ramirez/Daughter: Angela Gonzalez).

b5. JESUS LIBRADO GONZALEZ, baptized 17 August 1844, El Sagrario, Leon, Guanajuato, Mexico (Father: Luciano Gonzales/Mother: Santos Ramirez). Death/burial 20 August 1844, El Sagrario, Leon, Guanajuato, Mexico (Father: Luciano Gonzalez/Mother: Maria Santos Ramirez).

b6. JOSE FRANCISCO GONZALEZ, baptism 19 September 1845, El Sagrario, Leon, Guanajuato, Mexico (Father: Luciano Gonzales/Mother: Maria de los Santos Ramirez).

b7. MARIA SILVESTRE GONZALEZ, baptized 2 January 1849, El Sagrario, Leon, Guanajuato, Mexico (Father: Luciano Gonzalez/Mother: Maria Santos Ramirez). Married JOSE ANDRES FLORES (Father: Franquilino Flores/Mother: Maria de la Luz Serrano) on 24 February 1868, Leon, Guanajuato, Mexico (Father: Luciano Gonzalez/Mother: Santos Ramirez).

b8. MARIA de los ANGELES GONZALEZ, baptized 3 October 1853, El Sagrario, Leon, Guanajuato, Mexico (Father: Luciano Gonzales/Mother: Maria de los Santos).

~~~~~~~~

b1. Wife of FRANCISCO GONZALEZ - SERAPIA SERRANO (Father: Faustino Serrano/Mother: TEODORA MANRIQUE).

MARCIALA MANRIQUE (1817-1862)
m. RITO OJEDA
I
MARIA TEODORA OJEDA MANRIQUE (1837)
m. FRANCSICO GONZALEZ (1837-1909)

MARIA TEODORA OJEDA MANRIQUE, baptized 10 November 1837, El Sagrario, Leon, Guanajuato, Mexico (Father: Rito Ojeda/Mother: MARCIALA MANRIQUE).

MARCIALA MANRIQUE, burial 17 September 1862, El Sagrario, Leon, Guanajuato, Mexico (Spouse: Rito Ojeda) (born abt. 1817).

JOSE RITO OJEDA, baptism 26 May 1807, Leon, Guanajuato, Mexico (Father: Anastacio Ojeda/Mother: Maria Segura). Burial 29 January 1879, San Miguel de Leon, Guanajuato, Mexico.

The known children of Marciala Manrique and Rito Ojeda were:

a1. JUAN EVANGELISTA OJEDA, baptized 3 January 1835, El Sagrario, Leon, Guanajuato, Mexico (Father: Rito Ojeda/Mother: Marciala Manrique). Burial 19 September 1840, Nuestra Sonora de Guanajuato, Guanajuato, Mexico.

a2. MARIA TEODORA OJEDA MANRIQUE, baptized 10 November 1837, El Sagrario, Leon, Guanajuato, Mexico (Father: Vito Ojeda/Mother: Marciala Manrique).

a3, MARIA REFUGIO OJEDA MANRIQUE, baptism, El Sagrario, Leon, Guanajuato, Mexico

a4. MARIA ISADORA OJEDA MANRIQUE, born 1840, Leon, Guanajuato, Mexico. Burial 2 October 1840, Nuestra Senora de Guanajuato, Guanajuato, Mexico.

a5. JOSE TOMAS OJEDA MANRIQUE, baptism 8 March 1843, El Sagrario, Leon, Guanajuato, Mexico.

~~~~~~~

APPENDIX IV: BOCANEGRA

The children of Rita Antonia de la Luz Torres y Manrique and Jose Antonio Bocanegra, MARIA DOLORES BIBIANA BOCANEGRA and JOSE ANTONIO MAGDALENO BOCANEGRO married the children of JOSEPH URBANO MANRIQUE de LARA.

```
        BERNARDA MANRIQUE              JOSEPHA GOMEZ MANRIQUE de LARA
        m. DOMINGO de la CRUZ              m. NICOLAS de MEDINA
                   |                                  |
        PHELIPE MANRIQUE               GASPAR ANTONIO MANRIQUE de LARA
   (b. 8 October 1698, Leon, Gto, MX)    (b. 28 March 1702, Leon, Gto., MX)
   m. MARIA JOSEPHA ANTONIA de PINA      m. FRANCA. CALDERON HERRERA
                   |                                  |
        MARIA CECILIA MANRIQUE          JOSEPH MANUEL MANRIQUE de LARA
   (b. 27 November 1746, Leon, Gto, MX)  (b. 30 October 1734, Leon, Gto., MX)
        m. JOSE FRUETNOSO TORRES             m. ANA RITA ALCARAS
                   |                                  |
   RITA ANTONIA TORRES y MANRIQUE   JOSEPH URBANO MANRIQUE de LARA
      (b. 1776, Leon, Gto., MX)        (b. 26 May 1766, Leon, Gto., MX
        m. JOSE ANTONIO BOCANEGRA             m. MELCHORA LOPES
                   |                                  |
  MARIA DOLORES BIBIANA BOCANEGRA  ----    JOSE ISIDRO MANRIQUE
   (b. 2 December 1806, Leon, Gto., MX)    (b. 17 May 1804, Leon, Gto., MX)
                        Married 17 May 1804
 JOSE ANTONIO MAGDALENO BOCANEGRA  --  m. MARIA APOLONIA MANRIQUE
   (b. 27 July 1805, Leon, Gto., MX)       (b. 13 April 1814, Leon, Gto., MX)
                        Married 20 June 1830
```

~~~~~

BERNARDA MANRIQUE, born abt. 1678, Guanajuato, Mexico (*Unknown parentage*).
>   Married: DOMINGO de la CRUZ

The known child of Bernarda Manrique and Domingo de la Cruz:
PHELIPE MANRIQUE

PHELIPE MANRIQUE, christening 8 October 1698, Leon, Guanajuato, Mexico (Father: DOMINGO de la CRUZ/Mother: BERNARDA MANRIQUE) (Godmother: SEBASTIANA de la CRUZ*) (Witness: DIEGO de LARA) (*Leon de los Aldama. Baptism Records 1695-1704; Image 110-124*) (Phe. = Phelipe).

*Sebastiana de la Cruz was the godmother to Diego de la Cruz, Nicolas de Medina's father and Gaspar Antonio Manrique de Lara's grandfather.

>   Married (m1) ISABEL de ROCHA.

The known children of PHELIPE MANRIQUE (a) and (m1) ISABEL de ROCHA were:
a1. MARIA BERNARDA MANRIQUE de ROCHA, born 4 August 1712, Leon, Guanajuato, Mexico. Christening 21 September 1711, Leon, Guanajuato, Mexico (Father: Phe, Manrique/Mother: Isabel de Rocha) (Witnesses: Barme de Alcaras, Joseph Maldonado) (*Leon de los Aldama. Baptism records 1710-1715; Image 103/198*).
a2. GERTUDIS SAN (---), christening 1717, Santa Ana, Penjamo, Guanajuato, Mexico (Father: Phe. Manrique/Mother: Isabel de Rocha) (Witnesses: Juo. Antonio de Aguilar, Don Maldonado, Teresa).
a3. LUIS BERNARDINO MANRIQUE, baptized 2 June 1720, El Sagrario, Leon, Guanajuato, Mexico (Father: Phelipe Manrique/Mother: Ysabel de Rochas) (*Leon de los Aldama. Bautismos de indios, mulatos y mestizos 1717-1732*).
a4. CAYTANA ANTONIA MANRIQUE, baptized 22 September 1722, El Sagrario, Leon, Guanajuato, Mexico (Father: Phelipe Manrique/Mother: Isabel de Rochas) (*Leon de los Aldama. Bautismos de indios, mulatos y mestizos 1717-1732*).

Married (m2) MARIA JOSEPHA ANTONIA de PINA.

The known children of PHELIPE MANRIQUE (a) and (m2) MARIA JOSEPHA ANTONIA PINA were:
a5. THOMASA ANTONIA MANRIQUE, baptized 11 January 1728, El Sagrario, Leon, Guanajuato, Mexico. (Father: Phelipe Manrique/Mother: Josepha de Pina).
a6. MARIA JOSEPHA MANRIQUE, baptized 21 November 1730, El Sagrario, Leon, Guanajuato, Mexico (Father: Phelipe Manrique/Mother: Josepha Antonia de Pina) (*Leon de los Aldama. Bautismos de indios, mulatos y mestizos 1717-1732*).
a7. MARIA LORENSA MANRIQUE, baptized 16 August 1733, El Sagrario, Leon, Guanajuato, Mexico (Father: Phelipe Manrique/Mother: Josepha Pina) (*Leon de los Aldama. Bautismos de indios, mulatos y mestizos, 1732-1741*).
a8. MARIA DESIDERIA MANRIQUE, baptized 12 January 1739, Leon, Guanajuato, Mexico (Father: Phelipe Manrique/Mother: MA. Josefa Pina) (*Leon de los Aldama. Bautismos de indios, mulatos y mestizos 1732-1741*).
a9. SILVERIO JOSEPH MANRIQUE, son of Phe. Manrique and Maria Josepha) (*Leon. Baptism Records 1741-1745; Image 8/172*) baptized 16 August 1741, Leon, Guanajuato, Mexico (Father: Phe. Manrique/Mother: Maria Josepha de A-*guirre*) (*Leon de los Aldama. Bautismos de indios, mulatos y mestizos 1741-1749*).
a10. MARIA CECILIA MANRIQUE, christening 27 November 1746 (Espanola of the villa), Leon, Guanajuato, Mexico (Margin text: "Cecilia, of the villa. ...legitimate daughter of Phe. Manrique and Maria Josepha de Pina.") (Father: Phe. Manrique/Mother: Maria Josepha de Piria) (*Leon de los Aldama. Baptismal Records 1718-1748; Image 60/73*).
Married JOSE FRUETNOSO de TORRES. Burial (Jose Frutos Torres) 9 March 1785, Nuestra Senora de Guanajuato, Mexico. Spouse: Maria

Cecilia Manrique, Espanola) (*Leon. Death Certificates 1820-1823; Image 440/648*).

<u>Santa Ana Religious Marriage Investigation;</u> (*Files 1802/Image 17/218*)
    Don Pedro GALBAN (Witness) (ISABEL GALVAN married Baltasar Gomez Manrique de Lara)
    Don Joaquin Galban (born 1768; age 38) <u>married</u> to Dona Anna Getrudis Torres (age 23, born 1783), resident of Leon. Death/burial 31 December 1825, Santa Ana, Penjamo, Guanajuato, Mexico (Spouse: Dona Getrudis de Torres).
Don Jose Fausto de Torres and Dona Maria Cecilia Manrique (*Jose Fruetnoso de Torres' sister was Getrudis de Torres*))
    <u>Child</u>: JOSE SELBESTRE JUAN NEPOMUCENO IGNACIO de JESUS GALBAN
(Father: Don Joaquin Galban/Mother: Dona Gertrudis Torres), christening 2 January 1821, Santa Ana, Penjamo, Guanajuato, Mexico.

<u>The known children of Maria Cecilia Manrique (a) and Jose Fruetnoso de Torres were</u>:
- b1. JOSEPH FRANCO BERNABE TORRES MANRIQUE, christening 16 June 1768, Leon, Guanajuato, Mexico (Father: Joseph Frutos Torres/ Mother: Maria Cecilia Manrique, Espanoles).
- b2. **RITA ANTONIA de la LUZ TORRES y MANRIQUE**, christening 1776, Leon, Guanajuato, Mexico (Father: Joseph Fruto de Torres; Mother: Maria Cecilia) (Godparent: Pablo Manrique) (*Leon de los Aldama. Baptism Records 1775-1781; Image 62/310*). <u>Married</u> JOSE ANTONIO BOCANEGRA.
- b3. JOSE ANTONIO de TORRES, born abt. 1779. <u>Married</u> PAULA JOSEFA de TORRES on 27 June 1799, Nuestra Senora de Guanajuato, Guanajuato, Guanajuato, Mexico (Father: Jose Fruto Torres/ Mother: Maria Cecilia Manrique).
- b4. PAULA JOSEPHA de TORRES, born abt. 1782, Leon, Guanajuato, Mexico. <u>Married</u> JOSE ANTONIO de TORRES (son of Aparicio de Torres and Maria Velis) on 27 June 1799, Nuestra Senora de Guanajuato, Guanajuato, Guanajuato, Mexico (Father: Jose Fruto de Torres/Mother: Maria Cecilia Manrique).
- b5. ANTONIO ADAPTO TORRES, born abt. 1786, Leon, Guanajuato, Mexico. <u>Married</u> Dona MARIA GERTRUDIS MANRIQUE (born 1788) (Father: Don Telesforo Manrique/Mother: Dona Dolores Coronel) on 4 December 1804, Nuestra Senora de Guanajuato, Guanajuato, Guanajuato, Mexico (Father: Don Jose Torres/Mother: Dona Cecilia Manrique).

RITA ANTONIA de la LUZ TORRES y MANRIQUE, christening 1776, Leon, Guanajuato, Mexico (Father: Joseph Fruto de Torres/Mother: Maria Cecilia) (Godparent: Pablo Manrique) (Margin Text: "Rita Antonia de la Luz") (*Leon de los Aldama. Baptism Records 1775-1781; Image 62/310*).

Married: JOSE ANTONIO BOCANEGRA (Death/burial 20 September 1814, San Juan Bautista, Guanajuato, Mexico) (*San Juan Bautista Religious Death Records 181-1814; Image 198/203*).

The known children of Jose Antonio Bocanegra and Rita Antonia Torres y Manrique (b) were:

- c1. JOSE FELIX de JESUS BOCANEGRA TORRES, born 16 October 1791; christening 17 October 1791, Leon, Guanajuato, Mexico (Father: Jose Antonio Bocanegra/Mother: Antonia Torres) (*Leon de los Aldama. Baptism Records 1790-1794; Image 139/259*).
- c2. JOSE PONCIANO, christening November 1794, Leon, Guanajuato, Mexico (Father: Jose Antonio Bocanegra; Mother: Rita Antonia de Torres).
- c3. JOSE RAMON SATURNINO BOCANEGRA, baptism 1 December 1796, Leon, Guanajuato, Mexico (Father: Jose Antonio Bocanegra/ Mother: Rita de Torres).
- c4. JOSE GUADALUPE BOCANEGRA, born abt. 1798, Leon, Guanajuato, Mexico. Married MARIA JUANA GONZALEZ (daughter of Juan Gonzalez and Mariana Esparza) on 27 February 1827, Nuestra Senora de Guanajuato, Sante Fe, Guanajuato, Mexico (Father: Antonio Bocanegra; Mother: Rita Torres).
- c5. JOSE MARIA DOLORES BOCANEGRA, baptized 17 August 1800, Nuestra Senora de Guanajuato, Sante Fe, Guanajuato, Mexico (Father: Jose Antonio Bocanegra; Mother: Maria Rita Torres).
- c6. JOSE ANTONIO MAGDALENO BOCANEGRO, baptized 27 July 1805, Leon, Guanajuato, Mexico (*Bautismos de espanoles 1796-1809*) (Father: Jose Antonio Bocanegra; Mother: Maria Rita de Torres). Married MARIA APOLINA MANRIQUE (*sister of Jose Isidro Manrique*) (Father: Urbano Manrique; Mother: Melchora Lopes) on 20 June 1830, Nuestra Senora de Guanajuato, Leon, Guanajuato, Mexico.
- c7. **MARIA DOLORES BIBIANA BOCANEGRA**, born 2 December 1806; christening 7 December 1806, Nuestra Senora de Guanajuato, Leon, Guanajuato, Mexico (Father: Jose Antonio Bocanegra; Mother: Rita Antonia Torres) (Margin text: "Maria Dolores Vibiana ...infanta Espanola, de 5 dias... daughter of Don Jose Antonio Bocanegra and Dona Rita Antonia Torres Manrique.") (*Guanajuato. Baptism Records 1806 - 1808; Image 62/14*). Married **JOSE ISIDRO MANRIQUE** (baptized 17 May 1804, El Sagrario, Leon, Guanajuato, Mexico) on 27 February 1827, Sagrario Parroquia de San Sebastian de la Villa, Leon, Guanajuato, Mexico.

~~~~~~~~

APPENDIX V: ANA RITA ALCARAS (1730-)
(Wife of Joseph Manuel Manrique de Lara)

```
                                          Godparents of DIEGO de la CRUZ:
                                                FRANCISCO MARMOLEJO
                                              TOMASA GOMEZ of PORTUGAL
                                                           |
     LORENZO de ALCARAS (1650)           DIEGO de la CRUZ (1649, San Felipe)
        m. JUANA VALENZUELA                    m. MELCHORA de MEDINA
                  |                                        |
         LORENZO de ALCARAS                       NICOLAS de MEDINA
     (born abt. 1680, Salvatierra, Gto., MX)   (b. 1680, Salvatierra, Gto., MX)
            m. JUANA VARRERA                   m. JOSEPHA GOMEZ MdL (1677)      |
                                                           |
                  |                            GASPAR MANRIQUE de LARA
                  |                              (b. 1702, Leon, Gto., MX)
                  |                        m. FRANCA. CALDERON de HERRERA
                  |                                        |
ANA RITA ALCARAS (1730) married JOSEPH MANUEL MANRIQUE de LARA (1734)
                         (Godmother: RITA GETRUDIS MARMOLEJO)
```

~~~~~~

ANA RITA de ALCARAS, baptized 16 April 1730, El Sagrario, Leon, Guanajuato, Mexico (Father: LORENSO de ALCARAS/Spaniard. Mother: JUANA VARRERA) (Godparents: ALONSO VARRERA and ISABEL VARRREA).

LORENZO de ALCARAS (born abt. 1650) and JUANA VALENZUELA (born abt. 1660) married by 1687, Salvatierra, Guanajuato, Mexico.

The known children of Lorenzo Alcaras and Juana Varrera Valenzuela were:
a1. ISABEL de la VARRERA (ALCARAS), born abt. 1678, Salvatierra, Guanajuato, Mexico (Father: Lorenzo de Alcazar/Mother: Juana Valenzuela).
   Married JUAN ALTAMIRANO (Father: Miguel Altamirano/Mother: Augustina de los Reyes) on 13 April 1693, Salvatierra, Guanajuato, Mexico.
   The known children of Isabel Alcaras Valenzuela (a) and Juan Altamirano were:
   b1. JUAN JOSEPH ALTAMIRANO, christening 31 January 1694, Salvatierra, Guanajuato, Mexico (Father: Juan Altamirano/Mother: Isabel Valenzuela).
   b2. MARIA ANA de SAN JUAN ALTAMIRANO, born 22 June 1695, Salvatierra, Guanajuato, Mexico. Christening 26 June 1695, Salvatierra, Guanajuato, Mexico (Father: Juan Altamirano/Mother: Isabel de Valenzuela).

- b3. MARIA ANTONIA ALTAMIRANO de ALCARAS, born 13 June 1704 Salvatierra, Guanajuato, Mexico (Father: Juan Altamirano/Mother: Isabel de Alcaras).
- a2. LORENZO ALCARAS (*assumed*) (*born abt. 1680*).
  <u>Married</u> JUANA VARRERA.
  <u>The known children of Lorenzo Alcaras (a) and Juana Varrera were:</u>
  - b1. ASENCIO FRANCISCO de ALCARAS, born 25 April 1712, Leon, Guanajuato, Mexico. Christening 18 May 1712, El Sagrario, Leon, Guanajuato, Mexico (Father: Lorenzo de Alcaras/Mother: Juana Varrera) (Espanoles, married, of the villa) (Godparents: Nicolas Alcaras and Mariana Varrera) (Priest: BARTHE de ALCARAS - priest) (*Leon de los Aldama. Baptism Records 1691-1715; Image 79/128*).
  - b2. MARIA VALENTIN ALCARAS, christening 26 February 1714, El Sagrario, Leon, Guanajuato, Mexico (Father: Lorenzo Alcaras/Mother: Juana Varrera) (*Leon de los Aldama. Baptism Records 1710-1715; Image 163/198*).
  - b3. FRANCISCA JOSEPHA de ALCARAS, baptized 21 October 1717, El Sagrario, Leon, Guanajuato, Mexico (Father: Lorenzo de Alcaras/Mother: Juana Varrera).
  - b4. ANTONIO BASILIO de ALCARAS, 1727, El Sagrario, Leon, Guanajuato, Mexico (Father: Lorenzo de Alcaras/Mother: Juana Varrera).
  - b5. **ANA RITA de ALCARAS**, baptized 16 April 1730, El Sagrario, Leon, Guanajuato, Mexico (Father: LORENSO de ALCARAS/Spaniard. Mother: JUANA VARRERA) (Godparents: ALONSO VARRERA and ISABEL VARRREA). <u>Married</u> **JOSEPH MANUEL MANRIQUE de LARA** (born 1734).
  - b6. MARIA de los DOLORES de ALCARAS, baptism 23 April 1736, El Sagrario, Leon, Guanajuato, Mexico (Father: Lorenzo de Alcaras/Mother: Juana Varrera).
  - b7. JOSEPH BENITO ALCARAS, baptism 24 March 1737, Leon, Guanajuato, Mexico (Father: Lorenzo Alcaras/Mother: Juana).
- a3. GABRIELA ALCARAS (*assumed*) (born abt. 1704). <u>Married</u> **PABLO JOSEPH MANRIQUE de LARA** (Christening 21 January 1704, Nuestra Senora de la Soledad, Irapuato, Guanajuato, Mexico. Father: Joseph Manrique/Mother: Maria Ana Brito).
  <u>The known children of Pablo Manrique and Gabriela Alcaras (a) were:</u>
  - b1. MARIA EUGENIA MANRIQUE, baptized 30 November 1730, El Sagrario, Leon, Guanajuato, Mexico (Father: Pablo Manrique/Mother: Gabriela Alcaras, Mestizo) (Godparents: Ildephonso de *H-asa* and Francisca Villanueva) (*Leon. Baptism Records 1717-1721; Image 399/443*).
  - b2. JOSEPH DIONICIO MANRIQUE, baptized 15 April 1733, El Sagrario, Leon, Guanajuato, Mexico (Father: Pablo Manrique/ Mother: Gabriela Alcaras, married) (Godparents: Don Tomas Hernandez Cavado and Dona Maria Antonia Almeida) (Margin text: "Joseph

    Dionicio, espanol") (*Leon de Los Aldama. Baptism Records 1718-1748; Image 81/119*).

b3. FRANCISCO YLARIO MANRIQUE, baptized 22 November 1735, El Sagrario, Leon, Guanajuato, Mexico) (Father: Pablo Manrique and Xaviera Alcaras) (Godparents: Sebastian Orosco and Rosa Orosco) (Margin text: "Franco Ylario") (*Leon. Baptism Records 1732-1736; Image 125/147*). Married MARIA GUADALUPE de la PRESENTACION MEDRANO (Father: Pasqual Medrano and Juan Gertrudis de los Santos) on 22 July 1760, Nuestra Senora de Guanajuato, Guanajuato, Mexico) (Father: Pablo Manrique/Mother: Gabriela Alcaras).

b4. JOSEPH GERVACIO MANRIQUE, baptized 27 June 1738, El Sagrario, Leon, Guanajuato, Mexico (Father: Pablo Manrique/Mother: Gabriela Alcaras, married, Espanol, of the villa) (Godparents: Dona **RITA de MARMOLEJO**"---" espanoles and resident of the villa") (Margin Text: "Joseph Gervacio, espanol de la villa") (*Leon de los Aldama. Baptism Records 1718-1748; Image 107/119*).

b5. NICOLAS AMBROCIO MANRIQUE, baptized 12 November 1740, El Sagrario, Leon, Guanajuato, Mexico (Father: Pablo Manrique/ Mother: Gabriel Alcaras) (Godparents: Don Luis - and Dona Maria de Arze). Burial 18 December 1747, Nuestra Senora de Guanajuato, Guanajuato, Mexico (Father: Pablo Manrique/Mother: Gabriela de Alcaraz). (Margin text: "Nicolas Ambrocio, Casta de la villa") (*Leon. Baptism Records 1736-1741; Image 131/168*).

b6. JUANA de JESUS MANRIQUE, baptized 30 March 1745, El Sagrario, Guanajuato, Mexico (Father: Pablo Manrique/Mother: Gabriela de Alcaraz) (Godparents: Antonio Miranda and JOSEPHA de ALCARAS) (Margin text: "Juana de Jesus espanola de la villa") (*Leon de los Aldama. Baptism Records 1718-1748; Image 45/73*).

b7. DOMINGO de JESUS MANRIQUE, baptized 22 April 1743, El Sagrario, Leon, Guanajuato, Mexico (Father: Pablo Manrique/Mother: Gabriela Alcaras, "married, of the villa") (Margin text: "Domingo de Jesus, espanol de la villa") (*Leon de los Aldama. Baptism Records 1718-1748; Image 28/73*).

b8. MARIA de la LUZ MANRIQUE ALCARAS, christening 27 August 1747, Sante Fe, San Felipe, Guanajuato, Mexico (Father: Pablo Manrique de Lara/Mother: Gabriela Alcaras, "residents of the villa Leon") (Godparents: **DIEGO MANRIQUE de LARA** and MARIA ANA GOMEZ de BRITO, residents "de la villa las OMONEITO") (Margin text: "Maria de la Luz, espanola") (*Guanajuato Baptism Records 1746-1753; Image 51/176*).

~~~~~~~~~~~~~~~~~~~~

Only two Alcaras-Manrique de Lara marriages noted in Guanajuato, Mexico 1690-1750:

PABLO JOSEPH MANRIQUE de LARA (son of Joseph DIEGO Manrique de Lara and Maria Ana GOMEZ de Brito) married GABRIELA ALCARAS.

JOSEPH MANUEL MANRIQUE de LARA (son of Gaspar Antonio Manrique de Lara and Francisca Xaviera Calderon de Herrera) married ANA RITA ALCARAS.

~~~~~~~~~~~~~~~

The likely children of (MANRIQUE de LARA ALCARAS) of Joseph Maria Manrique de Lara (b) and Ana Rita Alcaras were:

c1. JOSEPH GREGORIO ENRIQUES ALCARAS, christening 29 April 1754, Marfil, Guanajuato, Mexico (Father: Joseph Maria Enriques/Mother: Rita de Alcaras - Espanoles) (Margin text: "Joseph Gregorio, espanol") (*FHL #004785560; Image 199/215*).

c2. FRANCO de la CRUZ MANRIQUE ALCARAS, christening 7 May 1758, Marfil, Guanajuato, Mexico (Father: Joseph Maria Manrique/Mother: Maria Rita Ana Alcaras) (Margin text: "Joseph Franco de la Cruz, Espanol") (*Marfil. Baptism Records; Image 300/519*).

c3. JOSEPH DIEGO MANRIQUEZ, baptism 10 October 1761, Marfil, Guanajuato, Mexico (Father: Joseph Maria ***Manriques de LARA***/Wife: Anna Rita de Alcaras) (Espanoles) (Godparents: Eusebio de la Trinidad Duran and Maria Josepha Zavala, Espanoles) (Margin text: "Joseph Diego, Espanol") (*Marfil. Baptism Records 1754-1774; Image 430/519*).

c4. MARIA JOSEPHA MARCELA MANRIQUE (Spaniard), born 30 October 1763, Guanajuato, Mexico. Baptized 31 October 1763, El Sagrario, Leon, Guanajuato, Mexico (Father: Joseph Maria Manrique/Mother: A. Rita Alcaras) (Godparents: Maria Nicolasa Duran and Manuel Anastacio Arias) (Margin text: "Maria Josepha Marcela, espanola de la villa") (*Leon de los Aldama. Baptism Records 1749-1777; Image 121/318*).

c5. **JOSEPH URBANO de la LUZ MANRIQUE de LARA,** b. 25 May 1768, Leon, Guanajuato, Mexico. Baptized 25 May 1768, El Sagrario Church, Leon, Guanajuato, Mexico (Father: Joseph Manuel Manrique/Mother: Anna Rita Alcaras).

c6. JOSEPH ANTONIO CIRIACO de la LUZ MANRIQUE, born 9 August 1770, Leon, Guanajuato, Mexico. Baptized 14 August 1770, San Jose y Santiago Church, Marfil, Guanajuato, Mexico (Father: Joseph MA Manrique/ Mother: Anna Rita Alcaras, both Spaniards) (Godparents: Antonio Miranda and his daughter, Anna Theresa) (Margin text: "Joseph Antonio Ciriaco de la Luz, espanol") (*Family Search #004002585; Image 274/457*).

c7. JOSEPH GUADALUPE SANTA MARIA MANRIQUE, born 19 October 1772, Leon, Guanajuato, Mexico. Baptized 25 October 1772, Sante Fe Church, Sante Fe, San Felipe, Guanajuato, Mexico (Father: Joseph Maria Manriquez/Mother: Ana Rita Alacala) (Godfather: Thomas Ventura Sierra) (Margin text: "Joseph Guadalupe Santa Maria, Espanol") (*Archivo de la Parroquia de Sante Fe, Guanajuato, Mexico, Vol. 48; Family Search Film #004791987; Image 533/543*). Engagement to MARIA RAFAELA VILLEGAS (dau. of MA Juana Guzman and Francisco Villegas) on 17 February 1810, Santa Fe Church, Sante Fe, Guanajuato, Mexico (Father: Jose Maria Manriquez/Mother: Ana Alcaras).

APPENDIX VI: MANUEL MANRIQUE

(Individuals given name, "Manuel," during 1729-1734 in Leon, Guanajuato, Mexico)

1.
JOSEPH MANUEL MANRIQUE de LARA, born 30 October 1734 (Page 13). Two of his children used "Manrique de Lara" as their surname. His father, Gaspar Manrique de Lara, married Francisca Xavier Calderon de Herrera. His grandmother was Josepha Gomez Manrique de Lara. His wife was 3 ½ years older which was unusual unless she was a widow. No marriage document discovered. Gabriela Alcaras, Manuel's wife's aunt, married Pablo Joseph Manrique de Lara.

2.
SALVADOR MANUEL MANRIQUE, baptized June 1726, El Sagrario, Leon, Guanajuato, Mexico (Father: Francisco Manrique/Mother: MANUELA de HERRERA) (Godparents: Sebastian de Orosco and Luisa de Aguirre) (Margin text: "Salvador Manuel") (*Leon de los Aldama. Baptism Records 1718-1748; Image 49/119*).

3.
MANUEL ANTONIO MANRIQUE, baptized 11 November 1731, El Sagrario, Guanajuato, Mexico (Father: Manuel Manrique/Mother: Jacinta de Aguilar Manrique) (Espanoles) (Residents of de la Paz de los Amolas) (Godparents: Manuel de la Fozze and Bernarda de Fozze) (Margin text: "Manuel Antonio de la Paz de los Amoles") (*Leon de los Aldama. Baptism Records 1718-1748; Image 67/119*).

4.
MANUEL ANTONIO MANRIQUEZ, baptism 6 December 1733, El Sagrario, Leon, Guanajuato, Mexico (Father: Matheo Manrique/Mother: Beatris de la Luz) (*Bautismos de indios, mulatos, y mestizos 1732-1741*).

~~~~~~~~

2. SALVADOR MANUEL MANRIQUE:

JULIO DABON m. FERNANDA MANRIQUE (abt. 1630)

JULIO CASMIRO DABON MANRIQUE (1655)　　　　　　　De HERRERA
　m. JOSEPHA GUERRERO (1656)　　　　　　　m. BERNARDA de BRAVO

FRANCISCO MANRIQUE (1693) m. MA. THERESA MANUELA de HERRERA (1709)

SALVADOR MANUEL MANRIQUE (1726)

FERNANDA MANRIQUE (born abt. 1630, Guanajuato, Guanajuato, Mexico)
　Married JULIO DABON (born abt. 1630, Guanajuato, Guanajuato, Mexico).
The known child of Fernanda Manrique and Julio Dabon was:

JULIO CASMIRO DABON MANRIQUE, baptized 1655, Nuestra de Senora, Guanajuato, Guanajuato, Mexico (Nuestra Senora de Guanajuato, Bautismos de espanoles) (Father: Julio Dabon/Mother: Fernanda Manrique) (Godmother: Teresa Manrique and Nicolas Gutierrez).

Godmother to JULIO CASMIRO DABON MANRIQUE: TERESA MANRIQUE

    TERESA MANRIQUE, born abt. 1630, Irapuato, Guanajuato, Mexico (Father: Garci Bravo de Lagunas/Mother: CATHALINA MANRIQUE) (*Daughter of Pedro Gomez and Catalina Manrique de Lara*).

    Married NICOLAS SEVILLANO (Father: Juan Sevillano Mother: Juana Rodriquez) on May 1648, Sante Fe, Guanajuato, Mexico.

Married JOSEPHA GUERRERO.

    JOSEPHA GUERRERO, christening 29 May 1656, Leon, Guanajuato, Mexico (Father: Joseph Guerrero/Mother: Maria de las Arenas) (Godparents: Lorenzo de Malpando and Antonia de la Vega) (Margin text: "Josepha, espanola") (*Leon de los Aldama. Baptism Records 1636-1673; Image 28/87*).

The known children of Julio Casmiro Manrique and Josepha Guerrero were:

a1. PHELIPE MANRIQUE, born 10 October 1688, Leon, Guanajuato, Mexico. Christening 22 October 1688, Leon, Guanajuato, Mexico (Father: Juan Manrique/Mother: Josepha Guerrero) (Godparents: Nicolas de la Fuente and Maria de Oleas) (Espanoles de la villa) (Margin text: "Phelipe") (*Leon de los Aldama. Baptism Records 1673-1691; Image 18-26*).

a2. MARIA JOSEPHA MANRIQUE, born 1690, (Father: Juo. Manrique/Mother: Josepha Guerrero) (Godparents: Antonio Chavesti and Rita de Quesada) (Margin text: "Maria Josepha") (Espanoles) (*Leon de los Aldama. Baptism Records 1673-1691; Image 23/26*).

a3. **FRANCISCO MANUEL MANRIQUE**, christening 9 April 1693, Leon, Guanajuato, Mexico (Father: Juo. - Julio Manrique/Mother: Josepha Guerrero) (Godparents: Luis de Acosta and Maria de Acosta) (Margin text: "Francisco, espanol"). Married TERESA MANUELA de HERRERA.

a4. JUANA GALINA MANRIQUE, born 24 March 1695, Leon, Guanajuato, Mexico. Christening April 1695, Leon, Guanajuato, Mexico (Father: Juo. Manrique/ Mother: Josepha Guerrero con Luxe---) (Godparents: Phe. - Phelipe Varrera-- and Dona MARIA MANRIQUE de LARA) (Document text: "Juana Galina espanola") (Margin text: "Juana de la villa") (*Leon de los Aldama. Baptism Records 1691-1715; Image 22/128*).

FRANCISCO MANUEL MANRIQUE, christening 9 April 1693, Leon, Guanajuato, Mexico (Father: Juo. - Julio Manrique/Mother: Josepha Guerrero) (Godparents: Luis de Acosta and Maria de Acosta) (Margin text: "Francisco, espanol"). Married THERESA MANUELA de HERRERA.

MARIA THERESA HERRERA, born 7 March 1709, Leon, Guanajuato, Mexico. Christening 1708, Leon, Guanajuato, Mexico (Father: de Herrera/Mother: Andrea Bernarda de Bravo) (Godparent: Antonio de Gaona) (Margin text: "Maria Josepha") (Document text: "Maria Theresa") (*Leon de los Aldama. Baptism Records 1706-1710; Image 56/148*).

The known children of Francisco Manrique and Theresa Manuela de Herrera were:

a1. JOSEPH FRANCISCO MANRIQUE, baptized 1721, El Sagrario, Leon, Guanajuato, Mexico (Father: Francisco Manuel Manrique/Mother: Theresa Manuela de Herrera, "Espanoles/Married/of the villa") (Godmother: Dona Isabel de Espejo) (*Leon de los Aldama. Baptism Records 1718-1748; Image 29/119*).
Isabel de Espejo, born 1659, Leon, Guanajuato, Mexico was the daughter of Juana Gomez de Espejo and Domingo Hernandez Gamino who married Juan Herrera Quintana. Isabel was the daughter of Juana Gomez de Espejo (1595-1653), the child of Juana Gomez of Portugal (1560) and Gaspar de Maldonado (1550).

a2. **SALVADOR MANUEL MANRIQUE**, baptized June 1726, El Sagrario, Leon, Guanajuato, Mexico (Father: Francisco Manrique/Mother: MANUELA de HERRERA) (Godparents: Sebastian de Orosco/Mother: Luisa de Aguirre) (Margin text: "Salvador Manuel") (*Leon de los Aldama. Baptism Records 1718-1748; Image 49/119*).

a3. JUSTO JOSEPH MANRIQUE, baptized 2 January 1729, Leon, Guanajuato, Mexico (Father: Francisco Manrique/Mother: Manuela de Herrera) (Godparents: Nicolas Nunez and Cayetana Espinosa) (Margin text: "Justo Joseph de la villa") (*Leon. Baptism Records 1717-1721; Image 349/443*).

a4. THOMASA ANTONIA MANRIQUE, baptized 1 April 1733, El Sagrario, Leon, Guanajuato, Mexico (Father: Francisco Manrique/Mother: Theresa Manuela de Herrera) (Godparents: Alonso de Herrera and Maria Lopez Ybarra) (Margin text: "Thomasa Antonia, espanola de la villa") (*Leon de los Aldama. Baptism Records 1718-1748; Image 80/119*).

Godparents to SALVADOR MANUEL MANRIQUE:
SEBASTIAN de OROSCO and LUISA MARIA de AGUIRRE
The known children of Sebastian de Orosco and Luisa de Aguirre were:

a1. ROSA MARIA, christening February 1710 (Father: Sebastian de Orsco/ Mother: Luisa Maria de Aguirre) (Godparents: Antonio Sanchez and Isabel Lopez) (Margin text: "Rossa Maria de la villa") (Espanola) (*Leon de los Aldama. Baptism Records 1691-1715; Image 96/128*).

a2. MARIA GUADALUPE, christening 20 December 1711, Leon, Guanajuato, Mexico (Father: Sebastian de Orosco/Mother: Luisa de Aguirres) (Godmother: Rita de Torres) (*Leon de los Aldama. Baptism Records 1710-1715; Image 68/198*).

a3. ESTEBAN JACINTO de OROSCO, baptized 11 March 1718, El Sagrario, Leon, Guanajuato, Mexico (Father: Sebastian de Orozco/Mother:

villa") (Godparents: Antonio de Aguirre and Rosa Morales) (*Leon de los Aldama. Baptism Records 1718-1748; Image 7/119*).
- a4. VICENTE FERRER de OROSCO, baptized 2 October 1728, El Sagrario, Leon, Guanajuato, Mexico (Father: Sebastian de Orosco/Mother: Luisa de Aguirre).

3.
MANUEL ANTONIO MANRIQUE, baptized 11 November 1731, El Sagrario, Guanajuato, Mexico (Father: Manuel Manrique/Mother: Jacinta de Aguilar Manrique) (Espanoles) (Residents of de la Paz de los Amolas) (Godparents: Manuel de la Fozze and Bernarda de Fozze) (Margin: "Manuel Antonio de la Paz de los Amoles") (*Leon de los Aldama. Baptism Records 1718-1748; Image 67/119*).

```
            SEBASTIAN MANRIQUE
        m.  THERESA ARIAS de AGUIRRE
                    |
            CATALINA MANRIQUE (1664)
            m. MANUEL FLORES
                    |
            MANUEL FLORES MANRIQUE (1684)
            m.  JACINTA de AGUILAR
                    |
            MANUEL ANTONIO MANRIQUE (1731)
```

SEBASTIAN MANRIQUE de LARA, son of Pedro Gomez and Catalina Manrique de Lara:

Married (m1) JUANA de CERVANTES.
The known child of Sebastian Manrique de Lara (a) and Juana de Cervantes was:
a1. MARIA MANRIQUE CERVANTES, christening 5 May 1650, Nuestra Senora de Soledad, Irapuato, Guanajuato, Mexico.

Married (m2) THERESA ARIAS de AGUIRRE.
The known children of Sebastian Manrique de Lara (a) and THERESA ARIAS de AGUIRRE were:
- a2. BEATRIZ MANRIQUE ARIAS, christening 8 November 1662, Leon, Guanajuato, Mexico (Father: Sebastian Manrique and Theresa Arias) Godparents: Juan Sanchez de Lara and Ines Arias) (Margin text: "Beatriz").
- a3. MARIA MANRIQUE de AGUIRRE, christening 1663, Leon, Guanajuato, Mexico (Father: Sebastian Manrique/Mother: Theresa de Aguirre) (Godparents: Martin de Olaz and Isabel Cortez) (Margin text: "Maria") (*Leon de los Aldama. Baptism Records 1636-1673; Image 51/87*).
- a4. **CATALINA MANRIQUE ARIAS**, christening 13 August 1664, Leon, Guanajuato, Mexico (Father: Sebastian Manrique/Mother: Teresa Arias) (Godparents: Eugenio Martinez Solora and Magdalena de MEDINA) (Margin text:

"Catalina") (*Leon de los Aldama. Baptism Records 1636-1673; Image 56/87*). Married (m1) Manuel Flores Manrique/(m2) Felipe Beltran.

a5. FRANCA MANRIQUE de AGUIRRE, christening 28 June 1669, Leon, Guanajuato, Mexico (Father: Sebastian Manrique/Mother: Teresa de Aguirre) (Godparents: Joseph de Torres Galban and Andrea/Yandia de MEDINA) (Margin text: "Franca.") (*Leon de los Aldama. Baptism Records 1636-1673; Image 68/87*).

MANUEL FLORES MANRIQUE, christening 23 April 1684, Leon, Guanajuato, Mexico (Father: Manuel Flores/Mother: CATALINA MANRIQUE) (Godparents: Diego de Cordoba and Theresa de Aguirre) (Margin text: "Manuel") (*Leon de los Aldama. Baptism Records 1673-1691; Image 4/26*).

CATALINA MANRIQUE ARIAS, christening 13 August 1664, Leon, Guanajuato, Mexico (Father: Sebastian Manrique/Mother: Teresa Arias) (Godparents: Eugenio Martinez Solora and Magdalena de MEDINA) (Margin text: "Catalina") (*Leon de los Aldama. Baptism Records 1636-1673; Image 56/87*).

The known children of CATALINA MANRIQUE and (m1) MANUEL FLORES were:

a1. JUAN MANRIQUE, christening October 1681, Leon, Guanajuato, Mexico (Father: Manuel Flores/Mother: Catalina Manrique) (Godparents: Diego de Cordova and Dona Josepha --Olloa (Margin text: "Ju.") (*Leon de los Aldama. Baptism Records 1673-1691; Image 27/39*).

a2. MANUEL FLORES MANRIQUE, christening 23 April 1684, Leon, Guanajuato, Mexico (Father: Manuel Flores/Mother: Catalina Manrique) (Godparents: Diego de Cordoba and Theresa de Aguirre) (Margin text: "Manuel") (*Leon de los Aldama. Baptism Records 1673-1691; Image 4/26*).

Married (m2) CATALINA ARIAS *MALDONADO* married FELIPE BELTRAN.
(*Juana GOMEZ of Portugal married Gaspar de Maldonado*)

The known children of CATALINA ARIAS *MALDONADO* and (m2) FELIPE BELTRAN were:

a3. MATHEO BELTRAN ARIAS, christening 7 October 1685, Irapuato, Guanajuato, Mexico (Father: Felipe Beltran/Mother: Catalina Arias).

a4. RITA BELTRAN MALDONADO, christening 3 May 1690, Nuestra Senora de la Soledad, Irapuato, Guanajuato, Mexico (Father: Felipe Beltran/Mother: Catalina Maldonado).

a5. CATHERINA BELTRAN MALDONADO, christening 31 January 1695, Irapuato, Guanajuato, Mexico (Father: Felipe Beltran/Mother: Catherina Maldonado).

~~~~~~~~

PEDRO GOMEZ (born abt. 1520) (Leon by 1560)
m. CATALINA MANRIQUE de LARA (born *abt. 1530*)
|
BALTASAR (1550) - GASPAR (1550) - LUCIA (1555)
m. MARIANA FERRER
|
(Irapuato) SEBASTIAN (1603)   CATALINA MdL (1605)
m. JUANA CERVANTES m. GARCI BRAVO de LAGUNAS
| |
FERNANDA MANRIQUE (1630) SEBASTIAN MdL (1640) MARIA MdL (1630)
m. JULIO DABON m. THERESA AGUIRRE ARIAS m. PEDRO AGUIRRE GONZALEZ
| | |
JULIO CASMIRO MANRIQUE (1655) CATALINA MANRIQUE (1664) JOSEPHA
m. JOSEPHA GUERRERO (1656)   m. MANUEL FLORES m. NICOLAS MEDINA
| | |
FRANCISCO MANRIQUE (1693) MATEO FLORES MdL (1684) GASPER MdL (1702)
m. MANUELA HERRERA(1709)-m. JACINTA AGUILAR- m.FRANCA HERRERA(1707)
| | |
SALVADOR MANUEL (1726) -MANUEL ANTONIO (1731) -JOSEPH MANUEL (1734)

Assumption: Catalina Manrique de Lara and Sebastian Manrique de Lara were children of Gaspar Antonio Gomez Manrique de Lara and Mariana Ferrer.

1) Lucia Manrique married (m1) SEBASTIAN AGUIRRE in Irapuato/(m2) CRISTOBAL CERVANTES in Salamanca.
2). Sebastian Manrique married (m1) JUANA CERVANTES/(m2) THERESA ARIAS de AGUIRRE.
3). Catalina (GOMEZ) Manrique de Lara married GARCI BRAVO de LAGUNAS. Their daughter Maria (GOMEZ) MdL married PEDRO GONZALES AGUIRRE. Child #13 was JOSEPHA (GOMEZ MdL) GONZALES BRAVO, christening 23 July 1677, Irapuato, Guanajuato, Mexico.

~~~~~~~~~

GASPAR ANTONIO MANRIQUE de LARA and FRANCA. de HERRERA children:
Godparents:
CARLOS VINCENTE de MEDINA, baptized 2 April 1733, El Sagrario, Leon, Guanajuato, Mexico (Father: Gasper de Medina/Mother: Franca. Herrera) (Godparents: Don Nicolas **Marmolejo** and Dona Maxiana Gonzales) (Espanol).
JOSEPH MANUEL MANRIQUE, born 30 October 1734, Leon, Guanajuato, Mexico. Baptized 5 November 1734, El Sagrario, Leon, Guanajuato, Mexico (Espanol) (Father: Gasper Manrique/Mother: Franca. de Herrera) (Godparent: **Rita Getrudis Marmolejo**, single, Spaniard (*Book of Baptisms of Spaniards 1746-1777, 1806-1814) (Family Search #4777478; Image 91/382).*
Married ANA RITA ALCARAS (1730).
MARIANA de la CRUZ MANRIQUE, baptized 27 September 1747, El Sagrario, Leon, Guanajuato, Mexico) (Father: Gaspar Antonio Manrique/Mother Franca. Xaviera Herrera, mestiza de la villa (Godparent: **DIEGO JOSEPH MANRIQUE** and

Mariana Lopez - *Maria Ana **Gomez of Portugal** de Brito*) (Margin text: "Mariana de la Cruz, Mestiza de la Villa") (*Leon. Baptism Records 1745-1749; Image 120/212*).

Godmother: Rita Getrudis Marmolejo (**Appendix VII**):

MARIA GETRUDIS MARMOLEJO BANALES, born September 1715 (Father: Pedro Marmolejo; Mother: Angela Banales). Margin text: "Maria Gertrudis, espanola of the villa." Record text: ..."legitimate daughter of Pedro Marmolejo and Dona Angela Banales del Castillo, espanoles." Godparent of the villa: Godmother: Dona Angela de Bustos (*Leon de los Aldama. Baptism Records 1691-1715; Image 127/128*).

Death/burial: 15 September 1753, Nuestra Senora de Guanajuato, Guanajuato, Mexico (Spouse: Don Gasper Garcia) Margin text: "Dona Rita Marmolejo, espanola de la Villa; married to Don Gaspar Garcia Diego" (*Leon. Death Certificates 1820-1823; Image 291-648*).

RITA MARMOLEJO's lineage connects to Diego GOMEZ of Portugal.

~~~~~~

JOSEPH DIEGO MANRIQUE de LARA married MARIA ANA GOMEZ BRITO.

The known children of Joseph Diego Manrique de Lara and Maria Ana GOMEZ BRITO were:

a1. MARIA MAGDALENA MANRIQUE de LARA (born abt. 1700) married FRANCISCO CAIETANO GUTIERRES (Father: Juan Alfonso Gutierres/ Mother: Maria de Busto) on 13 May 1720, La Soledad, Irapuato, Guanajuato, Mexico ("Francisco Caietano Gutierres espanol") to (Maria Magdalena Manrique de Lara, "espanola," "legitimate daughter of Joseph Manrique de Lara and spouse Maria Anna Gomez Brito") (Godparents: Antonio Musnado- and JUANA MANRIQUE de LARA, espanoles) (*Irapuato. Marriage Records 1717-1756; Image 11/500*).

a2. JUANA MANRIQUE de LARA, born abt. 1703. Married JOSEPH de SANDOBAL (Father: Diego de Sandobal/Mother: Maria Rossa Arias de Vmana) on 7 January 1722, La Soledad, Irapuato, Guanajuato, Mexico (Text: "Juana Manrique de Lara, espanola legitimate daughter of Joseph Manrique and his wife, Maria Ana de Brito, espanoles") (Godparents: Caietano and Magdalena Manrique) (*Irapuato. Marriage Records 1717-1756; Image 14/500*).

a3. PABLO JOSEPH MANRIQUE de LARA, christening 21 January 1704, Nuestra Senora de la Soledad, Irapuato, Guanajuato, Mexico (Father: Joseph Manrique/Mother: Maria Ana Brito). Married GABRIELA ALCARAS.

~~~~

JOSEPH GUTIERRES MANRIQUE de LARA, christening 1688, Irapuato, Guanajuato, Mexico (Father: Cristobal Gutierrez/Mother: Bernarda Manrique de Lara)
Possibly: JOSEPH DIEGO (GUTIERRES) MANRIQUE de LARA.

GARCI BRAVO de LAGUNAS (1595)
m. CATALINA MANRIQUE de LARA (1605)
daughter of PEDRO GOMEZ (1530) and CATALINA MANRIQUE de LARA (1555)
|
JUANA GARCI BRAVO de LAGUNAS (MANRIQUE de LARA) (1622-1681)
m. DOMINGO HERNANDEZ GAMINO y GOMEZ,
son of JUANA GOMEZ de ESPEJO (1595, Guanajuato - 16 June 1653, Leon, Gto., MX)
and Domingo Hernandez Gamino (1595, Spain - 13 October 1687, Leon, Gto., MX),

on 7 May 1642, Sante Fe, San Miguel de Allende, Guanajuato.
|
JOSEPH (*DIEGO*) GUTIERRES MANRIQUE de LARA (1688)

~~~~~~~~~

JOSEPH DIEGO MANRIQUE de LARA married MARIA ANA GOMEZ BRITO.

The only other GOMEZ de BRITO named individual (1600-1700) residing in Guanajuato, Mexico was: SIMON GOMEZ de BRITO.

SIMON GOMEZ de BRITO, born abt. 1618, Guanajuato, Mexico.
  Married: ANTONIA FARFAN.
The known children of Simon Gomez de Brito and Antonia Farfan were:
- a1. CLEMENCIA BRITO RODRIQUEZ, christening 29 November 1638, (Father: Simon Brito/Mother: Antonia Rodriquez de Farfan) (Godparent: Nicolas de Pardo) (*Guanajuato. Baptism Records 1605-1609; Image 61/155*).
- a2. CATALINA GOMEZ FARFAN, christening 3 September 1640, Inglesia Parrochial de esta Real de Santa, Guanajuato, Mexico (Father: Simon Gomez de Brito and Antonia Farfan) (Godparents: Joseph Diego de Sestomo - (*Guanajuato. Baptism Records 1605-1609; Image 68/155*).
- a3. JUANA GOMEZ de BRITO, christening 24 August 1646, Nuestra Senora de Guanajuato, Guanajuato, Mexico (Father: Simon Gomez de Brito/Mother: Antonia Farfan).
- a4. JOSEPH GOMEZ FARFAN, christening 8 April 1647, Nuestra Senora de Guanajuato, Guanajuato, Mexico (Father: Simon Gomez de Brito/Mother: Antonia Farfan).
- a5. GERONIMA GOMEZ FARFAN, christening 28 October 1648, Nuestra Senora de Guanajuato, Guanajuato, Mexico (Father: Simon Gomez de Brito/Mother: Antonia Farfan).
- a6. PETRONILA GOMEZ FARFAN, christening 10 July 1650, Nuestra Senora de Guanajuato, Guanajuato, Mexico (Father: Simon Gomez de Brito/Mother: Antonia Fanfan).

~~~~~

APPENDIX VII: RITA MARMOLEJO (1715-1753)
(Godmother to JOSEPH MANUEL MANRIQUE de LARA)

MARMOLEJO - Connection to Manrique de Lara lineage

~Carlos Vincente de Medina, baptized 2 April 1733, El Sagrario, Leon, Guanajuato, Mexico (Father: Gasper de Medina/Mother: Franca. Herrera) (Godparents: Don Nicolas **Marmolejo** and Dona Maxiana Gonzales) (Espanol).

~Joseph Manuel Manrique de Lara, born 30 October 1734, Leon, Guanajuato, Mexico. Baptized 5 November 1734, El Sagrario Church, Leon, Guanajuato, Mexico (Espanol) (Father: Gasper Manrique/Mother: Franca. de Herrera) (Godparent: **Rita Getrudis Marmolejo**, single, Spaniard) (*Book of Baptisms of Spaniards 1746-1777, 1806-1814*) (*Family Search #4777478; Image 91/382*).

Also godmother to:
    Joseph Gervacio Manrique, baptized 27 June 1738, El Sagrario, Leon, Guanajuato, Mexico (Father: Pablo Manrique/Mother: Gabriela Alcaras) (Godmother: Dona **Rita de Marmolejo**, espanola) (Margin text: "Joseph Gervacio, espanol de la villa") (*Leon de los Aldama. Baptism Records 1718-1748; Image 107/119*).

Note: Spelling of name "Getrudis"/"Gertrudis" varies per record.

~~~~~

    DIEGO **GOMEZ** of PORTUGAL (1566)   GASPAR GOMEZ MdL (abt. 1550)
      m. MARIA GARCIA de ARRONA (1570)   MARIANA *FERRER* (abt. 1560)
          | |
    MELCHORA **GOMEZ** de PORTUGAL (1615)   CATALINA MdL (1600, Leon)
    m. PEDRO de MARMOLEJO de PEDRAZA   m. GARCI BRAVO de *LAGUNAS*
               (1610, Leon)
          | | |
MARIA PEDRAZA   PEDRO MARMOLEJO   MARIA GOMEZ MdL (1632)
of PORTUGAL (1640)   de PEDRAZA (1630)   m. PEDRO GONZALES
m. CRISTOBAL HERRERA   m. JOSEPHA de BUSTOS   de AGUIRRE y RULES
                           | |
         PEDRO MARMOLEJO (1668)   JOSEPHA **GOMEZ** MdL (1677)
        m. ANGELA BANALES CASTILLO   m. NICOLAS de MEDINA
                     | |
         RITA GETRUDIS MARMOLEJO   GASPER MEDINA
               (1715-1753)   MANRIQUE de LARA (1702-1755)
                                      m. FRANCA. de HERRERA (1707)
                                                  |
                                     JOSEPH MANUEL MANRIQUE de LARA
                                      Godson to RITA GETRUDIS MARMOLEJO

MARIA GETRUDIS MARMOLEJO BANALES, born September 1715, Leon, Guanajuato, Mexico (Father: Pedro Marmolejo; Mother: Angela Banales) (Margin text: "Maria Gertrudis, espanola of the villa") (Record text: ..."legitimate daughter of Pedro Marmolejo and Dona Angela Banales del Castillo, espanoles") (Godparent of the villa: Godmother: Dona Angela de Bustos) (*Leon de los Aldama. Baptism Records 1691-1715; Image 127/128*).

Death/burial: 15 September 1753, Nuestra Senora de Guanajuato, Guanajuato, Mexico (Spouse: Don Gasper Garcia) (Margin text: "Dona Rita Marmolejo, espanola de la Villa; married to Don Gaspar Garcia Diego") (*Leon. Death Certificates 1820-1823; Image 291-648*).

RITA GETRUDIS MARMOLEJO BANALES
Married: GASPER GARCIA DIEGO.
The children of Rita Getrudis Marmolejo and Gasper Garcia Diego were:
- a1. FRANCISCO GASPAR MACEDONIA GARCIA MARMOLEJO, christening September 1740, Leon, Guanajuato, Mexico (Father: Gaspar Garcia Diego/Mother: Rita Marmolejo) (Margin text: "Fran. Gaspar Macedonia, Espanol of the villa") (Godparents: Jopal Marmolejo and Maria Teresa de Menchaca) (*Leon de los Aldama. Baptism Records 1749-1777; Image 11/318*).
- a2. MARIA FRANCISCA MANUELA de la HAGAS de JESUS DIEGO, baptized 2 February 1746, El Sagrario, Leon, Guanajuato, Mexico (Father: Don Gasper Garcia Diego/Mother: Dona Rita Marmolejo).
- a3. MARIA CATHARINA IGNACIA DIEGO, baptized 26 November 1747, El Sagrario, Leon, Guanajuato, Mexico (Father: Don Gasper Garcia Diego; Mother: Dona Rita Getrudis Marmolejo) (Margin text: "Maria Catharina Ignacia, espanola of the villa") (Godparents: Don Manuel Bonales and Dona Maria Josepha de Alcocer) (*Leon de los Aldama. Baptism Records 1718-1748; Image 65/73*).

~GOMEZ OF PORTUGAL~

CAPTAIN JUAN BEJAR de AVIZ y GOMEZ de PORTUGAL. Born 1536, Portugal. Christening 1537, Santa Maria de Garzaga, Navarre, Spain. Died 1610, Villa de los Lagos, Nueva Espana (Jalisco, Mexico).
CATALINA LOPEZ de XIMENA y de NAVA de JAEN. Born 1538, Badajoz, Extremadura, Spain/or born 16 May 1538, Toledo, Toledo, Castilla-La Mancha, Spain. Died Villa de los Lagos, Nueva Galicia, Nueva Espana (Jalisco, Mexico).

~7 children born Spain & Lagos de Moreno, Jalisco, Mexico~

CAPTAIN DIEGO GOMEZ of PORTUGAL (1566-1649) (4th child)
Married MARIA GARCIA de ARRONA y MIRANDA (1570-1652) on 8 January 1590, Santa Maria de los Lagos, Lagos de Moreno, Jalisco, Mexico.
13 children born - youngest child: MELCHORA GOMEZ de PORTUGAL (1615)

MELCHORA GOMEZ de PORTUGAL
(Born abt. 1615, Lagos de Moreno, Jalisco, Mexico)
Married
PEDRO de MARMOLEJO y de PEDRAZA
(Born abt. 1610, Leon, Gto, Mexico. Died 2 September 1660, Leon, Gto, Mexico)

Son of FRANCISCO de MARMOLEJO y MEJIA (1577)
Married MARIA de PEDRAZA (1590) abt. 1605, Mexico City, Mexico.

Grandson of DIEGO MARMOLEJO (1507)
Married FRANCISCA MEJIA VILLALOBOS (1530) abt. 1570, San Luis Potesi, Mexico.

The children of Melchora Gomez de Portugal and Pedro Marmolejo de Pedraza were:
(listed at Family Search tree - no documents)
1. MARIANA MARMOLEJO de PEDRAZA y PORTUGAL*
2. DIEGO MARMOLEJO de PEDRAZA y PORTUGAL*
3. JOSE MARMOLEJO de PEDRAZA y PORTUGAL*
4. MARCOS MARMOLEJO de PEDRAZA y PORTUGAL*
5. LORENZO MARMOLEJO
    Married: ISABEL de BUSTOS.
6. PEDRO de MARMOLEJO y de PEDRAZA, born abt. 1630, Leon, Guanajuato, Mexico.
    Married JOSEPHA de BUSTOS.

The known children of Pedro Marmolejo (a) and Josepha de Bustos were:
b1. ANA MARMOLEJO de BUSTOS, christening 6 April 1650, Leon, Guanajuato, Mexico (Margin text: "Ana") (Document text: christening of "Ana, hija de Pedro Marmolejo and Dona Josepha de Bustos") (Godparents: Lorenzo Marmolejo and Dona Isabel de Bustos) (*Leon de los Aldama. Baptism Records 1636-1673; Image 17/87*).
b2. JUAN MARMOLEJO, christening 1652, El Sagrario, Leon, Guanajuato, Mexico (*Bautismos de espanoles 1636-1715, 1718-1748; Image 20/598*).
b3. LORENZO MARMOLEJO, christening 30 September 1654, Leon, Guanajuato, Mexico (Father: Pedro Marmolejo/Mother: Josepha de Bustos).
b4. JOSEPHA MARMOLEJO, christening 11 May 1655, Leon, Guanajuato, Mexico (Father: Pedro Marmolejo/Mother: Josepha de Bustos) (Margin text: "JOSEPHA, Espanola") (Document text: "Baptism of Josepha, hija de Pedro Marmolejo and Dona Josepha de Bustos, of the villa") (Godparents: Antonio de Herrera and Maria de Vellon) (*Leon de los Aldama. Baptism Records 1636-1673; Image 26/87*).
b5. JOSEPH MARMOLEJO (born abt. 1657, Leon, Guanajuato, Mexico.
    Married JOSEPHA ROJAS.
    The known child of Joseph Marmolejo (b) and Josepha Rojas was:
    c1. JUAN MARMOLEJO de ROJAS, baptism 23 December 1673 (Father: Joseph Marmolejo/Mother: Josepha de Rojas) (Margin text: "Juan, Espanol" (Godparents: Pedro Marmolejo and Melchora Gomez) (*Leon de los Aldama. Baptism Records 1673-1691; Image 6/39*).

Christening 23 February 1676, Leon, Guanajuato, Mexico (Father: Joseph Marmolejo/Mother: Josepha de Rojas) (Margin text: "Juan") (Godfather: Pedro Marmolejo/Godmother: Melchora Gomez, "Espanoles and residents of the villa") (*Leon de los Aldama. Baptism Records 1673-1691; Image 11/39*).

Married JOSEPHA CANALES de BUSTOS.

The known children of Juan Marmolejo (c) and Josepha Canales de Bustos were:

d1. GETRUDIS MARMOLEJO. Baptized 5 June 1686, El Sagrario, Leon, Guanajuato, Mexico (Father: Juan Antonio Marmolejo/Mother: Josepha de Bustos) (Document text: "Getrudis, hija de Ju. Marmolejo y de Lugarda de Mestizos de la Canada de...") (*Leon. Baptism Records 1636-1686; Image 86/100*).

d2. ANTONIA MARMOLEJO, christening 1710, Leon, Guanajuato, Mexico (Father: Juan Marmolejo/Mother: Josepha Canales) (Margin text: "Antonia de la villa") (Godparents: Felipe Nunos and Rosa Maria) (*Leon de los Aldama. Baptism Records 1710-1715; Image 16/198*).

d3. LUISA MARMOLEJO CANALES, christening 7 July 1713, Leon, Guanajuato, Mexico (Father: Juan Marmolejo Rojas/Mother: Josepha Canales) (Margin text: "Luisa de la villa") (Godparents: Nicholas Perez and Maria Perez, "Espanoles de la villa") (*Leon de los Aldama. Baptism Records 1691-1715; Image 86/128*). Married JOSEF RANGEL (son of Juan Rangel and Herrera) on 10 January 1731, Santa Ana, Penjamo, Guanajuato, Mexico (Father: Juan Marmolejo/Mother: Josepha Canales) (Document text: "Joseph Rangel, Espanol, to Luisa Canales, Espanola, of the villa Leon, legitimate daughter of Juan Marmolejo and his spouse, Josepha Canales") (*Santa Ana. Baptism Records 1699-1852; Image 83/263*).

d4. DORTHEA MARMOLEJO, christening 20 February 1716, Manuel Doblado, Guanajuato, Mexico (Father: Juan Marmolejo/Mother: Maria Josepha Canales) (Margin text: "Dorthea espanola de la Canada de GALBAN") (Document text: "Dortea, legitimate daughter of Juan Marmolejo and Maria Josepha, Espanoles de la Canada de Galban...") (Godparents: Francisco Lozano Soltero and Maria Juana Arias, "Espanoles y villa casada/*Spaniards married in the villa* en La Canada") (*San Pedro Piedragorda. Baptism Records 1709-1759; Image 17/224*).

d5. JUANA BAPTA MARMOLEJO CANALES, baptism 17 July 1718, Santiago Apostol, Silao de la Victoria, Guanajuato, Mexico (Father: Juan Marmolejo/Mother: Josepha Canales) (Margin text: "Joa. Bap. Espanola") (Document text: "Juana

Bap., hija de Juan Maxmolejo and Josepha Canales, espanoles and married") (Godparents: Juan Antonio Ruiz and Josepha de Rojas GOMEZ) (*Silao de la Victoria. Baptism Records 1717-1748; Image 52/483*) (Bapt.= Bautista).

- b6. PEDRO MARMOLEJO, born abt. 1668.
  Married ANGELA BANALES de CASTILLO.
  The known child of Pedro Marmolejo and Angela Banales de Castillo was:
  - c1. MARIA (**RITA**) **GETRUDIS MARMOLEJO** BANALES, born September 1715 (Father: Pedro Marmolejo; Mother: Angela Banales) (Margin text: "Maria Gertrudis, espanola of the villa") (Document text: ..."legitimate daughter of Pedro Marmolejo and Dona Angela Banales del Castillo, espanoles") (Godparent: Dona Angela de Bustos) (*Leon de los Aldama. Baptism Records 1691-1715; Image 127/128*).
    Married GASPER GARCIA DIEGO.
    The known children of Rita Getrudis Marmolejo (b) and Gasper Garcia Diego were:
    - c1. FRANCISCO GASPAR MACEDONIA GARCIA MARMOLEJO, christening September 1740, Leon, Guanajuato, Mexico (Father: Gasper Garcia Diego Mother: Rita Marmolejo) (Margin text: "Fran. Gaspar Macedonia, Espanol of the villa") (Godparents: Jopal Marmolejo and Maria Teresa de Menchaca) (*Leon de los Aldama. Baptism Records 1749-1777; Image 11/318*).
    - c2. MARIA FRANCISCA MANUELA de la HAGAS de JESUS DIEGO, baptized 2 February 1746, El Sagrario, Leon, Guanajuato, Mexico (Father: Don Gasper Garcia Diego/Mother: Dona Rita Marmolejo).
    - c3. MARIA CATHARINA IGNACIA DIEGO, baptized 26 November 1747, El Sagrario, Leon, Guanajuato, Mexico (Father: Don Gasper Garcia Diego; Mother: Dona Rita Getrudis Marmolejo) (Margin text: "Maria Catharina Ignacia, espanola of the villa.") (Godparents: Don Manuel Bonales and Dona Maria Josepha de Alcocer) (*Leon de los Aldama. Baptism Records 1718-1748; Image 65/73*).
    Death/burial: 15 September 1753, Nuestra Senora de Guanajuato, Guanajuato, Mexico (Spouse: Don Gasper Garcia) (Margin text: "Dona Rita Marmolejo, espanola de la Villa; married to Don Gaspar Garcia Diego") (*Leon. Death Certificates 1820-1823; Image 291-648*).
- b7. JUAN MARMOLEJO, christening 1670 (Father: Pedro Marmolejo/Mother: Josepha Bustos) (*Archdiocesis de Michoacan, 1670-1681; Image 41/95*).

The children of Melchora Gomez de Portugal and Pedro Marmolejo de Pedraza were: (continued)

7. MARIA de PEDRAZA y PORTUGAL, born abt. 1640, Leon, Guanajuato, Mexico. Married CRISTOBAL de HERRERA QUINTANA on 17 October 1658, San Felipe Guanajuato, Mexico (*Archdiocesis de Morelia, Michoacan, Mexico-Matrimonial Acts 1658; Image 658/873*). Name: MARIA de PEDRAZO y PORTUGAL. Known also as: MARIA de MARMOLEJO.

The known children of Maria de Pedraza y Portugal (a) and Cristobal de Herrera were:

b1. AGUSTINA HERRERA PORTUGAL, christening 9 October 1659, San Jose y Santiago, Marfil, Guanajuato, Mexico (Father: Cristobal Herrera/Mother: Maria de Portugal).

b2. JUAN BAUTISTA de HERRERA de PORTUGAL, christening 27 July 1661, Marfil, Guanajuato, Mexico (Father: Cristobal Herrera/Mother: Maria de Portugal). Married MICHAELA CONTRERAS SALGADO (daughter of Joseph Salgado and Josepha de Contreras) on 25 November 1693 (Juan de Herrera Quintana) (Father: Cristobal de Herrera Quintana and Maria de Pedraza Marmolejo).

b3. NICOLASA HERRERA PEDRAZA, christening 19 June 1663, San Jose y Santiago, Marfil, Guanajuato, Mexico (Father: Cristobal Herrera Quintana/Mother: Maria de Pedraza).

b4. MARIA HERRERA PORTUGAL, christening 25 November 1664, San Jose y Santiago, Marfil, Guanajuato, Mexico (Father: Cristobal Herrera Quintana/Mother: Maria de Portugal).

b5. MARCELA HERRERA PORTUGAL, christening 11 July 1667, San Jose y Santiago, Marfil, Guanajuato, Mexico (Father: Cristobal Herrera Quintana/Mother: Maria de Portugal). Married JUAN ARIAS MALDONADO (son of Juan Arias Maldonado and Anna de Espinosa) on 25 April 1691, San Jose y Santiago, Marfil, Guanajuato, Mexico (Marcela de Pedraza Herrera) (Father: Cristobal de Herrera/Mother: Maria de Pedraza Marmolejo).

b6. MELCHORA QUINTANA de PORTUGAL, christening 12 December 1669, Marfil, Guanajuato, Mexico (Father: Cristobal Herrera Quintana/Mother: Maria de Portugal). Married AGUSTIN BUITRON de LESCANO (son of Francisco Buitron and Isabel de Armenta y Lescano) on 5 June 1691, San Jose y Santiago, Marfil, Guanajuato, Mexico (Melchora de Herrera) (Father: Cristobal de Herrera/Mother: Maria de Pedroza).

b7. MICHAELA de MARMOLEJO, christening 22 December 1673, Leon, Guanajuato, Mexico (Father: Cristobal/Mother: Maria de la O. de Marmolejo). Married NICOLAS de la ROSA (son of Nicolas de Rosa and Isabel Ramos) on 16 May 1705, San Jose y Santiago, Marfil, Guanajuato, Mexico (Michaela de Herrera) (Father: Cristobal de Herrera/Maria de Pedraza).

APPENDIX VIII:
Godparents for the children of
Gaspar Antonio Medina Manrique de Lara
(Son of Nicolas de Medina and Josepha Gomez Manrique de Lara)
and Francisca Xaviera Calderon de Herrera:

1. JUE (JOSUE/*JOSHUA*) ANTONIO MANRIQUE, baptized 16 June 1730, El Sagrario, Leon, Guanajuato, Mexico (Father: Gaspar Manrique/Mother: Franca de Herrera Manrique).
Godparents: Antonio Sanchez and Maria Herrera - *Undetermined*
(*Hypothesis: Maria Herrera = MARIA JOSEPHA de HERRERA*)

2. MARIA JOSEPHA ESTANISLAO MANRIQUE, baptized 25 November 1731, El Sagrario, Leon, Guanajuato, Mexico (Father: Gaspar Anto. Manrique/Mother: Franca de Herrera).
Godparents: Juan de Almaras and Dona Maria Herrera de O*xnafe* - *Undetermined*

3. CARLOS VINCENTE de MEDINA, baptized 2 April 1733, El Sagrario, Leon, Guanajuato, Mexico (Father: Gaspar de Medina/Mother: Franca. Herrera).
Godparents: Don Nicholas Marmolejo and Dona Mariana Gomez/ **(Dona Maria Ana Gomez de Portugal)** (*married spouses*):

    NICOLAS ANTONIO JOACHIN MARMOLEJO (son of Antonio Marmolejo and Juana Banales) married MARIA ANA VALENTIN GOMEZ of Portugal (daughter of Salvador Gomes of Portugal and Theresa Lopes Moreno) on 8 February 1722, Santa Maria de Los Lagos, Lagos de Moreno, Jalisco, Mexico.

4. **JOSEPH MANUEL MANRIQUE**, baptized 4 November 1734, El Sagrario, Leon, Guanajuato, Mexico (Father: GASPAR MANRIQUE/Mother: FRANCA. de ERRERA MANRIQUE).
Godparent: Rita Getrudis Marmolejo - (**APPENDIX VII**)

5. JOSEPH EUGENIO de MEDINA, baptized 19 September 1736, El Sagrario, Leon, Guanajuato, Mexico ("legitimate son") (Father: Gaspar de Medina, Espanol/Mother: Franca Xaviera, Mestiza).
Godparents: Mathias -- and Maria Antonia Manrique

    MARIA ANTONIA MANRIQUE
    a1. MARIA ANTONIA MANRIQUE, christening 1 October 1708, Leon, Guanajuato, Mexico (Father: Joseph Lorenzo de Chaves/Mother: Ana Maria Manrique) (Margin text: "Ma. Antonia, mestiza") (Godmother: Dona Estaphana de Obregon) (*Leon de los Aldama. Baptism records 1706-1710; Image 88/148*).

6. MARIA MAGDALENA MANRIQUE, baptized 29 July 1738, El Sagrario, Leon, Guanajuato, Mexico (Father: Gaspar Manrique/Mother: Geronima Herrera).
Godparents: Joseph Guzman and Maria de la Encarnacion - *Undetermined*

7. JOSEPH FRANCISCO MANRIQUE, baptized 9 May 1744, El Sagrario, Leon, Guanajuato, Mexico (Father: Gaspar Manriquez/Mother: Maria Franca. Herrera).
Godparents: Gregorio Infante and Getrudis Espinosa

    GREGORIO INFANTE
        a1. GREGO INFANTE, christening 1702, Apaseo el Grande, Guanajuato, Mexico (Father: Juan Infante).

    GETRUDIS ESPINOSA
        a1. GETRUDIS ESPINOSA MEDINA, christening 30 March 1695, San Juan Bautista, Apaseo el Grande, Guanajuato, Mexico (Father: Nicolas de Espinosa/Mother: Biolanta de Medina).
        a2. MARIA GETRUDIS ESPINOSA, baptism 6 April 1724, El Sagrario, Leon, Guanajuato (Mother: Eugenia Espinosa).

8. MARIA de JESUS MANRIQUE, baptized 26 May 1746, El Sagrario, Leon, Guanajuato, Mexico (Father: Gaspar Manrique/Mother: Franca Xaviera de Bierrara).
Godparents: Don Francisco Abrego and Dona Josepha Calvillo

    Burial: Dona JOSEPHA CALVILLO
    Spouse: Don FRANCISCO de ABREGO
    Date: 28 April 1759
    Location; Nuestra Senora de Senora de Guanajuato, Guanajuato, Mexico. *(Leon. Death Certificates 1820-1823; Image 308/648)*.

    JOSEPHA CALVILLO
        a1. VICTORIANA MARIA JOSEPHA MICHAELA ORTEGA CALVILLO, (espanola), christening 9 March 1779, San Nicolas del Monte, Guanajuato, Guanajuato, Mexico (Father: Joseph Maria de Ortega/Mother: Maria Ignacia) (Godparents: Don Manuel *Bennay* and Lorencia *Valvende*) (*Monte de San Nicolas. Baptism Records 1772-1805; Image 40/143*).

9. MARIANA de la CRUZ MANRIQUE, baptized 27 September 1747, El Sagrario, Leon, Guanajuato, Mexico (Father: Gaspar Antonio Manrique/Mother: Francisca Xaviera Herrera).
Godparents: Diego Joseph Manrique and Mariana Lopes

DIEGO JOSEPH MANRIQUE: Burial: 4 November 1761, El Sagrario, Leon, Guanajuato, Mexico. Spouse: Dona ANA MARIA LOPES.

- a1. DIEGO MANRIQUE, christening 21 November 1700, Nuestra Senora de Guanajuato, Guanajuato, Mexico (Father: Joseph Manrique). (*Bautismos de Espanoles 1699-1703; Image 246/701 - no listing at 21 November 1700*).
  (DIEGO JOSEPH MANRIQUE) Married ANA MARIA LOPES de LARA. (*possibly sister to Rosa Lopes de Lara*)
  The known children of Diego Joseph Manrique (a) and Ana Maria Lopes were:
  - b1. ISIDRO PHELIPE MANRIQUE, christening 7 February 1744, Leon de los Aldama, Guanajuato, Mexico (Father: Mother: Ana Lopez de Lara) (Margin text: "Joseph Phelipe Maria, Espanol de la Villa") (Godparents: **Gregario Infante** and Getrudis de Espinosa) (*Leon de los Aldama. Baptism Records 1718-1748; Image 34/73*).
  - b2. VINCENTE FERRER MANRIQUE, christening 14 October 1747, El Sagrario, Leon, Guanajuato, Mexico (Father: Diego Manrique/Mother: Mariana Lopez) (Margin text: "Vincente Ferrer, Espanol de la Villa") (Godparents: Juan de *Licano* and Dona Juana de Ulloa) (*Leon de los Aldama. Baptism Records 171801748; Image 64/73*).
  - b3. ANA MARIA MANRIQUE, burial 5 September 1748, El Sagrario, Leon, Guanajuato, Mexico (Father: Diego Manrique/Mother: Mariana Lopez) (Margin text: "Ana Maria, Espanola de la Villa") (*Leon. Death certificates 1820-1823; Image 266/648*).
  - b4. MARIA JOSEPHA GETRUDIS de los DOLORES MANRIQUE, baptism 20 November 1745, El Sagrario, Leon, Guanajuato, Mexico (Father: Diego Manrique/Mother: Maria Ana Lopes) (Margin text: "Maria Josepha Gertrudis de los Dolores, Espanola de la Villa") (Godparents: Caetano Manrique and Felipa de Acosta) (*Leon de los Aldama. Baptism Records 1718-1748; Image 51/73*).
  - b5. DIEGO JOSEPH MANRIQUE, born 20 August 1761, Leon, Guanajuato, Mexico (Father: Diego Manrique/Mother: Maria Lopez de Lara) (Margin text: "Diego Joseph, Espanol de la Villa") (Godparent: Bernardino Anastacio de *Austzi*) (*Leon de los Aldama. Baptism Records 1749-1777; Image 75/318*).

10. JOSEPH JOAQUIN MANRIQUE de HERRERA, christening date was 12 May 1749, Parroquia de Leon, Leon, Guanajuato, Mexico (Father: Gaspar Antonio Manriquez/Mother: Maria de Herrera).

Godparents: Don Juan Sanches and Maria de Herrera - *Undetermined*

11. JUAN de DIOS MANRIQUE, christening year was 1751, Leon, Guanajuato, Mexico (Father: Gaspar Manrique/Mother: Franca de Errera).

Godparents: <u>Don Ildephonso Navarrete and Dona (Maria) Rosa (Theodora) Lopez (de Lara)</u> (*possibly sister to Ana Maria Lopes de Lara*)

    a1. Don ILDEFONSO JOSEPH de NAVARRETE y ARGOTE
<u>Married</u> Dona MARIA ROSA THEODORA LOPEZ de LARA.
        (Known also as: MARIA ANTONIA)
<u>The known children of Ildefonso Joseph de Navarrete y Argote and Maria Rosa Lopez were</u>:

        b1. JOSEPH ARGOTE LOPES, christening 25 February 1731, San Jose y Santiago, Marfil, Guanajuato, Mexico (Father: Yldefonzo Joseph de Argote/Mother: Maria Lopes, "Espanoles") (Margin text: "Joseph, Espanol") (Godparents: Augustin Losano, and his wife, Maria Perez) (*Marfil. Baptism Records 1731-1736; Image 14/215*).

        b2. PABLO VINCENTE FERRER NAVARRETE, baptized 24 January 1735, El Sagrario, Leon, Guanajuato, Mexico (Father: Yldefonzo Nabarrete/Mother: Rosa Theodora Lopes) (Godparents: Donato Lopez de Lara and Juana B*ravo*) (*Leon. Baptism Records 1732-1736; Image 93/147*).

        b3. FELIZ MARIA de ARGOTE, baptized 1 December 1736, El Sagrario, Leon, Guanajuato, Mexico (Father: Ildefonso de Argote/Mother: Maria Lopez de Lara) (Margin text: "Feliz Maria, espanola") (Godparents: Don Andres Lopes and Dona Maria Vasquez) (*Leon de los Aldama. Baptism records 1718-1748; Image 99/119*).

        b4. JOSEPH IGNACIO MARIA ARGOTE, baptized 4 December 1740, El Sagrario, Leon, Guanajuato, Mexico (Father: Ildephonso Argote/Mother: Rosa Lopez de Lara) (Margin text: "Joseph Ygnacio Maria, Espanol de la Villa") (Godparents: Don Joseph Ygnacio *Camijo Vendi*) (*Leon de los Aldama. Baptism Records 1718-1748; Image 10/73*).

        b5. ANDRES MARIA de NAVARRETE y ARGOTE, burial 29 March 1749, El Sagrario, Leon, Guanajuato, Mexico (Father: Don Ildefonso Joseph de Navarrete y Argote/Mother: Dona Maria Rosa Lopez).

        b6. CRESPIN NABARRETE, born abt. 1750, Leon, Guanajuato, Mexico. Burial 18 January 1839, San Francisco de Guanajuato, Guanajuato, Mexico (Father: Yldefonso Nabarrete).

        b7. MARIA JOSEPHA ARGOTE, burial 4 September 1770, El Sagrario, Leon, Guanajuato, Mexico (Father: Ildephonso Argote/ Mother: Maria Antonia Argote).

Death/Burial: Don ILDEPHONSO de ARGOTE on 28 August 1771, El Sagrario, Leon, Guanajuato, Mexico. Spouse: Dona Maria Rosa Lopes.

~~~~~~

(Additional Details)

3. CARLOS VINCENTE de MEDINA, baptized 2 April 1733, El Sagrario, Leon, Guanajuato, Mexico (Father: Gaspar de Medina/Mother: Franca Herrera).
Godparents: Don Nicolas Antonio Joachin **Marmolejo** and Dona Mariana **Gomez/ (Maria Ana Gomez of Portugal)**

1698, birth of NICOLAS MARMOLEJO BANALES
Death record: Don Nicolas Marmolejo, Espanol de la villa, husband of Dona Anna Maria Gomez, Espanoles. Burial 18 December 1756, El Sagrario, Leon, Guanajuato, Mexico (*Leon. Death Certificates 1820-1823; Image 301/648*).

The parents of Maria Anna Valentin Gomez of Portugal were:
SALVADOR GOMES de Portugal and THERESA LOPES INFANTE MORENO.

NICOLAS ANTONIO JOACHIN MARMOLEJO (son of Antonio Marmolejo and Juana Banales) married **MARIA ANA VALENTIN GOMEZ of Portugal** (daughter of Salvador Gomes of Portugal and Theresa Lopes Moreno) on 8 February 1722, Santa Maria de Los Lagos, Lagos de Moreno, Jalisco, Mexico.

The known children of Nicolas Marmolejo and MARIA ANA GOMEZ of Portugal were:
- a1. JOSEPH ANASTACIO MARMOLEJO, born abt. 1726.
    Married: MARIA de ARRIETA (daughter of Joseph de Arrieta and Francisca Martines de Alarcon) on 2 February 1750, Santa Maria de los Lagos, Lagos de Moreno, Jalisco, Mexico (Father: Nicolas Joachin Marmolejo/Mother: Maria Ana Gomez of Portugal).
- a2. MARIA BERNARDA MARMOLEJO, baptized 26 May 1728, El Sagrario, Leon, Guanajuato, Mexico (Father: Don Nicolas Marmolejo/Mother: Dona Maria Anna Gomez of Portugal, "Married, Espanoles, residents of the villa") (Margin text: "Maria Bernarda") (Godparent: Pedro Marmolejo) (*Leon de los Aldama. Baptism Records 1718-1748; Image 55/119*).
- a3. JUAN ANTONIO MARMOLEJO, baptism 16 July 1730, El Sagrario, Leon, Guanajuato, Mexico (Father: Don Nicolas Antonio Marmolejo/ Mother: Dona Maria Anna Gomez of Portugal, "Married, Espanoles of the villa") (Godparents: Don Joseph de Bustos and Dona Lorenza Marmolejo) (*Leon de los Aldama. Baptism Records 1718-1748; Image 61/119*).
- a4. MARIA MARMOLEJO, born abt. 1733. Death/Burial 21 May 1772, El Sagrario, Leon, Guanajuato, Mexico (Document text: "Maria Marmolejo, Espanol, adulta, *daughter* of Don Nicolas Marmolejo

and Dona Maria Anna of Portugal") (*Leon. Death Certificates 1820-1823; Image 362/648*).
- a5. PETRA THERESA MARMOLEJO, baptized 25 October 1737, El Sagrario, Leon, Guanajuato, Mexico (Father: Don Nicolas Marmolejo and Maria Anna Gomez de Portugal, "Married legitimately, Espanoles and residents of the villa") (Margin text: "Petra Theresa of the Villa") (Godmother: Theresa Rabon, "resident of the villa") (*Leon de los Aldama. Baptism Records 1718-1748; Image 104/119*).
- a6. DIONISIO MANUEL MARMOLEJO, baptism 14 April 1739, El Sagrario, Leon, Guanajauto, Mexico (Father: Don Nicholas Joachin Marmolejo/Mother: Dona Maria Anna of Portugal, "Married, Espanoles, residents of the villa") (Margin text: "Dion Manuel, Espanol") (Godparents: Don Joseph de Ybarra and Dona Getrudis de Cos, "married, espanoles, residents of the villa") (*Leon de los Aldama. Baptism Records 1718-1748; Image 111/119*).

SALVADOR GOMES LOZANO, christening 20 June 1676, Santa Maria de los Lagos, Lagos de Moreno, Jalisco, Mexico (Father: Diego Gomez of Portugal/Mother: Josepha Losano) (*Santa Maria de los Lagos, Bautismos de hijos legitimos 1676-1707, 1766; Image 21/558*).

Married THERESA de LOPEZ y DIAZ INFANTE y MORENO. Parents: Alonso Lopez de Aguirre y Garrido (1645-) and Maria Diaz Infante y Moreno de Villegas, daughter of Diego Diaz Infante (1682-) (Married on 24 November 1651, Lagos de Moreno, Jalisco, Mexico) and Theresa Moreno de Ortega (1631).

The known children of Salvador Gomes Lozano and Theresa Lopes were:
- a1. MARIANA GOMES LOPEZ, christening 1 March 1700, Santa Maria de los Lagos, Lagos de Moreno, Jalisco, Mexico (Father: Salvador Gomez/Mother: Theresa Lopez).
NICOLAS ANTONIO JOACHIN MARMOLEJO (son of Antonio Marmolejo and Juana Banales) married **MARIA ANA VALENTIN GOMEZ of Portugal** (daughter of Salvador Gomes of Portugal and Theresa Lopes Moreno) on 8 February 1722, Santa Maria de Los Lagos, Lagos de Moreno, Jalisco, Mexico.
- a2. YSIDRO GOMEZ LOPEZ, christening 28 May 1702, Santa Maria de los Lagos, Lagos de Moreno, Jalisco, Mexico (Father: Salvador Gomez/Mother: Theresa Lopez *Infante*).
- a3. FRANCISCA XAVIERA (espanola), christening 13 October 1704, Santa Maria de los Lagos, Lagos de Moreno, Jalisco, Mexico (Father: Salvador Gomez/Mother: Theresa Lopez). Baptism 3 November 1704, Santa Maria de los Lagos, Lagos de Moreno, Jalisco, Mexico (Father: Salvador Gomez; Mother: Theresa Lopez *Infante*).
- a4. MARIA THERESA GOMEZ LOPEZ, christening 2 November 1706, Santa Maria de los Lagos, Lagos de Moreno, Jalisco, Mexico (Father:

Salvador Gomez/Mother: Theresa Lopez). (Maria Theresa Gomes of Portugal) married JUAN JOSEPH ROMERO (son of Joseph Romero and Anna de Bejar) on 18 January 1734, Santa Maria de los Lagos, Lagos de Moreno, Jalisco, Mexico.

a5. JULIO CAIETANO GOMEZ LOPEZ, christening 27 October 1708, Santa Maria de los Lagos, Lagos de Moreno, Jalisco, Mexico (Father: Salvador Gomez/Mother: Theresa Lopes).

~~~~~

JUAN de PORTUGAL (1536-1586)
CATALINA LOPEZ (1538)
|
Captain DIEGO GOMEZ de Portugal (1566-1649)
Married 8 January 1590, Lagos de Moreno, Jalisco, Mexico.
MARIA GARCIA de ARRONA y MIRANDA (1570-1652)
|
DIEGO GOMEZ de PORTUGAL GARCIA de ARRONA (1590-1665)
Married 1629, Lagos de Moreno, Jalisco, Mexico
ISABEL FLORES de la TORRE y SANDI (1623-1663)
|
DIEGO GOMEZ de PORTUGAL y FLORES de la TORRE (1643-1703)
Married 20 February 1670, Lagos de Moreno, Jalisco, Mexico.
JOSEFA de LOZANO y GONZALES (1652, Aguascalientes, AG, Mexico)
|
SALVADOR GOMEZ de Portugal y LOZANO (1676-)
THERESA de LOPEZ INFANTE y DIAS (1680-1737)
|
NICOLAS ANTONIO JOACHIN MARMOLEJO (1698-1756)
MARIA ANA VALENTIN GOMEZ of Portugal (1700-)
(*Godparents to Carlos Vincente Medina, son of Josepha Gomez Manrique de Lara*)

~~~~~

JUAN de PORTUGAL (1536-1586)
CATALINA LOPEZ (1538)
|
Captain DIEGO GOMEZ de Portugal (1566-1649)
Married 8 January 1590, Lagos de Moreno, Jalisco, Mexico.
MARIA GARCIA de ARRONA y MIRANDA (1570-1652)
|
MELCHORA GOMEZ of Portugal 1615-)
PEDRO de MARMOEJO de PEDRAZA (1610-)
|
PEDRO MARMOLEJO de PEDRAZA (1630-)
JOSEPHA de BUSTOS

PEDRO MARMOLEJO (1668-)
ANGELA BANALES CASTILLO
|
RITA GETRUDIS MARMOLEJO (1715-1753)
(*Godmother to Joseph Manuel Manrique de Lara, born 30 October 1734, Leon, the grandson of Josepha Gomez Manrique de Lara*)
(Godmother to Nicolas Marmolejo, b. 1735, son of Miguel Marmolejo)

~~~~~~~~

NICOLAS MARMOLEJO (*Not godfather to Carlos de Medina Manrique de Lara*)
- a1. NICOLAS IGNACIO MARMOLEJO, baptism 14 December 1735, El Sagrario, Leon, Guanajuato, Mexico (Father: Miguel Marmolejo/ Mother: Francisca Sebastiana).
  Married MARIA JOSEPHA de HERRERA.
  The known child of NICOLAS MARMOLEJO and MARIA JOSEPHA de HERRERA was:
  - b1. NICOLAS JOSEPH MARMOLEJO de HERRERA, christening 18 November 1716, El Sagrario, Leon, Guanajuato, Mexico (Father: Nicolas Marmolejo/Mother: Maria Josepha de Herrera) (Godparents: Lazaro *Hortiz/Flores* de Parada and Maria Josepha Munos del *Castigo/Castillo*).

  MARIA JOSEPHA de HERRERA-
  - a1. MARIA JOSEPHA de HERRERA, christening 1689, Leon, Guanajuato, Mexico (Father: Antonio de Herrera/Mother: Maria *Fernandez/Fer- Toro*) (Godfather: Gonzales Dias Delgado) (Witness: Joseph de Herrera) (*Leon de los Aldama. Baptism Records 1763-1691; Image 21/26*).

The parents of Nicholas Marmolejo (m. Maria Josepha de Herrera) were MIGUEL ANTONIO MARMOLEJO and FRANCISCA SEBASTIANA de ORNATE GAONA.

The known children of Miguel Antonio Marmolejo and Francisca Sebastiana de Ornate were:
- a1. FRANCA XAVIERA MARMOLEJO, baptism 22 November 1729, El Sagrario, Leon, Guanajuato, Mexico (Father: Don Miguel Marmolejo/Mother: Dona Anna de Gaona Marmolejo) (Margin text: "Franca Xaviera, Espanola de la villa") (Godparents: Don Manuel de Cos and Dona Maria Marmolejo) (*last entry for year 1729*) (*Leon de los Aldama. Baptism Records 1718-1748; Image 58/119*).
- a2. JUAN ANTONIO MARMOLEJO, baptism 1 November 1731, El Sagrario, Leon, Guanajuato, Mexico (Father: Don Miguel Marmolejo/Mother: Dona Franca de Ornette) (Margin text: "Juan Antonio, espanol de la villa")

(Godparents: Dona Magdalena de Gaona and Francisco Marmolejo) (*Leon de los Aldama. Baptism Records 1718-1748; Image 68/119*).

a3. MARIA FRANCISCA de la LUZ MARMOLEJO, baptism 21 September 1733, El Sagrario, Leon, Guanajuato, Mexico (Father: Don Miguel Marmolejo/ Mother: Dona Francisca de Ornate, "Espanola") (Godparents: Don Joseph de Zuniga and Dona Ana Marmolejo) (*Leon de los Aldama. Baptism Records 1718-1748*).

a4. NICOLAS IGNACIO MARMOLEJO, baptism 14 December 1735, El Sagrario, Leon, Guanajuato, Mexico (Father: Miguel Marmolejo/Mother: Francisca Sebastiana) (Margin text: "Nicolas Ignacio") (Godparents: Diego de *Cos* and **Rita Marmolejo**) (*Leon de los Aldama. Baptism Records 1718-1748; Image 96/119*).

a5. FRANCO ANTONIO ILDIFONIO MARMOLEJO, baptized 4 May 1743, El Sagrario, Leon, Guanajuato, Mexico (Father: Manuel de Juan Marmolejo and Maria Magdalena de Lara) (Margin text: "Francisco Antonio Ildifonio, Espanol de la villa") (Godparents: Don Alonso Arzate and Dona Rosa Lopes) (*Leon de los Aldama. Baptism Record 1718-1748; Image 27/73*).

a6. JOSEPH MIGUEL MARMOLEJO, baptism 28 October 1745, El Sagrario, Leon, Guanajuato, Mexico (Father: Don Miguel Marmolejo and Dona Franca. de *Ornate*) (Margin text: "Joseph Miguel, espanol de la villa") (Godparents: Don NICOLAS MARMOLEJO and Dona MARIA ANA GOMES de PORTUGAL, "married, residents and Spaniards of the villa") (*Leon de los Aldama. Baptism Records 1718-1748; Image 51/73*).

~~~~~~

APPENDIX IX: FRANCISCA XAVIER(A) CALDERON de HERRERA
(Born 18 December 1707, Aguascalientes, Aguascalientes, Mexico)

Paternal:

Don *LOPE RUIZ de ESPARZA (1569 -1651)*
  Married *ANA FRANCISCA de GABAY NAVARRO y MOCTEZUMA.*
BERNARDO RUIZ de ESPARZA (1608-1696)
  LEONOR LOSANA ISLA (1617-1670)
PETRONA RUIZ ESPARZA LOZANO (baptized 25 January 1635, AG, AG, MX)
  Married JUAN MEDINA.
FRANCISCA de MEDINA ESPARZA (born abt. 1663, AG, AG, MX)
  Married ANTONIO GONZALES CALDERON.
CRISTOBAL CALDERON (born 28 December 1685, AG, AG, MX)
  Married MANUELA HERRERA (1687, AG, AG, MX) 1707, AG, AG, MX.

Maternal:

FRANCISCO SOLTERO (born abt. 1595, DF, MX; died 1669, AG, AG, MX)
  Married CLARA JAEN (born abt. 1620, DF, MX; died 1683, AG, AG, MX).
MICHAELA SOLTERO JAEN (born abt. 1658, AG, AG, MX)
  Married JUAN HERRERA (born abt. 1658) on 25 September 1678, AG, AG, MX.
MANUELA HERRERA (born 14 June 1687, AG, AG, MX)
  Married CRISTOBAL CALDERON during 1707, AG, AG, MX.

The child of Cristobal Calderon and Manuela Herrera was:

FRANCISCA XAVIER(A) CALDERON de HERRERA
  Baptism: 18 December 1707, Aguascalientes, Aguascalientes, Mexico (Father: Cristobal Calderon/Mother: Manuela de Herrera) (Margin text: "Franca. Xavier, mestiza") (Godparents: Antonio Gonzales and Franca. de Medina) (*Asuncion Bautisos, Aguascalientes, Mexico. Vol. 8. Anos 1701-1701. Film #004339959; Image 202/511*).

Married: GASPAR ANTONIO MANRIQUE de LARA.

~~~~~~~

When the Spanish Manrique de Lara from branch settled in 1576 Leon, Guanajuato, Mexico and Gaspar Antonio Manrique de Lara married Francisca Xavier Calderon de Herrera, our Spanish lineage connected to Aguascalientes, Mexico Basque settlers and descendants of the Montezuma Aztec line. Lineage to the Aguascalientes Ruiz de Esparza family also takes place within Gaspar Gomez (born abt. 1550) Manrique de Lara's twin brother, Baltasar Gomez Manrique de Lara's line.

From this Aztec line, the lineage follows: Moctezuma I (1398-1469), the second Aztec emperor and the fifth king of Tenochtitlan - Moctezuma II (born abt. 1460-1520, ninth Aztec emperor - Pedro Moctezuma, a son of Montezuma II/Leonor Cortes Moctezuma (1509/1510-

1550/1551), daughter of Moctezuma II - Leonor Cortes Moctezuma (born abt. 1528-), daughter of Isabel Moctezuma and Hernan Cortes.

Aguascalientes, Mexico was originally titled, Village of Our Lady of the Assumption of the Hot Waters (Villa de Nuestra Senora de la Asuncion de las Aguas Calientes) by Spanish families leaving Lagos de Moreno in 1575. The area is still home to many thermal springs, thereby the given name. King Felipe II of Spain approved the town founding on 22 October 1575 via Don Geronimo de Orozco, the President of the Royal Audiencia and Governor of Nueva Galicia, the former state name. Military outposts like Aguascalientes were situated along the Silver Route to protect individuals along the merchant trails. Aguascalientes today consists of more than forty haciendas, large properties owned by colonial settlers.

As noted by fellow Heritage Books author, John P. Schmal, "by 1610 the small town of Aguascalientes had approximately 25 Spanish residents, settlers who began arriving after 1580 (From "*Aguascalientes: The Geographic Center of Mexico,*" by John P. Schmal for the Houston Institute of Culture.)." At the "Parroquia de la Asuncion" in Aguascalientes, Mexico, many of the sponsors or godparents from 1616 onward were from the Ruiz de Esparza family. The Ruiz de Esparza family was Basque, originally from the town named Esparza situated, near Pamplona, Navarre, Spain. Captain Lope II Ruiz de Esparza emigrated from Esparza, Navarre, Spain to Aguascalientes, Mexico.

> "The patriarch of the family in Mexico was Lope Ruiz de Esparza, who is documented by the *Catalogo de Pasajeros a Indias* (Vol. III- #2.633) as having sailed from Spain to Mexico on Feb. 8, 1593. Lope, who was the son of Lope Ruiz de Esparza and Ana Dias de Eguino, was a bachelor and a servant of Don Enrique Maleon. After arriving in Mexico, Lope made his way to Aguascalientes, where, about a year later he is believed to have married Francisca de Gabai Navarro y Moctezuma. In the following decades, the Ruiz de Esparza family intermarried extensively with other prominent Spanish families in early Aguascalientes, including, Romo de Vivar, Macias Valdez, and Tiscareno de Molina." (From "*Aguascalientes: The Geographic Center of Mexico,*" by John P. Schmal for the Houston Institute of Culture.)

Our connection to Aguascalientes, Mexico and directly to the Esparza line is through Francesca Xaviera Calderon de Herrera's father, Cristobal Calderon. To restate, Francisca Xaviera Calderon de Herrera was baptized at El Sagrario Church on 18 December 1707 in Aguascalientes, Aguascalientes, Mexico where her parents were recorded as Cristobal Calderon and Manuela de Herrera (*Asuncion Bautismos Aguascalientes, Mexico. Vol. 8. Years 1701-1709*).

FRANCISCA XAVIERA CALDERON de HERRERA was the daughter of:

CRISTOBAL CALDERON, born 13 December 1685, Villa Agelion, Palo Alto, Calvillo, Aguascalientes, Mexico. Christening 28 December 1685, El Sagrario, Aguascalientes, Aguascalientes, Mexico (Father: Antonio Calderon/Mother: Franca. de Medina) (Margin text: "Cristobal, mestizo") (Godparents: Juan de Arella and

Getrudis Dias) (*Asuncion de Maria, Aguascalientes Catholic Church Records, Aguascalientes Bautismos 1684-1701; Image 50/619*).

and

MANUELA HERRERA JAEN, born 27 May 1687, Palo Alto, Calvillo, Aguascalientes, Aguascalientes, Mexico. Christening on 14 June 1687, El Sagrario, Aguascalientes, Aguascalientes, Mexico (Father: JUAN de HERRERA. Mother: MICHAELA de JAEN) (Margin text: "Manuela, Espanola") (Godparents: Francisco Nunes and Gertrudis Nunes) (*Asuncion de Maria, Aguascalientes, Mexico Church Records, Bautismos 1684-1701; Image 88/619*).

Cristobal Calderon was the son of Antonio Calderon & Francisca de Medina, who was the daughter of Juan Medina and PETRONA ESPARZA, a descendant of Lope Ruiz de Esparza who settled in Aguascalientes, Mexico.

Manuela Herrera was the daughter of Juan Herrera and Michaela (Clara) Soltero Jaen, who was the daughter of Francisco Soltero and Clara Jaen [their eldest daughter, Francisca, married Martin Ruiz de Esparza (Junior), the grandson of Lope Ruiz de Esparza].

FRANCISCA XAVIERA CALDERON de HERRERA'S paternal CALDERON-MEDINA line is as follows: The father of Francisca Xaviera Calderon de Herrera was CRISTOBAL CALDERON MEDINA, who was christened on 28 December 1685 at El Sagrario Church in Aguascalientes, Aguascalientes, Mexico. Cristobal Calderon Medina's father was ANTONIO CALDERON and his mother was FRANCISCA de MEDINA.

The parents of Cristobal Calderon Medina were ANTONIO GONZALES CALDERON (born abt. 1660) and FRANCISCA de MEDINA (born abt. 1663) who married on 12 January 1680, El Sagrario, Aguascalientes, Aguascalientes, Mexico (*Archivo de la Parroquia del Sagrario Antes de la Asuncion, Aguascalientes, AGS, Matrimonios Volume Years 1663-1702*).

The known children of Antonio Gonzales Calderon (a) and Francisca de Medina Esparza were:
- a1. PETRONILA CALDERON MEDINA, christening 17 February 1683, El Sagrario, Aguascalientes, Aguascalientes, Mexico (Father: Antonio de Calderon/Mother: Franca. de Medina).
- a2. **CRISTOBAL CALDERON MEDINA**, christening 28 December 1685, El Sagrario, Aguascalientes, Aguascalientes, Mexico (Born Palo Alto, Calvillo, Aguascalientes, Mexico - Villa de Agelion) (Father: Antonio Calderon/Mother: Franca. de Medina).
- a3. ISABEL CALDERON, christening June 1688, Palo Alto, Calvillo, Aguascalientes, Aguascalientes, Mexico (Beynte) (Father: Antonio Calderon/Mother: *Banz* de Medina). Record #2: YSAVEL CALDERON, christening 27 June 1688, El Sagrario,

        Aguascalientes, Aguascalientes, Mexico (Father: Antonio Calderon/ Mother: Francisca de Medina).
- a4. DIOS ANTONIO CALDERON de MEDINA, christening December 1690, Canada Honda, San Francisco de los Romo, Aguascalientes, Aguascalientes, Mexico (Villa de Aguascalientes) (Father: Antonio Calderon/Mother: Francisca de Medina). Record #2: ANTTO. CALDERON MEDINA, christening 6 December 1690, El Sagrario, Aguascalientes, Aguascalientes, Mexico (Father: Antto. Calderon/ Mother: Franca. de Medina).
- a5. MARIA MANUELA CALDERON MEDINA, christening 7 February 1693, El Sagrario, Aguascalientes, Aguascalientes, Mexico (Father: Antto. Calderon/Mother: Franca. de Medina). Record #2: MARIA MANUELA CALDERON. Birthdate: 20 February 1692. Christening: 7 February 1693, Palo Alto, Calvillo, Aguascalientes, Mexico (Villa de Ags).
- a6. OLALLA CALDERA MEDINA, christening 2 March 1694, El Sagrario, Aguascalientes, Aguascalientes, Mexico (Father: Anttonio Calderon/ Mother: Franca. de Medina).
- a7. JUAN CALDERON MEDINA, christening 1 December 1698, El Sagrario, Aguascalientes, Aguascalientes, Mexico (Father: Antto. Calderon/ Mother: Franca. de Medina).
  <u>Married</u> MANUELA ARIAS.
  <u>The known child of Juan de Silva Calderon (a) and Manuela Arias was</u>:
  - b1. MARIA GERTRUDIS de SILVA CALDERON, Death/Burial: Aguascalientes, Aguascalientes, Mexico (Father: Juan de Silva Calderon/Mother: Manuela Arias. <u>Married</u> (Spouse) ANTONIO RAMOS (Race: I/ Ethnicity: *IRISH*).
- a8. PHELIPA de SILVA CALDERON, birth unknown. <u>Married</u> THADEO ESPARZA. Death: 2 July 1777, Aguascalientes (San Marcos), Mexico (Widow/Spouse of THADEO ESPARZA. Ethnicity: *CANADIAN* [Father: Antonio Calderon/ Mother: Francisca Medina]).

The birth records of the parents of Antonio Gonzales de Calderon and Francisca de Medina's father have yet to be confirmed. However, that Francisca Medina's mother was Petrona Esparza links this line to the Esparza family, as the name, "Petrona," denotes ties to Petronila Moctezuma (born abt. 1532) who married Martin Navarro de Gabay likely by 1571 in Mexico City, Mexico. Their daughter, Ana Francisca Navarro de Gabay y Moctezuma, was born by 1573, then married (1594-1595) Lope Ruiz de Esparza.

FRANCISCA de MEDINA ESPARZA (born abt. 1663) was buried 1745 in Aguascalientes, Mexico where she was noted as a widow and spouse of ANTONIO CALDERON. FRANCISCA MEDINA was the daughter of JUAN MEDINA and PETRONA ESPARZA. The margin text reads: "Franca. de Medina, Espanola, Widow." The document text reads: "Franca. de Medina Espanola Orginiaria, *legitimate* daughter of Juan de Medina and Petra de Esparsa and widow of Antonio Calderon..." (*Asuncion de Maria, Aguascalientes, Aguascalientes, Mexico. Defunciones 1736-1748; Image 375/505*).

Petrona de Esparza (born 25 January 1635, Aguascalientes, Mexico) was a descendant of the Lope RUIZ de ESPARZA line and Moctezuma lineages from two branches.

PETRONA de ESPARZA died 8 September 1697 and was buried at Asuncion de Maria, Aguascalientes, Aguascalientes, Mexico (*Asuncion de Maria, Aguascalientes, Aguascalientes, Mexico. Defunciones 1620-1752; Image 267/560*). The margin and entry text reads: "Petrona, espanola, widow of Juan de Medina."

Petrona de Esparza was christened on 25 January 1635 at El Sagrario, Aguascalientes, Aguascalientes, Mexico. The record did not include her first name, but only, "Ruis Losano, female." The father was listed as, BERNARDO RUIS de ESPARZA. The mother was recorded as, **LEONOR de LOSANO**. Curiously, Leonor de Lozano's sister, Catalina Lozano Isla married Bernardo Ruiz de Esparza. (*Asuncion de Maria, Aguascalientes, Aguascalientes, Mexico, Bautisos Aguascalientes, Mexico. Vol. 1. Years 1616-1662. Image 52/334*)

Leonor de Lozano Isla (1617-1670) was christened at El Sagrario, Aguascalientes, Aguascalientes, Mexico on 22 May 1617, the child of Cristobal Lozano and Maria de Isla. She later married Bernabe Marino on 8 December 1650 at El Sagrario, Aguascalientes, Mexico. Leonor's sister, Catalina de Lozano Isla was born about 1613 in Aguascalientes, Aguascalientes, Mexico. Catalina Lozano married BERNARDO RUIZ de ESPARZA on 27 February 1634, El Sagrario, Aguascalientes, Aguascalientes, Mexico. Their first recorded child was born 9 May 1640 (Maria Ruiz Lozano). Leonor and Catalina Lozano Isla's sister, Isla Juana Lozano, married PEDRO RUIZ de ESPARZA, the brother to Bernardo Ruiz Esparza, on 12 April 1636, Aguascalientes, Aguascalientes, Mexico. Adding to the Lozano Isla-Ruiz de Esparza family connection is the fact another Lozano Isla daughter, Maria Hernandez Lozano, married JUAN de Araiza MEDINA, then had a son named JUAN MEDINA (*who may have been the husband of PETRONA ESPARZA*) (**Appendix XI**).

The known children of Petrona de Esparza (a) and Juan Medina were:
b1.   MARIA de MEDINA ESPARZA, christening 27 September 1659, El Sagrario, Aguascalientes, Aguascalientes, Mexico (Father: Juan Medina/Mother: Petrona de ESPARZA) (Margin text: "Maria, mestiza") (Document: "Baptism of Maria, daughter of Juan de Medina and Petrona de Esparza") (Godparents: Nicolas de Contreras and Franca. Sanches) (*Asuncion de Maria, Aguascalientes, Aguascalientes, Mexico. Bautismos 1616-1662; Image 228/334*).
b2.   FRANCISCA MEDINA ESPARZA, born abt. 1663, Aguascalientes, Aguascalientes, Mexico (*No record found*).

Possibly, "Maria de Medina Esparza" was Maria Francisca Medina Esparsa as no birth record was found for Francisca Medina de Esparsa.

To search for the parentage of Petrona Esparza, a review was done of the Lope Ruiz de Esparza family, specifically children who married by 1620 and their children born between the years of 1630-1640. As per my research, Petrona Ruiz (Esparza) Lozano was the daughter of Bernardo (Salado) Ruiz de Esparza and Dona Leonor Lozano Isla, the daughter of Don Cristobal and Dona Maria Lozano Isla, but not the wife of Bernado Ruiz de Esparza, who was Catalina Lozano Isla, Leonor Lozana Isla's sister.

Don LOPE RUIZ de ESPARZA was born during 1569 in Pamplona, Navarre, Spain to a family of Basque royalty. Lope Ruiz de Esparza was documented in the *Catalogo de Pasajeros a Indias* (Vol. III - #2.633) as having sailed from Spain to Mexico on 8 February 1593. He married (ANA) FRANCISCA NAVARRO de GABAY y MOCTEZUMA. Don Lope Ruiz de Esparza died on 14 August 1651 in Aguascalientes, Mexico and was buried within the parish church under the alter of San Lorenzo. He was considered a Spanish nobleman and early settler of Aguascalientes, Mexico.

ANA FRANCISCA NAVARRO de GABAY y MOCTEZUMA (1573-1652) was the daughter of MARTIN NAVARRO de GABAY and Dona PETRONILA de MOCTEZUMA, who was a lineal descendant of the last emperor of the Aztecs, Moctezuma II.

Lope Ruiz de Esparza married Ana Francisca Navarro de Gabay y Moctezuma between the years 1573 and 1574 in Mexico City, Mexico. After marrying a descendant of Moctezuma, the status of Lope Ruiz de Esparza as landowner was secured, as was the financial situation of his family for generations because he married an Indigenous woman with Moctezuma II lineage, land and wealth, not to mention social standing. As is well documented, Lope II Ruiz de Esparza left Spain on 8 February 1593 as a servant for Don Enrique Maleon. Lope Ruiz de Esparza, and his wife, Ana Francisca Navarro de Gabay y Moctezuma, settled in the colony of Nueva Galicia which had been founded on 22 October 1575. During 1610, the Villa of Aguascalientes consisted of twenty-five Spanish residents. By 1601, marriages were recorded in the parish registers at the local church (La Parroquia de la Asuncion), baptisms after 1616, and deaths listed by 1620.

For the births of Lope Ruiz de Esparza and Ana Francisca Navarro de Gabay y Moctezuma children, all born Aguascalientes, Aguascalientes, Mexico, records were not found, therefore the years are listed as "abt." or approximately that year (**APPENDIX X**).

The known children, born Aguascalientes, Aguascalientes, Mexico, of Don LOPE RUIZ de ESPARZA (1559-1651) and ANA FRANCISCA de GABAY y MOCTEZUMA (1577-1652) were:

a1. SALVADOR RUIZ de ESPARZA (1595-1680).
  Married MARIA de VIELMA on 1618, Aguascalientes, Aguascalientes, Mexico.
a2. ANA TOMASINA RUIZ de ESPARZA (born abt. 1597- died abt. 1667).
  Married FRANCISCO SANCHEZ de MONTES de OCA on 25 November 1618, Aguascalientes, Aguascalientes, Mexico (Resident of Morcenique, Aguascalientes, Mexico).
a3. MARTIN RUIZ de ESPARZA (born abt. 1600-1674).

        Married Dona MARIA LOPEZ de ELIZALDE y BECCERRA (daughter of Juan Lopez de Elizalde and Leonor Beccerra y Sanchez de Mendoza), the widow of Don Juan de Luevana (born Spain), during 1625, Aguascalientes, Aguascalientes, Mexico.

a4.   LORENZA RUIZ de ESPARZA (born abt. 1602-1690).
        Married CAPTAIN LUIS de TISCARENO de MOLINA y MARQUEZ (born Triana, Seville, Spain, son of Juan de Tiscareno de Molina and Dona Elvira Marquez) on 16 May 1623 in Morcenique, Aguascalientes, Aguascalientes, Mexico.

a5.   JACINTO RUIZ de ESPARZA (born abt. 1604-1679).
        (known as, ESCRIBIANO REAL de AGUASCALIENTES)
        Married Dona JUANA LOPES de ELIZALDE (died 21 May 1682, Aguascalientes, Aguascalientes, Mexico) (daughter of Juan Lopez de Elizalde and Leonor Beccerra y Sanchez de Mendoza) during 1629 in Aguascalientes, Aguascalientes, Mexico.

a6.   PEDRO RUIZ de ESPARZA (born abt. 1605-1607/1609; died abt. 1700).
        Married (m1) JUANA LOZANO ISLA (1605-1688) (daughter of Don Cristobal and Dona Maria Lozano Isla) on 12 April 1636, Aguascalientes, Aguascalientes, Mexico.
        Married (m2) MARGARITA GONZALES GALLEGOS (daughter of Luis Gonzales and Beatriz Gallegos) on 13 March 1688, Aguascalientes, Aguascalientes, Mexico.

a7.   BERNARDO (SALADO) RUIZ de ESPARZA (1608- died abt. 1696).
        Married Dona CATALINA LOZANO ISLA (daughter of Don Cristobal and Dona Maria Lozano Isla) on 27 February 1634 in Morcenique, Aguascalientes, Aguascalientes, Mexico.

a8.   MARIA RUIZ de ESPARZA (1613-unknown).
        Married Don NICOLAS de ULLOA (1605-1689) during 1630, Aguascalientes, Aguascalientes, Mexico (Resided Teocaltiche, Jalisco, Mexico).

a9.   CRISTOBAL RUIZ de ESPARZA (1616-1672).
        Married Dona ISABEL de ALCARAS PEREZ (1625-1699) on 18 August 1646, Aguascalientes, Aguascalientes, Mexico.

a10.   BERNABE RUIZ de ESPARZA (1618-1672).
        Married Dona ANA ORTIZ RAMIREZ (1625-1688) (daughter of Pablo and Dona Catalina) (born Sierra de Pinos) on 11 May 1643, Aguascalientes, Aguascalientes, Mexico.

a11.   LORENZO RUIZ de ESPARZA (1620-1693).
        Don LOPE RUIZ de ESPARZA y de GABAY (born Morcenique), baptized 21 August 1620, Aguascalientes, Aguascalientes, Mexico).
        Married (m1) Dona ANTONIA del CASTILLO (daughter of Juan del Castillo de Contreras and Dona Maria Ruiz de Aldana) on 2 May 1647, Aguascalientes, Aguascalientes, Mexico.
        Married (m2) JOSEFA de SANDI y AGUILERA (widow of Juan Martinez Calvillo) (daughter of Alonso de Aguilera y Josefa de Sandi) on 1 August 1677, Aguascalientes, Aguascalientes, Mexico.

The parents of Lope Ruiz de Esparza Junior were LOPE RUIZ de ESPARZA and Dona ANA DIAS de EGUINO, both natives of Pamplona, Navarre, Spain. LOPE RUIZ de ESPARZA Senior had lordship over the palaces of Esparza and Zariquiegui, Navarre, Spain. The children of Lope Ruiz de Esparza and Ana Francesca Gabay Navarro y Moctezuma's children were not baptized in the Aguascalientes parish church until after 1618, therefore it is likely they were christened at their private Morcenique chapel, the records of which were lost.

FRANCISCA XAVIERA CALDERON de HERRERA'S maternal HERRERA-JAEN line was as follows: The mother of FRANCISCA XAVIERA CALDERON de HERRERA was MANUELA HERRERA JAEN/XAEN who was christened on 14 June 1687, El Sagrario, Aguascalientes, Mexico. The parents of MANUELA HERRERA JAEN were JUAN de HERRERA and MICHAELA SOLTERO de JAEN who married on 25 September 1678, Aguascalientes, Aguascalientes, Mexico.

The parents of MICHAELA (CLARA) SOTELO JAEN were FRANCISCO SOTELO (born abt. 1595, Mexico City, Mexico or abt. 1610, Zacatecas, Mexico, the son of JUAN SOTELO, born abt. 1578)) and CLARA JAEN (born abt. 1618, Mexico City, Mexico). Francisco Sotelo and Clara de Jaen married abt. 1635. FRANCISCO SOTELO died or was buried 8 October 1669 in Aguascalientes, Mexico at Asuncion de Maria, Aguascalientes, Mexico where documented noted he was a Spaniard and spouse of Clara de Jaen.

My hypothesis given few Spaniards resided in the Villa of Aguascalientes, Mexico by 1640, is FRANCISCO Arias de SOTELO y Cervantes, born 1595 Mexico City, Mexico was the son of Fernand Arias de Sotelo y Moctezuma, the brother of Petronila Sotelo y Moctezuma. Francisco Sotelo married Clara de Jaen who also was likely born Mexico City, Mexico.

CLARA de JAEN, whose surname was also spelled XAEN, was buried on 3 March 1683 in Aguascalientes, Mexico. She was noted as a widow of spouse FRANCISCO SOTELO and buried at Asuncion de Maria, Aguascalientes, Mexico. A Sotelo-Jaen daughter married the son of LOPE RUIZ de ESPARZA, Martin Esparza (Junior) and named a son, Joseph *RUIS ESPARZA*. Fernand Sotelo's sister, Ana Francisca, married Lopes Ruiz de Esparza. Many godparents of Sotelo-Jaen children were from the Ruiz de Esparza line.

The known children of FRANCISCO SOTELO (a) and CLARA JAEN were:
    a1.   FRANCISCA SOTELO XAEN, christening 24 August 1638, El Sagrario, Aguascalientes, Aguascalientes, Mexico (Father: Franc. Sotelo/Mother: Clara de Zaen) (Margin text: "Franca. Espanola") (Godparents: Franco. Fernandez and Maria de Amara) (*Family Search #004339956; Image 75/334*). Married MARTIN ESPARZA on 21 February 1658 (FRANCA. de los REIES to MARTIN de ESPARZA), El Sagrario, Aguascalientes, Aguascalientes, Mexico. Death/Burial 15 May 1691, Asuncion de Maria, Aguascalientes, Aguascalientes, Mexico (Married/White) (Spouse: Martin Ruiz de Esparza).
        The known children of Martin Esparza (b) and Francisca Sotelo y Xaen were:

- b1. MARIA de ESPARZA SOTELO, christening 27 August 1665, Aguascalientes, Aguascalientes, Mexico (Father: Martin de Esparza/Mother: Francisca Sotelo) (Godfather/Grandfather: Martin Ruiz de Esparza y Gabay Sotelo Moctezuma). Death/Burial for MARIA de ESPARZA de JAEN on 12 January 1673, Asuncion de Maria, Aguascalientes, Aguascalientes, Mexico (Father: Martin de Esparza/Mother: Francisca de Jean) ("Single/White").
- b2. CLARA ESPARZA JAEN, christening 8 November 1667, El Sagrario, Aguascalientes, Aguascalientes, Mexico (Father: Martin de Esparza/Mother: Franca. de Jaen).
- b3. JOSEPH RUIZ ESPARZA, christening (JOSEPH de ESPARZA de JAEN) on 29 May 1673, Aguascalientes, Aguascalientes, Mexico (Father: Martin de Esparza/Mother: Francisca de Jaen). Buried (JOSEPH RUIS ESPARZA) on 28 March 1744, Asuncion de Maria, Aguascalientes, Aguascalientes, Mexico (Father: Martin Esparza/Mother: Francisca Sotelo) (Married/White) (Spouse: JUANA NICOLAS).
- b4. MARTIN ESPARZA SOTELO, christening 2 July 1675, El Sagrario, Aguascalientes, Aguascalientes, Mexico (Father: Martin de Esparza/Mother: Franca. Sotelo y Xaen). Married MARIA de CASTANEDA on 5 May 1704 (MARTIN RUIZ de ESPARZA), Pinos San Matias, Zacatecas, Mexico.
- b5. JUANA ESPARZA JAEN, christening on 7 December 1677, El Sagrario, Aguascalientes, Aguascalientes, Mexico (Father: Martin de Esparza/Mother: Franca. de Jaen).
- b6. BLAS ESPARZA JAEN, christening on 19 February 1680, El Sagrario, Aguascalientes, Aguascalientes, Mexico (Father: Martin de Esparza/Mother: Franca. de Jaen). Married MICHAELA de AMADOR on 3 December 1707. Death/Buried 1741, Asuncion de Maria, Aguascalientes, Aguascalientes, Mexico (Father: Martin Esparza/Mother: Francisca Sotelo) (Married/White) (Spouse: MICAELA AMADOR).
- b7. YGNACIO ESPARZA, birth unknown, Aguascalientes, Aguascalientes, Mexico. Married YNES GARCIA. Death/Buried 1738, Asuncion de Maria, Aguascalientes, Aguascalientes, Mexico (Father: Martin Esparza/Mother: Francisca Sotelo) (Widow/White) (Spouse: YNES GARCIA).
- a2. ANTONIO SOTELO de JAEN, baptized December 1636, Guadalajara, Jalisco, Mexico (*Guadalajara, Jalisco 1614-1668; Image 252/706*). Death 29 January 1654, Guadalajara, Jalisco, Mexico (*Guadalajara, Jalisco, Mexico 1614-1668; Image 246/706*).
- a3. ELENA SOTELO JAEN, born 18 January 1639, Asiento, Aguascalientes, Aguascalientes, Mexico. Married IGNACIO RUIZ de ESPARZA on 5 August 1651, Aguascalientes, Aguascalientes, Mexico. Died 24

January 1673, Asuncion de Maria, Aguascalientes, Aguascalientes, Mexico (Widowed).

The known children of Ignacio Ruiz Esparza and Elena (a) Sotelo Jaen were:
- b1. TERESA RUIZ de ESPARZA.
- b2. MIGUEL RUIZ de ESPARZA.
- b3. SEBASTIAN RUIZ de ESPARZA.
- b4. JUAN RUIZ de ESPARZA.
- b5. MARIA de JAEN y ESPARZA.

a4. JOANA SOTELO JAEN, born 11 September 1640/christening 27 September 1640, El Sagrario, Aguascalientes, Aguascalientes, Mexico (Father: Franco. Sotelo/Mother: Clara de Jaen) (Margin text: "Joana, Espanola") (Godparents: Luis Tiscareno and Lorenza Ruis de Esparza) (*Family Search #004339956; Image 100/334*). Married YGNASIO CALVALLO on 19 January 1674, El Sagrario, Aguascalientes, Aguascalientes, Mexico. Died 11 February 1695, Aguascalientes, Aguascalientes, Mexico.

The known children of Ygnasio Calvallo and Joana (a) Sotelo Jaen were:
- b1. NICHOLAS CALVILLO SOTELO, christening 20 December 1675, El Sagrario, Aguascalientes, Aguascalientes, Mexico (Father: Ygnacio Calbillo/Mother: Jua. Sotelo).
- b2. SIMON CALVILLO SOTELO, christening on 10 November 1676, El Sagrario, Aguascalientes, Aguascalientes, Mexico (Father: Ygnasio Calvillo/Mother: Jua. Sotelo).
- b3. ANTONIA CALVILLO XAEN, christening 10 February 1681, El Sagrario, Aguascalientes, Aguascalientes, Mexico (Father: Ygnacio Calvillo/Mother: Juana de Xaen). Record #2: SANTO A. ANTONIA CALVILLO de JAEN, christening 20 February 1681, Canada Honda, San Francisco de los Romo, Aguascalientes (Villa de Aguascalientes), Aguascalientes, Mexico.

a5. JUAN SOTELO JAEN, christening 15 May 1644, El Sagrario, Aguascalientes, Aguascalientes, Mexico (Father: Francisco Sotelo/Mother: Clara de Jaen) (Margin text: "Juan, Espanol") (Godparents: Salvador de Esparza and Maria de Vielma) (*Family Search #004339956; Image 122/334*). Married MARIA de la CRUZ y GONZALEZ on 12 June 1673, El Sagrario, Aguascalientes, Aguascalientes, Mexico.

The known children of Juan Sotelo Jaen (a) and Maria de la Cruz Gonzales were:
- b1. JUANA SOTELO, christening 25 December 1674, El Sagrario, Aguascalientes, Aguascalientes, Mexico (Father: Juan Sotelo/Mother: Maria de la Cruz).
- b2. TERESA SOTELO GONZALEZ, christening 18 November 1676, El Sagrario, Aguascalientes, Aguascalientes, Mexico (Father: Juan Sotelo/Mother: Maria Gonzalez).

      b3.   ANDREA SOTELO, christening 1 December 1678, El Sagrario, Aguascalientes, Aguascalientes, Mexico (Father: Juan Sotelo/Mother: Maria de la Cruz) (*male*).

      b4.   MARIA SOTELO, christening 7 December 1685, El Sagrario, Aguascalientes, Aguascalientes, Mexico (Father: Jn. Sotelo/Mother: Ma. de la Cruz).

a6.   MARIA SOTELO XAEN, christening 2 October 1647, El Sagrario, Aguascalientes, Aguascalientes, Mexico (Father: Franco. Sotelo/Mother: Clara de Xaen) (Margin text: "Maria, Espanola") (Godparents: Salvador de Esparza and Maria de Vielma) (*Family Search #004339956; Image 149/334*). Married CEVASTIAN MERINO on 9 June 1680, El Sagrario, Aguascalientes, Aguascalientes, Mexico (MA. De JAEN). Death/Burial 8 April 1687, Asuncion de Maria, Aguascalientes, Aguascalientes, Mexico (Married/White) (Spouse: Sebastian Merino).

a7.   **MICHAELA (*CLARA*) SOTELO de JAEN**, born abt. 1658, Aguascalientes, Aguascalientes, Mexico. Married JUAN de HERRERA on 25 September 1678, El Sagrario, Aguascalientes, Aguascalientes, Mexico (*Mexico matrimonios, 1570-1950*).
(*Baptismal records of Sotelo/Jaen children list the mother as both Clara and Michaela Jaen*).

    The known children of Juan de Herrera and Michaela (a) Sotelo Jaen were:

      b1.   BARVARA HERRERA JAEN, christening 18 December 1678, El Sagrario, Aguascalientes, Aguascalientes, Mexico (Father: Juan de Herrera/Mother: Michaela de Jaen).

      b2.   JUANA HERRERA JAEN, christening 3 February 1680, El Sagrario, Aguascalientes, Aguascalientes, Mexico (Father: Juan de Herrera/Mother: Michaela de Jaen).

      b3.   MIGUEL HERRERA XAEN, christening 22 March 1681, El Sagrario, Aguascalientes, Aguascalientes, Mexico (Father: Juan de Herrera/Mother: Michaela de Xaen).

      b4.   YSABEL HERRERA JAEN, christening 6 August 1684, El Sagrario, Aguascalientes, Aguascalientes, Mexico (Father: Juan de Herrera/Mother: Clara de Jaen).

      b5.   **MANUELA HERRERA XAEN**, born 27 May 1687, Palo Alto, Calvillo, Aguascalientes, Aguascalientes, Mexico. Christening 14 June 1687, El Sagrario, Aguascalientes, Aguascalientes, Mexico (Father: Juan de Herrera/Mother: Michaela de Xaen). Married XPTO. CALDERON on 9 February 1707, El Sagrario, Aguascalientes, Aguascalientes, Mexico.

      b6.   MARIA HERRERA XAEN, christening 13 March 1690, El Sagrario, Aguascalientes, Aguascalientes, Mexico (Father: Juan de Herrera/Mother: Michaela de Jaen) (Born Palo Alto, Calvillo, Aguascalientes, Mexico).

a8. GERTRUDIS de JAEN, born abt. 1665, Aguascalientes, Aguascalientes, Mexico. <u>Married</u> AGUSTIN LOPES on 3 June 1685, El Sagrario, Aguascalientes, Aguascalientes, Mexico. Death/burial (GETRUDES de XAEN) 1699, Aguascalientes, Aguascalientes, Mexico (Married) (Spouse: Agustin Lopes).

<u>The known children of Agustin Lopes and Gertrudis (a) Soletro Jaen were:</u>

b1. MARIA LOPES JAEN, christening 29 December 1687, El Sagrario, Aguascalientes, Aguascalientes, Mexico (Father: Agustin Lopes/Mother: Gertrudis de Jean).

b2. JUANA LOPES JAEN, christening 11 March 1689, El Sagrario, Aguascalientes, Aguascalientes, Mexico (Father: Agustin Lopes/Mother: Gertrudis de Jaen).

b3. THERESA LOPES XAEN, christening 12 December 1690, El Sagrario, Aguascalientes, Aguascalientes, Mexico (Father: Augustin Lopes/Mother: Gertrudis de Xaen).

b4. ANDRES LOPES JAEN, christening 17 December 1691, El Sagrario, Aguascalientes, Aguascalientes, Mexico (Father: Agustin Lopes/Mother: Gertrudis de Jaen).

b5. JOSEPHA LOPES GAES, christening 4 December 1695, El Sagrario, Aguascalientes, Aguascalientes, Mexico (Father: Agustin Lopes/Mother: Gertrudis de Gaes).

b6. MARIA LOPES JAEN, christening 14 January 1698, El Sagrario, Aguascalientes, Aguascalientes, Mexico (Father: Agustin Lopes/Mother: Gertrudes de Jaen).

To repeat:

MICHAELA (CLARA) de JAEN (born abt. 1658) <u>married</u> JUAN de HERRERA (born abt. 1658) on 25 September 1678 at El Sagrario, Aguascalientes, Aguascalientes, Mexico. The witnesses to the marriage were Juan Antonio Sotelo and Nicholas Calvillo (*Family Search #00434890; Image 100/325*).

<u>The known children of Juan Herrera (a) and Michaela Sotelo Jaen were:</u>

a1. BARVARA HERRERA JAEN, christening 18 December 1678, El Sagrario, Aguascalientes, Aguascalientes, Mexico (Father: Juan de Herrera/Mother: Michaela de Jaen).

a2. JUANA HERRERA JAEN, christening 3 February 1680, El Sagrario, Aguascalientes, Aguascalientes, Mexico (Father: Juan de Herrera/Mother: Michaela de Jaen).

a3. MIGUEL HERRERA XAEN, christening 22 March 1681, El Sagrario, Aguascalientes, Aguascalientes, Mexico (Father: Juan de Herrera/Mother: Michaela de Xaen).

a4. YSABEL HERRERA JAEN, christening 6 August 1684, El Sagrario, Aguascalientes, Aguascalientes, Mexico (Father: Juan de Herrera/Mother: Clara de Jaen).

- a5. **MANUELA HERRERA XAEN**, christening 14 June 1687, El Sagrario, Aguascalientes, Aguascalientes, Mexico (Father: Juan de Herrera/Mother: Michaela de Xaen).
- a6. MARIA HERRERA XAEN, christening 13 March 1690, El Sagrario, Aguascalientes, Aguascalientes, Mexico (Father: Juan de Herrera/Mother: Michaela de Xaen).

MANUELA de HERRERA (born 14 June 1687, Palo Alto, Cavillo, Aguascalientes, Aguascalientes, Mexico) married (CRISTOBAL) XPTO. CALDERON (born December 1685, Palo Alto, Cavillo, Aguascalientes, Aguascalientes, Mexico) on 9 February 1707, El Sagrario, Aguascalientes, Aguascalientes, Mexico.

The known children of Cristobal Calderon (a) and Manuela Herrera Jaen were:
- a1. **FRANCA. XAVIERA CALDERON HERRERA**, christening 18 December 1707, El Sagrario, Aguascalientes, Aguascalientes, Mexico (Father: Cristobal Calderon/Mother: Manuela Jaen de Herrera) (*Mexico bautismos, 1590-1950*).
  Married GASPAR ANTONIO MANRIQUE de LARA by 1729, Leon, Guanajuato, Mexico.
  The child of Gaspar Antonio Manrique de Lara and Francisca Calderon Herrera (a) was:
  - b. **JOSEPH MANUEL MANRIQUE de LARA**, born 30 November 1734, Leon, Guanajuato, Mexico (Mother: Franc. Xaviera Calderon de Herrera) (*Possibly named for maternal grandmother, Manuela Jaen de Herrera*).
- a2. JUAN de SAN PEDRO CALDERON (HERRERA), christening 18 November 1708, El Sagrario, Aguascalientes, Aguascalientes, Mexico (Father: Xpl. de Calderon/Mother: Manuela de Herrera. Married JOSEPHA LABATO. Death/burial 1744, Asuncion de Maria, Aguascalientes, Aguascalientes, Mexico (Father: Cristobal Calderon. Mother: Manuela Herrera) (Race: I) (Married/Spouse: Josepha Lobato).
- a3A. MONICA CALDERA (*CALDERON*) HERRERA, christening 19 May 1711, El Sagrario, Aguascalientes, Aguascalientes, Mexico (Father: Cristobal Caldera - *Calderon*/Mother: *Salbadora* Herrera) (*Unconfirmed whether Calderon-Herrera child*).
- a3. FRANCISCO (CALDERON) de HERRERA, christened on 21 October 1711, El Sagrario, Aguascalientes, Aguascalientes, Mexico (Father: Cristobal de Calderon/Mother: Manuela de Herrera). Record #2: Christening 21 October 1711, Canada Honda, San Francisco de los Roma, Aguascalientes, Mexico (son) (Father: Cristobal de Calderon/Mother: Manuela de Herrera) (*twin?*).
- a4. FRANCA. YNES CALDERON, christening 21 October 1711, El Sagrario, Aguascalientes, Aguascalientes, Mexico (Father: Xptobal. De Calderon/ Mother: Manuela de Herrera) (daughter) (*twin?*).

~~~~~~

Francisca Xavier Calderon de Herrera
(born 18 December 1707, Aguascalientes, Aguascalientes, Mexico)

Paternal lineage:
Don LOPE RUIZ de ESPARZA (1569 -1651)
  Married ANA FRANCISCA de GABAY NAVARRO y MOCTEZUMA.
BERNARDO RUIZ de ESPARZA (1608-1696)
  LEONOR LOSANO ISLA (1617-1670)
PETRONA RUIZ ESPARZA LOZANO (baptized 25 January 1635, AG, AG, MX)
  Married JUAN MEDINA.
FRANCISCA MEDINA (born abt. 1663, AG, AG, MX)
  Married ANTONIO GONZALES CALDERON.
CRISTOBAL CALDERON (born 28 December 1685, AG, AG, MX)
  Married MANUELA HERRERA (1687, AG, AG, MX) 1707, AG, AG, MX.

Maternal lineage:
FRANCISCO SOLTERO (born abt. 1595, DF, MX; died1669, AG, AG, MX)
  Married CLARA JAEN (born abt. 1620, DF, MX; died 1683, AG, AG, MX).
MICHAELA SOLTERO JAEN (born abt. 1658, AG, AG, MX)
  Married JUAN HERRERA (born abt. 1658) on 25 September 1678, AG, AG, MX.
MANUELA HERRERA (born 14 June 1687, AG, AG, MX)
  Married CRISTOBAL CALDERON during 1707, AG, AG, MX.

~~~~~~

With Petrona Esparza the daughter of Bernardo Ruiz de Esparza and grandchild of Lope Ruiz de Esparza - Ana Francesca Gabay de Navarro y Moctezuma, ties to Aztec Mexican history enters the Manrique de Lara family line. It is also notable Petrona Ruiz de Esparza was related to Juana Navarro de Gabay y Moctezuma by both parents (Leonor Lozano Isa and Bernardo Ruiz de Esparza), as well as, named for her great-grandmother (Petronila Arias Sotelo Moctezuma) and aunt (Petrona de Isla Lavezarri Moctezuma). Both Cristobal Calderon and his daughter, Franca. Xaviera Calderon de Herrera were listed as mixed race, heritage from Ana Francesca Gabay de Navarro y Moctezuma.

Lope Ruiz de Esparza, "el menor," married a Moctezuma descendant, Ana Francesca Gabay Navarro y Moctezuma. Cristobal Martinez Lozano married Maria de Isla Lavezzari y Moctezuma, the daughter of Ana Francisca Gabay Navarro y Moctezuma's sister, Juana Gabay Navarro y Moctezuma. The history of the Moctezuma line follows:
MOCTEZUMA II XOCOYOSIN II (born abt. 1480), was the son AXAYACTL TLATOANIA, otherwise known as, "Water Mask/Face" who was the sixth Emperor of the Axtecs between the years 1469-1481 in Tenochtitlan, Mexico. Axayactl Tlatoania was grandson of Emperor Moctezuma I, who reigned from 1440-1469. Moctezuma II became Emperor of the Aztec Empire in 1502. He died during the fall of Tenochtitlan in 1520.

The Aztec history continues and is well documented, but to reference a starting point:

The parents of CIHUACOATL TLILPOTONCATZIN CUAUHTITLAN de TENOCHTITIAN were:
TLACOCHCALCATL TLACAELEL I (1397-1487)
MAQUITZIN (1410-1450)
Married 1417, Azteca, Tenochtitlan, Mexico.

The known children of TLACOCHCALCATL TLACAELEL I and MAQUITZIN were:
TLACOCHCALCATL CACAMATIZN (1422-)
XIUHPOPOCATZIIN (1432-)
MACUILXOCHGTIZIN (1435-)
QUAUHTLAMIYAHUALTZIN (1440-)
CIHUACOATL TLILPOTOCATZIN CUAUHTITLAN (1450/1477-1503)

The parents of **MOCTEZUMA XOCOYOTZIN** were:
TLATOANI MEXICA AXAYACAL (born 1449, Tenochtitlan, Mexico; died 1496, Tenochtitlan, Mexico) (Water Mask/Water Face) (6th Emperor of Aztecs - 1469-1481)
XOCHICUEYETL AZCALXOCHITL XOCHIQUETZAL de TEXCOCO (born abt. 1450, Tenochtitlan, Mexico; died 1510, Tenochtitlan, Mexico)

The children of TLATOANI MEXICA AXAYACAL and XOCHICUEYETL AZCALXOCHITL XOCHIQUETZAL de TEXCOCO were:
MOCTEZUMA XOCOYOTZIN II (1468-1520) (Emperor of Aztecs 1502-1520)
CUITLAHUAC (1480-1520)
FRANCISCO de XOCOYOTZIN (1485-)

The parents of TZIHUACXOCHITZIN ACATLAN were:
CIHUACOATL TLILPOTONCATZIN CUAUHTITLAN de TENOCHTITLAN (born abt. 1450-1477, Tenochtitlan, Mexico; died 1503, Tenochtitlan, Mexico)
XIUHTOZTZIN de TENCHTITLAN (born 1460, Amaquemecan, Chalco, Mexico: died abt. 1490, Tenochtitlan, Mexico)

The children of CIHUACOATL TLILPOTONCATZIN CUAUHTITLAN de TENOCHTITLAN and XIUHTOZTZIN de TENCHTITLAN were:
MICCACALCATL TLALTETECUINTZIN (1483-)
TZIHUACXOCHITZIN ACATLAN (1485-1520) (noble Mixtec woman from Acatlan)

The parents of MARIANA LEONOR de MOCTEZUMA were:
MOCTEZUMA XOCOYOTZIN (b. 29 June 1468, Tenochtitlan, Mexico; died 30 June 1520, Tenochtitlan, Mexico)
TZIHUACXOCHITZIN ACATLAN (born 1485, Tenochtitlan, Mexico; Died 1520, Tenochtitlan, Mexico)

The children of **MOCTEZUMA XOCOYOTZIN** and TZIHUACXOCHITZIN ACATLAN were:
TLALTECATZIN MOCTEZUMA (1501-1520)

FRANCISCA de MOCTEZUMA (1504-1570)
MARIANA LEONOR de MOCTEZUMA (1510-1550)

Mariana Leonor Moctezuma adopted Christianity as per influence by Hernan Cortez, then was given the "encomienda rights," or a grant by the Spanish Crown to colonize Ecatepec, to a town near Mexico City, thereby forcing inhabitants to work mines or plantations while demanding future crops and currency were properties of Spain.

Mariana Leonor de Moctezuma married (m1) JUAN PAEZ in 1527. Juan Paez, a conquistador, died in late August of 1529.

Mariana Leonor de Moctezuma married (m2) CRISTOBAL de VALDERRAMA. Don Cristobal de Valderrama was born in 1490 Burgos, Spain and was also a conquistador who served Michoacan, Colima and Zacatula, Mexico. He was given the "encomienda" rights to Tarimbaro (1526-1537) and Ecatepec. Because of their marriage, Leonor Moctezuma's father-in-law, X'poval (Cristobal) de Valderrama, was also listed on a 1574 Archive General Mexico ownership chart.

Mariana Leonor de Moctezuma and Cristobal de Valderrama married during 1531 and only had one child, LEONOR de VALDERRAMA y MOCTEZUMA, who was baptized during 1532 in Mexico.

The parents of DONA LEONOR VALDERRAMA y MOCTEZUMA were:
Conquistador CRISTOBAL de VALDERRAMA (1490-1537)
 MARIANA LEONOR de MOCTEZUMA (b. 11 July 1510, Tenochtitlan, Mexico; d. 9 July 1550, Mexico City, Mexico)
Married during 1531 in Tenochtitlan, Mexico.

The child of CRISTOBAL de VALDERRAMA and MARIANA LEONOR de MOCTEZUMA was:
Dona LEONOR VALDERRAMA de MOCTEZUMA (1532-1562)
    Married DIEGO ARIAS de SOTELO (1526-1566) about 1550, Mexico City, MX.

The parents of CRISTOBAL de VALDERRAMA were CRISTOBAL VALDERRAMA (born abt. 1450, Spain) and MARIA de URBINA (born abt. 1450, Spain).

Dona LEONOR de VALDERRAMA y MOCTEZUMA married DIEGO ARIAS de SOTELO (born 1525/1526, Zamora, Spain), the son of FERNANDO de SOTELO and MARIA de VILLASENOR. The known children of DIEGO ARIAS de SOTELO (a) and (m2) DONA LEONOR VALDERAMA MOCTEZUMA were PETRONILA ARIAS SOTELO de MOCTEZUMA (born abt. 1552, Mexico City, Mexico; Died 1628, Villa de Aguascalientes, Aguascalientes, Mexico), ANA MARINA ARIAS SOTELO de MOCTEZUMA (christened 7 September 1553, Mexico City, New Spain), Don FERNANDO ARIAS SOTELO de MOCTEZUMA, born abt. 1554 Mexico City, New Spain: died after 1604 and before 1618, Colma/DF, Mexico) and Don CRISTOBAL ARIAS SOTELO de

MOCTEZUMA (born abt. 1555-1562, Mexico City, New Spain. Died abt. 1607, Mexico City, New Spain).

Dona LEONOR de VALDERRAMA y MOCTEZUMA was the second "encomendera" of Tarimbaro and Ecatepec. She died at age thirty after marrying in 1550 DIEGO ARIAS de SOTELO, born 1525, Zamora, Spain, the son of FERNANDO de SOTELO and MARIA de VILLASENOR. Diego Arias de Sotelo arrived in Mexico by 1550 and assisted the Viceroy LUIS de VELASCO while serving as an "Alcalde Ordinario de Majico" in 1651. The couple, Diego and Leonor, were involved in many lawsuits which involved the properties in Ecatepec and Tlateloloco. By 1568 the Vice Royalty had exiled in Diego Arias Sotelo to Spain for crimes against New Spain and a plot against Don MARTIN CORTES. Diego Arias Sotelo's brother was executed for his crimes against the state.

Fernando Arias Sotelo y Moctezuma, the son of Leonor Moctezuma and Diego Aries Sotelo, became owner of the "encomienda of Ecatepec" after his father's exile.

To repeat:

The parents of Dona LEONOR VALDERRAMA de MOCTEZUMA were:
Conquistador CRISTOBAL de VALDERRAMA HARA y CESPEDES (born 1490 Burgos, Burgos, Castile-Leon, Spain; died November 1537, Mexico City, Mexico)
and

MARIANA LEONOR de MOCTEZUMA (b.11 July 1510, Tenochtitlan, Imperial Mexico; d. 9 July 1550, Mexico City, New Spain).

The child of Conquistador CRISTOBAL de VALDERRAMA HARA y CESPEDES and MARIANA LEONOR de MOCTEZUMA was:
Dona LEONOR VALDERRAMA de MOCTEZUMA (1532-1562)

The parents of DIEGO ARIAS de SOTELO y NUNEZ VELA were Captain ANTONIO ARIAS de SOTELO y CISNEROS (born 1490 Villa San Miguel de Ribera-Zamora, Spain; died 14 January 1548, Panama, Central America) and USENDA NUNEZ VELA (born 1492, Cuellar de la Sierra, Soria, Spain; died abt. 1544, Zamora, Leon, Spain).

The parents of CAPTAIN ANTONIO SOTELO y CISNEROS were PEDRO de SOTELO and INEZ BEATRIZ CISNEROS.

The known children of Captain ANTONIO ARIAS de SOTELO y CISNEROS and USENDA NUNEZ VELA were GASPAR de SOTELO (born abt. 1518, Spain), BALTASAR de SOTELO (born abt. 1519, Spain) and DIEGO ARIAS de SOTELO y NUNEZ VELA (born abt. 1526, Zamora, Castile-Leon, Spain; died 7 July 1566, Teocaltiche, Jalisco Mexico).

DIEGO ARIAS SOTELO y NUNEZ married twice, first to (m1) MARIA MANUEL of Portugal then to (m2) LEONOR VALDERRAMA de MOCTEZUMA in Mexico.

The known child of DIEGO ARIAS de SOTELO (a) and (m1) MARIA MANUEL of Portugal (a) was:
b1.   CRISTOBAL SOTELO of Portugal, born abt. 1546-1548, Spain.

A 1574 Archive General chart listed Leonor de Valderrama and Diego Arias Sotelo as the parents of Fernando Sotelo de Moctezuma and noted "other children of Diego Arias Sotelo," but did not provide the names. My hypothesis is FRANCISCO Arias de SOTELO y Cervantes, born 1595 Mexico City, Mexico, was the son of Fernand Arias de Sotelo y Moctezuma, brother of Petronila Sotelo y Moctezuma, who married Clara Jaen.

Leonor Valderrama y Moctezuma died in 1562. Diego Arias de Sotelo, her husband, died 7 July 1566.

The known children of DIEGO ARIAS de SOTELO and (m2) Dona LEONOR VALDERRAMA MOCTEZUMA (a) were:
b1.   PETRONILA ARIAS SOTELO de MOCTEZUMA, born abt. 1552, Mexico City, Mexico. Died 1628, Villa de Aguascalientes, Nueva Galicia, New Spain.
Married MARTIN GABAY de NAVARRO (1554-1610).
The known children of PETRONILA SOTELO de MOCTEZUMA (b) and MARTIN GABAY de NAVARRO were:
   c1.   JUANA NAVARRO de GABAY y ARIAS de SOTELO, born 1572, Aguascalientes, Aguascalientes, Mexico. Death: 28 December 1651, Teocaltiche, Jalisco, Mexico.
   Married FRANCISCO BENITO GONZALEZ de ISLA y LAVEZARRI.
   The known children of Francisco Benito Gonzales de Isla Lavezarri and Juana Navarro de Gabay y Arias de Sotelo (c) were:
      d1.   MAGDALENA de ISLA de LAVEZZARI y NAVARRO MOCTEZUMA.
      d2.   (MARIA) MAGDALENA de ISLA.
      d3.   PETRONA de ISLA y NAVARRO.
      d4.   MARIA GONZALES de ISLA y LAVEZZARI MOCTEZUMA.
      Married CRISTOBAL MARTINEZ LOZANO.
      The known children of Cristobal Martinez Lozano and Maria de Isla (d) were:
         e1.   LUISA de ISLA (1602-1676).
         e2.   JUANA LOZANO ISLA (1603-1688).
         e3.   JACINTO LOZANO ISLA (1610-1673).
         e4.   ISABEL LOZANO ISLA (1612-1676).
         e5.   CATALINA LOZANO ISLA (1613-1683).
         e6.   ANA MARIA HERNANDEZ LOZANO (1614-1659).
         e7.   ANA MARTINA LOZANO ISLA (1615-1716).
         e8A. LORENZO LOZANO ISLA (1617-?).
         e8B. LEONOR LOZANO ISLA (1617-1670).
         e9.   ISLA JUANA LOZANO (1618-).
         e10. MAGDALENA LOZANO ISLAS (1619-1666).

                e11.   CRISTOBAL LOZANO MARTINEZ de ISLA (1620-1683).
        d5.   BERNARDINO GONZALEZ de ISLAS y LAVEZZARI.
c2.   MARIA CONCEPTION NAVARRO de GABAY NAVARRO y MOCTEZUMA,
            born 1573, Aguascalientes, Aguascalientes, Mexico. Died 30 March
            1652, Aguascalientes, Aguascalientes, Mexico.
        Married (m1) SIORDIA/(m2) PEDRO FERNANDEZ de VAULUS.
        The known children of Maria Conception Navarro de Gabay Navarro y
        Moctezuma (c) and (m1) Siorda were:
        d1.   PETRONILA de SIORDIA (m1), born abt. 1558-1606.
               Married JUAN de PADILLA.
               The known child of Juan and Petronila (d) (de Siorda) Padilla was:
               e1.   ELVIRA de PADILLA y SIORDA.
        d2.   ANTONIO de SIORDIA (m1) (born abt. 1578-1626).
               Married MARIA de INIQUEZ.
               The known child of Antonio de Siorda (d) and Maria de Iniquez
               was:
               e1.   FRANCISCA de SORDIA.
        d3.   JUANA de SIORIA VAULUS y GABAY MOCTEZUMA.
               (Father: Pedro Fernandez de Vaulus - m2) (born abt. 1578-
               1602)
               Married DON FRANCISCO (el VIEJO) RODRIQUEZ-PONCE.
               The known children of Juana de Siora Vaulus y Gabay Moctezuma
               (d) and Francisco Rodriquez Ponce were:
               e1.   NICOLAS RODRIQUEZ-PONCE y SIORDIA.
               e2.   BERNARDA SALADO y SIORDIA.
        d4.   MARIA ISORIDIA (m2), daughter of PEDRO FERNANDEZ
               de VAULUS, born abt. 1563-1619).
               Married LUIS de MEDINA y VALDIVIA.
               The known children of Maria Isordia y Gabay Moctezuma (d) and
               Luis de Medina y Valdiva were:
               e1.   MARIA de MEDINA ISORDIA.
        d5.   MARTIN FERNANDEZ de VALDOUX (m2), son of Pedro
               Fernandez de Valulus, born abt. 1578-1618).
               Married ISABEL de VELASCO GRIJALBA.
               The known children of Martin Fernandez de Vaulus (d) and Isabel
               de Valasco Grijalba were:
               e1.   NICOLAS de SIORDA.
               e2.   CATALINA FERNANDEZ de VAULUS de VELASCO.
               e3.   ISABEL FERNANDEZ de VAULUS de VELASCO.
               e4.   JACINTHA FERNANDEZ de VAULUS.
               e5.   GERONIMA FERNANDEZ de VAULUS.
               e6.   PEDRO FERNANDEZ de VAULUS.
        d6.   JUAN FERNANDEZ de VAULUS, son of Pedro Fernandez
               de Vaulus born abt. 1572. Died 1657.
               Married LEONOR BECCERA.

The known children of Juan Fernandez de Vaulus (d) and Leonor Beccera were:
    e1.   LEONOR FERNANDEZ BECCERA.

c3.   ANA FRANCISCA de GABAY NAVARRO y MOCTEZUMA, born 1573-1577, Guadalajara, Mexico. Married 1594-1595. Died 30 March 1652, Aguascalientes, Aguascalientes, Mexico.
Married LOPE II RUIZ de ESPARZA y EGUINO.
The known children of Ana Francisca de Gabay Navarro y Moctezuma and Lope Ruiz de Esparza were:
- d1.   SALVADOR RUIZ de ESPARZA (1595-1679).
  Married MARIA de VIELMA.
- d2   ANA TOMASINA RUIZ de ESPARZA (1597-1667).
  Married FRANCISCO SANCHEZ MONTES de OCA.
- d3.   MARTIN RUIZ de ESPARZA (1600-1662).
  Married MARIA LOPEZ de ELIZALDE.
- d4.   LORENZA RUIZ de ESPARZA (1602-1690).
  Married CAPTAIN LUIS TISCARENO de MOLINA.
- d5.   JACINTO) RUIZ de ESPARZA (1604-1679).
  (ESCRIBANO REAL de AGUASCALIENTES)
  Married JUANA LOPES de ELIZALDE.
- d6.   PEDRO RUIZ de ESPARZA (born abt. 1605 to1609; died 1700).
  Married (m1) JUANA LOZANO ISLA)/(m2) MARGARITA GONZALES GALLEGOS.
- d7.   BERNARDO (SALADO) RUIZ de ESPARZA (1608-1696).
  Married CATALINA LOZANO ISLA.
- d8.   MARIA RUIZ de ESPARZA y GABAY SOTELO (1613-unknown).
  Married NICOLAS de ULLOA.
- d9.   CRISTOBAL RUIZ de ESPARZA (1616-1672).
  Married ISABEL de ALCARAS y PEREZ (1625-1669).
- d10.   BERNABE RUIZ de ESPARZA (1618-1672).
  Married ANA ORTIZ RAMIREZ.
- d11.   LORENZO (LOPE) RUIZ de ESPARZA (1620-1693).
  Married (m1) ANTONIA de CONTRERAS y CASTILLO/(m2) JOSEFA de SANDI y AGUILERA.

b2.   ANA MARINA ARIAS SOTELO de MOCTEZUMA, christening 7 September 1553, Mexico City, New Spain (Father: Diego Arias de Sotelo/Mother: Leonor de Valderrama). Died abt. 1628, Mexico City, Mexico. Ana Sotelo de Moctezuma became a nun.

b3.   Don FERNANDO ARIAS SOTELO de MOCTEZUMA, born abt. 1554 Mexico City, New Spain. Died after 1604 and before 1618, Colma/DF, Mexico.
Married MARIA de VILLASENOR CERVANTES y CORONA.
The known children of FERNANDO SOTELO de MOCTEZUMA (b) and MARIA de VILLASENOR CERVANTES y CORONA:
- c1.   JUAN de SOTELO y MOCTEZUMA (b. 1560, DF, MX; d. 11 November 1643, DF, MX).
  Married MARIA HURTADO de MENDOZA.

The known children of Juan de Sotelo y Moctezuma (c) and Maria Hurtado de Mendoza:
- d1. LORENZO SOTELO MOCTEZUMA (born abt. 1565-1625).
  Married ANA RIVERA.
- d2. MARIA de MOCTEZUMA y MENDOZA.
- c2. La REBERENDE MADRE ANA del ESPRITU SANTO ARIAS (born abt. 1559-1609).
- c3. LICENCIADO DIEGO ARIAS de SOTELO CERVANTEZ, CANONIGO de la CATEDRAL (born abt. 1559-1609).
- c4. SR. Pbro. ANTONIO ARIAS de SOTELO y CERVANTES.
- c5. La REBERENDA MADRE JERONIMA (born abt. 1559-1609).
- c6. FERNANDO ARIAS de SOTELO y CERVANTES (born abt. 1559-1609, DF, MX).
- c7. La REBERENDA MADRE CATALINA (born abt. 1559-1609).
- c8. La REVERENDA MADRE LEONOR de la TRINIDAD de SOTELO y CERVANTES (born 1592, DF, MX).
- c9. **FRANCISCO** ARIAS de **SOTELO** y CERVANTES (born 1595, DF, MX).
  (*Possibly married CLARA JAEN*).
- c10. ANDRES MALDONADO y SOLIS (born 1559-1609 DF, MX).
  Married JUANA de SAAVEDRA y ZAYAS.
- c11. DIEGO SOTELO MOCTEZUMA (born abt. 1559-1619, DF, MX).
- c12. JUAN SOTELO MOCTEZUMA (born 1559-1619, DF, MX).
- b4. Don CRISTOBAL ARIAS SOTELO de MOCTEZUMA (born abt. 1555-1562, Mexico City, New Spain; died abt. 1607, Mexico City, New Spain)
  Married JUANA HEREDIA PATINO during 1594, Mexico City, Mexico.

The known children of DIEGO ARIAS de SOTELO (1526-1566) were CRISTOBAL SOTELO of Portugal (born abt. 1546-1548, Spain), PETRONILA ARIAS SOTELO de MOCTEZUMA (born abt. 1552, Mexico City, Mexico), ANA MARINA ARIAS SOTELO de MOCTEZUMA (christening 7 September 1553, Mexico City, New Spain), Don FERNANDO ARIAS SOTELO de MOCTEZUMA (born abt. 1554 Mexico City, New Spain) and Don CRISTOBAL ARIAS SOTELO de MOCTEZUMA (born abt. 1555-1562, Mexico City, New Spain).

No marriage record exists for the assumed 1571 marriage between Petronila Sotelo Moctezuma to Martin Gabay de Navarro (Martin Navarro).

Teocaltiche, which in the Nahuatil language means, "place near the temple," was home to many Spanish conquistadors by 1546. Located in the state of Jalisco, Mexico, the church ("la Capilla") was built soon after the Spaniards settled amid Teocaltiche. The territory was conquered in 1530 by Cristobal de Onate and Manuel de Iberra on order of Nuno de Guzman (1490-1558), a conquistador. Nuno Betran de Guzman was born in Guadalajara, Spain, the son of a wealthy merchant. He later founded Guadalajara, Jalisco, Mexico. Once a bodyguard to Charles I of Spain, he was sent to upset the power of Hernan Cortez, the leader of the Spanish conquest of the Aztec Empire and link to individuals in our Moctezuma line. Arrested for treason in 1537, Guzman returned to Spain, thereby solidifying the historical legacy of his opponent, Hernan Cortes.

Given few Spaniards resided in the Villa of Aguascalientes, Mexico by 1640, it is likely FRANCISCO Arias de SOTELO y Cervantes, born 1595, Mexico City, Mexico was the son of Fernand Arias de Sotelo y Moctezuma, the brother of Petronila Sotelo y Moctezuma. This Francisco Sotelo likely married Clara Jaen. Their daughter, Francisca married into the Ruiz de Esparza line directly (Martin Ruiz de Esparza, grandson of Lope Ruiz de Esparza, son of Martin Ruiz de Esparza Junior) while their other daughter, from our line entered the Ruiz de Esparza line via her husband's lineage to the son of Lope Ruiz de Esparza (Bernardo Ruiz de Esparza's child, Petrona Esparza).

The parents of Captain MARTIN NAVARRO de GABAY (1554-1610) were PEDRO NAVARRO REDONDO (b. 1515, Pamploma, Navarre, Spain; d. 1610, Mexico) and UBALDA de GABAY MOYANO y de PEDROZA BELLO (b. 1522 Seca, Colmbra, Portugal; d. 1565, Teocaltiche, Jalisco, Mexico).

The children of PEDRO NAVARRO REDONDO and UBALDE de GABAY MOYANO y de PETROZA BELLO were JUAN de la CRUZ de NAVARRO de GABAY (b. 1548), PARBULO FRANCO NAVARRO de GABAY (b. 1551) and Captain MARTIN NAVARRO de GABAY (1554-1610).

The parents of UBALDA de GABAY MOYANO y PEDROZA BELLO were MIGUEL MOYANO MARTIN (born prior to 1507, Nuestra Senora de la Asuncion, La Seca, Valladolid, Castile, Spain) and ANA MARIA PEDROZA (born before 1509, Spain).

The parents of PEDRO NAVARRO REDONDO (1515-1610) were BERNABE NAVARRO LORENZO (b. 1490, Pamplona, Navarre, Spain; died Navarre, Spain) and FELICIANA REDONDO (b. 1490, Pamplona, Navarre, Spain; d. 1520, Spain).

The children of BERNABE NAVARRO LORENZO and FELICIANA REDONDO were MATILLA de los CANOS NAVARRO REDONDO (b. 1510, Pamplona, Navarre, Spain) and PEDRO NAVARRO REDONDO (born abt. 1515, Pamplona, Navarre, Spain; d. 1610, Mexico).

The parents of BERNABE NAVARRO LORENZO (b. 1490) were PEDRO NAVARRO RODRIQUEZ (born abt. 1460 Pamplona, Navarre, Spain) and AGUSTINA LORENZO (born abt. 1460 Pamplona, Navarre, Spain).

The parents of PEDRO NAVARRO RODRIQUEZ were PEDRO NAVARRO (born abt. 1440, Pamplona, Navarre, Spain) and ISABEL RODRIQUEZ de SANTANDER.

The parents of FELICANA REDONDO were ALONSO REDONDO (born abt. 1472, Spain) and BEATRIZ ROMAN (born abt. 1472, Spain).

To restate, Captain MARTIN NAVARRO de GABAY (1554-1610) married PETRONILA ARIAS SOTELO y VALDERRAMA (1552-1628).
<u>The children of Captain MARTIN NAVARRO de GABAY and PETRONILA ARIAS SOTELO y VALDERRAMA MOCTEZUMA (a) were:</u>

a1. JUANA NAVARRO de GABAY y ARIAS de SOTELO y VALDERRAMA MOCTEZUMA (1568-1651).
a2. MARIA NAVARRO de GABAY y ARIAS de SOTELO y VALDERRAMA MOCTEZUMA (1570-1688).
a3. CRISTOBAL NAVARRO de GABAY y ARIAS de SOTELO y VALDERRAMA MOCTEZUMA (1572-1648).
a4. ANA FRANCISCA NAVARRO de GABAY y ARIAS de SOTELO y VALDERRAMA MOCTEZUMA (1577-1652).

The parents of LOPE "el Menor" RUIZ de ESPARZA (1565-1651) were LOPE "El Mayor" RUIZ de ESPARZA y de ESPINOSA (1525-1604) and Dona MARIA ANA DIAZ de EQUINOA (1525-Deceased).

The children of LOPE "el Mayor" RUIZ de ESPARZA and Dona MARIA ANA DIAZ de EQUINOA were Captain ANDRES RUIZ de ESPARZA y EQUINOA, Captain LOPE II "El Menor" RUIZ de ESPARZA y EQUINOA (1569-1651), who married ANA FRANCISCA GABAY NAVARRO y MOCTEZUMA, and PEDRO RUIZ de ESPARZA y EQUINOA.

The parents of ANA FRANCISCA NAVARRO de GABAY y ARIAS de SOTELO y VALDERRAMA MOCTEZUMA (1577-1652) were Captain MARTIN NAVARRO de GABAY (1554-1610) and PETRONILA ARIAS SOTELO y VALDERRAMA MOCTEZUMA (1552-1628) who married abt. 1592, Nochistan, New Spain.

LOPE II RUIZ de ESPARZA's death and burial was recorded on 14 August 1651 at Asuncion de Maria, Aguascalientes, Aguascalientes, Mexico.

ANA FRANCISCA NAVARRO de GABAY y MOCTEZUMA's death and burial was recorded on 30 March 1652, Asuncion de Maria, Aguascalientes, Aguascalientes, Mexico where she was noted a widowed spouse of Lope Ruiz de Esparza.

The known children of Don Lope Ruiz de Esparza and Ana Francisca de Gabay Navarro y Moctezuma (a) were: (**APPENDIX X**)

a1. SALVADOR RUIZ de ESPARZA (1595-1680).
   Married MARIA de VIELMA.
a2 ANA TOMASINA RUIZ de ESPARZA (born abt. 1597- died abt. 1667).
   Married FRANCISCO SANCHEZ MONTES de OCA.
a3. MARTIN RUIZ de ESPARZA (born abt. 1600-1674).
   Married MARIA LOPEZ de ELIZALDE (daughter of Juan Lopez de Elizalde and Leonor Beccara y Sanchez de Mendoza).
a4. LORENZA RUIZ de ESPARZA (born abt. 1602-1690).
   Married CAPTAIN LUIS TISCARENO de MOLINA.
a5. JACINTO RUIZ de ESPARZA (born abt. 1604-1679).
   (ESCRIBANO REAL de AGUASCALIENTES)
   Married JUANA LOPES de ELIZALDE (daughter of Juan Lopez de Elizalde and Leonor Beccara y Sanchez de Mendoza).
a6. PEDRO RUIZ de ESPARZA (born abt. 1605-1607/1609; died after 1700).

        Married (m1) JUANA LOZANO ISLA (daughter of Don Cristobal Lozano and Dona Maria de Isla)/(m2) MARGARITA GONZALES GALLEGOS.
- a7. BERNARDO (SALADO) RUIZ de ESPARZA (1608- died abt. 1696).
  Married CATALINA LOZANO ISLA (daughter of Don Cristobal Lozano and Dona Maria de Isla).
- a8. MARIA RUIZ de ESPARZA y GABAY SOTELO (1613-unknown).
  Married NICOLAS de ULLOA.
- a9. CRISTOBAL RUIZ de ESPARZA (1616-1672).
  Married ISABEL de ALCARAS y PEREZ (1625-1669).
- a10. BERNABE RUIZ de ESPARZA (1618-1662).
  Married ANA ORTIZ RAMIREZ.
- a11. LORENZO (LOPE) RUIZ de ESPARZA (1620-1693).
  Married (m1) ANTONIA de CONTRERAS y CASTILLO/(m2) JOSEFA de SANDI y AGUILERA.

~~~~~

To restate, CRISTOBAL LOZANO MARTINEZ and MARIA de ISLA LAVEZZARI y MOCTEZUMA likely connects the MdL-Herrera line to Esparza and Moctezuma lineage.

Two Lope Ruiz II de Esparza sons (Pedro Ruiz de Esparza and Bernardo Ruiz de Esparza) married Lozano Isla sisters. Our line connects to Bernardo Ruiz de Esparza who had a daughter, Petrona Ruiz de Esparza, with a Lozano Isla family member who he did not marry, Leonor Lozano Isla.

Although early Aguascalientes, Mexico families are well documented, Petrona Esparza who married Juan Medina was not listed in online records of this lineage. My search for her parentage noticed three things - 1) Petrona Esparza's parents were Bernardo Ruiz de Esparza and Leonor de Lozano, 2) Catalina Lozano, Leonor's sister, married Bernardo Ruiz de Esparza, and 3) Petrona de Isla Lavezzari's sister, Maria de Isla Lavezzari, the mother of both Leonor and Catalina Lozano Isla, was a witness to Leonor Lozano's children's birth, a fact that leads to stating "Petrona" RUIZ ESPARZA was the child of Bernardo Ruiz de Esparza and Leonor Lozano Isla, as well as, an individual named for Leonor Lozano Isla's aunt. Petrona de Isla was Maria de Isla's sister and also Leonor Lozano Isla's godparent. Both Maria de Isla, wife of Cristobal Lozano Martinez, and her sister, Petrona de Isla, were children of Juana Navarro de Gabay y Arias de Sotelo Moctezuma (1568-1651). Juana Navarro de Gabay y Arias de Sotelo Moctezuma was sister to Ana Francisco de Gabay y Arias de Sotelo Moctezuma (born abt. 1573-1577) who married Lope Ruiz de Esparza. Both Juana Navarro and Ana Francisca were children of Dona Petronila Moctezuma and Martin Gabay Navarro. Essentially, Bernardo Ruiz de Esparza (born 1608) had a child with his second cousin or his cousin Maria de Isla's daughter, Leonor Lozano Isla (b. 1617) then married his second cousin's different daughter, Catalina Lozano Isla (born abt. 1613).

(PETRONA) RUIZ de ESPARZA was christened 25 January 1635 at El Sagrario, Aguascalientes, Aguascalientes, Mexico, the child of BERNARDO RUIZ de ESPARZA and LEONOR de LOSANO.

CATALINA de LOZANO married BERNARDO RUIZ de ESPARZA, 27 February 1634.
ISLA JUANA LOZANO married PEDRO RUIZ de ESPARZA, 12 April 1636.
LEONOR de LOZANO married BERNABE MERINO, 8 December 1650.

LORENZO and LEONOR LOZANO ISLA appear to be twins, but Lorenzo Lozano is often not listed historically as the son of Cristobal Lozano and Maria de Isla. However, both Lorenzo and Leonor Lozano Isla had the same witnesses: Francisco Gonzales, their grandfather (their mother, Maria de Isla's father), and Petrona de Isla, their aunt (mother's sister) and daughter of Francisco Gonzales.

LEONOR LOSANO ISLA was christened on 22 May 1617, El Sagrario, Aguascalientes, Aguascalientes, Mexico (Father: Cristobal Lozano/Mother: Maria de Isla). It is noted she resided in Xiconaque, an "estancia" which her father, Cristobal Lozano, also lived.

LORENZO LOZANO ISLA, christening May 1617, El Sagrario, Aguascalientes, Aguascalientes, Mexico (Father: Cristobal Lozano/Mother: Maria Isla) (Sister: LEONOR ISLA) (Godparent: FRANCISCO GONZALEZ) (*Francisco Gonzales was Maria de Isla's father and Lorenzo Lozano's grandfather*) **(Witnesses: PETRONA de ISLA).**

LEONOR LOZANO ISLA had a child at age eighteen with her sister's husband, Bernardo Ruiz de Esparza:

(A1.) **(PETRONA) RUIZ LOZANO,** christening 25 January 1635, El Sagrario, Aguascalientes, Aguascalientes, Mexico (Father: Berdo. Ruis de Esparza/Mother: **Leonor de Losano**).

Text reads: ".... hija de Bernardo de Esparza y de Leonor Losano ..."

There is no first or last name given in the margin of the book. The only text in the margin is a plus sign: "+." The record *(Family Search Film #004339956; Image 52/334)* is from "Archivo de la Parroquia del Sagrario Antes de la Asuncion Bautismos Aguascalientes, Mexico, Volume 1."

The name "Antonia" was placed at some genealogical sites for this unidentified daughter of Bernardo Esparza and Leonor Lozano. However, in honor of Leonor's aunt, the child was likely named, "Petrona" Ruiz (Esparza) Losano. Petrona Esparza married Juan Medina.

Leonor Lozano Isla named her child for the witness of her brother, Lorenzo: Petrona de Isla, *the sister of Maria de Isla, the mother of Leonor Lozano Isla* and Lorenzo Lozano Isla. Further speculation is whether LEONOR LOZANO ISLA had *two children* with Bernardo Ruiz de Esparza: Petrona Ruiz Lozano *and* Lope Ruiz de Esparza. The reason for this hypothesis is the witness for Lope Ruiz de Esparza born 1640 was "Petrona," and the surname of the mother appears to be Isla. There was a Maria India who lived in Aguascalientes in 1640, but she was married to Francisco Joseph. During this period, Maria India did not marry an Esparza. However, this supposition is possible:

(A2.) LOPE RUIZ de ESPARZA, christening 2 June 1640, El Sagrario, Aguascalientes, Aguascalientes, Mexico (Mother: MARIA INDIA/*ISLA*)
(Witness: **PETRONA**)

Pedro Ruiz de Esparza and (Isla) Juana Lozano, Leonor Lozano's sister, also named a son, LOPE, named after Pedro Ruiz de Esparza's father and grandfather:

LOPE ESPARZA LOZANO, christening 29 April 1655, El Sagrario, Aguascalientes, Aguascalientes, Mexico (Father: Pedro ESPARZA/ Mother: JUANA LOZANO). Death/Burial (of LOPE RUIZ de ESPARZA) on 31 July 1717, Asuncion de Maria, Aguascalientes, Aguascalientes, Mexico (Single/White).

LEONOR LOSANO (1617-1670) married BERNABE MERINO on 8 December 1650, El Sagrario, Aguascalientes, Aguascalientes, Mexico.

Leonor Lozano Isla was godmother to:

her brother, Jacinto Lozano's child-
JUANA LOZANO GONZALES, christening 21 July 1651, El Sagrario, Aguascalientes, Aguascalientes, Mexico (Father: Jacinto Lozano/Mother: Juana Gonzalez). **(Godmother: DONA LEONOR LOSANO)** *(Record #2 stated that 21 June 1651 was the baptism of JUANA, legitimate daughter of Jacinto Lozano and Juana Gonzalez. It also noted, "Ya difunta, fue madrinas Dona Leonor Lozano" or "already deceased was godmother, Dona Leonor Lozano...")*

and

her brother, Cristobal Lozano's child:
FELIPA LOZANO (son), christening 17 August 1679, Aguascalientes, Aguascalientes, Mexico (Father: Cristobal Lozano/Mother: Mariana Gonzalez) (**Witness: LEONOR LOZANO**).

It seems the translator put the text on the incorrect record (at *Family Search*). Leonor was deceased by 1679 at the christening of Felipa Lozano: "*Ya difunta, fue madrinas Dona Leonor Lozano*" or "*already deceased was godmother, Dona Leonor Lozano...*"

The children of Leonor Lozano Isla (a) and Bernabe Merino were:
b1. MARIA MERINO LOSANO, christening 12 November 1651, El Sagrario, Aguascalientes, Aguascalientes, Mexico (Father: Bernabe Merino/Mother: Leonor Lozano).
b2. MARIA JOSEPHA MERINO LOSANO, christening 12 November 1651, El Sagrario, Aguascalientes, Aguascalientes, Mexico (Father: Bernabe Merino/Mother: Leonor Losano).

b3. MATHIANA MERINO LOZANO, christening 16 March 1653, El Sagrario, Aguascalientes, Aguascalientes, Mexico (Father: Bernabe Merino/Mother: Leonor Lozano).

The death/burial of LEONOR LOSANO took place during 1670 at Asuncion de Maria, Aguascalientes, Aguascalientes, Mexico (Widowed) (Spouse: Bernabe Merino). (*Asuncion de Maria, Aguascalientes, Aguascalientes, Mexico. Defunciones 1620-1752; Image 121/560*).

CRISTOBAL LOZANO, father to Leonor Lozano and grandfather to Petrona Ruiz de Esparza (who married Juan Medina), was notable as an early Villa de Aguascalientes settler. Captain JUAN LOZANO and his wife INES MARTINEZ were parents of CRISTOBAL MARTIN LOZANO, also known as CRISTOBAL MARTINEZ LOZANO, who is assumed to be one of the founders of the Villa Nuestra Senora de la Asuncion of Aguascalientes in 1575, although genealogical research of his descendants offers zero exact proof of this reference. His death certificate, registered in the Parochial Archives of Aguascalientes and recorded before Joseph Altamirano de Castilla Alcade, mayor of Aguascalientes, designated his sons, Cristobal and Jacinto Lozano as executors of his estate. CRISTOBAL MARTINEZ LOZANO was married to MARIA de ISLA, sometimes referred to by the surname, GONZALES de ISLAS, the daughter of FRANCISCO GONZALES MARTINEZ and Dona MAGDALENA LAVEZARRI.

The Cristobal Lozano and Maria de Isla lineage is as follows:

The parents of Captain Juan Hernandez Lozano y de Zapata were:
ALONSO HERNANDEZ LOZANO (1513, Spain-)
MARIA ZAPATA (1515, Spain-).

Alonso Hernandez Lozano and Maria Zapata had one child, Juan Hernandez Lozano y Zapata.

CAPTAIN JUAN HERNANDEZ LOZANO y de ZAPATA (born abt. 1530, Lobon, Badajoz, Extremadura, Spain). Military service - Presidio de Sombrerete, Zacatecas, Mexico.

CAPTAIN JUAN HERNANDEZ LOZANO y de ZAPATA married INEZ MARTINEZ de VACA y GONZALES (born abt. 1551, Badajoz, Extremadura, Spain) by 1575 where they resided afterwards in Aguascalientes, Aguascalientes, Mexico.

The children of Captain Juan Hernandez Lozano y de Zapata and Inez Martinez de Vaca y Gonzales (a) were:
b1. **CRISTOBAL LOZANO MARTINEZ (1565-1646) m. Maria de Isla Lavezzari.**
b2. MARIA LOZANO MARTINEZ (1575, Sombrete, Zacatecas, Mexico-1647).
b3. FRANCISCO GONZALEZ MARTINEZ (b. 30 August 1578, Nochistlan de Mejia, Zacatecas, Mexico-). (Assumed) *Married Isabel de Frias (1586-)*
The children of Francisco Gonzales Martinez and Isabel de Frias were (c):
c1. *JUAN HERNANDEZ LOZANO y GONZALES (1612-1686).*

  c2. ANA HERNANDEZ LOZANO y GONZALEZ (1615-).
  c3. CATALINA LOZANO FRIAS (abt. 1616-).
b4. JACINTO HERNANDEZ LOZANO y MARTINEZ (1588-).

The parents of MARIA de ISLA de LAVEZZARI were:
FRANCISCO BENITO GONZALES de ISLA y LAVEZZARI (1558, Seville, Andalucia, Spain) and JUANA NAVARRO de GABAY y ARIAS de SOTELO MOCTEZUMA (1568, Mexico City, MX-1651).

The ISLA surname was also recorded as, ISLAS.

FRANCISCO BENITO GONZALES de ISLA y LAVEZZARI married JUANA NAVARRO de GABAY y ARIAS de SOTELO MOCTEZUMA during 1588, Nochistlan, Mexico.

The parents of Francisco Benito Gonzales de Isla y Lavezzari were:
 BERNARDINO GONZALES de ISLA y LAVEZZARI (1514-1558)
 MAGDALENA de LAVEZZARI y CHAVEZ ALVARADO (1518, Seville, Spain-)

Bernardino Gonzales de Isla y Lavezzari and Magdalena de Lavezzari y Chavez Alvarado married *27 April 1536, San Juan Bautista, Ostuncalco, Quezaltenango, Guatemala* (although location of Andalucia, Spain is noted in their children's births).

The children of Bernardino Gonzales de Isla y Lavezzari and Magdalena de Lavezzari y Chavez Alvarado (a) were:
b1. JUAN de ISLA de LAVEZZARI y CHAVEZ (1531, Andalucia, Spain-).
b2. BARTOLOME ISLA de LAVEZZARI (1535, Andalucia, Spain-).
b3. SEBASTIAN de ISLA de LAVEZZARI (1537, Andalucia, Spain -).
b4. MAGDALENA de LAVEZZARI y CHAVEZ ALVARADO (1540, Seville, Andalucia,
  Spain-).
b5. BERNARDINO de ISLA de LAVEZZARI (1545, Seville, Andalucia, Spain-).
b6. FRANCISCO BENITO GONZALEZ de ISLA (1558, Seville, Andalucia, Spain-
  died Teocaltiche, Jalisco, Mexico).

Parents of Juana Navarro de Gabay y Arias de Sotelo were:
Captain MARTIN NAVARRO de GABAY (b. 2 September 1554, Santa Cruz, Navarre,
 Spain- d.1610, Teocaltiche, Jalisco, Mexico).
PETRONILA ARIAS SOTELO y VALDERRAMA MOCTEZUMA (b. 1552, Nochistlan,
 Mexico- d.1628, Aguascalientes, Mexico).
The children of Martin Navarro de Gabay and Petronila Arias Sotelo y Valderrama Moctezuma (a) were:
b1. JUANA NAVARRO de GABAY ARIAS de SOTELO y MOCTEZUMA (1568-
  1651). Married Francisco Benito Gonzales de Isla.
b2. MARIA NAVARRO de GABAY ARIAS de SOTELO y MOCTEZUMA (1570-).
b3. CRISTOBAL NAVARRO de GABAY ARIAS de SOTELO y MOCTEZUMA (1572,
  DF, MX- 3 July 1648 Teocaltiche, Jalisco, Mexico).

b4. ANA FRANCISCA GABAY NAVARRO y ARIAS de SOTELO y MOCTEZUMA (1577-1652). Married Lope Ruiz Esparza.

JUANA NAVARRO de GABAY y ARIAS de SOTELO (b. 1568, DF, Mexico; d. 28 December 1651, Teocaltiche, Jalisco, Mexico) also used the surname, Gonzales de Isla y Lavezzari.

The children of Juana Navarro de Gabay y Arias de Sotelo (1568-1651) and Francisco Benito Gonzalez de Isla y Lavezzari (a) were:
b1. MAGDALENA GONZALES de ISLA (1585, Nochistlan, Zacatecas, Mexico-).
b2. MAGDALENA (MARIA) de LAVEZZARI (1590, Nochistlan, Zacadecas, Mexico-).
b3. **PETRONA GONZALES de ISLA y NAVARRO** (born abt. 1590, Nochistlan, Zacatecas, Mexico; d. Aguascalientes, Aguascalientes, Mexico).
b4. **MARIA de ISLAS de LAVEZZARI** (1597-1667). Born 1597 Nochistlan de Mejia. Zacatecas, Mexico; d. 18 June 1667, Aguascalientes, Aguascalientes, Mexico. Married **Cristobal Martinez Lozano.**
b5. BERNARDINO GONZALES de ISLAS (b. 30 May 1608, Nochistlan, Zacatecas, Mexico; d. 5 January 1681, Nochistlan, Zacatecas, Mexico).

As per previous text, JUANA NAVARRO de GABAY y ARIAS de SOTELO y MOCTEZUMA (1568-1651) was the child of Captain MARTIN NAVARRO de GABAY (1554-1610) and PETRONILA ARIAS SOTELO y VALDERRAMA MOCTEZUMA (1552-1628).

FRANCISCO BENITO GONZALEZ de ISLA y LAVEZZARI (1558-) married JUANA NAVARRO de GABAY y ARIAS de SOTELO y MOCTEZUMA (1568-1651) about 1588, Nochistlan, Nueva Galicia, Nueva Espana (Zacatecas, Mexico).

The known children of **JUANA NAVARRO de GABAY y ARIAS de SOTELO MOCTEZUMA** (1568-1651) and FRANCISCO BENITO GONZALES de ISLA y LAVEZZARI (1588-) (a) were:
b1. MAGDALENA GONZALES de ISLA de LAVEZZARI y NAVARRO (1585-).
b2. MAGDALENA (MARIA) GONZALES de ISLA de LAVEZARES (1590-).
b3. **PETRONA** GONZALES de ISLA de LAVEZZARI y NAVARRO (born abt.1590; d. Aguascalientes, Aguascalientes, Mexico).
b4. **MARIA de ISLA de LAVEZZARI** (1597-1667, Aguascalientes, Aguascalientes, Mexico). Married CRISTOBAL LOZANO MARTINEZ (1565-1646) abt. 1600, Aguascalientes, Aguascalientes, Mexico.
The known children of Maria de Islas (b) and Cristobal Martinez Lozano were:
    c1. LUISA de ISLA (1602-1676).
    c2. JUANA LOZANO ISLA (1603-1688).
    c3. JACINTO LOZANO ISLA (1610-1673).
    c4. ISABEL LOZANO ISLA (1612-1676).
    c5. CATALINA LOZANO ISLA (1613-1683).
    c6. ANA MARIA HERNANDEZ LOZANO (1614-1659).
    c7. ANA MARTINA LOZANO ISLA (1615-1716).
    c8A. LORENZO LOZANO ISLA (1617-).

        c8B.   LEONOR LOZANO ISLA (1617-1670).
        c9.   ISLA JUANA LOZANO (1618-).
        c10.   MAGDALENA LOZANO ISLAS (1619-1666).
        c11.   CRISTOBAL LOZANO MARTINEZ de ISLA (1620-1683).
b5.   BERNARDINO GONZALEZ de ISLAS y LAVESSARI (1608-1681).

The parents of Captain JUAN HERNANDEZ LOZANO were ALONSO HERNANDEZ LOZANO (1513-) and MARIA ZAPATA (1515-). The parents of INEZ MARTINEZ de VACA y GONZALEZ were FRANCISCO MARTINEZ de VACA (1524-) and ISABEL GONZALEZ (1520-1550).

The parents of CRISTOBAL LOZANO MARTINEZ (1565-1646) were: Captain JUAN HERNANDEZ LOZANO y ZAPATA (1530-) and INEZ MARTINEZ de VACA y GONZALEZ (1551-) who married abt. 1575, Aguascalientes, Aguascalientes, Mexico.

The known children of Captain JUAN HERNANDEZ LOZANO y ZAPADA (1530-) and INEZ MARTINEZ de VACA y GONZALEZ (1551-) (a) were:
b1.   **CRISTOBAL LOZANO MARTINEZ** (1565-1646).
      Married **MARIA de ISLA de LAVEZZARI** (1597-1667) abt. 1600, AG, MX.
      The known children of Cristobal Martinez Lozano (b) and Maria de Islas were:
        c1.   LUISA de ISLA (1602-1676).
        c2.   JUANA LOZANO ISLA (1603-1688).
        c3.   JACINTO LOZANO ISLA (1610-1673).
        c4.   ISABEL LOZANO ISLA (1612-1676).
        c5.   CATALINA LOZANO ISLA (1613-1683).
        c6.   ANA MARIA HERNANDEZ LOZANO (1614-1659).
        c7.   ANA MARTINA LOZANO ISLA (1615-1716).
        c8A.   LORENZO LOZANO ISLA (1617-).
        c8B.   LEONOR LOZANO ISLA (1617-1670).
        c9.   ISLA JUANA LOZANO (1618-).
        c10.   MAGDALENA LOZANO ISLAS (1619-1666).
        c11.   CRISTOBAL LOZANO MARTINEZ de ISLA (1620-1683).
b2.   MARIA LOZANO MARTINEZ (1575-1647).
b3.   FRANCISCO GONZALEZ MARTINEZ (1578-).
b4.   JACINTO HERNANDEZ LOZANO y MARTINEZ (1588-).

MARIA de ISLA de LAVEZZARI (1597-1667) was born 1597, Nochistian de Mejia, Zacatecas, Mexico. Her death/burial date was 19 June 1667, El Sagrario, Aguascalientes, Aguascalientes, Mexico. She was the grandchild of LEONOR VALDERRAMA y MOCTEZUMA and Captain DIEGO ARIAS de SOTELO. Her name was written many ways including Maria Martinez de Sotomayor, Maria de Yslas, *Maria de la Isla y Navarro de Gabay y Arias de Sotelo de Valderrama Moctezuma* and *Maria Gonzales de Isla y Lavezzari Moctezuma.*

The known children of Cristobal Martinez Lozano and Maria de Isla de Lavezzari (a), who married abt. 1600, Aguascalientes, Aguascalientes, Mexico, were:
b1.   LUISA de ISLA (1602-1676).
b2.   JUANA LOZANO ISLA (1603-1688).
b3.   JACINTO LOZANO ISLA (1610-1673).
b4.   ISABEL LOZANO ISLA (1612-1676).
b5.   CATALINA LOZANO ISLA (1613-1683).
b6.   ANA MARIA HERNANDEZ LOZANO (1614-1659).
b7.   ANA MARTINA LOZANO ISLA (1615-1716).
b8A. LORENZO LOZANO ISLA (1617-).
b8B. LEONOR LOZANO ISLA (1617-1670).
b9.   ISLA JUANA LOZANO (1618-).
b10. MAGDALENA LOZANO ISLAS (1619-1666).
b11. CRISTOBAL LOZANO MARTINEZ de ISLA (1620-1683).

The parents of FRANCISCO BENITO GONZALEZ de ISLA y LAVEZZARI were BERNARDO GONZALEZ de ISLA y LAVEZZARI (1514-1558) and MAGDALENA de LAVEZZARI y CHAVEZ ALVARADO (1518-) who married 27 April 1536, San Juan Bautista, Ostuncalco, Guezaltenango, Guatemala.

The known children of BERNARDO GONZALEZ de ISLA y LAVEZZARI (1514-1558) and MAGDALENA de LAVEZZARI y CHAVEZ ALVARADO (1518-) (a) were:
b1.   JUAN de ISLA de LAVEZZARI (1535-).
b2.   BERTOLOME ISLA de LAVEZZARI (1535-).
b3.   SEBASTIAN de ISLA de LAVEZZARI (1537-).
b4.   MAGDALENA de LAVEZZARI (1540-).
b5.   BERNARDO de ISLA de LAVEZZARI (1545-).
b6.   **FRANCISCO BENITO GONZALEZ de ISLA y LAVEZZARI** (1558-).

JUANA NAVARRO de GABAY y ARIAS de SOTELO y MOCTEZUMA (1568-1651) was the child of Captain MARTIN NAVARRO de GABAY (1554-1610) and PETRONILA ARIAS SOTELO y VALDERRAMA MOCTEZUMA (1552-1628).

FRANCISCO BENITO GONZALEZ de ISLA y LAVEZZARI (1558-) married JUANA NAVARRO de GABAY y ARIAS de SOTELO y MOCTEZUMA (1568-1651) about 1588, Nochistlan, Nueva Galicia, Nueva Espana (Zacatecas, Mexico).

The known children of **JUANA NAVARRO de GABAY y ARIAS de SOTELO MOCTEZUMA** (1568-1651) and FRANCISCO BENITO GONZALES de ISLA y LAVEZZARI (1588-) (a) were:
b1.   MAGDALENA GONZALES de ISLA de LAVEZZARI y NAVARRO (1585-).
b2.   MAGDALENA (MARIA) GONZALES de ISLA de LAVEZARRI (1590-).
b3.   **PETRONA** GONZALES de ISLA de LAVEZZARI y NAVARRO (1590; died, Aguascalientes, Aguascalientes, Mexico).

b4. **MARIA de ISLA de LAVEZZARI** (1597-1667, Aguascalientes, Aguascalientes, Mexico). Married CRISTOBAL LOZANO MARTINEZ (1565-1646) abt. 1600, Aguascalientes, Aguascalientes, Mexico.
b5. BERNARDINO GONZALEZ de ISLA y LAVEZZARI (1608-1681).

The parents of Captain JUAN HERNANDEZ LOZANO were ALONSO HERNANDEZ LOZANO (1513-) and MARIA ZAPATA (1515-). The parents of INEZ MARTINEZ de VACA y GONZALEZ were FRANCISCO MARTINEZ de VACA (1524-) and ISABEL GONZALEZ (1520-1550).

The parents of CRISTOBAL LOZANO MARTINEZ (1565-1646) were Captain JUAN HERNANDEZ LOZANO y ZAPEDA (1530-) and INEZ MARTINEZ de VACA y GONZALEZ (1551-) who married abt. 1575, Aguascalientes, Aguascalientes, Mexico.

The known children of Captain JUAN HERNANDEZ LOZANO y ZAPEDA (1530-) and INEZ MARTINEZ de VACA y GONZALEZ (1551-) (a) were:
a1. **CRISTOBAL LOZANO MARTINEZ** (1565-1646). Married **MARIA de ISLAS de LAVEZZARI** (1597-1667) abt. 1600, Aguascalientes, AG, MX.
a2. MARIA LOZANO MARTINEZ (1575-1647).
a3. FRANCISCO GONZALEZ MARTINEZ (1578-).
a4. JACINTO HERNANDEZ LOZANO y MARTINEZ (1588-).

The two following maps outline our early Mexico links: MAP A/MAP B

Map A

PETRONILA MOCTEZUMA
m. MARTIN NAVARRO de GABAY

ANA FRANCISCA NAVARRO de GABAY | JUANA NAVARRO de GABAY
(Born abt. 1573-1577/Married 1600 | (b. 1568/Married 1588
Aguascalientes, Aguascalientes, MX) | Zacatecas, MX)
LOPE RUIZ de ESPARZA | FRANCISCO BENITO GONZALEZ
 | de ISLA y LAVEZZARI

BERNARDO RUIZ de ESPZARA | PETRONA | MARIA
(b.1608, Aguascalientes, AG, MX) | de ISLA (b. 1590) | de ISLA (b. 1597)
 | | m. CRISTOBAL
 | | LOZANO MARTINEZ

--LEONOR LOZANO
ISLA (b. 1617)

PETRONA RUIZ de ESPARZA
(Christening 25 January 1635, El Sagrario, AG AG, MX)
(Witness: PETRONA de ISLA)
(Father: Bernardo Ruiz de Esparza/Mother: Leonor de Lozano)
Married JUAN de MEDINA
(Death/burial 1697, Asuncion de Maria, Aguascalientes, Aguascalientes, MX).

FRANCISCA MEDINA ESPARZA
(Born abt. 1663, AG, AG, MX/d. 1745, Aguascalientes, Aguascalientes, Mexico)
Married ANTONIO CALDERON GONZALEZ

CRISTOBAL CALDERON MEDINA
(Christening 28 December 1685, Aguascalientes, Aguascalientes, Mexico)
Married MANUELA HERRERA JAEN
(Christening 14 June 1687, El Sagrario, Aguascalientes, Aguascalientes, Mexico)
(Father: JUAN de HERRERA/ Mother: MICHAELA CLARA JAEN)

FRANCISCA XAVIERA CALDERON HERRERA
(Baptized 18 December 1707, El Sagrario, AG, AG, MX)
Married GASPAR ANTONIO (MEDINA y GOMEZ) MANRIQUE de LARA

JOSEPH MANUEL MANRIQUE de LARA (HERRERA)
(Born 30 October 1734, Leon, Guanajuato, Mexico)

Map B

MOCTEZUMA XOCOYOTZIN
Married TZIHUACXOCHITZIN ACATLAN

MARIANA LEONOR de MOCTEZUMA (1510-1550)
Married CHRISTOBAL de VALDERRAMA (b. 1490, Spain), 1531 Mexico City, MX

LEONOR de VALDERRAMA (1532, DF, MX; d. 1562, Mexico City, MX)
Married DIEGO ARIAS de SOTELO (1526, Zamora, Castile, Spain, Teocaltiche, Jalisco, Mexico -1566) during 1550, Mexico City, Mexico.

PETRONILA ARIAS SOTELO y VALDERRAMA de MOCTEZUMA (1552, Mexico City, MX; died 1628, Aguascalientes, Aguascalientes, Mexico)
Married MARTIN GABAY de NAVARRO (1554, Spain; died 1610, Mexico)

JUANA NAVARRO de GABAY ------------------------------ ANA FRANCISCA NAVARRO
y ARIAS de SOTELO y VALDERRAMA   de GABAY y ARIAS de SOTELO
MOCTEZUMA (1568-1651)   y VALDERRAMA MOCTEZUMA (1573-1652)
Married: FRANCISCO BENITO GONZALEZ   Married LOPE RUIZ de ESPARZA
         de ISLA y LAVEZZARI

PETRONA	MARIA	BERNARDO
de ISLA	de ISLA	RUIZ de ESPARZA
(1590)	(1597)	(1608-)
	m. CRISTOBAL	
	LOZANO	
	LEONOR LOZANO ISLA	
	(1617-)--	

PETRONA RUIZ de ESPARZA (1635-1697)
Married JUAN MEDINA

FRANCISCA de MEDINA (abt. 1663-1745)
Married ANTONIO CALDERON GONZALEZ

CRISTOBAL CALDERON MEDINA (1685-)
Married MANUELA HERRERA JAEN

FRANCISCA XAVIERA CALDERON HERRERA (1707-)
Married GASPAR ANTONIO MANRIQUE de LARA (1702)

JOSEPH MANUEL MANRIQUE de LARA (1734-)

APPENDIX X: RUIZ de ESPARZA

The children of Lope "el Menor" Ruiz de Esparza and Ana Francisca Gabay Navarro y Moctezuma were:

(a1) **SALVADOR RUIZ de ESPARZA (**1595-1680). Born abt. 1595, Aguascalientes, Aguascalientes, Mexico. Died 24 October 1680, Aguascalientes, Aguascalientes, Mexico.

(signed baptismal record for grandchild of Francisco Sotelo and Clara Jaen's grandchild, the son of MARTIN RUIZ de ESPARZA).

Married MARIA CUELLAR de VIELMA MORALES about 1618, Aguascalientes, Aguascalientes, Mexico.

MARIA CUELLAR de VIELMA MORALES was christened in April 1604, at Sagrario Metropolitano, Guadalajara, Jalisco, Mexico. She was the daughter of Pedro de Cuellar and Jhoana de Vielma. Maria de Vielma's death/burial was 29 September 1679, Asuncion de Maria, Aguascalientes, Aguascalientes, Mexico (Married/White) (Spouse: Salvador de Esparza).

The children of Salvador Ruiz de Esparza (a) and Maria de Vielma were:
b. *ANA ROMANCINA RUIZ, christening 1618, El Sagrario Aguascalientes, Aguascalientes, Mexico (Father: Lope Ruiz de Esparza/Mother FRANCISCA SABADO/ Sibling: Thomasina Ruiz/Sister Ana Thomasina Ruiz). This is a baptismal record which lists a correct sibling of Ana Thomasina Ruiz, but incorrect father/mother's name.*

b1. FRANCO. RUIZ VIELMA, christening 15 December 1619, El Sagrario, Aguascalientes, Aguascalientes, Mexico (Father: Salvador Ruiz de Esparza. Mother: Maria de Vielma).
Married SEBASTIANA del RIO.
The known children of Francisco Ruiz Vielma Esparza (b) and Sebastiana del Rio were:
    c1.   GERONIMA ESPARZA, christening 10 May 1665 San Diego de Alcala, Canatian, Durango, Mexico (Father: Francisco de Esparza/Mother: Sevastiana del Rio).
    c2.   JUAN de DIOS ESPARZA RIO, christening 21 March 1672, El Sagrario Metropolitano, Victoria de Durango, Durango, Mexico (Father: Franco. de Esparza/Mother: Sebastiana del Rio).
    c3.   MAGDALENA ESPARZA RIO, christening 29 September 1674, El Sagrario Metropolitano, Victoria de Durango, Durango, Mexico (Father: Franco. de Esparza/Mother: Sebastiana del Rio).
    c4.   FRANCISCA ESPARZA RIO, christening 14 March 1677, El Sagrario Metropolitano, Victoria de Durango, Durango, Mexico (Father: Franco. de Esparza/Mother: Sebastiana del Rio).

b2. ANDRES ESPARZA VIELMA, baptism 29 November 1620, Asuncion de Maria, Aguascalientes, Aguascalientes, Mexico (Andres de Esparza). Died 24 October 1680, Aguascalientes, Aguascalientes, Mexico.
Married (m1) CATALINA de la FUENTE, 7 April 1643, Asuncion de Maria, Aguascalientes, Aguascalientes, Mexico/(m2) VITORIA de SOTOMAYOR on 26 February 1675, El Sagrario, Aguascalientes, Aguascalientes, Mexico.
The known children of Andres Esparza Vielma (b) and Catalina de la Fuente were:
- c1. AMONDE ESPARZA, christening 1643, El Sagrario, Asuncion de Maria, Aguascalientes, Aguascalientes, Mexico (Father: Andres de Esparza/Mother Catalina de la Fuente) (Godparents: Salvador de Esparza/Mother: M. de Vielma).
- c2. SEBASTIANA ESPARZA, christening 19 February 1646, El Sagrario, Aguascalientes, Aguascalientes, Mexico (Father: Andres de Esparza/Mother: Caterina).
- c3. ANTONIO ESPARZA FUENTES, christening 8 July 1651, El Sagrario, Aguascalientes, Aguascalientes, Mexico (Father: Andres de Esparza/Mother: Catherina de Fuentes).
- c4. DIEGO ESPARZA FUENTES, christening 29 November 1654, El Sagrario, Aguascalientes, Aguascalientes, Mexico (Father: Andres de Esparza/Mother: Catalina de la Fuentes).
- c5. JUAN ESPARZA FUENTE, christening June 1657, El Sagrario, Aguascalientes, Aguascalientes, Mexico (Father: Andres de Esparza/Mother: Catharina de la Fuente).
- c6. DOMINGA ESPARZA FUENTE, christening 25 April 1659, El Sagrario, Aguascalientes, Aguascalientes, Mexico (Father: Andres de Esparza/Mother: Catarina de la Fuente).

Death/Burial: CATALINA de la FUENTE y ARIOLA on 11 October 1674, Asuncion de Maria, Aguascalientes, Aguascalientes, Mexico (Married) (Spouse. Andres de Esparza).
Married VITORIA de SOTOMAYOR on 26 February 1675, El Sagrario, Aguascalientes, Aguascalientes, Mexico (Spouse: Andres de Esparza).
The known children of Andres de Esparza (b) and Vitoria de Sotomayor were:
- c7. MARIA RUIZ de ESPARZA, christening 29 June 1675, christening, Asuncion de Maria, Aguascalientes, Aguascalientes, Mexico (Father: Andres de Esparza/ Mother: Vitoria de Soto Mayor). Died 10 September 1691, Asuncion de Maria, Aguascalientes, Aguascalientes, Mexico (Father: Andres de Esparza/Mother: Vitoria Sotomayor).
- c8. JOSEPHA ESPARZA SOTOMAYOR, christening 19 May 1678, El Sagrario, Aguascalientes, Aguascalientes, Mexico (Father: Andres de Esparza/Mother: Vitoria de Sotomayor).

Death: ANDRES RUIZ de ESPARZA on 24 October 1680, Aguascalientes, Aguascalientes, Mexico.

Death/Burial: VITORIA de SOTOMAYOR on 13 June 1690, Asuncion de Maria, Aguascalientes, Aguascalientes, Mexico (Married/White) (Spouse: Andres de Esparza).

- b3. ANA RUIZ de ESPARZA, born 3 November 1622, Aguascalientes, Aguascalientes, Mexico.
- b4. MARIA FRANCISCA ESPARZA VIELMA, born 10 February 1625/baptized 16 February 1625, El Sagrario, Aguascalientes, Aguascalientes, Mexico (Father: Salvador de Esparza/Mother: Ma. de Vielma). Married NICOLAS de la CERDA. Died/Buried 23 June 1657, Asuncion de Maria, Aguascalientes, Aguascalientes, Mexico (Father: Salvador de Esparza/ Mother: Maria de Bielma).
- b5. NICOLAS ESPARZA BIELMA, christening 28 October 1626, El Sagrario, Aguascalientes, Aguascalientes, Mexico (Father: Salvador de Esparza/ Mother: Maria de Bielma). Confirmation, 16 January 1627, Asuncion de Maria, Aguascalientes, Aguascalientes, Mexico. Christening, 1628, El Sagrario, Aguascalientes, Aguascalientes, Mexico. Died/Buried 21 October 1637, Asuncion de Maria, Aguascalientes, Aguascalientes, Mexico (Father: Salvador de Esparza).
- b6. MANUEL de ESPARZA, baptism 6 June 1634/5, Asuncion de Maria, Aguascalientes, Aguascalientes, Mexico (Father: Salvador de Esparza/ Mother: Maria de Bielma). Married MARIA RANGAL on 6 February 1670, Asuncion de Maria, Aguascalientes, Aguascalientes, Mexico.
- b7. JUAN JULIO RUIZ de ESPARZA VIELMA, christening 20 May 1636, El Sagrario, Aguascalientes, Aguascalientes, Mexico (Father: Salvador de Esparza/ Mother: Maria de Bielma) (Registered at *Parroquial Villa de Aguascalientes, Nueva Galicia, Nueva Espana*). Married JOSEPHA de la PUERTA on 10 December 1658, San Jose Hidalgo de Parral, Chihuahua, Mexico (Father: Salvador Ruis de Esparza/Mother: Maria de MORALES).
- b8. MATEO RUIZ de ESPARZA, born 9 October 1640, Aguascalientes, Aguascalientes, Mexico.
- b9. AMONDE ESPARZA, christening 1643, El Sagrario, Aguascalientes, Aguascalientes, Mexico (Father: Salvador de Esparza/Mother: M. de Vielma).
- b10. ANTONIO/A ESPARZA VIELMA, christening 11 October 1643, El Sagrario, Aguascalientes, Aguascalientes, Mexico (Father: Salvador de Esparza/ Mother: Maria de Vielma).

Death/Burial: MARIA de VIELMA, 29 September 1679, Asuncion de Maria, Aguascalientes, Aguascalientes, Mexico (Married/White) (Spouse: Salvador de Esparza).

Death/Burial: SALVADOR de ESPARZA, 24 October 1680, Asuncion de Maria, Aguascalientes, Aguascalientes, Mexico (Widow/Spouse: Maria de Vielma).

(a2) <u>**ANA TOMASINA RUIZ de ESPARZA**</u>, born abt. 1597, Aguascalientes, Aguascalientes, Mexico. Died abt. October 1667, Aguascalientes, Aguascalientes, Mexico (*no record*).

<u>Married</u> FRANCISCO RODRIQUEZ SANCHEZ de MONTES de OCA (1593-?) on 25 November 1618, Asuncion de Maria, Aguascalientes, Aguascalientes, Mexico.

<u>The known children of Francisco Rodriquez Sanchez Montes de Oca and Ana Tomasina Ruiz de Esparza (a) were:</u>

b. *ANA ROMANCINA RUIZ, christening 1618, El Sagrario, Aguascalientes, Aguascalientes, Mexico (Father: Lope Ruiz de Esparza/Mother FRANCISCA SABADO/ Sibling: Thomasina Ruiz/Sister Ana Thomasina Ruiz). This is a baptismal record which lists a correct name of Ana Thomasina Ruiz, but incorrect father/mother's name.*

b1. JOANA SANCHES RUIZ, christening 23 September 1619, El Sagrario, Aguascalientes, Aguascalientes, Mexico (Father: Frco. Sanches Montes de Oca/Mother: Ana Tomasina Ruiz de Esparza).

b2. FRANCISCA SANCHEZ, born abt. 1620, Aguascalientes, Aguascalientes, Mexico. <u>Married</u> ANTONIO de IBARRA on 17 August 1639, Asuncion de Maria, Aguascalientes, Aguascalientes, Mexico (Parents: Ana Ruiz de Esparza and Francisco Rodriquez de Montes de Oca).

b3. NICOLAS SANCHES RUIZ, christening 30 April 1621, El Sagrario, Aguascalientes, Mexico (Father: Franco. Sanches/Mother: Ana Thomasina Ruiz).

b4. LORENZO RUIZ, christening 24 September 1622, El Sagrario, Aguascalientes, Aguascalientes, Mexico (Mother: Ana Ruiz).

b5. ESTEBAN SANCHEZ RUIZ, christening 11 June 1623, El Sagrario, Aguascalientes, Aguascalientes, Mexico (Father: Franco. Sanches de Montes de Oca/Mother: Ana Thomasina Ruiz de Esparza).

(a3) <u>**MARTIN RUIZ de ESPARZA,**</u> born 3 August 1600, Aguascalientes, Aguascalientes, Mexico. Died 25 October 1674, Aguascalientes, Aguascalientes, Mexico.

<u>Married</u> MARIA LOPEZ de ELIZALDE was born abt. 1597, Aguascalientes, Aguascalientes, Mexico, the daughter of Juan Lopez de Elizalde and Leonor Beccerra y Sanchez de Mendoza. Maria Lopez de Elizalde was the widow of Don Juan de Luevana when she married Martin Ruiz de Esparza. Maria Lopez y Lizalde died 4 March 1678, Asuncion de Maria, Aguascalientes, Aguascalientes, Mexico (Widowed) (Spouse: Martin de Esparza).

Maria Lopez de Elizalde y Becerra <u>married</u> (m1) Don Juan de Luevana, born Spain.

The known child of Juan de Luevana and Maria Lopes de Elizalde (a) was:
- b1. JUAN de LUEVANA y LOPES de LIZALDE, christening 14 March 1618, El Sagrario, Aguascalientes, Aguascalientes, Mexico. Married MARIA de ALBARADO. Death/burial 1672, Asuncion de Maria, Aguascalientes, Aguascalientes, Mexico (Married/White) (Spouse: Maria de Albarado).

    The known children of Juan de Luebana (b) and Maria de Albarado were:
    - c1. FABIANA LUEBANA ALBARADO, christening 23 January 1646, El Sagrario, Aguascalientes, Aguascalientes, Mexico.
    - c2. JUAN LUEBANA ALBARADO, christening, 8 May 1647, El Sagrario, Aguascalientes, Aguascalientes, Mexico.
    - c3. LORENZA de LUEBANA de ALBARADO, christening 20 September 1649, El Sagrario, Aguascalientes, Aguascalientes, Mexico.
    - c4. NICOLAS LUEBANA ALBARADO, christening 14 September 1651, El Sagrario, Aguascalientes, Aguascalientes, Mexico.

Dona Maria Lopez de Elizalde married (m2) Martin Ruiz de Esparza about 1625, Aguascalientes, Aguascalientes, Mexico.

The known children of Martin Ruiz de Esparza (a) and Maria Lopez de Elizalde were:
- b1. IGNACIO RUIZ de ESPARZA y LOPEZ de LIZALDE. Married ELENA SOTELO JAEN (born abt. 1639, Aguascalientes, Aguascalientes, Mexico; Died 24 January 1673, Aguascalientes, Aguascalientes, Mexico) on 5 August 1651, El Sagrario, Aguascalientes, Aguascalientes, Mexico (Alternate spellings of names were YGNACIO de ESPARZA and HELENA SOTELO de JAEN). Died 24 January 1673, Aguascalientes, Aguascalientes, Mexico.

    The known children of Ignacio Ruiz de Esparza (a) and Elena Sotelo Jaen were:
    - c1. TERESA RUIZ de ESPARZA, christening 14 November 1652, El Sagrario, Aguascalientes, Aguascalientes, Mexico (Father: Ygnasio Ruiz de Esparza/Mother: Elena Sotelo).
    - c2. MIGUEL RUIZ de ESPARZA, (MIGUEL RUIS XAEN), christening 20 May 1654, El Sagrario, Aguascalientes, Aguascalientes, Mexico (Father: Ygnasio Ruis/Mother: Elena de Xaen). Record #2: MIGUEL RUIS XAEN, christening 26 May 1654, El Sagrario, Aguascalientes, Aguascalientes, Mexico (Father: Ygnasio Ruis/Mother: Elena de Xaen).
    - c3. MARIA de JAEN y ESPARZA, christening 1654, El Sagrario, Aguascalientes, Aguascalientes, Mexico (Father: Ignacio Ruiz). Died 9 March 1710, Aguascalientes, Aguascalientes, Mexico) (Text: "Maria Ruiz de Esparza y Sotelo Jaen." Daughter of Elena Sotelo Jaen and Ignacio Ruiz de Esparza).
    - c3. SEBASTIAN RUIZ de ESPARZA.
    - c4. JUAN RUIZ de ESPARZA.
- b2. MARTIN RUIZ de ESPARZA. Married FRANCISCA SOTELO JAEN (Christening 24 August 1638, El Sagrario, Aguascalientes, Aguascalientes, Mexico; d.

15 May 1691, Aguascalientes, Aguascalientes, Mexico) on 21 February 1658 (FRANCA. de los REIES to MARTIN de ESPARSA), El Sagrario, Aguascalientes, Aguascalientes, Mexico.

The known children of Martin Ruiz de Esparza (b) and Francisca Sotelo Jaen were:

- c1. MARIA de ESPARZA SOTELO, christening 27 August 1665, Aguascalientes, Aguascalientes, Mexico (Mother: Francisca Sotelo/Father: Martin de Esparsa) (Godfather/Grandfather: Martin Ruiz de Esparza y Gabay Sotelo Moctezuma). Death/Burial for MARIA de ESPARSA de JAEN on 12 January 1673, Asuncion de Maria, Aguascalientes, Aguascalientes, Mexico (Father: Martin de Esparza/Mother: Francisca de Jean) (Single/White).
- c2. CLARA ESPARZA JAEN, christening 8 November 1667, El Sagrario, Aguascalientes, Aguascalientes, Mexico (Father: Martin de Esparza/Mother: Franca. de Jaen).
- c3. JOSEPH RUIZ ESPARZA, christening (JOSEPH de ESPARZA de JAEN) on 29 May 1673, Aguascalientes, Aguascalientes, Mexico (Father: Martin de Esparza/Mother: Francisca de Jaen). Buried (JOSEPH RUIS ESPARZA) on 28 March 1744, Asuncion de Maria, Aguascalientes, Aguascalientes, Mexico (Father: Martin Esparza/ Mother: Francisca Sotelo) (Married/White) (Spouse: JUANA NICOLAS).
- c4. MARTIN ESPARZA SOTELO, christening 2 July 1675, El Sagrario, Aguascalientes, Aguascalientes, Mexico (Father: Martin de Esparza/Mother: Franca. Sotelo y Xaen). Married MARIA de CASTANEDA on 5 May 1704 (MARTIN RUIZ de ESPARZA), Pinos San Matias, Zacatecas, Mexico.
- c5. JUANA ESPARZA JAEN, christening on 7 December 1677, El Sagrario, Aguascalientes, Aguascalientes, Mexico (Father: Martin de Esparza/Mother: Franca. de Jaen).
- c6. BLAS ESPARZA JAEN, christening on 19 February 1680, El Sagrario, Aguascalientes, Mexico (Father: Martin de Esparza/Mother: Franca. de Jaen). Married MICHAELA de AMADOR on 3 December 1707, Death/Buried 1741, Asuncion de Maria, Aguascalientes, Aguascalientes, Mexico (Father: Martin Esparza/ Mother: Francisca Sotelo) (Married/White) (Spouse: MICAELA AMADOR).
- c7. YGNACIO ESPARZA, birth unknown, Aguascalientes, Aguascalientes, Mexico. Married YNES GARCIA. Death/Buried 1738, Asuncion de Maria, Aguascalientes, Aguascalientes, Mexico (Father: Martin Esparza/Mother: Francisca Sotelo) (Widow/White) (Spouse: YNES GARCIA).

Death/Burial: MARTIN (RUIZ) de ESPARZA on 25 October 1674, Asuncion de Maria, Aguascalientes, Aguascalientes, Mexico (Married/White) (Spouse: Maria Lopes).

Death/Burial: MARIA LOPES de LISALDI on 4 March 1678, Asuncion de Maria, Aguascalientes, Aguascalientes, Mexico (Widowed) (Spouse: Martin de Esparza).

(a4) LORENZA RUIZ de ESPARZA, born 1602, Aguascalientes, Aguascalientes, Mexico. Died June 1690, Aguascalientes, Aguascalientes, Mexico.

Married LUIS TISCARENO de MOLINA y MARQUEZ (1598-1660) on 16 May 1623, Asuncion de Maria, Aguascalientes, Aguascalientes, Mexico. The marriage took place in Morcenique, Aguascalientes, Mexico.

Luis Tiscareno de Molina y Marquez was born 1598, Triana, Castile, Spain. He died on 20 February 1660, Aguascalientes, Aguascalientes, Mexico.

The known children of Luis Tiscareno de Molina y Marquez and Lorenza Ruiz de Esparza (a) were:

b1. JUAN *(LUIS)* TISCARENO de MOLINA, born abt. 1624, Aguascalientes, Aguascalientes, Mexico.

b2. LUIS(A) (MARGARITA TISCARENO de MOLINA) de ESCARENO, baptized 4 March 1625, Aguascalientes, Aguascalientes, Mexico. Christening 24 March 1625, El Sagrario, Aguascalientes, Aguascalientes, Mexico (Father: Luis de Escareno/Mother: Lorenza de Esparza). Married ANDRES LOPES de NAVA on 3 September 1652, Aguascalientes, Aguascalientes, Mexico.

b3. ELVIRA de TISCARENO de MOLINA y MARQUEZ, baptism 11 May 1627, Asuncion de Maria, Aguascalientes, Aguascalientes, Mexico.

b4. LUISA de TISCARENO, born abt. 1630, Aguascalientes, Aguascalientes, Mexico. Confirmation 5 June 1634, Asuncion de Maria, Aguascalientes, Aguascalientes, Mexico.

b5. MARIA CARENO RUIZ (MARIA TISCARENO de MOLINA), christening 13 March 1634, El Sagrario, Aguascalientes, Aguascalientes, Mexico (Father: Luis Careno/Mother: Lorenza Ruiz).

b6. LORENZA TISCARENO RUIZ, christening 26 September 1636, El Sagrario, Aguascalientes, Aguascalientes, Mexico (Father: Luis Tiscareno/Mother: Lorenza Ruiz de Esparza).

b7. BEATRIZ TISCARENO RUIZ, christening 22 March 1639, Aguascalientes, Aguascalientes, Mexico (Father: Luis Tiscareno/Mother: Lorenza Ruiz). Married BALTHASAR DIAS on 2 March 1668, Aguascalientes, Aguascalientes, Mexico. Death/Burial 10 April 1734, Asuncion de Maria, Aguascalientes, Aguascalientes, Mexico (Widowed) (Spouse: Balthasar Dias) (Father: Luis de Tiscareno/Mother: Lorenza Ruiz de Esparza).

b8. MARGARITA TISCARENO RUIZ (TISCARENO de MOLINA), christening 27 January 1642, El Sagrario, Aguascalientes, Aguascalientes, Mexico (Father: Luis Tiscareno/Mother: Lorenza Ruiz). Baptized 27 June 1642, Aguascalientes, Aguascalientes, Mexico (Father: Luis Tiscareno de Molina y Marquez/Mother: Lorenza Esparza).

b9. JUANA TISCARENO RUIZ (TISCARENO de MOLINA) christening 20 August 1644, Aguascalientes, Aguascalientes, Mexico (Father: Luis Tiscareno de Molina y Marquez/Mother: Lorenza Esparza). Death/Burial 1565, Asuncion de Maria, Aguascalientes, Aguascalientes, Mexico (Father: Luis de Tiscareno/Mother: Lorenza Ruiz de Esparza).

Death/Burial: LUIS de TISCARENO on 20 February 1660, Asuncion de Maria, Aguascalientes, Aguascalientes, Mexico (Married/White) (Spouse: Lorenza Ruiz de Esparza).

Death/Burial: LORENZA RUIZ de ESPARZA on 3 June 1690, Asuncion de Maria, Aguascalientes, Aguascalientes, Mexico (Widowed) (Spouse: Luis Tiscareno).

(a5) JACINTO RUIZ de ESPARZA, born 1604, Aguascalientes, Aguascalientes, Mexico. Died 27 July 1679, Aguascalientes, Aguascalientes, Mexico.

Married Dona JUANA LOPES de ELIZALDE was born abt. 1610, Aguascalientes, Aguascalientes, Mexico and the daughter of Juan Lopez de Elizalde and Leonor Beccerra y Sanchez de Mendoza. She died on 21 May 1682, Aguascalientes, Aguascalientes, Mexico (Widowed/White) (Spouse: Jacinto Ruiz de Esparza).

The known children of Jacinto Ruiz Esparza (a) and Juana Lopez Elizalde were:
b1. MARIA RUIZ de ESPARZA, christening 5 June 1624, Aguascalientes, Aguascalientes, Mexico (Father: Jacinto Esparza/Mother: Juana Lopes). Married NICOLAS de la TORRE. Death/Burial (MARIA de ESPARZA) on 14 March 1672, Asuncion de Maria, Aguascalientes, Aguascalientes, Mexico (Married/White) (Spouse: Nicolas de la Torre).
b2. TERESA RUIZ de ESPARZA, christening 19 February 1636, Asuncion de Maria, Aguascalientes, Aguascalientes, Mexico (Mother: Ju. Lopez). Married JOSEPH ALONSO on 18 June 1666, El Sagrario, Aguascalientes, Aguascalientes, Mexico. Died abt. 1718, Aguascalientes, Aguascalientes, Mexico.
b3. PABLO RUIZ LISALDI, christening 10 December 1637, El Sagrario, Aguascalientes, Aguascalientes, Mexico. (Father: Jacintho Ruiz de Esparza/Mother: Jua. De Lisaldi). Married ANA de la CRUZ on 22 December 1690, Santa Maria del Marquesado, Oaxaca de Juarez, Oaxaca, Mexico (Father: Jacinto Ruiz/Mother: Juana Ruiz).
b4. NICOLASA ESPARZA LOPES, christening 11 April 1642, El Sagrario, Aguascalientes, Aguascalientes, Mexico (Father: Jacinto de Esparza Mother: Jua. Lopes de Lizaldi) (*twin*). Death/Burial 1674, Asuncion de Maria, Aguascalientes, Aguascalientes, Mexico (Father: Jacinto de Esparza/Mother: Juana Lizaldi).
b5. JOSEPH ESPARZA LOPES, christening 11 April 1642, El Sagrario, Aguascalientes, Aguascalientes, Mexico (Father: Jacinto de Esparza/

Mother: Jua. Lopes de Lizalde) (*twin*). Died prior to 1649, Aguascalientes, Aguascalientes, Mexico.

b6. THERESA ESPARZA LISARDI, christening 1 June 1645, El Sagrario, Aguascalientes, Aguascalientes, Mexico (Father: Jacinto de Esparza/ Mother: Joana de Lizaldi).

b7. JACINTO ESPARZA LISARDI, christening 31 March 1645, El Sagrario, Aguascalientes, Aguascalientes, Mexico (Farther: Jasinto de Esparza/ Mother: Juana de Lizaldi). Married MATHIANA GARCIA on 2 June 1679, Aguascalientes, Aguascalientes, Mexico. Died 4 November 1697, Aguascalientes, Aguascalientes, Mexico (Father: Jacinto de Esparza/ Mother: Juana de Lizaldi).

b8. LUISA ESPARZA LISARDI, christening 28 February 1648, El Sagrario, Aguascalientes, Aguascalientes, Mexico (Father: Jacinto de Esparza/ Mother: Juana de Lizalde).

b9. JOSEPH ESPARZA LISARDI, christening 4 October 1649, El Sagrario, Aguascalientes, Aguascalientes, Mexico (Father: Jacinto de Esparza/ Mother: Juana de Lisaldi). Death/Burial 15 December 1673, Asuncion de Maria Aguascalientes, Aguascalientes, Mexico (Father: Jacinto de Esparza/Mother: Juana de Lizaldi).

b10. DOMINGO RUIZ ESPARZA, born 1651, Aguascalientes, Aguascalientes, Mexico. Married NICOLASA de SESENA y ARIAS on 9 April 1681, El Sagrario, Aguascalientes, Aguascalientes, Mexico. Death 1740, Asuncion de Maria, Aguascalientes, Aguascalientes, Mexico (Father: Jacinto Esparza/Mother: Juana Lizalde) (Married/White) (Spouse: NICOLASA SESENO).

b11. FRANCA. ESPARZA LISALDI, christening 30 September 1655, El Sagrario, Aguascalientes, Aguascalientes, Mexico (Father: Jacinto de Esparza/ Mother: Juana de Lizaldi). Married (m1) NICOLAS DURAN on 5 March 1669, Aguascalientes, Aguascalientes, Mexico/(m2) JUAN ARANDA, Aguascalientes, Aguascalientes, Mexico. Died 1741, Aguascalientes, Aguascalientes, Mexico (Father: Jacinto Esparza/Mother: Juana Lizalde) (Married/White) (Spouse: Juan Aranda).

b12. JUANA ESPARZA LISALDI, christening 7 June 1658, El Sagrario, Aguascalientes, Aguascalientes, Mexico (Father: Jacinto de Esparza/Mother: Juana de Lisaldi). Death/Burial 1674, Asuncion de Maria, Aguascalientes, Aguascalientes, Mexico (Father: Jacinto de Esparza/Mother: Juana di Lizaldi).

(b13). ANA de ESPARZA de GUEVARA, christening 8 June 1640, El Sagrario, Aguascalientes, Aguascalientes, Mexico (Father: Jacinto de Esparza/ Mother: JULIA de GUEVARA.)

Death/Burial: JASINTO de ESPARZA during 1679, Asuncion de Maria, Aguascalientes, Aguascalientes, Mexico (Married/White) (Spouse: Juana de Lisaldi).

Death/Burial: JUANA de LISALDI on 21 May 1682, Asuncion de Maria, Aguascalientes, Aguascalientes, Mexico (Widowed/White) (Spouse: Jacinto de Esparza).

(a6) **PEDRO RUIZ de ESPARZA** (born abt. 1605-1607/1609; died after 12 January 1700, Aguascalientes, Aguascalientes, Mexico).

Prior to his first marriage, it appears Pedro Ruiz de Esparza had children with MARGARITA GONZALEZ GALLEGOS (born abt. 1606, Aguascalientes, Aguascalientes, Mexico). He later married Margarita Gonzales Gallegos after his first wife died. Most genealogical tracking website list Pedro Ruiz de Esparza with a birth year of 1611, but for his children to have been born by 1622, Pedro must have been born prior to 1611. There is no record of Pedro Ruiz de Esparza's Aguascalientes birth.

Married JUANA LOZANO ISLA (1605-1688) (daughter of Don Cristobal and Dona Maria Lozano Isla) on 12 April 1636, Aguascalientes, Aguascalientes, Mexico ("Po. de Esparza,"/Witnesses: Salvador de Esparza and Jacinto Lozano).

The known children of Pedro Ruiz de Esparza (a) and Juana Lozano Isla were:
b1. LUISA ESPARZA LOZANO, christening 6 February 1637, El Sagrario, Aguascalientes, Aguascalientes, Mexico (Father: Po. de Esparza/Mother: Luisa Esparza Lozano).
b2. NICOLAS ESPARZA LOZANO, christening 2 July 1639, El Sagrario, Aguascalientes, Aguascalientes, Mexico (Father: Po. de Esparza/Mother: Jua. Lozano).
b3. MARIA ESPARZA LOZANO, christening 29 December 1641, El Sagrario, Aguascalientes, Aguascalientes, Mexico (Father: Po. de Esparza/Mother: Jua. Lozano).
b4. NICOLASA ESPARZA LOZANO, christening 3 October 1644, El Sagrario, Aguascalientes, Aguascalientes, Mexico (Father: Pedro de Esparza/ Mother: Juana Losano).
b5. MATIANA de ESPARZA LOZANO, christening 18 March 1647, El Sagrario, Aguascalientes, Aguascalientes, Mexico (*Witness: FERNANDO CALDERON*).
b6. ANTONIO ESPARZA LOZANO, christening 19 December 1649, El Sagrario, Aguascalientes, Aguascalientes, Mexico (Father: Po. de Esparza/Mother: Jua. Lozano).
b7. JUAN ESPARZA LOZANO, christening 17 November 1652, El Sagrario, Aguascalientes, Aguascalientes, Mexico (Father: Po. de Esparza/Mother: Juana Lozano). Married ROSA MARTINES de SOTOMALLOR during 1702, Aguascalientes, Aguascalientes, Mexico. Death/Burial 23 September 1742, Asuncion de Maria, Aguascalientes, Aguascalientes, Mexico (Father: Pedro Ruiz Esparza/Mother: Juana Lozano).

b8. LOPE ESPARZA LOZANO, christening 29 April 1655, El Sagrario, Aguascalientes, Aguascalientes, Mexico (Father: Pedro de Esparza/Mother: Juana Lozano).

b9. PEDRO ESPARZA, born unknown date, Aguascalientes, Aguascalientes, Mexico. Death/Burial 1669, Asuncion de Maria, Aguascalientes, Aguascalientes, Mexico.

Death/Burial: JUANA LOZANO on 26 January 1688, Asuncion de Maria, Aguascalientes, Aguascalientes, Mexico (Married/White) (Spouse: Pedro de Esparza).

Married (m2) MARGARITA GONZALES GALLEGOS (daughter of Luis Gonzales and Beatriz Gallegos) on 13 March 1688, El Sagrario, Aguascalientes, Aguascalientes, Mexico (Spouse: Pedro Ruiz de Esparza).

Death/Burial: MARGARITA GONZALES on 12 January 1700, Asuncion de Maria, Aguascalientes, Aguascalientes, Mexico (Married/White) (Spouse: Pedro Ruiz de Esparza).

(Pedro Ruiz de Esparza must have died after 12 January 1700)

The assumed children of Pedro Ruiz de Esparza (a) and (m2) Margarita Gonzales Gallegos (born out of wedlock) were:

b10. MARIANA RUIZ de ESPARZA (GONZALES GALLEGOS), *christening 20 September 1622, El Sagrario, Aguascalientes, Aguascalientes, Mexico (Father: Pedro Ruiz de Esparza/Mother: Margarita Gonzales Gallegos) (Also listed: Luis Gonzales/Beatriz Gallegos, parents of Margarita Gonzales Gallegos) (Godfather: LOPE RUIZ de ESPARZA).*

b11. MARGARITA RUIZ de ESPARZA (GONZALES GALLEGOS), *baptized 24 November 1625, El Sagrario, Aguascalientes, Aguascalientes, Mexico (Father: Pedro Ruiz de Esparza/Mother: Margarita Gonzales Gallegos) (Also listed: Luis Gonzales/Beatriz Gallegos, parents of Margarita Gonzales Gallegos).*

b12. NICOLAS RUIZ de ESPARZA (GONZALES GALLEGOS), *christening 6 June 1634, El Sagario, Aguascalientes, Aguascalientes, Mexico (Father: Pedro Ruiz de Esparza/Mother: Margarita Gonzales Gallegos) (Also listed: Luis Gonzales/Beatriz Gallegos, parents of Margarita Gonzales Gallegos).*

(a7) <u>BERNARDO RUIZ de ESPARZA</u>, born 17 June 1608, Aguascalientes, Aguascalientes, Mexico. Died during 1696, Aguascalientes, Aguascalientes, Mexico.

Married CATALINA LOZANO ISLA (1613-1683) (daughter of Don Cristobal and Dona Maria Lozano Isla) on 27 February 1634, El Sagrario, Aguascalientes,

Aguascalientes, Mexico. Records note they married in the town of Morcenique, Aguascalientes, Aguascalientes, Mexico. Catalina Lozano Isla (1615-1683) was the older sister of Leonor Lozano Isla (1617-1670).

Catalina Lozano Isla was born about 1613 in Villa de Aguascalientes, Aguascalientes, Mexico, the daughter of Don Cristobal and Dona Maria Lozano Isla. She died on 26 July 1683, Aguascalientes, Aguascalientes, Mexico (Married) (Spouse: Bernardo Salado de Esparza).

Bernardo Ruiz de Esparza also used the name, BERNARDO SALADO ESPARZA.

The known child of Bernardo Ruiz (a) and Leonor (Lozano) was:
b1. **PETRONA** RUIZ LOSANO, christening 25 January 1635, El Sagrario, Aguascalientes, Aguascalientes, Mexico (Father: Berdo. Ruiz de Esparza/Mother: Leonor de Losano) (FEMALE) (*Record does not list female child's name, only text: Ruiz Losano.*) (**PETRONA RUIZ de ESPARZA**). Married JUAN MEDINA. Died 1687, Aguascalientes, Aguascalientes, Mexico.

The known children of Petrona de Esparza (b) and Juan Medina were:
   c1.   MARIA de MEDINA ESPARZA, christening 27 September 1659, El Sagrario, Aguascalientes, Aguascalientes, Mexico (Father: Juan Medina/Mother: Petrona de ESPARZA) (*Possibly "Maria Franca. de Medina Esparza*).

   c2.   **FRANCISCA MEDINA ESPARZA**, born abt. 1663, Aguascalientes, Aguascalientes, Mexico. FRANCISCA MEDINA. Married ANTONIO CALDERON. Death/burial during 1745 in Aguascalientes, Mexico (Widow/Spouse of ANTONIO CALDERON).

The known children of Antonio Calderon and Francisca Medina Esparza (c) were:
   d1.   PETRONILA CALDERON MEDINA, christening 17 February 1683, El Sagrario, Aguascalientes, Aguascalientes, Mexico (Father: Antonio de Calderon/Mother: Franca. de Medina) (*Named for mother, Petrona Ruiz de Esparza*).

   d2.   **CRISTOBAL CALDERON MEDINA**, christening 28 December 1685, El Sagrario, Aguascalientes, Aguascalientes, Mexico (and Palo Alto, Calvillo, Aguascalientes, Mexico - Villa de Agelion) (Father: ANTONIO CALDERON/Mother: FRANCA. de MEDINA). Married MANUELA HERRERA JAEN (christening 14 June 1687, El Sagrario, Aguascalientes, Aguascalientes, Mexico [Father: JUAN de HERRERA. Mother: MICHAELA de JAEN]) on 9 February 1707, El Sagrario, Aguascalientes, Aguascalientes, Mexico

The known children of Cristobal Calderon (d) and Manuela Herrera Jaen were:
   e1.   **FRANCA. XAVIERA CALDERON HERRERA**, christened on 18 December 1707, El Sagrario, Aguascalientes,

Aguascalientes, Mexico (Father: Cristobal Calderon/Mother: Manuela Jaen de Herrera) Married GASPAR ANTONIO (MEDINA y GOMEZ) MANRIQUE de LARA by 1729, Leon, Guanajuato, Mexico.

The known child of Gaspar Antonio Manrique de Lara and Franca Xaviera Calderon Herrera (e) was:

    f1.   **JOSEPH MANUEL MANRIQUE de LARA**, baptized 4 November 1734, Leon, Guanajuato, Mexico (Mother: Franca. de Herrera).

- e2. JUAN de SAN PEDRO CALDERON, christening 18 November 1708, El Sagrario, Aguascalientes, Aguascalientes, Mexico (Father: Xpl. de Calderon/Mother: Manuela de Herrera. Married JOSEPHA LABATO. Death/burial 1744, Asuncion de Maria, Aguascalientes, Aguascalientes, Mexico (Father: Crlstobal Calderon. Mother: Manuela Herrera. Race: I. Married/Spouse: Josepha Lobato).
- e3. FRANCISCO de HERRERA, christened on 21 October 1711, El Sagrario, Aguascalientes, Aguascalientes, Mexico (Father: Cristobal de Calderon/Mother: Manuela de Herrera) Record #2 Christening 21 October 1711, Canada Honda, San Francisco de los Roma, Aguascalientes, Mexico (son) (Father: Cristobal de Calderon/Mother: Manuela de Herrera) (*twin*).
- e4. FRANCA. YNES CALDERON, christening 21 October 1711, El Sagrario, Aguascalientes, Aguascalientes, Mexico (Father: Xptobal. de Calderon/Mother: Manuela de Herrera) (daughter) (*twin*).

d3. ISABEL CALDERON, christening in June of 1688, Palo Alto, Calvillo, Aguascalientes, Aguascalientes, Mexico (Beynte) (Father: Antonio Calderson/Mother: *Banz* de Medina). Record #2: YSAVEL CALDERON, christening 27 June 1688, El Sagrario, Aguascalientes, Aguascalientes, Mexico (Father: Antonio Calderon/Mother: Francisca de Medina).

d4. DIOS ANTONIO CALDERON de MEDINA, christening 6 December 1690, Canada Honda, San Francisco de los Romo, Aguascalientes, Aguascalientes, Mexico (Villa de Aguascalientes) (Father: Antonio Calderon/Mother: Francisca de Medina). Record #2: ANTTO. CALDERON MEDINA, christening 6 December 1690, El Sagrario, Aguascalientes, Aguascalientes, Mexico (Father: Antto. Calderon/Mother: Franca. de Medina).

d5. MARIA MANUELA CALDERON MEDINA, christening 7 February 1693, El Sagrario, Aguascalientes, Aguascalientes, Mexico (Father: Antto. Calderon/Mother: Franca. de Medina).

Record #2: MARIA MANUELA CALDERON. Birthdate: 20 February 1692. Christening: 7 February 1693, Palo Alto, Calvillo, Aguascalientes, Mexico (Villa de Ags).

- d6. OLALLA CALDERA MEDINA, christening 2 March 1694, El Sagrario, Aguascalientes, Aguascalientes, Mexico (Father: Anttonio Calderon/Mother: Franca. de Medina).
- d7. JUAN CALDERON MEDINA, christening on 1 December 1698, El Sagrario, Aguascalientes, Aguascalientes, Mexico (Father: Antto. Calderon/Mother: Franca. de Medina).

Married MANUELA ARIAS.

The known child of Juan de Silva Calderon (d) and Manuela Arias was:

- e1. MARIA GERTRUDIS de SILVA CALDERON, Death/Burial: Aguascalientes, Aguascalientes, Mexico (Father: Juan de Silva Calderon/Mother: Manuela Arias. Married [Spouse: Antonio Ramos]. Race: I. Ethnicity: *IRISH*).
- d8. PHELIPA de SILVA CALDERON, born abt. 1700. Death: 2 July 1777, Aguascalientes (San Marcos), Mexico (Widow/ Spouse of THADEO ESPARZA. Ethnicity: *CANADIAN* [Father: Antonio Calderon/ Mother: Francisca Medina]).

The known children of Bernardo Ruiz de Esparza (a) and Catalina Lozano Isla were:

- b2. JOAN BME (*BERNARDO*) SALADO LOZANO, christening 18 December 1636, El Sagrario, Aguascalientes, Aguascalientes, Mexico (Father: Bernardo Salado/Mother: Catalina Lozano).
- b3. MARIA RUIZ LOZANO, christening 9 May 1640, Nuestra Senora de los Dolores, Teocaltiche, Jalisco, Mexico (Father: Bernardo Ruiz de Esparza/Mother: Catalina Lozano) Record #2: Christening 9 May 1640, Aguascalientes, Aguascalientes, Mexico (Father: Bernardo Salado/Mother: Catalina Lozano) (*ethnicity listed as: Canadian*).

    Married: FRANCISCO FLORES (to *MARIA de RUIZ ESPARZA*) on 21 February 1666, Asuncion de Maria, Aguascalientes, Aguascalientes, Mexico. Record #2: Married FRANCO. FLORES to MARIA de ESPARZA on 21 February 1666, El Sagrario, Aguascalientes, Aguascalientes, Mexico.

    The known child of Francisco Flores and Maria Ruiz de Esparza (b) was:
- c1. MARIA FLORES RUIZ, christening 8 May 1668, Villa de Aguas, Aguascalientes, Mexico (Father: Francisco Flores/Mother: Maria Ruiz. Witnesses: BERNARDO SALADO and CATALINA JOSE).

Death/Burial: CATALINA LOSANO on 26 July 1683, Asuncion de Maria, Aguascalientes, Aguascalientes, Mexico (Married) (Spouse: Bernardo Salado de Esparza).

Death/Burial: BERNARDO RUIZ de ESPARZA, abt. during 1696, Aguascalientes, Aguascalientes, Mexico.

(a8) MARIA JUANA RUIZ de ESPARZA, born abt. 1613, Aguascalientes, Aguascalientes, Mexico. Death unknown.

Married NICOLAS de ULLOA MUNOZ de JEREZ (1605-) about 1630, Teocaltiche, Jalisco, Mexico.

The known children of Nicolas de Ulloa Munoz de Jerez and Maria (a) Ruiz de Esparza were:
- b1. BERNARDINA ULLOA RUYS, christening 1 September 1633, El Sagrario, Aguascalientes, Aguascalientes, Mexico (Father: Nicolas de Ulloa/Mother: Maria Ruiz de Esparza).
- b2. JUSEPA ULLOA RUIZ, christening 5 April 1637, El Sagrario, Aguascalientes, Aguascalientes, Mexico (Father: Nicolas de Ulloa/Mother: Maria Ruiz).
- b3. NICOLAS de ULLOA, christening 6 December 1638, El Sagrario, Aguascalientes, Aguascalientes, Mexico (Mother: Maria Ruiz).
- b4. JUAN -, christening 4 September 1639, El Sagrario, Aguascalientes, Aguascalientes, Mexico (Father: Nicolas/Mother: Maria).
- b5. FRANCISCA de ULLOA, christening 1640, El Sagario, Aguascalientes, Aguascalientes, Mexico (Father: Nicolas de Ulloa/Mother: Maria Ruiz).
- b6. RIBERA (?) (male), christening 1645, El Sagrario, Aguascalientes, Aguascalientes, Mexico (Father: Nicolas de Ulloa/Mother: Maria Ruiz).

(a9) CRISTOBAL RUIZ de ESPARZA (1616-1672) born 1616, Aguascalientes, Aguascalientes, Mexico. Died 21 October 1672, Aguascalientes, Aguascalientes, Mexico (*no record*).

Married ISABEL de ALCARAS y PEREZ (1625-1669) on 18 August 1646, El Sagrario, Aguascalientes, Aguascalientes, Mexico.

The known child of Cristobal Ruiz de Esparza (a) and Isabel de Alcaras y Perez was:
- b1. ISABEL ESPARZA PEREZ, christening 13 October 1656, El Sagrario, Aguascalientes, Aguascalientes, Mexico (Father: Cristobal de Esparza Mother: Isabel Peres).

Death/Burial: ISABEL PEREZ on 31 March 1669, Asuncion de Maria, Aguascalientes, Aguascalientes, Mexico (Married/White) (Spouse: Cristobal de Esparza).

(a10) BERNABE RUIZ de ESPARZA, christening 17 June 1618, El Sagrario, Aguascalientes, Aguascalientes, Mexico (Lope Ruiz de Esparza/Mother Franca.). Died 21 October 1662, Aguascalientes, Aguascalientes, Mexico.
Married ANA ORTIZ RAMIREZ (1625-1688) on 11 May 1643, Asuncion de Maria, Aguascalientes, Aguascalientes, Mexico (Parents: Lope Ruiz de Esparza & Francisca Gabay/Pablo Ortiz & Catalina Ramirez).
No known children were born to Bernabe Ruiz de Esparza and Ana Oriz Ramirez.

Death/Burial: Bernabe de Esparza on 21 October 1662, Asuncion de Maria, Aguascalientes, Aguascalientes, Mexico (Married/White) (Spouse: Ana Ortiz).

Death/Burial: Ana Oritz on 10 December 1688, Asuncion de Maria, Aguascalientes, Aguascalientes, Mexico (Widowed/White) (Spouse: Bernabe de Esparza).

(a11) LORENZO (LOPE) RUIZ de ESPARZA, christening 27 August 1620, El Sagrario, Aguascalientes, Aguascalientes, Mexico (Father: Luis Ruiz de Esparza/Mother: Francisca Gabadi). Died 30 October 1693, Aguascalientes, Aguascalientes, Mexico.

Married (m1) ANTONIA del CASTILLO y CONTRERAS (1631-1676) on 2 May 1647, Aguascalientes, Aguascalientes, Mexico.

The known child of Lorenzo Ruiz de Esparza (a) and (m1) Antonia del Castillo y Contreras was:

b1. ANTONIA del CASTILLO, christening on 1647, El Sagrario, Aguascalientes, Aguascalientes, Mexico (Witnesses: Francisca Gavadia, Jose Ruiz de Esparza, Pedro Ruiz de Esparza).

Death/Burial: Antonia de Contreras during 1676, Asuncion de Maria, Aguascalientes, Aguascalientes, Mexico (Married/White) (Spouse: Lorenzo Ruiz de Esparza).

Married (m2) JOSEPHA de SANDI y AGUILERA on 1 August 1677, El Sagrario, Aguascalientes, Aguascalientes, Mexico.

The known children of Lorenzo Ruiz de Esparza (a) and Josepha de Sandi y Aguilera were:

b2. LORENZO ESPARZA SANDI, christening 24 December 1678, El Sagrario, Aguascalientes, Aguascalientes, Mexico (Father: Lorenzo de Esparza/ Mother: Josepha de Sandi).

b3. ANA ESPARZA SANDI, christening August 1682, Palo Alto, Calvillo, Aguascalientes, Aguascalientes, Mexico (Father: Lorenzo de Esparza/ Mother: Josepha Sandi).

Death/Burial: Lorenzo de Esparza on 30 October 1693, Asuncion de Maria, Aguascalientes, Aguascalientes, Mexico (Married/White) (Spouse: Josepha de Aguilera).

~~~~~~

To repeat, the parents of Petronila Arias Sotelo y Valderrama were DIEGO ARIAS de SOTELO y NUNEZ (1526-1566) and DONA LEONOR VALDERRAMA (1532-1662) who married 1550, Mexico City, Mexico.

PETRONILLA ARIAS SOTELO y VALDERRAMA married Captain MARTIN NAVARRO de GABAY (1554-1610).

The child of MARTIN NAVARRO de GABAY and PETRONILLA ARIAS SOTELO y VALDERRAMA (1552-1628) was ANA FRANCISCA GABAY NAVARRO y ARIAS MOCTEZUMA (Born 1577, Nueva Galicia, New Spain. Died 30 March 1652, Aguascalientes, Mexico) who married Lope II Ruiz de Esparza and whose grandchild was PETRONA RUIZ de ESPARZA.

~~~~~~

APPENDIX XI - LOZANO-ISLA

MARIA de ISLA de LAVEZZARI was also known as MARIA GONZALES de ISLA y LAVEZARES. She was the daughter of FRANCISCO GONZALES MARTINEZ and Dona MAGDALENA LAVEZZARES (born abt. 1580-1597; died 18 June 1667, Aguascalientes, Aguascalientes, Mexico). MARIA de ISLA married CRISTOBAL LOZANO MARTINEZ (1565-1646) about 1600 in Aguascalientes, Aguascalientes, Mexico.

The parents of Cristobal Martin Lozano, also known as Cristobal Martinez Lozano, were Captain JUAN LOZANO and INEZ MARTINEZ.

Death/Burial CRISTOVAL MARTINEZ LOZANO on 5 May 1646, Asuncion de Maria, Aguascalientes, Aguascalientes, Mexico.

The known children of Cristobal Hernandez Lozano y Martinez de Vaca and Maria Gonzales de Isla de Lavezzari were:

b1. LUISA de ISLA, born abt. 1602, AG, AG, MX. Married ANTONIO de AGUAYO 25 February 1631, Zacatecas, Mexico.
The known children of Luisa de Isla (b) and Antonio de Aguayo were:
- c1. MARIA ANA de AGUAYO, born abt. 1620, Nochistlan, Nochistlan de Majia, Zacatecas, Mexico. Died July 1702, Nochistlan, Nochistlan de Majia, Zacatecas, Mexico.
- c2. ANDREA de AGUAYO, born abt. 1635, Nochistlan, Nochistlan de Majia, Zachetecas, Mexico. Married NICOLAS RODRIGUEZ on 5 June 1654, Nochistlan, Nochistlan de Mejia, Zacatecas, Mexico. Died July 1702, Nochistlan, Nochistlan de Majia, Zacatecas, Mexico.
- c3. JUAN AGUAYO de ISLA, christening 3 March 1635, Zacatecas, Mexico (Father: Antonio de Aguayo y Luisa de Ysla).
- c4. MAGDALENA AGUAYO, born abt. 1640. Zacatecas, Mexico.
- c5. LUISA DE AGUAYO, born abt. 1641, Zacatecas, Mexico.
- c6. AGUAYO ISLAS, christening 8 December 1650, Zacatecas, Mexico.

Death/burial: LUISA de ISLA on 2 October 1676, Zacatecas, Mexico (Widower: ANTONIO de AGUAYO).

b2. JUANA (MARTINEZ) LOZANO, born abt. 1603, Aguascalientes, Aguascalientes, Mexico) married HERNANDO de VELASCO on 1 April 1619, El Sagrario, Aguascalientes, Aguascalientes, Mexico.
The known children of Hernando de Velasco Salinas and Juana Martinez Lozano (b) were:
- c1. JOSEPH VELASCO MARTINEZ, christening 29 August 1622, El Sagrario, Aguascalientes, Aguascalientes, Mexico (Father: Hernando de Velasco Salinas/Mother: Juana *Martinez* Lozano).

  c2. XPOVAL. VELASCO MARTINEZ, christening 1 November 1624, El Sagrario, Aguascalientes, Aguascalientes, Mexico (Father: Hernando de Velasco/Mother: Juana *Martinez*).

b3. Captain JACINTO LOZANO ISLA (JACINTO de LOZANO GONZALES de ISLA), Born abt. 1610, Aguascalientes, Aguascalientes, Mexico. Died abt. 1673, Aguascalientes, Aguascalientes, Mexico. Married JUANA GONZALES de RUBALCABA y RODAS on 6 September 1632, Santa Maria de los Lagos, Lagos de Moreno (Father of groom: Cristobal Lozano) (Father of bride: Fulgenio Gonzales. Mother of bride: Maria Luisa).
The known children of Captain Jacinto Lozano Isla (b) and Juana Gonzales Rubalcaba y Rodas were:
  c1. JUANA LOZANO GONZALES, christening 7 May 1636, El Sagrario, Aguascalientes, Aguascalientes, Mexico (Father: Jacinto Lozano/Mother: Joana Gonzales).
  c2. YSIDRO LOZANO GONZALES, christening 19 June 1638, Santa Maria de Los Lagos, Lagos de Moreno, Jalisco, Mexico (Father: Jacinto Lozano/Mother: Juana Gonzales). Death/Burial 8 October 1665, Asuncion de Maria, Aguascalientes, Aguascalientes, Mexico (Single/White) (Father: Jacinto Lozano/Mother: Juana Gonzales).
  c3. JOSEPH LOZANO GONZALEZ, christening 26 October 1639, Santa Maria de los Lagos, Lagos de Moreno, Jalisco, Mexico (Father: Jacinto Lozano/Mother: Juana Gonzalez).
  c4. LUISA LOZANO GONZALES, christening 27 December 1645, El Sagrario, Aguascalientes, Aguascalientes, Mexico (Father: Jacinto Lozano/Mother: Juana Gonzalez).
  c5. MARIA LOZANO GONZALES, christening 25 May 1648, El Sagrario, Aguascalientes, Aguascalientes, Mexico (Father: Jacinto Lozano/Mother: Juana Gonzales).
  c6. JACINTO LOZANO GONZALES, christening 5 January 1650, El Sagrario, Aguascalientes, Aguascalientes, Mexico (Father: Jacinto Lozano/Mother: Juana Gonzales). Death/Burial 1656, Asuncion de Maria, Aguascalientes, Aguascalientes, Mexico (Father: Jacinto Lozano/Mother: Juana Gonzalez).
  c7. JUANA LOZANO GONZALES, christening 21 July 1651, El Sagrario, Aguascalientes, Aguascalientes, Mexico (Father: Jacinto Lozano/Mother: Juana Gonzalez). (*Godmother: DONA LEONOR LOSANO*).

b4. ISABEL de ISLA y MARTINEZ LOZANO, born 1612, Tlaltenango de Sanchez Roman, Zacatecas, Mexico. Married DIEGO DELGADO DIAZ GALLEGOS (1616-unknown) on 22 February 1637, El Sagrario, Aguascalientes, *Aguascalientes, Mexico (to YSABEL MARTINES LOZANO)*. Death/Burial 16 July 1676, Charcas, Charcas, San Luis Potosi, Mexico.
The known children of Isabel de Isla y Martinez Lozano (b) and Diego Delgado were:

- c1. JUAN DELGADO LOPEZ, christening 21 February 1638, Tlaltenago, de Sanchez Roman, Zacatecas, Mexico (Father: Diego Delgado/ Mother: Ysabel Lopez).
- c2. ANTONIO DELGADO LOPEZ, christening 1639, Tlaltenago de Sanchez Roman, Zacatecas, Mexico (Father: Diego Delgado/Mother: Isabel Lopez).
- c3. MARTIN DELGADO LOPEZ, christening 12 April 1643, Tlaltenego de Sanchez Roman, Zacatecas, Mexico (Father: Diego Delgado/ Mother: Isabel Lopez).
- c4. NICOLAS DELGADO LOPEZ, christening 8 April 1648, Tlaltenago de Roman, Zacatecas, Mexico.
- c5. MARIA DELGADO MARTINEZ, 1650, Tlaltenango de Sanchez, Zacatecas, Mexico (Father: Diego Delgado/Mother: Isabel Martinez) (Witness: Pedro Martinez Lozano).
- c6. MARIA DELGADO MARTINEZ, christening 20 October 1652, Tlaltenago de Sanches Roman, Zacatecas, Mexico (Father: Diego Delgado Mother: Ysabel Martinez).
- c7. FRANCISCA DELGADO LOPES, christening 4 August 1655, Tlaltenango de Sanches Roman, Zacatecas, Mexico (Father: Diego Delgado Mother: Ysabel Lopes).
- c8. MARCOS DELGADO LOPES, christening 22 June 1659, Tlaltenango de Roman, Zacatecas, Mexico (Father: Diego Delgado/Mother: Ysabel Lopes).

b5. CATALINA LOZANO GONZALES de ISLA, born abt. 1613, Aguascalientes, Aguascalientes, Mexico. Death/Burial on 26 July 1683 (CATALINA LOZANO) Asuncion de Maria, Aguascalientes, Aguascalientes, Mexico. (Spouse: BERNARDO SALADO de ESPARZA).

Married BERNARDO RUIZ de ESPARZA on 27 February 1634, Aguascalientes, Aguascalientes, Mexico.

~Daughter born to (sister) LEONOR de LOSANO and Berdo. Ruiz de Esparzo (Petrona) RUIS ESPARZA, 25 January 1635, Aguascalientes, Aguascalientes, Mexico.

The known child of CATALINA LOZANO GONZALEZ de ISLA (b) and BERNARDO RUIZ de ESPARZA was:
- c1. MARIA RUIZ LOZANO, born 9 May 1640, Nuestra Senora de los Dolores, Teocaltiche, Jalisco, Mexico. Married FRANCISCO FLORES.
  The known child of Maria Ruiz Lozano (c) and Francisco Flores was:
  - d1. BERNARDA FLORES y RUIZ de ESPARZA.

b6. ANA MARIA LOZANO de ISLA, born abt. (1611) April 1614, Aguascalientes, Aguascalientes, Mexico. Married JUAN de ARAIZA y MEDINA (born abt. 1610) abt. 1637, Aguascalientes, Aguascalientes, Mexico. Died 8 September 1659, Aguascalientes, Aguascalientes, Mexico.

The known children of Ana Maria Lozano de Isla (b) and Juan de Araiza y Medina were:

- c1. HERNANDO ARASCA ISLA, christening 23 August 1637, El Sagrario, Aguascalientes, Aguascalientes, Mexico (Father: Juan de Araiza Medina/Mother: Ana Maria de Isla).
- c2. CRISTOBAL AREYSA ISLA, christening 13 September 1639, El Sagrario, Aguascalientes, Aguascalientes, Mexico (Father: Juan de Araiza Medina/Mother: Maria de Isla).
- c3. GERTRUDIS ARAIZA ISLA, christening 4 August 1641, El Sagrario, Aguascalientes, Aguascalientes, Mexico (Father: Juan de Araiza/ Mother: Maria de Isla).
- c4. JUAN ARAIZA ISLA (SILVA), christening 21 December 1643, El Sagrario, Aguascalientes, Aguascalientes, Mexico (Father: Juan de Araiza/ Mother: Maria de Isla-*Silva*).
- c5A. THERESA ARAIZA ISLA, christening 7 March 1646, El Sagrario, Aguascalientes, Aguascalientes, Mexico (Father: Juan de Araiza/ Mother: Maria de Isla).
- c5B. TERESA ARAISA ISLA, christening 10 December 1647, El Sagrario, Aguascalientes, Aguascalientes, Mexico (Father: Juan de Araiza y Medina/Mother: Maria de Isla).
- c6A. GABRIEL ARAIZA LOSANO, christening 19 March 1650, El Sagrario, Aguascalientes, Aguascalientes, Mexico (Father: Juan de Araiza Medina/Mother: Maria Losano).
- c6B. GABRIEL ARAISA ISLA, christening 21 December 1651, El Sagrario, Aguascalientes, Aguascalientes, Mexico (Father: Juan de Araiza/ Mother: Maria de Isla).
- c7. MARIA de ARIASA, death/burial 1659, Asuncion de Maria, Aguascalientes, Aguascalientes, Mexico (Father: Juan de Araiza/Mother: Maria de Isla).

Death/Burial: MARIA de ISLA on 8 September 1659, Asuncion de Maria, Aguascalientes, Aguascalientes, Mexico (Married) (Spouse: Juan de Araiza Medina).

Death/Burial: JUAN de ARAISA MEDINA on 14 August 1665, Asuncion de Maria, Aguascalientes, Aguascalientes, Mexico (Widowed).

b7. ANA MARTINA MARTINEZ LOZANO y de ISLA, born abt. 1615, Aguascalientes, Aguascalientes, Mexico. Married FRANCISCO PRIETO GALLARDO. (Death/Burial *[assumed] 19 August 1716, Lagos de Moreno, Jalisco, Mexico*).

The known children of Ana Martina Martinez Lozano (b) and Francisco Prieto Gallardo were:

- c1. MARIA PRIETO LOZANO, christening 11 January 1634, El Sagrario, Aguascalientes, Aguascalientes, Mexico (Father: Franco. Prieto/ Mother: Ana Lozano).
- c2. ANA PRIETO LOZANO, christening 18 February 1636, El Sagrario, Aguascalientes, Aguascalientes, Mexico (Father: Francisco Prieto/Mother: Ana Lozano).
- c3. FRANCISCO PRIETO, christening 3 April 1638, El Sagrario, Aguascalientes, Aguascalientes, Mexico (Father: Franco. Prieto/ Mother: Ana Lozano). Death/burial: 1695, Asuncion de Maria, Aguascalientes, Aguascalientes, Mexico (Married) (Spouse: Luisa).
- c4 GONZALO PRIETO LOZANO, christening 28 December 1639, El Sagrario, Aguascalientes, Aguascalientes, Mexico (Father: Franco. Prieto/ Mother: Lozano).
- c5. INES PRIETO LOZANO, christening 14 April 1643, El Sagrario, Aguascalientes, Aguascalientes, Mexico (Father: Francisco Prieto Gallardo/Mother: Ana Martina Lozano).

Death/burial: FRANCISCO PRIETO during 1643, Asuncion de Maria, Aguascalientes, Aguascalientes, Mexico (Married) (Spouse: ANA LOZANO).

b8. LORENZO LOZANO ISLA, christening May 1617, El Sagrario, Aguascalientes, Aguascalientes, Mexico (Father: Cristobal Lozano/Mother: Maria Isla) (*Sister: LEONOR ISLA*) (*Godparent: FRANCISCO GONZALEZ, grandfather*) (Witness: **Petrona de Isla**) *(twin with Leonor Lozano Isla)*.

b9. **LEONOR LOSANO ISLA**, christening 22 May 1617, El Sagrario, Aguascalientes, Aguascalientes, Mexico (Father: Cristobal Lozano/Mother: Maria de Isla) *(twin with Lorenzo Lozano Isla)*. Resided Xiconaque, Aguascalientes, Mexico. Death/Burial 13 June 1670, Asuncion de Maria, Aguascalientes, Aguascalientes, Mexico (Widowed - LEONOR LOSANO) (Spouse: Bernabe Merino).

The child born to **LEONOR de LOSANO** (b) and Berdo. Ruiz de Esparza was:

(cA.) **(PETRONA) RUIZ LOZANO**, christening 25 January 1635, El Sagrario, Aguascalientes, Aguascalientes, Mexico (Father: **Berdo. Ruis de Esparza**/Mother: **Leonor de Lozano**) (*Leonor de Lozano age 18*).

(cB.) *LOPE RUIZ de ESPARZA, christening 2 June 1640, El Sagrario, Aguascalientes, Aguascalientes, Mexico (Mother: MARIA INDIA/ISLA)* (Witness: **PETRONA** ISLA) *(Hypothesis)*.

Married BERNABE MERINO on 8 December 1650, El Sagrario, Aguascalientes, Aguascalientes, Mexico.

The children of Leonor Lozano Isla (b) and Bernabe Merino were:
- c1. MARIA MERINO LOZANO, christening 12 November 1651, El Sagrario, Aguascalientes, Aguascalientes, Mexico (Father: Bernabe Merino/Mother: Leonor Lozano).
- c2. MARIA JOSEPHA MERINO LOZANO, christening 12 November 1651, El Sagrario, Aguascalientes, Aguascalientes, Mexico (Father: Bernabe Merino/Mother: Leonor Lozano).
- c3. MATHIANA MERINO LOZANO, christening 16 March 1653, El Sagrario, Aguascalientes, Aguascalientes, Mexico (Father: Bernabe Merino/Mother: Leonor Lozano).

b9. (ISLA) JUANA LOZANO, born April 1618, christening 1618, El Sagrario, Aguascalientes, Aguascalientes, Mexico (Father: Cristobal Lozano/Mother: Maria de Isla).

Married PEDRO RUIZ de ESPARZA on 12 April 1636, Aguascalientes, Aguascalientes, Mexico.

The known children of Pedro Ruiz de Esparza and Juana Lozano Isla (b) were:
- c1. LUISA ESPARZA LOZANO (Luisa de los Angeles de los Reyes Esparza Lozano), christening 6 February 1637, El Sagrario, Aguascalientes, Aguascalientes, Mexico (Father: Po. de Esparza/Mother: Luisa Esparza Lozano).
- c2. NICOLAS ESPARZA LOZANO, christening 2 July 1639, El Sagrario, Aguascalientes, Aguascalientes, Mexico (Father: Po. de Esparza/Mother: Jua. Lozano).
- c3. MARIA ESPARZA LOZANO, christening 29 December 1641, El Sagrario, Aguascalientes, Aguascalientes, Mexico (Father: Po. de Esparza/Mother: Jua. Lozano).
- c4. NICOLASA ESPARSA LOZANO, christening 3 October 1644, El Sagrario, Aguascalientes, Aguascalientes, Mexico (Father: Pedro de Esparza/Mother: Juana Lozano).
- c5. MATIANA de ESPARZA LOZANO, christening 18 March 1647, El Sagrario, Aguascalientes, Aguascalientes, Mexico (*Witness: Fernando Calderon*).
- c6. ANTONIO ESPARZA LOZANO, christening 19 December 1649, El Sagrario, Aguascalientes, Aguascalientes, Mexico (Father: Po. de Esparza/Mother: Jua. Lozano).
- c7. JUAN ESPARZA LOZANO, christening 17 November 1652, El Sagrario, Aguascalientes, Aguascalientes, Mexico (Father: Po. de Esparza/Mother: Juana Lozano). Married ROSA MARTINEZ de SOTOMAYOR during 1702, Aguascalientes, Aguascalientes, Mexico. Death/Burial 23 September 1742, Asuncion de Maria, Aguascalientes, Aguascalientes, Mexico (Father: Pedro Ruiz Esparza/Mother: Juana Lozano).

The known child of Juan Esparza Lozano (c) and Rosa Martinez Sotomayor was:
- d1. NICOLAS HILARIO RUIZ de ESPARZA y MARTINEZ de SOTOMAYOR, born 2 November 1716, Aguascalientes, Aguascalientes, Mexico. Died 30 March 1785, Aguascalientes, Aguascalientes, Mexico.

- c8. BEATRIZ RUIZ de ESPARZA, born 1653, Aguascalientes, Aguascalientes, Mexico (*no record*). Married PEDRO LOPES. Death/burial 2 January 1678, Asuncion de Maria, Aguascalientes, Aguascalientes, Mexico.

  The known child of Beatriz Ruis de Esparza (c) and Pedro Lopes was:
  - d1. MARIA ANTONIA de la TRINIDAD LOPES RUIS, christening 9 July 1707, El Sagrario, Aguascalientes, Aguascalientes, Mexico.

- c9. LOPE ESPARZA LOZANO, christening 29 April 1655, El Sagrario, Aguascalientes, Aguascalientes, Mexico (Father: Pedro de Esparza/Mother: Juana Lozano).

- c10. PEDRO ESPARZA, born unknown date, Aguascalientes, Aguascalientes, Mexico. Death/Burial 1669, Asuncion de Maria, Aguascalientes, Aguascalientes, Mexico.

b10. MAGDALENA LOSANO ISLA, christening 7 September 1619, El Sagrario, Aguascalientes, Aguascalientes, Mexico (Father: Cristobal Lozano /Mother: Maria de Isla). Married MIGUEL LOPEZ (de ELIZALDE) on 15 February 1635, El Sagrario, Aguascalientes, Aguascalientes, Mexico. *Death/burial 23 November 1666, Asuncion de Maria, Aguascalientes, Aguascalientes, Mexico.*

Death/Burial: MIGUEL LOPES de ELIZALDE during 1691, Asuncion de Maria, Aguascalientes, Aguascalientes, Mexico.

b11. CRISTOBAL LOZANO ISLA, born April 1620, Aguascalientes, Aguascalientes, Mexico. Married (*Engagement*): MARIANA GONZALES de BERMEJO (y PEREZ de GARDEA) on 20 March 1633, El Sagrario, Aguascalientes, Aguascalientes, Mexico (Xtpoval. Lozano to Mariana Gonzales). Marriage dates - (Cristobal Lozano to Mariana de Bermejo) 20 March 1643 then 21 April 1643. Death/burial CRISTOBAL MARTINEZ LOZANO, 5 May 1646, Asuncion de Maria, Aguascalientes, Aguascalientes, Mexico.

The known children of Cristobal Lozano Isla (b) and Mariana Gonzales de Bermejo y Perez de Gardea were:
- c1. JUAN LOZANO PEREZ, christening 14 February 1644, Asuncion de Maria, Aguascalientes, Aguascalientes, Mexico (Father: Cristobal Lozano/Mother: Mariana Perez Bermejo).
- c2. ISABEL LOZANO GONZALEZ, christening 7 June 1647, El Sagrario, Aguascalientes, Aguascalientes, Mexico (Father: Cristobal Lozano/Mother: Mariana Gonzales).

- c3. MARIA LOZANO GONZALEZ, christening 6 January 1650, El Sagrario, Aguascalientes, Aguascalientes, Mexico (Father: Cristobal Lozano/ Mother: Mariana Gonzalez).
- c4. JOSEFA LOZANO GONZALES (born abt. 1652), Palo Alto, Calvillo, Aguascalientes, Mexico (Father: Cristobal Lozano/Mother: Maria). Engagement to DIEGO GOMEZ of PORTUGAL, 25 March 1670, El Sagrario, Aguascalientes, Aguascalientes, Mexico. Married DIEGO GOMEZ of PORTUGAL on 1 June 1670, Santa Maria de los Lagos, Lagos de Moreno, Jalisco, Mexico (JOSEPHA MARTINEZ) (*Matrimonios 1663-1702; Image 36/325*).

The known children of Diego Gomez (b5) and Josepha Lozano were:
- d. JOSEPHA LOZANO, *born 1668 prior to marriage*. Married SEBASTIAN LUNA ORTIZ de ESQUIBEL (1659) abt. 1688, Zacatecas, Mexico.
- d1. MARIANA GOMES of PORTUGAL, born abt. 1671. Married Captain MIGUEL RODRIGUEZ of PORTUGAL (son of Francisco Rodriquez and Ana of Portugal) on 20 June 1689, Lagos de Moreno, Jalisco, Mexico (MARIANA GOMES of PORTUGAL - Father: Diego Gomes of Portugal/Mother: Josepha Losano).
- d2. SALVADOR GOMES LOSANO, christening 1676, Santa Maria de los Lagos, Lagos de Moreno, Jalisco, Mexico (Father: Diego Gomes Portugal/Mother: Josepha Losano). Married TERESA de LOPES y DIAZ (1680-1737).
- d3. MANUEL GOMES LOSANO, christening 1678, Santa Maria de los Lagos, Lagos de Moreno, Jalisco, Mexico (Father: Diego Gomes Portugal/Mother: Josepha Losano). Married: ISADORA de NABA y ARAUJO (daughter of Nicolas de Naba y Araujo and Ysidora de Naba y Araujo)(ISADORA CATHARINA NAVA de la FUENTE) (1697) on 27 February 1718, Santa Maria de los Lagos, Lagos de Moreno, Jalisco, Mexico (Father: Diego Gomes Portugal/Mother: Josepha Losano).
- d4. ROSA BEJAR GOMES LOSANO, christening 1680, Santa Maria de los Lagos, Lagos de Moreno, Jalisco, Mexico (Father: Diego Gomes Portugal/Mother: Josepha Losano).
- d5. GERTRUDIS GOMES LOSANO, christening 1683, Santa Maria de los Lagos, Lagos de Moreno, Jalisco, Mexico (Father: Diego Gomes Portugal/Mother: Josepha Losano). Married JOSE MORENO de ORTEGA ARUJO (1679-1706) on May 1701, Lagos de Moreno, Jalisco, Mexico.
- d6. MAGDALENA GOMES GONZALES, christening 4 August 1685, Santa Maria de los Lagos, Lagos de Moreno, Jalisco, Mexico (Father: Diego Gomes de Portugal/Mother: Josepha Gonzales Gardea). Married CRISTOBAL RODRIQUEZ

RAMIREZ y BEJAR de AVIS YSASSI (1678) on 11 September 1701, Lagos de Moreno, Jalisco, Mexico.
- d7. MANUELA GOMES LOSANO, christening 1688, Santa Maria de los Lagos, Lagos de Moreno, Jalisco, Mexico (Father: Diego Gomes Portugal/Mother: Josepha Losano).
- d8. JUAN CRISOSTOMO GOMEZ LOZANO, christening 18 February 1692, Santa Maria de los Lagos, Lagos de Moreno, Jalisco, Mexico (Father: Diego Gomes/Mother: Josepha Losano) (Espanol).
- d9. CRISTOBAL GOMEZ LOZANO, christening 3 August 1695, Santa Maria de los Lagos, Lagos de Moreno, Jalisco, Mexico (Father: Diego Gomes/Mother: Josepha Losano).

c5. PHELIPA LOZANO BERMEJO, christening 19 May 1654, El Sagrario, Aguascalientes, Aguascalientes, Mexico (Father: Cristobal Lozano/ Mother: Mariana Gonzalez).

c6. Captain ONOFRE LOZANO GONZALEZ, christening 8 June 1656, El Sagrario, Aguascalientes, Aguascalientes, Mexico (Father: Cristobal Lozano/Mother: Mariana de la Cruz). Married MARIA de ALBA y ESTRADA during 1689, Asuncion de Maria, Aguascalientes, Aguascalientes, Mexico.

c7. GERTRUDIS LOZANO GARDEA, christening 21 June 1660, El Sagrario, Aguascalientes, Aguascalientes, Mexico (Father: Cristobal Lozano/Mother: Mariana de Gardea). Married YSIDRO ESPARZA on 21 November 1730, Guadalajara, Jalisco, Mexico.

c8. RITA LOZANO, born abt. 1661, Aguascalientes, Aguascalientes, Mexico (*no record*). Married GASPAR de LARES on 5 May 1680, El Sagrario, Aguascalientes, Aguascalientes, Mexico.

The known child of Rita Lozano (c) and Gaspar de Lares was:
- d1. CRISTOBAL LARES LOZANO, christening 1684, Santa Maria de Los Lagos, Lagos de Moreno, Jalisco, Mexico.

c9. FELIPA LOZANO (son), christening 17 August 1679, Aguascalientes, Aguascalientes, Mexico (Father: Cristobal Lozano/Mother: Mariana Gonzalez) (**Witness: LEONOR LOZANO**).

APPENDIX XII

PEDRO GOMEZ
(born abt. 1520 - 1585, Nueva Espana)
CATALINA MANRIQUE de LARA
(born abt. 1530 - died abt. 1585-1587, Nueva Espana)

As per Josepha Gomez Manrique de Lara's surname combination, the search for ancestors in Leon took our lineage to Pedro Gomez who married Catalina Manrique (de Lara). While Catalina Manrique was listed without text of, "de Lara," her children and grandchildren took the entire "Manrique de Lara" surname. Unfortunately, the only genealogical information found in Mexico centered upon one of the twins, Baltasar Gomez Manrique rather than our ancestor, Gaspar Gomez Manrique (de Lara). Two biographies of Pedro Gomez were found: one written in 1961 and the other in 1990.

From: Fuente: Gonzalez Leal, Mariano. Leon Trayectoria y Destino. Pro Urbe. Leon 1990. Pages. 5 y 6.

> "He resided in this region at least since 1564, the year the Royal court of Mexico awarded him the site of the Cerro Gordo - on August 13th. In the corresponding document reference is made to his merits in the war against the Chichimecas. He came with his wife, Catalina Manrique and three children: Baltasar and Gaspar Gomez, twins, and Lucia Manrique.
>
> In the year 1581, Pedro Gomez held the position of Mayor of the First Church (…), a position that he held until his death in the year of 1584 or early 1585, and at least from 1582 to 1584 he was the ordinary mayor of the town of Leon as recorded in the protocol of the notary, Andres de Truijllo in the volumes corresponding to those years.
>
> In a document dated March 21, 1585, it is stated that Lucia Manrique, daughter of the founder and also founder, was married to PEDRO de ZAVALA, a resident of Irapuato.
>
> Baltasar Gomez, called "Old Man" because he has a son of the same name, was born around 1550. He was still alive in 1624. He declared his age in the famous "big lawsuit" between the Mayors' Offices of Leon and Lagos. He inherited the Cerro Gordo Ranch and owned the Palenque ranch, close to the towns of Rincon - San Francisco and Purisima and the border with Nueva Galicia. He was married to MARIA ISABEL GALVAN, and lest numerous descendants who later became linked to the AROCHA family."

As per the translation of, "Mayor of the First Church, according to Rodolfo Herrera Perez, Director of Leon's Archivo Historico, "stewards or treasurers of the Church were lay people who intervened in the economic life of the ecclesiastical corporations," ecclesiastical assets or financial matters upon which the clergy had no formal role. Pedro Gomez, as "Mayor of the First Church," was responsible for accounting expenses and assets of the church incurred by celebrations of the year and held an administrative role for church finances.

From a genealogical study listed in the <u>Memories of the Mexican Academy of Genealogy and Heraldry</u> (second period, Volume II, December 1961, pages 109-114), Lic. Gonzalo Torres Martinez outlined his lineal relationship to Pedro Gomez in: "Descendants of Pedro Gomez, Founder and First Settler of Villa de San Sebastian de Leon in Nueva Espana, today Leon, Guanajuato." From Martinez' research, it can be confirmed our line did not descend from either Baltasar Gomez Manrique or Lucia Manrique (de Lara), but instead from Gaspar Gomez Manrique (de Lara).

> "By Royal Decree given by the Audencia of Mexico on 13 August 1564, the Catholic Majesty of King Philip II rewarded the services rendered by Don Pedro Gomez in the war against the Chichimecas and Guachichiles in which he took part in providing men, arms and horses with his own money..." (*Martinez, Page 109*)

> "The lands that comprised the original mercy and others that were acquired later by the descendants of Don Pedro Gomez, were in the hands of his descendants *of Baltasar Gomez Manrique de Lara*) for three centuries..."(*Martinez, Page 109*)

> "When, by the order of the Viceroy of New Spain, Don Martin Enriquez de Almanza, what is now the city of Leon was founded on 20 January 1576, Don Pedro, together with his wife, Dona Catalina Manrique (de Lara) and his twin sons Don Baltasar and Don Gaspar Manrique, (who had) settled in Cerrogordo from the time it was granted, move to Leon, and in their capacity as Spaniards and first settlers they received plots of land in the layout of the new town to cultivate their houses and orchards." (*Martinez, Page 110*)

> ..."Elected councilors (during 1576 included) Pedro Gomez..." (*Martinez, Page 111*)

> "In the year 1581, Don Pedro Gomez held the position of Mayor Domo of the First Church that existed in Leon, a position that he held until his death in the year 1584 or early 1585, and at least from 1582 to 1584 he was ordinary mayor of the Villa de Leon as stated in the Protocol of Notary Andres de Trujillo in the volumes corresponding to those years." (*Martinez, Page 111*)

> "On 21 March 1585 Don Pedro Gomez, according to the declaration of his widow, Dona Catalina Manrique (de Lara) before the Notary Andres de Trujillo in notarial instrument of recognition of debt to her son-in-law Pedro de Zavala, a resident of Irapuato, by virtue of a clause in the will of Don Pedro Gomez that has not been found." (*Martinez, Pages 111-112*)

> "As the parish archives began in 1646, since the previous books were lost, it is not possible to establish the date of Don Pedro Gomez' death nor that of his wife and his children Don Baltasar and Don Gaspar Gomez Manrique appear as her children and

heirs, (individuals who) recognize(e) (their) brother-in-law Pedro de Zavala's credit on the estate." (*Martinez, Page 112*)

From Martinez' account of the Pedro Gomez family, we confirm Pedro Gomez and Catalina Manrique de Lara were Spaniards and records were lost prior to 1646. Additionally, Martinez outlines the inheritance of Pedro Gomez land (Cerro Gordo and others) to his son, Baltasar Gomez Manrique de Lara. There is no mention of Gaspar Gomez Manrique, although he is listed as an heir in Pedro Gomez' will. Given our verified ancestor, Josepha Gomez Manrique de Lara, carried the two surnames, and few individuals existed in Guanajuato with the Gomez-Manrique de Lara surname combination, as per onomastics, I have placed the Manrique-Hopkins branch within the Pedro Gomez and Catalina Manrique de Lara line.

~~~~~~

PEDRO GOMEZ - (born abt. 1520-1585). Military: War of Chichimaca. Resided in Leon post 1576. Royal Audencia awarded him Cerro Gordo, a Leon hacienda with a river named for the family, Rio Gomez, running through it. Councilor/Mayor of the First Church and patron of the parish of Villa de San Sebastian de Leon, Nueva Espana.
Married CATALINA MANRIQUE de LARA (born abt. 1530; died abt. 1585-1587, Nueva Espana; likely Leon, Guanajuato, Mexico).

The known children of Pedro Gomez (d. 1585) and Catalina Manrique de Lara (a) were:
b1. BALTASAR GOMEZ MANRIQUE (de LARA), born abt. 1550 (twin). (Died 1624)
      Married: MARIA ISABEL GALVIN.
b2. GASPAR GOMEZ MANRIQUE (de LARA), born abt. 1550 (twin).
      Married: *MARIANA FERRER.*
b3. LUCIA MANRIQUE (de LARA), born prior to 1565.
      Married PEDRO ZAVALA (by 21 March 1585) - *IRAPUATO*

~~~~~~

GOMEZ - MANRIQUE de LARA LINEAGE

Most Pedro Gomez/Catalina Manrique de Lara (MdL) branches have at least one generation missing between the years 1550 to the mid-1600s as per lost documents. However, it is verified Pedro Gomez and his wife, Catalina Manrique de Lara settled in 1576 Leon with children born by 1550. Pedro Gomez died (in Leon) by 1585. Gen2 Gomez/Manrique de Lara branches born 1575 onward would be the (great) grandchildren of Pedro Gomez and Catalina Manrique de Lara. The Gomez-Manrique de Lara surname combination was very unusual between 1550-1750 in Leon and Viceroyalty of New Spain (Guanajuato, Mexico) nor did it exist within the (Santa Maria de los Lagos) Kingdom of New Galicia (Jalisco, Mexico). As per verified birth/marriage and death records, our line descended from Gaspar Antonio

Manrique de Lara (1702-1755), the child of Josepha Gomez Manrique de Lara (1677-1718), the grandchild of Gaspar Antonio Gomez Manrique de Lara (born abt. 1550) and great-grandchild of Pedro Gomez and Catalina Manrique de Lara, Leon co-founders. Search for the wife of Gaspar Gomez Manrique de Lara (born abt. 1550) was inconclusive other than the first name, Mariana and various spellings of her surname *FERRER*. Given Josepha Gomez Manrique de Lara died in Mexico City, this branch had ties to Distrito Federal (DF) or Mexico City, Mexico which was over two hundred miles from Leon, Guanajuato.

PEDRO GOMEZ (born abt. 1510-1585)
CATALINA MANRIQUE de LARA (born abt. 1530 -)
| | | | |
BALTASAR GOMEZ (1550) - GASPAR GOMEZ (1550) - (LUCIA MdL) - (UNKNOWN)
MA. ISABEL GALVIN   MARIANA (*FERRER*)   PEDRO ZAVALA
|
CATALINA MANRIQUE de LARA (born abt. 1600)
GARCI BRAVO de LAGUNAS
|
MARIA MANRIQUE de LARA (born abt. 1630)
PEDRO GONZALES de AGUIRRE y RULES
|
JOSEPHA GOMEZ MANRIQUE de LARA
(born 1677, Irapuato, Guanajuato; died 1718, Mexico City, MX)
NICOLAS de MEDINA
|
GASPAR ANTONIO MANRIQUE de LARA
(born 1702, Leon, Gto., MX; died 1755 Leon, Gto., MX)

1. BALTASAR GOMEZ MANRIQUE de LARA (1550-1624+)
   Married MARIA ISABEL GALVAN by 1585 in Irapuato, Guanajuato, Mexico

Given Baltasar Gomez owned Palenque Ranch near the Nueva Galicia border and was involved in the "Great Lawsuit," a territorial dispute between the Viceroyalty of New Spain and the court of Nueva Galicia, it is assumed he resided not at Cerro Gordo near Leon, but instead by Purisma del Rincon and San Francisco. For this reason, it is unlikely that our ancestors came from this branch of the Pedro Gomez-Catalina Manrique de Lara line.

From Martinez' account: (Gen2) Don Baltasar Gomez Manrique, "founder and first settler and ordinary mayor of Leon, owner of Cerrogordo ranches near Leon and Palenque in the jurisdiction of Nueva Galicia (Comanja)." (*Martinez, Page 112*)

The (*assumed*) children of Baltasar Gomez and Maria Anna Isabel Galvan (a) were:
b1. MARIA GOMEZ (born abt. 1605).
    Married HERNANDO JOSEPH on 27 January 1630, San Luis Rey, San Luis de
    la Paz, Guanajuato, Mexico (Father: Baltasar Gomez/Mother: Anna
    Ysabel) ("... Maria, daughter of Don Baltasar Gomez..." Godparent:

        Lucia Ma [Maria/Manrique] and Juan Peralta) (*Archivo de la Parroquia de San Luis Rey en San Luis de la Paz, Guanajuato. Diocesis de Leon. Matrimonios. Vol. Num. 1. Years 1621-1644*) (*Film #004796572; Image 74/814*).

b2.   MARCOS GOMEZ (born abt. 1610).
       Married MARIA ANA on 26 January 1640, San Luis Rey, San Luis de la Paz, Guanajuato, Mexico (Father: Baltasar Gomez/Mother: Maria Ana) (*Archivo de la Parroquia de San Luis Rey en San Luis de La Paz, Guanajuato. Diocesis de Leon. Matrimonios. Vol. Num. 1. Years 1621-1644.*)

      The known children of Marcos Gomez (b) and Maria Ana were:

    c1.   JOANA MELCHORA GOMES, born abt. 1640.
          Married PASQUAL de VARGAS (son of Pedro Martin and Cecilia Maria Martin) on 25 May 1664, San Pedro, Guanajuato, Guanajuato, Mexico (daughter of Marcos Gomes and Ana Maria Gomes).

    c2.   DIEGO GOMEZ born 31 May 1647, San Luis Rey, San Luis de la Paz, Guanajuato, Mexico. Christening 10 June 1647, San Luis Rey, San Luis de la Paz, Guanajuato, Mexico (Father: Marcos Gomez/ Mother: Ana Maria) (Margin text: Diego Gomez) (Text: ..."son of Marcos Gomez and Ana Maria...") (Godparents: Francisco Hernandez and Maria Juana -Gomez) (*Archivo de la Parroquia de San Luis Rey en San Luis de la Paz, Guanajuato. Diocesis de Leon. Bautismos. Vol. Number 2. Years 1645-1660; Image 182/644*).

b3.   MARIA GOMEZ, christening 4 January 1626, Celaya, Celaya, Guanajuato, Mexico (Father: Baltasar Gomez/Mother: Ysabel Lucia).

b4.   ANDRES GOMEZ GALVIN (born abt. 1627-1673, San Luis Potosi, Mexico).
      Married CATALINA CABALLERO (born abt. 1627, Leon, Guanajuato, Mexico), daughter of Pedro Caballero de Los Olivos (b. 21 November 1592, Cigales, Valladolid, Castilla y Leon, Spain-1660, Nueva Leon, Mexico) and Maria Margarita Rodriquez (1595-1682) who married 29 April 1622, Tordesillas, Valladolid, Castilla y Leon, Spain.

during 1644, Leon, Guanajuato, Mexico.

"Inherited the Cerro Gordo Hacienda and several mines in Comanja, Nueva Galicia and in Charcas, San Luis Potosi, where he resided" until his death February 1673." (*Martinez, Pages 112-113*).

The known children of Andres Gomez Galvin (b) and Catalina Caballero were:

    c1.   ISABEL GOMEZ CABALLERO, born Leon 1645. Died Real de Charcas, San Luis Potosi on 19 December 1710.
        Married "Capitan de Caballos Corazas" Don FRANCISCO BERNAL LOBO, "treasurer and miner of Real de Minas de Nuestra Senora de las Charcas.

Inherited the Cerrogordo hacienda, several houses, a mill and an orchard in the town of Leon and some of the mines of said Real y de Comanja..." (*Martinez, Page 113)*

The known children of Isabel Gomez Caballero (c) and Francisco Bernal Lobo were:

- d1. JOSEPH BERNAL CABALLERO, christening 7 May 1644, El Sagrario, Aguascalientes, Aguascalientes, Mexico (Father: Franco. Bernal Lobo/Mother: Isabel Caballero).
- d2. JOSEPH BL CABALLERO, christening 25 December 1665, El Sagrario, Aguascalientes, Aguascalientes, Mexico (Father: Franco. B. Lobo/Mother: Isabel Caballero).
- d3. PEDRO BERNAL CABALLERO, christening 20 May 1681, San Francisco, Charcas, San Luis Potosi, Mexico (Father: Francisco Bernal/Mother: Ysabel Caballero).
- d4. FRANCISCA BERNAL CABALLERO, christening 1681, San Francisco, Charcas, San Luis Potosi, Mexico.
- d5. ISABEL CABALLERO, christening 1 May 1683, San Francisco, Charcas, San Luis Potosi, Mexico (Father: Franco. Bernal/Mother: Isabel Caballero).
- d6. MARIA SOLOME LOBO CABALLERO, christening 1 May 1686, San Francisco, Charcas, San Luis Potosi, Mexico (Father: Franco. Bernal Lobo/Mother: Isabel Caballero).
- d7. ANA MARIA de las NIEVES BERNAL GOMEZ CABALLERO, christening 13 December 1689, San Francisco, Charcas, San Luis Potosi, Mexico (Father: Franco. Bernal/Mother: Isabel Caballero). Died 1735, Leon, Guanajuato, Mexico. (*Martinez, Page 113.*)

  Married Don SEBASTIAN de HERRERA ARCOCHA (born Santander Montanas de Burgos on 20 January 1678; son of Joseph de Herrera y Coterillo y Maria de Arcocha y Garcia who married 26 August 1675) during 1711 at Real de Minas. Don Sebastian de Arcocha (Espanol) death/burial 13 March 1788, El Sagrario, Guanajuato, Mexico (*Leon. Death Certificates 1820-1823; Image 46/648*).

  The known children of Dona Ana Maria de las Nieves Bernal Gomez Caballero (d) and Don Sebastian de Herrera Arcocha were:
  - e1. FRAN. JOSEPH HERRERA NIEVES, christening 30 September 1717, San Francisco, Charcas, San Luis Potosi, Mexico (Father: Sebastian de Herrera y Acrocha/Mother: Maria Nieves).
  - e2. JOSE SANTIAGO de HERRERA ACROCHA y BERNAL GOMEZ, born 2 December 1725, Leon, Guanajuato, Mexico. Died 26 July 1786, Leon, Guanajuato, Mexico (*Martinez, Page 113).*

    Attorney general, councilor and ordinary mayor of Leon.

Owner of Hacienda Cerro Gordo.

Married Dona MARIA GERTRUDIS PEREZ FRANCO y GONZALEZ (daughter of Joseph Perez Franco y Gomez and Dona Maria de San Juan Gonzalez y Garcia, residents of Lagos de Moreno, Jalisco, Mexico) on 30 January 1757.

The known child of Jose Santiago de Herrera Arcrocha y Bernal Gomez (e) and Maria Gertrudis Perez Franco y Gonzales was:

f1. JOSE FRANCISCO de ARCOCHA y PEREZ FRANCO, born 7 January 1760, Leon, Guanajuato, Mexico. Died 1 December 1822, Leon, Guanajuato, Mexico (*Martinez, Page 114*).

Married Dona MARIA RITA SANCHEZ GUERRERO (Born Hacienda del Talayote in San Francisco del Rincon; daughter of Don Lorenzo Sanchez, owner of Hacienda del Talayote, San Francisco del Rincon, and Dona Juana B. Guerrero y Martinez) (born 28 May 1779, San Francisco del Rincon, Guanajuato, Mexico; died 21 February 1833, Leon, Guanajuato, Mexico) on 30 January 1791 in Leon, Guanajuato, Mexico.

Ensign of the Calvary of the III Company of the Provincial Regiment of the Prince, Regidor and Ordinary Mayor of Leon.

Inherited Hacienda Cerro Gordo, and other properties (estates of Echeveste, de San Jose al Alto, de la Canada de Juan Diaz, del Sauco, de los Gomez, de la Labor de Larzaro Gomez, del Cerrito de Jerez, de la de Nuestra Senora del Rosario, de la Patina, the mill at Arcrocha) (*Martinez, Page 114).*

The known children of Jose Francisco Arcocha Perez and Maria Rita Sanchez Guerrero were:

g1. MARIA IGNACIA PERICILLANA ARCOCHA (1791-1802).
g2. JOSE CAYETANO ARCOCHA SANCHEZ (1792-).
g3. FELIPE BLAS de JESUS ARCOCHA (1797-).
g4. MARIA GETRUDIS PANTALEON ARCOCHA (christening 28 July 1798, Leon, Guanajuato, Mexico).

- g5. YGNACIO FELIPE DOROTEO ARCOCHA (christening 5 February 1803, Leon, Guanajuato, Mexico).
- g6. IGNACIA ARCOCHA (1803-1833).
- g7. JOSE MARIA ATOJENES de la TRINIDAD (1804-1820).
- g8. JOSE CLEMENTE ARCOCHA (christening 25 November 1805, Leon, Guanajuato, Mexico).
- g9. GREGARIO ARCOCHA (1810-1853).
- g10. GETRUDIS ARCOCHA (born abt. 1811; burial 5 March 1826, Guanajuato, Guanajuato, Mexico).
- e3. ANNA ISABEL THERESA ARCOCHA, baptized 15 August 1728, El Sagrario, Guanajuato, Guanajuato, Mexico (Father: Don Sebastian Arcocha/Mother: Dona Maria Nieves Caballero) (Godparents: Don Cristobal Marmolejo and Dona Luisa Theresa Marmolejo) (Text: "Anna Isabel Theresa espanola de la Villa") (Margin text: "Anna Isabel") (*Leon de los Aldama. Baptism Records 1718-1748; Image 54/119*).
- d8. MARGARITA CABALLERO, christening 6 April 1691, San Francisco, Charcas, San Luis Potosi, Mexico (Mother: Isabel Caballero).
- c2. PHELIPE GOMEZ CABALLERO, christening 9 May 1647, El Sagrario, Leon, Guanajuato, Mexico (Father: Andres Gomez Galvan/ Mother: Cathalina Cavallero) (Text: "legitimate son of Andres Gomez Galvan and Cathailna Cavallero") (Godparents: Don de A-Durbitens- - and Dona ANA GOMEZ GALVIN) (Margin text: "Phelipe") (*Leon de los Aldama. Baptism Records 1636-1673; Image 11/87*).
- c3. AUGUSTIN GOMEZ CABALLERO, born 2 August 1649, Leon, Guanajuato, Mexico. Christening 3 August 1649, Leon, Guanajuato, Mexico.
- c4. MARIA CABALLERO GOMEZ, christening 29 March 1654, Leon, Guanajuato, Mexico.
- c5. SIMON GOMEZ CABALLERO, christening 5 November 1657, El Sagrario, Leon, Guanajuato, Mexico (Father: Andres Gomes de Galvin/ Mother: Catalina Caballero) (Godparents: Joseph Galban/Juan de Dios) (Margin text: "Simon") (*Leon de los Aldama. Baptism Records 1636-1673; Image 29/87*).
- c6. CARLOS GOMEZ CABALLERO, born 15 November 1658, Leon, Guanajuato, Mexico.
- c7. LORENZA GOMEZ CABALLERO, born abt. 1660, Leon, Guanajuato, Mexico.
- c8. CRISTOBAL GOMEZ CABALLERO, born 8 June 1661, Leon, Guanajuato, Mexico. Christening 9 June 1661, El Sagrario, Leon, Guanajuato, Mexico (Father: Andres Gomez/Mother: Catalina Caballero)

(Godparents: Don Rodrigo Lares and Dona Juana de Salcedo, espanoles de la villa) (Margin text: "Cristobal") (*Leon de los Aldama. Baptism Records 1636-1673; Image 45/87*).

    c9.   LUIS GOMES GALBAN, born abt. 1663, Leon, Guanajuato, Mexico.

    c10.   BALTASAR GOMEZ CABALLERO, born 9 February 1664, Leon, Guanajuato, Mexico. Christening 1664, Leon, Guanajuato, Mexico (Father: Andres Gomez/Mother: Dona Catalina Caballero) (Godparents: DOMINGO HERNANDEZ and Dona MAGDALENA MANRIQUE) (Margin text:" Baltasar") (*Leon de los Aldama. Baptism Records 1636-1673; Image 55/87*).

    c11.   FRANCISCA GOMEZ, (born abt. 17/18 October 1665, Leon, Guanajuato, Mexico) christening January 1666, El Sagrario, Leon, Guanajuato, Mexico (Father: Andres Gomez Galvin/Mother: Catalina Caballero) (Godparents: Don Domingo Hernandez and Dona Magdalena Caballero) (Margin text: "Francisca") (*Leon de los Aldama. Baptism Records 1636-1673; Image 61/87*).

    c12.   ANTONIA GOMEZ CABALLERO, christening 22 January 1669, El Sagrario, Leon, Guanajuato, Mexico (Father: Andres Gomes/Mother: Catalina Caballero) (Godparents: DOMINGO HERNANDEZ and Dona MAGDALENA CABALLERO) (Margin text: "Antonia") (*Leon de los Aldama. Baptism Records 1636-1673; Image 67/87*).

    c13.   FRANCISCO GOMEZ CABALLERO, born 16 August 1671, Leon, Guanajuato, Mexico. Christening 17 August 1671, Leon, Guanajuato, Mexico.

    c14.   *ANDRES GOMEZ GALVAN CABALLERO.*

b5.   ANA GOMEZ GALVIN (Mentioned in baptismal record of Andres Gomez Galvin's son, c1 - Phelipe Gomez Caballero).

b6.   JOSEPH GALVIN (Also in baptismal record of Andres' Gomez' Galvin's child, Simon c3).

2.   GASPAR ANTONIO GOMEZ MANRIQUE de LARA (born abt. 1550).
Married: *MARIANA (FERRER).*

As per onomastics, our line fits within the GASPAR GOMEZ MANRIQUE (1550-) branch. Given we know our ancestor was named GASPAR ANTONIO MANRIQUE de LARA (1702-1755) and he was buried inside Leon's El Sagrario church, he must have descended from the Gomez-Manrique de Lara line. That his mother, JOSEPHA GOMEZ MANRIQUE de LARA (1677-1718) carried the GOMEZ MANRIQUE de LARA name is significant given few individuals had such a surname combination. Gaspar Gomez Manrique de Lara (born abt. 1550) honored his mother, Catalina Manrique de Lara (born 1530), by naming his daughter, Catalina Manrique de Lara (born abt. 1600).

Gaspar Gomez Manrique likely married and resided in Mexico City when his father, Pedro Gomez, died in 1585 Leon. To honor his twin brother, Baltasar Gomez Manrique de Lara, Gaspar Gomez Manrique de Lara likely gave his son the same first name. Although few records exist until the mid-1600s, Mexico City held significance in our branch as Josepha Gomez Manrique de Lara was buried there in 1718. In addition, the name, "Gaspar Antonio" connects to Josepha Gomez Manrique de Lara's son, Gaspar Antonio Manrique de Lara to this line. Josepha Gomez Manrique de Lara's grandmother was Catalina Manrique de Lara (born abt. 1600, Guanajuato, Mexico), the child of Gaspar Gomez Manrique de Lara and Mariana Ferrer, whose Mexico City ties/marriage record has yet to be determined. Additionally, Lucia Manrique (de Lara), Gaspar Gomez Manrique de Lara's sister, resided in Irapuato where Josepha Gomez Manrique de Lara was born in 1677.

Married MARIANA (*YNERO, JENERE, PRERE,* FERRER, *FERRERO*).
(*Please note Mariana Ferrer's Mexico City ancestry is still being researched. Updates available at: Ancestry dot com - Gaspar Antonio MdL family tree.*)

The known children of Gaspar Gomez Manrique and Mariana *Ferrer* were:
b1.   BALTASAR GOMEZ, christening March 1583, Santa Catarina Martir, Santa Catarina-Mexico Ciudad, Distrito Federal, Mexico (Godparents: Esteban de *liMufin* and Leonor de *li Mufin* -Munoz?) (*Film # 004008996; Image 77/984*).
Married ANA MAGDALENA CECILIA (*assumed*).
The known children of Baltasar Gomez and Ana Maria were:
   c1.   ANNA MARIA GOMEZ, born abt. 1620. Married 5 February 1645, San Felipe, Guanajuato, Mexico (Father: Baltasar Gomez/Mother: Anna Cecilia) to JOAN ALONSO.
   c2.   MARIA MAGDALENA GOMEZ, born abt. 1625. Married MARTIN de la CRUZ on 19 April 1654, San Felipe, Guanajuato, Mexico.
   c3.   JUANA GOMEZ, christening 24 July 1635, San Miguel Arcangel, Guanajuato, Mexico.
   c4.   LUCAS GOMEZ, christening 19 October 1638, Nuestra Senora de la Soledad, Irapuato, Guanajuato, Mexico (son of Baltasar Gomez and Ana Magdalena -- de Franc Lopes) (Godparents: Domingo Hernandez and Clara -) (*Irapuato, Baptism Records 1633-1655; Image 67/406*).
b2.   MAGDALENA GOMEZ, christening July 1585, Santa Catarina Martir, Santa Catarina-Mexico Ciudad, Distrito Federal, Mexico (Father: Gaspar Gomez/Mother: Mariana Prere) (*Film #004008996; Image 104/984*).
b3.   **CATALINA MANRIQUE de LARA**, born abt. 1600 (*Leon*), Guanajuato, Mexico. *Died abt. before 22 May 1648, Guanajuato, Mexico (Family Search).*
Married GARCI BRAVO de LAGUNAS (born abt. 1600, Real de Sante Fe, Guanajuato, Mexico) *(born 1595, Leon de los Aldema, Leon, Guanajuato, Mexico)* (*Unknown relationship to Francisco Bravo de Lagunas, 1645 Salvatierra, Guanajuato founder*).
The known children of Garci Bravo de Lagunas and Catalina Gomez Manrique de Lara (b) were:
   c1.   JUANA GARCI BRAVO de LAGUNAS MANRIQUE, born 1622.
Married DOMINGO HERNANDEZ GAMINO y GOMEZ de ESPEJO to JUANA (y BRAVO de LAGUNAS) MANRIQUE (de LARA)

on 7 May 1642, Sante Fe, Guanajuato, Mexico.

DOMINO HERNANDEZ GAMINO de ESPEJO (born 1620). Son of Domingo Hernandez Gamino and Juana GOMEZ de Espejo. Brother to Diego Gomez de Espejo, Ana Gomez de Espejo, Juana Gomez de Espejo, Blas Gomez de Espejo, Isabel de Espejo, Juan Hernandez Gamino, Nicolas Hernandez Gamino and Cristobal Hernandez Gamino (m. Velasco).

The known children of Domingo Hernandez Gamino and Juana Garci Bravo de Lagunas Manrique de Lara (c) were:

- d1. FELIPE HERNANDEZ GAMINO, born abt. 1643 Irapuato, Guanajuato, Mexico. Married AGUSTINA de FONCESCA MONTENEGRA on 21 November 1669, Iraputato, Guanajuato, Mexico.

  The children of Felipe Hernandez Gamino (d) and Agustina de Foncesca Montenegra were:
  - e1. FELIPE GAMINO, christening 5 January 1671, Irapuato, Guanajuato, Mexico.
  - e2. JOSE HERNANDEZ GAMINO, christening 4 December 1762, Irapuato, Guanajuato, Mexico. Married JERONIMINA GARCIA de AREGON, on 27 July 1692, Irapuato, Guanajuato, Mexico.

    The known children of Jose Hernandez Gamino (e) and Jeronimina Garcia de Aregon were:
    - f1. ANDRES JERONIMO HERNANDEZ GAMINO, b. 4 December 1706, Irapuato, Guanajuato, Mexico.
    - f2. JUAN FRANCISCO HERNANDEZ GAMINO, b. 5 July 1740, Irapuato, Guanajuato, Mexico.
  - e3. LORENZA HERNANDEZ GAMINO.
  - e4. MARIA ROSA GAMINO.
  - e5. JUAN HERNANDEZ GAMINO.
  - e6. FRANCISCA HERNANDEZ GAMINO.
  - e7. NICOLAS CLEMENTE GAMINO.
  - e8. MARIA TERESA GAMINO.
- d2. HIPOLITO HERNANDEZ MANRIQUE, christening 29 August 1645, Irapuato, Guanajuato, Mexico (Father: Domingo Hernandez Mother: Juana Manrique).
- d3. MARIA HERNANDEZ BRAVO, christening 20 October 1647, Nuestra Senora de la Soledad, Irapuato, Guanajuato, Mexico (Father: Domingo Hernandez/Mother: Juana Bravo).
- d4. DOMINGO HERNANDEZ BRAVO, christening 20 August 1654, Nuestra Senora de la Soledad, Irapuato, Guanajuato, Mexico (Father: Domingo Hernandez Bravo/Mother: Juana Bravo).

d5. Captain ANTONIO HERNANDEZ GAMINO, born abt. 1655, Irapuato, Guanajuato, Mexico. Death/burial 16 November 1714, Hacienda de la Sauceda, Santa Maria de Los Lagos, Jalisco, Mexico.
Married ANTONIA GONZALEZ de RUBALCABA.
The known children of Captain Antonio Hernandez Gamino (d) and Antonia Gonzales Rubalcaba were:
e1. JUAN GAMINO.
e2. MARIA MANUELA BRAVO de LAGUNA.
e3. CATARINA HERNANDEZ GAMINO.
e4. ANTONIA HERNANDEZ GAMINO.
e5. IGNACIA GAMINO y GONZALEZ.
e6. JOSE HERNANDEZ GAMINO.
e7. JUANA GONZALEZ GAMINO.
e8. BERNARDO HERNANDEZ GAMINO, born abt. 1700, Hacienda de Cueramaro, Penjamo, Guanajuato, MX.

d6. LUIS HERNANDEZ GAMINO, born abt. 1656. Married GETRUDIS DAZA y BUSTAMANTE on 24 December 1681, Irapuato, Guanajuato, Mexico.

d7. JOSE HERNANDEZ GAMINO, born abt. 1657. Married EUSEBIA SARMIENTO PALOMINO on 14 April 1679, Irapuato, Guanajuato, Mexico.
The children of Jose Hernandez Gamino (c) and Eusebia Sarmiento Palomino were:
e1. JOSE HERNANDEZ GAMINO, b. 25 October 1676 Irapuato, Guanajuato, Mexico.
e2. VINCENTE HERNANDEZ GAMINO, b. 1700, Irapuato, Guanajuato, Mexico. Married FRANCISCA GUERRERO on 1 June 1731, Irapuato, Guanajuato, Mexico.

d8. JUANA BRAVO de ESPEJO, born abt. 1658. Married JOSEPH BARRETO de TABORA on 3 July 1678, La Soledad, Irapuato, Guanajuato, Mexico.

d9. ANTONIA MANRIQUE de LARA, born abt. 1660. Married JOSEPH de la FUENTE.
The known child of Antonia Manrique de Lara (d) and Joseph de la Fuente was:
e1. JUANA MANRIQUE de LARA, born abt. 1680. Married LORENSO AGUADO (son of Joseph de la Fuente and Micaela Rodriquez) on 7 January 1697, San Jose y Santiago, Marfil, Guanajuato, Mexico.

d10. AGUSTIN HERNANDEZ BRAVO, christening 18 January 1663, Nuestra Senora de la Soledad, Irapuato, Guanajuato, Mexico (Father: Domingo Hernandez Gamino/Mother: Juana Bravo). (Alternate record: AUGUSTIN GAMINO CASADO, son of DOMINGO HERNANDEZ GAMINO and

JUANA BRAVO (Espanoles) (*Salamanca. Baptism Records 26 February 1651 -1 January 1689/Image 292/505*).

d11. CATALINA GRAVINO BRAVO (MANRIQUE de LARA), christening 14 July 1666, Nuestra Senora de la Soledad, Irapuato, Guanajuato, Mexico (Father: Domingo Gravino (*Gamino*) Mother: Juana Bravo). (CATHARINA MANRIQUE)
Married PABLO LOPES de la FUENTE on 1 July 1684, Irapuato, Guanajuato, Mexico. Died 1716.

d12. BERNARDA HERNANDEZ y BRAVO de LAGUNAS MANRIQUE de LARA, christening 8 October 1668, Nuestra Senora de la Soledad, Irapuato, Guanajuato, Mexico (Father: Domingo Hernandez Gamino/Mother: Juana Manrique) (Listed on record: Manrique, Garcia Bravo Pelaguna, Godparent - Bernarda Manrique Espes, Joseph Antonio de Castilla).
Married CRISTOBAL GUTIERREZ NAVARRO on 7 September 1686, Guanajuato, Mexico.

The known children of Bernarda Manrique de Lara (d) and Cristobal Gutierrez Navarro were:

e1. JOSEPH GUTIERREZ MANRIQUE, christening 7 January 1688, Nuestra Senora de la Soledad, Irapuato, Guanajuato, Mexico (Father: Cristobal Gutierrez Navarro/Mother: Bernarda Manrique de Lara).

e2. MARIA THERESA GUTIERREZ MANRIQUE, christening 17 September 1690. Irapuato, Guanajuato, Mexico (Father: Cristobal Gutierrez/Mother: Bernarda Manrique de Lara).

e3. CATHERINA GUTIERREZ BRAVO, christening 13 December 1695, Nuestra Senora de la Soledad, Irapuato, Guanajuato, Mexico (Father: Cristobal Gutierrez/Mother: Bernarda Bravo).

e4. LORENZO GUTIERREZ, christening August 1700, Irapuato, Guanajuato, Mexico (Father: Cristobal Gutierrez Navarro) (Witnesses: Juana/B. Juan de Ribera, Antonia Navarro) (Espanoles).

e5. CRISTOBAL GUTIERREZ NAVARRO BRAVO, christening 1 January 1702, Nuestra Senora de la Soledad, Irapuato, Guanajuato, Mexico (Father: Cristobal Gutierrez/Mother: Bernarda Bravo). Married BEATRIZ LOPEZ.

The known child of Cristobal Gutierrez Navarro Bravo (d) and Beatriz Lopez was:

f1. MANUEL GUTIERREZ LOPEZ, christening December 1732, Irapuato, Guanajuato, Mexico (Father: Cristobal Gutierrez Navarro/Mother: Beatriz Lopes) (Witnesses: Cristobal Gutierrez Navarro and Bernarda Bravo).

- d6. JUANA GERTRUDIS GUTIERREZ MANRIQUE, christening 19 March 1704, Nuestra Senora de la Soledad, Irapuato, Guanajuato, Mexico (Father: Cristobal Gutierrez/Mother: Bernarda Manrique de Lara). Married (m1) Don JUAN JOSEPH de AGUILAR y ARTEAGA (son of Don Lucas de Aguilar Arteaga and Dona Juana de Sanabria) on 19 April 1723, La Soledad, Irapuato, Guanajuato, Mexico (Dona Juana Getrudiz Gutierrez Navarro, daughter of Don Cristobal Gutierrez Navarro and Dona Bernarda Bravo de Lagunas).
  (GETRUDIS BRAVO de LAGUNAS) Married (m2) JUAN CARRILLO ALTAMIRANO on 1 October 1713, Salvatierra, Guanajuato, Mexico. Spouse of JUAN CAMILLO died (GERTRUDIS BRAVO) on 27 June 1741, Salvatierra, Guanajuato, Mexico.
- d7. MARIA de la CONCEPTION GUTIERREZ MANRIQUE, christening 3 January 1706, Nuestra Senora de Soledad, Irapuato, Guanajuato, Mexico (Father: Cristobal Gutierrez Deraya/Mother: Bernarda Manrique de Lara) (Espanola).
- d8. JUAN MANRIQUEZ, christening 12 March 1724, Celaya, Guanajuato, Mexico (Mother: Bernarda Manrique de Lara) (Witnesses: Don Juan de Aguilar y Artega - spouse of daughter, Juana Getrurdis Gutierrez Manrique).
- d13. BENITO HERNANDEZ BRAVO, christening 25 May 1670, Nuestra Senora de la Soledad, Irapuato, Guanajuato, Mexico (Father: Domingo Hernandez/Mother: Juana Bravo). Married GERTRUDIS PEREZ RAMOS abt. 1718, Irapuato, Guanajuato, Mexico.

c2. TERESA MANRIQUE, born abt. 1630, Guanajuato, Mexico. Married NICOLAS SEVILLANO (son of Juan Sevillano and Juana Rodriquez) on 22 May 1648, Sante Fe, Guanajuato, Mexico (Father: Garci Bravo-*Bravo* de Lagunas/Mother: Cathalina Manrique).

The known child of Teresa Manrique (c) and Nicolas Sevillano was:
- d1. ANTONIO SEVILLANO MANRIQUE, christening 17 July 1648, Nuestra Senora de Guanajuato/Sante Fe - San Felipe, Guanajuato, Mexico (Father: Nicolas Sevillano/Mother: Teresa Manrique).

c3. **MARIA MANRIQUE de LARA**, born abt. 1631, Sante Fe, Guanajuato, Mexico; died abt. 1692. Married PEDRO GONZALES de AGUIRRE y RULES (son of Juan Gonzales de Aguirre and Casilda Rules) on 6 September 1651 (Father: Garcibrabo de Laguna/Mother: Cathalina Manrique), Sante Fe, Guanajuato, Guanajuato,

Mexico (other people on record: Juan Goncalves de Aguirre, Casilda Rules) (Espanoles - Sante Fe).
(Mother's name switches from Maria Manrique to Maria Bravo)
(Children's surnames: Gonzales Manrique, Aguirre Bravo, Aguirre Manrique, Gonzales Manrique de Laguna, Gonzalez Bravo)

The known children of Pablo Gonzales de Aguirre y Rules and Maria Manrique de Lara were (c):

- d1. JUAN GONZALES MANRIQUE, christening 21 November 1652, Sante Fe, San Felipe, Guanajuato, Mexico (Father: Pedro Goncalves de Aguirre/Mother: Maria Manrique)/23 November 1652, Nuestra Senora de Guanajuato, Mexico (Father: Pedro Gonzales de Aguirre/Mother: Maria Manrique). Married BERNARDINA GUZMAN SANCHES (christening 8 July 1650, Guanajuato, Mexico).

  The children of Juan Gonzales de Laguna and Bernardina Gusman Sanches (d) were:
  - e1. JUAN GONZALES SANCHES (born 1670).
  - e2. JUANA GONZALES SANCHES (born 1674).
  - e3. MAGDALENA GONZALEZ SANCHES (born 1676).
  - e4. JUANA GONZALEZ SANCHES (born 1679). Married BERNARDO de la HIGUERA.

- d2. CATHALINA GONZALES MANRIQUE, christening 14 July 1654, Sante Fe, San Felipe, Guanajuato, Mexico/Nuestra Senora de Guanajuato, Mexico (Father: Pedro Gonzales de Aguirre/Mother: Maria Manrique). Married JUAN QUINTANA de HOYAS.

- d3. CASILDA AGUIRRE MANRIQUE, christening 9 March 1656, Sante Fe, San Felipe, Guanajuato & Nuestra Senora, Guanajuato, Guanajuato, Mexico (Father: Pedro de Aguirre/Mother: Maria Manrique).

- d4. PEDRO AGUIRRE BRAVO, christening 16 July 1657, Sante Fe, San Felipe & Nuestra Senora, Guanajuato, Guanajuato, Mexico (Father: Pedro de Aguirre/Mother: Maria *Bravo*).

- d5. MARIA AGUIRRE MANRIQUE, christening 18 November 1658, Sante Fe, San Felipe & Nuestra Senora, Guanajuato, Guanajuato, Mexico (Father: Pedro de Aguirre/Mother: Maria Manrique). Married FRANCISCO CUELLAR de ACOSTA (to Maria Gonzalez de Aguirre), 1685, Morelia, Mexico.

- d6. GARCIA AGUIRRE MANRIQUE, christening 5 February 1660, Sante Fe, San Felipe & Nuestra Senora, Guanajuato, Guanajuato, Mexico (Father: Pedro de Aguirre/Mother: Maria Manrique Bravo). Known also as: *Garcibravo Gonzales de Laguna*.

- d7. BARBARA AGUIRRE BRAVO, christening 15 January 1665, Nuestra Senora de la Soledad, Irapuato, Mexico (Father:

Pedro de Aguirre/Mother: Maria de Bravo). Married FERMIN FEMATE.

- d8. CARLOS GONZALES BRAVO, christening 19 December 1666, Nuestra Senora de la Soledad, Irapuato, Guanajuato, Mexico (Father: Pedro Gonzales de Aguirre/Mother: Maria Bravo; Text: "Espanoles") (Witness: GARCIA BRAVO).
- d9. MARIA GONZALES de AGUIRRE, born 1667. Married FRANCISCO de ACOSTA on 21 APRIL 1685, Santiago Apostol, Silao de la Victoria, Guanajuato, Mexico.
- d10. NICOLAS de AGUIRRE BRAVO, christening 6 October 1668, Nuestra Senora de la Soledad, Irapuato, Guanajuato, Mexico (Father: Pedro de Aguirre/Mother: Maria Bravo) (Witnesses: Garcia Antonio, Joseph Antonio).
- d11, ALONSO GONZALEZ MANRIQUE (de LAGUNA), christening 24 April 1670, Nuestra Senora de la Soledad, Irapuato, Guanajuato, Mexico (Father: Pedro Gonzales de Aguirre/ Mother: Maria Manrique).
- d12. JUANA GONZALES MANRIQUE, christening 7 August 1673, Nuestra Senora de la Soledad, Irapuato, Guanajuato, Mexico (Father: Pedro Gonzales de Aguirre/Mother: Maria Manrique).
- **d13. JOSEPHA GONZALES BRAVO (GOMEZ MANRIQUE de LARA),** christening 23 July 1677, Nuestra Senora de la Soledad, Irapuato, Guanajuato, Mexico (Father: Pedro Gonzalez de Aguirre/Mother: Maria Bravo) (Margin text: "JOSEPHA, Espanola") (*Family Search film #004783806; Image 326/406*). (Mother's name: *MARIA BRAVO de LAGUNAS **GOMEZ MANRIQUE de LARA***)

    Married NICOLAS de MEDINA (Born 29 September 1680, Salvatierra, Guanajuato, Mexico. Died prior to March 1718).

    Death/Burial: 2 March 1718, Santa Veracruz, Mexico City, Mexico (JOSEPHA MANRIQUE, *Widow of Nicolas de Medina*).

    The known children of Nicolas de Medina and Josepha Gomez Manrique de Lara (d) were:

- e1. SEBASTIAN (MEDINA MANRIQUE de LARA), birthdate 20 January 1700/christening 1700, Leon, Guanajuato, Mexico (Father: Nicolas de Medina/Mother: JOSEFA **GOMEZ**, wife) (ESPANOLES) (Godfather: Nicolas Manrique/Godmother: Maria de Olaes - Ulloa) (Priest: R. Nicolas de Salazar) (*Leon de los Aldama. Baptism Records 1695-1704; Image 33/174*).

    Married MARIANA ANTONIA ARIAS.

    The known child of Sebastian Manrique (e) and Marina Antonia Arias was:

        f1.   ANDRES ANTONIO MANRIQUE ARIAS, christening 16 December 1729, San Jose y Santiago, Marfil, Guanajuato, Mexico.
Death/burial: 14 August 1749, El Sagrario, Leon, Guanajuato, Mexico (*Leon Death Certificates 1820-1823; Image 271/ 648*). Spouse: MARIANA ANTONIA ARIAS. Record text: "Sebastian Manrique, Espanol."

        e2.   **GASPAR ANTONIO (MEDINA) MANRIQUE de LARA,** born 28 March 1702, Leon Guanajuato, Mexico. Christened April 1702, Leon, Guanajuato, Mexico (Father: NICOLAS de MEDINA/Mother: JOSEPHA MANRIQUE de LARA) (Witnesses: **Gaspar**, Gaspar Antonio, Saval Manrique) (*Leon de los Aldema Baptismal Records book from 1691-1715; image 45/128*). Recorded in margin of book as: "Gaspar Antonio, Espanol." Married FRANCA. XAVIERA CALDERON HERRERA. Death/burial: 17 September 1755, El Sagrario, Leon, Guanajuato, Mexico.

        e3.   FELIPE de SANTIGO (MEDINA MANRIQUE de LARA), christened during 1707, Leon, Guanajuato, Mexico (Father: Nicolas de Medina/Mother: Josefa Manrique) (Witnesses: Joseph de Gaona, Manuela Manrique, Joseph de Lara, Julio de Dios Marquez Ramirez). Recorded in margin of book as, "Felipe de Santigo, Espanol."

c4.   BERNARDA BRAVO MANRIQUE, christening 30 August 1634, Irapuato, Guanajuato, Mexico (Father: Josef Bravo de la Penas/Mother: Catalina Manrique).

Married JUAN PABON de SEGURA (son of Francisco Sanches Pabon and Ysabel de Segura. Christening 11 September 1633, San Miguel Archangel, San Miguel de Allende, Guanajuato, Mexico) on 3 July 1651, Nuestra Senora de Guanajuato/Sante Fe, Mexico (Father: GARSIBRABO --*Bravo* de Laguna/Mother: CATHALINA MANRIQUE) (Event place: *Sante Fe, San Felipe, Guanajuato, Mexico*).

The known children of Bernarda Bravo Manrique de Lara and Joan Pabon de Segura were:

        d1.   FRANCISCO PABON MANRIQUE, christening 2 June 1652, Nuestra Senora de Guanajuato, Guanajuato, Mexico (Father: Juan Pabon de Segura/Mother: Bernarda Manrique) (Margin text: "Juan, espanol son of Juan Pabon de Segura and Maria Manrique") (Text: "...Francisco, espanol hijo de Juan Pabon de Segura y Bernarda Manrique") (Godparents: Lucas de Vico- Verelo) (*Nuestra Senora de Guanajuato, Guanajuato, Mexico. Bautismos de*

Espanoles/Mexico Guanajuato Catholic Church Records 1519-1984; Image 33/701).

  d2. JOAN CASIMIO PABON de SEGURA MANRIQUE de LARA, christening 22 March 1655, Nuestra Senora de Guanajuato, Guanajuato, Mexico (Father: Juan Pabon/Mother: Bernarda Manrique) (Born: Sante Fe, San Felipe, Guanajuato, Mexico) (Godparents: Nicolas Gutierrez P--es and --- Josefa Manrique) (Margin text: "Juan Casimiro, espanol, hijo Juan Pabon y Bernarda Manrique") (Text: "...espanol hijo legitimo de Juan Pabon y Bernarda Manrique") (*Nuestra Senora de Guanajuato. Bautismo de Espanoles. Volume Number S/N. Years 1646-1669; Image 50/701*). Applied for priesthood in 1679, Leon, Guanajuato, Mexico. Joan Pabon did his religious studies in Mexico City prior.

  d3. BERNARDA PABON BRAVO, christening 28 July 1657, Nuestra Senora de Guanajuato, Guanajuato, Mexico (Father: Juan Pabon/Mother: Bernardo Bravo) (Godparents: Don Garcia de Villas) (Margin text: Bernarda) (*Nuestra Senora de Guanajuato, Bautismos de Espanoles. Volume Number S/N. Years 1646-1649*) (*Family Search #004790239; Image 66/701*).

Sebastian Manrique de Lara has been placed within the Gaspar Antonio Gomez Manrique de Lara line because Josepha Gomez Manrique de Lara's son was named, Sebastian and he also married an ARIAS surnamed individual. Whether he was Josepha Gomez Manrique de Lara's uncle is undetermined, but he resided in Leon rather than Irapuato. Like Gaspar Antonio Manrique de Lara (1702-1755) and his brother, Sebastian Manrique (1700-1749), Sebastian Manrique de Lara took the surname of his father's mother - Catalina Manrique de Lara. There is a possibility he may have been the son of Lucia Manrique de Lara and Pedro Zavala, who also took the name of his mother, Lucia Manrique de Lara. If this was the case, the below marriage would be (m2).

b4. SEBASTIAN MANRIQUE de LARA, born abt. 1620-35, Leon, Guanajuato, Mexico. Married THERESA de AGUIRRE ARIAS.
The known children of Sebastian Manrique (b) and Theresa Arias de Aguirre were:
  c1. BEATRIZ MANRIQUE ARIAS, christening 8 November 1662, Leon, Guanajuato, Mexico (Father: Sebastian Manrique/Mother: Theresa Arias) (Godparents: Juan Sanchez de Lara and Ines Arias).
  c2. MARIA MANRIQUE de AGUIRRE, christening 1663, Leon, Guanajuato, Mexico (Father: Sebastian Manrique/Mother: Theresa Arias) (Godparents: Martin de Ollaz and Isabel Cortez).
  c3. CATALINA MANRIQUE ARIAS, christening 13 August 1664, Leon, Guanajuato, Mexico (Father: Sebastian Manrique/Mother: Teresa Arias) (Godparents Magdalena de Medina) (Witness: S. Francisco). CATALINA ARIAS married MANUEL FLORES.
The children of Manuel Flores and CATALINA ARIAS (c) were:

- d1. MANUEL FLORES MANRIQUE, christening 22 April 1684, Leon, Guanajuato, Mexico (Father: Manuel Flores/Mother: Catalina Manrique) (Godparents: Diego de Cordoba and Theresa de Aguirre).
- d2. JUAN MANRIQUE, christening October 1686, Leon, Guanajuato, Mexico (Father: Manuel Flores/Mother: Catalina Manrique).
- c4. FRANCA. MANRIQUE de AGUIRRE, christening 1669, Leon, Guanajuato, Mexico (Father: Sebastian Manrique/Mother: Juesa de Aguirre).
- c5. JUANA MANRIQUE de AGUIRRE (*assumed*) (born 1673).
  <u>Married</u> NICOLAS BARRETO de TABORA y TANARES 1694, Morelia, Archdiocesis de Morelia, Morelia, Michoacan, Mexico (*Image 87/1561*),
  <u>The known children of Nicolas Barreto and Juana Manrique de Aguirre were</u>:
  - d1. JUAN BARRETO MANRIQUE, christening 14 December 1694, Nuestra Senora de la Soledad, Irapuato, Guanajuato, Mexico (Father: Nicolas Barreto/Mother: Juana Manrique de Aguirre).
  - d2. PETRONILA BARRETO MANRIQUE, baptism 16 November 1701; christening 22 December 1701, Nuestra Senora de la Soledad, Irapuato, Guanajuato, Mexico (Father: Nicolas Barreto de Tavora/Mother: Juana Manrique de Aguirre).
  - d3. PETRONILA MANRIQUEZ, christening 1702, Irapuato, Guanajuato, Mexico (Father: Nicolas Barreto/Mother: Juana Manriquez de Aguirre).
  - d4. NICOLAS BARRETO AGUIRRE, christening 11 July 1703, Nuestra Senora de la Soledad, Irapuato, Guanajuato, Mexico (Father: Nicolas Barreto/Mother: Juana de Aguirre) (Godparents: Diego Barreto and Juana Bravo, Espanoles) (Margin text: "Nicolas, espanol") (*La Soledad. Baptism Records 1690-1707; Image 46/137*).

3. LUCIA MANRIQUE de LARA (born abt. 1555).
   <u>Married</u> PEDRO de ZAVALA by 21 March 1585.
   Resided Irapuato, Guanajuato, Mexico.

While the above reference noted that Pedro de Zavala married Lucia Manrique de Lara, there were zero records with the surname "Zavala" found in *Family Search* 1580-1600 records. There was, however, an individual named, Lucia Manrique de Lara who married in Irapuato. Without a birth record, the connection is undetermined, but likely, this Lucia Manrique de Lara was the child of Pedro de Zavala and Lucia Manrique de Lara, the daughter of Pedro Gomez and Catalina Manrique de Lara.

<u>The *assumed* child of Pedro de Zavala and Lucia Manrique de Lara (a) was</u>:

b1. LUCIA MANRIQUE de LARA (born abt. 1600).
Married (m1) SEBASTIAN LOPEZ AGUIRRE.
The known children of Lucia Manrique de Lara and Sebastian Lopez Aguirre were:
- c1. SEBASTINA de SOTO (born 1620).
- c2. LUIS LOPES MANRIQUE, christening 31 August 1633, Irapuato, Guanajuato, Mexico (Father: Sebastian Lopez de Aguirre/Mother: Lucia Manrique de Lara).
- c3. JORGE LOPES de AGUIRRE (- d. 1673).
  Married MARIA ORTIZ CALDERON.
  (Godparents to Juan, espanol - *Irapuato Baptism Records 1633-1655; Image 299/406*) (Juan's Record - father Juan de Villanueva Dias and mother Maria Ortiz Calderon)
  The known children of Jorge Lopes de Aguirre and Maria Ortiz Calderon were:
  - d1. THERESA LOPES ORTIZ, christening 15 November 1637, Nuestra Senora de la Soledad, Irapuato, Guanajuato, Mexico.
  - d2. JUAN LOPES, christening 1 December 1639, Nuestra Senora de la Soledad, Irapuato, Guanajuato, Mexico (Father: Jorge Lopes de Aguirre).
  - d2. JORGE LOPES ORTIZ, christening 13 April 1642, Nuestra Senora de la Soledad, Irapuato, Guanajuato, Mexico.
  - d3. SEBASTIAN LOPEZ ORTIZ, christening 9 November 1644, Nuestra Senora de la Soledad, Irapuato, Guanajuato, Mexico.
  - d4. JOSEPH LOPEZ ORTIZ, christening 27 April 1648, Nuestra Senora de la Soledad, Irapuato, Guanajuato, Mexico.
  - d5. ATHANASIO LOPES ORTIZ, christening 31 May 1651, Nuestra Senora de la Soledad, Irapuato, Guanajuato, Mexico.
- c4. LUCIA MANRIQUE de LARA (born abt. 1622).
  Married CRISTOBAL de CERVANTES.
  The known children of Lucia Manrique (c) and Cristobal de Cervantes were:
  - d1. JUAN CERVANTES MANRIQUE de LARA, christening 14 December 1649, Irapuato, Guanajuato, Mexico (Father: Cristobal de Cervantes/Mother: Lusia Manrique de Lara).
  - d2. JUAN CERVANTES MANRIQUE, christening 20 March 1657, Salamanca, Guanajuato, Mexico (Father: Cristobal de Cervantes/Mother: Lusia Manrique).
  - d3. ANTONIO CERVANTES MANRIQUE, christening 4 October 1658, Salamanca, Guanajuato, Mexico (Father: Cristobal de Cervantes/Mother: Lusia Manrique).

- d4. CRISTOBAL CERVANTES MANRIQUE, christening 6 March 1662, Salamanca, Guanajuato, Mexico (Father: Cristobal Cervantes Manrique/Mother: Lusia Manrique).
- d5. MARSELA CERVANTES MANRIQUE, christening 22 February 1666, Salamanca, Guanajuato, Mexico (Father: Cristobal de Cervantes/Mother: Lucia Manrique).
- d6. MATIANA/MARIANA, christening 15 October 1669, Salamanca, Guanajuato, Mexico (Father: Xptobal de Cervantes/Mother: Lucia Manrique) (Godparents: Ursula de Paz and Juan de Cervantes) (*Salamanca. Baptism Record Feb. 26, 1651-1689; Image 41/505*).

c5. SEBASTIAN MANRIQUE de LARA, born abt. 1625, Guanajuato, Mexico.

Married (m1) JUANA de CERVANTES.

The known child of Sebastian Manrique de Lara (c) and Juana de Cervantes was:
- d1. MARIA MANRIQUE de LARA CERVANTES, christening 5 May 1650, Nuestra Senora de la Soledad, Irapuato, Guanajuato, Mexico (Father: Sebastian Manrique de Lara/Mother: Juana de Cervantes).

APPENDIX XIII: MEDINA

De FRANCISCO MIGUEL (born abt. 1600-1620)
m. CATALINA de la CRUZ (born abt. 1600-1620)
|
DIEGO de la CRUZ (1649, San Felipe, Guanajuato, MX)
m. MELCHORA de MEDINA (abt. 1650)
|
NICOLAS de MEDINA
(1680, Salvatierra, Gto., MX. Death prior to 2 March 1718)
m. JOSEPHA GOMEZ MANRIQUE de LARA
(Born 1677, Iraputao, Guanajuato, Mexico;
Death/burial 2 March 1718, Mexico City, MX)
|
SEBASTIAN MANRIQUE (20 January 1700- 14 August 1749 Leon, Gto, MX)
GASPAR ANTONIO MANRIQUE (28 March 1702 - 17 September 1755, Leon, Gto.)
FELIPE de SANTIGO (christened during 1707, Leon, Guanajuato, Mexico)

~~~~~~~~~~

DIEGO de la CRUZ, christening 6 September 1649, San Felipe, Guanajuato, Mexico (Father: **de Franco. Miguel**/Mother: Catalina de la Cruz) (Godparents: FRANCISCO MARMOLEJO and Sebastiana de la Cruz) (*San Felipe. Baptism Records 1643-1670; Image 39/511*) (*Family Search* translated the surname "de Francisco Miguel" to Nicolas Miguel).

MELCHORA de MEDINA married DIEGO de la CRUZ on 17 July 1670, Salvatierra, Guanajuato, Mexico (*Mexico matrimonios, 1570-1950*).

The known child of Diego de la Cruz and Melchora de Medina was:
a1. NICOLAS MEDINA, Christening 29 September 1680, Salvatierra, Guanajuato, Mexico (Father: Diego de la Cruz/Mother: Melchora de Medina) (Godparents: Pablo de Caseras and Nicolas de Perez of the Valle de Santiago) (Margin text: Nicolas, of the villa) (*Salvatierra. Baptism Records August 28,1679-January 9, 1686; Image 28/120*).

~~~~~~~~~

The godfather of Diego de la Cruz was: FRANCISCO MARMOLEJO

FRANCISCO MARMOLEJO
married
TOMASA (GOMEZ) OF PORTUGAL

The known child of Francisco Marmolejo and Tomasa (Gomez) of Portugal was:
a1. ANTONIA MARMOLEJO, christening 22 January 1645, San Felipe, Guanajuato, Mexico (Father: Francisco Marmolejo/Mother: Tomasa de Portugal).

ANTONIA MARMOLEJO of PORTUGAL, baptized 20 February 1646, San Felipe, Guanajuato, Mexico (Father: Franco. Marmolejo/Mother: Tomasa of Portugal (*San Felipe. Baptism Records 1645-1670; Image 16/511*).

Godparents: Franco. Marmolejo and Tomasa of Portugal in 1689, (*Baptism Records 1682-1691, San Felipe; Image 101/147*) (Diego Cayetano Ybarra, son of Yberra and Josepha Sanchez, mulato).

~The youngest daughter of Captain Diego Gomez of Portugal (1566-1649) (4th child) and Maria Garcia de Arrona y Miranda (1570-1652) was Melchora Gomez of Portugal (born abt. 1615, Lagos de Moreno, Jalisco, Mexico) who married Pedro de Marmolejo y de Pedraza (born abt. 1610, Leon, Guanajuato, Mexico). They resided in Leon, Guanajuato, Mexico.

Melchora Gomez of Portugal was Rita Getrudis Marmolejo's great-grandmother *(Rita Getrudis Marmolejo was godmother to Joseph Manuel Manrique)* and married to Pedro de Marmolejo y de Pedrazza (**APPENDIX VII**).

Tomasa Gomez of Portugal was from the Gomez of Portugal line. Francisco Marmolejo may have been brother to Pedro de Marmolejo y de Pedrazza, son of FRANCISCO de MARMOLEJO y MEJIA (1577) and MARIA de PEDRAZA (1590, Mexico City, Mexico)/ grandson of DIEGO MARMOLEJO (1507)/FRANCISCA MEJIA VILLALOBOS (1530).

~~~~~~~~~

The godmother of Diego de la Cruz was: SEBASTIANA de la CRUZ.

Sebastiana de la Cruz was also godmother to: PHELIPE MANRIQUE.

PHELIPE MANRIQUE, christening 8 October 1698, Leon, Guanajuato, Mexico (Father: DOMINGO de la CRUZ/Mother: BERNARDA MANRIQUE) (Godmother: SEBASTIANA de la CRUZ*) (Witness: DIEGO de LARA) (*Leon de los Aldama Baptism Records 1695-1704; Image 110-124*) (Phe. = Phelipe).

This line connects to **APPENDIX IV**.

~~~~~~~

De FRANCISCO MIGUEL - possible connections

1. DIEGO de la CRUZ, christening 6 September 1649, San Felipe, Guanajuato, Mexico (Father: **de Francisco los Miguel**/Mother: Catalina de la Cruz.

APPENDIX XIV: MANRIQUE de LARA
(Individuals not included in other research)

1600-1699
Leon, Guanajuato, Mexico

GONZALO MANRIQUE de LARA, born abt.1660.
   Married MICHAELA GUTIERREZ de MENDOZA, Guanajuato, Guanajuato, Mexico.
   The known child of Gonzalo Manrique de Lara and Michaela Gutierrez de Mendoza was:
   a1.   FELIX MANRIQUE de LARA, born abt. 1680.
         Married MARIA YGLESIAS de AIBAR.

JUAN MANRIQUE de LARA, born abt. 1660.
   Married JOSEPHA de HERRERA.
   The known child of Juan Manrique de Lara and Josepha de Herrera was:
   a1.   MARIA MANRIQUE de LARA, born abt. 1682.
         Married HERNANDO PEREZ on 5 February 1708, Guanajuato, Mexico.

ANTONIA MANRIQUE de LARA, born abt. 1662.
   Married JOSEPH de la FUENTA.
   The known child of Antonia Manrique de Lara and Joseph la Fuenta was:
   a1.   JUANA MANRIQUE de LARA, born abt. 1682.
         Married LORENZO AGUADO on 7 January 1697, Marfil, Guanajuato, Mexico.
         The known children of Juana Manrique de Lara and Lorenzo de Aguado were:
         b1.   CATHARINA MANRIQUE, born abtl 1698, Marfil, Guanajuato, Mexico. Married JOSEPH de LLANOS on 25 November 1708, Marfil, Guanajuato, Mexico.
         b2.   JOSEPH AGUADO MANRIQUE, christening August 1701, Marfil, Guanajuato, Mexico.
         b3   MARIA GETRUDIS AGUADO FUENTAS, christening 10 September 1702, Marfil, Guanajuato, Mexico. Married PEDRO MANUEL del CAMPO on 10 November 1734, Marfil, Guanajuato, Mexico.
         b4.   BERNABE ANTONIO AGUADO MANRIQUE, christening 3 July 1707, Marfil, Guanajuato, Mexico.
         b5.   JOSEPH BAPTISTA AGUADO MANRIQUE, christening 16 July 1710, Marfil, Guanajuato, Mexico.
         b6.   MARIA JOSEPHA AGUADO FUENTE, christening 22 January 1713, Marfil, Guanajuato, Mexico.
         b7.   ANTONIA RITA AGUADO MANRIQUE de LARA, christening 20 January 1718, Marfil, Guanajuato, Mexico. Married JOSEPH MANUEL URBINA on 8 October 1745, Marfil, Guanajuato, Mexico.

The known children of Antonia Rita Manrique de Lara and Joseph Urbina were:
- c1. JOSEPH JOAQUIN URBINA MANRIQUE, christening 8 March 1746, Marfil, Guanajuato, Mexico.
- c2. JOSEPH RAFAEL URBINA, christening 24 September 1749, Marfil, Guanajuato, Mexico.

FELIX MANRIQUE de LARA, born abt. 1680.
Married MARIA YGLESIAS de AIBAR, 19 April 1708, Nuestra Senora de Guanajuato, Guanajuato, Mexico (Father: Gonzalo Manrique de Lara/Mother: Michaela Gutierrez de Mendoza).

JUAN FRANCISCO MANRIQUE de LARA, born abt. 1680.
Married GERTRUDIS LUIZ de SABEDRA on 16 January 1713, Salvatierra, Guanajuato, Mexico.

DIEGO MANRIQUE de LARA, born abt. 1685.
Married Vco GUITIERREZ.
The known child of Diego Manrique de Lara and Vco. Guitierrez was:
- a1. JUANA SANTA MARIA MANRIQUE, christening 1714, Leon, Guanajuato, Mexico (Witnesses: Geronimo de Silva, Joseph Manuel Gutierrez).

NICOLAS MANRIQUE de LARA, born abt. 1688.
Married JOSEPHA FRANCO on 8 February 1708, Marfil, Guanajuato, Mexico.

JUAN (MANRIQUE) de LARA, born abt. 1690.
Married GETRUDIS del CASTILLO.
Death/burial: 14 March 1754, Salvatierra, Guanajuato, Mexico.
The known children of Juan Manrique de Lara and Getrudis del Castillo were:
- a1. MARIA GETRUDIS GUADALUPE MANRIQUE de CASTILLA, christening 28 September 1713, Salvatierra, Guanajuato, Mexico.
- a2. TORIBIO RAFAEL de LARA, christening 19 April 1729, Salvatierra, Guanajuato, Mexico.
- a3. MARIA RITA ANTONIA de VALVENEDA MANRIQUE CASTILLO, christening 20 July 1735, Salvatierra, Guanajuato, Mexico.

MARIA MANRIQUE de LARA, born 1698.
Married MIGUEL de MEDINA VINCENTELO on 8 January 1724, El Sagrario Metropolitano, Morelia, Michoacan, Mexico.
Death/Burial: 30 November 1726, Parroquia de Patzcuaro, Michoacan, Mexico (Race: E. Ethnicity: English).
The known child of Miguel de Medina Vincentelo and Maria Manrique de Lara was:
- a1. JOSEPH MIGUEL de MEDINA VINCENTELO, christening 8 February 1725, Patzcuaro, Michoacan, Mexico).

ESTEFANIA MANRIQUE de LARA, born abt. 1699 (Espanola).
Married ANCELMO LORENZO (Lorencio).
Death/burial: 22 April 1752, Salvatierra, Guanajuato, Mexico.
The known children of Estefania Manrique de Lara and Ancelmo Lorenzo were:
- a1. MARIA de la ASENSION LAURENCIO MANRIQUE, christening 29 May 1715, Salvatierra, Guanajuato, Mexico.

- a2. JUANA MARIA LAURENCIO MANRIQUE, christening 11 May 1717, Salvatierra, Guanajuato, Mexico (Witnesses: Felipe de Santiago, Juana Maria de la Cruz).
- a3. FRANCISCA MARIA LAURENCIO MANRIQUE, christening 1721, Salvatierra, Guanajuato, Mexico.
- a4. MARIA NICOLASA LAURENCIO MANRIQUE, christening 9 February 1726, Salvatierra, Guanajuato, Mexico.

1700-1778

JOSEPH MANRIQUE de LARA, born abt. 1695, Mexico.
Married JOANA PAEZ de GUZMAN on 15 September 1710, El Sagrario, Durango, Durango, Mexico.
The known children of Joseph Manrique de Lara and Joana Paez de Guzman were:
- a1. MANUELA JOSEFA de los DOLORES, christening 22 June 1714, Sagrario Metropolitano (Santa Iglesia Catharina), Guadalajara, Jalisco, Mexico (*ESPANOLA*).
- a2. PEDRO JOSEPH VINCENTE MANRIQUEZ PAEZ, christening 16 July 1716, Sagrario Metropolitano, Guadalajara, Jalisco, Mexico.
- a3. LORENZO IGNACIO, christening 21 August 1718, Sagrario Metropolitano, Guadalajara, Jalisco, Mexico (*ESPANOL*).

PEDRO MANRIQUEZ de LARA. Born abt. 1708.
Married: NICOLASA GARCIA, 5 September 1731, Nuestra Senora de Guanajuato, Guanajuato, Mexico.
The known children of Pedro Manriquez de Lara and Nicolasa Garcia were:
- a1. PETRONILA FRANCISCA MANRIQUEZ GARCIA, christening 6 July 1732, Nuestra Senora de Guanajuato, Sante Fe, Guanajuato, Mexico.
- a2. PHILIPA MARSELINA MANRIQUES GARCIA, christening 26 September 1734, Nuestra Senora de Guanajuato/Sante Fe - San Felipe, Guanajuato, Mexico.
    Married EUGENIO GREGORIO VIELMA on 28 August 1754, Marfil, Guanajuato, Guanajuato, Mexico.
- a3. MARIA THEODORA MANRIQUEZ GARCIA, christening 15 August 1740, Sante Fe - San Felipe/Nuestra Senora, Guanajuato, Guanajuato, Mexico.
    Married FRANCISCO XAVIER DAMIAN LONA (son of Vincente Anastacio Lona and Maria Petra Betansas) on 16 November 1763, San Jose y Santiago, Marfil, Guanajuato, Mexico.

JUAN JOSE MANRIQUE de LARA, born abt. 1720.
Married AGUSTINA MARTINEZ.
The known child of Juan Jose Manrique de Lara and Agustina Martinez was:
- a1. JUAN JOSE MARIANO MANRIQUE de LARA, born abt. 1763. Married MARIA GUADALUPE de LEON.

LORENZO MANRIQUE de LARA, born abt. 1720.
    Married LUISA de RIVIERA.
    The known children of Lorenzo Manrique de Lara and Luisa de Riviera were:
        a1.   EUSTACHIA JOSEPHA MANRIQUE RIVIERA, born 20 September 1724; christening 25 September 1724, Sagrario Metropolitano, Morelia, Michoacan, Mexico.
        a2.   MIGUEL JUSTO MANRIQUE RIVIERA, christening 29 July 1726, Sagrario Metroplitano, Morelia, Michoacan, Mexico.
        a3.   MANUEL APOLONIO MANRIQUE RIVERA, christening 18 April 1742, Nuestra Senora de la Paz, Indaparapeo, Michoacan, Mexico.

PEDRO MANRIQUE de LARA, born abt. 1723.
    Married MATHIANA CHAMORRO, 26 February 1743, Santa Fe, Guanajuato, Guanajuato, Mexico.
    The known children of Pedro Manrique de Lara and Mathiana Chamorro were:
        a1.   PETRONILA FRANCISCA MANRIQUE de LARA.
        a2.   PHELIPA MARSELINA MANRIQUE de LARA.
        a3.   MARIA THEODORA MANRIQUE de LARA.
        a4.   EUGINIO GREGORIO MANRIQUE de LARA.
        a5.   FRANCISCO XAVIER MANRIQUE de LARA.

JUAN FRANCISCO MANRIQUE(S) de LARA, born abt. 1726.
    Married JOSEFA RODRIGUEZ.
    The known child of Juan Francisco Manrique de Lara and Josefa Rodriguez was:
        a1.   JOSEPH MARIANO MANRIQUES RODRIGUEZ, born 18 June 1746, Santa Veracruz, Mexico Ciudad, Distrito Federal, Mexico.

JUAN FRANCISCO MANRIQUE de LARA, born abt. 1726.
    Married MARIA JUANA de ARZE on 17 August 1746, Santa Veracruz, Mexico Ciudad, Distrito Federal, Mexico.
    The known children of Juan Francisco Manrique de Lara and Maria Juana de Arze were:
        a1.   ANNA MARIA del ORETO MANRIQUE ARZE, christening September 1749, Guerrero Sureste, Ciudad de Mexico. Distrito Federal, Mexico.
        a2.   MARIA AUGUSTINA MANRIQUE de LARA, born 1757.
                Married JOSEPH MANUEL ESPINOSA on 22 May 1777 Asuncion, Mexico, DF, Mexico.
        a3.   FERNANDO JOSEPH MARIA MANRIQUE ARZE, christening May 1758, Guerrero Sureste, Ciudad de Mexico, Distrito Federal, Mexico.

JUAN JOSE MARIANO MANRIQUE de LARA, born abt. 1740.
    Married MARIA GUADALUPE de LEON on 7 May 1783, Santa Catarina Martir, Santa Catarina, Mexico Ciudad, DF, Mexico.

MANUEL MANRIQUE de LARA, born abt. 1744.
    Married MARIA LOPEZ.
    The known children of Manuel Manrique de Lara and Maria Lopez was:
        a1.   MIGUEL MANRIQUE de LARA (born abt. 1764).
                Married ANNA JOSEFA OLVERA on 28 July 1784, Santa Veracruz, Distrito Federal, Mexico.

ANTONIO MANRIQUE de LARA, born abt. 1746.
> Married ANNA PAULA MELENDES.
> The known children of Antonio Manrique de Lara and Anna Paula Melendes was:
> a1.   JOSE LEANDRO MANRIQUE de LARA, born abt. 1766.
>> Married JUANA MARIA on 2 March 1791, Sante Fe, Guanajuato, Mexico.
> a2.   JOSE LEANDRO MANRIQUE de LARA, born 1767.
>> Married MARIA JOSEFA DIAS on 2 March 1791.

MARIA MANRIQUE de LARA, born abt. 1750.
> Married MANUEL PASTRANO.
> Death/Burial: 6 November 1800, Asuncion, Sagrario, Metropolitano, DF, MX

JOSEPH AUGUSTIN MARIANO MANRIQUE de LARA, born abt. 1750.
> Married MARIA PETRA MONTES de OCA.
> The known children of Joseph Agustin Mariano Manrique de Lara and Maria Petra Montes de Oca were:
> a1.   MARIANO RAFAEL AUGUSTIN MANRIQUE de LARA, baptized 13 December 1773, San Gabriel Arcangel, Tacuba, DF, Mexico.
>> Married MARIA LUGARDA NAJERA.
>> The known child of Mariano Rafael Agustin Manrique de Lara and Maria Lugarda Najera was:
>> b1.   MARIA IGNACIA MANRIQUE de LARA.
> a2.   MARIA CIPRIANA GUADALUPE MANRIQUE de LARA, born abt. 1775.
>> Married JOSE COSME DAMIAN RODRIQUEZ.
> a3.   JOSEPH CAYTANA MANRIQUE de LARA, born abt. 1776.
>> Married MARIA TOMASA RESILLAS on 19 June 1795, Santos Apostoles Felipe y Santiago, DF, Mexico.
> a4.   JOSEPH YGNASIO YNNOSENO MANRIQUE de LARA, born 28 December 1778, DF, Mexico. Christening 4 January 1779, DF, Mexico.
>> Married MARIA de la PENA.
>> The known child of Joseph Ygnasio Ynnoseno Manrique de Lara and Maria de la Pena was:
>> b1.   MARIA JOSEFA ANTONIA VINCENTA MANRIQUE de la PENA.
> a5.   JOSEPH MIGUEL MANRIQUE de LARA, born abt. 1780.
>> Married ANA GERTRUDIZ BAUTISTA MONTES de OCA (daughter of: Vincente Antonio Bautista and Maria Rita Montes de Oca, sister of Maria Petra Montes de Oca).
> a6.   THOMAS MARIA NEPOSMOSENO MONTES MANRIQUE de LARA, baptized 24 September 1783, San Cosmo, DF, Mexico. Death/Burial 27 September 1783, San Cosme y Damian, DF, Mexico.
> a7.   JOSEPH ANTHONIO VALERIANO MONTES MANRIQUE de LARA, baptized 20 April 1786, San Cosme, DF, Mexico. Death/Burial 18 September 1787, DF, Mexico.

a8. JOSEPH MANUEL ROMUALDO THOMAS MONTES MANRIQUE de LARA, baptized 10 February 1788, DF, Mexico.

MIGUEL MANRIQUE(Z) de LARA, born abt. 1755.
Death/Burial: 13 December 1852, San Miguel Arcangel, Guanajuato, Guanajuato, Mexico (*Don Miguel*) (age 97) (Spouse:DA).

JUAN de DIOS MANRIQUE de LARA, born abt. 1757.
Married MARIA JOSEFA de la BLANCA y VALENZUELA.
The known child of Juan de Dios Manrique de Lara and Maria Josefa de la Blanca was:
a1. MANUEL JOSE/JOSEPH MANRIQUE de LARA.
Married MARIA JOSEFA ANASTACIA GARDUNO.

GABRIELA PATRICIA MANRIQUE de LARA, born abt. 1757-67.
Married JOSEPH MATAIS MARTINEZ on 28 February 1787, Sante Fe, Guanajuato, Mexico.

JOSE MARIANO MANRIQUE de LARA, born abt. 1763.
Married MARIA GUADALUPE de LEON on 7 May 1783, Santa Catarina Martir Santa Catarina, Mexico Ciudad, DF, Mexico (Father: Juan Jose Manrique de Lara/Mother: Agustina Martinez).

MIGUEL MANRIQUE de LARA, born abt. 1764.
Married ANNA JOSEFA OLVERA on 28 July 1784, Santa Veracruz, DF, Mexico (Father: Manuel Manrique de Lara/Mother: Mara Lopez).

JOSE LEANDRO MANRIQUE de LARA, born abt. 1766.
Married (*Engagement*) MARIA JUANA JOSEFA DIAS on 12 December 1790, Nuestra Senora de Guanajuato, Mexico. Marriage 2 March 1791, Sante Fe, Guanajuato, Mexico (Father: Antonio Manrique(z) de Lara/Mother: Anna Paula Melendes).

MARIANA MANRIQUE de LARA, born abt. 1770.
Married JOSE ANTONIO RAFAEL LOSA y ESTRADA on 16 June 1790, Sante Fe, Guanajuato, Mexico.

JOSEPH CORNELIO MANRIQUE de LARA, Born abt. 1772.
Married JUANA MARIA VILLASNOR on 20 February 1792, Sante Fe, Guanajuato, Mexico.

JOSEPH MIGUEL MANRIQUE de LARA, born abt. 1772.
Married MARIA MANUELA QUINONES on 30 August 1792, Sante Fe, Guanajuato, Mexico.

JOSEPH MARIA MANRIQUE de LARA, born abt. 1777.
Married ROSA LOPES on 29 August 1792, Sante Fe, Guanajuato, Guanajuato, Mexico.

JOSEPH MANUEL MANRIQUE de LARA, born abt. 1777.
Married MARIANA JOSEFA VALDEZ on 14 June 1797, Sante Fe & Nuestra Senora de Guanajuato, Guanajuato, Mexico.

MANUEL JOSEPH/JOSE MANRIQUE de LARA, born 1777.
Married MARIA JOSEFA ANASTACUA GARDUNO.
Death/burial: 15 August 1836, San Sebastian Martir, Cuauhtemoc, Ciudad, de Mexico (Paternal grandparents: Don Juan Manrique de Lara and Dona Josefa Valenzuela) (7 known children born).

MARIA GERTRUDIS MANRIQUE de LARA, born abt. 1778.
    Married JOSE IGNACIO CHACON.

~~~~~~~

Miscellaneous

JOSEPHA named individuals born in Guanajuato, Mexico 1680-1685:

JOSEPHA, baptized November 1681, Leon de los Aldama (*Baptism Records 1673-1691; Image 28/39*), daughter of Diego de Man- and Mariana Munos y C/Gerez (Perez) (Godparents: Francisco Manrique and Juana de Lariz). Margin text: "Josepha."

JOSEPHA, baptized 30 January 1683, Leon de los Aldama (*Baptismal Record 1673 1691; Image 30/39*). "daughter of Espanoles"
(Father: MANRIQUE/ Mother: Maria de las ...) (Godparent: Alonso de Aguilar). Margin text: "Josepa/Jusepa."

JOSEPHA, christening 17 May 1681, Salvatierra, Guanajuato, Mexico.

JOSEPHA, christening 28 October 1684, Salvatierra, Guanajuato, Mexico "Josepha, daughter del la Inglesia. Godparent: Geronimina -- de Leon

JOSEPHA, christening 26 September 1685, Salvatierra, Guanajuato, Mexico "Josepha Espanola, daughter del al Inglesia. Godparent: Maria de Sandi y Ja- (*Image 8/676 - FH*).

~~~~~~~

Mexico City/Salvatierra, Guanajuato, Mexico

MARIA THERESA MANRIQUE de LARA (born abt. 1646).
    Married FRANCISCO de VERSOSA y LODENA on 10 August 1666, La Asuncion, Iztacalco, Ciudad de Mexico.

JUAN FRANCISCO MANRIQUE de LARA, born abt. 1685.
    Married GERTRUDIS LUIZ de SABEDRA on 16 January 1713, Salvatierra, Guanajuato, Mexico.

~~~~~~~~~

Miscellaneous

PHELIPE MANRIQUE de LARA (born abt. 1678) (Priest, Santa Veracruz, Guerrero, Cuahtemoc, Mexico City, Mexico 1698-1720.

LEONARDO MANRIQUE de LARA - Son of Rodrigo Manrique de Lara.
    From: Indice Geobiografico De Mas De 56 Mil Pobladores De La America Hispanica Volume 1 1493-1519 by Peter Boyd-Bowman (Published by Fondo de Cultura Economica Mexico): Leonardo Manrique de Lara, descendant of Rodrigo Manrique de Lara and Isabel de Molina.

~~~~~~~

MANRIQUE SURNAMES - LEON

FRANCISCA MANRIQUE (born 1627) married LORENZO PEREZ on 26 May 1647, Guanajuato, Guanajuato, Mexico.

AGUSTIN MANRIQUE married ISABEL JUAREZ GONZALES.
  The known children of Agustin Manrique and Isabel Juarez Gonzales were:
  - a1. JORGE MANRIQUE, baptized 2 January 1648, Leon, Guanajuato, Mexico (Father: Agustin Manrique/Mother: Isabel Juarez).
  - a2. MARIA MANRIQUE, baptized 24 October 1649, Leon, Guanajuato, Mexico (Father: Agustin Manrique/Isabel Gonzalez).
  - a3. LUIS MANRIQUE, baptized 21 December 1650, Leon, Guanajuato, Mexico (Father: Agustin Manrique/Isabel Gonzalez).
  - a4. AGUSTIN MANRIQUE, baptized 12 November 1652, Leon, Guanajuato, Mexico (Father: Agustin Manrique/Mother: Isabel Gonzales).

ANTONIA MANRIQUE GAVIENDOLE married JOSEPH de la FUENTE.
  The known children of Antonia Manrique Gaviendole and Joseph de la Fuente were:
  - a1. JOSEPH MANRIQUE, christening 1663, Leon, Guanajuato, Mexico (Father: Joseph de la Fuente/Mother: Antonia Manrique) (Godparents: Ambrosio Garcia and Bernardo de Lariz with --Ulloa).
  - a2. NICOLAS MANRIQUE, christening 20 June 1666, Leon, Guanajuato, Mexico (Father: Joseph de la Fuente/Mother: Antonia Manrique) (Godparents: *Nicolas Marmolejo* and Juana Obserbantz).

FRANCISCO XAVIER MANRIQUE, born 1677. Christening 29 December 1680, Leon, Guanajuato, Mexico (Father: Joseph Manrique/Mother: Maria).

FELIPE/FELIZ MANRIQUE married MARIA de OLLOA.
  The known children of Felipe/Felix Manrique and Maria de Olloa were:
  - a1. RUFINA MANRIQUE, christening 11 February 1672, Leon, Guanajuato, Mexico (Father: Felix Manrique/Mother: Maria de Olloa) (Godparent: Catalina de la Aguirre).
  - a2. AGUSTIN MANRIQUE, christening 13 September 1675, Leon, Guanajuato, Mexico (Father: Felipe Manrique/Mother: Maria de Olloa) (Godfather: Juan Bernal) (Godparents: Antonio de Aguillera and Maria de Aguillera).
  - a3. SEBASTIAN MANRIQUE, christening 1680, Leon, Guanajuato, Mexico (Father: Felipe Manrique/Mother: Maria de Olloa).

MANUEL GERTRUDIZ MALDONADO MANRIQUE, christening 20 March 1699, Leon, Guanajuato, Mexico (Father: Mathias Maldonado/Mother: -- Manrique).

ESTEBAN TORIBIO de la ROCHA MANRIQUE, christening September 1700, Leon, Guanajuato, Mexico (*Leon Baptism Records 1710-1715; Image 29/198*) (Father: Fernando de la Rocha/Mother: Maria Josepha Manrique) (Godparents; Juan Chavez and Margarita Lopez).

APPENDIX XV: MANRIQUE de LARA - Spain

Our link to a specific Manrique de Lara line remains unconfirmed since the parents of Catalina Manrique de Lara (born abt. 1530) are unknown. However, Catalina Manrique de Lara, the spouse of Pedro Gomez, likely descended from the following Manrique de Lara branches:

~DIEGO GOMEZ MANRIQUE de LARA, Seventh Lord of Amusco and Trevino (1355-1385)
~GARCI FERNANDEZ MANRIQUE de LARA (first-born son of the second marriage of Garci Fernandez Manrique de Lara and his wife, Teresa Vazquez de Toledo) (born abt. 1356; died abt. 1411)
~GABRIEL MANRIQUE de LARA (second son of Garci Fernandez Manrique de Lara and his wife Dona Aldonza de Aguilar) (born abt. 1356-)
~JUAN MANRIQUE de LARA (second son of Garci Fernandez Manrique de Lara and his wife Dona Teresa Vazquez de Toledo) (1398-)
~JUAN MANRIQUE de LARA (second son of Juan Manrique de Lara, Second Count of Castaneda, and his second wife Catalina Enriquez de Ribera) (born abt. 1430-)
~RODRIGO MANRIQUE de LARA (second son of Juan Manrique de Lara, Second Count of Castaneda, and his second wife Catalina Enriquez de Ribera)
~RODRIGO MANRIQUE de LARA, First Count of Paredes de Nava (second son of Pedro Manrique de Lara y Mendoza, Eighth Lord of Amusco and Trevino, and his wife Dona Leonor de Castilla). Married three times (1406-1476).
~GARCIA FERNANDEZ MANRIQUE de LARA y CASTILLA (eighth son of Pedro Manrique de Lara y Mendoza, Eighth Lord of Amusco, and his wife Leonor de Castilla), was Lord of Amayuelas. Married Aldonza Fajardo.

After reviewing Manrique de Lara lineage, it seems our Catalina Manrique de Lara, the spouse of Pedro Gomez, was a specifically a descendent of Juan Fernandez Manrique de Lara, the 3rd Marquis of Aguilar de Campoo, 5th Count of Castaneda, Major Chancellor of Castile, Major Hunter of Carlos V who married (m2) Dona BLANCA PIMENTEL de VELASCO (his second cousin, daughter of the Fifth Counts of Venavente). His youngest child was:

    a7.   MARIA MANRIQUE de LARA y PIMENTEL. Married MARTIN ENRIQUEZ, Lord of Valderrabano and Viceroy and Captain General of New Spain (Born abt. 1508; died 1583).

Martin Enriquez moved to New Spain and founded Leon, Guanajuato, Mexico. My hypothesis is Catalina Manrique de Lara was a child of MARTIN ENRIQUEZ de ALMANZA y ULLOA (died 13 March 1583), the 4th Viceroy of New Spain under Phillip II from 5 November 1568 - 3 October 1580. He was member of the House of Enriquez, one of the four cadet branches of the House of Burgundy, Castile.

His father was FRANCISCO ENRIQUEZ de ALMANZA, First Marquess of Alcanices, great-great-grandchild of Infante Fadique Alonso of Castile, the illegitimate child of Alonso XI of

Castile. Enrique Enriquez de Almanza's mother was ISABEL de ULLOA y CASTILLA, a Castilian royal on her mother's side. Born Toro, Zamora, Spain, Martin Enriquez de Almanza was the third son of Francisco Enriquez. His elder brother inherited the Marquisate of Alcanices.

In 1568, the King of Spain, Phillip II, convened the Council of Indies in Madrid. Martin Enriquez de Almanza became Viceroy of New Spain on 5 November 1568 at age sixty, a role he undertook for twelve years (until 3 October 1580). While in New Spain, he founded the town of Celaya in 1571 and San Felipe near San Luis de Potosi. **In 1576, Martin Enriquez de Almanza founded the Villa of Leon where Catalina Manrique de Lara, his assumed daughter, was also considered a founder, alongside her husband, Pedro Gomez and their three children - Baltasar and Gaspar Gomez Manrique de Lara (twins) and Lucia Manrique de Lara.**

Leon was founded by order of the Viceroy Don Martin Enriquez de Almanza. The "viceregal" mandate was granted on 12 December 1575 and fulfilled by Dr. Juan de Orozco on 20 January 1576, the day of the patron saint of the town, Saint Sebastian, is celebrated.

As Viceroy of the Council of the Indes, New Spain, Martin Enriquez de Almanza arrived first in Veracruz then went to Mexico City while working as a mediator between bishops and religious orders in New Spain. By 1570, he personally led an expedition between the Indian tribes that had been devastating the interior but did not give into demands for a total war against the Chichimeca, a war in which Pedro Gomez, the spouse of Catalina Manrique de Lara, was also involved, earning Cerro Gordo for his role by the Royal Audencia. Enriquez de Almanza founded the Villa de San Felipe, Guanajuato, as well as colleges. By 1573, he began the construction for the Cathedral of Mexico City.

While Viceroy of Peru, Martin Enriquez de Almanza died 1583 Lima, Peru after a stroke.

Married to Maria Manrique de Castilla (born abt. 1510), daughter of Juan Fernandez Manrique de Lara, 3rd Marquis of Aguilar de Campoo and 5th Count of Castandesa, the known children of Martin Enriquez and Maria Manrique de Castilla were:
- a1. FRANCISCO ENRIQUEZ de ALMANZA y MANRIQUE, 1st Marquis of Valderrabano
- a2. ENRIQUE ENRIQUEZ, Augustinian Bishop of Osma and Plasencia.
- a3. JUAN ENRIQUEZ, Priest.
- a4. ISABEL ENRIQUEZ de ALMANZA y MANRIQUE, mother of the 1st Count of Fuetiduena.

Studies about Martin Enriquez have been written such as: "Portrait of an American Viceroy: Martin Enriquez, 1568-1583. Cambridge University Press: 11 December 2015.

CATALINA MANRIQUE de LARA, founder of Leon, Guanajuato, born abt. 1530, has unknown parentage, but her estimated birth year fits within the timeframe of Martin Enriquez' New Spain arrival. This fact is supplemented with Pedro Gomez' connection to the War of the Chichamecas. Additionally, Pedro Gomez and Catalina Manrique de Lara, along with their twins, Baltasar and Gaspar Gomez Manrique de Lara, and daughter, Lucia Manrique de Lara, are considered 1576 founders of Leon, Guanajuato. For these reasons, my hypothesis is that Catalina Manrique de Lara, was likely was a child of Martin Enriquez de Almanza and Maria Manrique de Lara:

a1. ISABEL ENRIQUEZ de ALMANZA y MANRIQUE (de LARA). Married ALVARO de LUNA.
a2. FRANCISCO ENRIQUEZ de ALMANZA y MANRIQUE de LARA, First Marques de Valderrabano. Married MARIANA de ZUNIGA VELASCO y ARELLANO, sixth Contessa de Nieva (born abt. 1530).
a3. *CATALINA MANRIQUE de LARA (born abt. 1530). Married PEDRO GOMEZ.*
a4. ENRIQUE ENRIQUEZ de ALMANZA, Bishop of Osma and Palencia.
a5. JUAN ENRIQUEZ de ALMANZA y MANRIQUE (de LARA), priest.
a6. *MARIA MANRIQUE ENRIQUEZ de ALMANZA. Married PEDRO RUIZ de LEDESMA, Senior of Santis-Lamenar and Ramiro Nunez de Guzman, II, Senior.*

Regardless of Catalina Manrique de Lara's lineage, our Manrique de Lara line connects to the Lara Family.

Two books - "Enciclopeida Heraldica y Genealogica Hispanoamericana" (published 1919, Spain) by the Garcia Carraffa brothers and "Historia Genealogica De La Casa De Lara" (published 1696, Madrid) by Luis de Salazar y Castro provide most historically proven Manrique de Lara entries.

The basis for our Manrique de Lara line:

Pedro Gonzalez de Lara, Count of Lara, Medina & Torres, married Eva Perez de Trava, daughter of Count of Transtamara. Their son was named: Manrique de Lara. Pedro Gonzalez de Lara died 1130.

Manrique de Lara (born abt. between 26 November 1134 and 2 June 1137) became the Count of Lara and Viscount of Narbona. He married Hermesenda de Narbona. Manrique de Lara died at the Battle of Huete in 1164.

The son of Manrique de Lara and Hermesenda de Narbona was: Pedro Manrique de Lara. He was also called, Pedro de Molina or Peter of Lara. He married three times and was Viscount of Narbonne by 1192.

Pedro Manrique de Lara, Viscount of Narbona married Sancha de Navarra, daughter of the King of Navarra. The son of Pedro Manrique de Lara and Sancha de Navarra was Rodrigo Perez Manrique de Lara, Lord of Amusco, Pina and Amayuelas. Pedro Manrique de Lara died January 1202.

All Manrique de Lara branches extend from Lara lineage.

Lara was once a city of Ausina - "four leagues from the city of Burgos. It was destroyed by the Moors and rebuilt by the order of King Don Alonso 'the Catholic,' becoming the town of Lara," according to Fray Purdencio Sandoval, Bishop of Pamplona.

All information listed below in this Manrique de Lara chronology was taken from *Historia Genealogica de la Casa de Lara* by Don Luis de Salazar y Castro and translated by Madrid genealogist, Matthew Hovious. The first ancestors of the Lara family were:

1. "Amalaric, Gothic King of Spain in 515. Married Dona Cotilde, daughter of Clovis, first Christian King of the French.
    The known children of Amalaric and Dona Clotilde were:
    a1. Luvia I, King of the Goths.
    a2. Leovigildo, King of the Goths (in Spain). Died 586. Married Dona Teodosia (daughter of Severiano, Duke of Cartagena and his wife, Dona Teodora) de Cartagena.
    The known children of Leovigild, King of Goths, and Dona Teodosia de Cartagena were:
    b1. Hermengildo.
    b2. Recaerdo I, Gothic King of Spain.
    b3. Hermenegildo. Martyred in 595 for refusing communion. Married Mrs. Ingunda (Daughter of King of Austria). Known now as Saint Hermenegildo.
    b4. Atanagild. Married Dona Flavia Juliana (daughter of Peter Augustus, brother to the Emperor of Mauritius).
    b5. Paulo Ardavasto, husband of a relative of King Cindasiundo.
    b6. Ervigio, Gothic King of Spain. Died 687. Married Dona Luibigtohona, granddaughter of Recaredo.
    The known children of Ervigio and Dona Luibigtohona were:
    c1. Veremundo, Duke of Cantabria.
    c2. Cigilona, wife of Egica, Gothic King of Spain.
    The known children of Egica and Cigilona were:
    d1. Uvitiza, Gothic King of Spain. Died 710.
    d2. Count Don Julian Oppa, Archbishop of Toledo.
    b7. Pedro, Duke of Cantabria in 700. Married Unknown.
    The known children of Pedro, Duke of Cantabria, were:
    c1. Fruela, King of Spain in 766. Married daughter of Count Gudesindo.
    The known children of Fruela, King of Spain, and daughter of Count Gudesindo were:
    d1. Rodrigo Frolaz, Count of Castile in 762.
    d2. Aurelio, King of Asturias.
    d3. Dona Nuna.
    d4. Singerico.
    d5. Gonzalo, Lord of Lara.
    The known child of Gonzalo Lara was:
    e1. Dona Aragonta, Lady of Lara. Married Count Teudio.

c2. Alonso, the "Catholic," King of Asturias; son-in-law of Pelayo.

From here Counts of Castile and Viscounts of Narbonne, Lords of Molina and Mesa follow amongst the Lara branches. Our lineage descended from the son of Pedro Lara, Manrique de Lara.

"RAMIRO I
(born 790, Oviedo, Asturias, Espana; died 1 February 850, Oriedo, Asturias, Espana.
King of Asturias, Leon, Galicia 842 to 850)
Father: BERMUDO I "El Diacono" de Asturias.
(Grandparents: FRUELA de CANTABRIA and DESCONOCIDA GRUDESINDO)
Married: URRACA PATERNA, Countess of Castile
|
RODRIGO II, Count of Castile (Governed 850-862/873)
Married: Unknown
|
DIEGO RODRIQUEZ, 2nd Count of Castile (Governed 873-885)
Married: ASURA
|
FERNANDO DIAZ, Count of Castile (Governed 917-924, Lantaron & Cerezo)
Married: Unknown
|
GONZALO FERNANDEZ (born abt. 885-915), Count of Castile, Lord of Lara
Married: MUNIADUNA
|
FERNAN GONZALEZ, Sovereign Count of Castile, Alava and Lara
(born Burgos, Spain; died 970, Burgos, Spain)
Married: SANCHA de NAVARRA
(Daughter of the King Sancho Garcia II of Navarre)
|
GONZALO FERNANDEZ de LARA, Count of Lara and Bureba
First Lord of Aza
Married: NUNA de GUZMAN
(Sister of Count Rodrigo Nunez de Guzman)
|
NUNO GONZALEZ de LARA, Lord of the House of Lara,
Governor of Alava, Lanzaron and Cellorigo
Married: Dona DORDIA DIAZ
|
GONZALO NUNEZ MINAYA de LARA, Lord of the House of Lara
Married: Dona GONTRODA
|
Count NUNO GONZALEZ de LARA, Lord of the House of Lara,
Governor of Lara, Asturias and Mena
Married: Dona MUNIA HERMESENDA GONZALEZ de MAYA
(Daughter of Gonzalo Trastamirez de Maya, Lord of the lands of Maya)

GONZALO NUNEZ de LARA, Count and Lord of the House of Lara,
Governor of Lara and Osma
<u>Married</u>: Dona GODO GONZALEZ SALVADORES
(Daughter of Gonzalo Salvadores, nobleman and Patron of San Martin de Escalada)

Count PEDRO GONZALEZ de LARA, Lord of the House of Lara, Count of Lara, Medina de las Torres, Mormojon, Duenas and Tariego.
<u>Married</u>: Mrs. EVA PEREZ de TRAVA

Count MANRIQUE de LARA, Viscount of Narbonne, Lord of Molina and Mesa, Major Ensign of Emperor Alonso VII and Lord of the honors of Avila, Segovia, Baeza and Toledo. Tutor of King Alonso VIII of Castile and Governor of his Kingdoms.
<u>Married</u>: HERMESENDA de NARBONA, Viscountess of Narbonne
(daughter of Aymerico, third of the name, Viscount and Sovereign of Narbonne, and of Dona Hermengarda, his wife)

(Additional source for chart: <u>Enciclopedia Heraldica y Genealogica Hispanoamerica</u> by Arturo y Alberto Garcia Carraffa. Madrid, 1919. Volume 48. Pgs. 168-184).

As stated, our lineage descended from:

XXIII. Count MANRIQUE de LARA, Viscount of Narbonne, Lord of Molina and Mesa, Major Ensign of Emperor Alonso VII and Lord of the Honors of Avila, Segovia, Baeza and Toledo. Tutor to King Alonso VII of Castile and Governor of his Kingdoms. Fought many battles with the Moors. <u>Married</u> Dona HERMESENDA, Viscountess of Narbonne (daughter of Aymerico, third of name, Viscount and Sovereign of Narbonne and Dona Hermengarda, his wife).
<u>The known children of Count Manrique de Lara and Dona Hermesenda were</u>:
- a1. PEDRO MANRIQUE de LARA (*a1 = XXIV, follows below*).
- a2. AYMERICO (IV of name), Duke of Narbonne. No children.
- a3. GUILLERMO MANRIQUE de LARA.
- a4. MAJOR MANRIQUE de LARA (EMILIA). <u>Married</u> GOMEZ GONZALES, Lord of Manzanedo (House of Aza). Many children born; House of Villalobos.
- a5. MARIA MANRIQUE de LARA. <u>Married</u> DIEGO LOPEZ de HARO ("El Bueno"), Lord of Vizcaya.
- a6. SANCHA MANRIQUE de LARA.
- a7. ELVIRA MANRIQUE de LARA, Countess of Urgel and Subirats. <u>Married</u> (m1) ARMENGOL VIII, Count of Urgel, Lord of Valladolid, Lerida, Aytona, etc./(m2) GUILLEN de CERVERA, Lord of Juneda and Ricohombre of Catalonia.

XXIV. PEDRO MANRIQUE de LARA, second of the name, was Thirteenth Viscount of Narbonne, Second Lord of Molina and Mesa. Tutor to King Don Alonso VIII and Governor of Toledo and Extramadura. <u>Married</u> (m1) Dona

Sancha, Infante of Navarre, Widow of Gaston V., Count of Bearne/(m2) Countess Margarita/Margerina.

The known children of Pedro Manrique de Lara and (m2) Dona Sancha were:
- a1. AYMERICO, fifth of the name (*a1 = XXV, follows below*).
- a2. GONZALO PEREZ MANRIQUE de LARA, Third Lord of Molina and Mesa.
- a3. RODRIGO PEREZ MANRIQUE de LARA, Lord of Amusco and Pina.
- a4. GARCIA PEREZ de LARA, Lord (of half) of Molina by the time of his 1175 birth from his grandmother, Countess Hermesenda de Narbona.
- a5. NUNO PEREZ de LARA, Ricohombre and Lord of Bertavillo.

XXV. AYMERICO, fifth of the name, Fourteenth Viscount of Narbonne. Died 1 February 1239. Married (m1) Dona GUILLERMETA de MONCADA (daughter of Ramon de Moncada, Lord of Tortosa and Great Seneschal of Catalonia, and his wife, Dona Guillerma de Claramunt)/(m2) Dona MARGARITA de MARLY, Lady of the Villas of Vernuil, Moutstrueil and others.

The known children of Aymerico and (m2) Dona Margarita de Marly were:
- a1. AMALARICO, second of the name (*a1 = XXVI, follows below*), Viscount of Narbonne.
- a2. AYMERIC of Narbonne, Lord of Vernueil and other lands of his mother and Canon of Saint Paul of Narbonne.
- a3. MARGARITA de NARBONA.
- a4. ALIX of NARBONNE, Cistercian Order nun at Port-Royal Abbey.
- a5. HERMENGARDA de NARBONA. Married ROGER BERNARDO, Count of Fox, Viscount of Castelbou, during 1232. With succession.

XXVI. AMALARICO, second of the name, was Viscount of Narbonne. Married Dona FELIPA de ANDUCE.

The known children of Amalarico and Dona Felipa de Anduce were:
- a1. AYMERICO, sixth of the name (*a1 = XXVII, follows below*).
- a2. AMALARICO of Narbona, Baron of Talayran. Illustrious descendants.
- a3. GUILLERMO of Narbona, Lord of Vernueil and Archdeacon of Tolosa.
- a4. GALCERANDA of Narbona. Married WILLIAM of VAISINS. Illustrious succession in France.
- a5. MARGARET of Narbonne. Married ARNOLD ANTON, Viscount of Leomagne.

XXVII. AYMERICO, sixth of his name. Viscount of Narbonne. Married Mrs. SILBIA de FOX/FAX (eldest daughter of Roger Bernardo, Count of Fox, and Mrs. Brunisenda de Cardona).

The known children of Aymerico and Mrs. Silbia de Fox were:
- a1. AMALARICO, third of the name (*a1 = XXVIII, follows below*).
- a2. PEDRO de NARBONNA, Lord of Vernueil, etc.
- a3. BRUNISENDA de NARBONNA. Married LOPE DIAZ, Lord of Rada and Ricohombre de Navarra.
- a4. MARGARITA de NARBONA. Married Infante PEDRO de CASTILLA, Lord of Ledesma. With succession.
- a5. MAHALDA de NARBONA, Queen of Castile and Leon. Married ALONSO de la CERDA, King of Castile, the eldest son of Infante Don

Fernando, firstborn of King Don Alonso X "the Wise," and Queen Dona Violante, Infanta de Aragon.

XXVIII. AMALARICO, third of the name, was Viscount of Narbonne. Married Dona JUANA de la ISLA (daughter of Jordan, fourth of the name, Lord of the Island Jordan and Viceroy of Naples in 1262, and of Dona Faidida de Cassaubon, his first wife).

The known children of Amalarico and Dona Juana de la Isla were:
- a1. AYMERICO, seventh of the name (*a1 = XXIX, follows below*).
- a2. WILLIAM of NARBONNE, Lord of Martanhac, etc.
- a3. PEDRO of NARBONA, Bishop of Urgel.
- a4. JOAN of NARBONNE. Married DIOSDADO, Lord of Severac.
- a5. JAUSERANDA of NARBONNE.
- a6. CONSTANCE de NARBONNE, Viscountess de Talard.
- a7. SIBILA de NARBONA, Countess of Ampurias. Married MAUGALIN, Count of Ampurias.

XXIX. AYMERICO, seventh of the name, was Viscount of Narbonne. Married (m1) CATHERINE de POITIERS/(m2) TIBURGA de PUISALGUIER.

The known children of Aymerico and (m1) Catherine de Poitiers were:
- a1. AMALARICO, fourth of the name. Married (m1) Mrs. URIANDA de BELLEGARDE/(m2) Mrs. MARIA de CANET (only daughter of Ramon, Viscount of Canet and Mrs. Maria de Narbona).
- a2. AYMERICO, eighth of the name.

The known children of Aymerico and (m2) Tiburga de Puisalguier were:
- a3. AMALARIC of Narbonne.
- a4. GUILLERMO de NARBONA, Knight of the Order of St. John.
- a5. GASTON de NARBONNE.
- a6. ARNALDO de NARBONA.
- a7. SIBILIA de NARBONA. Married ANDRES de FENOLLET, Viscount of Illa, in 1353.
- a8. JOAN of NARBONNE, a nun.

The succession of Viscounts of Narbonne continues to William, third of the name, Viscount of Narbonne, Prince and Judge of Arborea, etc.

The **SECOND BRANCH** includes the Lords of Aza and Ayllon.

The **THIRD BRANCH** consists of Lords of the House of Ale Lara, of Alcala de Guadaira and Valdenebro. This line includes:

I. Count NUNO PEREZ de LARA, was Lord of Lara, Gama and other places, Major Ensign of Castile, Tutor of King Don Alonso VIII and Regent of his kingdoms. Married Mrs. TERESA FERNANDEZ de TRAVA, sister of King Henry I of Portugal (daughter of Fernando Perez de Trava, Count of Trastamara and Queen Teresa of Portugal, daughter of King Alonso VI). The eldest child of Nuno Perez de Lara and Mrs. Teresa Fernandez de Trava was Count Gonzalo Nunez de Lara, Lord of House of Lara.

The **FOURTH BRANCH** includes Senores of Molina y Mesa del Postigo in Ubeda. Gonzalo Perez Manrique de Lara (second son of Pedro Manrique de Lara, second of the name, Thirteenth Viscount of Narbona and Second Lord of Molina and Mesa, and his first wife, Infanta Dona Sancha de Navarra) became the Third Lord of Molina and Mesa. GONZALO PEREZ MANRIQUE de LARA <u>married</u> Dona Sancha Gomez, Lady of the County of Trastamara.

<u>The known children of Gonzalo Perez Manrique de Lara and Dona Sancha Gomez were:</u>
- a1. PEDRO GONZALEZ de MOLINA.
- a2. MANRIQUE de LARA, Ricohombre, who served King Fernando III, "the Saint," in the conquest of Seville.
- a3. GUILLERMO GONZALEZ de LARA.
- a4. GONZALO PEREZ de LARA.
- a5. GOMEZ GONZALEZ de MOLINA.
- a6. MAFALDA de LARA. Inherited the house. Was "letter" Senora de Molina y Mesa, a condition required for her marriage to the Infante Don Alonso, brother of San Fernando.

The **FIFTH BRANCH**: Lords of Amusco.

I. RODRIGO PEREZ MANRIQUE de LARA (third son of Pedro Manrique de Lara, Thirteenth Viscount of Narbonne, and of his first wife the Infanta of Narvarre Dona Sancha mentioned in XXIV of trunk branch) was Lord of Amusco, Pina, Amayuelas, Palacios de Benagel, Piedra de Vivel, San Martin de Helines, Renedo, Estar, Quintana, Escalada and other places. <u>Married</u> Mrs. TERESA GARCIA de BRAGANZA.

<u>The known children of Rodrigo Perez Manrique de Lara and Teresa Garcia de Braganza were:</u>
- a1. PEDRO RODRIQUEZ MANRIQUE (*a1=II, follows below*).
- a2. RODRIGO RODRIQUEZ MANRIQUE, Ricohombre and Lord of Lac, etc.
- a3. MILLA RODRIQUEZ, Senora de Caleruega.

II. PEDRO RODRIGUEZ MANRIQUE de LARA was Lord of Amusco, Sotopalacios, Pina, etc. <u>Married</u> Dona MARINA GARCIA de VILLAMAYOR.

<u>The known children of Pedro Rodriquez Manrique de Lara and Dona Marina Garcia de Villamayor were:</u>
- a1. GARCI FERNANDEZ MANRIQUE de LARA (a1 = III, follows below).

III. GARCI FERNANDEZ MANRIQUE de LARA was Lord of Amusco, Avia, Pina, Amayuelas, etc. <u>Married</u> BRUNISENDA de NARBONA (Daughter of AYMERICO, sixth of the name, Viscount of Narbona, and second cousin of the Knight mentioned).

<u>The known children of Garci Fernandez Manrique de Lara and Brunisenda de Narbona were:</u>
- a1. PEDRO GARCIA MANRIQUE de LARA (*b1= IV, follows below*).
- a2. JUAN MANRIQUE de LARA, Ricohombre and Lord of Oter de Moronta and Adelantado Mayor of Castile. <u>Married</u> Dona JUANA de ROJAS. With succession.

  a3. N. MANRIQUE de LARA. Married RODRIGO PEREZ de VILLALOBOS.
IV. PEDRO MANRIQUE de LARA was Lord of Amusco, Avia, Palacios de Benagel, etc. Married Dona TERESA de SOTOMAYOR.

The known children of Pedro Manrique de Lara and Dona Teresa de Sotomayor were:

a1. GARCI FERNANDEZ MANRIQUE de LARA (a1= V, follows below).

a2. GOMEZ MANRIQUE de LARA, Archbishop of Santiago and Toledo, Chancellor Major of Castile, etc. Before being ordained as a priest, he had a natural daughter:

The child of Gomez Manrique de Lara was:

  b1. TERESA MANRIQUE de LARA. Married MEN RODRIGUEZ de BENAVIDES, Lord of the houses of Benavides and Santisteban del Puerto. With succession.

V. GARCI FERNANDEZ MANRIQUE de LARA was Ricohombre, Lord of Amusco, Avia, Sotopalacios, Pina, etc. Mayor Major of Algeciras, Merino Mayor of Castilla and Alferez Mayor of the Infante Don Alonso. Married (m1) Dona URRACA de LEIVA (daughter of the Lord of Coruna and Valido del Rey Don Alonso XI, Juan Martinez de Leiva, and of his first wife Dona Guiomar)/(m2) Dona TERESA VASQUEZ de TOLEDO, of illustrious Aragonese house).

The known children of Garci Fernandez Manrique de Lara and (m1) Dona Urraca de Leiva were:

a1. PEDRO MANRIQUE de LARA (*a1= VI, follows below*).

a2. GOMEZ MANRIQUE de LARA, Lord of Malvecino, Sotopalacios and other places, etc.

a3. JUAN GARCIA MANRIQUE de LARA, Bishop of Orense, Siguenza and Coimbra, Archbishop of Santiago and elected of Braga, etc.

The known children of Garci Fernandez Manrique de Lara and (m2) Dona Teresa Vasquez de Toledo were:

a4. GARCI FERNANDEZ MANRIQUE de LARA, Ricohombre and Lord of Estar and Villanueva de Garamo.

a5. RODRIGO MANRIQUE de LARA, Ricohombre and Lord of Tor de Moronta, Fontoria and other places. No succession.

a6. DIEGO GOMEZ MANRIQUE de LARA, Ricohombre and Lord of Villamedian, Redecilla, Trevino, etc. Beginning of branches for the Counts of Trevino, Dukes of Najera from which the Counts of Paredes, Santa Gadea, Villazopeque, Amayuelas, Frigiliana and other illustrious houses were derived.

a7. TERESA MANRIQUE de LARA, Lady of Villarmentero. Married JUAN RAMIREZ de ARELLANO, "El Mozo," Lord of Dicastillo and Ricohombre of Navarre. With succession. Surname: Ramirez de Arellano.

VI. PEDRO MANRIQUE de LARA was the Sixth Lord of Amusco, Ovierna, Sotopalacios and other places. Major Adelantado of Castile, Major Merino of Guipuzcoa, General of the Army of Galicia and the Frontier of Navarre and Warden of Logrono and Viana. Married Dona TERESA de CISNEROS, from the illustrious family of Cisneros.

The known children of Pedro Manrique de Lara and Dona Teresa de Cisneros were:

- a1. GOMEZ MANRIQUE de LARA, Lord of Santa Gadea, Requena, Fromista, Sotopalacios and Adelantado Mayor de Castilla. Married Dona SANCHA de ROJAS, Lady of Santa Gadea, Villaveta, etc.

The known children of Gomez Manrique de Lara and Dona Sancha de Rojas were:

- b1. MENCIA MANRIQUE de LARA (b1= VIII follows below).
- b2. MARIA MANRIQUE de LARA, Lady of Fromista and Arcos.
- b3. TERESA MANRIQUE de LARA, Lady of Villarreal de Alava. Married JUAN de AVENDANO. With succession. Surname: Avendano.
- b4. JUANA MANRIQUE de LARA, Lady of Amaya, Peones, Ovierna and other places. Married PEDRO MANUEL, Lord of Montealegre and Menses; 1st cousin to Kings of Castile, Portugal and Navarre. With succession. Surname: Manuel.
- b5. ELVIRA MANRIQUE de LARA, Lady of Reuquena, Poza and Villaquiran. Married JUAN RODRIQUEZ de ROJAS, Lord of Pozas and Villaquiran. With succession. Surname: Rojas.

VIII. MENCIA MANRIQUE de LARA was Lady of Santa Gadea, Sotopalacios, Villaveta, Calatanazor and Coruna. Married JUAN de PADILLA, Head Chamberlain of King Juan II of Castile, in 1339. With succession. Surname: Padilla.

The **SIXTH BRANCH**: Lords of Ayala, Vizcaya, Belorado and Briones.

The **SEVENTH BRANCH**: Marquises of Aguilar de Campoo. Counts of Castaneda. Lords of Fuenteguinaldo.

I. GARCI FERNANDEZ MANRIQUE de LARA (first born son of the second marriage of Garci Fernandez Manrique de Lara to Dona Teresa Vazquez de Toledo - Paragraph V of the Fifth Branch) was Ricohombre of Castile, Lord of Estar, Villanueva de Garamo, San Martin de Helines and part of Amusco. Married Dona ISABEL ENRIQUEZ (last daughter of Enrique Enriquez, Lord of Vilava and Nogales and Justice Major of the King's House, and Dona Teresa de Haro).

The known children of Garci Fernandez Manrique de Lara and Dona Isabel Enriquez were:

- a1. GARCI FERNANDEZ MANRIQUE de LARA (a1 = II, follows below).
- a2. DIEGO MANRIQUE de LARA (tragic death).
- a3. ELVIRA MANRIQUE de LARA. Married (m1) MARTIN SANCHEZ de ROJAS, Lord of Monzon/(m2) GARCI FERNANDEZ SARMIENTO, Lord of Rivadavia, Mucientes, etc. With succession.
- a4. LEONOR MANRIQUE de LARA. Married BERENGUER CARROZ, Count of Quirra.

II. GARCI FERNANDEZ MANRIQUE de LARA, Richohombre of Castile, Lord of Estar, Villanueva and other places, First Count of Castaneda, Major Steward of the Infante Don Enrique and General Captain of the Border of Jaen. <u>Married</u> Dona ALDONZA de AGUILAR, daughter of the Lord of Aguilar.

<u>The known children of Garci Fernandez Manrique de Lara and Dona Aldonza de Aguilar were:</u>
- a1. JUAN MANRIQUE de LARA (*a1 = III, follows below*).
- a2. GABRIEL MANRIQUE de LARA (*mentioned later*).
- a3. BEATRIZ MANRIQUE de LARA, Lady of Celedilla, Villagre and Lobilla. <u>Married</u> SANCHO de ZUNIGA, Lord of Banares and Warden of the Castle of Burgos.

III. JUAN MANRIQUE de LARA, Second Count of Castaneda, Lord of many towns and places and General Captain of the Border of Jaen. <u>Married</u> (m1) Mrs. MENCIA ENRIQUEZ, sister of Fadrique Enriquez, Major Admiral of the Sea/(m2) Mrs. CATALINA ENRIQUEZ de RIBERA.

<u>The known children of Juan Manrique de Lara and (m2) Mrs. Catalina Enriquez de Ribera were:</u>
- a1. GARCI FERNANDEZ MANRIQUE de LARA (a1 = IV, follows below).
- a2. JUAN MANRIQUE de LARA, Lord of Fuenteguinaldo and Villalumbroso.
- a3. ALDONZA MANRIQUE de LARA. <u>Married</u> JUAN QUIJADA, Lord of Villagarcia.
- a4. ISABEL MANRIQUE de LARA. <u>Married</u> (m1) PEDRO VELASCO, Captain of one of the Companies of Castile/ (m2) SANCHO SANCHEZ de ULLOA, First Count of Monterrey.

<u>Out of wedlock, the known children of Juan Manrique de Lara were:</u>
- a5. ALONSO MANRIQUE de LARA.
- a6. GARCIA MANRIQUE de LARA.

IV. GARCI FERNANDEZ MANRIQUE de LARA, Third Count of Castenda, First Marquis of Aguilar de Campo, Lord of numerous towns and places and Major Chancellor of the King. <u>Married</u> (m1) Mrs. BEATRIZ de VELASCO, the house of the Dukes of Frias/ (m2) Mrs. BRAZAIDA de ALMADA, Portuguese Lady/ (m3) Mrs. LEONOR PIMENTEL (daughter of Alonso Pimentel, Third Count of Beavente, and of Mrs. Maria de Quinones).

<u>The known children of Garcia Fernandez Manrique de Lara and (m2) Mrs. Brazaida de Almada were:</u>
- a1. JUAN MANRIQUE de LARA, died as a child.
- a2. LUIS FERNANDEZ MANRIQUE de LARA (*a2 = V, follows below*).
- a3. CATALINA MANRIQUE de LARA. <u>Married</u> PEDRO LOPEZ de AYALA, Third Count of Fuensalida.
- a4. ALDONZA MANRIQUE de LARA. <u>Married</u> GONZALO RUIZ de la VEGA, Lord of Barcena and Knight of the Order of Santiago, during 1510.
- a5. BERNARDO MANRIQUE de LARA, religious of the Saint of Dominic and Bishop of Malaga.

- a6. ALDONZA MANRIQUE de LARA (*same name as sibling*). Married ANTONIO de MENESES, Lord of Villaverde and the Order of Santiago.

V. LUIS FERNANDEZ MANRIQUE de LARA, Second Marquis of Aguilar de Campo, Fourth Count of Castaneda, Chancellor of Castile and Lord of many towns and places. Married Dona MARIA MANRIQUE (daughter of Pedro Manrique, Second Count of Trevino and First Duke of Najera, and his wife, Dona Guiomar de Castro).

The known children of Luis Fernandez Manrique de Lara and Dona Maria Manrique were:
- a1. JUAN FERNANDEZ MANRIQUE de LARA (*a1 = VI, follows below*).
- a2. ALONSO MANRIQUE de LARA, killed in the siege of Naples.
- a3. PEDRO MANRIQUE de LARA, Bishop of Ciudad Rodrigo and Cordoba and Cardinal of the Roman Church.
- a4. INES MANRIQUE de LARA. Married PEDRO MANRIQUE de LARA, Fourth Count of Paredes de Nava.
- a5. ANA MANRIQUE de LARA, also known as ANA PIMENTEL. Married FERNANDO de TOLEDO (son of the First Duke of Alba).
- a6. CATALINA MANRIQUE de LARA, Lady of Isabel "the Catholic." Married ALVARO de AYALA (grandson of the First Dukes of Arevalo and Plasencia). With succession.
- a7. LUISA MANRIQUE de LARA. Married GOMEZ GONZALEZ de BUTRON y MOJICA, a noble Basque family.
- a8. MARIA MANRIQUE de LARA. Married JOSE de GUEVARA, Lord of Escalante.
- a9. ANA MANRIQUE de LARA, Abbess of the Monastery of Santa Clara de Aguilar.

Out of wedlock, the known child of Luis Fernandez Manrique de Lara was:
- a10. JUANA MANRIQUE de LARA. Married PEDRO RUIZ de AYALA, Lord of the House of Nogales.

VI. JUAN FERNANDEZ MANRIQUE de LARA was Third Marquis of Aguilar de Campoo, Fifth Count of Castaneda, Major Chancellor of Castile, Major Hunter of Carlos V, his Ambassador in Rome and Viceroy and General Captain of Catalonia. Married (m1) Dona MARIA de LUNA y SANDOVAL (his third cousin, daughter of Second Marquises of Denia, Counts of Lerma)/(m2) Dona BLANCA PIMENTEL de VELASCO (his second cousin, daughter of the Fifth Counts of Venavente) (Born abt. 1490. Died 14 October 1553).

The known child of Juan Fernandez Manrique de Lara and (m1) Dona Maria de Luna y Sandoval was:
- a1. ANA MANRIQUE de LARA y de LUNA. Married ANTONIO MANRIQUE de LARA, her first cousin, the Fifth Count of Paredes de Nava.

The known children of Juan Fernandez Manrique de Lara and (m2) Dona Blanca Pimentel de Velasco were:
- a2. LUIS FERNANDEZ MANRIQUE de LARA y PIMENTEL (*a2 = VII, follows later*) (Born abt. 1520; died 1585).

a3. ANTONIO MANRIQUE de LARA y PIMENTEL, Rector of the University of Salamanca and later Canon of Toledo.

a4. GARCIA MANRIQUE de LARA y PIMENTEL, who followed the career of arms.

a5. JUAN MANRIQUE de LARA y PIMENTEL, who went to Flanders with Philip II in 1548.

a6. ANA MANRIQUE de LARA y PIMENTEL. Married DIEGO SARMIENTO de VILLANDRADO y de la CERDA (son of the Third Count and Countess of Salinas).

a7. MARIA MANRIQUE de LARA y PIMENTEL (born abt. 1510). Married MARTIN ENRIQUEZ, Lord of Valderrabano and Viceroy and Captain General of New Spain.

> MARTIN ENRIQUEZ de ALMANZA y ULLOA (died 13 March 1583) 4th Viceroy of New Spain under Phillip II from 5 November 1568- 3 October 1580. Member of the House of Enriquez, one of the four cadet branches of the House of Burgundy, Castile.
>
> Father: FRANCISCO ENRIQUEZ de ALMANZA, First Marquess of Alcanices, great-great-grandchild of Infante Fadique Alonso of Castile, the illegitimate child of Alonso XI of Castile. Mother: ISABEL de ULLOA y CASTILLA, a Castilian royal on her mother's side.
>
> Born Toro, Zamora, Spain, the third son of Francisco Enriquez. His elder brother inherited the Marquisate of Alcanices.
>
> In 1568, the King of Spain, Phillip II, convened the Council of Indies and Martin Enriquez de Almanza became Viceroy of New Spain on 5 November 1568 - 1580. He founded the town of Celaya in 1571 and San Felipe near San Luis de Potosi. In 1576, he founded the Villa of Leon - where Catalina Manrique de Lara resided with husband, Pedro Gomez. From 1570 onward, he personally led an expedition between the Indian tribes that had been devastating the interior, but did not give into demand for a total war against the Chichimeca. By 1573, he began construction for the Cathedral of Mexico City. As Viceroy of Peru, he died Lima, Peru 1583 after a stroke.
>
> He married Maria Manrique de Castilla, daughter of Juan Fernandez Manrique de Lara, 3rd Marquis of Aguilar de Campoo and 5th Count of Castaneda.
>
> The known children of Martin Enriquez de Almanza and Maria Manrique de Lara y Pimentel were:

- a1. FRANCISCO ENRIQUEZ de ALMANZA y MANRIQUE de LARA, First Marques de Valderrabano. Married MARIANA de ZUNIGA VELASCO Y ARELLANO, VI Condesa de Nieva (born abt. 1530).
- a2. ENRIQUE ENRIQUEZ de ALMANZA, Augustinian Bishop of Osma and Palencia.
- a3. JUAN ENRIQUEZ de ALMANZA y MANRIQUE (de LARA), priest.
- a4. ISABEL ENRIQUEZ de ALMANZA y MANRIQUE, mother of the 1st Count of Fuetiduena. Married ALVARO de LUNA.

The *assumed* children of Martin Enriquez de Almanza and Maria Manrique de Lara y Pimentel were:
- a5. *CATALINA MANRIQUE de LARA (born abt. 1530). Married PEDRO GOMEZ. Died Leon, Guanajuato, Mexico.*

  The known children of Catalina Manrique de Lara and Pedro Gomez were:
  - b1. *BALTASAR GOMEZ MANRIQUE de LARA (twin) (1550).*
  - b2. *GASPAR GOMEZ MANRIQUE de LARA (twin) (1550).*
    - c1. *CATALINA GOMEZ MANRIQUE de LARA (1600.)*
      - d1. *MARIA GOMEZ MANRIQUE de LARA (1630).*
        - e1. *JOSEPHA GOMEZ MANRIQUE de LARA (child #13; b. 1677).*
          - f1. *GASPAR ANTONIO MANRIQUE de LARA (born 1702 Leon, Gto., MX; died 1755, Leon, Gto., MX).*
  - b3. *LUCIA MANRIQUE de LARA.*
- a6. *MARIA MANRIQUE ENRIQUEZ de ALMANZA (born abt. 1545-1589). Married PEDRO RUIZ de LEDESMA, Senior of Santis-Lamenar and Ramiro Nunez de Guzman, II, Senior.*

VII. LUIS FERNANDEZ MANRIQUE de LARA y PIMENTAL was Fourth Marquis of Aguilar de Campoo, Sixth Count of Castaneda, Major Chancellor of Castile, Major Hunter of Philip II, of his Councils of State and War, Commander of Socuellamos and Thirteenth of the Order of Santiago. Married Dona ANA de MENDOZA y ARAGON (daughter of the Fourth Duke and Duchess of Infantado).

The known children of Luis Fernandez Manrique de Lara y Pimentel and Dona Ana de Mendoza y Aragon were:
- a1. JUAN FERNANDEZ MANRIQUE de LARA y MENDOZA, Seventh Count of Castaneda, died without succession.
- a2. INIGO FERNANDEZ MANRIQUE de LARA y MENDOZA, also known as, INIGO de MENDOZA. Died in Salamanca studying for his ecclesiastical career.
- a3. BERNARDO MANRIQUE de LARA y MENDOZA (*a3 = VIII, follows below*).
- a4. LUIS MANRIQUE de LARA y MENDOZA, Knight of the Order of Alcantara. Married Dona FRANCISCA de ZUNIGA y AVILA, granddaughter and heiress of the Marquis de Miraval.

- a5. BLANCA MANRIQUE de LARA y MENDOZA. Married (m1) LUIS XIMENEZ de URREA, Fourth Count of Aranda/(m2) PEDRO ALVAREZ OSORIO y SARMIENTO, Eighth Marquis of Astorga, Count of Trastamara, Santa Marta and Villalobos. With succession.

VIII. BERNARDO MANRIQUE de LARA y MENDOZA was the Fifth Marquis of Aguilar de Campoo and Eighth Count of Castaneda, Major Chancellor of Castile and Lord of many towns and places. Married Dona ANTONIA de la CERDA y ARAGON (daughter of the Fifth Dukes of Medinaceli) in Medinaceli.

The known children of Bernardo Manrique de Lara y Mendoza and Dona Antonia de la Cerda y Aragon were:

- a1. JUAN LUIS FERNANDEZ MANRIQUE de LARA y la CERDA (a1 = IX, follows below).
- a2. ANA MANRIQUE de LARA y de la CERDA. Married GARCI MANRIQUE de LARA y ZAPATA, Seventh Count of Osorno.
- a3. CASILDA MANRIQUE de LARA y de la CERDA, died as a child.
- a4. ANTONIA MANRIQUE de LARA y de la CERDA, Marquise of Eliseda and Countess of Onate and Villamediana by marriage to RUY GOMEZ de SILVA y MENDOZA, First Marquis of Eliseda, Count of Galve, Alferez Mayor of Ciudad Rodrigo (third son of Ruy Gomez de Silva, Prince of Eboli and First Duke of Pastrana and Estermera, and of Dona Ana de Mendoza, Princess of Melito, Duchess of Francavila and Marchioness of Algecilla). Widowed on 30 January 1616. Married (m2) INIGO VELEZ de GUEVARA y TASSI, Eighth Count of Ornate and Villamediana, Great of Spain during 1621.

The known children of Antonia Manrique de Lara y de la Cerda and (m1) Ruy Gomez de Silva y Mendoza were:

- b1. BERNARDO de SILVA y MANRIQUE de LARA. Inherited Marquisate of Aguilar.
- b2. ANA de SILVA y MANRIQUE de LARA, Princess of Melito. Married (m1) FRANCISCO ANTONIO SILVESTRE de ULLOA ZUNIGO y VELASCO, Fourth Marquis of Mota and Eighth Count of Nieva/(m2) DIEGO de BENAVIDES y de la CUEVA, Eighth Count of Santisteban del Puerto, Marquis of Solera.

The known children of Antonia Manrique de Lara y de la Cerda and (m2) Inigo Velez de Guevara y Tassis were:

- b3. CATALINA VELEZ de GUERVARA y MANRIQUE de LARA, Countess of Onate y Villamediana, Marchioness of Guevara.
- b4. MARIANA VELEZ de GUEVARA y MANRIQUE de LARA. Married JUAN DOMINGO RAMIREZ de ARELLANO, Count of Aguilar.
- b5. LUIS MANRIQUE de LARA de la CERDA, Hieronymite monk.

IX. JUAN LUIS FERNANDEZ MANRIQUE de LARA y de la CERDA was the Sixth Marquis of Aguilar de Campoo and Ninth Count of Castaneda and Buelna, Major Chancellor of Castile, Lord of many towns and places and

Commander of Horajo in the Order of Santiago. He died 27 June 1653. Married (m1) JUANA PORTOCARRERO, Lady of Queen Margarita, known as Countess of Medellin (daughter of the First Marquis of Almazan and Count of Monteagudo)/(m2) BEATRIZ de HARO y AVELLANEDA (daughter of the Counts of Castillo).

The known children of Juan Luis Fernandez Manrique de Lara y de la Cerda and (m2) Beatriz de Haro y Avellaneda were:

 a1. BERNARDO MANRIQUE de LARA y de HARO (*a1 = X, follows below*) (legitimate son).

Born out of wedlock, the children of Juan Luis Fernandez Manrique de Lara and Dona Ana de Cosio were:

 a2. Fray JUAN JACINTO MANRIQUE de LARA, Rector of the University of Salamanca.

 a3. Friar JUAN ANTONIO MANRIQUE de LARA, Captain of Horses.

 a4. Fray JOSE MANRIQUE de LARA, also a Benedictine monk.

 a5. Fray PLACIDO MANRIQUE de LARA, of the same order.

 a6. ANA MANRIQUE de LARA, also known as ANA de COSIO, Abbess of Santa Clara in Aguilar de Campoo.

X. BERNARDO MANRIQUE de LARA y de HARO was the Seventh Marquis of Aguilar de Campoo and Tenth Count of Castaneda and Buelna and Major Chancellor of Castile. He died in infancy on 31 October 1662 and was succeeded by his first cousin.

XI. BERNARDO de SILVA y MANRIQUE de LARA was the Eighth Marquis of Aguilar de Campoo, Eleventh Count of Castaneda and Buelna, Major Chancellor of Castile, Marquis of the Eliseda, Thirteenth of the Order of Santiago and Gentleman of the Chamber of Felipe IV. Died 1672. Married Dona ANA MARIA de GUEVARA, Lady of the Queen Dona Isabel and full sister of his stepfather the Eighth Count of Onate, during 1629.

The known children of Bernardo de Silva y Manrique de Lara and Dona Ana Maria de Guevara were:

 a1. JUAN MANRIQUE de LARA y GUEVARA, died as a child.

 a2. BERNARDO MANRIQUE de LARA y GUEVARA (*a2 = XII, follows below*)

XII. BERNARDO MANRIQUE de LARA y GUEVARA was the Ninth Marquis of Aguilar de Campoo, Twelfth Count of Castandeda, Marquis of Aliseda, Major Chancellor of Castile and Gentilhombre de Camara of the King. Married Dona TERESA de BENEVIDES MANRIQUE y SILVA, his first cousin (daughter of the Counts of Santisteban del Puerto). No succession. Dona Teresa de Benevides Manrique y Silva's sister inherited the house.

XIII. FRANCISCA MANRIQUE de SILVA was the Tenth Marquise of Aguilar de Campoo, Thirteenth Countess of Castaneda y de Buelna, Marquise of Aliseda, etc. Married PEDRO de la CUEVA RAMIREZ de ZUNIGA, Third Marquis of Flores Davila.

The **EIGHTH BRANCH**: Counts of Trevino, Dukes of Najara.

I. DIEGO GOMEZ MANRIQUE de LARA was the Seventh Lord of Amusco and Trevino (third son of the second marriage of Garci Fernandez Manrique de Lara with Dona Teresa Vazquez de Toledo; 5th branch). Married Dona JUANA de MENDOZA, known in Castile as "la Rica Hembra," or sister of Diego Furtado de Mendoza, a Richohombre and Lord of Mendoza, Hita and Buitrago and Dukes of Infantado.

The known children of Diego Gomez Manrique de Lara and Dona Juana de Mendoza were:
a1. PEDRO MANRIQUE de LARA y MENDOZA (a1 = II, follows below).
a2. N. MANRIQUE de LARA y MENDOZA.

II. PEDRO MANRIQUE de LARA y MENDOZA was the Eighth Lord of Amusco, Trevino, Navarrete, Ocon, Redecilla, Paredes de Nava, the two Amayuelas and many other places, Captain General of the Border of Jaen and Warden of Davilillo. Born in 1381. Married Dona LEONOR de CASTILLA, first cousin of the Kings Enrique III of Castilla, Fernando I of Aragon and Dona Blanca of Navarra.

The known children of Pedro Manrique de Lara y Mendoza and Dona Leonor de Castilla were:
a1. DIEGO GOMEZ MANRIQUE de LARA (*a1 = III, follows below*).
a2. RODRIGO MANRIQUE de LARA, First Count of Paredes de Nava. Descendant of the line of the Counts of Paredes de Nava.
a3. PEDRO MANRIQUE de LARA, Lord of Valdescarey, Anguiano and Matute, who made the branch of the Adelantados of Castile, Counts of Santa Gadea.
a4. INIGO MANRIQUE de LARA, Bishop of Oviedo, Coria and Jaen, Archbishop of Seville, and President of the Council of the Catholic Monarchs.
a5. GOMEZ MANRIQUE de LARA, Lord of Villazopeque, Belbimbre and Cordovilla, Worden and Corregidor of Toledo, and of the Council of Catholic Monarchs. Married Dona JUANA MENDOZA (daughter of Diego Hurtado de Mendoza, First Lord of Canete, and Dona Teresa de Guzman, m2).

The known children of Gomez Manrique de Lara and Dona Juana Mendoza were:
b1. LUIS MANRIQUE de LARA y MENDOZA, Knight of the Order of Santiago and Lord of Villazopeque. Married Dona INES de CASTILLA (daughter of Sancho de Castilla, First Lord of Herrera, and his wife Dona Beatriz Enriquez, descendants of King Alfonso XI of Castilla).

The known child of Luis Manrique de Lara y Mendoza and Dona Ines de Castilla was:
c1. ANA MANRIQUE de LARA y CASTILLA, Lady of Villazopeque and other places. Married RODRIGO MENDOZA, Third Count of Castrogeriz. With succession. Other surnames.

- c2. MARIA MANRIQUE de LARA y MENDOZA, Abbess of the Calabazanos Monastery.
- c3. CATALINA MANRIQUE de LARA y MENDOZA, Lady of Mejorada, Seguirilla and Cervera. Married DIEGO GARCIA de TOLEDO, Seventh Lord of Mejorada. With succession.

a6. JUAN MANRIQUE de LARA, Archdeacon of Valpuesta, Apostolic Protonotary and the Council of King Enrique IV.

The known child of Juan Manrique de Lara was:
- b1. CATALINA MANRIQUE de LARA, Lady of Requena. Married JUAN RODRIQUEZ de ROJAS, Fourth Lord of Requena, brother of Antonio (le Rojas, Archbishop of Granada and President of Castile). Trunk of long succession to the Lordship of Requena. Surname: Rojas.

a7. FADIQUE MANRIQUE de LARA, Lord of Banos, Hito, Menjivar, Torrecampo and other places. Major Sheriff of Ecija, of the Council of the King and Commander of the Azuago in the Order of Santiago. Married Dona BEATRIZ de FIGUEROA, Lady of the House of Rebolledo de la Torre and full sister to the First Count of Feria.

The known children of Fadique Manrique de Lara and Dona Beatriz de Figueroa were:
- b1. ELVIRA MANRIQUE de LARA y FIGUEROA, Lady of Banos, el Hito, Quintanilla, etc. Married FRANCISCO ENRIQUEZ, Lord of Vega de Rui Ponce, Warden of Velez, Malaga and General of the Navy. With succession.
- b2. FRANCISCA MANRIQUE de LARA y FIGUEROA. Married LOUIS PORTOCARRERO, Seventh Lord of Palma and Almenara and Commander of Azuaga. With succession. Surname: Portocarrero.
- b3. MARIA MANRIQUE de LARA y FIGUEROA, Senora de Sotosgudo, Rebolledo de la Torre y Alvala, and Duchess of Sessa, Terranova and Saint Angelo. Married GONZALO FERNANDEZ de CORDOVA, the First Duke of Terranova. With succession. Other surnames used.
- b4. LEONOR MANRIQUE de LARA y FIGUEROA, Senora de Salazar, Palazuelos, Santillan, etc. Married PEDRO CARRILLO de CORDOBA. With succession.

a8. GARCI FERNANDEZ MANRIQUE de LARA, Lord of Amayuelas de Abajo and de Arriba, Belliza, Espinosa, Jiquena, Alhama and Tirieza, of the Council of the Catholic Monarchs, Captain of his people of war, first Warden, Major Justice and Captain of Malaga and Commander of the Corral de Almaguer in the Order of Santiago. Trunk for the branch of Counts of the Amayuelas.

a9. BEATRIZ MANRIQUE de LARA. Married PEDRO FERNANDEZ de VELASCO, First Count of Hara. With succession.

- a10. JUANA MANRIQUE de LARA. <u>Married</u> FERNANDO de SANDOVAL y ROJAS, Second Count of Castro, of Denla and Adelantado Major of Castile. With succession.
- a11. LEONOR MANRIQUE de LARA. <u>Married</u> ALVARO de ZUNIGA, First Duke of Arevalo, Plasencia and Bejar, Count of Ledesma and Major Justice of Castile.
- a12. INES MANRIQUE de LARA. <u>Married</u> JUAN HURTADO de MENDOZA, Second Lord of Canete. Trunk for the Marquises of Canete.
- a13. MARIA MANRIQUE de LARA. <u>Married</u> RODRIGO de CASTANEDA, Lord of Fuentiduena.
- a14. ISABEL MANRIQUE de LARA. <u>Married</u> PEDRO VELEZ de GUEVARA, Ricohombre and Lord of Ornate.
- a15. ALDONZA MANRIQUE de LARA, Abbess of the Monastery of Santa Clara de Calabazanos.

III. DIEGO GOMEZ MANRIQUE de LARA was Ninth Lord of Amusco, Redecilla, Navarrete and other towns and places. Adelantado Mayor, Notary Major of the Kingdom of Leon and First Count of Trevino. <u>Married</u> Dona MARIA de SANDOVAL (daughter of Diego de Sandoval, First Count of Castro, and Dona Beatriz de Avellaneda, Lady of Gumeil).

<u>The known children of Diego Gomez Manrique de Lara and Dona Maria de Sandoval were:</u>

- a1. PEDRO MANRIQUE de LARA y SANDOVAL (*a1 = IV, follows below*).
- a2. DIEGO MANRIQUE de LARA y SANDOVAL, Notary Major of the Kingdom of Leon.
    <u>The known children of Diego Manrique de Lara y Sandoval were:</u>
    - b1. ALONSO MANRIQUE de LARA.
    - b2. PEDRO MANRIQUE de LARA.
- a3. JUANA MANRIQUE de LARA y SANDOVAL. <u>Married</u> INIGO de GUEVARA, First Count of Onate. With succession. Surname: Guevara.
- a4. LEONOR MANRIQUE de LARA y SANDOVAL. <u>Married</u> SANCHO de BAZAN (son of the First Viscounts of Valduerna).
- a5. BEATRIZ MANRIQUE de LARA. <u>Married</u> JUAN MANRIQUE de LARA, Lord of Fuenteguinaldo and brother of Garcia Manrique de Lara, First Marquis of Aguilar de Campoo; branch of the Marquises of Aguilar de Campoo.

IV. PEDRO MANRIQUE de LARA y SANDOVAL (born 1443) was the Second Count of Trevino and First Duke of Najera, Tenth Lord of Amusco, Navarrete and other towns and places, Major Treasurer of Vizcaya, Major Notary of the Kingdom of Leon, General Captain of the Frontiers of Aragon, Navarre and Jaen and of the Army of Navarre. <u>Married</u> Dona GUIOMAR de CASTRO, of the House of Castro.

<u>The known children of Pedro Manrique de Lara y Sandoval and Dona Guiomar de Castro were:</u>

a1. MANRIQUE de LARA y CASTRO, died young.
a2. ANTONIO MANRIQUE de LARA y CASTRO (a2 = V, follows below).

a3. LEONOR MANRIQUE de LARA y CASTRO. Married FRANCISCO de ZUNIGA y GUZMAN, Count of Ayamonte and Lord of Lepe, later Marquis of Ayamonte, his second cousin.
The known child of Leonor Manrique de Lara y Castro and Francisco de Zuniga y Guzman was:
   b1. TERESA de ZUNIGA y MANRIQUE de LARA, Marquise of Ayomonte, Duchess of Bejar, Countess of Banares. Married FRANCISCO de SOTOMAYOR, Fifth Count of Belalcazar, Viscount of Puebla de Alcocer. With succession.
a4. JUANA MANRIQUE de LARA y CASTRO, Lady of Zalduendo. Married VICTOR de GUEVARA, first-born son of the House of Onate (son of Inigo, First Count of Onate and of Dona Beatriz de Guzman, m1). With succession.
a5. BRIANDA MANRIQUE de LARA y CASTRO. Married LUIS de BEAUMONT, Third Count of Lerin, Constable and Grand Chancellor of Navarre. With succession.
a6. GUIOMAR MANRIQUE de LARA y CASTRO. Married FELIPE de CASTRO y PINOS, "the Posthumous," Lord of Baronies of Castro, Pinos Peralta and Guimera, Viscount of Illa and Canet (son of Felipe de Castro, "the Good," and his wife, Dona Maria Hurtado de Mendoza).
a7. MARIA MANRIQUE de LARA y CASTRO, died young.
a8. FRANCISCA MANRIQUE de LARA y CASTRO. Married FRANCISCO FOLCH de CARDONA, Second Duke of Cardona, Count of Prades, Marquess of Pallars, etc. With succession.
a9. ISABEL MANRIQUE de LARA. Abbess of the monastery of Las Huelgas de Burgos.

Out of wedlock, the known children of Pedro Manrique de Lara y Sandoval, the First Duke of Najera were:
a10 ALVARO MANRIQUE de LARA.
a11. LUIS MANRIQUE de LARA. Lord of Alesanco, Commander of the houses of Cordoba, in the order of Calatrava, whose mother was Dona MARIA de SANDOVAL, first cousin with his father. With succession.
a12. FRANCISCO MANRIQUE de LARA. Chaplain of Carlos V and Bishop of Orense, Salamanca and Siguenza.
a13. JORGE MANRIQUE de LARA.
a14. FELIPE MANRIQUE de LARA, Commander of Ballesteros and Warden of the Almaden in the Order of Calatrava.
a15. JUAN MANRIQUE de LARA, called "Boquinete." Accompanied Charles V in the conquest of Tunisia.
a16. GARCIA MANRIQUE de LARA. Canon and Treasurer of the Cathedral of Toledo.
a17. PEDRO MANRIQUE de LARA. Lord of Azofra. Married Dona ISABEL de MENDOZA (daughter of Pedro Carrillo de Albornoz, Lord of Torralba, Beteta and other places and of Dona Mencia de Mendoza).

The known children of Pedro Manrique de Lara and Dona Isabel de Mendoza were:
- b1. DIEGO MANRIQUE de LARA y MENDOZA, Commander of Mora of the Order of Santiago.
- b2. JUANA MANRIQUE de LARA y MENDOZA, Lady of Bedmar. Married ALONSO de la CUEVA y BENAVIDES, First Lord of Bedmar. Trunk of the Lords of Bedmar.

- a18. CLAUDIO MANRIQUE de LARA. Commander of Badajoz and Villasbuenas in the Order of Alcantar and Steward of Queen Mary of Hungary.
- a19. Commander LORENZO MANRIQUE de LARA.
- a20. ANA MANRIQUE de LARA.
- a21. CATALINA MANRIQUE de LARA, Abbess of the monastery of Santa Clara, Burgos, and six other daughters, all nuns in Santa Clara, Burgos.

V. ANTONIO MANRIQUE de LARA y CASTRO was the Second Duke of Najera, Third Count of Trevino, Eleventh Lord of Amusco, Major Treasurer of Vizcaya, Knight of the Golden Fleece and Viceroy and Captain General of Navarre. Married Dona JUANA de CARDONA, sister of the Duke of Cardona and first cousin of Fernando "the Catholic" (daughter of the First Duke and Fourth Count of Cardona, and of Dona Aldonza Enriquez, sister of Queen Dona Juana Enriquez, mother of the Catholic King).

The known children of Antonio Manrique de Lara y Castro and Dona Juana de Cardona were:
- a1. MANRIQUE de LARA y CARDONA (*a1 = VI, follows below*).
- a2. JUAN MANRIQUE de LARA y CARDONA, Lord of San Leonardo and other villas and Clavero de Calatrava, Major Accountant of Castile, Ambassador Extraordinary in Rome, Viceroy of Naples and Steward of Carlos V. Married (m1) Dona JUANA de CASTRO y de NORONA, Lady of the Empress Dona Isabel with whom he passed from Portugal to Castile/(m2) Dona ANA FAJARDO, Lady of the Queen Dona Isabel de la Paz (and daughter of the First Marquis of the Velez).

    The known children of Juan Manrique de Lara y Cardona and Dona Ana Fajardo were:
    - b1. ANTONIO MANRIQUE de LARA y FAJARDO, Lord of San Leonardo.
    - b2. JUANA MANRIQUE de LARA y FAJARDO, Lady of San Leonardo and Countess of Valencia. Married (her nephew) MANRIQUE de LARA GIRON, Count of Valencia, Viceroy and Captain General of Catalonia.
    - b3. ISABEL MANRIQUE de LARA y FAJARDO, nun in the Agustinas de Gracia, in Avila.

- a3. RODRIGO MANRIQUE de LARA y CARDONA.
- a4. BERNARDINO MANRIQUE de LARA y CARDONA, Commander of Herrera in the Order of Calatrava. Married Dona ANA de

CASTRO (daughter of Hernando de Castro, Warden of the Fortress of Bolanos, and of Dona Leonor de Hueva).

The known children of Bernardino Manrique de Lara y Cardona and Dona Ana de Castro were:

- b1. ALDONZA MANRIQUE de LARA y CASTRO. Did not marry.
- b2. GUIOMAR MANRIQUE de LARA y CASTRO. Married ALVARO de BAZAN, Second Marquis of Santa Cruz, First Marquis del Vivo. With succession.
- b3. JUANA MANRIQUE de LARA y CASTRO.

a5. ALDONZA MANRIQUE de LARA y CARDONA. Did not marry.
a6. GUIOMAR MANRIQUE de LARA Y CARDONA. Married ANTONIO MANRIQUE de LARA, Fifth Count of Paredes de Nava in 1542. Succession to the branch of the Counts of the Paredes of Nava.
a7. MARIA MANRIQUE de LARA y CARDONA, Chambermaid of the Empress Maria, wife of Emperor Maximilian II of Austria, Infanta of Spain and sister of Felipe II.

VI. MANRIQUE de LARA y CARDONA was the Third Duke of Najera, Fourth Count of Trevino and Valencia, Twelfth Lord of Amusco, Major Treasurer of Vizcaya and Knight of the Golden Fleece. Married Dona LUISA de ACUNA y MANUEL (daughter of Enrique de Acuna, Fourth Count of Valencia, and of Dona Aldonza Manuel).

The known children of Manrique de Lara y Cardona and Dona Luisa de Acuna y Manuel were:

- a1. MANRIQUE de LARA y ACUNA (*a1 = VII, follows later*).
- a2. ENRIQUE MANRIQUE de LARA y ACUNA. Married (first cousin) INES MANRIQUE de LARA, Sixth Countess of Paredes de Nava.

Out of wedlock, the known children of Manrique de Lara y Carbona were:

- a3. MANRIQUE de LARA, Gentleman of King Phillip II.
- a4. JUAN BAUTISTA MANRIQUE de LARA, Canon of Toledo.
- a5. ANTONIO MANRIQUE de LARA, Clergyman.
- a6. ALONSO MANRIQUE de LARA, of the Society of Jesus.

VII. MANRIQUE de LARA y ACUNA was the Fourth Duke of Najera, Fifth Count of Trevino, Sixth Count of Valencia, Thirteenth Lord of Amusco, Commander of Herrera in the Order of Calatrava, Major Treasurer of Vizcaya, Viceroy and General Captain of Valencia and of the Council of State. He died 5 June 1600 in Madrid. Married Dona MARIA GIRON (daughter of Juan Giron, Fourth Count of Urena, and of his wife, Dona Maria de la Cueva).

The known children of Manrique de Lara y Acuna and Dona Maria de la Cueva were:

- a1. MANRIQUE de LARA y GIRON, Count of Valencia and Viceroy and Captain General of Catalonia. Married Dona JUANA MANRIQUE de LARA FAJARDO, his aunt, first cousin of his father, Third Lady of San Leonardo (daughter of Juan Manrique de Lara, Lord of San Leonardo, and his wife, Dona Ana Fajardo).

The known child of Manrique de Lara y Giron and Dona Juana Manrique de Lara Fajardo was:

    b1. MARIANA MANRIQUE de LARA y MANRIQUE de LARA, nun in La Concepcion, Torrijos.
  a2. JUAN MANRIQUE de LARA y GIRON, Sixth Count of Trevino and Commander of Herrera in the Order of Calatrava. <u>Married</u> Dona MARIA de QUINONES (daughter of Luis de Quinones, Fifth Count of Luna, and of Dona Francisca de Beaumont). He died, as did his older brother, before his father, without children.
  a3. LUISA MANRIQUE de LARA y GIRON (*a3 = VIII, follows below*).
  a4. RODRIGO MANRIQUE de LARA y GIRON. Died young.
  a5. PEDRO MANRIQUE de LARA y GIRON. Died young.

<u>With Dona MENCIA de UBIERNA, Manrique de Lara y Acuna, the 4th Duke of Najera, had two children:</u>
  a6. JUAN MANRIQUE de LARA y UBIERNA.
  a7. ISABEL MANRIQUE de LARA y UBIERNA.

VIII. LUISA MANRIQUE de LARA y GIRON was the Fifth Duchess of Najera, Duchess of Maqueda, Seventh Countess of Maqueda, Sixth of Trevino, Fourteenth Lady of Amusco, etc. <u>Married</u> BERNARDINO de CARDENAS, Third Duke of Maqueda, in whose house the titles of this branch of Lara were incorporated. With succession. Surname: Cardenas.

The **NINTH BRANCH**: Lara family from Segovia.

Rama Once: Lords of Ontoria, Ortizuela and Torre de Zubaran.

The **TWELFTH BRANCH**: Counts of Osorno - Dukes of Galisteo.

I. GABRIEL MANRIQUE de LARA (second son of Garci-Fernandez Manrique de Lara and his wife Aldonza de Aguilar, mentioned seventh branch, Marquises of Aguilar de Campoo) was the First Count of Osorno, Duke of Galisteo, Major Commander of Castile, Thirteen of the Order of Santiago and Lord of Maderuelo, Fuenteguinaldo, San Martin del Monte and other towns and places. <u>Married</u> (m1) Mrs. MENCIA DAVALOS y GUERVARA, Lady of Orsorno (daughter of Ruy Lopez Davalos, Count of Rivadeo, and of Mrs. Elvira de Guevara, his second wife)/(m2) Mrs. ALDONZA de VIVERO (eldest daughter of Alonso Perez de Vivero, Lord of Vivero and Major Accountant of Castile, and of Mrs. Ines de Guzman, Duchess of Villalva).

<u>The known children of Gabriel Manrique de Lara and (m1) Mrs. Mencia Davalos y Guervara were:</u>
  a1. TELLO MANRIQUE de LARA y DAVALOS, died young.
  a2. GARCIA MANRIQUE de LARA y DAVALOS, died young.

<u>The known children of Gabriel Manrique de Lara and (m2) Mrs. Aldonza de Vivero were:</u>
  a3. PEDRO MANRIQUE de LARA y VIVERO (*a3 = II, follows below*).

- a4. JUAN MANRIQUE de LARA y VIVERO, Commander of Montemolin in the Order of Santiago. Married Dona ISABEL de la CUEVA, sister of Beltran de la Cuerva, First Duke of Albuquerque, Count of Ledsma.
  The known children of Juan Manrique de Lara y Vivero and Dona Isabel de la Cueva were:
  - b1. GARCI FERNANDEZ MANRIQUE de LARA y de la CUEVA. Married Dona LUISA de PEREA y FIGUEROA.
    The known children of Garci Fernandez Manrique de Lara y de la Cueva and Dona Luisa de Perea y Figueroa were:
    - c1. GABRIEL MANRIQUE de LARA y PEREA.
    - c2. JUAN MANRIQUE de LARA y PEREA, Knight and Attorney General of the Order of Santiago.
    - c3. FRANCISCO MANRIQUE de LARA y PEREA.
    - c4. ISABEL MANRIQUE de LARA y PEREA.
    - c5. ELVIRA MANRIQUE de LARA y PEREA.
  - b2. MAYOR MANRIQUE de LARA y de la CUEVA.
  - b3. CATALINA MANRIQUE de LARA y de la CUEVA.
  - b4. ISABEL MANRIQUE de LARA y de la CUEVA.
- a5. MARIA MANRIQUE de LARA y VIVERO. Married GONZALO CHACON, First Lord of Casarrubies and Arroyomolinos. No succession.
- a6. BEATRIZ MANRIQUE de LARA y VIVERO, Abbess of the Monastery of Santa Clara de Carrion de los Condes.
- a7. ALDONZA MANRIQUE de LARA y VIVERO. Married GOMEZ CARRILLO de Acuna, Lord of Pinto and Caracena.
- a8. LEONOR MANRIQUE de LARA y VIVERO. Married GARCIA de TOLEDO, Lord of Horcajo and cousin of the Catholic King (fifth son of Garcia Alvarez de Toledo, First Duke of Alba and Count of Salvatierra, and of Dona Maria Enriquez).

II. PEDRO MANRIQUE de LARA y VIVERO was Second Count of Osorno, Duke of Galisteo and Major Commander of Castile in the Order of Santiago. Married (m1) Dona TERESA de TOLEDO, first cousin of the Catholic King (daughter of Garcia Alvarez de Toledo, First Duke of Alba, and of Dona Maria Enriquez)/(m2) Dona MARIA de CABRERA y BOBADILLA, sister of the Second Marquis of Moya and of the First Count of Chinchon.

The known children of Pedro Manrique de Lara y Vivero and (m1) Dona Teresa de Toledo were:
- a1. GARCI FERNANDEZ MANRIQUE de LARA y TOLEDO (a1 = III, follows below).
- a2. GABRIEL MANRIQUE de LARA y TOLEDO, Lord of Villacis, and trunk of the Counts of Villanueva de Canedo.
- a3. PEDRO MANRIQUE de LARA y TOLEDO, religious of Santo Domingo.
- a4. JUAN MANRIQUE de LARA y TOLEDO, religious of Santo Domingo.
- a5. ALDONZA MANRIQUE de LARA y TOLEDO. Married PEDRO de LUNA, Third Lord of Fuentiduena and full brother of Dona Maria de Luna, by her marriage Third Countess of Osorno.
- a6. MARTA MANRIQUE de LARA y TOLEDO, nun in Santa Clara de Carrion.

       a7.   BEATRIZ MANRIQUE de LARA y TOLEDO, nun in Santa Clara de Carrion.

The child of Pedro Manrique de Lara y Vivero and (m2) Dona Maria de Cabrera y Bobadilla was:

       a8.   PEDRO MANRIQUE de LARA y BOBADILLA, Commander of Benfayan, in the Order of Alcantara.

            The known children of Pedro Manrique de Lara y Bobadilla were:

            b1.   PEDRO MANRIQUE de LARA, monk at the Carthusian monastery of Granada.

            b2.   ANTONIA MANRIQUE de LARA.

III.   GARCI FERNANDEZ MANRIQUE de LARA y TOLEDO was the Third Count of Orsorno, Duke of Galisteo, Commander of Ribera and Monreal and Thirteenth of the Order of Santiago, of the Council of Indies, Captain General of Seville and of the Council of State. Married (m1) Dona JUANA ENRIQUEZ, his aunt, Lady of Vega de Ruiponce/(m2) Dona MARIA de LUNA (daughter of Alvaro de Luna, Second Lord - de Fuentiduena, and of Dona Isabel de Bobadilla).

The known children of Garci Fernandez Manrique de Lara y Toledo and (m2) Dona Maria de Luna were:

       a1.   PEDRO MANRIQUE de LARA y LUNA (*a1 = IV, follows below*).

       a2.   ALONSO MANRIQUE de LARA y LUNA, Commander of Ribera in the Order of Santiago, Lord of Las Graneras and trunk of the Candes de Montehermoso.

       a3.   JUAN MANRIQUE de LARA y LUNA, Dominican religious.

       a4.   MARIA MAGDALENA MANRIQUE de LARA y LUNA. Married HURTADO de MENDOZA, Second Marquis de Canete, during 1532.

       a5.   ISABEL MANRIQUE de LARA y LUNA. Married GASPAR GASTON de la CERDA y MENDOZA, Lord of Pastrana, during 1539.

       a6.   CATALINA MANRIQUE de LARA y LUNA. Married GARCI LOPEZ de CARVAJAL, Lord of Torrejon el Rubio and Knight of the Order of Santiago.

IV.   PEDRO MANRIQUE de LARA y LUNA was the Fourth Count of Osorno, Duke of Galisteo, Commander of Ribera and Monreal and Thirteenth of the Order of Santiago. Married Mrs. ELVIRA ENRIQUEZ de CORDOVA, daughter of the First Marquises of Regio, during 1529/(m2) Mrs. MARIA de VELASCO y ARAGON, Lady of Villavla del Alcor and daughter of the Fifth Lords of Moron, during 1539.

The children of Pedro Manrique de Lara y Luna and (m1) Mrs. Elvira Enriquez de Cordova were:

       a1.   GARCI MANRIQUE de LARA y ENRIQUEZ (*a1 = V, follows below*).

       a2.   PEDRO MANRIQUE de LARA y ENRIQUEZ, died as a child.

       a3.   MIGUEL MANRIQUE de LARA y ENRIQUEZ, Gentleman of Phillip II and Treasurer of the Mint of Mexico and Santo Domingo.

       a4.   GABRIEL MANRIQUE de LARA y ENRIQUEZ, Knight of the Order of Santiago.

- a5. ALVARO MANRIQUE de LARA y ENRIQUEZ, Knight of the Order of Calatrava.
- a6. MARIA MANRIQUE de LARA y ENRIQUEZ. Married PEDRO PIMENTEL, First Marquis of Viana. With succession.
- a7. CATALINA MANRIQUE de LARA y ENRIQUEZ.
- a8. TERESA MANRIQUE de LARA y ENRIQUEZ, nun in the Covent of Santa Clara, Cabazanos.
- a9. ELVIRA MANRIQUE de LARA y ENRIQUEZ. Married SUERO de VEGA. Commander of Sancti-Spiritus in the Order of Alcantara (daughter of the Fourth Lords of Grajal).

The children of Pedro Manrique de Lara y Luna and (m2) Dona Maria de Velasco y Aragon were:

- a10. PEDRO MANRIQUE de LARA y VELASCO.
- a11. JUAN MANRIQUE de LARA y VELASCO.
- a12. JULIANA ANGELA MANRIQUE de LARA y VELASCO, nun in the Descalzas Reales of Madrid.
- a13. MARIA MANRIQUE de LARA y VELASCO, died as a child.
- a14. JUANA MANRIQUE de LARA y VELASCO. Married ANTONIO GOMEZ de BUTRON y MUJICA during 1583 in Valladolid.
- a15. ANGELA MANRIQUE de LARA y VELASCO, nun in the Descalzas Reales of Madrid.
- a16. LUISA MANRIQUE de LARA y VELASCO, a nun in Belen de Valladolid.

V. GARCI MANRIQUE de LARA y ENRIQUEZ was the Fifth Count of Osorno. Duke of Galisteo. Lord of several towns and places and Knight of the Order of Santiago. Married Dona TERESA ENRIQUEZ, of the House of the Counts of Alba de Liste.

The known children of Garci Manrique de Lara y Enriquez and Dona Teresa Enriquez were:

- a1. PEDRO MANRIQUE de LARA y ENRIQUEZ (a1 = VI, follows below).
- a2. DIEGO MANRIQUE de LARA y ENRIQUEZ, died as a child.
- a3. ANTONIO MANRIQUE de LARA y ENRIQUEZ. Married Dona ANA de LUNA, Third Countess of Morata.

  The known children of Antonio Manrique de Lara y Enriquez and Dona Ana de Luna were:
  - b1. JOSE MANRIQUE de LARA y LUNA, First Marquis of Viluena, who did not marry.
  - b2. ANTONIO MANRIQUE de LARA y LUNA, Fourth Count of Morata, and Second Marquis of Vineula. Entered the Order of Santiago.
  - b3. MIGUEL MANRIQUE de LARA y LUNA.
  - b4. ANA POLONIA MANRIQUE de LARA y LUNA, Fifth Countess of Morata and Third Marquise of Vinuela, who became the Eighth Countess of Osorno.

- a4. ELVIRA MANRIQUE de LARA y ENRIQUEZ. Married ANTONIO GOMEZ MANRIQUE de MENDOZA, Fifth Count of Castrogeriz.
- a5. CATALINA MANRIQUE de LARA y ENRIQUEZ, nun in Villanueva del Rio.

- a6. MARIA MANRIQUE de LARA y ENRIQUEZ. <u>Married</u> FERNANDO ENRIQUEZ de RIBERA, Second Marquis of Villanueva del Rio. With succession. Surname: Enriquez de Ribera.
- a7. JUANA MANRIQUE de LARA y ENRIQUEZ. <u>Married</u> PEDRO ESTEBAN DAVILA, Third Marquis of Las Navas and Count of El Risco. With succession.

VI. PEDRO MANRIQUE de LARA y ENRIQUEZ was the Sixth Count of Osorno, Duke of Galisteo and Lord of several towns and places. <u>Married</u> Dona CATALINA ZAPATA de MENDOZA, sister of the Second Count of Barajas (and daughter of Francisco de Zapata Cisneros, First Count of Barajas, and Dona Maria de Mendoza).

<u>The children of Pedro Manrique de Lara y Enriquez and Dona Catalina Zapata de Mendoza were:</u>
- a1. GARCI MANRIQUE de LARA y ZAPATA (*a1 = VII, follows below*).
- a2. FRANCISCO MANRIQUE de LARA y ZAPATA, Knight of Alcantara. Without succession.

VII. GARCI MANRIQUE de LARA y ZAPATA was the Seventh Count of Osorno, Duke of Galisteo, Perpetual Major constable of the Chancery of Valladolid and Major Guardian of the Inquisition of Valladolid. <u>Married</u> Dona ANA MANRIQUE de LARA de la CERDA (eldest daughter of Bernardo Manrique de Lara y Mendoza, Fifth Marquis of Aguilar de Campoo, Count of Castaneda and Buelna, and of Dona Antonia de la Cerda y Aragon of the branch of Marquises of Aguilar de Campoo, Counts of Castaneda).

<u>The known child of Garci Manrique de Lara y Zapata and Dona Ana Manrique de Lara de la Cerda was:</u>
- a1. ANTONIO MANRIQUE de LARA y MANRIQUE de LARA (*a1 = VIII, follows below*).

VIII. ANTONIO MANRIQUE de LARA y MANRIQUE de LARA died young. He passed the house with his titles to Ana Polonia Manrique de Lara y Luna.

IX. ANA POLONIA MANRIQUE de LARA y LUNA (fourth daughter of Antonio Manrique de Lara y Enriquez and Dona Ana de Luna). <u>Married</u> BALTASAR BARROSO de RIVERA, Third Marquis of Malpica and First Count of Navalmoral. She had no children and passed her titles to ANTONIO ALVAREZ de TOLEDO, Seventh Duke of Alba, her nephew and grandson of the Marquise of Villanueva del Rio Dona Maria Manrique, sister of the Count, her father.

The **THIRTEENTH BRANCH** - Gentleman of Fuenteguinaldo.

I. JUAN MANRIQUE de LARA (second son of Juan Manrique de Lara, Second Count of Castaneda, and of his second wife Catalina Enriquez de Ribera, mentioned in the seventh branch of the Marquises of Aguilar de Campoo, Counts of Castaneda), was the First Lord of Fuenteguinaldo, Villalumbroso, Villatoquite, Revenga and Villarmentero and Captain of Men-at-Arms of the Guards of Castile. <u>Married</u> Dona BEATRIZ MANRIQUE de LARA, sister of Pedro Manrique de Lara, First Duke of

Najara and Count of Trevino (and both sons of Diego Gomez de Manrique de Lara, First Count of Trevino, all mentioned in the branch of the mentioned titles).

The known children of Juan Manrique de Lara and Dona Beatriz Manrique de Lara were:

- a1. FADIQUE MANRIQUE de LARA y MANRIQUE de LARA (*a1 = II, follows below*).
- a2. JUANA MANRIQUE de LARA y MANRIQUE de LARA. <u>Married</u> PEDRO de SILVA, Alderman of Ciudad Rodrigo.
- a3. MARIA MANRIQUE de LARA y MANRIQUE de LARA, a nun.
- a4. BRIANDA MANRIQUE de LARA y MANRIQUE de LARA. <u>Married</u> ALONSO NINO de CASTRO, Lord of Castroverde, Merino Mayor and Alderman of Valladolid. With succession.

II. FADIQUE MANRIQUE de LARA y MANRIQUE de LARA was Marshal of Castile, Second Lord of Fuenteguinaldo and of the other previously mentioned towns and places. <u>Married</u> Dona ANTONIA de VALENCIA, Lady of this house, originally from the Royal House of Castile.

The known children of Fadique Manrique de Lara y Manrique de Lara and Dona Antonia de Valencia were:

- a1. JORGE MANRIQUE de LARA y VALENCIA (*a1 = III, follows below*).
- a2. JUAN MANRIQUE de LARA. <u>Married</u> ANA de CARDONA.
- a3. FADIQUE MANRIQUE de LARA y VALENCIA, Corregidor of Ubeda and Baeza. <u>Married</u> Dona LEONOR MANRIQUE (sister of Francisco de Guzman, First Marquis of Algaba, both sons of Luis de Guzman Fourth Lord of Algaba, and of Dona Leonor Manrique de Lara y Fajardo, sister of the Fourth Count of Paredes de Nava) in Seville.
- a4. ANTONIO MANRIQUE de LARA y VALENCIA, Bishop of Pamplona.
- a5. ANA MANRIQUE de LARA y VALENCIA. <u>Married</u> JERONIMO de MENDOZA, Lord of Arroyo, in Valladolid.
- a6. MARIA MANRIQUE de LARA y VALENCIA. <u>Married</u> JUAN de AYALA, Second Lord of the town of Pero Moro. With succession.
- a7. JUANA MANRIQUE de LARA y VALENCIA. <u>Married</u> GARCIA MANRIQUE, third of the name, Lord of the Towers of Alozaina, her uncle, second cousin of her father, as great-grandchildren of Pedro Manrique de Lara, Lord of Amusco, Trevino and Navarrete, during 1525.
- a8. FRANCISCA MANRIQUE de LARA y VALENCIA, Abbess of Las Huelgas de Burgos.
- a9. BEATRIZ MANRIQUE de LARA y VALENCIA, a nun at Las Huelgas de Burgos.
- a10. CATALINA MANRIQUE de LARA y VALENCIA.

III. JORGE MANRIQUE de LARA y VALENCIA was Marshal of Castile, Third Lord of Fuenteguinaldo and other towns and places and Alderman of Zamora. <u>Married</u> Dona LEONOR de ZUNIGA (daughter of the Sixth Lords of Autillo).

The known children of Jorge Manrique de Lara y Valencia and Dona Leonor de Zuniga were:

      a1.   ANTONIA MANRIQUE de LARA y ZUNIGA (*a1 = IV, follows below*).
      a2.   JUANA MANRIQUE de LARA y ZUNIGA, died as a child.
      a3.   INES MANRIQUE de LARA y ZUNIGA, died as a child.

IV.   ANTONIA MANRIQUE de LARA y ZUNIGA was Fourth Lady of Fuenteguinaldo and of the House of Valencia. <u>Married</u> Don FADRIQUE de VARGAS, Lord of this house in Madrid and Knight of the Order of Santiago.

<u>The known children of Antonia Manrique de Lara y Zuniga and Don Fadrique de Vargas were:</u>

    a1.   FRANCISCO de VARGAS MANRIQUE de LARA y VALENCIA (*a1 = V, follows below*).

    a2.   FADRIQUE de VARGAS MANRIQUE de LARA, who was Marshal of Castile and Lord of the House of Vargas. <u>Married</u> (m1) Dona MARIA DAVILA (daughter of Gonzalo de Bracamonte, Commander of Campo de Criptana in the Order of Santiago, and of Dona Teresa de Valderrabano, Lady of Naharros)/(m2) Dona MARIA de TOLEDO y SILVA, sister of Fernando de Toledo, Marquis of the Floresta and Knight of Calatrava. Succession from first marriage who took the title of Marquis of San Vincente.

    a3.   DIEGO de VARGAS MANRIQUE de LARA, Knight of the Order of Alcantara. <u>Married</u> MARIANA de TAPIA.

<u>The known children of Diego de Vargas Manrique de Lara and Mariana de Tapia were:</u>

      b1.   ANTONIO MANRIQUE de LARA y TAPIA, First Marquis of Chavela and Knight of the Order of Santiago. <u>Married</u> Dona EUFRASIA de BAZAN y MENDOZA (natural daughter of Alonso de Bazan, Commander of Viso and Santa Cruz and brother of the First Marquis of Santa Clara).

      <u>The known children of Antonio Manrique de Lara y Tapia and Eufraisia de Bazan y Mendoza were:</u>

        c1.   DIEGO MANRIQUE de LARA y BAZAN, Second Marquis of Chavela. <u>Married</u> Mrs. RAIMUNDA PUCH in Catalonia.
        c2.   GONZALO MANRIQUE de LARA y BAZAN.
        c3.   ANDRES MANRIQUE de LARA y BAZAN.

      b2.   ANA MANRIQUE de LARA y BAZAN. <u>Married</u> INIGO LOPEZ de MENDOZA, Fifth Marquis of Mondejar, Count of Tendilla.

      b3.   CATALINA MANRIQUE de LARA y TAPIA. <u>Married</u> FRANCISCO BRAVO de GUZMAN, Knight of the Order of Santiago and Governor of Ocana.

V.   FRANCISCO de VARGAS MANRIQUE de LARA was Marshal of Castile, Fifth Lord of Fuenteguinaldo and Knight of the Order of Alcantara. <u>Married</u> (m1) Dona MARIA de GUZMAN (daughter of the Lord of Pejamo)/(m2) Dona BEATRIZ de GUZMAN, sister of Alonso de Guzman, First Count of Penaranda de Bracamonte/(m3) Dona FRANCISCA CHACON, sister of the First Count of Casarrubios.

<u>The known children of Francisco de Vargas Manrique de Lara and (m3) Dona Francisca Chacon were:</u>

- a1. FADRIQUE MANRIQUE de LARA y CHACON, First Marquis of San Vicente.
- a2. FRANCISCO MANRIQUE de LARA y CHACON, died as a child.
- a3. ANTONIO MANRIQUE de LARA y CHACON. <u>Married</u> Mrs. De VILLAVIUDAS.
- a4. ALDONZA MANRIQUE de LARA y CHACON, nun in Santo Domingo el Real de Toledo.

THE FOURTEENTH BRANCH: Counts of Paredes de Nava.

I. RODRIGO MANRIQUE de LARA was the First Count of Paredes de Nava (second son of Pedro Manrique de Lara y Mendoza, Eighth Lord of Amusco and Trevino, etc. and his wife Dona Leonor de Castilla, mentioned in the eighth branch, Counts of Trevino and Dukes of Najera), was the First Count of Paredes de Nava, Constable of Castilla, Master of the Order of Santiago and Lord of numerous towns and cities. <u>Married</u> (m1) Mrs. MENCIA de FIGUEROA, his second cousin, sister of the First Count of Feria (daughter of Gomez Suarez de Figueroa, First Lord of Zafra, Feria and other towns, and of Mrs. Elvira Laso de Mendoza, his wife)/(m2) Dona BEATRIZ de GUZMAN (daughter of Diego Hurtado de Mendoza, First Lord of Canete and Major Montero of the King Don Juan II, and of the Dona Teresa de Guzman, his second wife)/(m3) Dona ELVIRA de CASTANEDA (eldest daughter of Pedro Lopez de Ayala, First Count of Fuensalida, and of Dona Maria de Silva, sister of the First Count of Cifuentes).

<u>The known children of Rodrigo Manrique de Lara and (m1) Mrs. Mencia de Figueroa were:</u>
- a1. PEDRO MANRIQUE de LARA (*a1 = II, follows below*).
- a2. DIEGO MANRIQUE de LARA y FIGUEROA.
- a3. RODRIGO MANRIQUE de LARA y FIGUEROA, Commander of Yeste and Taivilla and Thirteenth of the Order of Santiago, Governor of the province of Leon, Warden of Purchena, Corregidor of Baza, Guadix and Almeria and Steward of Queen Juana. <u>Married</u> Dona MENCIA de BENAVIDES, his third cousin (daughter of Dia Sanches de Benavides, First Count of Santisteban del Puerto and Major Caudillo of the Bishopric of Jaen, and of his wife, Dona Maria Carrillo de Perea).

    <u>The known children of Rodrigo Manrique de Lara and Dona Mencia de Benavides were:</u>
    - b1. DIEGO MANRIQUE de LARA y BENAVIDES, Commander of Yeste and Taivilla in the Order of Santiago.
    - b2. RODRIGO MANRIQUE de LARA, y BENAVIDES, Commander of Manzanares in the Order of Calatrava.
    - b3. PEDRO MANRIQUE de LARA y BENEVIDES, Provisor of his uncle the Bishop of Cordoba, Alonso Manrique de Lara y Quinones.
    - b4. FADRIQUE MANRIQUE de LARA y BENAVIDES.

- b5. FRANCISCA MANRIQUE de LARA y BENAVIDES, Lady of Villaverde and the Galapagares. Married FRANCISCO de AGUAYO, Lord of Villaverde and Galapagares, and one of the most illustrious gentlemen of Andalusia. With succession. Surname: Aguayo.
- b6. LEONOR MANRIQUE de LARA y BENEVIDES, Lady of Carlete and Benimodol. Married GALCERAN de CASTELLVI, Lord of Carlete and Benimodol. Succession used the title Count of Carlete and surname, Castellvi.
- b7. ANA MANRIQUE de LARA y BENAVIDES.
- b8 MENCIA MANRIQUE de LARA y BENAVIDES.
- b9. ISABEL MANRIQUE de LARA y BENAVIDES. Married DIEGO VACA de SOTOMAYOR, Gentleman of Carlos V, in Alcaraz.

a4. JORGE MANRIQUE de LARA y FIGUEROA, Lord of Belmontejo, Commander of Montizon in the Order of Santiago, Thirteenth of the same Order and Captain of Men-at-Arms. Married Dona GUIOMAR de MENESES, sister of Dona Elvira de Castaneda, his stepmother.

The known child of Jorge Manrique de Lara y Figueroa and Dona Guiomar de Menses was:

- b1. ISABEL MANRIQUE de LARA y MENESES. Married MANUEL de BENAVIDES, Third Lord of Jabalquinto, Espeluy, Almanzora and other towns, and both parents of the Marquises of Jabalquinto.

a5. FADRIQUE MANRIQUE de LARA y FIGUEROA, Lord of Jarafe. Married Dona MARIA de MOLINA, Lady of the Fortress and term of Jarafe, in Ubeda. Without succession.

a6. LEONOR MANRIQUE de LARA y FIGUEROA, Countess of Cartagena. Married PEDRO FAJARDO. Succession earned title of Marquises of Velez.

a7. ELVIRA MANRIQUE de LARA y FIGUEROA. Married GOMEZ de BENAVIDES, Marshal of Castile, Lord of Fromista. With succession.

The known children of Rodrigo Manrique de Lara and (m3) Dona Elvira de Castaneda were:

a8. ENRIQUE MANRIQUE de LARA y CASTANEDA, Lord of the entailed estate of Rielves and Commander of Carrizosa in the Order of Santiago. Married Dona JUANA de QUINONES (daughter of Gonzalo Davila, Lord of Navalmorcuende, Villatoro and other towns, and Dona Leonor de Quinones, sister of the First Count of Luna).

The known children of Enrique Manrique de Lara y Castaneda and Dona Juana de Quinones were:

- b1. FRANCISCO MANRIQUE de LARA y QUINONES. Married Dona TERESA de BAZAN.

        b2.   ALONSO MANRIQUE de LARA y QUINONES, Archdeacon of Carmona in the church of Seville.
        b3.   INES MANRIQUE de LARA y QUINONES. Married ALONSO ENRIQUEZ de SEVILLA, Seventh Lord of Villalva de los Llanos. Parents of the Marquiese of Valdefuentes.
        b4.   ELVIRA MANRIQUE de LARA y QUINONES, nun in Madre de Dios, Toledo.
        b5.   CATALINA MANRIQUE de LARA y QUINONES, nun in Madre de Dios, Toledo.
        b6.   ISABEL MANRIQUE de LARA y QUINONES, nun in Madre de Dios, Toledo.
        b7.   ANA MANRIQUE de LARA y QUINONES, nun in Santa Isabel, Toledo.
    a9.   ALONSO MANRIQUE de LARA y CASTANEDA, Cardinal of the Roman Church, Bishop of Tortosa, Badajoz and Cordoba, Archbishop of Seville and Inquisitor General.
    a10.   RODRIGO MANRIQUE de LARA y CASTANEDA, Commander of Manzanares in the Order of Calatrava, and later of Villarrubia in the Order of Santiago and of the Council of Charles V.

II.   PEDRO MANRIQUE de LARA y FIGUEROA was the Second Count of Paredes de Nava, Lord of Villapalacios, Villaverde and other places, Commander of Segura and Thirteenth of the Order of Santiago. Married Dona LEONOR de ACUNA (daughter of Pedro de Acuna, First Count of Buendia, High Guard of Kings Juan II and Enrique IV, and of Dona Ines de Herrera).

The known children of Pedro Manrique de Lara y Figueroa and Dona Leonor de Acuna were:
    a1.   DIEGO GOMEZ MANRIQUE de LARA y ACUNA, died.
    a2.   RODRIGO MANRIQUE de LARA y ACUNA (a2 = III, follows below).
    a3.   INES MANRIQUE de LARA y ACUNA. Married JUAN CHACON, Adelantado and Captain Major of the Kingdom of Murcia and Lord of the city of Cartagena.
    a4.   MARIA MANRIQUE de LARA y ACUNA. Married GOMEZ GONZALEZ de BUTRON y MOJICA. With succession.
    a5.   MAGDALENA MANRIQUE de LARA y ACUNA, Lady of the Catholic Queen. Married PEDRO FAJARDO y MANRIQUE de LARA, Marquis de los Velez.
    a6.   ALDONZA MANRIQUE de LARA y ACUNA, nun in Calabazanos.
    a7.   CATALINA MANRIQUE de LARA y ACUNA, a nun.

III.   RODRIGO MANRIQUE de LARA y ACUNA was the Third Count of Paredes de Nava and Commander of Alhambra and La Solana in the Order of Santiago. Married Dona ISABEL FAJARDO y MANRIQUE de LARA, his niece, sister of Pedro Fajardo y Manrique de Lara, First Marquis of the Velez (children both of Leonor Manrique de Lara y Figueroa, and of her husband Pedro Fajardo)/(m2) Dona ANA de JAEN.

The known children of Rodrigo Manrique de Lara y Acuna and (m1) Dona Isabel Fajardo were:

a1. PEDRO MANRIQUE de LARA y FAJARDO (*a1 = IV, follows below*).
a2. JUAN MANRIQUE de LARA y FAJARDO, Knight of the Order of Santiago.
a3. RODRIGO MANRIQUE de LARA y FAJARDO, Commander of Briedma in the Order of Santiago. Illegitimate children with Dona CATALINA LOPEZ.

The known children of Rodrigo Manrique de Lara y Fajardo and Dona Catalina Lopez were:

    b1. FRANCISCO MANRIQUE de LARA, Knight of the Order of Santiago, Page of Philip II and General Overseer of his Royal Treasury.
    b2. JORGE MANRIQUE de LARA, Knight of the Order of Santiago, Ombudsman of the Audiences of Panama and Charcas, in Peru. Married Mrs. MENCIA de SILVA y CORDOVA.

    The known children of Jorge Manrique de Lara and Mrs. Mencia de Silva y Cordova were:

        c1. FRANCISCO MANRIQUE de LARA y SILVA, Officer of the Holy Office and Collegiate of the distinguished College of the Manrique family in Alcala.
        c2. ANA MANRIQUE de LARA y SILVA.
        c3. JUANA AGUSTINA MANRIQUE de LARA y SILVA.
    b3. FERNANDO MANRIQUE de LARA.
    b4. FRANCISCO MANRIQUE de LARA.
    b5. MARIA MANRIQUE de LARA. Married DIEGO de TEVES MANRIQUE, Field Master of the Chilean Army.
    b6. LUISA MANRIQUE de LARA.
    b7. CATALINA MANRIQUE de LARA.
a4. JORGE MANRIQUE de LARA y FAJARDO.
a5. LEONOR MANRIQUE de LARA y FAJARDO. Married LUIS de GUZMAN, Fourth Lord of Algaba. Succession earned title of Marquises of Algaba.
a6. LUISA MANRIQUE de LARA, nun in Calabazanos.
a7. ISABEL MANRIQUE de LARA, nun in Calabazanos.
a8. MENCIA MANRIQUE de LARA FAJARDO. Married LUIS VICH, Third Lord of Laurin and Matada, in the Kingdom of Valencia.
a9. MARIA MAGDALENA MANRIQUE de LARA y FAJARDO. Married FRANCISCO de MONROY, First Count of Deleitosa, in 1534.

The known children of Rodrigo Manrique de Lara y Acuna and (m2) Dona Ana de Jaen were:

a10. BERNARDINO MANRIQUE de LARA y JAEN, Dean of Granada.
a11. JUAN MANRIQUE de LARA de JAEN, died as a child.
a12. BERNARDINO MANRIQUE de LARA y JAEN, died as a child.
a13. JUAN MANRIQUE de LARA y JAEN.
a14. RAFAEL MANRIQUE de LARA y JAEN, First Count of Burgo-Labezar, Lord of Villaverde, Knight of the Order of Santiago and Governor and Castilian of Cremona. Married UNKNOWN.

The known children of Rafael Manrique de Lara y Jaen and Unknown were:
- b1. RODRIGO MANRIQUE de LARA, Second Count of Burgo-Labezar and Lord of Villaverda. No succession.
- b2. JORGE MANRIQUE de LARA, Third Count of Burgo-Labezar. Married Dona MAGDALENA CIGONA from Milan.
  The known child of Jorge Manrique de Lara and Magdalena Cigona was:
  - c1. RODRIGO MANRIQUE de LARA y CIGONA, Fourth Count of Burgo-Labezar and Lord of Villaverde. Without succession.
- b3. HIPOLETA MANRIQUE de LARA, Fifth Countess of Burgo-Labezar and Lady of Villaverde. Married JUAN DIAZ ZAMORANO, Sergeant Major of the Tercio de Lombardia. With succession.

a15. JUANA MANRIQUE de LARA y JAEN. Married JERONIMO de ALIAGA, Conqueror of Peru.

IV. PEDRO MANRIQUE de LARA y FAJARDO was the Fourth Count of Paredes de Nava, Lord of several towns and places and Knight of the Order of Santiago. He died on 28 May 1539. Married Dona INES MANRIQUE de LARA y PIMENTEL (daughter of Luis Fernandez Manrique de Lara, Second Marquis of Aguilar de Campoo, Count of Casteneda, and his wife Dona Ana Pimentel - from the branch of Marquises of Aguilar de Campoo).

The known children of Pedro Manrique de Lara y Fajardo and Dona Ines Manrique de Lara y Pimentel were:
- a1. ANTONIO MANRIQUE de LARA y MANRIQUE de LARA (*a1 = V, follows below*).
- a2. FRANCISCO MANRIQUE de LARA y MANRIQUE de LARA, Commander of Villafranca and Bienvenida in the Order of Santiago, Thirteenth of this same Order, Gentilhombre de boca of Felipe II and the Chamber of Prince Don Carlos.
  The known children of Francisco Manrique de Lara y Manrique de Lara and unknown were:
  - b1. RODRIGO MANRIQUE de LARA, Captain General of the Artillery in Sicily. Married Mrs. VIOLANTE MARIELLO. No succession.
  - b2. ISABEL MANRIQUE de LARA, a nun in Calabazanos.
  - b3. INES MANRIQUE de LARA, a nun in Calabazanos.
- a3. ISABEL MANRIQUE de LARA y MANRIQUE de LARA, Lady of the Empress Isabel. Married GONZALO MESIA CARRILLO, the First Marquis de la Guardia and Commander of Penausende in the Order of Santiago. With succession. Surname: Carrillo.
- a4. MARIA MANRIQUE de LARA y MANRIQUE de LARA, a nun in Calabazanos.
- a5. ANTONIA MANRIQUE de LARA y MANRIQUE de a LARA, a nun in Calabazanos.

- a6. FRANCISCA MANRIQUE de LARA y MANRIQUE de a LARA, a nun in Calabazanos.
- a7. MARGARITA MANRIQUE de LARA y MANRIQUE de a LARA, a nun in Calabazanos.
- a8. JUANA MANRIQUE de LARA y MANRIQUE de a LARA. <u>Married</u> FADRIQUE ENRIQUEZ GIRON, Commander of the Monastery and Queen and Thirteenth of the Order of Santiago, during 1545.

V. ANTONIO MANRIQUE de LARA y MANRIQUE de LARA was the Fifth Count of Paredes de Nava. <u>Married</u> (m1) Dona ANA MANRIQUE de LARA y LUNA, his first cousin (daughter of Juan Fernandez Manrique de Lara, Third Marquis of Aguilar de Campoo and Fifth Count of Castaneda, and of his first wife, Dona Maria de Luna, mentioned prior)/(m2) Dona GUIOMAR MANRIQUE de LARA y CARDONA (daughter of Antonio Manrique de Lara, Second Duke of Najera, Count of Trevino, and of his wife, Dona Juana de Cardona, mentioned in the branch of the Dukes of Najera, Counts of Trevino)/(m3) Dona FRANCISCA de ROJAS y SANDOVAL, who was a first cousin of his first wife (daughter of Luis de Sandoval y Rojas, Third Marquis of Denia, Count of Lerma and brother of Dona Maria de Luna, Third Marquise of Aguilar de Campoo, and of Dona Catalina de Zuniga, his wife). From (m1) and (m3) he had no succession.

<u>The known child of Antonio Manrique de Lara y Manrique de Lara and (m2) Dona Guiomar Manrique de Lara y Cardona was:</u>
- a1. INES MANRIQUE de LARA y MANRIQUE de LARA (*a1 = VI, follows below*).

VI. INES MANRIQUE de LARA y MANRIQUE de LARA was the Sixth Countess of Paredes de Nava and Lady of many towns and places. <u>Married</u> ENRIQUE MANRIQUE de LARA y ACUNA (second son of Manrique de Lara y Cardona, the Third Duke of Najera and Count of Trevino, and of his wife, Dona Luisa de Acuna, Fifth Countess of Valencia, mentioned prior), her cousin and Lord of Villapalacios, Bienservida and Villaverde and Commander of Mohernando in the Order of Santiago.

<u>The known children of Ines Manrique de Lara y Manrique de Lara and Enrique Manrique de Lara y Acuna were:</u>
- a1. ANTONIO MANRIQUE de LARA y MANRIQUE de LARA (*a1 = VII, follows below*).
- a2. PEDRO MANRIQUE de LARA y MANRIQUE de LARA (*a2 = VIII, follows below*).
- a3. FRANCISCO MANRIQUE de LARA y MANRIQUE de LARA, Knight of the Order of Santiago.
- a4. MANUEL MANRIQUE de LARA y MANRIQUE de LARA (*a4 = IX, follows below*).
- a5. ENRIQUE MANRIQUE de LARA y MANRIQUE de LARA, Knight of the Order of Santiago.
- a6. FRANCISCA MANRIQUE de LARA y MANRIQUE de LARA, Lady of the Infanta Isabel Clara Eugenia.
- a7. JUANA MANRIQUE de LARA y MANRIQUE de LARA.

- a8. LUISA MANRIQUE de LARA y MANRIQUE de LARA, Lady of Queen Margarita, wife of Philip III. <u>Married</u> FELIPE RAMIREZ de ARELLANO, Seventh Count of Aguilar, Lord of the Cameros, during 1604.
- a9. MARGARITA MANRIQUE de LARA y MANRIQUE de LARA, a nun in Calabazanos.

VII. ANTONIO MANRIQUE de LARA y MANRIQUE de LARA was the Seventh Count of Paredes de Nava and Lord of Villapalacios, Bienservida, Villaverde and Commander of the Houses of Plasencia and Fuentiduena, in the Order of Calatrava. He died along with his brother, Francisco Manrique de Lara y Manrique de Lara, in a shipwreck of the Invincible Armada along the coast of England, without leaving succession, and his brother then inherited his title.

VIII. PEDRO MANRIQUE de LARA y MANRIQUE de LARA was the Eighth Count of Paredes de Nava, Lord of the mentioned villas, Commander of the Houses of Plasencia in the Order of Calatrava and of Portezuela and the Magdalena in that of Alcantara and Ayo of the King Don Felipe IV. <u>Married</u> CATALINA FERNANDEZ de CORDOVA, Lady of the Infanta Isabel Clara and sister of the Second Marquis of Carpio, during 1592. They did not have children, which passed the house to his brother.

IX. MANUEL MANRIQUE de LARA y MANRIQUE de LARA was the Ninth Count of Paredes de Nava, Lord of previously mentioned towns, Commander Major of Montalban and Bienvenida, in the Order of Santiago, and Steward of Queen Margarita. <u>Married</u> LUISA MANRIQUE ENRIQUEZ, his second cousin, sister and heir of Fadrique Enriquez de Lujan, Commander of Eliche and Castilleja in the Order of Alcantara, and of the Councils of War and Chamber of the Indies.

<u>The known children of Manuel Manrique de Lara y Manrique de Lara and Luisa Manrique Enriquez were:</u>
- a1. MARIA INES MANRIQUE de LARA y MANRIQUE (*a1 = X, follows below*)
- a2. ISABEL MANRIQUE de LARA y MANRIQUE. <u>Married</u> FRANCISCO de OROZCO y RIBERA, Second Marquis of Mostara and First Marquis of Olias.
- a3. ANTONIA MANRIQUE de LARA y MANRIQUE, died as a child.

X. MARIA INES MANRIQUE de LARA y MANRIQUE was the Tenth Countess of Paredes de Nava and Lady of previously mentioned towns. <u>Married</u> VESPASIANO GONZAGA, Sovereign Duke of Guastala, Luzara and Rechiolo, Gentilhombre de Camara of Kings Philip IV and Charles II, Great of Spain, Viceroy of Valencia and Commander of Villahermosa and Castrotoras in the Order of Santiago, during 1646.

<u>The known children of Maria Ines Manrique de Lara y Manrique and Vespasiano Gonzaga were:</u>
- a1. JOSE MANRIQUE de LARA y GONZAGA, died at a young age.
- a2. MARIA LUISA MANRIQUE de LARA y GONZAGA (*a2 = XI, follows below*).

- a3. ISABEL GONZAGA y MANRIQUE de LARA, who died as Lady of the Queen Mariana de Austria.
- a4. JOSEFA GONZAGA y MANRIQUE de LARA. Married ANTONIO GASPAR PIMENTEL BARROSO de RIBERA y DAVILA, Fourth Marquis of Malpica and Sixth Povar and Count of Navalmoral.

XI. MARIA LUISA MANRIQUE de LARA y GONZAGA put her mother's surname before her father's surname for reasons of inheritance and was the Eleventh Countess of Paredes de Nava, Marquise of La Laguna and Head Chamberlain of Queen Mariana of Austia. Married TOMAS de la CERDA y ENRIQUEZ de RIBERA, Third Marquis of La Laguna (son of Antonio Juan Luis de la Cerda, Seventh Duke of Medinaceli, and his wife Dona Ana Maria Luisa Enriquez de Ribera, Fifth Duchess of Alcala). By this marriage, the title of Count of Paredes de Nava was incorporated into the House of Medinaceli, passing later to the Guzman, Marquises of Montealegre, then to the Zavala, Marquises of Sierra-Bullones and finally to the Garcia Sancho, Counts of Consuegra. The title of Countess of Paredes de Nava was eventually held by Dona Trinidad Garcia Sancho y Zabala, Tenth Countess, Grande of Spain, Lady of the Order of Maria Luisa who married Juan Bustamante y Campuzano, Marquis of Herrera.

The FIFTEENTH BRANCH: Counts of Santa Gadea.

I. PEDRO MANRIQUE de LARA y CASTILLA (third son of Pedro Manrique de Lara y Mendoza, Eighth Lord of Amusco, and of his wife, Leonor de Castilla, mentioned of the eighth branch), was Lord of Valdescaray, Anguiano, Matute and Escamilla, and Doncel of King Juan II of Castilla. Married (m1) Dona ISABEL de QUINONES (daughter of the Lord of Luna)/(m2) Dona CONTESINA de LUNA, the Fourth Lady of Escamilla.

The known children of Pedro Manrique de Lara y Castilla and (m1) Dona Isabel de Quinones were:
- a1. PEDRO GOMEZ MANRIQUE de LARA y QUINONES (*a1 = II, follows below*).
- a2. INIGO MANRIQUE de LARA y QUINONES, Bishop of Leon.
- a3. LEONARDO MANRIQUE de LARA y QUINONES. Married Dona INES CARRILLO de ACUNA, of the house of the Counts of Buendia. No succession.
- a4. LEONOR MANRIQUE de LARA y QUINONES. Married RUY DIAZ de MENDOZA, Lord of Mendivil, Nanclares and other towns.

The known child of Pedro Manrique de Lara y Castilla and (m2) Dona Contesina de Luna was:
- a5. BERNABE MANRIQUE de LARA y LUNA, Lord of Villamadorni, Escamilla and other places and Councilman of Burgos. Married (m1) Dona CATALINA de TOLEDO/(m2) Dona CATALINA de la TORRE.

The known child of Bernabe Manrique de Lara y Luna and (m1) Dona Catalina de Toledo was:

       b1.   JUAN MANRIQUE de LARA y TOLEDO, Knight of the Order of Santiago and Mayor of Burgos.

The known children of Bernabe Manrique de Lara y Luna and (m2) Dona Catalina de la Torre were:

- b2. PEDRO MANRIQUE de LARA de la TORRE.
- b3. RODRIGO MANRIQUE de LARA y de la TORRE, Knight of the Order of San Juan.
- b4. JORGE MANRIQUE de LARA y de la TORRE, Knight of the Order of Santiago.
- b5. GARCIA MANRIQUE de LARA y de la TORRE, Treasurer and Canon of Toledo.
- b6. MARIA MANRIQUE de LARA, Lady of Estepar and Frandovinez.
- b7. ANGELA MANRIQUE de LARA y de la TORRE.
- b8. BLANCA MANRIQUE de LARA y LUNA, Lady of Queen Juana. Married JUAN ACUNA PORTOCARRERO, Third Lord of Pajares, in 1306. With succession.

II. PEDRO GOMEZ MANRIQUE de LARA y QUINONES was the Second Lord of Valdescaray, Anguiano, Matute, Escamilla, etc. and Adelantado Mayor of the Catholic Monarchs and their Council. Married (m1) Mrs. LEONOR de LEIVA, Lady of Redecilla del Campo/(m2) Mrs. ELVIRA LASO MANUEL (daughter of Juan Manuel Laso Lord of the County of Cangas de Tineo and Belmonte de Campos, and of Mrs. Aldonza de la Vega).

The known children of Pedro Gomez Manrique de Lara y Quinones and (m2) Mrs. Elvira Laso Manuel were:

- a1. PEDRO MANRIQUE de LARA y LASO, died as a child.
- a2. ANTONIO MANRIQUE de LARA y LASO (*a2 = III, follows below*).
- a3. MANUEL MANRIQUE de LARA y LASO.

III. ANTONIO MANRIQUE de LARA y LASO was Adelantado Mayor of Castilla, Third Lord of Valdescaray, Santurde and other places. Married Dona LUISA de PADILLA (daughter of Antonio de Padilla, Lord of this house and of Santa Gadea, Sotopalacios, etc, and of Dona Ines Enriquez de Acuna, first cousin of the Catholic King).

The known children of Antonio Manrique de Lara y Laso and Dona Luisa de Padilla were:

- a1. JUAN MANRIQUE de LARA y PADILLA, also called Juan de Padilla (*a1 = IV, follows below*).
- a2. MARTIN MANRIQUE de LARA y PADILLA (*a2 = V, follows below*).
- a3. GOMEZ MANRIQUE de LARA y PADILLA, Commander of Lopera in the Order of Calatrava.
- a4. PEDRO MANRIQUE de LARA y PADILLA, Canon of Toledo.
- a5. ANGELA MANRIQUE de LARA y PADILLA.
- a6. ISABEL MANRIQUE de LARA Y PADILLA, Lady of the Princess Juana of Portugal. Married JUAN de MENDOZA y LUNA, Second Marquis of Castil de Vayuela.
- a7. LUISA MANRIQUE de LARA y PADILLA. Married LUIS PORTOCARRRO y BOCANEGRA, Second Count of Palma.

IV. JUAN MANRIQUE de LARA y PADILLA was the Fourth Lord of Valdescaray and other places and Adelantado Mayor of Castile. <u>Married</u> Dona MARIA de ACUNA, his aunt, cousin of his mother.

The known children of Juan Manrique de Lara y Padilla and Dona Maria de Acuna were:
- a1. ANTONIO MANRIQUE de LARA y ACUNA, who would have succeeded but joined the Society of Jesus.
- a2. LUISA MANRIQUE de LARA y ACUNA (*a2 married V, follows below*).
- a3. CASILDA MANRIQUE de LARA y ACUNA, nun in Burgos.
- a4. MARIA MANRIQUE de LARA y ACUNA, nun in Burgos.

V. MARTIN MANRIQUE de LARA y PADILLA was the First Count of Santa Gadea, Seventh Count of Buendia, Adelantado Mayor of Castilla, Fifth Lord of Valdescaray and Great of Spain. <u>Married</u> Dona LUISA MANRIQUE de LARA y ACUNA, his niece, the daughter of his brother, Juan Manrique de Lara y Padilla.

The known children of Martin Manrique de Lara y Padilla and Dona Luisa Manrique de Lara y Acuna were:
- a1. JUAN MANRIQUE de LARA y MANRIQUE de LARA (*a1 = VI, follows below*).
- a2. MARCO ANTONIO MANRIQUE de LARA y MANRIQUE de LARA, died young.
- a3. MARTIN MANRIQUE de LARA y MANRIQUE de LARA, Society of Jesus.
- a4. EUGENIO MANRIQUE de LARA y MANRIQUE de LARA (*a4 = VII, follows below*).
- a5. MARIANA MANRIQUE de LARA y MANRIQUE de LARA, Duchess of Uceda and Marquise of Cea. <u>Married</u> CRISTOBAL GOMEZ de SANDOVAL y ROJAS, First Duke of Uceda, Marquis of Cea and Caballerizo Major of Felipe II. With succession. Surname: Sandoval.

    The known child of Maria Manrique de Lara y Manrique de Lara and Cristobal Gomez de Sandoval y Rojas was:
    - b1. FRANCISCO GOMEZ de SANDOVAL MANRIQUE de LARA, inherited title of Manrique de Lara house of Gadea.
- a6. ANA MARIA MANRIQUE de LARA y MANRIQUE de LARA. <u>Married</u> FRANCISCO FERNANDEZ de la CUEVA, Marquis of Cuellar and Seventh Duke of Alburquerque.
- a7. LUISA MANRIQUE de LARA y MANRIQUE de LARA. <u>Married</u> ANTONIO XIMENEZ de URREA, Fifth Count of Aranda.

VI. JUAN MANRIQUE de LARA y MANRIQUE de LARA was the Second Count of Santa Gadea, of Cifuentes and Buendia, Sixth Lord of Valdescaray, Commander of Zalamea, Adelantado Major of Castile and Great of Spain. <u>Married</u> Dona ANA de SILVA, Eighth Countess of Cifuentes. No succession so his brother Eugenio Manrique de Lara y Manrique de Lara inherited the house.

VII. EUGENIO MANRIQUE de LARA y MANRIQUE de LARA was the Third Count of Santa Gadea and Buendia, Seventh Lord of Valdescaray, Gentleman of

Chamber of Felipe II, Commander of Zalamea in the Order of Alcantara and Great Spain. <u>Married</u> Dona LUISA de ARAGON y MONCADA (daughter of the Third Dukes of Bibona).

<u>The known child of Eugenio Manrique de Lara y Manrique de Lara and Dona Luisa de Aragon y Moncada was:</u>

a1. MARTIN MANRIQUE de LARA y ARAGON, died as a child.

The titles of this house passed to FRANCISCO GOMEZ de SANDOVAL MANRIQUE de LARA, the first-born son of MARIA MANRIQUE de LARA y MANRIQUE de LARA and Cristobal Gomez de Sandoval y Rojas, First Dukes of Uceda.

The SIXTEENTH BRANCH: Lords and Counts of Amayuelas.

I. GARCIA FERNANDEZ MANRIQUE de LARA y CASTILLA (eighth son of Pedro Manrique de Lara y Mendoza, Eighth Lord of Amusco, and his wife, Leonor de Castilla, mentioned in eighth branch of Counts of Trevino and Dukes of Najera) was Lord of two Amayuelas, de Abajo and de Arriba, Belliza Espinosa and other places, of the Council of Catholic Kings, Major Justice and Captain of Malaga and Commander of Corral de Almaguer, in the Order of Santiago. <u>Married</u> Dona ALDONZA FAJARDO.

<u>The known children of Garcia Fernandez Manrique de Lara y Castila and Dona Aldonza Fajardo were:</u>

a1. BERNARDINO MANRIQUE de LARA y FAJARDO (*a1 = II, follows below*).

a2. RODRIGO MANRIQUE de LARA y FAJARDO, Master of Cordoba and Archdeacon of Almunecar in Granada.

a3. FRANCISCO MANRIQUE de LARA y FAJARDO, Knight of the Order of San Juan.

a4. PEDRO MANRIQUE de LARA y FAJARDO.

a5. INIGO MANRIQUE de LARA y FAJARDO, First Lord of Frigilana and of the Tower of Alozaina. Trunk of the lines of Lords of the Towers of Alozaina and of the Counts of Frigilana and Aguilar, Marquises of Hinojosa.

a6. GOMEZ MANRIQUE de LARA y FAJARDO, Commander of the Houses of Plasencia and Fuetiduena in the Order of Calatrava.

a7. GUIOMAR MANRIQUE de LARA y FAJARDO, Lady of Isabel "the Catholic." <u>Married</u> DIEGO FERNANDEZ de CORDOBA, Lord of Salzarejo and Commander of Alqueza.

a8. LEONOR MANRIQUE de LARA y FAJARDO, nun in Calabazanos.

a9. ALDONZA MANRIQUE de LARA y FAJARDO, nun in Calabazanos monastery.

a10. CLARA MANRIQUE de LARA y FAJARDO, religious sister.

a11. MENCIA MANRIQUE de LARA y FAJARDO, Lady of the Catholic Queen. <u>Married</u> SANCHO de la CABALLERIA.

II. BERNARDINO MANRIQUE de LARA y FAJARDO was Commander of the Tiendas in the Order of Santiago, Maestresala of the Catholic Kings, of his Council and Contador Mayor de Despensa y Raciones. <u>Married</u> ISABEL

ORDONEZ de GUZMAN, Lady of Sagrada, Terrados and other places (daughter of Antonio Nunez, native of Ciudad Rodrigo and Major Accountant of King Enrique IV, and of Maria Ordonez de Villaquiran) in 1487.

The known children of Bernardino Manrique de Lara y Fajardo and Isabel Ordonez were:

- a1. GARCI FERNANDEZ MANRIQUE de LARA y ORDONEZ (*a1 = III, follows below*).
- a2. ALONSO MANRIQUE de LARA y ORDONEZ, who served Charles V in Flanders.
- a3. DIEGO MANRIQUE de LARA y ORDONEZ, Captain of one of the ships of the Armada of Charles V.
- a4. GABRIEL MANRIQUE de LARA y ORDONEZ, Chaplain of honor of Felipe II.
- a5. JORGE MANRIQUE de LARA y ORDONEZ, Captain of the ship, "Santa Maria del Parral," of the Armada of Charles V.
- a6. MARIA MANRIQUE de LARA y ORDONEZ. Married MARTIN de ROJAS, Lord of the Tower of Mazuelo, during 1509.
- a7. LEONOR MANRIQUE de LARA y ORDONEZ, nun in Calabazanos.
- a8. ALDONZA MANRIQUE de LARA y ORDONEZ, nun in Sancti-Spiritus, Salamanca.
- a9. ISABEL MANRIQUE de LARA y ORDONEZ, Abbess of Calabazanos.
- a10. CATALINA MANRIQUE de LARA y ORDONEZ, Benedictine nun in Nuestra Senora la Serrana de Vega.
- a11. MENCIA MANRIQUE de LARA y ORDONEZ, nun in Calabazanos.

III. GARCI FERNANDEZ MANRIQUE de LARA y ORDONEZ was the Third Lord of Amayuelas and other places. Married (m1) Dona FRANCISCA de BENAVIDES, sister of Gomez de Benavides, Marshal of Castile and Lord of Fromista/(m2) Dona CONSTANZA de BAZAN (daughter of Guiterre de Robles, Second Lord of Valdetrigueros and sister of the First Marquis of Alcanizas).

The known children of Garci Fernandez Manrique de Lara y Ordonez and (m1) Dona Francisca de Benavides were:

- a1. BERNARDO MANRIQUE de LARA y BENAVIDES (*a1 = IV, follows below*).
- a2. ANTONIO MANRIQUE de LARA y BENAVIDES, died young.
- a3. FRANCISCO MANRIQUE de LARA y BENAVIDES.
- a4. ALDONZA MANRIQUE de LARA y BENAVIDES, nun in Portaceli, a town of Zarzosa.
- a5. LEONOR MANRIQUE de LARA y BENAVIDES, a nun in Portaceli, a town of Zarzosa.
- a6. ISABEL MANRIQUE de LARA y BENAVIDES. Married PEDRO ORDONEZ de VILLAQUIRAN, "el Mozo," Alderman of Salamanca, in 1535.
- a7. FRANCISCA MANRIQUE de LARA, a nun in Zarzosa.

The known children of Garci Fernandez Manrique de Lara y Ordonez and (m2) Dona Constanza de Bazan were:
- a8. GABRIEL MANRIQUE de LARA y BAZAN.
- a9. N. MANRIQUE de LARA, who died as a child.

IV. BERNARDINO MANRIQUE de LARA y BENAVIDES was the Fourth Lord of the Amayuelas and Gentilhombre of Felipe II. Married Dona ISABEL de MENDOZA, Lady of the Empress Isabel and sister of the Second Marquis of Canete, during 1542.

The known children of Bernardino Manrique de Lara y Benavides and Dona Isabel de Mendoza were:
- a1. GARCI FERNANDEZ MANRIQUE de LARA y MENDOZA (a1 = V, follows below).
- a2. ALONSO MANRIQUE de LARA y MENDOZA, Licentiate in Canons.
- a3. LUIS MANRIQUE de LARA y MENDOZA.
- a4. DIEGO MANRIQUE de LARA y MENDOZA, priest.
- a5. ANTONIO MANRIQUE de LARA y MENDOZA, priest.
- a6. MIGUEL MANRIQUE de LARA y MENDOZA, Governor of Toronto, Barleta, Aversa and Rijoles, in the Kingdom of Naples, who made the line of the Lords of Graneras.
- a7. FRANCISCA MANRIQUE de LARA y MENDOZA, a nun in Calabazanos.
- a8. BERNARDINA MANRIQUE de LARA y MENDOZA, a nun in Calabazanos.

V. GARCI FERNANDEZ MANRIQUE de LARA y MENDOZA was the Fifth Lord of the Amayuelas. Married (m1) Dona CATALINA de FONSECA y TOLEDO (daughter of Pedro de Fonseca, Lord of the Cube)/(m2) Dona MARIA de VELASCO.

The known children of Garci Fernandez Manrique de Lara y Mendoza and (m1) Dona Catalina de Fonseca y Toledo were:
- a1. BERNARDINO MANRIQUE de LARA y FONSECA (a1 = VI, follows below).
- a2. GASPAR MANRIQUE de LARA y FONSECA.
- a3. ISABEL MANRIQUE de LARA y FONSECA. Married JUAN ALONSO de SOLIS, Third Lord of Retortillo and La Granja, during 1593.

VI. BERNARDINO MANRIQUE de LARA y FONSECA was the Sixth Lord of Amayuelas, La Sagrada, Ambroz and other places. Married Dona ANTONIA del AGUILA (daughter of Diego del Aguila, Lord of Villaviciosa, and Dona Ana de Acuna).

The known children of Bernardino Manrique de Lara y Fonseca and Dona Antonia del Aguila were:
- a1. GARCIA MANRIQUE de LARA y del AGUILA (a1 = VII, follows below).
- a2. DIEGO MANRIQUE de LARA y del AGUILA, Knight of the Order of Santiago and Alderman of Salamanca.
- a3. PEDRO MANRIQUE de LARA y del AGUILA, died unmarried in Naples.
- a4. CATALINA MANRIQUE de LARA y del AGUILA. Married FRANCISCO LOPEZ de ZUNIGA y de la CERDA, Second Marquis of Baldes.

VII. GARCIA MANRIQUE de LARA y del AGUILA was the Seventh Lord of Amayuelas and Sixteenth Lord of Amusco and Redecilla, Knight of the Order of Alcantara and Alderman of Salamanca. Married Dona FRANCISCA NICOSTRATA de BARRIENTOS, Lady of the towns of Serranos de la Torre and Zapardiel de la Canada (daughter of Pedro Francisco de Barrientos Colona, Lord of the mentioned towns, and of Dona Beatriz Pacheco de Barrientos).

The known children of Garcia Manrique de Lara y del Aguila and Dona Francisca Nicostrata de Barrientos were:

    a1. BERNARDINO MANRIQUE de LARA y BARRIENTOS (a1 = VIII, follows below).

    a2. JOSE MANRIQUE de LARA y BARRIENTOS, Knight of the Order of Calatrava and Captain of the Guard of the Viceroy of Naples, Marquis of Astorga. Married Dona LEONOR FERNANDEZ de ARGUELLO.

    The known children of Jose Manrique de Lara y Barrientos and Dona Leonor Fernandez de Arguello were:

        b1. JOSE MANRIQUE de LARA y ARGUELLO.

        b2. MARIA MANRIQUE de LARA y ARGUELLO, a nun in the convent of Jesus, Salamanca.

    a3. BALTASAR MANRIQUE de LARA y BARRIENTOS, Menino of the Queen Mariana of Austria, Captain of Infantry of the Navy of the Ocean, and religious in San Agustin.

    a4. TERESA MANRIQUE de LARA y BARRIENTOS. Married ANTONIO JOSE del CASTILLO y PORTOCARRERO, Fourth Lord of the town of Fermoselle, Knight of the Order of Santiago and Alderman of Salamanca, in 1656. With succession.

    a5. ANTONIA MANRIQUE de LARA y BARRIENTOS, a nun.

    a6. MARIA MANRIQUE de LARA y BARRIENTOS. Married FELIX de SOLIS, of the noble family of Salamanca. With succession.

    a7. BEATRIZ MANRIQUE de LARA y BARRIENTOS, nun in the Augustinian Recollect Nuns of Salamanca.

    a8. CATALINA MANRIQUE de LARA y BARRIENTOS, nun in the Augustinian Recollect Nuns of Salamanca.

VIII. BERNARDINO MANRIQUE de LARA y BARRIENTOS was the First Count of the Amayuelas and Seventeenth Lord of Amusco, perpetual Curator of the University of Salamanca and Alderman of this city. The King Felipe IV made him merced of the County of the Amayuelas in 1658. Queen Mariana of Austria named him Governor of Cajamarca, in Peru, and he passed to that Kingdom, where he died before taking possession. Married LUISA de IBARRA y CARDONA, sister of the Second Marquise of Taracena.

The known children of Bernardino Manrique de Lara y Barrientos and Luisa de Ibarra y Cardona were:

    a1. GARCI FERNANDEZ MANRIQUE de LARA y IBARRA (a1 = IX, follows below).

a2. CARLOS MANRIQUE de LARA y IBARRA (a2 = X, follows below).
a3. JOSE MIGUEL MANRIQUE de LARA y IBARRA (a3 = XI, follows below).
a4. LEONOR PETRONILA MANRIQUE de LARA y IBARRA, Lady of Queen Mariana of Austria. Married GASPAR de VILLACIS QUIJADA y OCAMPO, Third Count of Penaflor who was widowed twice: the first time, of Dona Maria Antonia Manrique de Lara, sister of Rodrigo, Second Count of Frigiliana and Aguilar, and the Second, of Dona Aldonza Maria Ponce de Leon, widowed Countess of Cedillo.
a5. ANTONIA MANRIQUE de LARA y IBARRA, Carmelite nun at the Encarnacion de Avila.
a6. BLANCA MANRIQUE de LARA, Carmelite nun at the Encarnacion de Avila.
a7. DIEGO MANRIQUE de LARA y IBARRA, died as a child.
a8. MARIA MANRIQUE de LARA y IBARRA, died as a child.

IX. GARCI FERNANDEZ MANRIQUE de LARA y IBARRA was the Second Count of the Amayuelas, Eighteenth Lord of Amuseco, etc. He died without taking state, so he was succeeded by his brother.

X. CARLOS MANRIQUE de LARA y IBARRA was the Third Count of the Amayuelas and Nineteenth Lord of Amusco. He served in the Army of Lombardy and died on 3 July 1683 without children, passing the house to his third brother.

XI. JOSE ANGEL MANRIQUE de LARA y IBARRA was the Fourth Count of Amayuelas, Lord of Amusco, Gentilhombre de Camara of the King and Curator of the University of Salamanca. Married Dona CASILDA TERESA de RIVADENEIRA NINO de CASTRO, Lady of Queen Mariana of Austria (daughter of Baltasar de Rivadeneira y Zuniga, First Marquis de la Vega and Viscount of la Laguna, and Dona Ines Nino de Castro).

The known children of Jose Angel Manrique de Lara y Ibara and Dona Casilda Teresa de Rivandeneira Nino de Castro were:
a1. DOMINGO BENITO MANRIQUE de LARA y RIVADENEIRA, died.
a2. MARIA ANTONIA MANRIQUE de LARA y RIVADENEIRA, died very young.

The **SEVENTEENTH BRANCH**: Lords of the Towers of Alozaina.

I. INIGO MANRIQUE de LARA y FAJARDO (fifth son of Garcia Fernandez Manrique de Lara y Castilla and his wife, Aldonza Fajardo, mentioned in branch sixteen of Lords and Counts of the Amayuelas) was, as previously noted, First Lord of Frigiliana and Nerja, of the Towers of Alozaina, Commander of Almaguer in the Order of Santiago, Warden of Captain of Malaga, Corregidor of Granada, Maestresala of Prince Don Juan and of the Empress Dona Isabel, etc. Married Dona ISABEL CARRILLO (eldest daughter of Sancho de Rojas, Lord of Casapalma, and his wife Dona Margarita de Lomos) in 1498. He died on 27 January 1536 in Granada.

The known children of Inigo Manrique de Lara y Fajardo and Dona Isabel Carrillo were:
a1. GARCIA MANRIQUE de LARA y CARRILLO (a1 = II, follows below).

- a2. Commander RODRIGO MANRIQUE de LARA y CARRILLO, member of the line of the Counts of Frigiliana.
- a3. GUIOMAR MANRIQUE de LARA y CARRILLO. <u>Married</u> Commander GUTIERRE LASO de la VEGA, Knight of the Order of Santiago and Lord of Puertollano.
- a4. ISABEL MANRIQUE de LARA y CARRILLO, nun of Santa Clara, in Malaga.
- a5. ALDONZA MANRIQUE de LARA y CARRILLO. <u>Married</u> DIEGO de CORDOBA PONCE de LEON, Lord of La Campana, perpetual Major Ensign of Cordoba and Knight of the Order of Santiago.
- a6. MARIA MANRIQUE de LARA y CARRILLO. <u>Married</u> DIEGO de ROJAS (second son of Juan de Rojas, first Marquis of Poza).

II. GARCIA MANRIQUE de LARA y CARRILLO was Second Lord of the Towers of Alozaina and Warden, Captain and Alderman of Malaga. <u>Married</u> JUANA MANRIQUE de LARA y VALENCIA, Lady of Queen Leonor of Portugal (daughter of Fadrique Manrique de Lara, Marshal of Castile and Second Lord of Fuenteguanaldo, and of Antonia Valencia, mentioned in the Lords of Fuenteguinaldo branch), during 1525.

<u>The known children of Garcia Manrique de Lara y Carrillo and Juana Manrique de Lara y Valencia were:</u>
- a1. INIGO MANRIQUE de LARA y MANRIQUE de LARA (*a1 = III, follows below*).
- a2. FADRIQUE MANRIQUE de LARA y MANRIQUE de LARA.
- a3. FELIPE MANRIQUE de LARA y MANRIQUE de LARA.
- a4. FRANCISCA MANRIQUE de LARA y MANRIQUE de LARA.

III. INIGO MANRIQUE de LARA y MANRIQUE de LARA was the Third Lord of the Towers of Alozaina, of the inheritance of Malaga and of the entailed estate of Casa-Ubas, Alderman of Malaga and Menino of the Queen. <u>Married</u> Dona ANA de BAZAN of the House of the Viscounts of Valduerna.

<u>The known child of Inigo Manrique de Lara and Dona Ana de Bazan was:</u>
- a1. FRANCISCA FERNANDEZ MANRIQUE y BAZAN.

IV. FRANCISCA FERNANDEZ MANRIQUE y BAZAN who was the Fourth Senora de las Torres de Alozaina. <u>Married</u> RODRIGO MANRIQUE de LARA y AGUAYO, her second cousin (mentioned in the line of Lords and Counts of Frigiliana), during 1587.

The EIGHTEENTH BRANCH: Lords and Counts of Frigiliana.

I. Commander RODRIGO MANRIQUE de LARA y CARRILLO (second son of Inigo Manrique de Lara y Farjardo and his wife Dona Isabel Carrillo, mentioned in Lords of the Towers of Alozaina) was the Second Lord of Frigiliana and Nerja, Knight of the Order of Santiago, Contino of the House of Carlos V and Warden and Captain of Malaga. <u>Married</u> Mrs. CATALINA PACHECO y ARRONIZ, Lady of Esperilla and Fuente la Higuera (daughter of Luis Pacheco de Arroniz, Mayor Bailiff of Granada, and of Mrs. Luisa de Valderrabano).

The known children of Commander Rodrigo Manrique de Lara y Carrillo and Mrs. Catalina Pacheco y Arroniz were:
- a1. LUIS MANRIQUE de LARA y PACHECO (a1 = II, follows below).
- a2. JUAN MANRIQUE de LARA y PACHECO, who was in the battle of Lepanto and died in the assault of Mastrique.
- a3. DIEGO MANRIQUE de LARA y PACHECO, trunk of the line of the Lords of the Mayorazgo de Cazalla and Casa de la Madera.
- a4. ISABEL MANRIQUE de LARA y PACHECO, also known as Dona ISABEL CARRILLO, nun in Santa Clara, in Malaga.
- a5. MARIANA MANRIQUE de LARA y PACHECO, nun in Santa Clara, in Malaga.

II. LUIS MANRIQUE de LARA y PACHECO was Third Lord of Frigiliana and Nerja and of the repartimiento of the House of Arronz, in Malaga. Married Mrs. MENCIA MANRIQUE (daughter of Diego de Aguayo, Lord of Villaverde and the Galapagares and Knight of the Order of Santiago, and of Mrs. Maria Carrillo) in 1562 Seville.

The known child of Luis Manrique de Lara y Pacheco and Mrs. Mencia Manrique was:
- a1. RODRIGO MANRIQUE de LARA y AGUAYO (a1 = III, follows below).

III. RODRIGO MANRIQUE de LARA y AGUAYO was the Fourth Lord of Frigiliana and Nerja, and Warden and Captain of the city of Malaga. Married Dona FRANCISCA FERNANDEZ MANRIQUE de LARA y BAZAN, his second cousin and Fourth Senora de las Torres de Aloizaina, mentioned previously, which united both Lordships.

The known children of Rodrigo Manrique de Lara y Aguayo and Dona Francisco Fernandez Manrique de Lara y Bazan were:
- a1. INIGO MANRIQUE de LARA y MANRIQUE de LARA (a1 = IV, follows below).
- a2. JOSE MANRIQUE de LARA y MANRIQUE de LARA.
- a3. SABINIANO MANRIQUE de LARA y MANRIQUE de LARA, Knight of the Order of Calatrava and Captain General of the Philippine Islands.
- a4. BERNARDO MANRIQUE de LARA y MANRIQUE de LARA, Captain of Spanish Infantry in the Galleys of Spain. Married Dona ELVIRA de MONROY, daughter of the Lords of Tahena. No succession.
- a5. PEDRO MANRIQUE de LARA y MANRIQUE de LARA, who did not take state.
- a6. FRANCISCO MANRIQUE de LARA y MANRIQUE de LARA, who also pursued a military career.
- a7. GABRIEL MANRIQUE de LARA y MANRIQUE de LARA.
- a8. ANA MANRIQUE de LARA y MANRIQUE de LARA, nun in Malaga.
- a9. MENCIA MANRIQUE de LARA y MANRIQUE de LARA, a nun.
- a10. MARIA MANRIQUE de LARA y MANRIQUE de LARA, who did not take state.

IV. INIGO MANRIQUE de LARA y MANRIQUE de LARA was the First Count of Frigiliana and Viscount of the Source, Warden of the Malaga fortress, General Superintendent of the Frontiers of Badajoz, Governor of Cadiz,

Steward of the Queen and Knight of the Order of Alcantara. <u>Married</u> Dona MARIA de TABORA y SOUZA, Lady of Queen Isabel (daughter of Gaspar de Souza, Governor of Brazil and of the Council of State of Portugal, and of Dona Maria de Meneses).

<u>The known children of Inigo Manrique de Lara y Manrique de Lara and Dona Maria de Tabora y Souza were:</u>

- a1. RODRIGO MANUEL MANRIQUE de LARA y TABORA *(a1 = V, follows below)*.
- a2. GASPAR FRANCISCO MANRIQUE de LARA y TABORA, General of the Army of Milan and Knight of Santiago.
- a3. FRANCISCA MARIA MANRIQUE de LARA y TABORA. <u>Married</u> DIEGO FRANCISCO EUGENIO de SILVA y MENDOZA de la CERDA, Seventh Count of Galvez.
- a4. MARIA ANTONIA MANRIQUE de LARA y TABORA. <u>Married</u> GASPAR DOMINGO de VILLACIS QUIJADA de OCAMPO, Third Count of Penaflor. With succession.
- a5. TERESA MARIA MANRIQUE de LARA y TABORA. Married name: Princess of Barbanzon, Duchess of Arenberg and Countess de la Roche.

V. RODRIGO MANRIQUE de LARA y TABORA was the Second Count of Frigiliana, Viscount of La Fuente, Lord of Camares, Marquis of Hinojosa, of the Councils of State and War, Viceroy of Valencia, Captain General of Andalusia and Great of Spain. <u>Married</u> Dona MARIA ANTONIA de VALVANERA RAMIREZ de ARELLANO MENDOZA y ALVARADO, Tenth Countess of Aguilar and Villamor, Marquise of Hinojosa and Lady of the Queen Mariana of Austria (daughter of Juan Domingo Ramirez de Arellano and his wife Dona Mariana de Guevara, Ninth Count of Aguilar; great-granddaughter of Dona Luisa Manrique de Lara y Manrique de Lara, Seventh Countess of Aguilar, and her husband Felipe Ramirez de Arellano, and third maternal granddaughter of Enrique Manrique de Lara, son of the Third Duke of Najera and Dona Lucia de Acuna, and his wife Dona Ines Manrique de Lara, Sixth Countess of Paredes de Nava).

<u>The known children of Rodrigo Manrique de Lara y Tabora and Dona Maria Antonia de Valvanera Ramirez de Arellano Mendoza y Alvarado were:</u>

- a1. INIGO de la CRUZ MANRIQUE de LARA y RAMIREZ de ARELLANO *(a1 = VI, follows below)*.
- a2. MARIA TERESA MANRIQUE de LARA y RAMIREZ de ARELLANO, died as a child.

VI. INIGO de la CRUZ MANRIQUE de LARA y RAMIREZ de ARELLANO was the Eleventh Count of Aguilar, by gathering in him three of the branches of the House of Lara, Fifth Marquis of Hinojosa, Count of Villamor, Lord of the Cameros and other villas, Great of Spain and Knight of the Golden Fleece. <u>Married</u> ROSA MARIA de ARAGON y PIGNATELLI (daughter of Andres Fabricio de Pignatelli, Seventh Duke of Monleon, and his wife Teresa Pimentel, Duchess of Hijar).

The NINTEENTH BRANCH: Lords of the Mayorazgo de Cazalla and Casa de la Madera.

I. DIEGO MANRIQUE de LARA y PACHECO (third son of Commander Rodrigo Manrique de Lara y Carrillo, Second Lord of Frigiliana, and of his wife Dona Catalina Pacheco y Arroniz, mentioned in the Lords and Counts of Frigiliana) was Lord of the entailed estate of Cazalla and of the Casa de la Madera. Married Dona MARIA de CAZALLA y GUZMAN (daughter of Juan Bautista de Cazalla, Payador General de las Armadas y Fronteras de Malaga, and of his wife, Dona Leonor de Guzman y Sandoval).

The known children of Diego Manrique de Lara y Pacheco and Dona Maria de Cazalla y Madera were:
- a1. JUAN MANRIQUE de LARA y CAZALLA (a1 = II, follows below).
- a2. LUIS MANRIQUE de LARA y CAZALLA, Knight of the Order of Santiago and Gentilhombre of Prince Cardenal Don Fernando.

II. JUAN MANRIQUE de LARA y CAZALLA was Lord of the entailed estate of Cazalla and Casa de la Madera. Married Dona ISABEL MADERA GODINEZ (daughter of Licenciado Lopez Madera, Knight of the Order of Santiago and of the Royal Council of Castile and Lord of the House of Madera in Asturious).

The known children of Juan Manrique de Lara y Cazalla and Dona Isabel Madera Godinez were:
- a1. JUAN MANRIQUE de LARA y MADERA.
- a2. ANTONIO MANRIQUE de LARA y MADERA (a2 = III, follows below).

III. ANTONIO MANRIQUE de LARA y MADERA was the Lord of the mayorazgo of Cazalla and of the Casa de la Madera and Knight of the Order of Santiago. Married Mrs. INES COLLADO PACHECO.

The known children of Antonio Manrique de Lara y Madera and Mrs. Ines Collado Pacheco were:
- a1. FRANCISCO MANRIQUE de LARA y COLLADO, died young.
- a2. MARIA MANRIQUE de LARA y COLLADO (a2 = IV, follows below).
- a3. FRANCISCA MANRIQUE de LARA y COLLADO. Married ANDRES de la CONCHA y ZAPATA, Knight of the Order of Calatrava and President of the Chancery of Valladolid.
- a4. MARIANA MANRIQUE de LARA y COLLADO, nun in the Carmelitas Descalzas de Malaga.

IV. MARIA MANRIQUE de LARA y COLLADO was the Lady of the entailed estate of Cazalla and of the Casa de la Madera. Married FRANCISCO CHACON ENRIQUEZ, the First Count of Molina, Alderman of Antequera and Knight of the Order of Calatrava.

The known children of Maria Manrique de Lara y Collado and Francisco Chacon Enriquez were:
- a1. FERNANDO CHACON y MANRIQUE de LARA (a1 = V, follows below).
- a2. ANTONIO CHACON y MANRIQUE de LARA, who did not take state.
- a3. FRANCISCO CHACON y MANRIQUE de LARA, who did not take state.
- a4. BARTOLOME CHACON y MANRIQUE de LARA, who did not take state.

    a5.   INES CHACON y MANRIQUE de LARA. <u>Married</u> FRANCISCO de CARVAJAL y MENDOZA, Knight of the Order of Alcantara.
    a6.   MARTINA CHACON y MANRIQUE de LARA. <u>Married</u> FRANCISCO MIGUEL de PUEYO, Knight of the Order of Santiago, in Ubeda. With succession.
V.   FERNANDO CHACON y MANRIQUE de LARA, Lord of Cazalla.

Houses of Lara that continued were:

    The Laras of Sevilla
    The Laras of Los Hinojosos
    The Laras of Cartagena
    The Laras of Avila (Gentlemen of Torralvo)

Related to the House of Lara:

Lords of Pergola and Gurgo, Sicily; Lords of the Tower of Cuadros, Seville; Lords of the Guillena and estate of Palomares, Seville; Marquises of Santiago, Cervera del Rio Pisuerga (Palencia) and Tarazona (Zaragoza); Lords of Magana, Granada; Lords of Nogales, Quintana and Torres de Tobalina; House of Solis Manrique de Lara, Madrid; Lords of Sotilla, Guadalajara; Viscounts of Ambite, Madrid and Viscounts of Fenollet, Catalonia.

The House of Lara in the country of Columbia extends from "Gutierrez de Lara" lineage.

Research for this "Manrique de Lara" lineage text was taken from the "History of the House of Lara" written by Don Luis de Salazar y Castro, 1697, Madrid, Spain.

"Manrique de Lara" text by Don Luis de Salazar y Castro was translated from Spanish to English by Matthew Hovious, Madrid, Spain genealogist.

Ricohombre" = ("Richman") High Ranking Nobility:
    A title used during the Medieval Kingdoms of Spain and Portugal. It was replaced by the title,"Grandee" during 1400-1500. Ricohombres were advisors to rulers as per their noble birth status, significance beginning in Castile by the12th century. The number of "Ricohombes" were few (12-18) as they represented the highest nobility by birth or merit.

Order of Santiago = Religious and military order founded in 1170 by the Royal House of Bourbon. It was named for the patron Saint fo Spain: Santiago (St. James the Greater). It includes three other military orders: Order of Calatrava, Order of Alcantara and Order of Montesa.

APPENDIX XVI: GOMEZ
Births/Marriages of Gomez Surnames

The search for Baltasar Gomez and Gaspar Gomez, twins (born abt. 1550) of Pedro Gomez and Catalina Manrique de Lara, and their descendants found these similar names but unknown connections:

BALTASAR GOMEZ:

Possible children of Baltasar Gomez, the son of Baltasar Gomez born abt. 1550:

1. BALTASAR GOMEZ.
    Married MARIA ANGELINA ETZONI.
    The known children of Baltasar Gomez and Maria Angelina were (born Morelia):
    - a1. FRANCISCO GOMEZ ETZONI, christening 21 September 1621, Celaya, Celaya, Guanajuato, Mexico (Father: Baltasar Gomez/Mother: Angelina Etzoni).
    - a2. DIEGO GOMEZ ETZONI, christening 16 November 1624, Celaya, Celaya, Guanajuato, Mexico (Father: Baltasar Gomez/Mother: Angelina de Etzoni).
    - a3. SEBASTIAN GOMEZ, christening 2 April 1627, Celaya, Celaya, Guanajuato, Mexico (Father: Baltasar Gomez/Mother: Maria Angelina).

2. BALTASAR GOMEZ.
    Married (assumed) ANNA CECILIA.
    The known children of Baltasar Gomez (a) and Anna Cecilia were:
    - b1. ANNA MARIA GOMEZ, born abt. 1625.
        Married JOAN ALONSO (Father: Joan Martin/Mother: Lucia Ynes) on 5 February 1645, San Felipe, Guanajuato, Mexico).
    - b2. MARIA MAGDALENA GOMEZ, born abt. 1630.
        Married MARTIN de la CRUZ (Father: Juan Gabriel/Mother: Ana Maria de la Cruz) on 19 April 1654, San Felipe, Guanajuato, Mexico) (Father: Balthasar Gomez/Mother: Ana Cecilia).

3. BALTASAR GOMEZ.
    Married MARIA (MAGDALENA) GIACANI (de ROSAS) on 26 August 1630, Apaseo el Grande, Guanajuato, Mexico.
    The known children of Baltasar Gomez and Maria Magdalena Giacani de Rosas were:
    - a1. ANDRES JOAN GOMES married JUANA GARCIA (de Rosas) on 3 February 1636, Apaseo el Grande, Guanajuato, Mexico (Father: Baltasar Gomez/Mother: Magdalena de Rosas).
        The known children of Andres Joan Gomes (a) and Juana Garcia de Rosas were:

- b1. MARIA GOMES de ROSAS, born August 1636; christening 23 December 1636, Apaseo el Grande, Guanajuato, Mexico (Father: Andres Gomez/Mother: Juana de Rosas).
- b2. ANDRES GOMES GARCIA, christening 9 December 1638, Apaseo el Grande, Guanajuato, Mexico (Father: Andres Gomez/Mother: Juana Garcia). Died prior to 1643.
- b3. AGUSTINA GOMEZ GARCIA, christening 2 September 1640, Apaseo el Grande, Guanajuato, Mexico (Father: Andres Gomez/Mother: Joana Garcia).
- b4. ANDRES GOMES, christening 1 March 1643, Apaseo el Grande, Guanajuato, Mexico (Father: Andres Gomez/Mother: Juana Deni).
- a2. SEBASTIAN GOMEZ ROSAS, christening 22 January 1632, Apaseo el Grande, Guanajuato, Mexico (Father: Baltasar Gomez/Mother: Magdalena Rosas).
- a3. JUAN GOMEZ, christening 17 October 1632-14 November 1632, Apaseo el Grande, Guanajuato, Mexico (Father: Baltasar Gomez/Mother: Maria Magdalena de Rosas).
- a4. MARIA GOMES ROSAS, christening 7 January 1634, Apaseo el Grande, Guanajuato, Mexico (Father: Baltasar Gomez/Mother: Magdalena de Rosas).
- a5. LUCAS GOMEZ, christening 19 October 1638, Irapuato, Guanajuato, Mexico (Father: Baltasar Gomez/Mother: Anna Magdalena).
- a6. LUIS GOMEZ, christening 23 June 1647, Irapuato, Guanajuato, Mexico (Father: Baltasar Gomez/Mother: Ana Maria).
- a7. PEDRO GOMES, christening 7 November 1643, Apaseo el Grande, Guanajuato, Mexico (Father: Baltasar Gomes/Mother: Magdalena de Rosas).

GASPAR GOMEZ:

(*Possible connections to Gaspar Gomez born abt. 1550*):

1. GASPAR GOMEZ.
    Married MARIA MEXIA (Indio).
    The known children of Gaspar Gomez and Maria Mexia were:
    - a1. GASPAR GOMEZ, christening 22 May 1581, Santa Veracruz, Guerrero Sureste, Distrito Federal, Mexico (Father: Gaspar Gomez/Mother: Maria Mexia) (Margin text: Gaspar) (*Archivo de la Parroquia de la Santa Veracruz Mexico, Bautismo de Espanoles Vol. 2 1576-1601*) (*Film#004237306; Image 81/708*).
        Married FRANCISCA MEXIA (daughter of Goncalo Sanches and Mari Mexia) on 14 June 1637, Apaseo el Grande, Guanajuato, Mexico.
        The known children of Gaspar Gomez (a) and Francisca Mexia were:

- b1. THERESA GOMEZ MEXIA, christening 2 November 1640, Alpaseo el Grande, Guanajuato, Mexico (Father: GASPER GOMES Mother: Francisca Mexia).
- b2. JOANA GOMEZ married GREGORIA de MEDINA on 8 November 1644, Apaseo el Grande, Guanajuato, Mexico (Father: GASPAR GOMEZ).
- b3. NICOLAS GOMEZ MEXIA, christening 25 February 1648, Apaseo el Grande, Guanajuato, Mexico (Father: GASPAR GOMEZ Mother: Francisca Mexia).
- b4. GASPAR GOMEZ.
  Married ANA MARIA on 16 May 1660, San Juan Bautista, Apaseo el Grande, Guanajuato, Mexico.
  The known child of Gaspar Gomez (b) and Ana Maria was:
  - c1. MAGDALENA GOMEZ, christening 3 June 1665, San Juan Bautista, Apaseo el Grande, Guanajuato, Mexico.

2. GASPER GOMEZ, christening 24 June 1633, Comonfort, Guanajuato, Mexico (*possible grandson of Gaspar Gomez, born abt. 1550*).
3. GASPAR GOMEZ, born abt. 1610 (*possible son of Gaspar Gomez born 1550*)
   Married LINA de la CRUZ.
   The known child of Gaspar Gomez (a) and Lina de la Cruz was:
   - b1. GASPAR GOMEZ, christening 1637, Comonfort, Guanajuato, Mexico.
4. GASPAR GOMEZ, born abt. 1625 (*possible son of Gaspar Gomez born 1550*)
   Married CATANA.
   The known child of Gaspar Gomez (b) and Catana was:
   - c1. GASPAR GOMEZ, christening 25 September 1644, Yuriria, Guanajuato, Mexico.
5. GASPAR ANTONIO GOMEZ, born abt. 1625 (*possible son of Gaspar Gomez born 1550*).
   Married CATALINA MARIA/CATHARINA MARTA SOTO.
   The known child of Gaspar Gomez and Catalina Maria was:
   - b1. GOMEZ SOTO (hijo/hija), christening 28 September 1645, Apaseo el Grande, Guanajuato, Mexico (Father: ANTONIO GASPAR GOMEZ Mother: Catalina Maria Soto, of Apaceo Grande el alto) (Godfather: Gabriel Ximenes and Diego) (Witness: Juo. De Orellana) (*San Juan Bautista Baptism Records 1605-1639; Image 188/234*).
   - b2. FRANCISCO GOMEZ, born 1698. Burial 23 March 1738, Santurario de Guadalupe, Valle de Santiago, Guanajuato, Mexico (Father: ANTONIO GASPAR GOMEZ/Mother: Catharina Marta) (Spouse: Casilda de la Cruz) (*Santuario de Guadalupe, Valle Death records 1738-1748; Image 30/536*).
6. GASPAR GOMEZ, born abt. 1625 (*possible son of Gaspar Gomez born 1550*).
   Married ANA de QUESADA on 11 April 1649, Lagos de Moreno, Jalisco, Mexico.
   The known child of Gaspar Gomez and Ana de Quesada was:
   - b1. PO. (PEDRO) GOMEZ QUESADA, christening Santa Maria de Los Lagos, Lagos de Moreno, Jalisco, Mexico.

7. GASPER GOMEZ, born abt. 1630 (*Possible son of Gaspar Gomez born 1550*).
    Married MARIA ISABEL.
    The known child of Gasper Gomez and Maria Isabel was:
    b1.　ASEBASTIANA GOMEZ, christening 26 January 1674, Guanajuato, Mexico. Margin text: Espanola, Asebastiana/Arebolastiana, hija de GASPER GOMEZ and Maria Isabel with godmother, Juliana Luisa (*San Nicolas de Tolentino. Baptism Records 1661-1681; Image 78/90*).
8. GASPAR GOMEZ, born abt. 1640 (*Possible son of Gaspar Gomez born 1550*).
    Married ELENA de CRUZ on 29 April 1669, San Juan Bautista, Apaseo el Grande, Guanajuato, Mexico.
    The known children of Gaspar Gomez and Elena de la Cruz were:
    b1.　JUANA GOMEZ, christening 21 March 1670, San Juan Bautista, Apaseo el Grande, Guanajuato, Mexico.
    b2.　LORENCO GOMEZ, christening 30 October 1671, San Juan Bautista, Apaseo el Grande, Guanajuato, Mexico.
9. GASPER GOMEZ, born 1650 (*Possible grandson of Gaspar Gomez born 1550*).
    Married MARIA RODRIQUEZ on 23 April 1679, Salvatierra, Guanajuato, Mexico. (*Matrimonios de Naturales y Castas. Vol. S.N. 165301713*) (*FH # 00480634/Image 103-107/517*).

~~~~~~~

GOMEZ SURNAMES
Guanajuato, Mexico
(1580-1700)

San Miguel de Allende
(1580-1589)

GEORGE GOMEZ, born 1580. Burial (age two) 26 June 1582, Nuestra Senora de la Luz, San Luis de la Paz, Guanajuato, Mexico (Father: Martin/Mother: Eligia Gomez).

ANA GOMEZ, christening 17 July 1581, San Miguel Archangel, San Miguel de Allende, Guanajuato, Mexico (Father: Pedro Gomez/Mother: Ana Gomez).

MARIA GOMEZ, christening 16 November 1582, San Miguel Archangel, San Miguel de Allende, Guanajuato, Mexico (Father: Francisco/Mother: Maria Gomez).

JUAN GOMEZ, christening 3 February 1589, San Miguel Archangel, Guanajuato, Mexico (Father: Melchor Gomez/Mother: Francisca).

FRANCISCA GOMEZ, christening 7 May 1589, San Miguel Archangel, San Miguel de Allende, Guanajuato, Mexico (Father: Francisco Gomez/Mother: Magdalena).

Leon
(1575-1700)

LIDIA GERTRUDIS GOMEZ MORENO, born 24 August 1547. Christening 1590, Parroquia del Sagrario, Leon, Guanajuato, Mexico (Father: Evardo Gomez/Mother: Lidia Moreno).

ROMANA NAVARRO GOMEZ, born 1588. Christening 18 September -, Parroquia del Sagrario, Leon, Guanajuato, Mexico (Father: Jose Navarro/Mother: Angela Gomez).

NICOLAS GOMES de VALENCIA, christening 1600, Leon, Guanajuato, Mexico (Father: Pedro Gomez/Mother: Juana de Valencia) (Godfather: Antonio Gomes).

MARIA GOMEZ, christening 3 January 1646, Leon, Guanajuato, Mexico (Father: Antonio del Savesta/Mother: Isabel Gomez).

GOMEZ, son of *Melesion* Gomez of Terra Blanca and Ana -- of San Simon. Godparents: _ of Leon. 1616, San Juan Bautista, Victoria, Guanajuato, Mexico *(San Juan Bautista. Baptism Records 1590-1659; Image 163/314)*.

FRANCISCO GOMES, christening 12 November 1640, Irapuato, Guanajuato, Mexico (Father: Pedro Gomez/Mother: Catalina).

DOMINGO GOMEZ, baptism 6 April 1645, Leon, Guanajuato, Mexico (Father: Apoli- Gomez/Mother: Petra Diaz).

DOMINGO GOMEZ, baptism 6 April 1645, Leon, Guanajuato, Mexico (Mother: Juana Gomez).

ANA GOMEZ ORTIZ, born 23 December 1646; christening December 1646, Leon, Guanajuato, Mexico (Father: Antonio Gomez/Mother: Maria Ortiz).

MARIA DIAZ GOMEZ, christening 20 April 1647, Leon, Guanajuato, Mexico (Father: Domingo Dias/Mother: Juana Gomez).

APASEO el GRANDE (San Juan Bautista)
(1610-1648)

JUAN de GOMEZ (born abt. 1610) married JUSEPA SANCHES de la TORRE.
The known children of Juan de Gomez and Jusepa Sanches were:
    a1. HERM. GOMEZ SANCHES, christening 6 June 1628, Apaseo el Grande, Guanajuato, Mexico (Father: Juan de Gomez/Mother: Jusepa Sanches).
    a2. ANDRES GOMES SANCHES, christening 18 December 1629, Apaseo el Grande, Guanajuato, Mexico (Father: Juan de Gomez/Jusepa Sanches).
    a3. NICOLAS GOMEZ SANCHES, christening 17 November 1631, Apaseo el Grande, Guanajuato, Mexico (Father: Juan de Gomez/Mother: Jusepa Sanches de la Torre).

JOAN de GOMEZ married (m1) LEONOR RAMIREZ REYES/(m2) INES de ROSAS.
The known children of Joan de Gomez and (m1) Leonor Ramirez Reyes were:
    a1 LUISA GOMES RAMIREZ, christening 12 September 1635, Apaseo el Grande, Guanajuato, Mexico (Father: Joan de Gomez/Mother: Leonor Ramirez).

a2. LEONOR GOMEZ REYES, christening 24 July 1637, Apaseo el Grande, Guanajuato, Mexico (Father: Juan de Gomez/Mother: Leonor de los Reyes).

The known child of Joan de Gomez and (m2) Ines de Rosas was:

a3. AUGUSTIN GOMEZ, christening 26 August 1643, Apaseo el Grande, Guanajuato, Mexico (Father: Joan de Gomes/Mother: Ines de Rosas).

JUAN GOMEZ married MARIA de la CRUZ on 14 September 1620, Apaseo el Grande, Guanajuato, Mexico.

MARIA GOMEZ SAN MIGUEL, christening 29 May 1634, Apaseo el Grande, Guanajuato, Mexico (Father: Mateo Gomez/Mother: Magdalena de San Miguel).

DIEGO PENA GOMEZ, christening 4 September 1634, Apaseo el Grande, Guanajuato, Mexico (Father: Juan de Pena/Mother: Juana Gomez).

JUANA MALAGON GOMEZ, christening 8 July 1637, Apaseo el Grande, Guanajuato, Mexico.

SIMON GOMEZ, christening 15 November 1640, Apaseo el Grande, Guanajuato, Mexico.

DIEGO GOMEZ married LORENSA de LICAMA on 26 August 1640, San Juan Bautista, Apaseo el Grande, Guanajuato, Mexico.

SIMON LOPES GOMES, christening 15 November 1641, Apaseo el Grande, Guanajuato, Mexico (Father: Diego Lopes/Mother: Ynes Gomez).

AUGUSTIN de GOMEZ married ANNA MARIA RODRIQUEZ on 17 August 1643, Apaseo el Grande, Guanajuato, Mexico.

MARIA GOMEZ, christening October 1644, Apaseo el Grande, Guanajuato, Mexico.

GOMEZ, christening 28 September 1645, Alpaseo el Grande, Guanajuato, Mexico.

GOMEZ SOTO, christening 28 September 1645, Apaseo el Grande, Guanajuato, Mexico.

JUANA GOMEZ MEXIA, christening 4 July 1646, Apaseo el Grande, Guanajauto, Mexico (Father: Hernan Gomez/Mother: Juana Mexia).

NICOLAS GOMEZ, christening 1647, Apaseo el Grande, Guanajuato, Mexico.

ANA MARIA de GOMEZ, christening April 1647, Apaseo el Grande, Guanajuato, Mexico (Father: Juan de Gomez).

JOSEFA GOMEZ, christening 4 November 1647, Irapuato, Guanajuato, Mexico (Father: Manuel Gomez).

PHELIPE GOMEZ married (unknown) on 14 September 1648, Apaseo el Grande, Guanajuato, Mexico (Father: Pedro Gomez Barragan/Mother: Geronima de la Cruz).

GUANAJUATO
1610-1648

BERNARDINO GOMEZ, married ANNA de SANTIAGO ALTAMIRANO on 17 August 1631, Guanajuato, Guanajuato, Mexico.

The known child of Bernardo Gomez and Anna de Santiago Altamirano was:
a1.   JOSEPHA GOMEZ, christening 28 March 1632, Guanajuato, Guanajuato, Mexico (Father: Bernardino Gomez/Mother: Ana de Santiago).

(Single listings)
JULIANA GOMEZ ORTIZ, christening 11 November 1620, Guanajuato, Guanajuato, Mexico (Father: Francisco Gomez. Spouse: Isabel Ortiz).
DIEGO GOMEZ, christening 1627 (Mother: Anna Ramirez).
LUGO GOMEZ, christening 1629, Guanajuato, Guanajuato, Mexico.
DIEGO GOMEZ, christening 1630, Guanajuato, Guanajuato, Mexico.
PEDRO GOMEZ, baptism 7 July 1630, Guanajuato, Mexico (Father: Juan Rodrigo/ Mother: Geronima).
DIEGO GOMEZ, christening 18 May 1631, Guanajuato, Guanajuato, Mexico.
SEBASTIAN GOMEZ, christening 22 January 1633, Guanajuato, Guanajuato, Mexico (Father: Bernabe Gomez/Mother: Ana de San Juan).
ISABEL GOMES married FRANCISCO de BARGAS CHAMICO on 10 January 1637, Guanajuato, Guanajuato, Mexico.
CATHALINA GOMEZ, christening 3 September 1640, Guanajuato, Mexico.
CATHALINA GOMEZ, christening 25 November 1640, Guanajuato, Guanajuato, Mexico (Father: PEDRO GOMEZ/Mother: Maria).
De MARIA GOMES de SANTIAGO, christening 15 July 1641, Guanajuato, Guanajuato, Mexico (Father: Bernardino Gomez/Mother: Ana de Santiago).
SALVADOR GOMEZ, christening 6 January 1642, Guanajuato, Guanajuato, Mexico (Father: PEDRO GOMEZ/Mother: ISABEL).
MARIA GOMEZ married BERNABE GONCALVES on 24 January 1645, Guanajuato, Guanajuato, Mexico.
HERNANDEZ GOMEZ, baptism 11 April 1648, Guanajuato, Guanajuato, Mexico.

IRAPUATO
(1614-1649)

JUAN GOMEZ, born abt. 1614
   Married BEATRIZ.
   The known children of Juan Gomez and Beatriz were:
   a1.   MARIA GOMEZ, christening 25 July 1634, Irapuato, Guanajuato, Mexico (Father: Juan Gomez/Mother: Beatriz).
   a2.   AGUSTINA GOMEZ, christening 24 May 1641, Irapuato, Guanajuato, Mexico (Father: Juan Gomez/Mother: Beatriz).
CATALINA GOMEZ, born abt. 1615.
   Married JACINTO de BARRIOS.
   The known children of Catalina Gomez and Jacinto Barrios were:
   a1.   JASINTHA BARRIO GOMEZ, christening 3 June 1633, Irapuato, Guanajuato, Mexico (Father: Jasintho de Barrio/Mother: Catalina Gomez).

a2. MARIA BARRIOS GOMEZ, christening 30 December 1636, Irapuato, Guanajuato, Mexico (Father: Jacinto de Barrios/Mother: Catalina Gomez).

DIEGO GOMEZ, born abt. 1618.
   Married MARIA LUISA MAGDALENA.
   The known children of Diego Gomez and Maria Magdalena were:
   a1. MARIA GOMEZ, christening 8 April 1636, Irapuato, Guanajuato, Mexico (Father: Diego Gomez/Mother: Maria Magdalena).
   a2. MARIA GOMEZ, christening 4 July 1638, Irapuato, Guanajuato, Mexico (Father: Diego Gomez/Mother: Luisa Magdalena).

FRANCISCA RAMIREZ GOMEZ, christening 8 March 1633, Irapuato, Guanajuato, Mexico (Father: Gabriel Ramirez/Mother: Francisca Gomez).

GOMEZ HERNANDEZ, christening 6 February 1633, Irapuato, Guanajuato, Mexico (Father: Juan Gomez/Mother: Magdalena Hernandez).

ANA GOMEZ SANTOYO, christening 5 November 1634, Irapuato, Guanajuato, Mexico (Father: Manuel Gomez Tabeos/Mother: Maria de Santoyo).

JUANA AGUILAR GOMEZ, christening 10 June 1635, Irapuato, Guanajuato, Mexico (Father: Antonio de Aguilar/Mother: Isabel Gomez).

JUAN GOMEZ, christening 1636, Irapuato, Guanajuato, Mexico (Father: Nuel Gomez).

MARIA GOMEZ, christening 1637, Irapuato, Guanajuato, Mexico.

TERESA LOPES GOMEZ, christening 19 October 1637, Irapuato, Guanajuato, Mexico (Father: Francisco Lopes de Aguirre/Isabel Gomez).

JUAN GOMEZ, christening 20 October 1640, Irapuato, Guanajuato, Mexico (Father: Juan Gomez/Mother: Cecilia).

JULIO GOMEZ, christening 16 July 1640, Irapuato, Guanajuato, Mexico (Father: Juan Gomez/Mother: Juana).

AGUSTIN GOMEZ, christening 12 November 1640, Irapuato, Guanajuato, Mexico (Father: Matheo Gomez/Mother: Lusana Maria).

FRANCISCO GOMEZ, christening 12 November 1640, Irapuato, Guanajuato, Mexico (Father: Pedro Gomez/Mother: Catalina).

ISABEL GOMEZ CERVANTES, christening 16 July 1640, Irapuato, Guanajuato, Mexico (Father: Lucas Gomes/Mother: Maria de Cervantes).

JOSEPH GIL GOMEZ, christening 14 November 1641, Irapuato, Guanajuato, Mexico (Father: Isidro Gil/Mother: Mariana de Gomez).

ANDRES GOMEZ, christening 6 December 1642, Irapuato, Guanajuato, Mexico.

PASQUALA GOMEZ, christening 10 May 1648, Irapuato, Guanajuato, Mexico (Father: Andres Gomez/Mother: Francisca Juana).

ANTONIO MEDINA GOMEZ, christening 28 February 1649, Irapuato, Guanajuato, Mexico (Father: Diego Hernandez/Mother: Isabel Gomez).

PHELIPE TORRES GOMEZ, christening 28 May 1649, Irapuato, Guanajuato, Mexico (Father: Francisco de Torres/Mother: Elena Gomez).

CATHALINA GOMEZ MAYORGA, christening 19 December 1649, Irapuato, Guanajuato, Mexico (Father: Juan Gomez/Mother: Antonia Mayorga).

~~~~~~

SALVATIERRA

FRANCISCA GOMEZ, christening 2 August 1650, Salvatierra, Guanajuato, Mexico (Mother: Mariana Gomez).

~~~~~~~~~

From Leon Founders's Surname List: Rodrigo and Cristobal MARTIN
(Possible *MARTIN Leon founder relations*)

BALTASAR GOMEZ married MARIA GICANI on 26 August 1630, San Juan Bautista, Apaseo el Grande, Guanajuato, Mexico.

FRANCISCO MARTIN married MARIA GICANI on 26 March 1631, San Juan Bautista, Apaseo el Grande, Guanajuato, Mexico.

LUCAS MARTIN married MARIA GICANI on 29 July 1631, San Juan Bautista, Apaseo el Grande, Guanajuato, Mexico.

JUAN MARTIN married MARIA GICANI on 26 October 1632, San Juan Bautista, Apaseo el Grande, Guanajuato, Mexico.

GASPAR GOMEZ married FRANCISCA MEXIA on 14 June 1637, Apaseo el Grande, Guanajuato, Mexico.

~~~~~~~~~

LOPEZ de AGUIRRE

JOSEPHA LOPEZ AGUIRRE, christening 31 October 1644, Nuestra Senora de la Soledad, Irapuato, Guanajuato, Mexico (Father: Lorenzo Lopez/Mother: Antonia de Aguirre).

PEDRO LOPEZ de AGUIRRE (1650).
　　Married MARIA de HERRERA BOLANOS.
The known children of Pedro Lopez de Aguirre and Maria de Herrera Bolanos were:
- a1. ANDREA LOPEZ de AGUIRRE (1664), baptism 9 December 1664, San Francisco de Asis, Comonfort, Guanajuato, Mexico (Residence: Chamacuero de Comonfort, Guanajuato, Mexico).
- a2. MANUEL LOPEZ de AGUIRRE (1668).
- a3. ANTONIA de BOLANOS.
- a4. PETRONA de HERRERA.

RAFAEL LOPEZ de AGUIRRE, baptism 12 April 1663, Nuestra Senora de Guanajuato, Guanajuato, Mexico (Father: Don Juan Lopes de Mexia/Dona Maria Estafania de Aguirre) (Godparents: Benito Puday Aruanujo and his wife, Dona Maria Francisca de Concha) (*Guanajuato. Baptism Records 1762-1769; Image 22/322*).

APPENDIX XVII: GOMEZ of PORTUGAL

The parents of JUANA GOMEZ de PORTUGAL y LOPEZ de NAVA (1560) were:

CAPTAIN JUAN BEJAR de AVIZ y GOMEZ de PORTUGAL
Born 1536, Portugal.
Christening 1537, Santa Maria, Gargota, Navarra, Espana.
Died 1610, Villa de los Lagos, Nueva Galicia (Jalisco, Mexico).
CATALINA LOPEZ de XIMENA y de NAVA de JAEN
Born 1538, Badajoz, Extramadura, Spain.
Born 16 May 1538, Toledo, Toledo, Castilla-La Mancha, Spain.
Died Villa de los Lagos, Nueva Galicia (Jalisco, Mexico).

The known children of Captain Juan Gomez de Portugal and Catalina Lopez de Ximena de Nava were:
1. JUANA GOMEZ de PORTUGAL y LOPEZ de NAVA (1560).
   Born 1560, Spain.
   Married GASPAR de MALDONADO (1550).
   Died Acambaro, Acambaro, Guanajuato, Mexico.
   The known child of Juana Gomez of Portugal y Lopez de Nava and Gaspar de Maldonado was:
   a1. ISABEL GOMEZ MALDONADO.
       Married MIGUEL DOMINGUEZ de ESPEJO during 1596, San Juan Bautista, Apaseo el Grande, Guanajuato, Mexico.
       The children of ISABEL GOMEZ MALDONADO (a1) and MIGUEL DOMINGUEZ de ESPEJO:
       b1. JUANA GOMEZ de ESPEJO (1595-1653).
           Born abt. 1595, Celaya, Guanajuato, Mexico
           Died 16 June 1653, Leon, Guanajuato, Mexico.
           Married DOMINGO HERNANDEZ GAMINO (1595-1687).
           Born abt. 1595 Guadalupe, Caceres, Extramadura, Spain.
           Died 13 October 1687, Leon, Guanajuato, Mexico.

       The parents of DOMINGO HERNANDEZ GAMINO (1595-1687) were:
           JUAN "EL ESCRIBANO" HERNANDEZ GAMINO (1570-1632)
           ANA VELAZQUEZ CORREA (1573-1633)
       Married 14 February 1593, Canamero, Caceres, Extramadura, Spain.

       Three sons married DOMINGUEZ sisters born Aguascalientes, Aguascalientes, Mexico:
       BLAS HERNANDEZ GAMINO GOMEZ de ESPEJO (1630, Leon)
           married LUISA ALONSO de los HINOJOS ULLOA.
       JUAN HERNANDEZ GAMINO (1635, Leon)
           married ANA HINOJOS DOMINGUEZ.
       DIEGO BARTHOLME HERNANDEZ (1642, Leon)
           married ANA MARIA DOMINGUEZ de los HINOJOS.

Children of: Captain PEDRO ALONSO de los HINOJOS y de SANCHEZ de ULLOA (1595-1660) who married ANA DOMINGUEZ (1600-1675) on 3 May 1620, San Matias, Pinos, Zacatecas, Mexico).

Children of JUANA GOMEZ de ESPEJO (b1) and DOMINGO HERNANDEZ GAMINO:
c1. NICOLAS HERNANDEZ GAMINO y DOMINQUEZ de ESPEJO (1621), born abt. 1621, Leon, Guanajuato, Mexico.
c2. ISABEL HERNANDEZ GAMINO y DOMINGUEZ de ESPEJO (1624, Aguascalientes, Aguascalientes, Mexico). Married ANTONIO de ECHAVESTI (1616, Guipuzcoa, Pais Vasco, Spain) abt. 1643, El Sagrario, Aguascalientes, Aguascalientes, Mexico.
Children of Isabel Hernandez de Espejo (c2) and Antonio Echavesti:
  d1. JUANA CHAVESTI y GOMEZ de ESPEJO, born 2 January 1644, Leon, Guanajuato, Mexico.
  d2. MARIANA CHAVESTI y GOMEZ de ESPEJO, born 25 September 1646; christening 26 September 1646, Leon, Guanajuato, Mexico. Married ALONSO MARTIN BALLEJO on 26 May 1667, Leon, Guanajuato, Mexico.
  The known child of Mariana Chavesti (d2) and Alonso Martin:
    e1. JUAN MARTIN y CHAVESTI, born 14 February 1672, Leon, Guanajuato, Mexico; christening 15 February 1672, Leon, Guanajuato, Mexico.
  d3. SEBASTIANA CHAVESTI y GOMEZ de ESPEJO, born 25 January 1649, Leon, Guanajuato, Mexico; christening 26 January 1649, Leon, Guanajuato, Mexico. Married LUCAS GAONA.
  The children of Sebastiana Chavesti Gomez (d3) and Lucas Gaona:
    e1. LUCAS de GAONA y CHAVESTI, born 9 January 1673, Leon, Guanajuato, Mexico; christening 10 January 1673, Leon, Guanajuato, Mexico.
    e2. MARIA de GAONA y CHAVESTI, born 19 November 1674, Leon, Guanajuato, Mexico; christening 20 November 1674, Leon, Guanajuato, Mexico. Married PEDRO SARDENETA MUNOZ (1670) February 1690, Leon, Guanajuato, Mexico.
    e3. ANDRES de GAONA y CHAVESTI, born 2 January 1677, Leon, Guanajuato, Mexico; christening 3 January 1677, Leon, Guanajuato, Mexico.
    e4. JUAN de GAONA y CHAVESTI, born 2 January 1677; christening 3 January 1677, Leon, Guanajuato, Mexico.
    e5. MAGDALENA de GAONA y CHAVESTI, born 29 August 1679, Leon, Guanajuato, Mexico; christening 30 August 1679, Leon, Guanajuato, Mexico.

- e6. ANTONIO GABRIEL de GAONA y CHAVESTI, born 16 April 1681; christening 17 April 1681, Leon, Guanajuato, Mexico.
- d5. MAGDALENA CHAVESTI y GOMEZ de ESPEJO, born 25 January 1656, Leon, Guanajuato, Mexico; christening 26 January 1656, Leon, Guanajuato, Mexico.
- d6. ISABEL CHAVESTI y GOMEZ de ESPEJO, born 18 April 1659, Leon, Guanajuato, Mexico; christening 19 April 1659, Leon, Guanajuato, Mexico. Married JUAN de HERRERA QUINTANA.

The children of Isabel Chavesti Gomez (d6) and Juan Herrera Quintana:
- e1. MARIA JOSEFA de HERRERA y CHAVESTI, born 6 July 1687; christening 22 July 1687, Leon, Guanajuato, Mexico.
- e2. JUAN de HERRERA y CHAVESTI, born 19 July 1688, Leon, Guanajuato, Mexico; christening 20 July 1688, Leon, Guanajuato, Mexico.
- e3. FRANCISCO de HERRERA y CHAVESTI, born 22 October 1694, Leon, Guanajuato, Mexico; christening 31 October 1694, Leon, Guanajuato, Mexico.
- d7. ANTONIO CHAVESTI y GOMEZ de ESPEJO, born 21 March 1662, Leon, Guanajuato, Mexico; christening 22 March 1662, Leon, Guanajuato, Mexico. Married RITA de MENDOZA.

The children of Antonio Chavesti Gomez (d7) and Rita Mendoza:
- e1. GERTRUDIS CHAVESTI y MENDOZA, born 13 March 1696, Leon, Guanajuato, Mexico; christening 14 March 1696, Leon, Guanajuato, Mexico.
- e2. MARCO ANTONIO CHAVESTI y MENDOZA, born 25 April 1700, Leon, Guanajuato, Mexico; christening 13 May 1700, Leon, Guanajuato, Mexico.
- d8. MARIA de ESPEJO y CHAVESTI, born Leon, Guanajuato, Mexico. Married FRANCISCO de OJEDA LUNA.

The known children of Maria Espejo Chavesti (d8) and Francisco Ojeda:
- e1. MAGDALENA de OJEDA y CHAVESTI, born 10 August 1676, Leon, Guanajuato, Mexico; christening 11 August 1676, Leon, Guanajuato, Mexico. Married MANUEL GONZALES.
- e2. ROSA MARIA de OJEDA ESPEJO y CHAVESTI, born 1680, Leon, Guanajuato, Mexico. Married JOSE SARDENETA y LEGASPI MUNOZ (1677-1741) on 3 May 1698, Guanajuato, Mexico.

c3. DOMINGO HERNANDEZ GAMINO GOMEZ de ESPEJO (born 1626/1627). Married JUANA GARCI BRAVO de LAGUNAS, daughter of GARCI de LAGUNAS and CATALINA MANRIQUE de LARA (daughter of GASPER GOMEZ MANRIQUE de LARA and MARIANA FERRER, born abt. 1600, Leon, Guanajuato, Mexico) on 7 May 1642, Santa Fe, San Miguel Allende, Guanajuato, Mexico.

The known children of Domingo Hernandez Gamino (c3) and Juana Garci Bravo:

d1. FELIPE HERNANDEZ GAMINO, born 1643, Irapuato, Guanajuato, Mexico. <u>Married</u> AGUSTINA de FONSECA MONTENEGRO (christening 5 December 1651, Salamanca, Guanajuato, Mexico). <u>The known children of Felipe Hernandez Gamino (d1) and Agustina Fonseca</u>:
- e1. MARIA ROSA HERNANDEZ FONSECA, christening 20 April 1676, Nuestra Senora de la Soledad, Irapuato, Guanajuato, Mexico.
- e2. LUISA HERNANDEZ de FONSECA, 1678, Irapuato, Guanajuato, Mexico. <u>Married</u> DIEGO MARTIN de IBARRA (1675) on 6 January 1697, Irapuato, Guanajuato, Mexico.
- e3. JUAN HERNANDEZ FONSECA, christening 22 May 1680, Irapuato, Guanajuato, Mexico.
- e4. FRANCISCA HERNANDEZ FONSECA, christening 2 November 1682, Nuestra Senora de la Soledad, Irapuato, Guanajuato, Mexico.
- e5. NICOLAS CLEMENTE HERNANDEZ FONSECA, christening 11 December 1684, Nuestra Senora de la Soledad, Irapuato, Guanajuato, Mexico. <u>Married</u> Senora FONSECA (1687).
- e6. MARIA TERESA HERNANDEZ FONSECA, christening 9 December 1686, Nuestra Senora de la Soledad, Irapuato, Guanajuato, Mexico.

d2. HIPOLITO HERNANDEZ GAMINO BRAVO, christening 29 August 1645, Nuestra Senora de la Soledad, Irapuato, Mexico.

d3. MARIA HERNANDEZ BRAVO, christening 20 October 1647, Nuestra Senora de la Soledad, Irapuato, Mexico.

d4. DOMINGO HERNANDEZ BRAVO, christening 20 August 1654, Nuestra Senora de la Soledad, Irapuato, Guanajuato, Mexico. <u>Married</u> ANTONIA de ROJAS on 22 May 1673, Mexico.

d5. ANTONIO HERNANDEZ GAMINO, born abt. 1657, Irapuato, Guanajuato, Mexico. <u>Married</u> ANTONIA GOMEZ de RUBALCABA (christening 14 October 1659, Santa Maria de los Lagos, Lagos de Moreno, Jalisco, Mexico; died 20 August 1727, Lagos de Moreno, Jalisco, Mexico). Death/burial on 15 November 1714, Lagos de Moreno, Jalisco, Mexico.

d6. CATALINA HERNANDEZ BRAVO, christening 14 July 1666, Irapuato, Guanajuato, Mexico. Death/burial on 5 February 1716, Irapuato, Guanajuato, Mexico.

d7. BERNARDA HERNANDEZ y BRAVO de LAGUNAS MANRIQUE, christening 8 October 1668, Nuestra Senora de la Soledad, Irapuato, Guanajuato, Mexico. <u>Married</u> CRISTOBAL GUTIERREZ NAVARRO on 7 September 1686, La Soledad, Irapuato, Guanajuato, Mexico.

d8. BENITO HERNANDEZ BRAVO, christening 25 May 1670, Nuestra Senora de la Soledad, Irapuato, Guanajuato, Mexico. <u>Married</u> GERTRUDIS RAMOS MEXIA (christening 21 October 1691,

Salamanca, Guanajuato, Mexico) on 20 December 1717, Irapuato, Guanajuato, Mexico.
- d9. JUAN HERNANDEZ GAMINO BRAVO. Married EUSEBIA SARMIENTO PALOMINO on 14 April 1679, Sante Fe, San Miguel de Allende, Guanajuato, Mexico.
- d10. JUANA HERNANDEZ GAMINO BRAVO LAGUNAS married JOSEPH BARRETO de TABORA on 3 July 1678, La Soledad, Irapuato, Guanajuato, Mexico.
- d11. LUIS HERNANDEZ GAMINO BRAVO married GERTRUDIS DAZA y BUSTAMANTE on 24 December 1681, Irapuato, Guanajuato, Mexico.

c4. DIEGO HERNANDEZ GAMINO y DOMINQUEZ GOMEZ de ESPEJO, born abt. 1627, San Antonio de Padua; christening San Agustin, Tlajomulco de Zuniga, Jalisco, Mexico. Married MENICA RUIZ de HARO y NUNEZ de SOTOMAYOR (born abt. 1641 El Chico, Ayotlan, Jalisco, Mexico; died 4 May 1723, Tepatitlan, Jalisco, Mexico.

The known children of Diego Hernandez Gamino (c4) and Menica Ruiz Haro:
- d1. MARGARITA GOMEZ HERNANDEZ GAMINO y RUIZ de HARO, christening 30 May 1663, Ayo el Chico, Ayotlan, Jalisco, Mexico. Married PEDRO de ACEVES y BECERRA GALINDO (1655-1727) on 4 February 1679, Ayotlan, Jalisco, Mexico.

  The known children of Margarita Gomez Hernandez (d1) and Pedro Aceves were:
  - e1. PEDRO de ACEVES FERNANDEZ y HERNANDEZ DOMINGUEZ (1690-1729). Married LEONOR de ARIAS MALDONADO y de la MORA de HERMOSILLO (1700) on 2 June 1719, Ocotlan, Jalisco, Mexico.
  - e2. MARIA ACEVES y HERNANDEZ GOMEZ de ESPEJO, born 20 February 1693; christening 20 April 1693, Tapatitlan de Morales, Jalisco, Mexico. Married DIEGO GUTIERREZ GALINDO y CAMARENA (1688) on 13 February 1715, Tepatitlan de Morales, Jalisco, Mexico.
  - e3. MENCIA de ACEVES y GOMEZ de ESPEJO, born 9 July 1695; christening 8 August 1695, Tepetitlan, de Morelos, Jalisco, Mexico. Married MATHEO NAVARRO de la MORA (1692). Died abt. 2 March 1769, Tepatitlan de Morelos, Jalisco, Mexico.
- d2. MARIA HERNANDEZ y RUIZ de HARO, born abt. 1665, Ayo El Chico, Ayotlan, Jalisco, Mexico.
- d3. LUGARDA HERNANDEZ GOMEZ de ESPEJO y RUIZ DE HARO, born abt. 1669, Ayo El Chico, Ayotlan, Jalisco, Mexico. Married SEBASTIAN de ACEVES FERNANDEZ (1659) on 6 May 1689, Ayotlan, Jalisco, Mexico.
- d4. ANTONIA HERNANDEZ y RUIZ de HARO, born abt. 1671, Ayo El Chico, Ayotlan, Jalisco, Mexico. Died 17 March 1722, Jalisco, Mexico.

- d5. FELIX GOMEZ, born 1673, Ayo El Chico, Jalisco, Mexico. Married GERTRUDIS GONZALEZ (1678).
- d6. JUANA MARIA GOMEZ BELASCO, christening 1679, San Agustin, Tlajomulco de Zuniga, Jalisco, Mexico. Married PEDRO GONZALEZ (1674) on 10 May 1700 San Agustin, Tlajomulco de Zuniga, Jalisco, Mexico.

c5. CRISTOBAL HERNANDEZ GAMINO y DOMINGUEZ GOMEZ, born abt. 1628, Leon, Guanajuato, Mexico. Married MARIA de los ANGELES RUIZ de HARO y NUNEZ del PRADO (born 1634, Ayo El Chico, Jalisco, Mexico) on 23 February 1653, Leon, Guanajuato, Mexico. Died 1703, Ayo El Chico, Ayotlan, Jalisco, Mexico.

The known children of Cristobal Hernandez Gamino Dominquez (c5) and Maria Haro were:

- d1. MAGDALENA HERNANDEZ VELASQUEZ y RUIZ de HARO, born abt. 1654, Ayo el Chico, Ayotlan, Jalisco, Mexico. Married JOSEPH de ACEVES FERNANDEZ de HIGAR (1653-1700) (*Children born post 1687*).
- d2. JOSEFA de VELASCO HERNANDEZ GAMINO, born abt. 1661, Ayo El Chico, Ayotlan, Jalisco, Mexico. Married JUAN de PADILLA LOMELLINI (1660) on 15 February 1684, San Agustin, Tlajomulco de Zuniga, Jalisco, Mexico (*Children born post 1693*).
- d3. MIGUEL HERNANDEZ GAMINO, christening 31 January 1663, Ayo El Chico, Ayotlan, Jalisco, Mexico. Married ANGELA CASILLAS y CABRERA (1685) abt. 1703, Ayotlan, Aottlan, Jalisco, Mexico.
- d4. CLEMENTE de HERNANDEZ GAMINO y RUIZ de HARO, christening 31 December 1664, El Carrizal, Ayo El Chico, Jalisco, Mexico. Married JOSEFA de HERNANDEZ de LIEVANO (1675).
- d5. DIEGO HERNANDEZ VELAZQUEZ y RUIZ de HARO, born abt. 1666, Ayo El Chico, Jalisco, Mexico. Married MARIA FRANCO de la CUEVA de REBOLLAR y de GUTIERREZ HERMOSILLO (1676-1701) on 17 February 1697, Guadalajara, Jalisco, Mexico.
- d6. CRISTOBAL HERNANDEZ GAMINO Y VELASCO, born 5 May 1667; christening 8 May 1667, Ayo El Chico, Ayotalan, Jalisco, Mexico. Married MARIA NICOLASA AYALA de ALBA (1680) on 12 May 1691, San Agustin, Tlajomulco de Zuniga, Jalisco, Mexico. Died September 1754, La Barca, Jalisco, Mexico.
- d6. JOSE HERNANDEZ VELASCO, christening 11 June 1669, San Agustin, Tlajomulco de Zuniga, Jalisco, Mexico. Married MARIA BALDIVIA.
- d7. DIEGO HERNANDEZ GAMINO, christening 1671, San Agustin, Tlajomulco de Zuniga, Jalisco, Mexico. Married GERTRUDIS CASSILAS y RAMIREZ de MENDOZA.
- d8. ROSA HERNANDEZ GAMINO de VELASCO, born 1672, Ayo el Chico, Ayotlan, Jalisco, Mexico. Married JOSE JUAN ASCENCIO de LEON JIMENEZ (1676) on 26 September 1695, San Agustin, Tlajomulco de Zuniga, Jalisco, Mexico.

- d9. MARIA de los ANGELES HERNANDEZ GAMINO y RUIZ de HARO, christening 22 February 1674, Tlajomulco, Jalisco, Mexico. Married JOSE TELLO de OROZCO y de LUEVANO abt. 1678, Ayotlan, Ayoltan, Jalisco, Mexico.
- d10. JOSE DOMINGO HERNANDEZ GAMINO y VELASCO, christening 23 August 1676, El Carrizal, Ayo El Chico, Jalisco, Mexico. Married MARIANA de VALDIVIA GUTIERREZ on 26 May 1704, San Francisco de Asis, Tepatlan, Jalisco, Mexico.
- c6. BLAS HERNANDEZ GAMINO y GOMEZ de ESPEJO, born abt. 1630, Leon, Guanajuato, Mexico. Married LUISA ALONSO de los HINOJOS y MEDEI DOMINGUEZ (christening 15 May 1633, El Sagrario, Aguascalientes, Aguascalientes, Mexico) on 19 July 1654, El Sagrario, Aguascalientes, Aguascalientes, Mexico. Died 1688, Aguascalientes, Aguascalientes, Mexico.

The known children of Blas Hernandez Gamino Gomez (c6) and Luisa Hinojos were:
- d1. PEDRO HERNANDEZ GAMINO y DOMINGUEZ, christening 28 May 1655, El Sagrario, Aguascalientes, Aguascalientes, Mexico. Married VIOLANTE RUIZ de VELASCO ACEVES (1657-1772) during 1678, Aguascalientes, Aguascalientes, Mexico (*Sons born 1679, 1680, 1689*).
- d2. LUCIA HERNANDEZ de los HINOJOS, christening 2 February 1659, El Sagrario, Aguascalientes, Aguascalientes, Mexico.
- d3. JOSEFA HERNANDEZ HINOJOS, death/burial 1660, Asuncion de Maria, Aguascalientes, Aguascalientes, Mexico.
- d4. LUISA HERNANDEZ de HINOJOS, christening 26 February 1664, El Sagrario, Aguascalientes, Aguascalientes, Mexico. Married NICOLAS de SANTOS y BUSTOS CHAVEZ (1673-1742) on 12 June 1696, Aguascalientes, Aguascalientes, Mexico.
- d5. MIGUEL HERNANDEZ HINOJOS, christening 13 November 1666, El Sagrario, Aguascalientes, Aguascalientes, Mexico. Married JUANA MACIAS LOPEZ (1675) on 15 February 1699, El Sagrario, Aguascalientes, Aguascalientes, Mexico.
- c7. CATHALINA HERNANDEZ y GOMEZ de ESPEJO (1628-1703), born abt. 1632, Leon Guanajuato, Mexico. Married FRANCISCO VELAZQUEZ (born abt. 1620, Guanajuato, Mexico) on 26 January 1650, Leon, Guanajuato, Mexico.

The known children of Cathalina Hernandez Gomez (c7) and Francisco Velazquez were:
- d1. ISABEL VELASQUEZ HERNANDEZ, christening 7 May 1647, El Sagrario, Leon, Guanajuato, Mexico. Married JUAN de ACEVES FERNANDEZ y BECERRA GALLINDO (1658) on 20 January 1676, Sagrario Metropolitano, Guadalajara, Jalisco, Mexico.
- d2. JUAN VELAZQUEZ HERNANDEZ, christening 26 January 1650, El Sagrario, Leon, Guanajuato, Mexico.
- d3. ANTONIO VELAZQUEZ HERNANDEZ, born 24 April 1652; christening 25 April 1652, Leon, Guanajuato, Mexico.

c8. JUAN HERNANDEZ GAMINO, born abt. 1635, Mexico. Married ANA de los HINOJOS ULLOA y de MEDIA DOMINGUEZ (christening 10 January 1639, El Sagrario, Aguascalientes, Aguascalientes, Mexico) abt. 1664 Aguascalientes, Aguascalientes, Mexico. Death/burial 22 February 1688, Aguascalientes, Aguascalientes, Mexico.

The known children of Juan Hernandez Gamino (c8) and Ana Hinojos Ulloa were:

    d1. JUANA HERNANDEZ y GOMEZ de ESPEJO DOMINGUEZ, christening 11 April 1665, El Sagrario, Aguascalientes, Aguascalientes, Mexico. Married JUAN MACIAS VALDEZ de ORAN y VEGA on 12 June 1683, Aguascalientes, Aguascalientes, Mexico.

    d2. JOSEPH HERNANDEZ DOMINGUEZ, christening 12 December 1666, El Sagrario, Aguascalientes, Aguascalientes, Mexico.

    d3. MARIA HERNANDEZ DOMINGUEZ, born 13 November 1670; christening 13 November 1670, El Sagrario, Aguascalientes, Aguascalientes, Mexico.

    d4. BARTOLOME HERNANDEZ DOMINGUEZ, christening 28 September 1675, El Sagrario, Aguascalientes, Aguascalientes, Mexico. Married MARIA ISABEL RAMIREZ MARTINEZ (1690-1773) on 12 January 1710, Aguascalientes, Aguascalientes, Mexico.

    d5. MARIANA HERNANDEZ DOMINGUEZ, christening 6 October 1677, El Sagrario, Aguascalientes, Aguascalientes, Mexico.

    d6. TERESA HERNANDEZ DOMINGUEZ, christening 18 December 1678, El Sagrario, Aguascalientes, Aguascalientes, Mexico. Married JUAN CHAVARRIA LOZANO (1683-1743) on 22 October 1709, Aguascalientes, Aguascalientes, Mexico.

    d7. ANA HERNANDEZ DOMINGUEZ, christening 4 July 1680, El Sagrario, Aguascalientes, Aguascalientes, Mexico. Married JINES CALVILLO LOPES (1664) on 30 May 1696, El Sagrario, Aguascalientes, Aguascalientes, Mexico.

    d8. ANA HERNANDEZ DOMINGUEZ, death/burial 29 August 1675, Aguascalientes, Aguascalientes, Mexico.

c9. ANA HERNANDEZ GAMINO y DOMINGUEZ de ESPEJO, born abt. 1636, Aguascalientes, Aguascalientes, Mexico. Married JOSE SALCEDO (born abt. Aguascalientes, Aguascalientes, Mexico) abt. 1649, Aguascalientes, Aguascalientes, Mexico.

The known child of Ana Hernandez Gamino Dominguez (c9) and Jose Salcedo was:

    d1. MARIA SALCEDO HERNANDEZ y DOMINGUEZ ESPEJO, born abt. 1650, Aguascalientes, Aguascalientes, Mexico.

c10. JUANA HERNANDEZ GAMINO y DOMINGUEZ de ESPEJO, born abt. 1639, Puruandiro, Michoacan, Mexico. Married GONZALO AVALOS HURTADO (born Valladolid, Michoacan, Mexico) on 10 October 1650, Santa Ana, Penjamo, Guanajuato, Mexico.

The known children of Juana Hernandez Gamino (c10) and Gonzalo Avalos Hurtado were:

- d1. GONZALO de VILLASENOR, christening 1636, Puruandiro, Michoacan, Mexico. Married TERESA de ALBA ESTRADA (1650) March 1683, El Sagrario, Aguascalientes, Aguascalientes, Mexico. Died 6 August 1733, Aguascalientes, Aguascalientes, Mexico.
- d2. BALTAZAR De AVALOS y ESPEJO, born 21 January 1653; christening 22 January 1653, Leon, Guanajuato, Mexico.
- d3. JOSE de VILLASENOR y ESPEJO, born 14 April 1655; christening 15 April 1655, Leon, Guanajuato, Mexico.
- d4. GONZALO de VILLASENOR y ESPEJO, born 17 January 1660; christening 18 January 1660, Leon, Guanajuato, Mexico.

c11. LUISA GOMEZ ESPEJO (1639).

c12. ANTONIA LUCIA HERNANDEZ y GOMEZ de ESPEJO, born 1641, Ayo El Chico, Jalisco, Mexico. Married LUIS ANTONIO de SALCEDO (born 1637, Ayo El Chico, Jalisco, Mexico; died Tijuana, Baja California) during 1662, Ayotlan, Ayotlan, Mexico.

The children of Antonia Hernandez Gomez (c12) and Luis Salcedo were:
- d1. LORENZO ANTONIO de SALCEDO, born 1663, Ayo El Chico, Jalisco, Mexico. Married JUANA QUINTERO y ARIAS de AVELLANEDA (1667) on 16 December 1689, Sagrario Metropolitano, Guadalajara, Jalisco, Mexico.
- d2. TOMAS SALCEDO y GOMEZ ESPEJO, born 1666, Ayo El Chico, Jalisco, Mexico. Married ANTONIA VALDIVIA y HERMOSILLO (1676) on 27 February 1696, Tepatitlan de Moreno, Jalisco, Mexico. Died 13 September 1701.
- d3. DOMINGO HERNANDEZ SALCEDO, born 1670, Ayotlan, Jalisco, Mexico.

c13. DIEGO BARTOLOME HERNANDEZ y GOMEZ de ESPEJO, born 1642, Leon, Guanajuato, Mexico. Married ANA MARIA DOMNGUEZ de los INOJOAS (January 1639, Aguascalientes, Aguascalientes, Mexico; died 14 August 1675, El Sauz de los Macias, Aguascalientes, Aguascalientes, Mexico). Died 1692, Ayo el Chico, Jalisco, Mexico.

The known children of Diego Hernandez Gomez (c13) and Ana Dominquez were:
- d1. JUANA GOMEZ de ESPEJO y DOMINGUEZ, born 1654, San Nicolas de Penuelas, Aguascalientes, Aguascalientes, Mexico.
- d2. BARTOLOME HERNANDEZ GAMINO y DOMINGUEZ, born 1657, San Nicolas de Penuelas, Aguascalientes, Aguascalientes, Mexico.
- d3. TERESA HERNANDEZ DOMINGUEZ, died 22 May 1743, Mexico.
- d4. JOSE HERNANDEZ, born December 1666, Mexico.

c14. MARIA HERNANDEZ y GOMEZ de ESPEJO, born abt. 1643, Aguascalientes, Mexico, Married ANTONIO MARTINEZ de ROSAS (1629) during 1658, Celaya, Guanajuato, Mexico.

The known children of Maria Hernandez Gomez (c14) and Antonio Martinez were:
- d1. JOSEPHA MARTINEZ y GOMEZ de ESPEJO, born 25 March 1659; christening 26 March 1659, Leon, Guanajuato, Mexico.

    d2.   PEDRO MARTINEZ y GOMEZ de ESPEJO, born 9 August 1660; christening 10 August 1660, Leon, Guanajuato, Mexico.

    d3.   MIGUEL MARTINEZ de ROSAS, christening 6 November 1667, San Francisco de Asis, Comonfort, Guanajuato, Mexico.

c15.   TOMAS HERNANDEZ GAMINO y GOMEZ de ESPEJO, christening 3 June 1692, San Agustin, Ayo el Chico, Jalisco, Mexico. Married GERONIMA de LIEBANO y de LEON (christening 3 June 1692, San Agustin, Ayo El Chico, Jalisco, Mexico) during 1664, Ayotlan, Ayotlan, Jalisco, Mexico.

The known children of Tomas Hernandez Gamino (c15) and Geronima Liebano were:

    d1.   CLEMENTE de HERNANDEZ GAMINO y RUIZ de HARA, christening 31 December 1664, Ayo El Chico, Jalisco, Mexico. Married JOSEFA de HERNANDEZ de LIEVANO (1675) abt. 1686, Ayotlan, Ayotlan, Jalisco, Mexico.

    d2.   TOMAS HERNANDEZ GAMINO de LIEBANA, christening 7 January 1678, Ayo El Chico, Ayotlan, Jalisco, Mexico. Married MARIA LEONOR di LOMELLINI de CORTEZ BENAVIDES on 30 March 1703, Ayotlan, Ayotlan, Jalisco, Mexico.

c16.   ELVIRA HERNANDEZ y GOMEZ de ESPEJO, born 1648, Leon, Guanajuato, Mexico. Died 16 November 1691, Leon, Guanajuato, Mexico.

c17.   MARIA MARGARITA HERNANDEZ GAMINO GOMEZ de ESPEJO, born abt. Mexico City, Mexico.

The children of ISABEL GOMEZ MALDONADO (a1) and MIGUEL DOMINGUEZ de ESPEJO were:)(Continued)

    b2.   MARIA DOMINGUEZ de ESPEJO y MALDONADO BEJAR y GOMEZ, born abt. 27 October 1602, Mexico City, Mexico Died Mexico.

    b3.   JULIO GOMEZ, christening 11 June 1606, Apaseao el Grande, Guanajuato, Mexico (Father: Miguel Dominguez/Mother: Isabel Gomez) (Father: Diego Felipe/Brother: Miguel Dominquez).

    b4.   MIGUEL DOMINQUEZ de ESPEJO y MALDONADO BEJAR GOMEZ (1606) Christening 11 June 1606, San Juan Bautista, Apaseo el Grande, Guanajuato, Mexico (Miguel Dominguez Gomez) (Father: Miguel Dominguez/Mother: Isabel Gomez).

(The known children of Captain Juan Gomez de Portugal and Catalina Lopez de Ximena de Nava were:) (Continued)

2.   MANUEL GOMEZ de PORTUGAL y LOPEZ de NAVA (1561-1600).
    Born abt. 1561, Villa de Torrijos de los Olivos, Maueda, Toledo, Spain.
    Christening abt. 1561, Coina, Barreiro, Setubal, Portugal.
    Married ANA VICENTE (1540-1580).

Died abt. 1600 Coina, Barreiro, Setubal, Portugal.
3. THOMASA GOMEZ de PORTUGAL y LOPEZ de NAVA (1563).
Born abt. 1563, Villa de Constantina, Sevilla, Spain.
Died before 1626, New Spain.
<u>Married</u> JUAN XIL (b. 1550,) son of FRANCISCO GIL (1520, Seville, Andalusia, Spain) and ISABEL GUTIERREZ de RIVAS (1520, Seville, Andalucia, Spain) on 28 April 1583, Santa Maria de Los Lagos, Lagos de Moreno, Jalisco, Mexico (Father: Juan of Portugal/Mother: Catalina Lopez).

4. CAPTAIN DIEGO GOMEZ de PORTUGAL y LOPEZ de NAVA (1566-1649).
Born 6 May 1566, Lagos de Moreno, Jalisco, Mexico.
Christening 31 July 1580, Pinel de Abajo, Valladolid, Castille y Leon, Spain.
Died 28 February 1649, Lagos de Moreno Jalisco, Mexico.
<u>Married</u> MARIA GARCIA de ARRONA (1570-1652) (Born 24 April 1570, Lagos de Moreno, Jalisco, Mexico; Died 2 July 1652, Lagos de Moreno, Jalisco, Mexico) on 8 January 1590, Santa Maria de Los Lagos, Lagos de Moreno, Jalisco, Mexico.

<u>The known children of Captain Diego Gomez of Portugal (4) and Maria Garcia Arrona were</u>:

a1. MAGDALENA GOMEZ of PORTUGAL y GARCIA de ARRONA (1588-1646).

a2. DIEGO GOMEZ of PORTUGAL y GARCIA de ARRONA (1590-1665)
Born 1590, Abrantes, Santarem, Portugal. Christening 31 July 1590, Pinel de Abajo, Valladolid, Castilla y Leon, Spain.
Death/burial 31 October 1665, Santa Maria de los Lagos, Lagos de Moreno, Jalisco, Mexico.
<u>Married</u> ISABEL FLORES de la TORRE y de SANDI (1610-1680) 1629, Santa Maria de los Lagos, Lagos de Moreno, Jalisco, Mexico.

<u>The known children of Diego Gomez (a2) and Isabel Flores de la Torre y de Sandi were</u>:

b1. ANGELINA GOMEZ de PORTUGAL y FLORES de la TORRE (1630).

b2. JUSEPA GOMEZ FLORES, christening 13 September 1638, Santa Maria de los Lagos, Lagos de Moreno, Jalisco, Mexico (Father: DIEGO GOMEZ PORTUGAL/Mother: Isabel Flores) (JUSEPA GOMEZ de PORTUGAL)
"JOSEPA, "…christening 13 September 1638, "Jusepa, daughter of DIEGO GOMEZ PORTUGAL and DONA ISABEL FLOREZ. (Godparents: Jacinto de Lara and Maria de Azzona).
(Margin text: "Jusepa") (*Family Search #004002307/Image# 66/523*).

b3. ANA GOMEZ de PORTUGAL y FLORES de SANDI (1639-1712).
<u>Married</u> DOMINGO MARTIN LANDEROS (1640) on 28 July 1666, Santa Maria de los Lagos, Lagos de Moreno, Jalisco, Mexico.

The known children of Ana Gomez (b2) and Domino Martin Landeros were:

- c1. AGUSTIN LANDEROS GOMEZ de PORTUGAL (1660-1701). Married JUANA GONZALEZ de RUBALCAVA (1670) on 9 June 1690, Lagos de Moreno, Jalisco, Mexico.
- c2. MAGDALENA LANDEROS GOMEZ de PORTUGAL (1667-1713). Married Captain ANDRES de SANROMAN y SERRANO on 9 February 1682, Lagos de Moreno, Jalisco, Mexico.
- c3. JUANA LANDEROS (1670). Married JOSEPH MANUEL RAMOS XIMENES (1665) on 30 January 1689, Tlaquepaque, Jalisco, Mexico.
- c4. MARIA LANDEROS de PORTUGAL (1675-1699). Married JOSE de la MORA y ZAMORA, on 8 May 1690, Lagos de Moreno, Jalisco, Mexico.

b4. JUANA GOMEZ de PORTUGAL (1640). Married BLAS SANCHES ARIAS de LARA (BLAS SANCHES ARIAS de LARA to JUANA of PORTUGAL) on 3 September 1658, Santa Maria de los Lagos, Lagos de Moreno, Jalisco, Mexico.

b5. DIEGO GOMEZ de PORTUGAL y FLORES de la TORRE (1643-31 October 1665, Lagos de Moreno, Jalisco, Mexico).
Married (DIEGO GOMEZ of PORTUGAL) JOSEPHA LOZANO, Asuncion de Maria, Aguascalientes, Mexico (*Matrimonios 1663-1702; Image 36/325*).

DIEGO GOMEZ de PORTUGAL (engagement to) JOSEPHA LOSANO on 25 March 1670, El Sagrario, Aguascalientes, Aguascalientes, Mexico.

Dona JOSEPHA de LOZANO y GONZALES, born 1652 (JOSEPHA LOZANO GONZALES MARTINEZ GARDEA).

Confirmation Record: Palo Alto, Calvillo, Aguascalientes, Mexico. Margin name: "MARIA". (JOSEPHA LOSANO GONZALES) (Father: CRISTOBAL LOZANO/Mother: MARIANA GONZALES) (*Christening, Mexico, Aguascalientes, Catholic Church Records 1601-1962*).

Married JOSEPHA MARTINEZ (to DIEGO GOMES of PORTUGAL) on 1 June 1670, Santa Maria de los Lagos, Lagos de Moreno, Jalisco, Mexico.

The known children of Diego Gomez (b5) and Josepha Lozano were:
- c. JOSEPHA LOZANO, *born 1668 prior to marriage*.

           <u>Married</u> SEBASTIAN LUNA ORTIZ de ESQUIBEL (1659) abt. 1688, Zacatecas, Mexico.

c1.   MARIANA GOMES of PORTUGAL, born abt. 1671.
<u>Married</u> Captain MIGUEL RODRIGUEZ of PORTUGAL (son of Francisco Rodriquez and ANA of PORTUGAL) on 20 June 1689, Lagos de Moreno, Jalisco, Mexico (MARIANA GOMES of PORTUGAL - father: DIEGO GOMES of PORTUGAL; Mother: JOSEPHA LOSANO).

c2.   SALVADOR GOMES LOSANO, christening 1676, Santa Maria de los Lagos, Lagos de Moreno, Jalisco, Mexico (Father: DIEGO GOMES PORTUGAL; Mother: JOSEPHA LOSANO). <u>Married</u> TERESA de LOPES INFANTE (1680-1737) (Christening 3 June 1680, Nuestra Senora de la Soledad, Irapuato, Guanajuato, Mexico; Father: Alonso Lopes de Aguirre/Mother: Maria Infante de Villegas**).

<u>The known children of Salvador Gomez of Portugal and Teresa Lopes Infante were</u>:

    d1.   MARIANA GOMEZ LOPES, christening 1 March 1700, Lagos de Moreno, Jalisco, Mexico (Father: Salvador Gomez and Teresa Lopes) (Godparents: Miguel Rodriquez de la- and Maria Dias Infante) (Margin Text: "Mariana, Espanola") (*Santa Maria de los Lagos, Bautismos de hijos legitimos 1690-1701: Image 306/368*).

    d2.   ISIDRO GOMEZ LOPES, christening 28 May 1702, Santa Maria de los Lagos, Lagos de Moreno, Jalisco, Mexico (Father: Salvador Gomez; Mother: Theresa Lopes).

    d3.   FRANCISCA XAVIERA GOMEZ LOPEZ, born 3 November 1703; christening 13 October 1704, Santa Maria de los Lagos, Lagos de Moreno, Jalisco, Mexico (Father: Salvador Gomez/Mother: Theresa Lopes Infante) (Godparent: Antonio Rodriquez) (Margin text: "Franca. Xaviera, Espanola legitima") *(Bautismos de hijos legitmos 1701-1718; Image 119/693)*.

    d4.   MARIA THERESA GOMEZ LOPEZ, christening 2 November 1706, Santa Maria de los Lagos, Lagos de Moreno, Jalisco, Mexico (Father: Salvador Gomez/Mother: Theresa Lopes).

    d5.   JUAN CAIETANO GOMEZ LOPEZ, christening 27 October 1708, Santa Maria de los Lagos,

Lagos de Moreno, Jalisco, Mexico (Father: Salvador Gomez/Mother: Theresa Lopez) (Godparents: Don Alonso Lopez and Dona Josepha Losano de Gardea) (Margin text: "Ju Caitano, Espanol Legitimos") (*Bautismos de hijos legitimos 1701-1718; Image 266/693*).
Married JOSEPHA MORENO MARMOLEJO.
The known child of Juan Cayetano Gomez Portugal and Maria Josepha Moreno Marmolejo was:

 e1. ISABEL ANTONIA GOMEZ MORENO, born 7 June 1733; christening 13 July 1733, Santa Maria de los Lagos, Lagos de Moreno, Jalisco, Mexico (Godparents: Salvador Gomez Portugal and Theresa Lopes de Aguirre, residents of the Hacienda Oetabascoya) (Margin text: "Isabel Antonia, espanola of Aalisocoya") (*Santa Maria de los Lagos. Baptism Records 1729-1734; Image 309/368*).

c3. MANUEL GOMES LOSANO, christening 1678, Santa Maria de los Lagos, Lagos de Moreno, Jalisco, Mexico (Father: Diego Gomes Portugal/Mother: Josepha Losano).
Married ISADORA de NABA y ARAUJO (daughter of Nicolas de Naba and Ysidora de Naba y Araujo) (ISADORA CATHARINA NAVA de la FUENTE) (1697) on 27 February 1718, Santa Maria de los Lagos, Lagos de Moreno, Jalisco, Mexico (Father: Diego Gomes Portugal/Mother: Josepha Losano).

c4. ROSA BEJAR GOMES LOSANO, christening 1680, Santa Maria de Los Lagos, Lagos de Moreno, Jalisco, Mexico (Father: Diego Gomes/Mother: Josepha Losano).

c5. GERTRUDIS GOMES LOSANO, christening 1683, Santa Maria de los Lagos, Lagos de Moreno, Jalisco, Mexico (Father: Diego Gomes Portugal/Mother: Josepha Losano). Married JOSE MORENO de ORTEGA ARUJO (1679-1706) on May 1701, Lagos de Moreno, Jalisco, Mexico.

c6. MAGDALENA GOMES GONZALES, christening 4 August 1685, Santa Maria de los Lagos, Lagos de Moreno, Jalisco, Mexico (Father: Diego Gomes de Portugal/ Mother: Josepha Gonzales Gardea) (Witness: Gasper de Padilla y de Medina). Married CRISTOBAL

                RODRIGUEZ RAMIREZ y BEJAR de AVIS YSASSI (1678) on 11 September 1701, Lagos de Moreno, Jalisco, Mexico.
- c7. MANUELA GOMES LOSANO, christening 1688, Santa Maria de los Lagos, Lagos de Moreno, Jalisco, Mexico (Father: Diego Gomes Portugal/Mother: Josepha Losano).
- c8. JUAN CRISOSTOMO GOMEZ LOZANO, christening 18 February 1692, Santa Maria de los Lagos, Lagos de Moreno, Jalisco, Mexico (Father: Diego Gomes Mother: Josepha Losano) (Espanol).
- c9. CRISTOBAL GOMEZ LOZANO, christening 3 August 1695, Santa Maria de los Lagos, Lagos de Moreno, Jalisco, Mexico (Father: Diego Gomes/Mother: Josepha Losano).

b6. NICOLAS GOMEZ de PORTUGAL FLORES (1646).
<u>Married</u> MARIA RENTERIA de ISSAZI de DIAS ABREGO (1660) on 14 November 1674, Tlaquepaque, Jalisco, Mexico.
<u>The known children of Nicolas Gomez (b5) and Maria Renteria Issazi were:</u>
- c1. JOSEPHA GOMEZ de PORTUGAL y ISSASI (1675).
- c2. JUANA GOMEZ de PORTUGAL de ISSASI (1676).
  <u>Married</u>: NICOLAS de ASPEYTIA de RAMIREZ (1670) on 8 November 1718, Tlaquepaque, Jalisco, Mexico).
- c3. GASPAR GOMEZ de PORTUGAL (1678) <u>married</u> MARIA de LEON de ASPEYTIA (1685) on 12 May 1716, Tlaquepaque, Jalisco, Mexico.
- c4. ROSA MARIA GOMEZ YASSI (1679).
- c5. ANA GOMEZ of PORTUGAL y ISSASI (1681).
- c6. PETRONILLA BEJAR de AVIS y de ISSASI (1683).
- c7. PASQUELA BEJAR de AVIS y de ISSASI de DIAS (1684).
- c8. CLARA BEJAR de AVIS y de ISSASI (1686).
- c9. JUAN BEJAR DE AVIS y de ISSASI (1687).
- c10. GERONIMA BEJAR de AVIS de ISSASI (1690).
- c11. ALEJANDRO CAYTANO BEJAR de AVIS (1693).

b7. PEDRO GOMEZ de PORTUGAL y FLORES de la TORRE (abt. 1655). <u>Married</u> MARIA RENTERIA de IZZASI de DIAS ABREGO on 2 June 1680, Tlaquepaque, Jalisco, Mexico.
<u>The known child of Pedro Gomez (b7) and Maria Renteria Issazi was:</u>
- c1. PASQUEALA GOMEZ de YSASI, christening May 1684, Villa de Santa Maria de los Lagos, Lagos de Moreno, Jalisco, Mexico (Father: Pedro Gomez/Mother: Maria de Ysasi) (Witnesses: Santiago de la Cruz,

      Isabel Hernandez, Gaspar de Padilla de y Medina, Cristiana).
      <u>Married</u> NICOLAS GONZALES DURAN (1673) on January 1698, Lagos de Moreno, Jalisco, Mexico.
  b8. JUAN JUO. GOMEZ de PORTUGAL, born abt. 1656.
a3. Capt. JUAN GOMEZ of PORTUGAL y GARCIA de ARRONA (1593-1640)
  <u>Married</u> MICHAELA RAMIREZ de OVALIE (1650-1705) on 14 June 1666, Santa Maria de los Lagos, Lagos de Moreno, Jalisco, Mexico (*Juan Gomez of Portugal*).
  Death/burial: 22 October 1640, Santa Maria de Los Lagos, Jalisco, Mexico (son of Captain Diego Gomez of Portugal and Lopez de Nava).
<u>The known children of Capt. Juan Gomez (a3) and Michaela Ramirez were</u>:
  c1. ISABEL GOMEZ RAMIREZ, christening 1676, Santa Maria de los Lagos, Lagos de Moreno, Jalisco, Mexico (Father: Jn. Gomes/Mother: Micheala Ramires).
  c2. JUAN GOMEZ de PORTUGAL y RAMIREZ, christening 1678, Santa Maria de los Lagos, Lagos de Moreno, Jalisco, Mexico (Father: Jn. Gomes/Mother: Michela Ramirez)
    <u>Married</u>: LUISA LOPEZ de ACALA (daughter of Antonio Ponze de Leon and Petronila de Olivares) on 26 April 1690, Santa Maria de los Lagos, Lagos de Moreno, Jalisco, Mexico (Spouse's father: Juan Gomes Portugal) (Spouse's mother: Luisa Lopes de Acala) (engagement)/Marriage: 24 April 1691, LUISA LOPEZ de ACALA (daughter of Antonio Ponse de Leon/Mother: Petronila de Olivares) to JUAN GOMES PORTUGAL (son of Juan Gomez and Michaela Ramirez).
  c3. ANA GOMEZ de PORTUGAL y RAMIREZ, christening 1682, Santa Maria de los Lagos, Lagos de Moreno, Jalisco, Mexico (Father: Juan Gomes Portugal/Mother: Michaela Ramirez).
  c4. DIEGO GOMEZ de PORTUGAL y RAMIREZ (1689) Christening 7 August 1689. Lagos de Moreno, Jalisco, Mexico (Father: Juan Gomes Portugal /Mother: Michaela Ramirez). <u>Married</u> ESTEPHANIA MARQUES (Daughter of Gregorio Marques and Isabel de Espinosa) on 25 August 1720, Santa Maria de Los Lagos, Lagos de Moreno, Jalisco, Mexico (Spouse's father: Juan Gomes Portugal) (Spouse's mother: Michaela Ramirez).
  c5. MARIA ROSA de PORTUGAL, born abt. 1666. <u>Married</u> GERONIMO de PEDRAZA (son of Ygnacio de

      Pedraza and Antonia de Guzman) on 6 September 1688, Lagos de Moreno, Jalisco, Mexico (Spouse's father: Juan Gomes Portugal/Mother: Michaela Ramirez).

a4. PEDRO GOMEZ of PORTUGAL y GARCIA de ARRONA (1593-1669)
<u>Married</u> ISABEL ORTIZ de ANDA, daughter of Captain Pedro de Anda Altamirano (1540-1619) and Ortiz Pardo on 18 June 1613, Lagos de Moreno, Mexico.

<u>The known children of Pedro Gomez (a4) and Isabel Ortiz Anda were:</u>

b1. MAXIMA BEJAR GOMEZ y ORTIZ de ANDA, born 1 February 1614, Villa de los Lagos, Jalisco, Mexico. <u>Married</u> MIGUEL MUNOZ, on 1 February 1634 (Maxima Gomez), Santa Maria de Los Lagos, Lagos de Moreno, Jalisco, Mexico) (Father: Pedro Gomez/Mother: Isabel Ortiz).

<u>The known child of Maxima Gomez Ortiz (b1) and Miguel Munoz was:</u>

  c1. ANTONIO MUNOZ GOMEZ, christening 28 August 1636, Santa Maria de Los Lagos, Lagos de Moreno, Jalisco, Mexico (Father: Miguel Munoz/Mother: Ma. Gomez).

b2. JUANA BEJAR GOMEZ y ORTIZ de ANDA (1616).
  Born 30 October 1616, Villa de los Lagos, Lagos de Moreno, Jalisco, Mexico. Christening (JUANA GOMEZ ORTIZ) 1616, Santa Maria de Los Lagos, Lagos de Moreno, Jalisco, Mexico (Father: Pedro Gomez/Mother: Isabel Ortiz).

b3. DIEGO BEJAR GOMEZ y ORTIZ de ANDA (1619).
  (DIEGO GOMEZ of PORTUGAL)
  DIEGO GOMEZ ORTIZ, christening 10 November 1619, Santa Maria de los Lagos, Lagos de Moreno, Jalisco, Mexico) (Father: Pedro Gomez/Mother: Isabel Oritz).
<u>Married</u> (DIEGO GOMEZ PORTUGAL) PETRONA HERNANDEZ on 4 November 1657, Santa Maria de los Lagos, Lagos de Moreno, Jalisco, Mexico).

<u>The known children of Diego Gomez Ortiz (b3) and Petrona Hernandez were:</u>

  c1. SEBASTIAN GOMEZ HERNANDEZ, christening 8 February 1658, Santa Maria de los Lagos, Lagos de Moreno, Jalisco, Mexico (Father: Diego Gomez/Mother: Petrona Hernandez) (Witness: Antonio Ximenes). <u>Married</u> JUANA de la CRUZ on 4 February 1679, Santa Maria de los Lagos, Lagos de Moreno, Jalisco, Mexico (Father: Diego Gomez/Mother: Petrona Hernandez).

  c2. NICOLASA GOMEZ HERNANDEZ, born 19 February 1660 - christening 11 March 1660, Santa Maria de los Lagos, Lagos de Moreno, Jalisco, Mexico (Father: Diego

                Gomez/Mother: Petrona Hernandez) (Witness: Catalina de Castro). Married JOSEPH GONZALES de HERMOSILLO (son of Matheo de Hermosillo and Geronima de Villalva) on 15 January 1680 Lagos de Moreno, Lagos de Moreno, Jalisco Mexico (Spouse's father: Diego Gomez) (Spouse's mother: Petrona Hernandez).

        c3.   ISABEL GOMEZ HERNANDEZ, born 10 May 1663 - christening 11 June 1663, Santa Maria de los Lagos, Lagos de Moreno, Jalisco, Mexico (Father: Diego Gomez/Mother: Petrona Hernandez) (Witnesses: Vincente Hernandez, Catalina Dias & Bernabe de Ysasti).

b4.   JUAN BEJAR GOMEZ y ORTIZ de ANDA (1635).
        Baptized 2 January 1635, Santa Maria de los Lagos, Lagos de Moreno, Jalisco, Mexico (JUAN GOMEZ ORTIZ) (Father: Po. Gomez/Mother: Ysabel Ortiz).

b5.   LUISA BEJAR GOMEZ y ORTIZ de ANDA, christening 3 February 1637, Lagos de Moreno, Jalisco, Mexico (Father: Pedro Gomez/Mother: Isabel Ortiz). Married NICOLAS MASIAS on 1 February 1661, Santa Maria de los Lagos, Lagos de Moreno, Jalisco, Mexico.

The known children of Luisa Gomez Ortiz (b5) and Nicolas Masias were:

        c1.   MARIA MASIAS GOMEZ, born 30 January 1660/christening February 1660, Lagos de Moreno, Jalisco, Mexico (Father: Nicholas Macias/Mother: Luisa Gomez) (Witnesses: Pedro Gomez & Isabel Juana Gomez) (Espanola).

        c2.   MARIA MASIAS GOMEZ, christening 21 February 1662, Santa Maria de los Lagos, Lagos de Moreno, Jalisco, Mexico (Father: Nicolas Masias/Mother: Luisa Gomez).

        c3.   PETRONA MASIAS GOMEZ, christening 21 February 1664, Santa Maria de los Lagos, Lagos de Moreno, Jalisco, Mexico (Father: Nicolas Masias/Mother: Luisa Gomez).
                Married NICOLAS de TORRES (son of Juan de Torres and Juana Perez) on 1 July 1681, Santa Maria de los Lagos, Lagos de Moreno, Jalisco, Mexico (Father: Nicolas Macias/Mother: Luisa Gomez).

        c4.   RITA MACIAS GOMEZ, born 15 July 1666/christening 1666, Santa Maria de Los Lagos, Lagos de Moreno, Jalisco, Mexico (Father: Nicolas Macias/Mother: Luisa Gomez).

b6.   PEDRO GOMEZ de PORTUGAL y ORTIZ de ANDA (1639).

Christening 13 April 1639, Santa Maria de Los Lagos, Lagos de Moreno, Jalisco, Mexico (Father: Pedro Gomez Portugal/ Mother: Isabel Ortiz) (Godparents: Alvaro de Ornales and Mariana Gomez). Married ANA de AGUIRRE (PEDRO GOMEZ PORTUGAL) (Father: Pedro Gomez Portugal/ Mother: Isabel Ortiz) on 22 May 1679, Santa Maria de los Lagos, Lagos de Moreno, Jalisco, Mexico).

The known children of Pedro Gomez Ortiz (b6) and Ana Aguirre were:

- c1. AMBROSIO GOMEZ AGUIRRE, christening 11 July 1684, Santa Maria de los Lagos, Lagos de Moreno, Jalisco, Mexico (Father: Pedro Gomez; Mother: Ana de Aguirre).
- c2. LUISA GOMES AGUIRRE, christening 1685, Santa Maria de los Lagos, Lagos de Moreno, Jalisco, Mexico (Father: Pedro Gomez/Mother: Ana de Aguirre).
- c3. MICHAELA GOMEZ AGUIRRE, christening 1688, Santa Maria de los Lagos, Lagos de Moreno, Jalisco, Mexico (Father: Pedro Gomez/Mother: Ana de Aguirre).
- c4. PEDRO GOMEZ AGUIRRE, christening 10 May 1695, Santa Maria de los Lagos, Lagos de Moreno, Jalisco, Mexico (Father: Pedro Gomez/Mother: Ana de Aguirre). Married JOSEFA PONCE on 7 November 1715, Santa Maria, Tlaquepaque, Jalisco, Mexico.
- c5. JUAN JOSE GOMEZ PORTUGAL (Father: Pedro Jose Gomez Portugal/Mother: Catarina Flores). Married MARIA VICTORIANA BELOS on 24 June 1781, Lagos de Moreno, Jalisco, Mexico).

b7. CATALINA BEJAR GOMEZ y ORTIZ de ANDA (1640-1680). Death/burial: 13 June 1680, San Francisco de Rincon, Guanajuato, Mexico. Married DIEGO de QUESADA, (CATALINA LOPEZ) on 29 June 1653, Santa Maria de los Lagos, Lagos de Moreno, Jalisco, Mexico).

The known children of Catalina Gomez Ortiz (b7) and Diego Quesada were:

- c1. ANDREA QUESADA GOMEZ, christening 28 December 1659, Santa Maria de los Lagos, Lagos de Moreno, Jalisco, Mexico (Father: Diego de Quesada/Mother: Catalina Gomez) (Witness: Isabel Ortiz).
- c2. MARIANA QUESADA GOMEZ, christening 15 August 1655, Santa Maria de los Lagos, Lagos de Moreno, Jalisco, Mexico (Father: Diego de Quesada/Mother: Catalina Gomez).
- c3. GERONIMO de QUESADA GOMEZ, christening 3 March 1658, Santa Maria de los Lagos, Lagos de Moreno, Jalisco, Mexico.

        c4.   JUAN de QUESADA GOMEZ, born 18 April 1660, christening May 1660, Lagos de Moreno, Jalisco, Mexico (Father: Diego de Quesada/Mother: Catalina Gomez) (Witness: Joseph Gomez).
- b8. CAPTAIN JOSEF BEJAR GOMEZ ORTIZ (1650-1697)
  <u>Married</u> MARIA de ESPINOSA, 2 July 1664, Jalisco, Mexico. (Text: "Jose Gomez, son of Pedro Gomez Portugal and Isabel Ortiz Parada and Maria de Espinosa, daughter of Francisco de Espinosa and Maria de Salazar, both native of the Villa de los Lagos were married on 2 July 1664").
- b9. DIEGO GOMEZ PORTUGAL, christening 1657, Lagos de Moreno, Jalisco, Mexico (Father: Pedro Gomez Portugal/Mother: Isabel Ortiz) (Godparents: Joseph Moreno de Ortega/Fabiana Ximenez de Castro) (Witness: Petrona Hernandez).

<u>(The known children of Captain Diego Gomez of Portugal (4) and Maria Garcia Arrona were:)</u> *(Continued)*
- a5. CATALINA GOMEZ of PORTUGAL y GARCIA de ARRONA (1594-1648).
- a6. MANUEL GOMEZ of PORTUGAL y GARCIA de ARRONA (1595-1633).
- a7. GERONIMO GOMEZ of PORTUGAL y GARCIA de ARRONA (1600-1669).
- a8. JOSEPH GOMEZ of PORTUGAL y GARCIA de ARRONA (1602).
- a9. TEODORA GOMEZ of PORTUGAL y GARCIA de ARRONA (1604).
- a10. ANGELINA GOMEZ of PORTUGAL y GARCIA de ARRONA (1605).
- a11. ANA GOMEZ of PORTUGAL y GARCIA de ARRONA (1611).
- a12. MARIANA GOMEZ of PORTUGAL y GARCIA de ARRONA (1613).
- a13. MELCHORA GOMEZ of PORTUGAL y GARCIA de ARRONA (Born abt. 1615, Lagos de Moreno, Jalisco, Mexico).
  <u>Married</u> PEDRO de MARMOLEJO y de PEDRAZA (Born abt. 1610, Leon, Guanajuato, Mexico. Died 2 September 1660, Leon, Guanajuato, Mexico) (Son of FRANCISCO de MARMOLEJO y MEJIA (1577)
  <u>Married</u> MARIA de PEDRAZA (1590) abt. 1605, Mexico City, Mexico.
  Grandson of DIEGO MARMOLEJO (1507)
  <u>Married</u> FRANCISCA MEJIA VILLALOBOS (1530) abt. 1570, San Luis Potesi, Mexico.

<u>The children of Melchora Gomez de Portugal and Pedro Marmolejo de Pedraza were:</u>
(listed at Family Search tree - no documents)
- b1. MARIANA MARMOLEJO de PEDRAZA y PORTUGAL*
- b2. DIEGO MARMOLEJO de PEDRAZA y PORTUGAL*
- b3. JOSE MARMOLEJO de PEDRAZA y PORTUGAL*
- b4. MARCOS MARMOLEJO de PEDRAZA y PORTUGAL*
- b5. LORENZO MARMOLEJO.
  <u>Married</u>: ISABEL de BUSTOS.

b6. PEDRO de MARMOLEJO y de PEDRAZA, born abt. 1630, Leon, Guanajuato, Mexico.
Married JOSEPHA de BUSTOS.
The known children of Pedro Marmolejo (a) and Josepha de Bustos were:
- c1. ANA MARMOLEJO de BUSTOS, christening 6 April 1650, Leon, Guanajuato, Mexico (Margin text: "Ana." Record text: christening of "Ana, hija de Pedro Marmolejo and Dona Josepha de Bustos") (Godparents: Lorenzo Marmolejo and Dona Isabel de Bustos) (*Leon de los Aldama. Baptism Records 1636-1673; Image 17/87*).
- c2. JUAN MARMOLEJO, christening 1652, El Sagrario, Leon, Guanajuato, Mexico (*Bautismos de espanoles 1636-1715, 1718-1748; Image 20/598*).
- c3. LORENZO MARMOLEJO, christening 30 September 1654, Leon, Guanajuato, Mexico (Father: Pedro Marmolejo/Mother: Josepha de Bustos).
- c4. JOSEPHA MARMOLEJO, christening 11 May 1655, Leon, Guanajuato, Mexico (Margin text: " JOSEPHA, Espanola. "Baptism of Josepha, hija de Pedro Marmolejo and Dona Josepha de Bustos, of the villa") (Father: Pedro Marmolejo/Mother: Josepha de Bustos) (Godfather: Antonio de Herrera and Maria de Vellon) (*Leon de los Aldama. Baptism Records 1636-1673; Image 26/87*).
- c5. JOSEPH MARMOLEJO (born abt. 1657, Leon, Guanajuato, Mexico).
Married JOSEPHA ROJAS.
The known child of Joseph Marmolejo and Josepha Rojas was:
- d1. JUAN MARMOLEJO de ROJAS (Margin text: "Juan, Espanol"), baptism 23 December 1673 (Father: Joseph Marmolejo/Mother: Josepha de Rojas) (Godparents: Pedro Marmolejo and Melchora Gomez) (*Leon de los Aldama. Baptism Records 1673-1691; Image 6/39*).
  JUAN (Margin text), christening 23 February 1676, Leon, Guanajuato, Mexico. (Father: Joseph Marmolejo/Mother: Josepha de Rojas) (Godfather: Pedro Marmolejo/Godmother: Melchora Gomez) (Margin text: "Espanoles and residents of the villa" -Leon) (*Leon de los Aldama. Baptism Records 1673-1691; Image 11/39*).
Married JOSEPHA CANALES de BUSTOS.

The known children of Juan Marmolejo (c) and Josepha Canales de Bustos were:

e1. GETRUDIS MARMOLEJO, Mestizo. Baptized 5 June 1686, El Sagrario, Leon, Guanajuato, Mexico (Record text: "Getrudis, hija de Ju. Marmelejo y de Lugarda de Mestizos de la Canada de...") (Father: Juan Antonio Marmolejo/ Mother: Josepha de Bustos). *Leon. Baptism Records 1636-1686; Image 86/100).*

e2. ANTONIA MARMOLEJO, christening 1710, Leon, Guanajuato, Mexico (Father: Juan Marmolejo/Mother: Josepha Canales) (Godparents: Felipe Nunos and Rosa Maria) (Margin text: "Antonia de la villa") (*Leon de los Aldama. Baptism Records 1710-1715; Image16/198).*

e3. LUISA MARMOLEJO CANALES, christening 7 July 1713, Leon, Guanajuato, Mexico (Father: Juan Marmolejo Rojas/Mother: Josepha Canales) (Godparents: Nicholas Perez and Maria Perez, Espanoles de la villa) (Margin text: "Luisa de la villa") (*Leon de los Aldama Baptism Records 1691-1715; Image 86/128).* Married JOSEF RANGEL (Espanol) (son of Juan Rangel and Herrera) on 10 January 1731, Santa Ana, Penjamo, Guanajuato, Mexico (Father: Juan Marmolejo Mother: Josepha Canales) (Record text: "Joseph Rangel, Espanol, to Luisa Canales, Espanola, of the villa Leon, legitimate daughter of Juan Marmolejo and his spouse, Josepha Canales) (*Santa Ana. Baptism Records 1699-1852; Image 83/263).*

e4. DORTHEA MARMOLEJO, christening 20 February 1716, Manuel Doblado, Guanajuato, Mexico (Father: Juan Marmolejo/Mother: Maria Josepha Canales) (Witness: Francisco Lozano) (Margin text: "Dorthea espanola de la Canada de GALBAN." "Dortea, legitimate daughter of Juan Marmolejo and Maria Josepha, Espanoles de la Canada de Galban...") (Godparents: Francisco Lozano Soltero and Maria Juana Arias, "Espanoles y villa casada- *Spaniards married in the villa*- en La Canada.") (Witness: Max-- Sibriente) (*San Pedro Piedragorda. Baptism Records 1709-1759; Image 17/224*).

    e5.   JUANA BAPTA MARMOLEJO CANALES, baptism 17 July 1718, Santiago Apostol, Silao de la Victoria, Guanajuato, Mexico (Father: Juan Marmolejo/Mother: Josepha Canales) (Margin text: "Joa. Bap. Espanola.") (Record text: "Juana Bap., hija de Juan Maxmolejo and Josepha Canales, espanoles and married...") (Godparents: Juan Antonio Ruiz and Josepha de Rojas Gomez) (*Silao de la Victoria. Baptism Records 1717-1748; Image 52/483*) (Bapt.= Bautista).

c6.   PEDRO MARMOLEJO, born abt. 1668.
Married ANGELA BANALES de CASTILLO.
The known child of Pedro Marmolejo and Angela Banales de Castillo was:
    d1.   MARIA GETRUDIS MARMOLEJO BANALES, born September 1715 (Father: Pedro Marmolejo; Mother: Angela Banales) (Margin text: "Maria Gertrudis, espanola of the villa.") (Record text: ..."legitimate daughter of Pedro Marmolejo and Dona Angela Banales del Castillo, espanoles. Godparents of the villa: Godmother: Dona Angela de Bustos) (*Leon de los Aldama. Baptism Records 1691-1715; Image 127/128*).
Married GASPER GARCIA DIEGO.
The known children of Rita Getrudis Marmolejo (b) and Gasper Garcia Diego were:
    e1.   FRANCISCO GASPAR MACEDONIA GARCIA MARMOLEJO, christening September 1740, Leon, Guanajuato, Mexico (Father: Gasper Garcia Diego Mother: Rita Marmolejo) (Godparents: Jopal Marmolejo and Maria Teresa de Menchaca) (Margin text: "Fran. Gaspar Macedonia, Espanol of the villa.") (*Leon*

                      de los Aldama. Baptism Records 1749-1777; Image 11/318).

          e2.   MARIA FRANCISCA MANUELA de la HAGAS de JESUS DIEGO, baptized 2 February 1746, El Sagrario, Leon, Guanajuato, Mexico (Father: Don Gasper Garcia Diego/Mother: Dona Rita Marmolejo).

          e3.   MARIA CATHARINA IGNACIA DIEGO, baptized 26 November 1747, El Sagrario, Leon, Guanajuato, Mexico (Father: Don Gasper Garcia Diego; Mother: Dona Rita Getrudis Marmolejo) (Godparents: Don Manuel Bonales and Dona Maria Josepha de Alcocer) (Margin text: "Maria Catharina Ignacia, espanola of the villa.") (*Leon de los Aldama. Baptism Records 1718-1748; Image 65/73).*

        Death/burial: 15 September 1753, Nuestra Senora de Guanajuato, Guanajuato, Mexico (Spouse: Don Gasper Garcia) (Margin text: "Dona Rita Marmolejo, espanola de la Villa; married to Don Gaspar Garcia Diego) (*Leon Death Certificates 1820-1823; Image 291-648).*

      c7.   JUAN MARMOLEJO, christening 1670 (Father: Pedro Marmolejo/Mother: Josepha Bustos) (*Archdiocesis de Michoacan, 1670-1681; Image 41/95).*

b7.   MARIA de PEDRAZA y PORTUGAL, born abt. 1640, Leon, Guanajuato, Mexico.

    Married CRISTOBAL de HERRERA QUINTANA on 17 October 1658, San Felipe Guanajuato, Mexico (*Archdiocesis de Morelia, Michoacan, Mexico-Matrimonial Acts 1658; Image 658/873).*

    Name: MARIA de PEDRAZO y PORTUGAL or MARIA de MARMOLEJO.

The known children of Maria de Pedraza y Portugal and Cristobal de Herrera were:

    c1.   AGUSTINA HERRERA PORTUGAL, christening 9 October 1659, San Jose y Santiago, Marfil, Guanajuato, Mexico (Father: Cristobal Herrera/Mother: Maria de Portugal).

    c2.   JUAN BAUTISTA de HERRERA de PORTUGAL, christening 27 July 1661, Marfil, Guanajuato, Mexico (Father: Cristobal Herrera/Mother: Maria de Portugal).

        Married MICHAELA CONTRERAS SALGADO (daughter of Joseph Salgado and Josepha de Contreras) on 25 November 1693 (Juan de Herrera

                Quintana) (Father: Cristobal de Herrera Quintana and Maria de Pedraza Marmolejo).
- c3. NICOLASA HERRERA PEDRAZA, christening 19 June 1663, San Jose y Santiago, Marfil, Guanajuato, Mexico (Father: Cristobal Herrera Quintana/Mother: Maria de Pedraza).
- c4. MARIA HERRERA PORTUGAL, christening 25 November 1664, San Jose y Santiago, Marfil, Guanajuato, Mexico (Father: Cristobal Herrera Quintana/Mother: Maria de Portugal).
- c5. MARCELA HERRERA PORTUGAL, christening 11 July 1667, San Jose y Santiago, Marfil, Guanajuato, Mexico (Father: Cristobal Herrera Quintana/Mother: Maria de Portugal). Married JUAN ARIAS MALDONADO (son of Juan Arias Maldonado and Anna de Espinosa) on 25 April 1691, San Jose y Santiago, Marfil, Guanajuato, Mexico (Marcela de Pedraza Herrera) (Father: Cristobal de Herrera/Mother: Maria de Pedraza Marmolejo).
- c6. MELCHORA QUINTANA de PORTUGAL, christening 12 December 1669, Marfil, Guanajuato, Mexico (Father: Cristobal Herrera Quintana/Mother: Maria de Portugal) (Witness: Nicolas de Bustos). Married AGUSTIN BUITRON de LESCANO (son of Francisco Buitron and Isabel de Armenta y Lescano) on 5 June 1691, San Jose y Santiago, Marfil, Guanajuato, Mexico (Melchora de Herrera) (Father: Cristobal de Herrera/Mother: Maria de Pedraza).
- b7. MICHAELA de MARMOLEJO, christening 22 December 1673, Leon, Guanajuato, Mexico (Father: Cristobal Mother: Maria de la O. de Marmolejo). Married NICOLAS de la ROZA (son of Nicolas de Rosa and Isabel Ramos) on 16 May 1705, San Jose y Santiago, Marfil, Guanajuato, Mexico (Michaela de Herrera) (Father: Cristobal de Herrera/Maria de Pedraza).

(The known children of Captain Juan Gomez de Portugal and Catalina Lopez de Ximena de Nava were:) (Continued)
5. CATALINA GOMEZ de PORTUGAL y LOPEZ de NAVA.
6. JUAN GOMEZ de PORTUGAL y LOPEZ de NAVA.
7. MECLHORA GOMEZ de PORTUGAL.

~~~~~~~~

The parents of Captain JUAN GOMEZ de PORTUGAL (1536-1610) were:

INFANTE Don LUIS de PORTUGAL 5th Duke of BEJA (1506-1555)

YOLANDE FERNANDEZ GOMEZ de Portugal MADEIROS y MENDOZA
LARRALDE GONZALES de HERMISSILO (1505-1568)

The parents of CATALINA LOPEZ de XIMENA y de NAVA (1538) were:
CAPTAIN JUAN GOMEZ de XIMENA (1498-1550)
    Son of: ALONSO LOPES de JIMENA de MORALES (1480)
                  JUANA de la CUADRA (1485)
FRANCISCA de NAVA de LOPEZ (1516)
    Daughter of: CAPTAIN ANTONIO de NAVA (1480)
                   MARIA ANTONIA LOPEZ FERNANEZ (1483)
Married 1500, Escalona, Falcon, Venezuela.

The parents of INFANTE Don LUIS de PORTUGAL 5th Duke of BEJA (1506-1555) were:
KING MANUEL 1 of PORTUGAL (1469-1521)
QUEEN of PORTUGAL, MARIA de ARAGON y CASTILLA (1482-1517)

The parents of YOLANDE FERNANDEZ GOMEZ de Portugal MADEIROS y MENDOZA
LARRALDE GONZALES de HERMISSILO (1505-1568) were:

PEDRO LUIS FERNANDEZ GOMEZ de EVORA y MEDEIROS (1485-1559)
VICTORIA MENDOZA LARRALDE y GONZALES de HERMISILLO (1470-1555)

~~~~~~

PEDRO I, King of PORTUGAL (1320-1367)
INES CASTRO VADALARESS (1320-1355)
|
JOAO I de AVIS KING of PORTUGAL (1357-1433)
PHILIPPA of LANCASTER (1360-1415),
daughter of JOHN of GAUNTE, 1ST Duke of LANCASTER (1340-1388)
and BLANCHE of LANCASTER (1342-1368)
|
King DOM DUARTE, "O ELOQUENTE," of PORTUGAL and ALGARVE (1391-1438)
Dona LEONOR de ARAGON (1402-1455)
Married 4 November 1428, Colmbra, Colmbra, Portugal
|
Duke FERNANDO of VISEU and BEJA (1433-1470)
INFANTA BEATRIZ of PORTUGAL (1430-1506),
daughter of INFANTE JOAO of PORTUGAL (1400-1442)
and Lady ISABEL of BRAGANCA (1402-1465)
Married 1447, Alcacovas, Viana do Alentejo, Evora, Portugal
|
KING MANUEL I of PORTUGAL (1469-1521)
QUEEN of PORTUGAL, MARIA de ARAGON and CASTILLA (1482-1517) ***
Married 30 October 1500, Portugal
|

INFANTE Don LUIS de PORTUGAL 5th Duke of BEJA (1506-1555)
YOLANDA FERNANDEZ GOMEZ of PORTUGAL MADEIROS and MENDOZA
LARRALDE GONZALEZ of HERMOSILLO (1505-1568),
daughter of PEDRO LUIS FERNANDEZ GOMEZ of Evora & Medeiros (1485-1559) and
VICTORIA MENDOZA ARRALDE y GONZELES de HERMOSILLO (1470-1555)
|
Captain JUAN GOMEZ of PORTUGAL (1536-1610)**
CATALINA LOPEZ de XIMENA y de NAVA (1538)
|
GASPAR de MALDONADO (1550)
JUANA GOMEZ of PORTUGAL and LOPEZ de NAVA (1560)
|
ISABEL GOMEZ MALDONADO
MIGUEL DOMINGUEZ de ESPEJO (1575)
Married 1596, Apaseo el Grande, Gto., MX
|
JUANA GOMEZ
m. DOMINGO HERNANDEZ
~~~~~~
***
QUEEN of PORTUGAL, MARIA de ARAGON y CASTILLA (1482-1517) ***
KING MANUEL I of PORTUGAL (1469-1521)

KING ALFONSO XI of CASTILLA (1311-1350)
LEONOR NUNEZ de GUZMAN y PONCE de LEON (1310-1351)
|
KING ENRIQUE II de CASTILLA (1334-1379)
JUANA MANUEL VILENA NUNEZ de LARA (1339-1381),
daughter of PRINCE JUAN MANUEL de CASTILLA de VILENA SABOYA (1282-1348)
and BLANCA NUNEZ de la CERDA y LARA (1317-1347)
Married January 1329, Spain
|
KING JUAN I of CASTILLA (1358-1390) ~~~
LEONOR de ARAGON (1358-1382) ~~~~
Married 18 June 1375, Soria, Castille y Leon, Spain
~~~
KING of CASTILLA ~~~
(1358-1390)

KING FERNANDO IV of CASTILLA (1285-1312)
CONSTANZA de PORTUGAL (1290-1313),
daughter of DOM DINIS, KING OF PORTUGAL and the ALGARVE (1261-1325)
and SANTA ISABEL de ARAGAO (1271-1336)
Married 23 January 1302, Valladolid, Castilla y Leon, Spain
|
KING ALFONSO XI de CASTILLA (1311-1350)

LEONOR NUNEZ de GUZMAN y PONCE de Leon (1310-1350)
|
KING ENRIQUE II of CASTILLA (1334-1379)
JUANA MANUEL VILLENA NUNEZ de LARA,
daughter of PRINCE JUAN MANUEL de CASTILLA de VILENA SABOYA (1282-1348)
and BLANCA NUNEZ de la CERDA y LARA (1317-1347)
|
KING JUAN of CASTILLA (1358-1390)
LEONOR de ARAGON (1358-1382)
~~~~~
LEONOR de ARAGON ~~~~
(1358-1382)

KING PEDRO III of ARAGON (1240-1285)
CONSTANCE de SICILIA, QUEEN CONSORT of ARAGON (1249-1302)
|
SEGUBDO JAIME el JUSTO of ARAGON (1267-1327)
BLANCA D'ANJOU, QUEEN CONSORT of ARAGON (1280-1310),
daughter of CHARLES d'ANJOU II, KING of NAPLES (1245-1309)
and MARIA ARPADHAZI of HUNGARY, QUEEN of NAPLES (1257-1323)
Married 29 October 1295, Alt. Emporda, Girona, Catalonia, Spain
|
KING ALFONS IV d' ARAGON y VALENCIA (1299-1336)
THERESE VON MONTPELLIER GRAVIN VAN URGEL y AGER (1300-1337)
Married 1314 Lleida, Catalonia, Spain

KING PEDRO IV of ARAGON (1319-1387)
PRINCESS LEONORA of SICILIA (1325-1375),
daughter of PIETRO II of SICILIA (1305-1342)
and ELIZABETTA di CARINZIA (1298-1350)
Married 1345, Aragon, Spain
|
LEONOR de ARAGON (1358-1382)
KING JUAN I of CASTILLA (1358-1390)
Married 18 June 1375, Soria, Soria, Castilla y Leon, Spain

~~~~~

Wife of Salvador Gomez of Portugal: THERESA LOPES de AGUIRRE y INFANTE

The parents of Theresa Lopes de Aguirre were: ALONSO LOPES de AGUIRRE y GARRIDO (1645) and MARIA DIAS INFANTE y MORENO de VILLEGAS (1657) who were engaged 1677 (*Archdiocesis de Morelia, Michoacan; Information matrimonial y actas diversas 1677; Image 655/831*) then married 10 January 1678, Lagos de Moreno, Jalisco, Mexico (*Santa Maria de los Lagos, Matrimonios 1677-1697; Image 20/436*).

ALONSO LOPES de AGUIRRE (son of Francisco Lopes de Aguirre and Maria Garrido) married MARIA INFANTE de VILLEGAS (daughter of Diego Dias Infante and Theresa Moreno de Ortega) on 10 January 1678, Santa Maria de los Lagos, Lagos de Moreno, Jalisco, Mexico

The known children of Alonso Lopes de Aguirre y Garrido and Maria Dias Infante were:
a1. THERESA LOPES de AGUIRRE INFANTE (1680), christening 3 June 1680, Nuestra Senora de la Soledad, Irapuato, Guanajuato, Mexico (Father: Alonso Lopez de Aguirre/Mother: Maria Infante de Villegas) (Godparents: Juan Joseph) (Margin text: "Theresa, espanola from the villa Quintana") (*Irapuato. Baptism Records 1633-1655; Image 347/406*).
a2. NICOLAS LOPES de AGUIRRE y DIAS INFANTE (1681).
a3. CASMIRO LOPES INFANTE (1682), christening 10 June 1682, Nuestra Senora de la Soledad, Irapuato, Guanajuato, Mexico (Father: Alonso Lopes de Aguirre/Mother: Maria Infante).
a4. FRANCISCO FELIZ LOPES de AGUIRRE, christening 18 July 1686, Nuestra Senora de la Soledad, Irapuato, Guanajuato, Mexico (Father: Alonso Lopez Garrido/Mother: Maria Infante de Villegas) (*La Soledad. Bautismos de hijos legitimos 1633-1655, 1664-1688; Image 390/406*).
a5. ANTONIA MANUELA LOPEZ VILLEGAS, christening 30 March 1693, Nuestra Senora de Guanajuato, Guanajuato, Mexico (Father: Alonso Lopes de Aguirre/Mother: Maria Infante de Villegas)/ANTONIA MANUELA LOPES INFANTE, christening Sante Fe, San Felipe, Guanajuato, Mexico (Father: Alonso Lopes de Aguirre/Mother: Maria Infante de Villegas).

The parents of Alonso Lopes de Aguirre were: FRANCISCO LOPES de AGUIRRE (1625-1678) and MARIA GARRIDO (1625).
The known children of Francisco Lopes de Aguirre and Maria Garrido were:
a1. ANNA LOPEZ GARRIDO (1641).
a2. ALONSO LOPES de AGUIRRE y GARRIDO.

The parents of Maria Dias Infante y Moreno were: DIEGO DIAZ INFANTE (-1682) and THERESA MORENO de ORTEGA y de VILLEGAS (1631-).
The known children of Diego Diaz Infante and Theresa Moreno de Ortega were:
a1. MARIA DIAZ INFANTE y MORENO de VILLEGAS (1657).
a2. NICOLAS DIAZ de INFANTE y MORENO de ORTEGA (1660).
a3. JOSEPH DIAS INFANTE (1666).
a4. THERESA INFANTE MORENO (-).

~~~~~~

```
Captain DIEGO GOMEZ of Portugal          FRANCISCO de MARMOLEJO
   MARIA GARCIA de ARRONA                   MARIA de PEDRAZA
                  |                                 |
              PEDRO de MARMOLEJO y de PEDRAZA
              MELCHORA GOMEZ de Portugal (1615)
                              |
         MARIA de PEDRAZA y (GOMEZ de) PORTUGAL MARMOLEJO
                  CRISTOBAL de HERRERA QUINTANA
           Married 17 October 1658, San Felipe, Guanajuato, Mexico
```

The known children of Maria de Pedraza Portugal Marmolejo and Cristobal de Herrera Quintana were:

a1. AGUSTINA HERRERA PORTUGAL, christening 9 October 1659, San Jose y Santiago, Marfil, Guanajuato, Mexico (Father: Cristobal de Herrera Mother: Maria de Portugal).

a2. JUAN BAUTISTA de HERRERA de PORTUGAL, christening 27 July 1661
Married MICHAELA de CONTRERAS SALGADO (daughter of Joseph Salgado and Josepha de Contreras) on 25 November 1693, Marfil, Guanajuato, Mexico.

a3. NICOLASA HERRERA PEDRAZA, christening 19 June 1663 (Father: Cristobal de Herrera Quintana/Mother: Maria de Pedraza).

a4. MARIA HERRERA PORTUGAL, christening 25 November 1664, (Father: Cristobal de Herrera Quintana/Mother: Maria de Portugal).

a5. MARCELA HERRERA PORTUGAL, christening 11 July 1667, (Father: Cristobal de Herrera Quintana/Mother: Maria de Portugal).
Married JUAN ARIAS MALDONADO (Son of Juan Arias Maldonado and Anna de Espinosa) on 25 April 1691, Marfil, Guanajuato, Mexico.

a6. MELCHORA QUINTANA de PORTUGAL, christening 12 December 1669 (Father: Cristobal de Herrera Quintana/Mother: Maria de Portugal) (Godparent: Nicolas de Bustos).
Married AUGUSTIN BUITRON de LESCANO (son of Franco. Buitron and Isabel de Armenta y Lescano) on 5 June 1691, Marfil, Guanajuato, Mexico.

a7. MICHAELA de MARMOLEJO, christening 22 December 1673, Leon, Guanajuato, Mexico (Father: Cristobal de Herrera/Mother: Maria de la O. Marmolejo) (Godmother: Maria Rubio, of the villa) (Margin text: "Michaela, espanola") (*Leon de los Aldama. Baptism Records 1673-1691; Image 6/39*).

APPENDIX XVIII: MARIA CATALINA MANRIQUE de LARA y ARIAS de GUZMAN (born abt. 1585-1608)

There was an individual named, "Maria Catalina Manrique de Lara" who married in Irapuato during 1645. While the connection has not been confirmed, from our Gaspar Gomez Manrique de Lara line, Sebastian Manrique de Lara married Theresa de Aguirre Arias.

Hypothesis: JORGE MANRIQUE de LARA possibly a sibling to Catalina Manrique de Lara, wife of Pedro Gomez, and named his daughter to honor his sister, Catalina Manrique de Lara.

JORGE MANRIQUE de LARA
    Married JACINTA ARIAS de GUZMAN MALDONADO (born abt. 1585-1608), daughter of Juan Arias Maldonado (1560) and de Guzman.
    The known children of JORGE MANRIQUE de Lara and Jacinta Arias de Guzman Maldonado were:
- a1. **MARIA CATALINA MANRIQUE de LARA** y ARIAS de GUZMAN (1625/1626, Leon/Irapuato, Guanajuato, Mexico; died 27 May 1692, Guanajuato, Mexico).
- a2. JOSE MANRIQUE de LARA y ARIAS de GUZMAN (1625).
- a3. JOSEPH MANUEL MALDONADO (married 1652, Irapuato, Gto., MX).
- a4. ANDRES ARIAS MALDONADO.

    Married FRANCISCO MARTIN GALLARDO (1615) on 5 November 1645, Irapuato, Guanajuato, Mexico.

The known children of Jorge Manrique de Lara and Jacinta Arias de Guzman Maldonado were:
- a1. **MARIA CATALINA MANRIQUE de LARA y ARIAS de GUZMAN MALDONADO.** (*Born 1625/1626, Leon/Irapuato, Guanajuato, Mexico). Died 27 May 1692, Guanajuato, Mexico*)

    Married FRANCISCO MARTIN GALLARDO de RODAS (to CATALINA de GUZMAN MALDONADO) on 5 November 1645, Irapuato, La Soledad (*Matrimonios 1633-1706; Image 51/505*).

        FRANCISCO MARTIN GALLARDO born abt. 1615, Villa de los Lagos, Jalisco, Mexico.

The known children of Francisco Martin Gallardo and Catalina Manrique de Lara (a) were:
- b1. FRANCISCO MARTIN GALLARDO, christening September 1642, Irapuato, Guanajuato, Mexico (Father: Francisco Martin Gallardo/ Mother: Catalina) (Witness; Joseph Manrique).
- b2. JACINTO GALLARDO MANRIQUE de LARA, christening 28 August 1646, Nuestra Senora de la Soledad, Irapuato, Guanajuato, Mexico

(Father: Francisco Martin Gallardo/Mother: Catalina Manrique de Lara). Married GERTRUDIS NAVARRO on 9 June 1686, Irapuato, Guanajuato, Mexico.

The children of Jacinto Gallardo and Gertrudis Navarro were:
- c1. JUANA GALLARDO NAVARRO, born 1695.
- c2. FRANCISCA GALLARDO, died 1742.

b3. INES GALLARDO MANRIQUE, born 26 August 1646, Lagos de Moreno, Jalisco, Mexico. Died 19 August 1716, Lagos de Moreno, Jalisco, Mexico) (Mother: Maria Catalina Manrique de Lara).

b4. FRANCISCO GALLARDO GUSMAN, christening 4 September 1648, Nuestra Senora de la Soledad, Irapuato, Guanajuato, Mexico (Father: Francisco Martin Gallardo/Mother: Catalina Guzman Maldonado).

b5. JUANA CLARA GALLARDO MANRIQUE, christening 8 September 1650, Nuestra Senora de la Soledad, Irapuato, Guanajuato, Mexico (Father: Francisco Martin Gallardo/Mother: *ORNA* Catalina Manrique).

b6. JOSEPH GALLARDO MANRIQUE, christening 3 September 1652, Nuestra Senora de la Soledad, Irapuato, Guanajuato, Mexico (Father: Francisco Martin Gallardo/Mother: Maria Catalina Manrique Maldonado). Married TERESA ANGELA CAMACHO RIQUELME (1649-1711) during 1675, Jalostotitlan, Jalisco, Mexico). Died 9 February 1723, Lagos de Moreno, Jalisco, Mexico.

The known children of Joseph Gallardo Manrique and Teresa Riquelme were:
- c1. JOSEFA MARTIN GALLARDO Y CAMACHO (born 1660).
- c2. MARIA CATHALINA MARTINEZ GALLARDO (born 1677).
- c3. ALEJO GALLARDO CAMACHO RIQUELME (born 1680).

b7. ANTONIA GALLARDO, christening 17 June 1655, Nuestra Senora de la Soledad, Irapuato, Guanajuato, Mexico (Father: Francisco Martin Gallardo/Mother: Catalina). Married JOSEPH de PERES y ESCAMILLA (Son of Joseph de Peres and Maria de Escamilla) on 16 April 1679, Santa Maria de Los Lagos, Lagos de Moreno, Jalisco, Mexico (Antonia GALLARDO y GUZMAN) (Parents: Francisco Gallardo and Catalina Manrique de Guzman).

b8. JUAN ANTONIO GALLARDO MANRIQUE, born abt. 1660, Irapuato, Guanajuato, Mexico. Married JUANA BERNARDA de REYNOSA (Daughter of Francisco de Reynosa y Padilla and Josepha de Renterila y Baldes) on 6 January 1682, Santa Maria de los Lagos, Lagos de Moreno, Jalisco, Mexico (Son of Francisco Martin Gallardo and Cathalina Manriques). Death/burial (Juan Antonio Gallardo) 9 February 1723, Lagos de Moreno, Jalisco, Mexico.

The known children of Juan Antonio Gallardo Manrique (b) and Juana Bernarda de Reynosa Renteria were:
- c1. MARIA ANDREA GALLARDO REINOSO, christening 10 January 1683, Santa Maria de los Lagos, Lagos de Moreno, Jalisco,

Mexico (Father: Juan Antonio Gallardo/Mother: Juana Bernarda de Reinosa y Padilla) (Witnesses: D. Francisco, Josefa de Renteria, Reynoso y Padilla).

c2. CATHARINA GALLARDO REYNOSA, christening 1683, Santa Maria de los Lagos, Lagos de Moreno, Jalisco, Mexico (Father: Juan Antonio Gallardo/Mother: Juana de Reynoso y Padilla).

c3. JUAN ANTONIO GALLARDO REYNOSA, christening 1685, Santa Maria de los Lagos, Lagos de Moreno, Jalisco, Mexico (Father: Juan Gallardo/Mother: Juana Reynosa y Renteria). Married LUISA de RODAS (Spanish widow of Antonio Ramirez y Mendoza and daughter of Dionicio Sanches de Rodas y Francisca Martin del Campo) on 21 November 1712, Nuestra de la Asuncion, Jalostotitlan, Jalisco, Mexico (Espanoles) (Son of Juan Antonio Gallardo Manrique and Juana Bernarda de Reynoso Renteria). Death/burial, LUISA de RODAS, 14 February 1726, Nuestra Senora de la Asuncion, Jalostotitlan, Jalisco, Mexico (wife of Juan Antonio Gallardo).

c4. GERTRUDES GALLARDO REYNOSA, christening 27 April 1686, Santa Maria de los Lagos, Lagos de Moreno, Jalisco, Mexico (Father: Juan Gallardo/Mother: Dona Juana de Reynoso y Renteria).

c5. FRANCISCO DOMINGO GALLARDO REYNOSO, christening 15 September 1687, Santa Maria de los Lagos, Lagos de Moreno, Jalisco, Mexico (Father: Juan Antonio Gallardo/ Mother: Juana de Reinoso y Padilla) (Witnesses: Francisco, Padilla, Josefa de Renteria) (Espanol).

c6. DOMINGO GALLARDO REINOSO, christening 11 August 1690, Santa Maria de los Lagos, Lagos de Moreno, Jalisco, Mexico (Father: Juan Antonio Gallardo/Mother: Juana de Reynoso y Padilla) (Espanol).

c7. JOSEPHA GALLARDO REINOSO, christening 6 March 1691, Santa Maria de los Lagos, Lagos de Moreno, Jalisco, Mexico (Father: Juan Antonio/Mother: Juana Lorenza). Died 1772 in Mexico.

c8. MIGUEL GALLARDO REYNOSO, christening 13 October 1694, Santa Maria de los Lagos, Lagos de Moreno, Jalisco, Mexico (Father: Juan Antonio Gallardo/Mother: Juana Reynoso). Death/burial 4 June 1729, San Juan Bautista, San Juan de los Lagos, Jalisco, Mexico.

c9. MARIANA GALLARDO de REYNOSO, christening 11 March 1696, Nuestra Senora de la Asuncion, Jalostotitlan, Jalisco, Mexico (Father: Julio Gallardo/Mother: Juana de Reynoso y Venteria) (Witness: Ignacio Gallardo).

- c10. NICOLAS YSIDRO GALLARDO REINOSO, christening 23 May 1697, Nuestra Senora de la Asuncion, Jalostotitlan, Jalisco, Mexico (Father: Juan Gallardo/Mother: Juana Reinoso).
- c11. JUAN BAPTISTA GALLARDO REINOSO, christening 8 July 1698, Santa Maria de los Lagos, Lagos de Moreno, Jalisco, Mexico (Father: Juan Antonio Gallardo/Mother: Juana Reinoso y Renteria). Married MARIA CATHERINA de ALCALA y MORENO (daughter of Cristobal de Acala y Moreno and Maria de Anda y Moreno) on 24 May 1722, Santa Maria de los Lagos, Lagos de Moreno, Jalisco, Mexico (son of Juan Gallardo and Juana Reynosa y Renteria).

b9. YGNASIO GALLARDO ARIAS (MANRIQUE), christening 15 October 1662, Nuestra Senora de la Soledad, Irapuato, Guanajuato, Mexico (Father: Francisco Martin Gallardo/Mother: Catarina Arias Maldonado) (*Bautismos de hijos legitimos 1660-1674*).
Married HIPPOLITA CASIANA de GUEBARA on 13 August 1720, La Asuncion, Iztacalco, Ciudad de Mexico, Mexico.

The known children of Ygnacio Gallardo Arias Manrique (b) and Hippolita Casiana de Guebara were:
- c1. YGNACIO DOROTEO GALLARDO GUEBARA, christening 10 June 1721, Sagrario Metropolitano, Cuauhtemoc, Ciudad de Mexico, Mexico (Father: Ygnacio Gallardo/Mother: Hippolita Caciana Guebara).
- c2. MARIA TERESA GALLARDO GUEBARA, christening 14 October 1723, Asuncion, Distrito Federal, Mexico (Father: Ygnacio Gallardo/Mother: Hipolita de Guebara).
- c3. FABIAN SEBASTIAN GALLARDO de GUEBARA, birthdate 20 January 1727/christening February 1727, La Asuncion, Iztacalco, Ciudad de Mexico, Mexico (Father: Ygnacio Gallardo/Mother: Hipolita Casiana de Guebara).

b10. ROSA MARGARITA GUZMAN y MARTIN GALLARDO, born abt. 1664, Irapuato, Guanajuato, Mexico (Mother: Maria Catarina Manrique Maldonado)

b11. DIEGO GALLARDO MANRIQUE, christening 5 January 1666, Santiago, Queretaro, Mexico (Father: Francisco Martin Gallardo/Mother: Dona Catalina Manrique) (*Bautismos de espanoles 1636-1670*). Death 1739, Guanajuato, Mexico.
(*Known also as*, JOSEPH DIEGO GALLARDO MANRIQUE)
Married MARIA ANA GOMEZ BRITO (*GOMEZ de BRITO**).
MARIA BUSTOS BRITO, christening 22 September 1669, Sante Fe, San Felipe, Guanajuato, Mexico (Father: Joseph de Bustos/ Mother: Maria Brito. "IGNACIO GOMEZ, de santorio con la sencia del, "legitimate daughter of JOSEPH de BUSTO and DONA MARIA... "MARIA BRITO, espanoles, ...de la villa...)

(Godparents: Nicolas de Soto) (Margin text: "MARIA, espanola") (*Family Search #004791971; Image 23/604*).

The known children of (*Joseph*) Diego Gallardo Manrique de Lara (b) and Mariana Gomez Brito were:

c1. DIEGO GALLARDO MANRIQUE de LARA, born abt. 1686.

Married (m1) Unknown GUTIERREZ by 1714.

The known child of Diego Manrique de Lara (c) and Gutierrez was:

d1. JUANA SANTA MARIA MANRIQUE de LARA, christened in Leon, Guanajuato during 1714 (Father: Diego Manrique de Lara/Mother: -- GUTTIERES) (Godfather: Joseph Manuel Gutierrez) (Witness: Geronimo de Silva) (Baptismal book margin reads: "JUANA MARIA, Espanola de la villa") (*Leon de los Aldama Baptism Records 1691-1715; Image 89/128*) (Juana Santa Maria was the "legitimate daughter" of "*C. L.*" Gutierrez, whose first name was recorded in illegible initials).

Married (m2) MARIA ANTONIA MOSQUEDA.

The known children of Diego Gallardo Manrique de Lara and Maria Antonia Mosqueda were:

d2. JUAN ANTONIO GALLARDO MOSQUEDA, christened on 27 April 1734, Nuestra Senora de la Soledad, Irapuato, Guanajuato, Mexico (Father: Diego Gallardo/Mother: Antonia Mosqueda).

d3. JOSEPH GALLARDO MOSQUEDA, christened 22 March 1733, Nuestra Senora de la Soledad, Irapuato, Guanajuato, Mexico (Father: Diego Gallardo/Mother: Antonia Mosqueda).

d4. DIEGO ANCELMO GALLARDO, christened on 26 April 1742, Nuestra Senora de la Soledad Irapuato, Guanajuato Mexico ("Legitimate" son of Diego Gallardo and Maria Antonia Mosqueda) **(Godparent: *CATHARINA GALLARDO*, Diego Gallardo Manrique de Lara's grandmother)** (*Irapuato. Baptism Record 1804-1810; image 181/550*).

d5. JOSEPH THOMAS GALLLARDO MOSQUEDA, christened on 29 December 1744, Nuestra Senora de la Soledad, Guanajuato, Mexico (Father: Diego Gallardo/Mother: Antonia Mosqueda).

d6. JOSEPHA CLEMENTA GALLARDO MOSQUEDA, christened 16 November 1747, Nuestra de la Soledad, Guanajuato, Mexico (Father: Diego Gallardo/Mother: Antonia Mosqueda).

d7. MARIA MARTINA GALLARDO MOSQUEDA, christening 2 February 1749, Nuestra de la Soledad, Guanajuato,

Mexico (Father: Diego Gallardo/Mother: Antonia Mosqueda).

c2. MARIA MAGDALENA MANRIQUE de LARA, born abt. 1695, Irapuato, Guanajuato, Mexico (Father: Joseph Manrique de Lara/Mother: Maria Anna Gomez Brito). <u>Married</u> FRANCISCO CAIETANO GUTIERREZ (Espanol) (legitimate son of Juan Alfonso Gutierrez and Maria de Busto) on 13 May 1720, La Soledad, Irapuato, Guanajuato, Mexico (Margin text for Maria Magdalena Manrique de Lara: "Espanola hija legitima de Joseph Manrique de Lara and his wife Maria Anna Gomez Brito") (*Irapuato. Marriage Records 1717-1756; Image 11/500*).

c3. JUANA MANRIQUE de LARA, born abt. 1699. <u>Married</u> JOSEPH de SANDOBAL (Espanol) (son of Diego de Sandobal and Maria Rosa Arias de Vmana) on 7 January 1722, La Soledad, Irapuato, Guanajuato, Mexico (Father: Joseph Manrique de Lara/Mother: Maria Ana de Brito) (Margin text: "Juana Manrique de Lara, Espanola hija legitima de Joseph Manrique de Lara and Maria Ana de Brito, Espanoles") (Witness: Magdalena Manrique).

c4. DIEGO JOSEPH MANRIQUE, christening 21 November 1700, Nuestra Senora de Guanajuato, Mexico (Father: Joseph Manrique) (Godmother: Dona Maria Mathiana de Busto Witness: Alonso de Busto Moreno).

<u>Married</u> Dona ANA MARIA LOPEZ.

Death/Burial: 4 November 1761, Sagrario, Guanajuato, Guanajuato, Mexico.

<u>The known children of Diego Joseph Manrique and Ana Maria Lopez were:</u>

d1. ISIDRO PHELIPE MANRIQUE, baptized 7 February 1744, El Sagrario, Guanajuato, Guanajuato, Mexico.

d2. MARIA JOSEPHA GERTRUDIS de los DOLORES MANRIQUE, baptized 20 November 1745, El Sagrario, Guanajuato, Guanajuato, Mexico.

d3. VINCENTE FERRER (MANRIQUE LOPEZ), christening 14 October 1747, El Sagrario, Guanajuato, Guanajuato, Mexico.

d4. ANA MARIA MANRIQUE, death/burial 5 September 1748, El Sagrario, Guanajuato, Guanajuato, Mexico.

c5. PABLO JOSEPH MANRIQUE BRITO, christening 21 January 1704, Nuestra Senora de la Soledad, Irapuato, Mexico (Father: Joseph Manrique/Mother: Maria Ana Brito).

c6. JULIAN FULGENCIO MANRIQUE GOMEZ, christening 19 January 1706, Irapuato, Guanajuato, Mexico (Father: Joseph Manrique de Lara/Mother: Mariana Gomez) (Witness: Julia Manrique).

  c7. PHELIPPE TADEO MANRIQUE BRITO, christening 11 May 1707, Nuestro de Senora de la Soledad, Irapuato, Guanajuato, Mexico (Father: Joseph Manrique de Lara/Mother: Mariana de Brito).
 b12. TERESA GALLARDO, christening 14 January 1669, Santiago, Queretaro, Mexico (Father: Francisco Gallardo/Mother: Dona Catalina de Guzman) (*Bautismos de espanoles, 1636-1670*).
 b13. CATARINA ARIAS MALDONADO MANRIQUE, born Queretaro 1668 or Irapuato, Guanajuato, Mexico after 1669.
 Married FELIPE BELTRAN.
 The known children of Felipe Beltran and Catalina Manrique (b) were:
  c1. MATHEO BELTRAN ARIAS, christening 7 October 1685, Irapuato, Guanajuato, Mexico (Father: Felipe Beltran/Mother: Catalina Arias).
  c2. RITA BELTRAN MALDONADO, christening 3 May 1690, Nuestra Senora de la Soledad, Irapuato, Guanajuato, Mexico (Father: Felipe Baltran/Mother: Catalina Maldonado).
  c3. CATHERINA BELTRAN MALDONADO, christening 31 January 1695, Irapuato, Guanajuato, Mexico (Father: Felipe Beltran Mother: Catherina Maldonado).
 b14. ALEGO (ALEJO) GALLARDO MANRIQUE, christening 19 July 1682, Nuestra Senora de la Soledad, Irapuato, Guanajuato, Mexico (Father: Francisco Gallardo/Mother: Cathalina Manrique).

(Note: In Santiago, Queretaro resided Maria Gerturdis Manrique de Lara. The Maria Catalina Manrique de Lara and Francisco Martin Gallardo family resided in Santiago, Queretaro between 1666 and 1669.)

 Marriage: 5 November 1722, marriage between Don Prudencio de Pozados and Dona MARIA GERTRUDIS MANRIQUE de LARA, Santiago, Queretaro, Mexico) (Ethnicity: Canadian) (Margin text: "Prudencio de Pozados") (Godparents Domingo Urbano and Maria Luisa Lopes (*Santiago de Queretaro Marriage records 1712-1736; Image 94/747 -MDLS*).

 The known child of Maria Gertrudis Manrique de Lara (a) and Don Prudencio (Fredrico Dias) de Pozados was:
 b1. ROSA PRUDENCIA DIAS MANRIQUE, baptized 5 September 1723, Espiritu Santo, Queretaro, Queretaro, Mexico (Father: Fredrico Dias de Posada; Mother: Maria Gertrudis Manrique de Lara) (*Bautismos de espanoles 1720-1770*).

(Between 1670-1681, two to three children likely were born in either Santiago, Queretaro, Mexico or Irapuato, Guanajuato, Mexico. Possibly, the family moved to Spain between the years 1669 and 1683).

(?) LORENZA GALLARDO, born Nunoa, Spain (Mother: Maria Catalina Manrique Maldonado).
(?) THOMAS GALLARDO, born Murcia, Spain (Mother: Maria Catalina Manrique Maldonado).

~~~~~~

*SIMON GOMEZ de BRITO - Possible relation to Maria Ana Gomez de Brito, previously mentioned.

SIMON GOMEZ de BRITO married ANTONIA RODRIQUEZ FARFAN on 11 January 1638, Guanajuato, Guanajuato, Mexico.
The known children of Simon Gomez de Brito and Antonia Rodriquez Farfan were:
- a1. JOSEPH GOMEZ FARFAN, christening 8 April 1647, Sante Fe, San Felipe, Guanajuato, Mexico.
- a2. CATHALINA GOMEZ FARFAN, christening 3 September 1640, Guanajuato, Guanajuato, Mexico.
- a3. GERONIMA GOMEZ FARFAN, christening 28 October 1648, Guanajuato, Guanajuato, Mexico.
- a4. ISABEL GOMEZ FARFAN, christening 7 July 1642, Guanajuato, Guanajuato, Mexico.
- a5. JUANA GOMEZ FARFAN, christening 24 August 1645, Guanajuato, Guanajuato, Mexico.

APPENDIX XIX: HISTORY of LEON, GUANAJUATO, MEXICO

Synopsis of article
by D. A. Brading and Celia Wu
"Population Growth and Crisis: Leon, 1720-1860"
Journal of Latin American Studies, Vol. 5 No.1 (May 1973), pp. 1-36
Published by Cambridge University Press. (JSTOR)

Historically, the first few Manrique de Lara generations of Leon, Guanajuato, Mexico resided in a developing society.

The population of Leon between 1720-1860 was studied by researchers D. A. Brading and Cecilia Wu and their findings included in this synopsis put into context our Manrique de Lara branch amid a region which included silver mining, agriculture and epidemics like smallpox and typhus. "Founded in 1576, Leon was a town which encompassed twenty-five by thirty-seven miles of fertile land on the north and mountain ranges to the west. By 1742, Leon was a parish of seven thousand people divided among 15% Spaniards (1,050) and the rest of the population (85%) castas and Indians. Guanajuato was a mining town a day of travel away. The Parish of Leon by 1781 consisted of 1,585 Spaniards," including Joseph Manuel Manrique de Lara and Joseph Urbano Manrique de Lara. "The total number of Spaniards in both Haciendas y ranchos and Villa de Leon by 1781 totaled 3,204. In contrast, the population of Villa de Leon in 1781 was 5,507 (including 378 Indians and 3,544 Castas)."

"Diseases like the Matlazahuatl epidemic (1737-1739) killed numerous residents. The smallpox epidemics (1779-80, 1798 and 1804 - Jose Isidro Manrique de Lara's birth year) meant eighteen percent of children died. During the 1780 smallpox epidemic, 2,049 deaths in Leon were recorded. Famine also caused deaths, especially the corn disaster of 1785-6, a corn disaster in Silao, known as the agricultural heartland of Leon."

"Marriage records for Spaniards and castas began in Leon during 1711. After 1746, records for all three series (Spaniards, castas, Indians) were intact until 1821. Spaniards who married Spaniards were always in one book while Indians who married Indians were in another. Those who intermarried were listed in the casta registrar (Mestizos, Mulattos, Indians)."

In this area of Mexico, two separate societal groups existed - one for Indians, mulattos and some mestizos, and the other was comprised of Spaniards and most mestizos. Nearly all infants born in Leon, except those who died shortly after birth, were baptized. Spaniards, one-sixth of the population in Leon and one-third of the population in Guanajuato, married one another and retained homogeneity for generations.

"The average age to marry in 1782-1785 was sixteen followed by fifteen for females while during 1858-60, the average age was fifteen followed by sixteen. For men during the years of 1782-5, twenty percent of men ages 21-25 were married (229 out of 743) then by 1786-1788, the age rose to 21 (136 of 391)."

"Marrying amongst one's ethnic group was most common. For example, in 1782-1785, 75.5% of Espanoles (102) married Espanolas - while 17% Espanoles (23) married Mestizas and 6.7 Espanoles (9) married Mulatas with only 1 Espanoles or .8% marrying an Indian. The total number of marriages were 135 with an intermarriage rate of 24.5%.

By 1792-3, 76.4% of Espanoles married Espanolas (81), 6.6% of Espanoles (7) married Mulatas, 17% Espanoles (18) married Mestizas and zero married Indians totaling 106 marriages and an intermarriage rate of 23.6%."

Unlike Gaspar Manrique de Lara's burial inside El Sagrario, there was little "incentive to pay for a church burial" (page 6, Brading/Wu). Burial notations often only noted place of residence, not birth city or country. It is for this reason emigration recorded in the "Council of Indes" proved more helpful to determine early Spanish settler's origins.

The year of Urbano Manrique de Lara's birth (1768) there were 6,360 baptisms (1766-1770) whereas in 1751-1755, there had only been 3,734. As per Baptisms of Spaniards, when Joseph Manuel Manrique de Lara was born (1734) it was recorded (1731-1735) that 293 Spaniards were born during those years or 11% of the total 3,616 babies (including Castas & Indians). The year of Urbano Manrique de Lara's birth (1768) there were 811 (during 1766-1770) Spaniards born or 15,38% of total 5,278 babies (including Castas & Indians). By the year of Isidro's birth (1804) there were 1,137 Spaniards born (1801-1805) or 12.8% of the total 8,883 babies born (including Castas & Indians). The records Brading and Wu studied were found at the Archivo Parroquial de Leon Registro de Bautismos, the same ones *Family Search* scanned. Marriages like the one between Gaspar Manrique de Lara and Francisca Xaviera Calderon Herrera's marriage by 1728 was not found as only sixty-seven marriages (1726-1730) between Spaniards were recorded. By the time of Urbano Manrique de Lara's marriage in 1799, 182 marriages (1796-1800) were listed. Because Spaniards were recorded in separate books and married within their race, the homogeneity of the line was preserved, so much so this Manrique de Lara branch of Leon, Guanajuato from 1734 to 1891 was accurately determined genealogically.

(All above listed "*text*" and data regarding years and percentages of Spaniards was sourced from the previously mentioned article by D. A Brading and Cecilia Wu.)

APPENDIX XX: NEW SPAIN HISTORY

When I began my paternal ancestor search, I believed they emigrated to Mexico from Spain during the late-1800s. However, after learning my ancestors arrived in Guanajuato prior to 1600, I began researching Colonial Mexico via published articles available at JSTOR (established in1995, JSTOR stores 2,000 academic journals), including: "Spanish Colonization of the New World: Cultural Continuity and Change in Mexico" by Karl W. Butzer. Published by Erdkunde, Archive for Scientific Geography, Bd. 45.H.3 (September 1991), pp. 205-219 (15 pages). "By 1600, 6,800 Spaniards lived in Nueva Galicia (Aguascalientes, Guanajuato, Colima, Jalisco, Nayarit and Zacatecas) with 4,2000 in mining centers" (Butzer, p. 206). "Ninety percent of immigrants were Castillans (Butzer, p. 209") with "very few Spanish women (Butzer, p. 207)," a factor that led to a low population rate.

Although my maternal (Quaker) ancestors settled in 1634 Dover, New Hampshire, USA, academics have noted there were differences between Colonial America and Colonial Mexico. For instance, the "275,000 Spaniards (Butzer, p. 205)" who came to New Spain settled across "one and a half continents" was "double the average number of immigrants to British and French North America between 1630 and 1700 (Butzer, p. 209). However, the population of Spaniards born in New Spain was "well below averages for Anglo and French North America" as "(a)mong Spanish colonists, women accounted for only 6% (of emigrants) before 1540, rising to 16% by 1550 and only 28% after 1560 (Butzer, p. 209)." Additionally, whereas immigrants to America came to farm and to own property, by "1600, 75% of all the original land grants in settlement cores of New Spain had been awarded (Butzer, p. 210)." In Nueva Galicia, which included Aguascalientes, Guanajuato, Colima, Jalisco and Nayerit, the Spanish population from 1560-1640 totaled only 6,800. Even by 1793 Spanish settlers represented only twenty-nine percent of the Guanajuato, Mexico population.

While the Colonial American population grew larger while residing separately from Indigenous groups, Spaniards remained a minority of New Spain even during the 18th century. "As such, Spanish control focused on political and socioeconomic restructuring, leading to partial economic displacement, two-way assimilation, and significant indigenous ethnic survival (Butzer, p. 213)." "Like other Mediterranean nations, the Spaniards had long experience with other peoples and other cultures, a familiarity that North Americans did not share. More importantly yet, Catholicism is a universalist religion that was 'inclusive' and imbued with missionary zeal..., (a factor) which brought together the conquerors and the conquered to worship within one roof (Butzer, p. 213)."

> "In 1600 some 49% of the *espanoles* in the new World lived in large cities or mining centers, many of which rivaled the smaller cities of Castile in size. It was in these administrative centers that several, flexible constellations vied for power: the Castilian officials and (lawyers) *letrados,* the Sevillan petty bureaucrats and merchants and a landed gentry derived from many parts of Castile. Below the upper crust were the heterogeneous, middle echelons of (servants) *criados* or personal assistants, craftsmen, vendors, and skilled workers still privileged to live in the

'Spanish' city. Beyond that there were various urban and exurban (neighborhoods) *barrios* for a much larger population of Indians and growing mixed ranks of (races) *castas*. Despite these obvious contradictions, these multiracial cities, in a perverse sort of way, came to symbolize Spanish culture, and, somewhat ironically, serve to fossilize the external mores of the sixteenth century Peninsular society from which the colonists had derived their roots." "These multiracial cities had no counterparts in French or British North America (Butzer, p. 214)."

"The resulting Spanish policy of a dual - Spanish and Indian - society favored residential segregation and separate but interdigitated economies, as it sought to preserve at least part of the indigenous heritage and patrimony. While indigenous socioeconomic configurations were marginalized, a long process of economic, social, and cultural fusion ... led to mutual assimilation and the creation of a new, hybrid society. (Butzer, p. 214)"

Yet, from the early 1500s onward, the Spanish introduced sheep and cattle, which devastated the environment. Ecologically, during this period, land was overused, while epidemics and famines took place. Yet, our Gomez Manrique de Lara line resided in Leon, Guanajuato from at least 1575, and returned from 1702-1905.

The Garcia Carraffa brothers, Alberto and Arturo Garcia Carraffas, created (from 1919 to 1963) the "Encyclopedia of Spanish-American Heraldry, an encyclopedia ("Diccionario Heraldico y Genealogico de Apellidos Espanoles y Americanos") of Spaniards who emigrated to New Spain based upon the work of 15,000 genealogies. Later, Endika de Mogrobejo added additional information to the incomplete work to bring the listing to 17,000. The chapter on "Manrique" (Appendix A) remains separate from the "Manrique de Lara" branch, which was included with the "Lara" history.

Garcia Carrafa encyclopedia (excerpt) of MANRIQUE de LARA
(Volume 2) (Section 24):
"Pedro Manrique de Lara, the second of that name, was the 13 hereditary Viscount of Narbonna, the second Lord of Molina and Mesa, Tutor of King Alonso VIII, and governor of Toledo and Extremedura. He celebrated two marriages, the first with the Lady Sancha, Princess of Navarra, widow of Gaston V, Count of Bearne, and the second with the Countess Margarita or Margerina. Of the first liaison were born 1. Aymerico, fifth of the name, whose details follow, 2. Gonzalo Perez Manrique de Lara, third Lord of Molina and Mesa and trunk (i. e. paterfamilias) of the 4th branch, the Lords of Molina and Mesa, which will return to cite, 3. Rodrigo Perez Manrique de Lara, Lord of Amusco and Pina and trunk of the 5th branch, which will we will also return to site...."

Based upon onomastics and the fact each New Spain villa had at most twenty-five Spanish/Portuguese family groups, our line connects to both the Gomez and Manrique de Lara family lines, specifically an individual who fought in the Chichimeca War (1550-1590), and as such, received property from the Royal Audencia in Leon, Guanajuato. The forty-year war was between the Chichimeca natives fighting against the Spaniards who began living on their lands post silver ore mining discovery. As roads were built to transport the silver from Zacatecas and Queretaro, Chichemecan warriors would attack. The Chichimeca people, a population of about sixty thousand people, were nomads who traveled sixty-two thousand miles from Durango to Guanajuato to Guadalajara. They consisted of four ethnic groups: Guachichiles (San Luis Potosi), Pames (Queretaro), Guamares (Guanajuato) and Zacatecos (Zacatecas and Durango). Excellent nomadic warriors, their arrows could penetrate Spanish armor. As the treatment of Chichmecans punished by the war was seen a major reason for the continuation of the standoff, the 7th Viceroy of New Spain, Alvaro Manrique (de Lara) de Zuniga removed Spanish soldiers from their land and advocated against military operations. Instead, he supplied the Chichmecas with food, clothing and tools. By initiating a "Purchase of Peace" mission, the roads along the Silver Route became safe. Because of this program, the Chichimecas ended their nomadic life patterns and became Catholic. It is noted this Spanish series of measures which comprised of peace and welcoming, Catholic conversion, advocating settlements and providing food and other goods fostered the Chichmecas assimilation into implemented Spanish culture.

Leon, Guanajuato was founded on 20 January 1576 after fifty residents committed to staying for ten years. Once established, Villa de Leon became the fourth viceroy of New Spain. Founding Leon resident included Pedro Gomez who arrived in New Spain by 1564 with the intention to fight the Chichimeca Indians. Because of his efforts during the War of the Chichmecas, the Royal Court of Mexico awarded Pedro Gomez land in Leon named Cerro Gordo. Rio de los Gomez, which went through Leon, was named for the family as it also traversed Cerro Gordo, then a large ranch on a hill above the city. Pedro Gomez, his wife Catalina Manrique de Lara and their children, Balthasar Gomez, Gaspar Gomez and Lucia Manrique de Lara were founding members of Villa Leon and ancestors of the Manrique-Hopkins line.

The list of 1575 Leon settlers (from Spain and Portugal) included: Juan Alonso de Torres, Ana Ruiz Baron, Luis Alonso Torres, Isabel Baron, Pedro Gomez, Catalina Manrique (de Lara), Baltasar Gomez, Gaspar Gomez, Lucia Manrique (de Lara), Jorge Duarte, Juana de Leon, Juan Duarte, Isabel Duarte, Cristobal Martin, Juan Martin de la Rosa, Rodrigo Martin, Pedro Lopez, Antonio Rodriquez de Lugo, Diego Martinez, Alonso Lopez Guzman, Tadeo Alvarez, Diego Hinojosa Valderrama, Antonio de Silva, Diego Frausto d'Aponte, Agustin de Chagoya, Ruy Diaz, Alonso Espino, Hernando Alonso Cortes, Leonor de Silva, Padre Juan de Cuenca, Padre Maestro Cristobal de Soria, Francisco Ballesteros, Diego Hernandez, Tomas Hernandez, Captain Juan Cordillo, Miguel Ramirez, Alvaro Sanchez, Marcos Francisco and Diego Vasquez Lara.

Historically, few "Manrique de Lara" named individuals are found in New Spain history. As per Alvaro Manrique de Zuniga (1525, Seville, Andalucia, Spain-3 March 1604, Seville, Andalucia, Spain), his mother Teresa de Zuniga y Manrique de Lara, the III Duquesa of Bejar. Alvaro Manrique de Zuniga was New Spain's 7th Viceroy and governed New Spain from 17 October 1585 to 26 January 1590 at the behest of King Phillip 1. Alvaro Manrique de Zuniga was a son of the 4th Duke of Bejar, Francisco de Zuniga y Sotomayor, and was given the title Marques de Villamanrique by King Philip I of Spain in 1575. He was known for ending the War of Chichimecas by having Spanish soldiers removed from the area, ending capture of the Indians and provided the Chichimecas with land, food and clothing. By 1590, for the first time in forty years, the war ended.

By the 1700s, the Manrique de Lara surname became very unusual. In rare instances, the surmame appear on documents. When "Caballeros de Carlos 3 (1771-1847)" records were reviewed in a Joseph Manrique de Lara (1785) was found residing with his family in Mexico City. However, given the first name, "Joseph," lineage remains undefined:

> Don JOSEPH MANRIQUE, in the 1785 Company of the Prince: 1785 edition of the Gazette of Mexico, a periodical of government and business (Bottom page 119 - #199. Under section "Empleos" - Employment):
> "Ranks and honors obtained by the officials of the militias of the internal provinces by the grace of the King." The subtitle reads, "Captains" in which the second name is recorded as: SIR JOSEPH MANRIQUE, OF THE NINTH COMPANY OF THE PRINCE" ("NOVENA CONPENIA DEL CUERPO DE DRAGONES PROVINCIALES DEL PRINCIPE" = Ninth Company of the Corps of Provincial Dragoons of the Prince)."

The article was initiated with a number 30 by Jacobo Ugarte (and Loyola_, the commanding general of Internal Provinces). During this period, permanent units were paid for by the colonial governments and were known as, Viceroyalty of New Spain (Virreinato de Nueva Espana). Mexico City had eight to nine Infantry units which were also described as, dragoons. As per *HathiTrust:* "(Organization of Mexico's Colonial Militia) (Title: Provisional Regulation for the Regimentation, Governance and Establishment of the Companies of Militias on the Southern coast of the Kingdom of New Spain):

> (Page 6, Paragraph 19) - "The officers of all (companies) shall be precisely Spaniards, except in the Party of Acapulco, their elections resting with subjects located within the demarcation of the same companies, and having additionally the circumstances of decent birth, good conduct, age and resources to support themselves with the required decorum."

As stated previously, MANRIQUE de LARA was a prominent noble family of Spain. MANRIQUE was the first name of the person who began the Manrique de Lara branch of the LARA noble family. His surname was PEREZ de LARA, Perez being the son of Pedro.

MAP OF GUANAJUATO, MEXICO

                                                                                       San Luis Potosi,
                                                                                       San Luis Potosi, Mexico

Aguascalientes,
Aguascalientes, Mexico
o

                                       San Felipe
                                           o

                                                                                       San Luis de la Paz
                                                                                           o

Lagos de Moreno
Jalisco, Mexico
o

                                         Dolores Hidalgo
                                                 o

                    LEON
                      o

                                         Guanajuato
San Francisco del
Rincon   o
    o   **Silao de la Victoria**
                           o   **San Miguel de Allende**
                                                             o

                 Irapuato
                 o

                                                                   Santiago de Queretaro,
                                                                   Queretaro, Mexico o
                         Salamanca
                            o

                               Celaya
                               o

                               Salvatierra
                                o

<u>Distances (2024) in miles:</u>

Leon to Silao de Victoria:	21 miles	Leon to Aguascalientes:	81 miles
Leon to Guanajuato:	35.5 miles	Leon to Mexico City:	238 miles
Leon to Irapuato:	45 miles	Leon to San Luis Potosi:	114 miles
Leon to San Felipe:	61 miles	Leon to Queretaro:	113 miles
Leon to Salvatierra:	103 miles	Leon to Lagos de Moreno:	27 miles

Text from 1799 marriage of Joseph Urbano Manrique de Lara to Maria Melchora Lopes:

In the congregation of Silao on the 18th of May of the year 1790, I the Bachelor Don Rafael de Servantes with permission from the Priest on duty, having preceded without impediment the three notices of the Council (of Trent) of Josef Maria Manrique, Spaniard by origin and resident of Rancho de Bonillas, and Doña Maria Melchora Lopes, Spaniard by origin and resident of La Cañada de Amargura of this Parish, and being present in the Parish Church of said Congregation, I solemnly married and veiled in accordance with the order of our Holy Mother Church, having determined the mutual consent of both, and being Witnesses Don Josef Maria Araujo and Josef Joaquin Garrea (?) Spaniards of this neighborhood, and Godparents Francisco Manrique and Maria Catarina, residents of Rancho de Bonillas, and to certify I signed along with the Priest on duty. Signatures of Francisco (illegible) and Rafael Servantes

9 June 1864 Island of St. Helena marriage of Charles Essex to Catherine Harriet Hopkins (Island of St. Helena Archives document).

Mary Hopkins' birth announcement for Sunday, 29 July 1900 as noted on page 11 in the Tuesday, 31 July 1900 edition of The San Francisco Call, "Births-Marriages-Deaths" section.

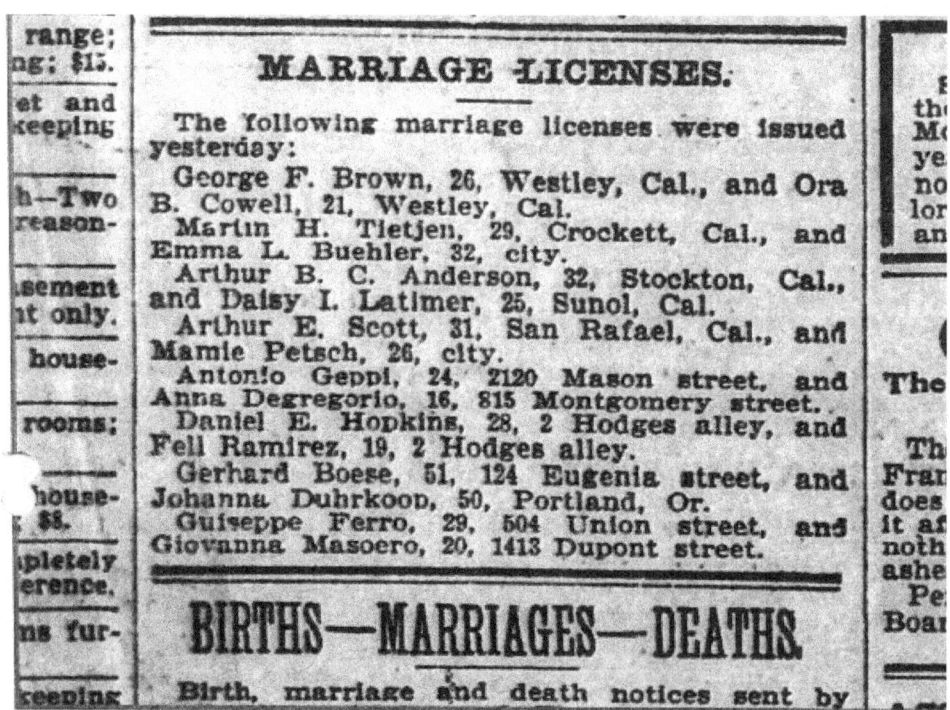

Marriage license dated Thursday, 24 October 1901 in San Francisco for Daniel E. Hopkins and Fell Ramirez as noted on page 13 in the Friday, 25 October 1901 edition of The San Francisco Call, "Marriage-Licenses" section.

Daniel Edwin Hopkins (sailor/musician), San Francisco, California, USA – 1902

Daniel Edwin, Flora (Ramirez) and Mary Hopkins (age 2) abt. 1902
San Francisco, California.

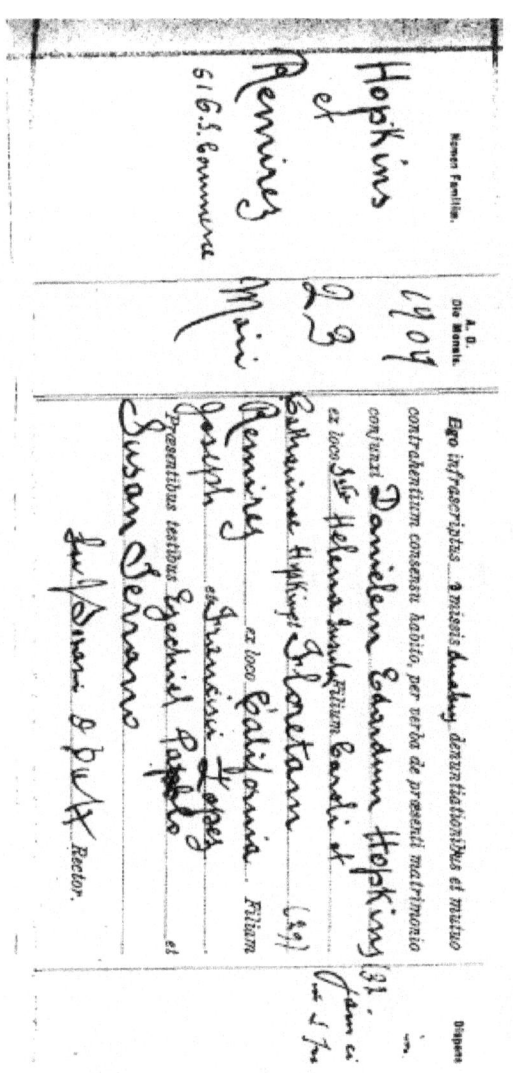

23 May 1909 St. Mary's Stockton Catholic church marriage certificate of Daniel and Flora (Ramirez) Hopkins (*certified on 6 June 2017 when an official copy was made on that date*).

> The remains are at Warren & Smith's
> HOPKINS— In Stockton, November 2,
> 1918. Flora Hopkins, wife of D. E.
> Hopkins, mother of Mrs. S. Manrique
> of Oakdale, Robert, Carrie, Lupe and
> Dave Hopkins of Stockton, a native
> of California, aged 36 years and 22
> days.
> [The funeral will take place Tuesday,
> November 5, 1918, at 2 p. m., from St.
> Mary's church. Interment in San Joa-
> quin cemetery. Services private. Re-
> mains at Warren & Smith's.]

Stockton Record newspaper obituary for Flora (Ramirez) Hopkins:

"HOPKINS - In Stockton, November 2, 1918, Flora Hopkins, wife of D. E. Hopkins, mother of Mrs. S Manrique of Oakdale, Robert, Carrie, Lupe and Dave Hopkins of Stockton, a native of California, aged 36 years and 22 days. The funeral will take place Tuesday, November 5, 1918 at 2 pm from St. Mary's church. Internment in San Joaquin cemetery. Services private. Remains at Warren & Smith's."

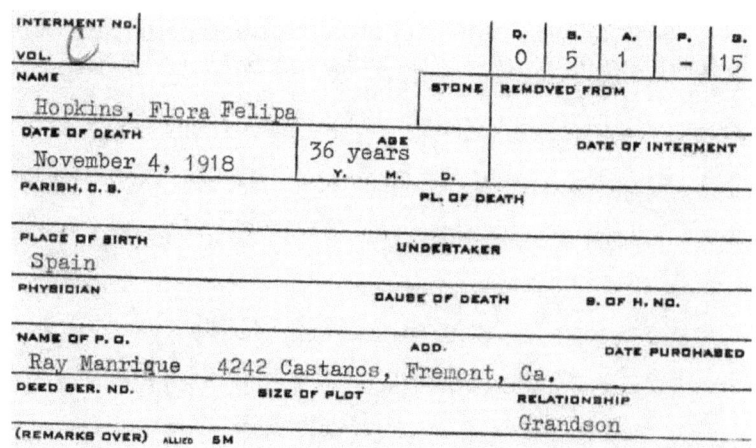

San Joaquin Cemetery card for Flora Felipa (Ramirez) Hopkins. States born: "Spain."

Oakdale, California Laughlin Road vineyard. (2017)

Former Serapio Manrique Oakdale Farmland
(Tree planted in by author's Grandfather)

(Back row, left to right) Linda, Joe, *(Middle)* Julius, *(Bottom row, left to right)* Tony, Alice, Edward and *(Sitting)* Madeline Violet Manrique.   North 5th farmhouse, 1942, Oakdale, California, USA.

(Left to right) Joseph, Mary (Hopkins), Lawrence & Serapio Manrique, Robert Hopkins Jr. (Mary's nephew).

Manrique Family (1950s)

(Back row, left to right) Julius, Edward, Richard, Joe, Tony and Lawrence Manrique
(Front row, left to right) Vincent, Alice, Mary (Hopkins), Linda, Primo and Raymond Manrique 1958, North 5th house, Oakdale, California, USA.

(Top Row, left to right) Vincent, Lawrence, Joseph, Julius and Raymond Manrique.
(Middle Row, left to right) Alice, Linda, Mary (Hopkins), and Dolores (m1).
(Bottom Row, left to right) Primo (m1), Richard, Tony, and Edward Manrique.

World War II Honoree

World War II Veteran

Lawrence Manrique

BRANCH OF SERVICE
U.S. Army Air Forces

HOMETOWN
Fremont, CA

HONORED BY
Mr. Julius C. Manrique, Brother

World War II Honoree

World War II Veteran

Joseph H. Manrique

BRANCH OF SERVICE
U.S. Army

HOMETOWN
Modesto, California

HONORED BY
Mr. Julius C. Manrique

RELATIONSHIP
Brother

World War II Honoree

World War II Veteran

Vincent Manrique

BRANCH OF SERVICE
U.S. Army Air Forces

HOMETOWN
San Leandro, CA

HONORED BY
Mr. Julius C. Manrique, Brother

ACKNOWLEDGMENTS

This genealogical account would not be complete without a special thank you to Jane Knowles Lindsey, a California Genealogical Society genealogist, who located Mary Hopkins' 1900 newspaper birth announcement. My genealogical research (1702-1799) was kindly confirmed by Debbie Gurtler, AG, a *Family Search* librarian. Also, a note of appreciation to my father, Julius Clement Manrique, for proofing family history related to the Oakdale, California, USA branch. With each document I found, my dad would respond "no one is ever going to believe this." Prior to his death, he learned Pedro Gomez and Catalina Manrique de Lara were founders of 1576 Leon, Guanajuato and our branch's emigration year from Spain likely was 1560. Additionally, thanks acknowledged to Madrid's DAR National Vice Chair for Spanish Research, Molly Fernandez de Mesa, and DAR's Henrietta Martinez Christmas, for seeking American Revolutionary ties via a Spanish soldier association to this established 1730 Leon, Guanajuato, Mexico family given Joseph Manuel Manrique de Lara was born during 1734 in Leon, Guanajuato, Mexico, the same year as my maternal DAR Patriot, Abijah Pinkham, was born in Dover, New Hampshire, USA. Please note this family story focused upon ancestry prior to 1940 with the aim to discover my grandfather's ancestors and their Spain to Mexico emigration year which was assumed to be the late 1870s.

Much research on Manrique de Lara to Esparza-Lozano lineage was from *Family Search* volunteers, information which helped organize records with historical timelines. A note of thanks is also extended to Stockton St. Mary's Catholic Church for locating Hopkins-Ramirez' baptismal and marriage records. *Family Search* digitized St. Helena records and St. Helena Island Archives emailed documents confirmed St. Helena ties.

The "de Villiers/Pama System" labels letters to generations. Created by Christoffel Coetzee de Villiers and Dr. Cornelis (Cor) Pama, the system was initially used in South Africa during the 19th century. I recorded the Manrique de Lara-Hopkins descendants using this method as additional members of this line will be added in the future.

As per the difference between the terms christening and baptism, a "Christening" involves a naming ceremony followed by a baptism, but a baptism does not include a naming ceremony. The purpose of a christening is "to christen" or "give name to" whereas a baptism is one of the seven sacraments in the Catholic Church.

GENEALOGICAL NUMBERING SYSTEM USED:
(*Please note Manrique generations are numbered beginning with Gaspar MdL*)
Generation1/JOSEPHA; Generation2/GASPAR - a; Generation3/MANUEL - b; Generation4/URBANO - c; Generation5/ISIDRO - d; Generation6/SIMON - e; Generation7/CLEMENTE - f; Generation8/SERAPIO - g; Generation9/JULIUS CLEMENT - h; Generation10/ANNE - i.

BIBLIOGRAPHY

"A Legacy for Generations to Come." *Vision*, Spring 2013, pp.16-17.

Brading, D. A. and Wu, Cecilia. "Population Growth and Crisis: Leon, 1720-1860," Journal of *Latin American Studies*, Vol. 5, No. 1 (May 1973), pp. 1-36. Published by Cambridge University Press.

Butzer, Karl W. "Spanish Colonialization of the New World: Cultural Continuity and Change in Mexico." Published by Erkunde, Archive for Scientific Geography. Bd.45.H.3 (Sep., 1991), pp. 205-219.

Fuente: Gonzales Leal, Mariano. *Leon Trayectoria y Destino*. Pro. Urbe. Leon 1990. Pp 5-6.

Garcia Carraffa, Alberto and Garcia Carrafa, Arturo. *Enciclopedia Heraldica Hispano-Americana*. 88 Volumes (Lara - Volume 48; page 165/Manrique de Lara - Volume 2; page 128). Published Madrid, 1919 (-1963).

Manrique, J. C. (2023) [Unpublished manuscript]. "From 157 North Fifth Avenue to College Avenue and the Many Miles Between." Pages 1-2; 5-6.

Manrique, Julius C., Ed.D. *My Mother's Garden*. 1st Books Library, 1999. Pages 4 & 6.

Martinez, Lic. Gonzalo Torres. "Descendancy of Don Pedro Gomez, Founder and First Settler of the Villa de San Sebastian de Leon of New Spain." *Memories of the Mexican Academy of Genealogy and Heraldry*, second period, Volume II, December 1961, pp 109-114.

Salazar y Castro, Don Luis de. *Historia Genealogica de la Casa de Lara, Justificada con Instrumentos y Escritores de Inviolable Fe*. Madrid. Published at the Imprenta Real by Mateo de Llanos y Guzman. 1697. (Ano de M.DC.XCVII) (#45302699-322) (586 pages) Volume 3 (Tomo III).

Santos, Robert LeRoy, "Mexicans in Stanislaus County Part 2: Pre-Bracero Period, 1850-1941" by Robert LeRoy Santos. *Stanislaus Historical Quarterly*, Vol. 7, Number 1, Spring 2014, Page 614. Alley-Cass Publications.

Schmal, John P. "Aguascalientes, including Romo de Vivar, Macias, Valdez, and Tiscarno..." from "Aguascalientes: The Geographic Center of Mexico." Houston Institute of Culture. 2004.

Schmal, John P. "Moctezuma's Descendants in Aguascalientes." September 7, 2022 from indigenousmexico dot org.

~~~~~

Archivo Historico de Leon, Guanajuato, Mexico.

California Genealogical Society, Oakland, California, USA.

Island of St. Helena Archives - Marriage/birth records not digitized by *Family Search*.

St. Mary's Catholic Church, Stockton, California, USA - Baptismal/marriage records.

Ancestry (dot com) - Birth/marriage/death records from California, USA.

Family Search - Birth/marriage/death records from Mexico & Island of St. Helena, UK.

Bob Bordier website - Noblezaseminario.com/TreeManriqueLara.

Matthew Hovious, genealogist, Madrid, Spain - Translated Manrique de Lara section from *Historia Genealogica de La Casa de Lara* by Don Luis de Salazar y Castro into English.

Rodolfo Herrera Perez, Director of Leon's Archivo Historico (2023)

Newspapers: *The Daily Review, Oakdale Leader, Modesto Bee, Modesto News-Herald, Stockton Record and The San Francisco Call.*

ALM - Updated 29 July 2024

NOTES

www.ingramcontent.com/pod-product-compliance
Lightning Source LLC
Chambersburg PA
CBHW080535300426
44111CB00017B/2728